CHAUCER
NAME DICTIONARY

Garland Reference Library
of the Humanities
(Vol. 709)

CHAUCER
NAME DICTIONARY

A Guide to Astrological, Biblical,
Historical, Literary, and Mythological
Names in the Works of Geoffrey Chaucer

Jacqueline de Weever

GARLAND PUBLISHING, INC. • NEW YORK & LONDON
1996

Maps 1, 2, and 5 were drawn by the author;
Maps 4 and 6 were drawn by Gregory Frazer.

Library of Congress Cataloging-in-Publication Data

de Weever, Jacqueline, 1932–
  Chaucer name dictionary.

  (Garland reference library of the humanities; vol. 709)
  Bibliography: p.
  1. Chaucer, Geoffrey, d. 1400—Dictionaries, indexes. 2. Chaucer,
Geoffrey, d. 1400—Knowledge—Occultism. 3. Chaucer, Geoffrey,
d. 1400—Knowledge—Literature. 4. Chaucer, Geoffrey, d. 1400—
Knowledge—Folklore, mythology. 5. Names, Personal, in literature—
Dictionaries. 6. Astrology in literature—Dictionaries. 7. Mythology
in literature—Dictionaries. 8. Allusions—Dictionaries. I. Title.
II. Series.
PR1903.D4   1988   821'.1   87-21236
ISBN 0-8240-8306-7 (alk. paper)
ISBN 0-8153-2302-6 (pbk.)

Hardcover design by Mary Beth Brennan
Paperback cover design by Lawrence Wolfson Design, New York
Photograph research by Marjorie Trenk
Cover photograph courtesy of The Bettman Archive

Printed on acid-free, 250-year-life paper
Manufactured in the United States of America

In memory of my mother and father

Contents

Foreword

We live in an age of wonderful reference books. Those Renaissance scholars who first edited Chaucer and asked the basic questions about his meanings lacked our concordances, dictionaries, gazetteers, and source guides. But then we and our students lack their classical education and ready familiarity with mythology and late medieval biography. So we need reference books as they have never been needed before.

Two years ago, Garland Publishing asked me to serve as a reader for this book, and I surreptitiously photocopied de Weever's typescript before I returned it with my comments. I needed her name dictionary *then*, not later, and have used it constantly since. This volume allows us to look up arcane information scattered through thousands of notes in editions variously available, and it updates citations to more modern (and accessible) editions and reference books. It also explains astronomical and astrological terms in ways I can understand, tying them to names and stories.

Professor de Weever has designed this volume for easy access by scholars and beginners, specialists and nonspecialists alike. You do not need to know the answer to find the answer, as in so many reference books in the medieval field. For example, she lists the names under their main Chaucerian spellings, on the assumption that most seekers will proceed from a reference in Chaucer's text. But she also cross-references heavily from other spellings, including modern ones. So we find "Augustin" cross-referenced from "Augustine," even though the two names sit side by side in her alphabetical listing. The best reference books assume very little.

This book goes far beyond answering questions about particular references occurring in Chaucer. For instance, I wondered if Chaucer had read Bede's *Ecclesiastical History*, so I looked up the key names: Bede,

Caedmon, Edwin, Hilda, Aidan, and Cuthbert. De Weever lists only the last, and her apparatus tells me that Chaucer did not need to know Bede to have the scholars in the *Reeve's Tale* ask for hospitality in the saint's name.

My typescript version has gotten a little dog-eared from use, and I look forward to replacing it with my own printed copy. On behalf of medieval scholars and students, I thank Professor de Weever for placing so much rich information at our fingertips.

Donald K. Fry
Poynter Institute for Media Studies
St. Petersburg, Florida

Acknowledgments

It gives me pleasure to acknowledge my indebtedness to the late Professor Robert A. Pratt, Professor Emeritus of the University of Pennsylvania, who suggested a segment of this project to me as a doctoral dissertation. I am especially grateful for his encouragement and support during work on this *Name Dictionary*. I would also like to thank Professor Ruth J. Dean and Professor Siegfried Wenzel for reading portions of the manuscript and for offering valuable suggestions for its improvement. Very special thanks to Professor Donald K. Fry, Poynter Institute for Media Studies, for rescuing me from the pit of error in several places. My thanks to the Research Foundation of the City University of New York for a grant while the work was in progress. Two colleagues have been particularly helpful. The late Samuel A. Moore read a very large portion of the typescript and pointed out infelicities of style, and I am very sorry indeed that he is not here to see the finished work. Professor Nancy Black read my Introduction and indicated places for further development. My deep gratitude goes to my friend and neighbor, Anne Itkin, for holding my hand and pulling me out when I found myself in the slough of despond. The librarians at the Brooklyn College Library have been models of patience with my requests and wizards at locating books at other libraries. To all of them my hearty thanks.

Introduction

This *Name Dictionary* brings together in a convenient form information on personal names in Chaucer's works and on the names of gods and goddesses in their mythological and planetary aspects. Names of books, *e.g.*, *Anteclaudian* and *Eneydos*, are considered under the entries for their authors, whose names are also mentioned. Names in square brackets at the beginning of entries, *e.g.*, **[JEAN DE MEUN]**, indicate that Chaucer mentions not the name but the work, *e.g.*, *Le Roman de la Rose.* To keep the emphasis on personal names, those of allegorical figures, such as Fame, Fortune, and Nature are not included. Place names are excluded because they have been dealt with in *A Chaucer Gazetteer,* by Francis P. Magoun, Jr. (Chicago: 1961).

The present work is addressed both to students—who may turn to it to find out where and in what context a given name occurs and to find out, at a glance, Chaucer's use of a given author, *e.g.*, Lucan—and to those readers who are interested in etymological sources, *e.g.*, the origin, formation, and development of Chaucer's names. The *Name Dictionary* thus supplements the notes of modern editions and goes beyond older indices, such as Corson's *Index of Proper Names and Subjects to Chaucer's Canterbury Tales* (London: 1911) and, more recently, Dillon's *Dictionary of Proper Names in the Works of Geoffrey Chaucer* and Scott's *Who's Who in Chaucer,* both published in 1974.

The listings are in Chaucerian spellings, *e.g.*, *Ladomya* instead of *Laodomia*, the classical spelling, to make it easier for the reader to find. In addition to using French, Italian, and modified Latin spellings, Chaucer modified names, without radically changing them, to suit the needs of rhyme and meter and to fit stress patterns.[1] Thus *May* occurs in medial and final rhyming positions, but *Mayus* occurs four times in various positions with initial syllabic stress in *The Merchant's Tale*;[2] *Griselde* becomes

Grisildis as stress and rhyme demand in *The Clerk's Tale*. Latin *Colatinus* is contracted to Middle English *Colatyn* for the same reasons. Sometimes Chaucer uses several variants of the same name, *e.g., Eneas* or *Enee*. *Eneas* is Middle English, French, and Italian; *Enee* appears for the sake of the rhyme. Position in the line, determined by the necessities of meter, in turn determines the form of the name; syllabic stress is shifted to meet the needs of metrical stress, and the shifted emphases are noted where they occur. Since *i/y*, *ch/th*, *c/k* are generally interchangeable in medieval manuscripts, no explanations are given for such variation.

Each entry has four sections. Biographical, historical, or mythological information is presented in the first paragraph, and names are given in classical spelling, *e.g., Laodomia*. Chaucer's use of the name appears in the second paragraph. Any particular connection, implication, or meaning of the name in the context in which it appears is discussed, with allegorical interpretation where appropriate, and names are given in Chaucerian spelling, *e.g., Ladomya, Laodomya*, and *Laudomia*. The third paragraph considers the etymology of the name, gives concordance occurrences for each form of the name, lists variant spellings, and takes note of the final -*e* where it occurs. Some names, like *Criseyde*, have final syllabic -*e* at the end of the line but elided final -*e* in the middle of a line before a word beginning with a vowel or unaspirated -*h*.[3] Since the form of the name generally bears some relation to its place in the line, these are discussed where appropriate. The fourth paragraph is a bibliography of all sources used in the entry as well as important articles on the person or the Tale. The exception is Migne's *Patrologia Latina*, whose designation, *e.g., PL* 23: 175, appears immediately next to the work identified in the text. Sources are listed in alphabetical order. Those most frequently used are listed by their abbreviated titles, *e.g., The Riverside Chaucer,* ed. L. Benson; *RR*, ed. E. Langlois. Articles are given full bibliographical treatment, *e.g.,* G. Dempster, "Chaucer at Work on the Complaint in *The Franklin's Tale.*" *MLN* 52 (1937): 6–16. Periods after Roman numerals in the entry indicate books within a book, or parts, followed by line numbers, *e.g., Iliad* II.695–699. In the sources that follow the entry, Roman numerals indicate volume numbers, followed by a colon and page numbers, *e.g.,* Homer, *Iliad*, ed. and trans. A.T. Murray, I: 102–103.

Cross-references appear in bold face and square brackets, *e.g.,* **[Dorigen]**. Index numbers distinguish several persons with the same name, *e.g.,* **Robin[1], Robin[2], Robin[3]**, each a different person. The following is a sample entry:

LADOMYA, LAODOMYA, LAUDOMIA. Laodomia was the wife of Protesilaus, who was killed when the Greeks landed at Troy, even before the main battles began (*Iliad* II.695–699). Laodomia killed herself when he did not return (*Heroides* XIII). Jerome mentions her among faithful wives, *Epistola adversus Jovinianum (Letter Against Jovinian)* I.45 (*PL* 23: 275).

The Man of Law lists a story of Ladomya among Chaucer's works, *MLI* 71, but no story exists. Dorigen thinks Laodomya is exemplary of wifely virtue, *FranklT* 1445; Laudomia appears in the catalogue of love's martyrs, *LGW F* 263, *LGW G* 217. **[Dorigen: Protheselaus]**

The forms appear to be scribal variants, all with four syllables. *Ladomya* occurs in final rhyming position, *MLI* 71; *Laodomya* appears in medial position, *FranklT* 1445; and *Laudomia* occurs medially, *LGW F* 263, *LGW G* 217.

G. Dempster, "Chaucer at Work on the Complaint in *The Franklin's Tale*." *MLN* 52 (1937): 6–16; Homer, *Iliad*, ed. and trans. A.T. Murray, I: 102–103; K. Hume, "The Pagan Setting of *The Franklin's Tale* and the Sources of Dorigen's Cosmology." *SN* 44 (1972): 289–294; Ovid, *Her*, ed. and trans. G. Showerman, 158–171.

It must be noted that the nameless pilgrims on the ride to Canterbury are referred to with capital initial letters, *e.g.*, the Knight, the Merchant, the Clerk, the Friar, the Summoner. The people in the Tales who have similar occupations are given lower-case initial letters, *e.g.*, the merchant (*The Shipman's Tale*), the clerk (*The Franklin's Tale*), the friar (*The Summoner's Tale*), the summoner (*The Friar's Tale*).

A key to abbreviations precedes the dictionary itself. It is divided as follows:

I. Chaucer's Works
II. Editions of Chaucer
III. Journals, Periodicals, and Reference Books
IV. Books and Other Abbreviations

An appendix at the end contains a short glossary of medieval astronomical and astrological terms, a Ptolemaic map of the universe, and diagrams of the zodiacal signs. There is a full bibliography, divided into primary and secondary sources.

I have used the Loeb editions of Greek and Latin authors wherever possible and medieval commentaries on mythological works for interpretation of figures and etymologies of names. The most important of these are Isidorus Hispalensis, *Etymologiarum sive Originum Libri XX* (ed. W.M. Lindsay, Oxford: 1911, 1972); Fulgentius, *Mitologiarum libri tres* in *Mythographi Latini* (ed. T. Munckerus, Amsterdam: 1681); Petrus Berchorius, *Reductorium morale, Liber XV: Ovidius moralizatus, Cap. i, De formis figurisque deorum, Brux. Bibl. Reg. 863–869* (Utrecht: 1966); *Ovide Moralisé* (ed. C. de Boer, Amsterdam: 1915-1938), and John Gower, *Confessio Amantis* (ed. G.C. Macaulay, Oxford: 1911). For astronomical and astrological names I have used Ptolemy's *Tetrabiblos*. J.D. North has shown that this work was Chaucer's principal source for knowledge about the heavens and that the work was very well known during the period.[4] For Chaucerian variants of Biblical names, the Latin Vulgate is the source.

The modern texts used for this work are *The Complete Works of Geoffrey Chaucer,* ed. W.W. Skeat (Oxford: 1894–1897); *The Riverside Chaucer,* ed. Larry Benson (Boston: 1987); *The Text of the Canterbury Tales,* ed. J.M. Manly and E. Rickert (Chicago: 1940); *The Tales of Canterbury,* ed. Robert A. Pratt (Boston: 1974); *A Parallel Text Print of Chaucer's Troilus and Criseyde,* put forth by F.J. Furnivall (Chaucer Society Publications, nos. 63, 64, 87, 88, London: 1881–1882), and *The Book of Troilus and Criseyde,* ed. R.K. Root (Princeton: 1926). I use mainly those spellings found in *The Riverside Chaucer,* but compare them with Manly-Rickert. Chaucer refers to the diversity of English dialects in the fourteenth century in *Troilus* V.1793–1798, and the variations found in the eighty-four manuscripts of *The Canterbury Tales* underscore his warning. In his discussion of the spelling of those manuscripts, J.M. Manly points out that there is no means of reconstructing the spelling systems of the ancestral scribe. Yet "conspicuous words, such as dialect forms, unusual words, proper names, and rhyme spellings are likely to be retained, and these only irregularly."[5] He cautions, therefore: "It is not wise, then, to conclude, as has sometimes been assumed or suggested, . . . that because the spellings of the MSS having the best texts agree in general, these MSS reproduce the spelling of the original." The term "Chaucerian spelling" used throughout this *Name Dictionary* refers to the forms as scribes have rendered them. The line numbers follow the fragment divisions of *The Riverside Chaucer.*

In addition to the prefaces and notes of the editions mentioned above, I am also indebted to *A Concordance to the Complete Works of Geoffrey Chaucer and to the Romaunt of the Rose,* by J.S.P. Tatlock and A.G. Kennedy (Washington, D.C.: 1927, 1963); *A Chaucer Gazetteer,* by F.P. Magoun, Jr. (Chicago: 1961); *A Dante Dictionary,* by Paget Toynbee, revised by Charles Singleton (Oxford: 1968); *The Oxford Dictionary of Saints,* by David Hugh Farmer (Oxford: 1978, 1979); *Medieval Science and Technology: A Selected, Annotated Bibliography,* by Claudia Kren (New York: 1985); *Chaucer Source and Analogue Criticism: A Cross-Referenced Guide,* by Lynn King Morris (New York: 1985). For the etymology and system of Roman names, *Cassell's Latin Dictionary* has been invaluable.

Notes

1. N.E. Eliason, "Personal Names in *The Canterbury Tales.*" *Names* 21 (1973): 137.
2. *May* occurs twenty-six times, *Mayus* four times in various positions. Emerson Brown, Jr., suggests that *Maius,* the month favorable to physicians, connects May with Damyan, who, with May, heals Januarie, *"The Merchant's Tale:* Why Is May called *Mayus?" Chaucer Review* 2 (1968): 273–277. He admits, however, that such a connection does not account for the form of the name.
3. For a full discussion of Chaucer's final -*e,* see E.T. Donaldson, "Chaucer's Final -*e.*" *PMLA* 63 (1948): 1101–1124; 64 (1949): 609; and Ian Robinson, *Chaucer's Prosody: A Study of the Middle English Verse Tradition* (Cambridge: 1971), 82–108.
4. J.D. North, "Kalendered Enluymned Ben They." *Review of English Studies,* new series 20 (1969): 134.
5. *The Text of the Canterbury Tales,* ed. John M. Manly and Edith Rickert. 8 vols. (Chicago: 1940), I: 560.

Abbreviations

I.   Chaucer's Works. The abbreviations used are modifications of those found in *The Riverside Chaucer*, ed. Larry Benson (Boston: 1987).

Adam	*Adam Scriveyn*
Anel	*Anelida and Arcite*
Astr	*A Treatise on the Astrolabe*
BD	*The Book of the Duchess*
Bo	*Boece*
Buk	*Lenvoy de Chaucer a Bukton*
CkP, CkT	*The Cook's Prologue, The Cook's Tale*
ClP, ClT	*The Clerk's Prologue, The Clerk's Tale*
Compl d'Am	*Complaynt d'Amours*
CYP, CYT	*The Canon's Yeoman's Prologue, The Canon's Yeoman's Tale*
Form Age	*The Former Age*
FranklP, FranklT	*The Franklin's Prologue, The Franklin's Tale*
FrP, FrT	*The Friar's Prologue, The Friar's Tale*
Gen Prol	*The General Prologue*
HF	*The House of Fame*
KnT	*The Knight's Tale*
LGW	*The Legend of Good Women*
MancP, MancT	*The Manciple's Prologue, The Manciple's Tale*
Mars	*The Complaint of Mars*
Mel	*The Tale of Melibee*
MerchP, MerchT	*The Merchant's Prologue, The Merchant's Tale*
MillP, MillT	*The Miller's Prologue, The Miller's Tale*
MkP, MkT	*The Monk's Prologue, The Monk's Tale*
MLI, MLP, MLT	*The Man of Law's Introduction, The Man of Law's Prologue, The Man of Law's Tale*
NPP, NPT	*The Nun's Priest's Prologue, The Nun's Priest's Tale*

PardI, PardP, PardT *The Pardoner's Introduction, The Pardoner's Prologue,*
                     The Pardoner's Tale
    ParsP, ParsT *The Parson's Prologue, The Parson's Tale*
              PF *The Parliament of Fowls*
           PhysT *The Physician's Tale*
         PrP, PrT *The Prioress's Prologue, The Prioress's Tale*
           Purse *The Complaint of Chaucer to his Purse*
         RvP, RvT *The Reeve's Prologue, The Reeve's Tale*
            Scog *L'envoy de Chaucer a Scogan*
       SNP, SNT *The Second Nun's Prologue, The Second Nun's Tale*
           ShipT *The Shipman's Tale*
        SqI, SqT *The Squire's Introduction, The Squire's Tale*
            Sted *The Lak of Stedfastnesse*
     SumP, SumT *The Summoner's Prologue, The Summoner's Tale*
    ThopP, Thop *The Prologue of Sir Thopas, The Tale of Sir Thopas*
              Tr *Troilus and Criseyde*
             Ven *The Complaint of Venus*
      WBP, WBT *The Wife of Bath's Prologue, The Wife of Bath's Tale*
        Wom Unc *Against Woman Unconstant*

II. Editions of Chaucer

           Manly *The Canterbury Tales,* ed. John M. Manly (New York:
                  1928).
   Manly-Rickert *The Text of the Canterbury Tales,* ed. John M. Manly
                  and Edith Rickert (Chicago: 1940).
            Pratt *The Tales of Canterbury,* ed. Robert A. Pratt (Boston:
                  1974).
Riverside Chaucer *The Riverside Chaucer,* ed. Larry Benson, based on
                  The Works of Geoffrey Chaucer, ed. F.N. Robinson.
                  2nd ed. (Boston: 1987).
         Robinson *The Works of Geoffrey Chaucer,* ed. F.N. Robinson.
                  2nd ed. (Boston: 1957).
            Skeat *The Complete Works of Geoffrey Chaucer,* ed. W.W.
                  Skeat. 7 vols. (Oxford: 1894–1897).

III. Journals, Periodicals, and Reference Books

          AN&Q *American Notes and Queries*
            AnM *Annuale Mediaevale*
          Archiv *Archiv für das Studium der neueren Sprachen und Lit-*
                  eraturen
            C&M *Classica et Mediaevalia*

CC	*Corpus Christianorum*
CE	*College English*
ChauR	*Chaucer Review*
CL	*Comparative Literature*
DA	*Dictionary of Angels*
DD	*Dante Dictionary*
DNB	*Dictionary of National Biography*
DSB	*Dictionary of Scientific Biography*
EI	*Encylopaedia of Islam*
EJ	*Encyclopaedia Judaica*
ELH	*Journal of English Literary History*
ELLMA	*European Literature in the Latin Middle Ages*
ELN	*English Language Notes*
EM	*English Miscellany*
ES	*English Studies*
ESC	*English Studies in Canada*
ESO	*Early Science at Oxford*
Etym	*Etymologiarum sive originum libri XX*
FCS	*Fifteenth Century Studies*
JEGP	*Journal of English and Germanic Philology*
JMRS	*Journal of Medieval and Renaissance Studies*
JWCI	*Journal of the Warburg and Courtauld Institutes*
MAE	*Medium Aevum*
MLN	*Modern Language Notes*
MLQ	*Modern Language Quarterly*
MLR	*Modern Language Review*
MP	*Modern Philology*
MRS	*Medieval and Renaissance Studies*
MS	*Mediaeval Studies*
N&Q	*Notes and Queries*
NCE	*New Catholic Encyclopedia*
NM	*Neuphilologische Mitteilungen*
OCCL	*Oxford Companion to Classical Literature*
OCD	*Oxford Classical Dictionary*
ODECN	*Oxford Dictionary of English Christian Names*
PG	*Patrologia Graeca*
PL	*Patrologia Latina*
PMASAL	*Papers of the Michigan Academy of Science, Arts, and Letters*
PMLA	*Publications of the Modern Language Association*
PMPA	*Publications of the Modern Philological Association*
PMRS	*Progress of Medieval and Renaissance Studies in the U.S. and Canada*
PQ	*Philological Quarterly*

RES Review of English Studies
RLC Revue de littérature comparé
RR Le Roman de la Rose (The Romance of the Rose) by
      Guillaume de Lorris and Jean de Meun
S&A Sources and Analogues to Chaucer's Canterbury Tales
SLL Studies in Language, Literature and Culture of the
      Middle Ages and Later
SN Studia Neophilologica
SP Studies in Philology
SSF Studies in Short Fiction
TLS Times Literary Supplement
WHR Western Humanities Review
WVUPP West Virginia University Philological Papers

IV. Books and Other Abbreviations

Les Arts Poétiques Les Arts Poétiques du XIIe et XIIIe siècle
AT Arthurian Tradition and Chrétien de Troyes
CFT Chaucer and the French Tradition
CFW Concerning Famous Women
CMS Chaucer and the Mediaeval Sciences
CRP Chaucer and the Roman Poets
DND De natura deorum
EETS Early English Text Society
Ex ser Extra series
Froissart Froissart's Chronicles
GL The Golden Legend
HDT Historia destructionis Troiae
Her Heroides
HMES A History of Magic and Experimental Science
IAC Iconographie de l'art chrétien
Inf Inferno
ITC The Indebtedness of Chaucer's Troilus and Criseyde
      to Guido delle Colonne's Historia destructionis
      Troiae
LA Legenda Aurea
MAME The Matter of Araby in Medieval England
ME Middle English
Met Metamorphoses
Metr Metrum
NH Natural History
OF Old French
OM Ovide Moralisé

OS   Original series
Par   *Paradiso*
PC   *A Preface to Chaucer*
Purg   *Purgatorio*
SATF   *Société des anciens textes français*
SHMS   *Studies in the History of Mediaeval Science*
SII   *Studies in Iconology*
Tes   *Il Teseide delle Nozze d'Emilia*

The Dictionary

The Prisoner

AARON was Moses's brother. He and his sons were consecrated the first priests of Israel. The Lord commanded that they refrain from wine and strong drink when they went into the tabernacle, lest they die (Leviticus 8–10).

The Friar says that Aaron governed the priests of the temple. They refrained from drinking any drink that would make them drunk when they prayed for the people in the temple. They prayed in abstinence, lest they die, *SumT* 1894–1901. **[Elye: Moses]**

The name appears once in Chaucer's works, initially, *SumT* 1894.

ABIGAIL: [ABIGAYL]

ABIGAYL, ABYGAIL. Abigail was Nabal's wife. She pacified David when she delivered several asses laden with food, and the king called off his raid on Nabal's farm. She saved Nabal's life without telling him at what price and spoke slightingly of him to David. When Nabal died, David married her (I Kings 25). Albertanus Brixiensis mentions her among *femmes de bon conseil,* or women of good counsel, *Liber consolationis et consilii,* V.

Januarie cites Abigayl as her husband's savior, *MerchT* 1369–1371. Prudence cites Abygail as a woman who gave good counsel, *Mel* 1099–1100. **[David: Januarie: Nabal: Prudence]**

The forms are spelling variants. *Abigayl* appears in medial position, *MerchT* 1369; *Abygail* occurs in *Mel* 1099.

Albertanus Brixiensis, *Liber consolationis,* ed. T. Sundby, 17.

ABRADATES: [HABRADATES]

ABRAHAM migrated from Ur of the Chaldees into the land of Canaan and became the first patriarch of the people of Israel (Genesis 11:27–32; 12–26).

Dame Alys cites Abraham as a holy man who had more than two wives, *WBP* 55–58. Jovinian, in his argument against celibacy and virginity, mentions Abraham, who had two wives, as proof that marriage did not diminish virtue. Jerome answers Jovinian in *Epistola adversus Jovinianum (Letter Against Jovinian)* I.7 *(PL* 23: 219). **[Sarra: Ysaac]**

The name appears once, *WBP* 55.

B.J. Whiting, "Jerome's *Epistola adversus Jovinianum.*" *S&A*, 208.

ABSALON, ABSOLON¹, David's favorite son, was the most beautiful man in Israel. He was noted for his extraordinary hair, which was cut and weighed once a year. Achitophel encouraged him to rebel against David and gave him a plan for the rebellion. When Achitophel saw that his counsel was not followed, he set his house in order and hanged himself. Joab halted the insurrection, and as Absalom fled on his mule, his hair caught in the branches of an oak. Here Joab's men found him and slew him. David wept and mourned for him, lamenting, "Oh Absalom! My son, my son!" (II Kings 14–18).

The Parson, in his homily on anger, mentions wicked counsel that leads to treachery; Chaucer adds a gloss, *"ut Achitofel ab Absolonem,"* *ParsT* 638–640. Absolon, with his blond hair, must make way for Alceste, *LGW F* 249, *LGW G* 203. By the twelfth century blond hair was an attribute of beauty; in Peter Riga's *Aurora, Liber Secundus Regum (The Second Book of Kings),* 41–50, Absolon has blond hair. The God of Love refers to the first lines of the *balade, LGW F* 539. **[Achetofel: David: Joab]**

Absalon/Absolon are Latin forms. *Absalon* appears in *LGW G* 203; *Absolon* in *LGW F* 249.

P.E. Beichner, "Chaucer's Hende Nicholas." *MS* 14 (1952): 151–153; Peter Riga, *Aurora,* ed. P.E. Beichner, I: 273.

ABSOLON² is the parish clerk who loves Alison in *The Miller's Tale.* He is the village dandy. His shoes have a design like that of the windows of St. Paul's church; his kirtle is light blue; his stockings are red; and his hair is abundant, *MillT* 3312–3338. P.E. Beichner points out that Hugo of St. Victor *(Wisdom* IX.15) equates abundant hair with excess. **[Alison¹: Gerveys: John²: Nicholas¹]**

The name never occurs initially. It appears twenty-two times in medial positions, *KnT* 3339, 3353, 3387, 3389, 3394, 3398, 3657, 3671, 3714, 3723, 3730, 3733, 3741, 3744, 3749, 3764, 3767, 3772, 3783, 3793, 3852, 3856; ten times in final rhyming position, *KnT* 3313, 3348, 3366, 3371, 3657, 3688, 3711, 3719, 3766, 3804.

P.E. Beichner, "Absolon's Hair." *MS* 12 (1950): 223; A. MacDonald, "Absolon and St. Neot." *Neophilologus* 48 (1964): 235–237.

ACADEMICIS: [ACHADEMYCIS]

ACHADEMYCIS. Plato founded his Academy c. 385 B.C. His followers were sometimes called the Academics.

Lady Philosophy commands the Muses to leave Boethius, who has been nourished by studies of the Eleatics and the Academics, *Bo* I, *Prosa* 1.68. **[Eleatics: Parmanydes: Plato: Zeno]**

Achademycis is Chaucer's transliteration of *Academicis*, Latin dative plural of *Academici.*

Boethius, *De consolatione philosophiae*, ed. and trans. S.J. Tester, note *a*, 134–135.

ACHALEOUS, ACHELEOUS, ACHELOYS. Achelous, a river god, was one of Dejanira's suitors. Hercules challenged him to combat, and Achelous changed himself into different forms, last of all into a bull. Hercules broke off one of his horns, defeated him, and won Dejanira (*Met* IX.4–88; *OM* IX.1–872).

The Monk mentions the breaking of Achelous's horn, *MkT* 2106. Lady Philosophy also tells of the fight, *Bo* IV, *Metr* 7.43–50.

The forms are variants of OF *Acheloüs. Acheloys* appears in medial position, *MkT* 2106; *Achaleous* occurs in *Bo* IV, *Metr* 7.43, and *Acheleous* appears in *Bo* IV, *Metr* 7.45.

Ovid, *Met*, ed. and trans. F.J. Miller, II: 2–9; *OM*, ed. C. de Boer, III, deel 30, no. 3: 221–242.

ACHATE, ACHATES was the faithful companion who went with Aeneas from burning Troy to Italy (*Aeneid* I.188). Virgil generally refers to him as *fidus Achates*, "faithful Achates."

Chaucer calls Achates a knight, *HF* I.226; Achates is a knight, *LGW* 964. Eneas's companions are called *chevaliers* and *barons* throughout the twelfth-century *Eneas*. Achates appears in the first half of the *Legend of Dido, LGW* 964–1136. **[Eneas]**

Achate occurs once in final rhyming position, *HF* I.226; *Achates* occurs medially, *LGW* 976, 1136, and in final rhyming position, *LGW* 964, 1023, 1129.

Eneas, ed. J.-J. Salverda de Grave; Virgil, *Aeneid*, ed. and trans. H.R. Fairclough, I: 254–255.

ACHELEOUS: [ACHALEOUS]
ACHELOYS: [ACHALEOUS]

ACHILLE, ACHILLES was the son of Peleus, grandson of Aeacus, and the leader of the Myrmidons against the Trojans in Homer's *Iliad*. The oracle foretold that he would be celebrated but would die young. So his mother Thetis dipped him in the Styx, holding him by the heel, to make him immortal (Statius, *Achilleid*, I.134). During his youth Chiron was his schoolmaster. Thetis, knowing that he would be killed at Troy, hid him among the daughters of Lycomedes, king of Skyros. Here Odysseus identified him and persuaded him to join Agamemnon's forces. Homer presents him as a warrior of ungovernable and implacable temper. The very first lines of the *Iliad* announce the poem's theme: the wrath of Achilles and the devastation it works. Ovid calls him fierce and bloodier than war *(ferox belloque cruentior, Met* XII.592–593). His death by Paris and Apollo is foretold in *Iliad* XXII.359–360.

Dictys of Crete, in *Ephemeridos belli Troiani (A Journal of the Trojan War)* I.14, and Guido delle Colonne, in *Historia destructionis Troiae (A History of the Destruction of Troy)* XXVII, emphasize Achilles's anger and cruelty. The prophecy that he would be killed either by Apollo or by Paris is treated vividly: Achilles falls in love with Polyxena, Priam's daughter, and arranges to meet Hecuba and Paris in the temple of Apollo Thrymbraeus in Troy. Paris and Deiphebus ambush him when he arrives, and they kill him. Fulgentius associates the incident with Achilles's lust, *Mythologies* III.7; Dante places Achilles in the Circle of the Lustful, *Inf* V.65–66.

The stars foretell the death of Achilles, *MLT* 198. The wonderful sword of the strange knight is compared with Achilles's spear, which wounded and healed King Telephus, *SqT* 236–240. On the way to Troy the Greeks attacked Mysia, and in the battle Achilles wounded the king, Telephus. When his wound would not heal, Telephus sought out Achilles in the camp at Aulis, for the oracle had said that the wounder would be the healer. Achilles and the sons of Aesculapius healed the king (Dictys Cretensis, *Ephemeridos belli Troiani* II.1–10). Later tradition added that the rust from the spear healed Telephus; Dante uses this part of the story in *Inf* XXXI.4–6. Andromacha's dream, a *visio* that foretells coming events, shows her Hector's death by Achilles, *NPT* 3142–3148. This dream appears in Dares, *De excidio Troiae historia (The Fall of Troy, a History)* 24, but Chauntecleer's account follows *Renart le Contrefait* 31323–31340. The story of Achilles at Troy is painted on the walls of the temple of glass, *BD* 329. The hardiness of Achilles, slain for love, *BD* 1067, is a medieval *topos* or commonplace topic. Benoît's account appears in *Roman de Troie* 21838–22334. Achilles appears in the catalogue of false lovers, *HF* I.397–398; Breseida bewails his treachery in Ovid's *Heroides* III. Statius (in his *Achilleid*) holds up the fame of cruel Achilles, *HF* III.1460–1463. Achilles is among love's martyrs, *PF* 290. Criseyde says she had trusted that Pandarus would have had no mercy on her had she loved either Hector or Achilles, *Tr* II.416. Troilus says that, if he lie, may Achilles's spear cleave his heart, *Tr* III.374–375. Achilles slays

Hector, *Tr* V.1559–1561, and kills Troilus, *Tr* V.1806. **[Eacides: Ector: Polixena: Thelopus: Thetis: Troilus]**

Achille occurs once, in final rhyming position, *Tr* V.1806; *Achilles* occurs five times in medial positions, *SqT* 239; *BD* 329, 1066; *Tr* III.374; *Tr* V.1559; six times in final rhyming position, *MLT* 198; *NPT* 3148; *PF* 290; *Tr* II.416; *HF* I.398; *HF* III.1463.

Dares Phrygius, *De excidio Troiae historia*, ed. F. Meister, 28–30; Dictys Cretensis, *Ephemeridos belli Troiani libri*, ed. W. Eisenhut, 3–29; Dares Phrygius and Dictys Cretensis, *The Trojan War*, trans. R.M. Frazer, 30, 152; Fulgentius, *Fulgentius the Mythographer*, trans. L. Whitbread, 91; Guido de Columnis, *HDT*, ed. N.E. Griffin, 206–208; Guido delle Colonne, *HDT*, trans. M.E. Meek, 198–203; Ovid, *Her*, ed. and trans. G. Showerman, 32–43; *ibid.*, *Met*, ed. and trans. F.J. Miller, II: 222–223; Benoît, *Roman de Troie*, ed. L. Constans, III: 373–399.

ACHITOFEL. Achitophel the Gilonite was one of David's counselors. He encouraged Absalom to rebel against his father. When he saw that his treacherous advice was not followed, he went home and hanged himself (II Kings 14–17).

In the homily on wicked counsel, *ParsT* 638–640, Achitofel is an example of the wicked counselor. The Man in Black says that he would be worse than Achitofel if he repented of his love, *BD* 1116–1119. **[Absolon[1]: David]**

The name occurs in *ParsT* 638 and *BD* 1118.

ACTEON: [ATTHEON]

ADAM[1] was the first man. There are two stories of his creation. The first tells that God created man in his image, male and female together (Genesis 1: 27), and Adam is not named in this version. The second tells that God created Adam from the dust of the ground, breathed into his nostrils, and he became a living soul (Genesis 2: 7). The commandment not to eat of the Tree of the Knowledge of Good and Evil is given to Adam (Genesis 2: 7–17). Isidore explains that man is named *homo* because he is made of *humus* or earth (*Etym* VII.vi.4).

Alys of Bath uses the term "the mark of Adam" to refer to male human beings, *WBP* 695–696. God made Eve for Adam's comfort, *MerchT* 1325–1332. Adam fell through gluttony, *PardT* 505–511; gluttony is the first sin (Jerome, *Epistola adversus Jovinianum [Letter Against Jovinian]* II.15, [*PL* 23: 305–306]). God made Adam but said that it was not good for him to be alone, *Mel* 1103–1105. A short stanza on Adam begins the Monk's series of tragedies, *MkT* 2007–2014. The Nun's Priest, following the tradition of Biblical exegesis, says that woman's counsel caused Adam's loss of Paradise, *NPT* 3256–3259. Sin entered the world through Adam when he broke God's commandment, *ParsT* 320–324. Adam and Eve were in a state of innocence when they were naked in Paradise, *ParsT* 325. Adam represents reason consenting to the delights of the flesh, *ParsT* 330–335. Since all people have the same parents, Adam and Eve, they should trust each other, *ParsT* 515–517. The first state conducive to love is the state of innocence, such as Adam's before he fell, *ParsT* 680–682. The sin of Adam and Eve is gluttony, *ParsT* 818–821. God made woman from Adam's rib so that she is his companion or "felawe," *ParsT* 925–929. The Dreamer invokes God, who made Adam, *HF* II.970. Behind the God of Love, the Dreamer sees such a procession of women that he had not thought possible since God made Adam out of earth, *LGWF* 282–289. The poet prays to Mary, the bright Lady who has been merciful to the seed of Adam, *ABC* 181–184. **[Caym: Eva]**

Adam occurs once initially, *PardT* 575; eight times in medial positions, *MkT* 2007, 2112; *NPT* 3258; *PardT* 508; *WBP* 696; *MerchT* 1325; *ABC* 182; *LGW F* 286; once in final rhyming position, *HF* II.970; and in the prose of the *Parson's Tale.*

P. Aiken, "Vincent of Beauvais and Chaucer's Monk's Tale." *Speculum* 18 (1942): 56–68; Isidore, *Etymologiae,* ed. W.M. Lindsay, I.

ADAM². Adam Scriveyne, or Adam the scrivener, was Chaucer's copyist. Several Adams have been suggested: Adam Stedeman, a London goldsmith, employed by John Walsshe to write his will, c. 1360–1475; Adam Acton; and Adam Pinkhurst. Adam may also be a generic name for all scriveners, following a tradition that made Adam the inventor of letters.

Chaucer wishes the "scalle," a disease of the scalp, on Adam, his scrivener, if he does not copy *Boece* or *Troilus* more accurately than hitherto, *Adam* 1–7.

The name appears initially, *Adam* 1.

R. Bressie, *TLS,* May 9, 1929: 383; Chaucer, *The Minor Poems, Part One,* ed. G.B. Pace and A. David, 133–134; R.E. Kaske, "*Clericus Adam* and Chaucer's *Adam Scriveyn,*" *Chaucerian Problems and Perspectives,* ed. E. Vasta and Z.P. Thundy, 114–118; J.M. Manly, *TLS,* May 16, 1929: 403; B.M. Wagner, *TLS,* June 13, 1929: 474.

ADMETUS: [AMETE]
ADONIS: [ADOON]

ADOON, ADOUN. Adonis was the son of Cinyras, king of Cyprus, by an incestuous union with his daughter Myrrha. The young man was so beautiful that Venus fell in love with him, preferring his company to the gods'. He ignored her advice not to hunt the boar and met his death when he attacked a particularly ferocious boar, which gored him to death. Venus, in love and grief, caused anemones to spring from his blood (*Met* X.298–518; *OM* X.1960–2493; *RR* 15668–15750).

Palamon invokes Venus by her love for Adoon, *KnT* 2224, and Troilus asks Venus to pray her father to turn all bad aspects of Mars or Saturne to grace for love of Adoun, *Tr* III.720–721. **[Mirra: Venus]**

The form seems to be Chaucer's own. *Adone* appears in *Tes* VI.42.1 and VII.43.5. *Adoon* occurs in final rhyming position, *KnT* 2224, and *Adoun* medially, *Tr* III.721.

Boccaccio, *Tutte le Opere*, ed. V. Branca, II: 432, 460; Ovid, *Met*, ed. and trans. F.J. Miller, II: 84–100; *OM*, ed. C. de Boer, II, deel 37, 58–70; *RR*, ed. E. Langlois, IV: 114–117; *RR*, trans. C. Dahlberg, 265–266.

ADRASTUS, king of Argos, was the leader of the Seven Against Thebes. His daughters married Polynices and Tydeus. Adrastus led the attack on behalf of Polynices's claim to the Theban throne, after Eteocles refused to give it up. Adrastus was the only survivor of the siege *(Thebaid* XI.424–446; *Roman de Thèbes* 9729–10230).

After the siege of Thebes and the deaths of the brothers Eteocles and Polynices, Adrastus goes home, and Thebes is desolate, *Anel* 57–63. **[Amphiorax: Campaneus: Ethiocles: Hemonydes: Parthonope: Polymyte: Tydeus]**

Roman de Thèbes, ed. L. Constans, I: 481–507; *Roman de Thèbes (The Story of Thebes)*, trans. J.S. Coley, 229–240; Statius, *Thebaid,* ed. and trans. J.H. Mozley, II: 420–423.

ADRIANE, ADRYANE. Ariadne, daughter of Minos and Pasiphae, fell in love with Theseus when he arrived in Crete. She saved his life by providing him with a ball of thread. He took the thread with him into the Labyrinth when he went to slay the Minotaur. After he killed the monster, Theseus followed the thread back to the entrance of the Labyrinth. Ariadne sailed away with him, but he abandoned her on the island of Naxos. Bacchus pitied her and made her his wife, and the gods set her crown among the stars *(Her* X; *Met* VIII.169–182; *OM* VIII.1083–1394).

The Man of Law says that Chaucer has written the complaint of Adriane, *MLI* 67, a reference to *LGW* 1886–2227. Theseus would have been devoured had not Adriane helped him and had pity on him, *HF* I.407–427. Adriane appears in the catalogue of faithful women, *LGW F* 268, *LGW G* 222. **[Dedalus: Minos: Phasipha: Phedra: Theseus]**

Adriane, OF variant by metathesis, occurs also in Machaut's *Le Jugement dou Roy de Navarre*, 2707–2806, which Chaucer knew. *Adryane* is a spelling variant.

The name never occurs initially. It appears ten times in medial positions, *MLI* 67; *HF* I.411; *LGW F* 268, *LGW G* 222; *LGW* 1969, 1927, 2078, 2171, 2175, 2545; five times in final rhyming position: *HF* I.407; *LGW* 2146, 2158, 2181, 2460.

Guillaume de Machaut, *Oeuvres*, ed. E. Hoepffner, I: 230–233; S.B. Meech, "Chaucer and the *Ovide Moralisé*—A Further Study." *PMLA* 46 (1931): 183–184; Ovid, *Her*, ed. and trans. G. Showerman, 120–130; *ibid.*, *Met*, ed. and trans. F.J. Miller, I: 418–419; *OM*, ed. C. de Boer, III, deel 30, no. 3: 134–142.

AEACIDES: [EACIDES]
AEETES: [OETES]
AEGEUS: [EGEUS]
AEGYPTUS: [EGISTE]
AENEAS: [ENEAS]
AEOLUS: [EOLUS]
AESCULAPIUS: [ESCULAPIUS]
AESON: [ESON]
AESOP: [ISOPE]

AFFRICAN, AFFRIKAN, AFFRYCAN. Publius Cornelius Scipio, Africanus Major (236–184/183 B.C.), invaded Africa in 206 B.C., while he was consul, and decisively defeated Hasdrubal and Hannibal in 203. Peace was negotiated when he captured Carthage; when Hannibal attacked again, Scipio defeated him at Zama. For these victories Scipio was given the *agnomen* or title *Africanus.* He was the grandfather of Scipio Africanus Minor, hero of the Third Punic War. Cicero's *Somnium Scipionis (The Dream of Scipio)* is told by Africanus Minor to a group of friends who have been discussing the nature of dreams and the belief in the afterlife. Scipio the Younger tells how he had visited the Numidian king, Masinissa, with whom he had discussed the elder Scipio, and how he had dreamed of his ancestor that night.

Chaucer refers to Africanus Major as *Affrican* throughout his work. Scipio the Younger dreams of the Affrican, *BD* 286–288; Affrycan appears to Scipio in a dream, *PF* 29–84. Affrican appears to the poet in a dream and leads him into a park, *PF* 106–170. **[Cipioun: Macrobeus: Massynisse: Tullyus]**

The contraction *Affrican/Affrikan* appears in medial positions, *PF* 41, 44, 52, 96, 107, 120, 153, and in final rhyming position, *BD* 287.

B.K. Cowgill, "The *Parlement of Foules* and the Body Politic." *JEGP* 74 (1975): 315–335; H.H. Scullard, *Scipio Africanus: Soldier and Politician.*

AFRICANUS: [AFFRICAN]
AGAMEMNON: [AGAMENON]

AGAMENON, AGAMENOUN. Agamemnon, son of Atreus, was the high king of Mycenae and the brother of Menelaus. His high-handed taking of Briseis away from Achilles caused the latter to sulk in his tent, while the Trojans wreaked havoc on the Greeks. After Hector killed Patroclus, Achilles emerged from his tent to avenge Patroclus's death and killed Hector. This is the story of Homer's *Iliad.*

Troilus says that he would rather be "caitif to cruel kyng Agamenoun" than lie to Criseyde, *Tr* III.382. Agamenon is mentioned four times in *Bo* IV, *Metr* 7.1–17, two of which are Chaucer's glosses. Chaucer identifies Agamenon as Menelaus's brother and explains that Agamenon allowed his daughter to be sacrificed at Aulis so that the gods would send a wind to blow the fleet to Troy. Boethius's Latin reads *ultor Attrides,* which Chaucer translates "the wrekere Attrides *(that is to seyn, Agamenon)."* [**Attrides: Clitermystra**]

Agamenon appears in *Bo* IV, *Metr* 7.1, 6, 8, 14. *Agamenoun,* a variant of OF *Agamenon,* occurs in final rhyming position, *Tr* III.382.

V.L. Dedeck-Héry, "Boethius' *De Consolatione* by Jean de Meun." *MS* 14 (1952): 256.

AGATHON: [AGATON]

AGATON. Agaton (c. 448–c. 402 B.C.) was the Greek tragic poet for whom the banquet is held in Plato's *Symposium,* to celebrate his first dramatic victory at the Lenaea in 416 B.C. *(Symposium* 172A). His tragedy, *Antheus,* departed from the custom of taking characters and plot from legend.

Chaucer credits Agaton with the saying that Jove placed Alceste among the stars because of her goodness, *LGW F* 521–526, *LGW G* 511–514.

Agaton suggests derivation from Dante's *Agatone, Purg* XXII.107.

Dante, *Divine Comedy,* ed. and trans. C.S. Singleton, II, 1: 240–241; *OCD,* 25; Plato, *Symposium,* ed. and trans. W.R.M. Lamb, 180–181.

AGENOR(ES). Agenor, king of Tyre, was the father of Cadmus and Europa. Jupiter fell in love with Europa and wooed her in the form of a white bull. She playfully leaped on his back, and he ran off with her to Crete *(Met* II.834–875; *OM* II.4937–5084).

The beast carrying off Agenor's daughter was adorned with daisies, *LGW F* 114. Ovid says that the garland was made of fresh flowers, *sertis novis, Met* II.867–868. [**Cadme: Europe**]

Agenores is the ME genitive case.

Ovid, *Met,* ed. and trans. F.J. Miller, I: 118–121; *OM,* ed. C. de Boer, I, deel 15: 276–279.

AGLAUROS: [AGLAWROS]

AGLAWROS. Aglauros was the daughter of Cecrops, the Athenian king. Mercury fell in love with her sister Herse and asked Aglauros to help him. Aglauros demanded gold, and Pallas Athena, patroness of Athens, was displeased with her cupidity, sending Envy to infect Aglauros's heart. Then Aglauros forbade Mercury to visit Herse. The god touched her with his magic wand, and Aglauros slowly turned to stone *(Met* II.722–832; *OM* II.3777–3898, 4044–4076).

Troilus invokes Mercury's help for the love of Hierse, because of which Pallas was angry with Aglawros, *Tr* III.729–735. **[Hierse: Mercurie: Pallas]**

The spelling *Aglawros* suggests that the form is derived through pronunciation.

Ovid, *Met*, ed. and trans. F.J. Miller, I: 110–115; *OM*, ed. C. de Boer, I, deel 15: 252–254; 257–258.

AHASUERUS: [ASSUER]
ALAIN DE LILLE: [ALEYN²]
ALANUS DE INSULIS: [ALEYN²]

ALAYN, ALEYN¹ is the Northumbrian student studying at Cambridge in *The Reeve's Tale*. Aleyn gets into the bed of the miller's daughter, while John, his fellow student who has accompanied him to the mill, cuckolds the miller to get even with the miller for stealing their corn. **[John³: Malyne: Simkin]**

H.D. Hinton suggests that the name is derived from French *alignier* meaning "to align" and is thus part of Aleyn's characterization, since he makes the miller's punishment fit the crime by stealing his daughter's maidenhead.

Alayn occurs four times, twice medially, *RvT* 4031, 4073, and twice finally, *RvT* 4188, 4273; *Aleyn* occurs seven times initially, *RvT* 4022, 4024, 4040, 4168, 4192, 4234, 4249; nine times in medial positions, *RvT* 4013, 4016, 4018, 4076, 4084, 4089, 4091, 4160, 4198, 4305, 4316; and once in final rhyming position: *RvT* 4108.

H.D. Hinton, "Two Names in *The Reeve's Tale*." *Names* 9 (1961): 117–120.

ALBAN: [ALBON]
ALBINUS: [ALBYN]

ALBON. St. Alban was the first martyr to Christianity in Britain. His name became a generic name for monks during the period. He died before A.D. 209 (Bede, *Ecclesiastical History*, I.7).

Harry Bailly wonders if the Monk's name is Daun John, Daun Thomas, or Daun Albon, *MkP* 1928–1930. **[John⁴: Piers: Thomas³]**

The name occurs once, in final rhyming position, *MkT* 1930.

Bede, *Ecclesiastical History of the English Nation*, ed. and trans. J.E. King, I: 34–44; *The South-English Legendary*, ed. C. D'Evelyn and A.J. Mill, I: 238–241.

ALBYN. Albinus (fl. sixth century A.D.) was a patrician and a councillor at Rome in Theodoric's court. Cassiodorus mentions him in *Epistolae Theodoricianae Variae* IV.30.

Boece says he defended Albyn when Cyprian accused him falsely, *Bo* I, *Prosa* 4.97–102. When the king tried to shift to the Senate the charges of which Albyn had been accused, Boece defended them all, *Bo* I, *Prosa* 4.212–219. [**Boece: Cyprian**]

Albyn is the English contraction of Latin *Albinus.*

Cassiodorus, *Cassiodori Senatoris Variae,* ed. Th. Momsen, I: 127.

ALCABITIUS: [ALKABUCIUS]

ALCEBIADES, ALCIBIADES, ALCIPYADES. Alcibiades (c. 450–404 B.C.) was the son of Cleinlas, Athenian general and statesman. His beauty was proverbial even in his own lifetime, as was his instability of character. Yet he was drawn to Socrates, shared a tent with him in battle, and generally revered the philosopher. When the Spartan general Lysander captured Athens in 404 B.C., Alcibiades fled to Bithnia with his mistress, Timandra, a courtesan. Lysander sent his men after them to kill the pair. The murderers did not enter Alcibiades's house but set it afire. When Alcibiades rushed out to fight the attackers, they ran off, shooting him with arrows until he fell. Timandra wrapped Alcibiades in her garments and buried him (Plutarch, *Life of Alcibiades*). Jerome tells the story of Timandra in *Epistola adversus Jovinianum (Letter Against Jovinian)* I.44 (*PL* 23: 274).

Dorigen thinks the mistress of Alcebiades exemplifies loyalty, *FranklT* 1439–1441. The beauty of Alcipyades, a medieval commonplace, appears in *BD* 1056–1057. Lady Philosophy comments on the outward beauty and inward corruption of Alcibiades, *Bo* III, *Prosa* 8.44045. [**Socrates**]

Alcebiades, a spelling variant, occurs in final rhyming position, *FranklT* 1439; *Alcipyades,* occurring in final rhyming position, *BD* 1057, is the OF variant, found in *RR* 8943, where Jean de Meun quotes Boethius.

Plutarch, *Parallel Lives,* ed. and trans. B. Perrin, IV: 2–115; *RR,* ed. E. Langlois, III: 102; *RR,* trans. C. Dahlberg, 162.

ALCESTE. Alcestis, the most beautiful of King Pelias's daughters, married Admetus of Thessaly after he passed the test her father had set him: to yoke together a wild boar and a lion. When his time came to die, Admetus asked his parents to die in his stead, but they refused. Then Alcestis offered herself in his stead, and he accepted her offer. But Persephone refused her sacrifice and sent her back to earth (Fulgentius, *Mythologies* I.22). In Euripides's play, *Alcestis,* Hercules rescues her from Hades. Alcestis is one of the four noble wives in Gower's *Confessio Amantis* VII.1917–1949, VIII.2640–2646.

Alceste is the image of the perfect wife; she appears in the Man of Law's catalogue of heroines, *MLI* 75, and she is on Dorigen's list of virtuous women, *FranklT* 1442. Cassandra tells Troilus the story of Alceste, *Tr*

V.1527–1533. The poet says that he would more gladly write of Penelope's loyalty and of good Alceste than of Criseyde, *Tr* V.1772–1785. Alceste surpasses other famous women who have died for love, *LGW G* 203–223. In Chaucer's vision the God of Love leads forth Alceste, who wears a crown made of "flourons smale," *LGW F* 217; she is clothed in green and crowned with white, *LGW F* 241–246, *LGW G* 173–174. Alceste pleads for the poet before the God of Love, *LGW F* 431–441, *LGW G* 421–431. The God of Love says that the poet has a book that tells the story of Alceste, how she chose to die for her husband and how Hercules rescued her, *LGW F* 510–518, *LGW G* 498–506. [Amete: Cibella]

Alceste appears three times initially, *LGW G* 209, 216, 223; five times in medial positions, *FranklT* 1442, *LGW G* 179, 317, *LGW F* 432, *LGW G* 532; eight times in final rhyming position: *MLI* 75; *Tr* V.1527, 1778; *LGW F* 511, 518, *LGW G* 499, 506, 530.

P. Clogan, "Chaucer's Cybele and the *Liber Imaginun Deorum.*" *PQ* 43 (1964): 272–274; Fulgentius, *Mythographi Latini*, ed. T. Munckerus, II: 62–64; *ibid.*, *Fulgentius the Mythographer*, trans. L.Whitbread, 62–63; John Gower, *Complete Works*, ed. G.C. Macaulay, III: 458.

ALCHABITIUS: [ALKABUCIUS]
ALCIBIADES: [ALCEBIADES]

ALCIONE, ALCYONE. Alcyone, daughter of Aeolus, was the wife of Ceyx, king of Trachis. When her husband did not return from his trip to Delphi, Alcyone prayed continually to Juno, goddess of married women, to help her in her distress. Juno pitied her and sent Morpheus in the guise of Ceyx to tell Alcyone that Ceyx had drowned at sea (*Met* XI.419–748; *OM*, XI.2996–3787).

The Man of Law says that in his youth Chaucer told the story of Ceys and Alcione, *MLI* 57. The full story, told in *BD* 62–220, was a favorite with medieval writers. Machaut tells it in *La Fonteinne Amoureuse* 539–1034, and Gower in *Confessio Amantis* VIII.2647–2656. [Ceys: Juno: Morpheus]

Alcione, a spelling variant, occurs twice in medial positions, *BD* 220, 1326; and four times in final rhyming position, *MLI* 57; *BD* 145, 196, 264. *Alcyone* occurs once, in final rhyming position *BD* 65.

John Gower, *The Complete Works*, ed. G.C. Macaulay, III: 458; Guillaume de Machaut, *Oeuvres*, ed. E. Hoepffner, III: 162–180; Ovid, *Met*, ed. and trans. F.J. Miller, II: 150–173; *OM*, ed. C. de Boer, IV, deel 37: 190–210; J.I. Wimsatt, "The Sources of Chaucer's 'Seys and Alcyone.'" *MAE* 36 (1967): 231–241.

ALCIPYADES: [ALCEBIADES]
ALCMENA: [ALMENA]
ALCYONE: [ALCIONE]
ALDABERAN: [ALDEBERAN]

ALDEBERAN. Aldaberan is the alpha or brightest star in the constellation Taurus. The name was originally given to the five stars of Taurus, and the brightest star was called in Arabic *Na'ir-al-Daberan*, "the bright one of the follower," because it follows the Pleiades. The first edition of the Alfonsine Tables (1252), a set of astronomical tables that were made for Alfonso the Wise of Castile and Leon, applied the name only to the alpha star.

Aldeberan is called the star of the south because it lies south of the ecliptic, or the path of the sun, but since it is north of the equator, it rises in the northeast, *Astr* I.21.13–17. **[Taur]**

Aldeberan means "the follower."

R.H. Allen, *Star Names and their Meanings,* 383–384; W.W. Skeat, ed., *A Treatise on the Astrolabe,* 78–79.

ALDIRAN. The term refers to the star in one of the forepaws of the lion in the constellation Leo. In an old Parisian list of stars Aldiran is described as *in fronte leonis,* in front of the lion. The Arabs applied the grammatical dual form *al dhira'an,* "the two paws," to the brightest and second brightest stars of Gemini because they stood 4 1/2 degrees apart. The astronomer al-Biruni says that the alpha or brightest star of Gemini is in the outstretched paw of Leo and that the second brightest or beta star is in the paw not stretched out. The ancient Arabs extended the figure far beyond the limits assigned to the constellation in modern astronomy.

The constellation Leo is ascending with its Aldiran when Cambyuskan rises from table, *SqT* 263–267. The sun has left its meridional angle or tenth house, so it is very much past noon. Leo begins to rise at noon and is fully risen about a quarter to three. **[Cambyuskan: Leo]**

The name occurs in final rhyming position, *SqT* 265.

al-Biruni, *The Chronology of Ancient Nations,* trans. C.E. Sachau, 345; *Riverside Chaucer,* ed. L. Benson, 893.

ALETE. Allecto, one of the Furies, was the sister of Megaera and Tisiphone, and a daughter of the Night. Virgil describes her with snakes in her hair (*Aeneid* VI.554–556, 570–572).

Alete and her sisters, daughters of the Night, complain endlessly in pain, *Tr* IV.22–24. The lines may have been influenced by Dante, *Inf* IX.37–51. **[Herenus: Megera: Thesiphone]**

The form of the name is the Italian variant.

Dante, *Divine Comedy,* ed. and trans. C.S. Singleton, I, 1: 90–91; J.L. Lowes, "Chaucer and Dante." *MP* 14 (1917): 142–148; Virgil, *Aeneid,* ed. and trans. H.R. Fairclough, I: 544–547.

ALEXANDER, ALISANDRE, ALISAUNDRE, ALIXANDRE, ALYSAUNDRE. Alexander III, the Great (356–323 B.C.), was the son of Philip

II of Macedon and Olympias of Epirus. Philip invited Aristotle to be Alexander's tutor; Aristotle accepted and stayed in Macedonia until 336 B.C., the year his pupil set out to conquer the world. First Alexander invaded Persia and defeated the Persian army, but he did not remain to consolidate the conquest. In 331 he conquered Egypt, then returned to Persia to inflict the final defeat on Darius. After Darius's death Alexander assumed the title "The Great King," or *Basileus*; he married the Sogdian princess Roxanne, then set off on further conquest. By 325 he had subdued India and overrun the Punjab. On the way back to Greece, he died of a fever at the age of thirty-three. Arrian's *Anabasis* describes his life and conquests.

The ultimate source for the life of Alexander during the medieval period is the romance-biography by one Pseudo-Callisthenes. D.J.A. Ross lists 120 derivatives, the last one, *The Wars of Alexander*, dating from the early fifteenth century. The romances appear not only in European vernaculars (English, French, German, Greek [Byzantine], Italian, Old Bulgarian, Serbian, Spanish), but also in oriental languages (Ethiopian, Hebrew, Persian, Syriac), both in verse and in prose. The most important derivative work is the Latin version by Julius Valerius, *Res Gestae Alexandri Macedonis,* written in the early fourth century A.D., from which most European redactions descend. During the twelfth century several important French redactions appear: *Roman d'Alexandre*, by Pfaffe Lamprecht; *Le Roman d'Alexandre, Fuerre de Gadres* by Eustache; *Le Roman d'Alexandre*, by Lambert le Tort of Chateaudun, which emphasizes the marvels and monsters of the East, *Le Roman d'Alexandre*, by Alexandre de Paris, including the Candace episode that gives the hero a romantic experience. *Le Roman de Toute Chevalerie* (1174–1182), by Thomas of Kent, presents Candace in the antifeminist tradition, and this work forms the basis of the Middle English *Kyng Alisaunder* (thirteenth century). The most popular romance of the fourteenth century is *Les Voeux du Payon,* by Jacques de Longuyon, written for Thibaut de Bar, Bishop of Liège, in 1312. Here Alexander appears as one of the Nine Worthies. He is also one of the Nine in the alliterative *Parlement of the Thre Ages*, 332–404 (c. 1352), in the monologue of Old Age. Romances telling of revenge for Alexander's death also appear during the twelfth century. The most important are the anonymous *Venjance Alixandre* and the *Venjement Alixandre*, by Gui de Cambrai. In addition, there are romances describing Alexander's celestial and submarine voyages.

The Monk tells a short life of Alisaundre, *MkT* 2631–2670. The anecdote told of Alisaundre, *MancT* 226–234, may have come from the *Gesta Romanorum* 146, or from Higden's *Polychronicon* III.19. The worthiness of Alysaundre is a medieval commonplace, *BD* 1059–1060. Alixandre Macedo is a celestial voyager, *HF* II.914–915. The goddess Fame wears the armor of Alexander and Hercules, *HF* III.1407–1413. **[Aristotle: Candace: Darius²]**

The variants are Old French. *Alexander* occurs once, *HF* III.1413; *Alisandre* occurs once medially, *MkT* 2658; *Alisaundre* occurs in medial position, *MkT* 2631; *MancT* 226; *BD* 1026; *Alixandre* occurs once in medial position, *HF* II.915; *Alysaundre*, a spelling variant, occurs medially, *BD* 1059.

Arrian, *Anabasis Alexandri*, ed. and trans. E.I. Robson, 2 vols.; *Gesta Romanorum*, trans. C. Green, 253; *Gesta Romanorum*, ed. H. Oesterly, 504–505; R. Higden, *Polychronicon*, ed. Babington and Lumley, III: 422–423; *Parlement of the Thre Ages*, ed. M.Y. Offord, 14–19; *Riverside Chaucer*, ed. L. Benson, 954; D.J.A. Ross, *Alexander Historiatus*, 5–65.

ALEYN: [ALAYN]

ALEYN[2]. Alanus de Insulis or Alain de Lille, a Cistercian, was professor at Paris and Montpellier. The traditional date of his birth, c. 1128, has been revised to 1116 or 1117. Alain died between April 14, 1202, and April 5, 1203. He was called *Doctor Universalis* because of his great learning. His two great works, *De planctu Naturae* and *Anticlaudianus de Antirufino*, were popular during the Middle Ages and influenced Jean de Meun and Chaucer. *De planctu Naturae* shows Boethian influence in its form, a mixture of prose and poetry, and in its conception of Dame Natura, who is modeled on Lady Philosophy. Alain's Natura is also kin to Natura in Bernard Silvester's *Microcosmos*. In Bernard's work Natura creates Man at Providence's command, assisted by Urania and Physis; Mercury creates hermaphrodites in his sphere of Cyllenius. Alain's *Anticlaudianus de Antirufino*, written about 1182, is a counterpart to Claudian's *In Rufinum* (A.D. 396). Alain describes his poem as a scientific one, an amalgam of the Seven Arts.

The lines from *CYT* 962–965 and *HF* I.272 are influenced by *Parabolarum* III.1. In contrast to Natura, who laments man's unfruitfulness in *De planctu Naturae*, Chaucer's Dame Nature presides over the birds' mating in *The Parlement of Foules*. She sits on a hill, exactly as Aleyn describes her, *PF* 316–318. Chaucer mentions the *Anticlaudianus* as if it were the name of the author, *HF* II.985–990; the flight of allegorical figures appears in *Anticlaudianus* IV.

Aleyn is mentioned once, in medial position, *PF* 316; the *Anteclaudian*, the English form for Latin *Anticlaudianus*, appears in HF II.986, in final rhyming position; the *Pleynt of Kynde*, the English translation of the Latin *De planctu Naturae*, appears in *PF* 316.

Alanus de Insulis, *Anticlaudianus*, ed. R. Bossaut; Alan of Lille, *Anticlaudianus, or The Good and Perfect Man*, trans. with commentary by J.J. Sheridan; Alain de Lille, *De planctu Naturae*, ed. N.M. Häring. *Studi Medievali*, 3, serie 19, 2 (1978): 797–879; *ibid.*, *The Plaint of Nature*, trans. and commentary by J.J. Sheridan (Toronto: 1980); W.W. Skeat, *The Complete Works of Geoffrey Chaucer*, V: 428; J. Ziolkowski, *Alan of Lille's Grammar of Sex*.

ALGARSIF, ALGARSYF is Cambyuskan's elder son in *The Squire's Tale*.
The Squire promises to tell how Algarsyf won Theodora for his wife, *SqT* 663–664, but the tale remains unfinished. **[Cambalo: Cambyuskan: Canacee[2]: Elpheta: Theodora]**

Dorothee Metlitzki suggests that *Algarsyf* has been transposed from Arabic *saif-al-jabbar,* meaning "the sword of the powerful one," the Arabic name for one of the three stars forming Orion's sword. *Algarsif* occurs in final rhyming position, *SqT* 663; *Algarsyf* occurs also in final rhyming position, *SqT* 30. The forms are spelling variants.

H.S.V. Jones, *S&A*, 364–374; D. Metlitzki, *The Matter of Araby in Medieval England,* 78–80.

ALGOMEYSE is the name sometimes applied to both the brightest and the second brightest stars of the constellation *Canis Minor* or the Little Dog. In the 1521 edition of the Alfonsine Tables, a set of astronomical tables made for Alfonso the Wise in 1252, the alpha or brightest star is called *Algomeysa.* The Arabs tell that the two dog stars were sisters of Canopus, another bright star, and that they were once together. When Canopus descended to the south (where it is today), Sirius, the greater dog star, followed. The third star remained in her place and wept for the loss of her two sisters until her eyes became infected with *ghumsa,* the white froth that collects in the inner corner of the eye. Thus, she is called *al-Ghumaisa.* Canopus is now seen only in the skies of the southern hemisphere.

Like Aldebaran, Algomeyse lies south of the ecliptic, the path of the sun, and is called a star of the south; since it is also north of the equator, it rises to the north of the eastern point of the horizon, *Astr* I.21.13–17. **[Alhabor: Syrius]**

Algomeyse is the ME descendant of Arabic *al-Ghumaisa,* "the frothy-eyed one."

R.H. Allen, *Star Names and their Meanings,* 133–134; W.W. Skeat, ed., *A Treatise on the Astrolabe,* 78–79.

ALHABOR is the Arabic name for Sirius, the brightest star in the constellation *Canis Major* or the Greater Dog.

Alhabor, a fair white star, is one of the fixed stars and lies 18 degrees on the west of the midday line; this is calculated on the back side of the rule or narrow revolving plate on the back of the astrolabe, used for measuring and taking altitudes, *Astr* II.3. 41–49. **[Algomeyse: Sirius]**

Alhabor is derived from the first part of the Arabic phrase *al-'abur al-Yamaniyyah* or "the passage of the South," a reference to the route taken by Canopus in the Arabic version of the myth of Canopus and Sirius.

R.H. Allen, *Star Names and their Meanings,* 121; W.W. Skeat, ed., *A Treatise on the Astrolabe,* 78, 81.

ALHAZEN: [ALOCEN]
'ALI: [HALY]

ALISON[1], ALISOUN[1] is the sexy young wife of John the Carpenter in *The Miller's Tale*. At eighteen years old she is an evocation of spring, compared with blossoming pear trees and frisky young animals. **[Absolon[2]: John[1]: Nicholas[1]: Robyn[1]]**

Both forms of the name are OF, meaning "of delight." *Alison* appears in medial positions only, *MillT* 3366, 3653, 3678, 3790, 3824; *Alisoun* appears medially, *MillT* 3577, 3617, 3649, and in final rhyming position, *MillT* 3401, 3523, 3639, 3698, 3832.

K.S. Kiernan, "The Art of the Descending Catalogue, and a Fresh Look at Alisoun." *ChauR* 10 (1975–1976): 1–16.

ALISOUN[2] is the name of Alys of Bath's "gossib" or close woman friend, with whom clerk Jankyn boards, *WBP* 525–530. **[Alisoun[3]: Alys[1]: Janekyn: Jankyn[2]]**

The name appears in final rhyming position, *WBP* 530.

ALISOUN[3] lives just outside Bath. The first portrait, *Gen Prol* 445–476, presents the outward appearance of this famous lady. The Prologue to her tale forms the second portrait, particularly *WBP* 603–620, where she provides astrological data to explain her personality, a dual character, "a marital and a martial nature," as B.F. Hamlin says.

Alisoun/Alison may be linked with the word *Aleison* from the mass, as it appears in the popular lyric, coupled with Jankyn in the lines: "Iankyn syngyt merie,/with 'aleyson.'" This is the refrain of a popular song, "Jolly Jankin," found in Sloan MS 2593. Chaucer's mating of Alison and Jankyn follows popular tradition. **[Alys[2]: Janekyn: Jankyn[2]: Mars: Mida: Pisces: Taur: Valerie: Valerius: Venus]**

Alisoun as the Wife of Bath's name appears only once, *WBP* 804.

W.C. Curry, *Chaucer and the Mediaeval Sciences*, 91–118; B.F. Hamlin, "Astrology and the Wife of Bath: A Reinterpretation." *ChauR* 9 (1973–1974): 153–165; R.H. Robbins, ed., *Secular Lyrics of the XIVth and XVth Centuries*, 21: 27.

ALKABUCIUS, Abu-l-Saqr 'Abd-al-Aziz ibn-Uthman ibn-'Ali-al-Qabisi (fl. first half of the tenth century), known in Latin as *Alchabitius*, was a famous Muslim astronomer. He was known for his treatise *al-Madkhal ila Sina 'at Ahkam al-Nudjum (Introduction to the Science of Astronomy)*, translated into Latin by John of Seville as *Inductorium ad Scientiam Judicialem Astronomial, Differentia Prima,* in the first half of the twelfth century and published in Venice in 1481. He is said to have written poetry, and a poem on the rainbow has been credited to him.

Chaucer says that he quotes Alkabucius, *Astr* I.8.13, referring to the treatise mentioned above.

Alkabucius is the ME variant of Latin *Alchabitius*, derived from the astronomer's patronymic, *Ibn 'Ali-al'Qabisi.*

Encyclopedia of Islam, II: 593, 1954–1960; G. Sarton, *Introduction to the History of Science,* I: 669.

AL-KHWARIZMI: [ARGUS[3]]
ALKMENA: [ALMENA]

ALLA, ALLE. Aella, king of Deira in Northumbria, ruled A.D. 559–588. Bede tells how Gregory determined to send missionaries to convert Britain when he heard the king's name (*Ecclesiastical History* II.1). In Trevet's *Les Chroniques Ecrités pour Marie d'Angleterre, fille d'Edward I,* Alle, a brave king, wins his battles against the Scots and the Picts (*S&A* 176).

Alla becomes Custance's second husband in *The Man of Law's Tale.* He slays his mother Donegild when he discovers that she has caused Custance and her child Maurice to be set adrift in the sea. Then, following his repentance, he travels to Rome to be absolved from his sin and there finds Custance his wife and their son Maurice. **[Custance: Donegild: Hermengyld: Maurice]**

Alla occurs twice in initial position, *MLT* 876, 1096; twenty-six times in medial positions, 578, 604, 610, 659, 688, 691, 893, 897, 984, 988, 996, 1003, 1006, 1014, 1016, 1022, 1032, 1045, 1046, 1051, 1073, 1088, 1100, 1128, 1141, 1144. *Alle*, Trevet's form, occurs once, in final rhyming position, *MLT* 725.

Bede, *Ecclesiastical History,* ed. and trans. J.E. King, I: 184–203; M. Schlauch, *S&A* 172–181.

ALLECTO: [ALETE]

ALMACHE, ALMACHIUS was the Roman prefect who questioned Cecilia, Tiburtius, and Valerian and ordered their deaths when they refused to observe the rites of the pagan religion (*LA* CLXIX).

Almachius performs his functions as prefect in *The Second Nun's Tale.* **[Cecile: Maximus: Tiburce: Valerian]**

Almache, the ME contraction of Latin *Almachius,* occurs twice initially, *SNT* 431, 458; and once medially, *SNT* 362; *Almachius* occurs twice initially, *SNT* 421, 435, and five times in medial positions, *SNT* 405, 410, 468, 487, 524.

Jacobus de Voragine, *GL,* trans. G. Ryan and H. Ripperger, 693–698; *ibid., LA,* ed. Th. Graesse, 774–777.

ALMENA. Alkmena, wife of Amphitryon, was mother of Hercules by Jupiter. Amphitryon had gone on a raid to avenge the deaths of Alkmena's brothers. While he was away, Jupiter came to Alkmena in Amphitryon's shape. He commanded Hermes to hold the moon in the sky and to prevent the sun from rising for the space of three days while he made love to her (*Met* IX.275–323; *OM* IX.1030–1179).

Troilus wishes that his first night with Criseyde would last as long as the night when Jove lay with Almena, *Tr* III.1428. **[Ercules: Jove]**

Almena is the medieval variant, used by Boccaccio in *Tes* IV.14.7; it occurs once medially, *Tr* III.1428.

Boccaccio, *Tutte le Opere*, ed. V. Branca, II: 357; Ovid, *Met*, ed. and trans. F.J. Miller, I: 22–25; *OM*, ed. C. de Boer, III, deel 30, no. 3: 246–249.

ALNATH is the alpha or brightest star of the constellation Aries in medieval star maps. The name is also given to the first mansion of the moon. Modern astronomers give the name to the beta or second brightest star of Taurus, in the tip of one horn. It is also the gamma or third brightest star of Auriga, the Charioteer, located in his left ankle, which overlaps with the horn of Taurus.

The magician from Orleans finds the moon's position by calculating the distance between Alnath in the head of Aries in the eighth sphere and the head of the fixed Aries above it in the ninth sphere or *primum mobile* above it, *FranklT* 1281–1284. **[Aries: Ram: Taur]**

The name is the ME variant of Arabic *al-nath*, the butting one, derived from the verb *nataha*, to butt with the horns.

R.A. Allen, *Star Names and their Meanings*, 80–81, 390; *Riverside Chaucer*, ed. L. Benson, 899.

ALOCEN. Abu 'Ali al-Hasan ibn-al-Haitham, known in Latin as *Alhazen* (c. A.D. 965, fl. 996–1002), was born in Basra and died in Cairo, c. 1039. His work on optics, *Kitab al-Manazir*, or *The Book of the Telescope*, was translated into Latin and greatly influenced medieval science, especially the work of Roger Bacon. His greatest contributions were on the subjects of spherical and parabolic mirrors, refraction, and the study of the atmosphere. He was the earliest user of *camera obscura*, "the dark chamber," the principle on which cameras function. The Polish physicist Witelo translated the work on optics, and a combined edition, *Alhazeni et Vitellonis Opticae (The Optics of Alhazen and Witelo)*, was printed in Basel in 1572.

The magic mirror, in which the future is reflected, reminds the people at Cambyuskan's court of Alocen, Vitulon, and Aristotle, who have written about mirrors, *SqT* 232. **[Aristotle: Vitulon]**

Alocen is the ME variant of Latin *Alhazen*, derived from the Arabic patronymic, *ibn-al-Haitham*. It appears medially, *SqT* 232.

Alhazen (ibn-al-Haytham). *De aspectibus*, ed. F. Risner; G. Sarton, *Introduction to the History of Science*, I: 721–722.

ALPHONSUS, PETRUS: [PIERS[2] ALFONCE]

ALYS[1]. Another name for Dame Alys's "gossib," Alison, *WBP* 548. [**Alisoun**[2]]

ALYS[2]. Another name for Dame Alison of Bath, *WBP* 320. [**Alisoun**[3]]

AL-ZARQALA: [ARSECHIEL(ES)]

AMBROSE (saint), c. A.D. 340–397, was born at Treves in north central Gaul and died in Milan. He studied law in Rome and was appointed governor of Ligures and Aemilia in A.D. 370. When Bishop Auxentius of Milan died, Ambrose was elected bishop, although he was not a priest, not even baptized. Consecrated in 374, he soon became one of the learned doctors of the church. He baptized Augustine of Hippo in his thirtieth year, while Augustine was in Milan as a teacher of rhetoric in 387. Several hymns of the western church are attributed to him, such as *Splendor Paternae*, hymns for the offices of Terce, Sext, None, and *Te Lucis Ante*. The spirits in Purgatory chant the beginning of the last hymn, *Purg* VIII.13–14. His treatise, *De virginitate (On Virginity)*, was widely read during the Middle Ages (*NCE* I: 373–375).

The Second Nun says that St. Ambrose is the source for the story of the two crowns in the *Legend of St. Cecilia, SNT* 271, referring perhaps to the mass for St. Cecilia's Day in the Ambrosian liturgy. The Parson quotes from Pseudo-Ambrose, *Sermo* XXV.1 in *ParsT* 84 (*PL* 17: 677). [**Augustine: Cecile**]

Dante, *Divine Comedy*, ed. and trans. C.S. Singleton, II, 1: 76–77; Jacobus de
    Voragine, *GL*, trans. G. Ryan and H. Ripperger, 24–33; *ibid.*, *LA*, ed. Th. Graesse,
    250–259; J.S.P. Tatlock, "St. Cecilia's Garlands and their Roman Origin." *PMLA*
    45 (1930): 169–170.

AMETE. Admetus, king of Pherae in Thessaly, succeeded in the seemingly impossible tasks set him by King Pelias and married the king's daughter, Alcestis. When his time came to die, he asked his old parents to die in his stead, and they refused. Then Alcestis offered herself, and he accepted. Persephone, Queen of the Underworld, would not accept Alcestis and sent her back to the light (Fulgentius, *Mythologies* I.22).

Pandarus mentions the daughter of King Amete, *Tr* I.659–665. Neither Ovid nor Boccaccio makes mention of this daughter. Chaucer may have learned of her from a gloss in Filippo Ceffi's Italian translation of *Heroides* V. [**Alceste**]

Amete is a variant of Italian *Ameto*, in Boccaccio's *Tes* vi.55.1.

Boccaccio, *Tutte le Opere*, ed. *V. Branca*, II: 437; Fulgentius, *Fulgentius the
    Mythographer*, trans. L. Whitbread, 62–63; *ibid.*, *Mythographi Latini*, ed. T.
    Munckerus, II: 62–64; S.B. Meech, "Chaucer and an Italian Translation of the
    Heroides." *PMLA* 45 (1930): 113.

AMPHIARAUS: [AMPHIORAX]
AMPHION: [AMPHIOUN]

AMPHIORAX. Amphiaraus was an Argive seer who married Eriphyle. He knew he would die if he accompanied Polynices to the siege of Thebes, so he hid when the latter came to fetch him. His wife, however, showed Polynices the hiding place in return for a golden necklace. Amphiaraus went reluctantly and was swallowed up by an earthquake (*Thebaid* IV.187–213; *Roman de Thèbes* 4711–4918).

Jankyn uses this story to illustrate the wickedness of wives, *WBP* 740–746. The manner of Amphiorax's death appears in *Anel* 5; *Tr* II.105. Criseyde calls him a "bisshop" because he was an augur, a term suggested perhaps by the French term *arcevesque*, archbishop, in *Roman de Thèbes*, 2276. Cassandra summarizes the story of the siege and of Amphiorax's death when she interprets Troilus's dream of the boar, *Tr* V.1485–1505. **[Adrastus: Clitermystra: Eryphylem: Phasipha]**

Amphiorax, the ME development of Latin *Amphiaraus,* is perhaps a variant pronunciation in *-x* in English for words where it represents etymologically an *-s* or *-us.* The final *-x* is also a French plural ending for singulars ending in *-u. Amphiorax* appears twice initially, *WBP* 741; *Tr* II.105; and twice medially, *Anel* 57; *Tr* V.1500.

Riverside Chaucer, ed. L. Benson, 814; *Roman de Thèbes*, ed. L. Constans, I: 230–241; *Roman de Thèbes (The Story of Thebes)*, trans. J.S. Coley, 111–115; Statius, *Thebaid*, ed. and trans. S.H. Mozley, I: 520–523.

AMPHIOUN. Amphion was the son of Jupiter and Antiope and the husband of Niobe. He became king of Thebes and built the walls of the city by the magic of his lyre (*Met* VI.177–183; *OM* VI.973–997).

Arcite bewails his predicament because now the royal house of Cadmus and Amphioun has been brought to confusion by his imprisonment, *KnT* 1545–1549. Not even the music of Amphioun and Orpheus can equal the music at Januarie's wedding, *MerchT* 1716. Amphioun, who built the walls of Thebes, cannot sing half as well as Phoebus, *MancT* 116–118. **[Nyobe: Tantale]**

Amphioun appears only in final rhyming position, *KnT* 1546; *MerchT* 1716; *MancT* 116.

Ovid, *Met*, ed. and trans. F.J. Miller, I: 300–301; *OM*, ed. C. de Boer, II, deel 21: 311–319.

ANAXAGORAS: [ANAXAGORE]

ANAXAGORE. Anaxagoras (c. 500–428 B.C.) was born in Clazomenae in Ionia and went to Athens about 460 B.C., where he became one of Pericles's tutors. His book *On Nature* was the first on solar eclipses; he held that Mind was the animating principle in the cosmic universe. During the war with Sparta Anaxagoras was charged for holding impious doctrines; since he had explained solar eclipses, they lost their religious significance. He was fined and left Athens for Lampsacus, where he established a school (Diogenes Laertius, II.7).

Lady Philosophy tells Boece that, if he does not know about Anaxagore's exile, of Socrates's poisoning, or of Zeno's torture, he has certainly heard of men like the followers of Seneca and of Canius, and of Soranus, *Bo* I, *Prosa* 3.53–59. **[Canyus: Seneca: Socrates: Soranas: Zeno]**
The form is the French variant, found in Jean de Meun's translation.

V.L. Dedeck-Héry, "Boethius' *De Consolatione* by Jean de Meun." *MS* 14 (1952): 175; Diogenes Laertius, *Lives of the Eminent Philosophers,* ed. and trans. R.D. Hicks, I: 134–145.

ANCHISES, ANCHYSES. Anchises was Aeneas's father and Venus's husband. Aeneas bore him on his back as they fled from burning Troy *(Aeneid* I.679–729). He died before they reached Italy. When Aeneas visited the underworld, he met his father's shade in a green valley, where Anchises showed him the spirits of their descendants, including Julius Caesar, and his son Iulus *(Aeneid* VI.679–702).

Anchises's flight with Eneas appears on the brass tablet in the temple of Venus, *HF* I.166–197. Eneas finds his father Anchyses in hell, *HF* II.440–444. Eneas bears Anchises on his back, *LGW* 943–944, in the brief prologue to Dido's story. Dido recognizes her guest, Eneas, as the son of Venus and Anchises, *LGW* 1086. **[Dido: Eneas: Venus³]**

Anchises never occurs initially; it appears once medially, *HF* I.171, and three times in final rhyming position, *HF* I.168, *LGW* 944, 1086. *Anchyses,* a spelling variant, occurs once, medially, *HF* I.442.

Virgil, *Aeneid,* ed. and trans. H.R. Fairclough, I: 340–343, 552–702.

ANDROGEOS: [ANDROGEUS]

ANDROGEUS was the son of Minos and Pasiphae, the king and queen of Crete. He was killed treacherously when he excelled at the Pan-Athenian Games *(Heroides* X.99).

Chaucer says that Androgeus was killed because of envy of his philosophical attainments, *LGW* 1894–1899. S.B. Meech points out that glosses on the *Metamorphoses* contributed to the medieval tradition that Androgeus's scholastic excellence brought about his death. Chaucer may have used the references in Geoffrey of Vinsauf, *Documentum de modo de arte dictandi et versificandi* I.2–8, as well. There is a short reference in Machaut, *Le jugement dou roy de Navarre,* 2702–2712. **[Adriane: Minos: Phasipha: Phedre: Theseus]**

E. Faral, *Les arts poétiques,* 265–266; Guillaume de Machaut, *Oeuvres,* ed. E. Hoepffner, I: 230; S.B. Meech, "Chaucer and the *Ovide Moralisé*—A Further Study." *PMLA* 46 (1931): 186–187; Ovid, *Her,* ed. and trans. G. Showerman, 128–129.

ANDROMACHA. Andromache, daughter of Eetion of Thebes, was Hector's wife and the mother of Astyanax.

Chauntecleer recalls Andromacha's dream of Hector's death, *NPT* 3141–3147. R.A. Pratt points out that his version closely follows that in *Renart le Contrefait* 31323–31340. Benoît gives a version in *Roman de Troie* 15263–15355; Dares summarizes the dream, *De excidio Troiae historia (The Fall of Troy, a History)*, 24. [Ector]

Andromacha occurs once, *NPT* 3141.

Benoît, *Roman de Troie*, ed. L. Constans, III: 20–26; Dares, *De excidio*, ed. F. Meister, 28–30; *ibid.*, *The Trojan War*, trans. R.M. Frazer, 152–153; R.A. Pratt, "Three Old French Sources of the Nonnes Preestes Tale." *Speculum* 47 (1972): 649.

ANDROMACHE: [ANDROMACHA]

ANELIDA, ANELYDA is the twenty-four-year-old queen of Ermony in Chaucer's fragment, *Anelida and Arcite*.

Anelida complains that Arcite's treachery has left her *mased* or confused: sometimes she complains, sometimes she is amused, a condition described in *Chaunte-pleure, Anel* 320–322. She refers to the thirteenth-century French poem, *La Pleurechante*, a moral poem. Of the fourteen manuscripts of this poem, three are of English origin.

Margaret Galway speculates that *Anelida* is derived from Joh-ann-a Lidd-el and identifies Anelida with Joan of Kent, thus connecting the poem with the court. Frederick Tupper connects the poem with Anne Welle, Countess of Ormonde, and makes Ermony a variant of Ormond.

The name appears in a variety of spellings in the earliest printed editions: *Analide, Anelyda, Annelada, Annelida. Anelida,* the form in the text of the *Riverside Chaucer*, occurs medially only, *Anel* 11, 49, 71, 139, 147, 167, 198, 204, 349, 351.

M. Galway, "Chaucer's Sovereign Lady: A Study of the Prologue to the *Legend* and Related Poems." *MLR* 33 (1938): 180–181; E.P. Hammond, *Chaucer: A Bibliographical Manual*, 356–357; P. Meyer, "Notice et Extraits du MS 8336 de la Bibliothèque de Sir Thomas Phillipps, No. 12." *Romania* 13 (1885): 510–511; F. Tupper, "Chaucer's Tale of Ireland." *PMLA* 36 (1921): 190.

ANNA: [ANNE]

ANNE[1]. Anna was Dido's sister and confidante. She advised Dido to accept Aeneas as lover since she had no husband and could not love Iarbus, the Gaetulian king *(Aeneid* IV.1–53).

Dido blames Anne for her suffering when Eneas secretly sails away, *HF* I.364–371; *LGW* 1343–1350. [Dido: Eneas]

The name appears twice in medial positions, *LGW* 1178, 1182; three times in final rhyming position, *HF* I.367, *LGW* 1168, 1343.

Virgil, *Aeneid*, ed. and trans. H.R. Fairclough, I: 396–399.

ANNE[2] (saint). Anne is the traditional name for the Virgin's mother. There is no scriptural or historical reference to the Virgin's parents; however, they are mentioned in the Apocryphal Gospels of Pseudo-Matthew, Protoevangelicon; the *Legenda Aurea* CCXXII gives a life of St. Anne.

St. Anne is the Virgin's mother in Chaucer's works. **[Marie[1]]**

The name occurs in final rhyming position, *MLT* 641; *FrT* 1613; *SNP* 70.

Jacobus de Voragine, no trans., in G. Ryan and H. Ripperger's edition; *ibid.*, *LA*, ed. Th. Graesse, 934–935; *The Middle English Stanzaic Versions of the Life of St. Anne*, ed. R.E. Parker; "The Protoevangelion," *Lost Books of the Bible*, 24–37; M.V. Ronan, *St. Anne: Her Cult and Her Shrines*.

ANSELM (saint), c. A.D. 1035–1109, was born at Aosta near Lombardy. He became a monk in 1060 at the Abbey of Bec, where he was later prior and abbot. He became Archbishop of Canterbury in 1093 but left in 1097 for Rome because of disputes with William Rufus. He remained in Rome until Henry I recalled him in 1100. He died at Canterbury in 1109, and his cult was known as early as 1165. Dante places him in the Heaven of the Sun, *Par* XII.137.

The Parson's paraphrase of Anselm's homily on the Last Judgment, *ParsT* 169, comes from *Meditatio Secunda* (*PL* 158: 724).

Dante, *Divine Comedy*, ed. and trans. C.S. Singleton, III, 1: 136–137; *The Life of St. Anselm, Archbishop of Canterbury, by Eadmer*, ed. and trans. R.W. Southern; R.W. Southern, *St. Anselm and his Biographer*; P. Toynbee, *A Dictionary of Proper Names . . . in the Works of Dante*, rev. C.S. Singleton, 41.

ANTEUS: [ANTHEUS]
ANTECLAUDIAN: [ALEYNE[2]]

ANTECRIST. Antichrist is God's adversary in *The Book of the Apocalypse*.

After pride, the sin of Lucifer and Antecrist, the worst sin is the sale of sacred things, *ParsT* 785–790.

Antecrist is the ME form.

R.K. Emmerson, *Antichrist in the Middle Ages: A Study of Medieval Apocalypticism, Art, and Literature*; *The Play of Antichrist*, trans. with introd. by J. Wright.

ANTENOR, ANTENORE, ANTHENOR. Antenor was the Trojan hero who betrayed Troy to the Greeks. Dictys of Crete, *Ephemeridos belli Troiani* IV.21–22, V.1–14, and Dares the Phrygian, *De excidio Troiae historia* 39–43, describe Antenor's treachery. Dante calls the second division of the Ninth Circle "Antenora," where traitors are punished, *Inf* XXXII.88.

The Man in Black says that, if he repents of his love, he would be worse than Anthenor, who betrayed Troy, *BD* 1117–1120. Antenor is a friend of the false Poliphete, *Tr* II.1466–1474. The Greeks capture him, in spite of the brave fighting of many Trojans, *Tr* IV.50–56. The Trojan Parliament decides to exchange Criseyde for Antenor, *Tr* IV.133–665, 792–795, 876–879. Criseyde says that when she returns in ten days' time Troilus would have won both Antenor and herself, *Tr* IV.1315–1316. Antenor returns and Troilus greets him, *Tr* V.71–77. Diomedes assures Criseyde that Calcas would not have exchanged Antenor for her had he not known that Troy would be destroyed, *Tr* V.904–987. **[Creseyde: Monesteo: Phebuseo: Polite: Polydamas: Rupheo: Santippe: Sarpedon: Troilus]**

The name never occurs initially. *Antenor* occurs fifteen times in medial positions, *Tr* I.1474, *Tr* IV.133, 137, 149, 177, 189, 196, 203, 212, 347, 378, 792, 878; *Tr* V.77, 905; *Antenore* appears once medially, *Tr* IV.1315, and once in final rhyming position, *Tr* IV.665; *Anthenor* appears once, in medial position, *BD* 1119.

Dante, *Divine Comedy*, ed. and trans. C.S. Singleton, I, 1: 344–345; Dares, *De excidio*, ed. F. Meister, 47–52; Dictys, *Ephemeridos*, ed. W. Eisenhut, 98–101; Dares Phrygius and Dictys Cretensis, *The Trojan War*, trans. R.M. Frazer, 100–102, 164–168.

ANTHEUS. Antaeus, the giant of Libya famous for his strength, prevailed against Hercules in their wrestling match as long as his feet touched the earth, his mother. Hercules heaved the giant into the air and held him aloft until his strength failed him; then he slew him (Lucan, *Pharsalia* IV.583–660). The giant is not to be confused with Antaeus the Latin, one of the foremost of Turnus's warriors, *Aeneid* X.561.

The slaying of Antheus is one of Hercules's feats, *MkT* 2108; *Bo* IV, *Metr* 7.50–52. **[Ercules]**

The form is the OF variant, in Jean de Meun's translation of Boethius.

V.L. Dedeck-Héry, "Boethius' *De Consolatione* by Jean de Meun," *MS* 14 (1952): 256; Lucan, *Pharsalia*, ed. and trans. J.D. Duff, 218–223; Virgil, *Aeneid*, ed. and trans. H.R. Fairclough, II: 208–209.

ANTHIOCHUS IV, called Epiphanes (c. 215–163 B.C.) became king of the Seleucid empire, including Syria and Judea, in 175 B.C. The Jews resisted his attempts to hellenize them and became nationalistic instead. Led by Judas Machabees, they revolted, and Antiochus sent out a force against them. Judas Machabees defeated the Roman generals, Nicanor and Timotheus, and the news was sent to Antiochus at Ecbatana. As Antiochus rushed off towards Jerusalem, his horses went out of control, and he was thrown from his chariot. Every bone in his body was broken, and his men had to carry him in a litter. Then he developed a strange disease and gave off a terrible smell of decay. The army deserted him and left him at Tabae in the Judaean mountains, where he died in 163 B.C. (II Maccabee, ix; *OCD*, 72)

The fall of Anthiochus is among the Monk's tragedies, *MkT* 2575–2630. **[Nichanore[2]: Thymothee[1]]**

Anthiochus occurs in final rhyming position, *MkT* 2575.

ANTICHRIST: [ANTECRIST]

ANTIGONE is Criseyde's niece who sings a song of love as she walks in the garden with Criseyde, Tharbe, and Flexippe, *Tr* II.813–875. This scene is Chaucer's invention; it does not appear in Boccaccio's *Il Filocolo* or *Il Filostrato*. Certain ideas and phrases in the song resemble Troilo's song in *Il Filostrato* III.73–89. Antigone and Tharbe accompany Criseyde to dinner at Deiphebus's house, *Tr* II.1562–1563, 1716. Antigone and nine or ten others accompany Criseyde to supper at Pandarus's house, *Tr* III.596–598. **[Creseyde: Flexippe: Tharbe]**

Antigone appears twice initially, *Tr* II.879, 1563; twice in medial positions, *Tr* II.824, 887; and three times in final rhyming position, *Tr* II.816, 1716; *Tr* III.597.

M.C. Borthwick, "Antigone's Song as 'Mirour' in Chaucer's *Troilus and Criseyde*." *MLQ* 22 (1961): 227–235; K. Young, *The Origin and Development of the Story of Troilus and Criseyde,* 173–175.

ANTILOCHUS: [ANTYLEGYUS]

ANTIOCHUS, the king, developed an incestuous passion for his daughter in the romance, *Apollonius of Tyre*. Gower tells his version in *Confessio Amantis* VII.271–2008.

The Man of Law says that Chaucer has not told this story, *MLI* 81–88, and gives a brief summary. The detail that Antiochus threw his daughter 'upon the pavement' is not in Gower's version of the story. **[Gower: Tyro Appollonius]**

The name occurs in final rhyming position, *MLI* 82.

John Gower, *The Complete Works,* ed. G.C. Macaulay, III: 393–440; *Riverside Chaucer,* ed. L. Benson, 856.

ANTONINUS: [ANTONYUS]

ANTONIUS, ANTONY[1]. Marcus Antonius (c. 82–30 B.C.), one of Rome's greatest generals, ruined his career through his affair with Cleopatra, queen of Egypt. Octavius Caesar, his rival for power in the Roman world, turned Antony's infatuation to his advantage and defeated him at the Battle of Actium in 31 B.C. (Suetonius, *The Deified Augustus*).

The death of Antonius appears on the walls of Mars's temple, *KnT* 2031–2039. This short passage, like *MLT* 197–203, is a reworking of a passage in Bernard Silvester's *Megacosmos*. Antonius is a senator sent by Rome to conquer towns and kingdoms in *The Legend of Cleopatra*. He falsely leaves his wife, Cesar's sister, and makes Cleopataras his wife. This action causes Octavian's war against Antony, who loses the war and stabs himself through the heart in despair. Boccaccio's Antonius is a pawn in Cleopatra's games of love and conquest; he gives her kingdoms in return for her love, *De claris mulieribus,* LXXXVI. Chaucer may have also used Vincent of Beauvais as a source for the story of Antony's death. [**Cesar²: Cleopataras: Octavyan**]

Antonius appears once initially, *LGW* 629; twice in medial positions, *LGW* 588, 684; and once in final rhyming position, *KnT* 2032. *Antony* appears once initially, *LGW* 652; three times in medial positions, *LGW* 625, 657, 701, never in final rhyming position.

P. Aiken, "Chaucer's *Legend of Cleopatra* and the *Speculum Historiale.*" *Speculum* 13 (1938): 232–236; Bernard Silvester, *Megacosmos,* ed. C.S. Barach and J. Wrobel, 16; Boccaccio, *De claris mulieribus,* ed. V. Zaccaria, 344–356; *ibid., CFW,* trans. G. Guarino, 192–197; Suetonius, *De vita Caesarum,* ed. and trans. J.C. Rolfe, 123–287.

ANTONY² (saint), c. A.D. 251–356, was born in Egypt and is said to have died in the Egyptian desert. He is regarded as the founder of eastern monasticism *(NCE* I: 594–596).

In his homily on *Superbia,* the Parson describes the medieval fashion of the tight codpiece, made of two colors to emphasize the shape and size of the "privee members" in such a way as to suggest that the private parts are swollen with the "fir of Seint Antony," *ParsT* 425–428. This image refers to the disease called "erysipelas," an acute eruption of the skin, marked by spreading inflammation. An epidemic of erysipelas broke out in the Dauphiné during the thirteenth century, and the sick were tended by the monks of St. Antony. Afterwards the disease was known as St. Antony's fire.

The saint appears only once, *ParsT* 425.

Athanasius, *Vita Sancti Antonini, PG* 26: 835–978; *PL* 73: 125–170; *ibid., La plus ancienne version Latine de la vie de S. Antoine;* Jacobus de Voragine, *GL,* trans. G. Ryan and H. Ripperger, 99–103; *ibid., LA,* ed. Th. Graesse 104–107; François Villon, *The Complete Works,* ed. J. Nicolson, 256–258.

ANTONYUS. Septimus Severus renamed his first son, Julius Bassianus, Marcus Aurelius Antoninus in A.D. 195, when the child was seven years old, thus borrowing for his son the names of the famous Antonine emperor. Because he wore a Gallic cloak called a *caracallus,* the soldiers called the boy Caracalla. His reign, A.D. 211–217, was marked by brutality. Spartianus Aelius tells that Caracalla ordered his soldiers to cut Papinianus, the noted jurist, into pieces *(Scriptores historiae Augustae* IV.i).

Lady Philosophy recalls such instances of imperial brutality, *Bo* III, *Prosa* 5.49–51. [**Papynian**]

Scriptores historiae Augustae, ed. and trans. D. Magie, II: 11.

ANTYLEGYUS. Antilochus accompanied Achilles to Apollo's temple, where they expected to meet Polyxena, whom Achilles expected to marry there. Instead, they met the Trojans, who slew them. The incident appears in Dares, *De excidio Troiae historia* 34, and Benoît, *Roman de Troie* 21838–22334.

The Man in Black tells how Achilles and Antylegyus were slain in a temple in revenge for Hector's death, as narrated by Dares Phrygius, *BD* 1069–1070. [**Achilles: Dares Frygius: Ector: Polixena**]

The form is a Chaucerian variant and occurs in final rhyming position, *BD* 1069.

Benoît, *Roman de Troie*, ed. Constans, III: 373–399; Dares Phrygius, *De excidio*, ed. F. Meister, 40–42; *ibid.*, *The Trojan War*, trans. R.M. Frazer, 160–161.

APELLES, a painter, flourished in the fourth century B.C. in Colophon and Ephesus. The Elder Pliny says that he surpassed all painters who preceded him and all who were to come after him. His superiority was acknowledged in his own lifetime by the public and by other painters. His Aphrodite Anadyomene (rising from the sea) was said to be an extraordinary work. Pliny lists several allegorical paintings featuring Alexander the Great (*NH* XXXV.xxxvi.79–97).

Nature boasts that not even Pigmalion, Apelles, or Zanzis could challenge her creation, Virginia, *PhysT* 16–18. In *RR* 16149–16183, the poet says that Pigmalion, Apelles, and Zeuzis have all failed to portray the form of Nature. [**Pigmalion: Zanzis**]

Apelles occurs initially, with initial stress on the vowel, *PhysT* 16.

Pliny, *NH*, ed. and trans. H. Rackham, IX: 318–333; *RR*, ed. E. Langlois, IV: 135–136; *RR*, trans. C. Dahlberg, 273–274.

APIUS. Apius Claudius felt savage lust for Verginia, a maiden who lived with her father Verginius. He hired a villain, Marcus Claudius, to swear in his court that Verginia was Claudius's slave, taken from him by Verginius. Apius intended to award Verginia to Claudius, who would then give her to Apius (Livy, *Ab urbe condita liber* III.xliv-lviii). Livy places the story in 449 B.C. Jean de Meun tells the story to illustrate that judges too often commit outrages: Appius hires a sergeant, Claudius, to lie in court that Virginia is his slave, *RR* 5589–5634. Gower's version shows Apius as governor and king of Rome; he plots with his brother Marcus Claudius to summon Virginia to court while her father fights at the front, *Confessio Amantis*, VII.5131–5306.

Chaucer follows Livy and Jean de Meun in making Apius a judge in *The Physician's Tale*. The people imprison him after Virginia's death, and he slays himself. [**Claudius: Livius: Virginia: Virginius**]

The form *Apius* indicates a long initial vowel, in contrast with Livy's *Appius*, where the doubled consonant indicates a short initial vowel. The name never occurs initially; it appears three times in medial positions,

PhysT 128, 227, 267; and four times in final rhyming position, *PhysT* 154, 204, 265, 270.

John Gower, *The Complete Works,* ed. G.C. Macaulay, III: 377–382; Livy, *Ab urbe condita libri,* ed. and trans. B.O. Foster, II: 142–199; *RR,* ed. E. Langlois, II: 263–265; *RR,* trans. C. Dahlberg, 114.

APOLLO, APOLLOO, APPOLLO. Phoebus Apollo, son of Leto and Jupiter, twin brother of Artemis/Diana, was the quintessential Greek god. He slew Python, the immense dragon of Delphi, and established his oracle there. Thus he assumed the title *Delphicus.* His priestess at Delphi, known as "Pythoness," prophesied through divination as she sat in a trance. Apollo fell in love with Daphne, but she fled from him; as he gained on her, she appealed to her father Peneus to save her, and she became a laurel tree. Thereafter, Apollo adopted the laurel as his emblem (*Met* I.452–567; *OM* I.2737–3064). Apollo is also god of prophecy, medicine, archery, and music (*Etym* VIII.xi.53). Petrus Berchorius describes Apollo as a youth of marriageable age. In one hand Apollo carries a bow, arrows, and quiver; in the other, a cithar (a stringed instrument). He is pictured with the huge, monstrous serpent he had decapitated (*De formis figurisque deorum,* fol. 4ᵛ a. 29–31, 43–45). Marsyas, a satyr of Phrygia, challenged Apollo to a musical contest. Apollo agreed but stipulated that each should be able to play his instrument upside down. Since Apollo played the lute and Marsyas the flute, Apollo won; then he flayed Marsyas alive for his insolence (*Met* VI.382–400; *OM* VI.1921–1980).

The Dreamer invokes Apollo as god of science and light, *HF* III.1092–1109, inspired by Dante, *Par* I.13–27. Marsia lost her skin because she undertook to pipe better than Apolloo, *HF* III.1229–1232. Here Chaucer follows a tradition in which Marsyas is feminine. *Marse* appears in an interpolation of forty lines in several manuscripts of the *Roman de la Rose,* 10830–10831. Calcas is the priest of Appollo Delphicus, *Tr* I.70–72. Criseyde calls Apollo "stoon of sikerness," rock of certainty, *Tr* II.843. The laurel quakes when the god answers Troilus, *Tr* III.540–546; Chaucer is the only poet to make Apollo speak from the tree. Appollo has told Calcas that Troy will fall, *Tr* IV.113–119. Criseyde intends to enchant her father so much that he will pay no attention to Appollo's *amphibologies* or ambiguities, *Tr* IV.1394–1407. In his agony, Troilus curses Apollo, *Tr* V.207–209, 1853.

Apollo is also the name for the planet Sol (*Etym* VIII.xi.53).

Aurelius appeals to Appollo as the sun, *FranklT* 1031–1043, whose declination or latitude changes from day to day. Apollo appears in an unfinished astrological periphrasis, which states the time, *SqT* 671–672. Apollo is also the sun, *MLI* 7–15, *MerchT* 2220–2224; *SqT* 48–51, 263–267; *FranklT* 124512–124548; *PhysT* 37–38; *MkT* 2745–2746, and throughout *Boece* and *Troilus and Criseyde.* **[Dane: Marcia: Phebus]**

Apollo occurs twice initially, *SqT* 671; *HF* III.1092; four times in medial positions, *Tr* II.842; *Tr* III.541, 543, 546; *Apolloo*, with extra long final vowel occurs in final rhyming position, *HF* III.1232; *Appollo* occurs once initially, *Tr* IV.114; five times in medial positions, *FranklT* 1031; *Tr* I.70; *Tr* IV.1397; *Tr* V.207, 1853; and once in final rhyming position, *Tr* I.72.

Petrus Berchorius, *Reductorium morale, Liber XV: Ovidius moralizatus,* ed. J. Engels, 17; Dante, *Divine Comedy,* ed. and trans. C.S. Singleton, III.1:14–17; A. David, "How Marcia Lost her Skin: A Note on Chaucer's Mythology." *The Learned and the Lewed,* ed. L.D. Benson, 19–29; Isidore, *Etymologiae,* ed. W.M. Lindsay, I; Ovid, *Met,* ed. and trans. F.J. Miller, I: 34–43, 314–317; *OM,* ed. C. de Boer, I, deel 15: 120–126; II, deel 21: 330–332; *RR,* ed. E. Langlois, III: 305–307; *RR,* trans. C. Dahlberg, 392.

APOLLONIUS OF TYANA: [BALLENUS]
APOLLONIUS OF TYRE: [TYRO APOLLONIUS]

APPELLES was a Jewish artist who designed and built a tomb for Satira, wife of Darius. At Alexander's command, he made a tomb for Darius also (Gautier de Châtillon, *Alexandreis* IV.176–274; VII.379–430).

Alys of Bath says that her fourth husband's tomb was not as elaborate as the tomb Appelles made for Darius, *WBP* 497–499. **[Alisoun³: Darius²]**.

Appelles occurs medially, *WBP* 499; the doubled consonants indicate a short preceding vowel.

Gautier de Châtillon, *Alexandreis,* ed. Mueldner, 84–87, 163–165.

AQUARIUS, the constellation the Water Carrier, is the eleventh sign of the zodiac, lies in the southern hemisphere between Capricorn and Pisces, and is the night house of Saturn *(Tetrabiblos* I.17, 29).

Aquarius is one of the signs of the zodiac, *Astr* I.8. It lies directly opposite Leo, *Astr* II.6.17, and obeys the sovereign or western sign Scorpio, *Astr* II.28.38. **[Scorpio]**

Ptolemy, *Tetrabiblos,* ed. and trans. F.E. Robbins, 81.

AQUILON: [EOLUS]
ARCHEMORUS: [ARCHYMORIS]

ARCHYMORIS. Archemorus was the infant son of Lycurgus, king of Nemea. When the Seven Chieftains were marching toward Thebes, they stopped at Nemea, and the infant's nurse left him alone to guide the warriors to a spring. While she was gone, a serpent killed the infant. The Seven gave him a splendid funeral *(Thebaid* V.499–679; *Roman de Thèbes* 2083–2630).

Cassandra summarizes the story when she interprets Troilus's dream of the boar, *Tr* V.1497–1505.

Archymoris is the Latin genitive singular. It appears once, *Tr* V.1499.

Roman de Thèbes, ed. L. Constans, I: 106–131; *Roman de Thèbes (The Story of Thebes)*, trans. J.S. Coley, 49–62; Statius, *Thebaid*, ed. and trans. J.H. Mozley, II: 38–53.

ARCITA, ARCITE is the young knight in *The Knight's Tale* and *Anelida and Arcita*. In *The Knight's Tale* Arcita falls in love with Emily; in *Anelida and Arcita* he loves and betrays Anelida.

Arcita is very much like Palamon, his cousin and 'felawe' or close friend, in *The Knight's Tale*. Theseus imprisons both knights after he has defeated Creon, but Arcita breaks out of prison on the third of May. Like Palamon, he has fallen in love with Emily, the young Amazon who is Theseus's sister-in-law. Returning to Thebes, Arcita suffers from *hereos* or love-sickness, and he returns to Athens after a year or two, taking the name Philostrate, which means "destroyed by love." By then, Palamon has also broken out of prison, and he encounters Arcita on May Day, as he observes May Day ceremonies in the woods. The two fight over Emelie. Here Theseus finds them up to their ankles in blood and decrees a tournament for the love of Emelye. Arcita is devoted to Mars, and Theseus builds an altar and oratory to the god in his honor. Here Arcita prays for victory in the tournament, and he wins. Saturn sends a fury from Pluto's realm to frighten Arcita's horse, and Arcita falls. He dies later from his injuries, and thus he loses his life and Emelye. W.C. Curry points out that Chaucer follows medieval astrology in building Arcita's character as a personality influenced by Mars. In *Anelida and Arcite* the hero is no longer faithful in love but causes the young queen Anelida great distress; he is portrayed as "the fals Arcite." [**Anelida: Argus[1]: Emelie: Mars: Palamon: Philostrate**]

Chaucer took the name from Boccaccio's *Il Teseide delle Nozze d'Emilia*; Boccaccio, in his turn, may have found the name in the Byzantine epic, *Digenis Akritas,* where the name *Akrites* is a Byzantine designation of knights who defended their country against the Muslims. The form *Arcita* occurs eleven times, only in *The Knight's Tale,* always in medial positions, *KnT* 1013, 1281, 1336, 1497, 2155, 2256, 2258, 2421, 2424, 2428, 2761. *Arcite* occurs seven times in *The Knight's Tale* with initial stress on the second syllable and elided final -e, thus giving the word two syllables, *KnT* 1116, 1628, 2368, 2436, 2582, 2658, 2815; thirty-one times in medial positions, sometimes with final syllabic -e, sometimes without, depending on the stresses in the line to even out the meter, *KnT* 1080, 1112, 1126, 1145, 1152, 1211, 1276, 1344, 1348, 1355, 1393, 1488, 1525, 1528, 1540, 1580, 1596, 1627, 1636, 1698, 1791, 2315, 2676, 2688, 2705, 2743, 2855, 2858, 2939, 2951, 3059; nineteen times in final rhyming position, *KnT* 1031, 1202, 1210, 1333, 1379, 1449, 1519, 1557, 1657, 1724, 1871, 2094, 2628, 2633, 2639, 2673, 2742, 2873, 2891. The name occurs once initially in *Anelida and Arcite, Anel* 333; it appears nine times in medial positions, *Anel* 91, 106, 140, 141, 155, 168, 179, 323, 349; and seven times in final rhyming position, with silent final -e, Anel

11, 49, 109, 175, 198, 210, 264. "The Love of Palamon and Arcite," *LGW F* 420, *LGW G* 408, appears in a short list of Chaucer's works and is a reference to *The Knight's Tale.*

W.C. Curry, *Chaucer and the Mediaeval Sciences,* 121–124, 131–134; R.L. Hoffmann, "Two Notes on Chaucer's Arcite." *ELN* 4 (1967): 172–175; H. and R. Kahane, "Akritas and Arcita: A Byzantine Source of Boccaccio's *Teseide.*" *Speculum* 20 (1945): 415–425; D. Metlitzki, *MAME,* 145; H. Savage, "Arcite's Maying." *MLN* 55 (1940): 207–209.

ARCTOUR, ARCTURUS is the alpha or brightest star of the constellation Artophylax or the Bear Driver, lying at the North Pole. The name was applied to the whole constellation as early as Hesiod *(Works and Days,* 564–567).

Boethius comments on the regularity of the seasons of the year: the seeds sown when Arcturus shines grow into tall crops under the heat of Sirius, *Bo* I, *Metr* 5.27. He who does not know how the stars of Arctour move near the pole of heaven will wonder at the law of high heaven, *Bo* IV, *Metr* 5.2. [**Boëtes: Syrius: Ursa**]

Both forms occur only in the *Boece.*

R.A. Allen, *Star Names and their Meanings,* 98; Hesiod, *Complete Works,* ed. and trans. H.G. Evelyn-White, 44–45.

ARGONAUTYCON: [VALERIUS FLACCUS]
ARGIA: [ARGYVE²]

ARGUS¹. Argos Panoptes, "all-eyed Argus," was so called because of his hundred eyes. Juno set him to guard Io, Jupiter's mistress, whom Jupiter had changed into a heifer to protect her from Juno's wrath. Argos tied her with a halter and fed her with bitter herbs. Jupiter decided to release Io from her torment. He commanded Mercury to slay Argos, an almost impossible task since the hundred eyes were never all closed at the same time. Mercury, however, charmed Argos to sleep with his magic wand and his flute music. When all the eyes were closed, he beheaded Argos and escaped with Io. Juno placed the eyes in the tail of her favorite bird, the peacock *(Met* I.668–723; *OM* I.3448–3752). The watchfulness of the hundred eyes became proverbial.

Mercury, dressed as he was when he slew Argus, appears to Arcite, *KnT* 1389–1390; that is, he wears his magic cap and his winged sandals and carries his magic wand. Not even Argus with his hundred eyes can keep watch on Alys, *WBP* 358. Despite his hundred eyes, with which he could examine closely and pry into matters, Argus was blinded, *MerchT* 2111. Troilus calls Calcas "Argus-eyed," *Tr* IV.1459. [**Alisoun³: Arcita: Mercurie**]

R.L. Hoffman, "Mercury, Argus, and Chaucer's Arcite: *Canterbury Tales* I (A), (1384–1390)." *N&Q* 210 (1965): 128–129; *ibid.,* "Ovid's Argus and Chaucer." *N&Q*

12 (1965): 213–216; Ovid, *Met*, ed. and trans. F.J. Miller, I: 48–53; *OM*, ed. C. de Boer, I, deel 15: 135–141.

ARGUS² was the Thespian who built the ship Argo for Jason and his companions, called the "Argonauts" *(Argonauticon* I.91–99).
Argus builds ships for Jason, *LGW* 1453. **[Jason]**
The name appears once.

Valerius Flaccus, *Argonauticon*, ed. and trans. J.H. Mozley, 11.

ARGUS³. Muhammad ibn-Musa al-Khwarizmi (fl. c. 840) wrote a series of astronomical tables. About 1126 Adelard of Bath, working from the Spanish versions, produced a Latin version of al-Khwarizmi's astronomical tables, and about 1149 Robert of Ketton revised Adelard's version, turning into Latin many Arabic words retained in the text. Al-Khwarizmi's work, *Hisab al-Djabr wa 'l-Mukabala*, was translated by Gerard of Cremona between 1176 and 1187 with the Latin title *Al-Goritmi de numero indorum*, or *The Book of Addition and Subtraction*. The word *al-djabr* of the Arabic title gives us our word *algebra*.
The passage mentioning Argus, the noble counter, *BD* 434–442, is a paraphrase of *RR* 12790–12810.
Chaucer's *Argus* is derived from OF *Algus*. The French variant is derived from *algorism*, a development of *al-Khwarizmi*, which means in Arabic the Khwarizmian or the man from Khwarizmi. Nicholas has placed his *augrim* or arithmetic stones, marked with the numerals of *algorism*, neatly spaced on shelves above his bed's heads, *MillT* 3210. *Nombres in augrim*, or arithmetic numbers, appear in *Astr* I.9.3. **[Gerard of Cremona: Nicholas¹]**

al-Khwarizmi, *The Astronomical Tables of al-Khwarizmi*, ed. H. Suter; *EI*, II: 912–913; C.H. Haskins, *Studies in the History of Medieval Science*, 22–23, 122–123; L.C. Karpinsky, "Robert of Chester's Latin Translation of the *Algebra* of al-Khowarizmi." *Contributions to the History of Science*, 1–164; E.S. Kennedy and Walid Ukashah, "Al-Khwarizmi's Planetary Latitude Tables." *Centaurus* 14 (1969): 86–96; *RR*, ed. E. Langlois, III: 256–257; *RR*, trans. C. Dahlberg, 222.

ARGYVE¹ is the name of Criseyde's mother, *Tr* IV.762.
Neither Boccaccio nor Benoît mentions a mother for Criseyde.
Chaucer may have taken the name from Statius's *Thebaid* V.1509. Susan Schibanoff suggests that medieval etymology linked *Argia/Argyve* with a synonym for *providentia*. It is thus a *redendnama*, or "speaking name," which reveals the character of the person named. **[Calcas: Criseyde]**

S. Schibanoff, "Argus and Argive: Etymology and Characterization in Chaucer's *Troilus*." *Speculum* 51 (1976): 647–658.

ARGYVE². Argia was the daughter of Adrastus, king of Argos. She married Polynices, Oedipus's son. When Eteocles refused to give up the

Theban throne to Polynices, Adrastus gathered an army together to besiege the city on behalf of his son-in-law (*Thebaid* V).

Cassandra tells of Argyve's distress and her weeping at her husband's death, *Tr* V.1509. [**Adrastus: Polymyte**]

Argyves is the ME genitive case. *Argyvam,* Latin accusative of *Argyva,* appears in a stanza inserted in the *Troilus* manuscript; *Argia* appears in one of the Latin arguments of the *Thebaid.* Chaucer may have derived the name from either form.

F.P. Magoun, Jr., "Chaucer's Summary of Statius's *Thebaid* II–XII." *Traditio* 11 (1955): 418; *Riverside Chaucer,* ed. L. Benson, 1177; Robinson, 912; Statius, *Thebaid,* ed. and trans. J.H. Mozley, II: 2–59.

ARIADNE: [ADRIANE]

ARIES, ARIETE. Aries, the constellation the Ram and the first sign of the zodiac, is the hot and dry sign and the night house of Mars (*Confessio Amantis* VII.989–992). It is the starting point of the zodiac, since the sun enters Aries at the spring equinox—March 12 in Chaucer's day, March 21 in modern times—and creates excessive moisture and the rains of spring. It is the exaltation or sign of maximum power of the sun and the depression or sign of minimum power of Saturn (*Tetrabiblos* I.19). It lies in the northern hemisphere near Taurus, exactly opposite Libra.

Phebus, the sun, is just past his exaltation or point of greatest influence in Aries, the choleric, hot sign, also known as the "mansion" or first face of Mars, on Cambyuskan's birthday, *SqT* 48–51. It is March 15, three days after March 12, the spring equinox. The magician finds the moon's position by calculating the distance between Alnath in the head or the beginning of Aries in the eighth sphere and the ninth sphere above it, *FranklT* 1281–1284. Criseyde promises Troilus that she will return before the moon passes out of Aries beyond Leo, *Tr* IV.1590–1593. The moon passes through Taurus, Gemini, Cancer, and Leo in nine days' time. Criseyde thus promises to return on the tenth day. The heads or beginnings of Aries and Libra turn on the equinoctial circle; when the sun enters the heads of Aries and Libra, moving northward, the days and nights are of equal length, *Astr* I.17.16–28. To calculate the tide on March 12, 1391 (Chaucer's date), the astrolabe is turned over; then the rete or topmost plate is allowed to revolve westward until the first point of Aries is just within the altitude circle marked 25, *Astr* II.3.23–25. Every degree of Aries is set directly opposite every degree of Libra when one is calculating dawn and twilight in the spring, *Astr* II.6.14–15. The longitude of a celestial body is measured in the ecliptic, from the beginning of Aries to the end of Pisces, *Astr* II.17.23–25. The difference between the meridian altitudes of a given degree of any sign of the zodiac and of the first point of Aries is the declination or latitude of that degree,

Astr II.20, 22, 25. Aries is a northern sign; since it is also an eastern sign, it is an "obedient" one and obeys Virgo in the west, *Astr* II.28.27. The sun never rises due east unless it is in the head or beginning of Aries or Libra, *Astr* II.31.3–6. **[Libra: Ram]**

Ariete is the Italian form.

John Gower, *Complete Works*, ed. G.C. Macaulay, III: 259–260; Ptolemy, *Tetrabiblos*, ed. and trans. F.E. Robbins, 61, 81, 89; W.W. Skeat, II: 494.

ARION: [ORION]

ARIONIS HARPE. Arion's Harp is the constellation Lyra, lying in the northern hemisphere, partly in the Milky Way.

The learned eagle points out the constellation to the frightened dreamer as they fly by, *HF* II.1000–1006. Gower uses Arion's harping as a trope for peacemaking, *Confessio Amantis, Prol.* 1054—1088. **[Orion]**

Arionis is the Latin genitive singular of *Arion*.

John Gower, *Complete Works*, ed. G.C. Macaulay, II: 33–34.

ARISTOCLIDES, tyrant of Orchomenos, had a passion for the maiden Stymphalides. On the night her father was murdered, Stymphalides, fearing the tyrant, fled to Diana's temple and clung to the altar, where she was slain. Jerome includes her in his list of virtuous pagan women, *Epistola adversus Jovinianum (Letter Against Jovinian)* I.41 (*PL* 23: 272).

Aristoclides the tyrant appears as the villain, *FranklT* 1387–1394. Chaucer does not make quite clear his part in the story. **[Stymphalides]**

The form of the name is the Greek patronymic and occurs in final rhyming position, *FranklT* 1387.

G. Dempster, "Chaucer at Work on the Complaint in the *Franklin's Tale*." *MLN* 52 (1937): 16–23; K. Hume, "The Pagan Setting of the *Franklin's Tale* and the Sources of Dorigen's Cosmology." *SN* 44 (1972): 289–294.

ARISTOTILE, ARISTOTLE. Aristotle of Stagira, 384–322 B.C., was the son of Nicomachus, physician to Amyntas II, king of Macedonia. He was Plato's pupil from 367 until Plato's death in 347 B.C. In that year Philip destroyed Stagira, and in 342 he invited Aristotle to Macedonia to become Alexander's tutor. When Alexander started out for Persia in 335, Aristotle returned to Athens, where he opened a school of philosophy and natural sciences. He was charged with impiety after Alexander's death in 323 and left Athens. He died in Chalcis the following year at the age of sixty-three (Diogenes Laertius V.i).

Medieval scholars knew a number of Aristotle's works. Michael Scot (c. 1175–c. 1235) translated from Arabic into Latin at Toledo, before 1220, the *Liber animalium (The Book of Animals)*, *De caelo et mundo (On the*

Heavens), and *De anima (On the Soul)* from ibn-Rushd's commentaries. At the same time, Alfredus Anglicus did a version of three chapters forming an appendix of the fourth book of the *Meteorology*, translated from ibn-Sina's Arabic *Shifa*, or *The Healing*. Alfred's translation of *On Plants* was the only Latin version known in the West. Gerard of Cremona did a version of *The Physics* and the *Posterior Analytics* in the twelfth century. Alexander Neckham used Michael Scot's translation of *Liber animalium* in his *De natura rerum*, completed in 1217. Medieval scholars thus knew more of Aristotle than of Plato, and Dante termed him *il maestro di color che sanno*, the master of those who know (*Inf* IV.131). Aristotle was so popular that he was identified simply as "the Philosopher." But the Arab elements in the Latin translations of his works were soon found to be irreconcilable with Christian doctrine, and the Paris Council forbade the teaching of Aristotle's works on natural philosophy in 1210. The prohibition was extended to the *Metaphysics* in 1215. Pope Gregory clarified the ban in 1231, but the statutes of the Faculty of the University of Paris mention several works as subjects for examinations in 1254. The prohibition did not extend further than Paris. Aristotelian studies flourished at Toulouse, and the *Parva naturalia*, a collection of essays on the senses and on sleep and dreams, was a prescribed text in the arts curriculum at Oxford after 1340.

The Clerk would rather have twenty books of Aristotle than fiddle and psaltery, *Gen Prol* 293–296, a collection that would have included texts with commentaries. The cost of such a library would have been forty pounds in medieval currency and about $8,000 in modern money. The magic mirror, which the strange knight presents to Cambyuskan, reminds the courtiers of Aristotle, who wrote on mirrors, *SqT* 232–235, a reference to Aristotle's *Physics*. Dante mentions this work in *Inf* XI.101. Aristotle and Plato are mentioned as writers on the law stating that every object has a natural place that it tries to reach, *HF* II.757–764, the medieval explanation of the law of gravity. The passage probably refers to Aristotle's *Physics*, VIII.3, 4. The definition of sound, *HF* II.765–781, is a possible rendering of a similar theory found in St. Thomas Aquinas's commentary on Aristotle's *On the Soul* II.viii.445–446. Aristotle appears as a source for the idea that if men had eyes like the lynx, they would be able to preceive things hidden from mortal eyes, *Bo* III, *Prosa* 8.40. Pindar's *Nemean Ode* X.61 tells the story of Lynceus, who was famous for his keen eyesight, and perhaps Boethius means Lynceus and not the lynx. No source for this idea has been found in Aristotle. Lady Philosophy discusses final cause and chance, *Bo* V; *Prosa* 1.62, and gives a brief summary of Aristotle's *Physics*, II.4–5. Lady Philosophy also quotes Aristotle, *Bo* V, *Prosa* 6.30, on the eternity of the world from *On the Heavens (De caelo)* I.279B: the world never began and it will never cease. Aristotle here reverses the opinions of two previous philosophers, Empedocles and Heraclitus. The lines "Vertu is the mene/As Etik says," *LGW F* 165–166, seem to refer to the *Nichomachean Ethics*, in which

Aristotle discusses happiness and virtue. Gower refers to Aristotle's advice to Alexander to keep the mean between avarice and prodigality (*Confessio Amantis* VII.2025–2057), another possible reference in contemporary writing to the *Ethics*. John Norton-Smith shows that Chaucer could have known Aristotle's *Ethics* in at least five versions in Latin, several Latin and vernacular adaptations, and one good complete translation in Old French. Robert Grosseteste did the first Latin translation of all ten books of the *Vetus Translatio* of the *Ethics* c. 1245, and Walter Burley wrote a commentary between 1340 and 1345, which Chaucer could have known. The *Ethics* could also be found in summary and verbatim quotations in Vincent of Beauvais, *Speculum Doctrinale* IV.x.xvi.

Much of Aristotle's work on dreams, memory and recollection, sleeping, and waking in his *Parva naturalia* appear in ibn-Sina's *Qanun*, or *Canon*; *On Dreams* III is paraphrased in ibn-Sina's *Commentary on the Soul,* and in Vincent of Beauvais, *Speculum naturale*, XXVI.i. If Chaucer was not familiar with the *Parva naturalia* itself, he could have become acquainted with its ideas from Vincent of Beauvais, for he seems to have known other aspects of Vincent's work. The Squire's definition of sleep as "the norice of digestion," *SqT* 347, appears in *On Sleeping and Waking* III. Pertelote says that when humors are abundant in a man, the fumes of overeating determine the images that appear in dreams, *NPT* 2923–2925; this notion echoes *On Dreams* III. Pertelote remarks that some dreams are caused by melancholy, which produces black images in sleep, *NPT* 2933–2936; Aristotle says that dreams are morbid in the melancholic, the feverish, and the intoxicated, *On Dreams* III. The dream that follows the narrator's reading of Africanus is caused by his activity during waking hours, *i.e.*, his reading of *The Dream of Scipio,* as well as by mental disturbance, *PF* 85–98. The "wery huntere" stanza that follows, inspired by Claudian's preface to *De raptu Proserpinae*, also illustrates Aristotle's definition of dreams: they are mental pictures arising from sense impressions during the day, *On Dreams* III, and some mental pictures that appear in sleep are associated with waking actions, *On Prophecy in Sleep* I. Pandarus says that Troilus's dream is produced by melancholy, *Tr* V.358–360; he asserts that some people say dreams come through impressions, having something in mind, *Tr* V.372–374, a paraphrase of Aristotle, that dreams are sense impressions occurring in sleep, *On Dreams* III. [**Alocen: Averrois: Avycen: Vitulon**]

Aristotile occurs in *Boece* V, *Prosa* 6.30, and the form suggests derivation through pronunciation; *Aristotle* occurs medially, *Gen Prol* 295; *SqT* 233; *HF* II.759, and in *Bo* III; *Prosa* 8.40; *Bo* V, *Prosa* 1.62.

P. Aiken, "Vincent of Beauvais and Dame Pertelote's Knowledge of Medicine." *Speculum* 10 (1935): 281–287; D.J. Allan, "Mediaeval Versions of Aristotle. *De caelo* and the Commentary of Simplicius." *Mediaeval and Renaissance Studies* 2 (1950): 82–120; Aristotle, *On the Soul*, ed. and trans. W.S. Hett; *ibid., Posterior Analytics,* ed. and trans. H. Tredennick; *ibid., On the Heavens,* ed. and trans. W.K.C. Guthrie; *ibid., Historia animalium*, ed. and trans. A.L. Peck; *ibid., Parva naturalia*, ed. and trans. W.S. Hett, 341, 363, 369, 379; J.A.W. Bennett, *Chaucer's Book of Fame*, 78–79; W.F. Boggess, "Aristotle's *Poetics* in the Fourteenth Century." *SP* 67 (1970): 278–294; R.R. Bolgar, *The Classical Heritage*, 179–181; Dante, *Divine Comedy*, ed. and trans. C.S. Singleton, I, 1, 42–43, 114–115; Diogenes Laertius, *Lives of the Eminent Philosophers*, ed. and trans. R.D. Hicks, I: 444–482; R.C. Fox, "Chaucer and Aristotle." *N&Q* 203 (1958): 523–524; John Gower, *Complete Works*, ed. G.C. Macaulay, III, 288; C.H. Haskins, *Studies in the History of Medieval Science*, 368; D. Metlitzki, *The Matter of Araby in Medieval England*, 40–41, 262, n. 157; J. Norton-Smith, *Geoffrey Chaucer*, 253–254, n. 18; F.E. Peters, *Aristotles Arabus*, 17, 33; *Riverside Chaucer*, ed. L. Benson, 983; S.D. Wingate, *The Medieval Latin Versions of the Aristotelian Scientific Corpus*, 60.

ARNALD OF THE NEWE TOUN. Arnoldus de Villanova, c. 1235–1314, was a Catalan theologian and alchemist. Arnold was so renowned that Peter III of Aragon asked for his services when he became ill; as a reward for curing him, Peter gave Arnold a castle in Tarragon. Arnold probably taught at Montpellier, which was under the jurisdiction of Aragon. In 1292 he wrote his *Tetragrammaton*, a treatise of four books in Hebrew and Latin, and published *De conservatione juventutis et retardatione senectutis (On the Conservation of Youth and the Retarding of Old Age)* in 1309. In 1299 the Inquisition in Paris arrested him for his works on alchemy, but he was immediately released. In 1305 the Inquisitor in Valencia forbade the possession or the reading of his books, and five years after his death, in 1319, the Inquisitor and Provost at Tarragon declared his writings heretical. His works on alchemy include *Rosarium philosophorum (The Philosopher's Rosary)* and *De lapide philosophorum (On the Philosopher's Stone)*.

The Canon's Yeoman says that he refers to Arnold's *Rosarium* for his knowledge of the alchemical properties of mercury, *CYT* 1428–1432. J.L. Lowes points out that the quotation comes from the chapters *De secretis naturae (On Nature's Secrets)* of the treatise *De lapide philosophorum*, II–V. E.H. Duncan shows how Chaucer manipulates passages on alchemy, using "sardonic humor and harsh invective" to satirize alchemists so that the treatises seem to condemn alchemy when they actually encourage investigation and experiment. [**Hermes**]

The form is the English translation of the name and occurs in final rhyming position, *CYT* 1428.

E.H. Duncan, "The Literature of Alchemy and Chaucer's *Canon's Yeoman's Tale*: Theme, Framework, and Characters." *Speculum* 43 (1968): 633–656; *ibid.*, "Chaucer and 'Arnald of Newe Toun': A Reprise." *Interpretations* (1977): 7–11; J.L. Lowes, "The Dragon and his Brother." *MLN* 28 (1913): 229; M.R. McVaugh, "The *Experimenta* of Arnald of Villanova." *Journal of Medieval and Renaissance Studies* 1 (1971): 107–118; L. Thorndike, *A History of Magic and Experimental Science*, II: 841–861.

ARNALDUS DE VILLANOVA: [ARNALD OF THE NEWE TOUN]

ARRIUS had a friend, Latumyus, who owned a beautiful, lush tree on which his wives hanged themselves. He eagerly begged Latumyus for a cutting to plant in his own garden, hoping for similar results. The story appears in Walter Map's *Dissuasio Valerii ad Rufinum philosophum ne uxorem ducat, De nugis curialium* IV.3 (c. 1180–1183).

Jankyn tells Dame Alys, his wife, this story from his collection, *WBP* 757–764. [**Latumyus: Valerie[2]**]

Arrius appears in final rhyming position, *WBP* 758, 762.

Walter Map, *De nugis curialium, Courtiers Trifles,* ed. and trans. M.R. James, rev. C.N.L. Brooke and R.A.B. Mynors, 202–203; R.A. Pratt, "Jankyn's Book of Wikked Wives: Medieval Antimatrimonial Propaganda in the Universities." *AnM* 3 (1962): 5–27.

ARSECHIELE(S). Abu Ishaq Ibrahim ibn-Yahya al-Naqqash, better known as ibn al-Zarqala or al-Zarqali, and whose Latin name was Arzachel, flourished at Cordova, c. 1029–1089. He was the best observer of the heavens in his time. His observations are dated 1061 and 1080. He invented an improved astrolabe called *Safiha flatus* or *saphaea Arzachelis*, the flat sphere or Arzachel's sphere, and his description of it was translated into Latin, Hebrew, and many vernaculars. He was the first to calculate explicitly the motion of the solar apogee, the point most distant from the earth, with reference to the stars. He also edited the so-called *Toledan Tables*, planetary tables based on observations made at Toledo and published by him and other Muslim and Jewish astronomers. These tables were translated into Latin by Gerard of Cremona during the twelfth century and enjoyed much popularity, but they were rendered obsolete by the *Alfonsine Tables*, made for Alfonso the Wise of Castile and Leon in 1272. One of the moon's craters is named *Arzarchel.*

The astronomer and magician of Orleans brings out his *Tables Tolletanes*, adapted to Orleans, *FranklT* 1273–1274. In *Astr* II.45.2 they are called Arsechiele's tables. [**Gerard of Cremona**]

Arsechieles is the ME genitive case of *Arsechiele*, the modification of Latin *Arzachel*, formed from Arabic *al-Zarqali al-Naqqash*, meaning "the engraver."

R.W.T. Gunther, *Early Science at Oxford*, 200–201, 384; F.P. Magoun, Jr., *A Chaucer Gazetteer*, 157; G.J. Toomer, "A Survey of the Toledan Tables." *Osiris* 15 (1968): 5–174.

ARTEMESIA: [ARTHEMESIE]

ARTHEMESIE. Artemesia II was the sister and wife of Mausolaus, satrap of Caria, 377–353 B.C. The satrap died in 353, and Artemesia ruled the country. She completed the colossal statue and tomb that her husband had begun. The finished mausoleum, adorned with friezes executed by the most famous sculptors of the day, reached a total height of about 134 feet.

It was one of the Seven Wonders of the World. Jerome tells that Artemesia promoted a literary competition every year in honor of her husband's memory, attended by all the most famous rhetoricians of the day, *Epistola adversus Jovinianum (Letter Against Jovinian)* I.44 (*PL* 23: 274).

To Dorigen, Arthemesie is exemplary of perfect wifehood, *FranklT* 1451. **[Dorigen]**

The form of the name is modified for the rhyme; intrusive *h* after *t* was not pronounced. The original name, *Arthemisia,* is an extended variant of *Artemis.*

G. Dempster, "Chaucer at Work on the Complaint in *The Franklin's Tale.*" *MLN* 52 (1937): 16–23; K. Hume, "The Pagan Setting of the *Franklin's Tale* and the Sources of Dorigen's Cosmology." *SN* 44 (1972): 289–294; *OCD,* 127.

ARTHOUR, ARTHUR(ES) was the son of Uther Pendragon, king of England, and Igraine, wife of the duke of Cornwall. He became king of England when he pulled the sword out of the stone, a feat no other knight could accomplish. With the help of Merlin the magician, he got his sword, Excalibur, from the Lady of the Lake. Against Merlin's advice, he married Guenevere, daughter of Leodegrance, king of Camelerd, who gave Arthur the Round Table, accompanied by a hundred knights. Arthur and his knights held high ideals of chivalry and courtesy. Among the knights of the Round Table were Lancelot, Gawain, Kay, Bedevere, Perceval, and Yvain. Guenevere and Lancelot fell in love, and their passion caused much strife in the kingdom. In a battle with his son Mordred, Arthur received his death wound. He commanded Sir Lucan to cast his sword into the water of a nearby lake, but twice Sir Lucan did not do so and came back to Arthur with a lie. But Arthur insisted, and when the sword was thrown into the water, a hand came up, met it, and caught it, shook it three times, and brandished it. Then hand and sword vanished into the water. Then Lucan and Bedevere took Arthur down to the lake and found a barge there with many fair ladies in it. They placed the king in the barge, and Arthur told them that he was going to Avalon to heal his wounds. But the next day Bedevere found a new grave near a chapel and hermitage, and the hermit told him that the night before he had buried a corpse brought to him by many fair ladies.

The story of Arthur had Celtic origins and belongs to Welsh and Cornish traditions. Arthur appears in the written tradition as early as c. A.D. 800, in Nennius's *Historia Brittonum* and in the *Annals of Wales* compiled c. 950. The Welsh *Mabinogion* (c. 1060) contains an Arthurian analogue in *Kulwch and Olwen*, perhaps the earliest Arthurian story. The Arthurian story was given wide currency by Breton *conteurs* at Anglo-Norman courts during the early years of the twelfth century. Then, c. 1137, Geoffrey of Monmouth published his *Historia Regum Britanniae* or *History of the Kings of Britain,* which, he claimed, he had translated into Latin from an old book. The fourth book of this work is called *Prophetae Merlini* and is derived mainly from the oral tradition of the Breton *conteurs*. Wace, an Anglo-Norman poet, made a paraphrase of Geoffrey's work c. 1155 in *Le Roman de Brut*, and from this Layamon made his *Brut* c. 1200 in English. The twelfth century also saw the creation of the cream of Arthurian romances in the work of Chrétien de Troyes: *Erec et Enide, Cligés, Le Chevalier de la Charrette, Yvain, Le Conte de Graal*. Chaucer's *Wife of Bath's Tale* and the anonymous *Sir Gawain and the Green Knight* appear between 1386 and 1400. Gower's *Tale of Florent* in *Confessio Amantis* I.1407–1861 is an Arthurian tale. English romances of the Arthurian cycle, known as the "matter of Britain," are *Sir Launfal, Sir Tristrem, Libeaus Desconus, Sir Percyvell of Galles, Yvain and Gawain, Alliterative Morte Arthur*, culminating in Malory's *The Book of King Arthur and his Noble Knights*, which Caxton published under the title *Le Morte d'Arthur*. In the preface to his edition Caxton points out that Arthur is one of the Nine Worthies, an appellation that appears in the *Parlement of the Thre Ages*, 462–512. A medieval tapestry hanging in The Cloisters collection of the Metropolitan Museum of Art in New York portrays Arthur as one of the Nine Worthies, his standard showing the three crowns of England, Scotland, and Brittany. The fifteenth-century poem *The Weddynge of Sir Gawen and Dame Ragnell* is Arthurian and an analogue of the *Wife of Bath's Tale*.

Dame Alys places her tale in the mythical past, in the days of King Arthour, *WBT* 857. The rapist-knight belongs to Arthour's house, *WBT* 882–883, and Arthour condemns the knight for his deed, *WBT* 889–892. The Old Wife's question—Is this Arthur's house?—indicates that Arthur's house is famous for its courtesy, *WBT* 1089. [**Gaufride: Gawayn: Launcelot**]

Arthour, the OF variant, appears in final rhyming position, *WBT* 882, 890. *Arthures,* the ME genitive case, occurs medially, *WBT* 1089. Both forms are derived from Latin *Artorius*. Intrusive *h* after *t* was not pronounced.

Geoffrey of Monmouth, *Historia Regum Britanniae*, ed. J. Hammer; *ibid., History of the Kings of Britain,* trans. with introd. L. Thorpe; N.J. Lacy, ed., *The Arthurian Encyclopedia*; Layamon, *Brut*, ed. G.L. Brook; R.S. Loomis, *Arthurian Literature in the Middle Ages*; *ibid.*, "Verses on the Nine Worthies." *MP* 15 (1917): 19–27; *Parlement of the Thre Ages*, ed. M.Y. Offord, 20–25; Wace, *Le Roman de Brut*, ed. A.S. Holden.

ARTOPHYLAX: [ARCTOUR]

ARVERAGUS is the young knight who becomes Dorigen's husband in *The Franklin's Tale*. He and Dorigen enter upon a contract to regard each other as friends in marriage and to allow each other utmost freedom. Dorigen rashly promises Aurelius, the young clerk who loves her, to return his love if he can make the black rocks on the coast disappear. Aurelius engages a magician from Orleans who accomplishes the task, to Dorigen's great distress. When Arveragus learns of her dilemma, he orders Dorigen to keep her promise but to let no one know, thus cancelling their contract of utmost freedom. Dorigen meets Aurelius in the garden, and when he sees her distress, he releases her from her promise. Geoffrey of Monmouth tells the story of Arviragus, who loves his wife Genuissa above all else, *Historia Regum Britanniae* IV.12–16. **[Aurelius: Dorigen: Gaufride]**

Arveragus is the ME modification of Latin *Arviragus*. The name does not appear in Boccaccio's *Il Filocolo*, the principal source for the story, so it appears that Chaucer has taken the name from Geoffrey. Jerome Archer suggests Juvenal's *Satire* IV.127 as well. *Arveragus* occurs twice initially, *FranklT* 1087, 1551; four times in medial positions, *FranklT* 837, 1460, 1517, 1595; and six times in final rhyming position, *FranklT* 808, 814, 969, 1351, 1424, 1526.

J.W. Archer, "On Chaucer's Source for 'Arveragus' in the *Franklin's Tale*." *PMLA* 65 (1950): 318–322; Geoffrey of Monmouth, *Historia Regum Britanniae*, ed. J. Hammer, 80–82; *ibid.*, *History of the Kings of Britain*, trans. L. Thorpe, 119–123; J.S.P. Tatlock, *The Scene of the Franklin's Tale Visited*, 62–74.

ARZACHEL: [ARSECHIELE(S)]

ASCALAPHUS: [ESCAPHILO]

ASCANIUS, ASCANYUS, ASKANIUS was the son of Aeneas and Creusa. When Aeneas arrived at Carthage, he left his son behind with the ships and went ashore. Later, he sent messengers to fetch the boy, and Venus substituted Cupid in his place. Thus Cupid arrived at the palace in the guise of Ascanius, and he caused Dido to fall passionately in love with Aeneas (*Aeneid* I.657–722; IV.105).

When Chaucer tells the story, *HF* I.171–180, he adds Askanius as a second son of Eneas, "eke Askanius also," Iulo being the first son. Eneas flees with his son Ascanius and his father Anchises from burning Troy, *LGW* 941. Eneas sends Achates to bring Ascanyus to Dido's court, *LGW* 1128–1133. **[Creusa: Dido: Eneas: Iulo]**

Ascanius occurs in final rhyming position, *LGW* 941, 1138; *Ascanyus* also occurs finally, *LGW* 1138; *Askanius* occurs medially, *HF* I.178.

Virgil, *Aeneid*, ed. and trans. H.R. Fairclough, I: 338–343, 396–397.

ASSUER, ASSUERE, ASSUERUS is the Persian title of Xerxes I, who reigned from 486 to 464 B.C. The Book of Esther tells how his prime minister, Haman, persuaded the king to set a date, the thirteenth day of Adar, when the Jews in his kingdom would be slaughtered. Esther, however, advised by her uncle Mordecai, outwitted Haman and persuaded the king to grant permission for the Jews to slay their enemies on that day.

Ester caused Assuere to elevate her uncle Mardochee, *MerchT* 1371–1374. May is as demure as Ester at Assuer's court, *MerchT* 1744–1745. In the reign of Assuerus, Ester exalted the people of God by her good counsel, *Mel* 1100. **[Ester]**

The forms appear in the Latin Vulgate *Liber Hester. Assuer* occurs in medial position, *MerchT* 1745; *Assuere* occurs in medial position, *MerchT* 1374, with elided final *-e; Assuerus* occurs in the prose of *Mel* 1100.

ATALANTA: [ATHALANTE]

ATHALANTE[1]. Atalanta, daughter of King Schoeneus of Boeotia, was famous for her beauty and for her swift feet. Warned by the oracle against marriage, she refused to wed any except the man who won the race against her. Helped by Venus, Hippomenes won by dropping three golden apples in her path, then passing her when she stooped to pick them up. She married him. Cybele changed the couple into lions when they slept together before her statue *(Met* X.560–707; *OM* X.2094–2437).

Athalante is one of love's martyrs, *PF* 286. **[Atthalante]**

The form, with final silent *-e*, occurs in final rhyming position, *PF* 286. Intrusive *h* after *t* was not pronounced.

Ovid, *Met*, ed. and trans. F.J. Miller, II: 104–115; *OM*, ed. C. de Boer, IV, deel 39: 61–69.

ATHALANTE[2]. Atlas was the giant of North Africa who held up the heavens on his shoulders. The Seven Pleiades were his daughters *(Met* VI.174–175).

The learned eagle points out the seven daughters of Atlas to the frightened poet, *HF* II.1007.

Athalantes, the ME genitive case, is a variant of *Atlantiades*, the Greek patronymic that appears in Latin. Here it is applied to Atlas himself. Intrusive *h* after *t* was not pronounced. The name occurs in medial position.

Ovid, *Met*, ed. and trans. F.J. Miller, I: 300–301.

ATHALUS. Attalus III, Philometer, c. 170–133 B.C., was king of Pergamum. He was a cruel ruler to his subjects and confiscated the estates of those who displeased him. He left a famous will in which he bequeathed his kingdom to Rome (Livy, Summary, *Ab urbe condita liber* LVIII).

Chaucer says that Athalus invented chess, *BD* 663–664, following *RR* 6689–6698. Jean de Meun cites *Policraticus* as his source, but John of Salisbury says that Atticus Asiaticus invented dice playing and reviews the evils inherent in all games of chance *(Policraticus* I.5). **[Demetrius: Stilboun]**

The form, the ME variant, occurs in medial position, *BD* 663. Intrusive *h* after *t* was not pronounced.

John of Salisbury, *Policraticus*, ed. J.P. Pike, 28–29; Livy, *Ab urbe condita libri*, ed. and trans. A.C. Schlesinger, XIV: 63, 65; *RR*, ed. E. Langlois, III: 14–15; *RR*, trans. C. Dahlberg, 129.

ATHAMANTE. Athamas was the son of Aeolus and king of Thebes. His wife, Ino, nursed the infant Dionysus, son of her sister Semele and Jupiter, thus incurring Juno's wrath. Juno drove both Athamas and Ino mad; Athamas killed his son Learchus, and Ino jumped off a cliff with a second son, Melicertes (*Met* IV.464–530; *OM* IV.2804–3963).

Criseyde tells Troilus that if ever she be false to him, may Juno, through her might, make her as mad as Athamante, *Tr* IV.1534–1540. **[Creseyde]**

Athamante, occurring medially, has syllabic final *-e* and seems a modification to fit the number of stresses in the line, *Tr* IV.1539. Intrusive *h* after *t* was not pronounced.

Ovid, *Met,* ed. and trans. F.J. Miller, I: 210–215; *OM*, ed. C. de Boer, II.71–95.

ATHAMAS: [ATHAMANTE]

ATITERIS. This person appears in company with those who play flutes, pipes, and horns in *The House of Fame*. Robinson and Skeat suggest that Chaucer means Tityrus, an old shepherd who plays the reed pipes in Virgil's *Eclogues* I and VI. Since, in Fame's house, Atiteris stands with Pseustis, a flute player representing paganism in the anonymous tenth-century poem *Ecloga Theoduli*, it is more likely that Chaucer means Alethia. Alethia represents Christianity in the *Ecloga Theoduli* and enters a contest with Pseustis, who loses to her.

Atiteris and Pseustis stand with Marsyas, who lost a contest to Apollo, *HF* III.1227–1229. **[Apollo: Marcia: Pseustis]**

The name appears in final rhyming position, *HF* III.1227.

Ecloga Theoduli, ed. J. Östernacher, 31–55; *Riverside Chaucer*, ed. L. Benson, 986; W.W. Skeat, III: 269.

ATRIDES: [ATTRIDES]

ATROPOS, ATTROPOS. Atropos was the last and most important of the Three Fates, daughters of Night. Clotho spun the thread of life and was responsible for birth; Lachesis drew out the thread and apportioned the length of life; Atropos cut the thread and decided the time of death (Hesiod, *Theogony* 217–222; Isidore, *Etym* VIII.11.93).

Troilus calls on Atropos to prepare his bier, *Tr* IV.1205–1211, when he learns that Criseyde is to be exchanged for Antenor. Criseyde asks Atropos to break in pieces her thread of life if she is false to Troilus, *Tr* IV.1545–1546. **[Lachesis: Parcas]**

Atropos means "not to be averted" or "the inevitable." Both forms are pronounced alike, the doubled consonant indicating an initial unstressed vowel, and may be scribal variants. *Atropos* occurs in medial position, *Tr* IV.1208; *Attropos* occurs also in medial position, *Tr* IV.1546.

Hesiod, *The Homeric Hymns and Homerica*, ed. and trans. H.G. Evelyn-White, 94–95; Isidore, *Etymologiae*, ed. W. Lindsay, I.

ATTALUS: [ATHALUS]

ATTHALANTE. Atalanta of Tegea was the huntress who joined the Calydonian boar hunt. Her arrow was the first to draw blood from the boar, and when Meleager slew it, he offered her a share of the spoils, the boar's head. As a huntress, she was devoted to Diana. Ovid differentiates between Arcadian Atalanta of the boar hunt (*Met* VIII.319–333; *OM* VIII.2170–2359) and Boeotian Atalanta of the swift feet (*Met* X.560–707; *OM* X.2094–2437).

The boar hunt of Atthalante and Meleagre appears on the walls of Diana's oratory, *KnT* 2070–2072. Chaucer may have used the *Ovide Moralisé* for Cassandra's version of the boar hunt, *Tr* V.1464–1484, when she interprets Troilus's dream of the boar. [**Athalante: Meleagre**]

Atthalante occurs medially, *KnT* 2070. The doubled consonants indicate an initial unstressed vowel; intrusive *h* after *t* was not pronounced.

Ovid, *Met*, ed. and trans. F.J. Miller, I: 428–429; II: 104–115; *OM*, ed. C. de Boer, III, deel 30: 161–166; IV, deel 37: 61–67; B.L. Wittlieb, "Chaucer and the *Ovide Moralisé*." *N&Q* 217 (1970): 204.

ATTHEON. Acteon, son of Aristaeus and Autonoë, was a skilled huntsman. One day he accidentally came upon Diana bathing with her nymphs. In her wrath, the goddess changed him into a stag; as he ran from the lake, his companions and their hounds thought him fair game and pursued him until the hounds tore him to death (*Met* III.143–252; *OM* III.273–570).

The story of Attheon is painted on the walls of Diana's oratory, *KnT* 2065–2068. Altheon endured Diana's anger, *KnT* 2302–2303. [**Diana**]

The form appears in Boccaccio's *Tes* VII.79.5. The name appears medially, *KnT* 2065, 2303. The doubled consonant indicates an initial unstressed vowel; intrusive *h* after *t* was not pronounced.

Ovid, *Met*, ed. and trans. F.J. Miller, I: 134–143; *OM*, ed. C. de Boer, I, deel 15: 305–311.

ATTILA. Attilla the Hun, fl. fifth century A.D., conqueror of most of western Europe, overran the western Roman Empire with his troops. In A.D. 453 he died of a stroke on his wedding night after he had gone to bed drunk (*The Gothic History* XLIX).

Attila represents drunken intemperance, *PardT* 579–582.

The name appears medially, *PardT* 579.

Jordanes, *The Gothic History*, trans. C.C. Mierow, 123.

ATTILLA: [ATTILA]

ATTRIDES. Chaucer uses the Greek patronymic as a name for Agamemnon, *Bo* IV, *Metr* 7.1. Boethius writes *ultor Atrides*, the avenger of Atreus. **[Agamenon]**

The doubled consonant in *Attrides* indicates an initial unstressed vowel.

ATTROPOS: [ATROPOS]

AUGUSTIN, AUGUSTINUS, AUGUSTYN, AUSTYN (saint). Aurelius Augustinus (A.D. 354–430) was born in Tagaste in Numidia (now called Souk Ahras, Algeria). His mother Monica was a devout Christian who prayed earnestly for his conversion; his father Patricius was a pagan. Augustine was first a Neo-Platonist, then a Manichaean, teaching rhetoric at Tagaste, then at Rome. When he moved to Milan, he came under St. Ambrose's influence. He became a Christian and was baptized in 387. In 391 he went to Hippo (Bone, Algeria), where he was ordained, and he became bishop of the city in 396. He died on 28 August 430, during the Vandal invasion of the city, at the age of seventy-six. In his *Retractationes (Retractions)* of 427 Augustine lists a total of ninety-three works. The most famous of these are *Confessions* (c. 397–400), describing his dissolute life, his emotional and psychological struggles, his religious conversion, and *De civitate Dei* or *The City of God* (413–426), written to answer the charge that the Christians caused the fall of the empire. He is one of the four greatest doctors of the Roman Catholic church, the others being Ambrose, Jerome, and Gregory the Great. Dante places him in the Celestial Rose, seated below St. Bernard and St. Francis, *Par* XXXII.35.

After his ordination at Hippo, Augustine established a monastery within the church confines. When he was consecrated bishop in 396, he had to leave the monastery. By the time of his death he had established many other monasteries for both men and women, which formed a rich heritage for the North African Church. The Rule of St. Augustine comes probably from Spain, written between the sixth and the eighth centuries. Its authenticity has not been established. The Augustinian Friars began canonically in the thirteenth century, but they trace their lineage to Augustine (*NCE* I: 1071–1072).

The Monk sees no reason to work with his hands as Austyn bids, *Gen Prol* 186–188; he does not give a "pulled hen" for the text that says that hunters are not holy men. St. Augustine, *De civitate Dei (The City of God)* XVI.4, defines the word "hunter" to mean "entrapper, persecutor, murderer of earthly creatures." A tradition grew up in medieval scriptural exegesis that, although fishermen had been holy (Peter, James, John, and Andrew), no hunters were holy. This tradition began with Aelfric's pastoral letters and the homilies of Wulfstan. The *Decretals* of Ivo of Chartres, a series of compilations written between 1140 and 1151, elaborate the tradition. Thus monks were required to abstain from hunting. Dame Prudence quotes from Augustine, *Mel* 1617, a quotation that has not been identified, and from his *Sermon* CCCLV.1 (*PL* 39: 1568), *Mel* 1643. Augustine is an authority on the doctrine of God's foreknowledge and man's free will, *NPT* 3241. Although Chaucer does not say that the monk in the *Shipman's Tale* is an Augustinian canon, he probably belongs to that order since he sends the merchant on his way with a blessing from the saint, *ShipT* 259. The Parson quotes Augustine's *Sermon* CCCLI.2 (*PL* 39: 1537), *ParsT* 97; *Epistle* CCLXV.8 (*PL* 33: 1089), *ParsT* 101; Augustine's *Sermon* IX.16 (*PL* 38: 87), *ParsT* 150; he quotes Pseudo-Augustine, *Liber de vera et falsa poenitentia (The Book of True and False Penitence)*, IX.24 (*PL* 40: 1121), *ParsT* 303. *ParsT* 329–460 appears to be an Augustinian interpretation of the secret punishment of evil. The Parson quotes from Augustine's *Sermon* CCCLIII.1 (*PL* 39: 1561), *ParsT* 484, 678; from *De civitate Dei (The City of God)*, XIV.15.2 (*PL* 41: 424), *ParsT* 535, 741; from Augustine, *De bono coniugali (On the Good Marriage)*, 20–21 (*PL* 40: 387), *ParsT* 921; from *Liber de vera et falsa poenitentia (The Book of True and False Penitence)*, X.25 (*PL* 40: 1122), *ParsT* 985, 1026. The following citations have not been identified: *ParsT* 230, 269, 368, 383, 630, 831, 844. The narrator points out, ironically, Augustine's "greet compassyoun" for Lucretia, *LGW* 1690–1691, but, in fact, Augustine emphasizes the inappropriateness of her suicide. In *De civitate Dei (The City of God)* I.18, Augustine devotes a section to the comparison of pagan virtue to Christian virtue with Lucretia's story as illustration.

Augustin/Augustyn are scribal variants influenced by pronunciation and appear in the prose works, *Mel* 1617, 1643; *ParsT* 97, 100, 150, 230, 269, 301, 368, 383, 484, 535, 630, 675, 678, 690, 740, 765, 830, 845, 920, 955, 985, 1020, 1025. *Augustinus* appears in a gloss, *ParsT* 750. The English form, *Austyn,* occurs in medial positions, *Gen Prol* 187, 188; *ShipT* 259; *LGW* 1690; it appears as a rhyming tag, *PrP* 441.

Peter R.L. Brown, *Augustine of Hippo*; A.L. Kellogg, "An Augustinian Interpretation of Chaucer's Pardoner." *Speculum* 26 (1951): 465–481; *ibid.*, "St. Augustine and the Parson's Tale." *Traditio* 8 (1952): 424–430; R. Willard, "Chaucer's 'Text that seith that hunters ben nat hooly men.' " *Studies in English* (1947): 209–251.

AUGUSTINE: [AUGUSTIN]

AURELIAN. Lucius Domitius Aurelianus, c. A.D. 215–275, became Roman emperor on the death of Claudius in 270. Two Roman emperors had failed to defeat Zenobia, queen of Palmyra, but Aurelian succeeded in 273. The city was reduced to a village, and Aurelian led Zenobia in his triumph through the streets of Rome. When he was criticized in the Senate for treating her like a conquered general instead of like a woman, Aurelian praised her military prowess (Flavius Vospiscus, *Divus Aurelianus* XXII–XXX, in *Scriptores historiae Augustae*).

The Monk narrates the life of Cenobia, a famous woman defeated by Fortune, *MkT* 2247–2274. Chaucer's sources are very likely Boccaccio, *De claris mulieribus*, XCVIII, and *De casibus virorum illustrium*, VIII.6. [**Cenobia: Odenake**]

Aurelian, the English variant of Latin *Aurelianus,* occurs once initially, *MkT* 2351, and once in final rhyming position, *MkT* 2361.

Boccaccio, *CFW,* trans. G. Guarino, 226–230; *ibid., De casibus,* ed. P.G. Ricci and V. Zaccaria, 678–682; *ibid., De claris mulieribus,* ed. V. Zaccaria, 406–414; *Scriptores historiae Augustae,* ed. and trans. D. Magie, III: 193–294.

AURELIE, AURELIUS, AURELYUS is the young squire who loves Dorigen in *The Franklin's Tale*. He sees her first on the 6th of May, as she dances with her friends in a public garden. For more than two years he loves her as secretly as Pamphilles loved Galatea. He is a servant of Venus and devoted to Apollo. Rashly promising to return his love if he makes the rocks disappear from the seacoast, Dorigen is appalled when Aurelius engages a magician who performs the feat. But her husband Arveragus insists that she keep her word, and all ends well. [**Apollo: Arveragus: Dorigen: Galathee: Pamphilles: Phebus**]

Aurelie appears four times initially, *FranklT* 929, and medially *FranklT* 989, 1007, 1037; *Aurelius* occurs nine times initially, *FranklT* 1006, 1188, 1226, 1241, 1256, 1297, 1514, 1557, 1592; four times in medial positions, *FranklT* 1020, 1100, 1183, 1235; and six times in final rhyming position, *FranklT* 938, 965, 970, 979, 1303, 1499. *Aurelyus,* a spelling variant, occurs once, in final rhyming position, *FranklT* 1102.

A.T. Gaylord, "The Promises in *The Franklin's Tale*." *ELH* 31 (1964): 331–365; W.E.H. Rudat, "Aurelius' Quest for Grace: Sexuality and the Marriage Debate in *The Franklin's Tale*." *CEA Critic* 45 (1982): 16–24; J.S.P. Tatlock, "Astrology and Magic in Chaucer's *Franklin's Tale*." *Anniversary Papers by Colleagues and Pupils of George Lyman Kittredge*, 339–350.

AURORA: [PETER[1] RIGA]
AUSTER: [EOLUS]
AVERROES: [AVERROIS]

AVERROIS. Abu-al-Walid Muhammad ibn-Ahmad ibn-Muhammad ibn-Rushd, 1126–1198, was born in Cordova and died in Marrakesh. He became a judge in both Seville and Cordova and, in 1182, physician to the Almohad caliph, Abu-Ya'qub Yusuf at Marrakesh. His prominence lasted until the reign of the following caliph, with whom he held a favorable position at first. In 1195, however, Caliph Ya'qub al-Mansur banished ibn-Rushd back to Cordova and ordered his writings, except the strictly scientific ones, burnt. The caliph seems to have changed his mind subsequently, for ibn-Rushd was back in Marrakesh in 1196, where he died in 1198. His chief works are a *Compendium* (a translation of Aristotle's *Posterior Analytics*) in 1170, short and middle-length commentaries or paraphrases on Aristotle's *De caelo et mundo (On the Heavens), Physica (Physics), De generatione et corruptione (On Generation and Corruption), De anima (On the Soul), De sensu et sensibilibus (On the Senses and Sensibilities),* and *Meteorologica (Meteorology),* composed in 1177, and a *Great Commentary* on many of the same works, including the *Metaphysica (Metaphysics),* composed in 1186. The Arabic commentary on *The Great Commentary* is lost but remains extant in Michael Scot's Latin translation, done between 1217 and 1220 at Toledo before he moved to Italy. Ibn-Rushd also wrote commentaries on Galen's *Treatise on Fevers.* Herman the German's translations of ibn-Rushd's commentaries on Aristotle date from 1240 and 1254. Merton College had, between 1360 and 1385, a manuscript of Averroes's work called *Liber universalis de medicina (The Universal Book of Medicine),* translated from the Arabic *Kitab-al-Kulliyat.*

Averrois appears in the Doctor's catalogue of authorities, *Gen Prol* 433.
[Aristotle: Avycen]

Averrois is the ME variant of Latin *Averroes,* a development from the Arabic patronymic, *ibn-Rushd.*

J.B. Allen, "Herman the German's Averroistic Aristotle and Medieval Literary Theory." *Mosaic* 9 (1976): 67–81; Averroes (ibn-Rushd), *On Aristotle's* De generatione et corruptione: *Middle Commentary and Epitome,* trans. S. Kirkland; F.J. Carmody, "The Planetary Theory of Ibn Rushd." *Osiris* 10 (1952): 556–586; *EI,* III: 910–911; O.B. Hardison, "The Place of Averroes' Commentary on the *Poetics* in the History of Medieval Criticism." *Medieval and Renaissance Studies* 4 (1970): 57–81; F.E. Peters, *Aristoteles Arabus: The Oriental Translation and Commentaries on the Aristotelian Corpus,* 36; F.M. Powicke, *The Medieval Books of Merton College,* 139.

AVYCEN. Abu-'Ali al-Husain ibn-'Abdullah ibn-Sina, 980–1037, was born in the Persian province of Kharmaithan, where his father was governor. In a short autobiography, he tells that by the time he was sixteen he had mastered all his teachers could teach him, and that he was practicing medicine by the time he was eighteen. He dismissed his last teacher, Nateli, who admitted he had nothing more to give. After that, ibn-Sina taught himself everything he needed to know: logic, natural sciences, medicine, and philosophy. While serving as vizier to Shams al-Dawlah, emir of Hamadan (997–1021), ibn-Sina experienced the most productive period of his life. He began his *Qanun,* or *The Canon of Medicine,* an immense medical encyclopedia, and from c. 1020 to 1030 completed his *Kitab al-Shifa,* or *The Book of Healing,* incorporating Aristotle's *Physica (Physics), De generatione et corruptione (On Generation and Corruption), De caelo et mundo (On the*

Heavens), and *Liber animalium (The Book of Animals)*; Section 9 of Part IV is devoted to Aristotle's treatment of poetry. Michael Scot translated and abbreviated his commentary on the *Liber animalium* for Frederick II before 1232. Gerard of Cremona translated the *Qanun* in the second half of the twelfth century.

Avycen appears in the Doctor's catalogue of authorities, *Gen Prol* 432. The Pardoner refers to the *Qanun* and its chapters on poisons, Book IV, fen vi (a *fen* is a subdivision of a book), *PardT* 889–892. Merton College Library owned a copy of this work between 1360 and 1385. [**Aristotle: Averrois**]

Avycen is the ME development of Latin *Avicenna*, derived from the Arabic patronymic, *ibn-Sina*, by way of Hebrew *Aven Sina*. The contraction appears in final rhyming position, *Gen Prol* 432, *PardT* 889.

S.M. Afnan, *Avicenna, his Life and Works*, 57–69; Avicenna, *The General Principles of Avicenna's* Canon of Medicine, ed. and trans. M.H. Shah; Marie-Thérèse d'Alverny, "L'explicit du 'De animalibus' d'Avicenne, traduit par Michel Scot." *Bibliothèque de l'Ecole des Chartes*, 115 (1957): 32–42; F.E. Peters, *Aristoteles Arabus*, 89; F.M. Powicke, *The Medieval Books of Merton College*, 138.

B

BACCHUS: [BACHUS]

BACHUS, BACUS. Bacchus is a Lydian name for Dionysus, the Thracian fertility god. A son of Jupiter, he later became the god of wine. Jupiter visited Semele, princess of Thebes, at night, and when she became pregnant, she asked to see his face. As he showed himself in thunder and lightning, she caught afire; thereupon, Jupiter ripped the infant out of her womb and placed him in his thigh, where he remained until he reached maturity. Ovid calls Bacchus "son of the thunderbolt, twice born" *(Met* IV.9–17; *OM* IV.1–118).

Alys of Bath observes that after wine comes Venus, for a "likerous mouth moste han a likerous tayl," *WBP* 464–466, echoing *The Art of Love (Ars Amatoria)* I.229–244. Petrus Berchorius says that ardor has a womanly face and the desires of women are born wine in drunkenness *(De formis figurisque deorum,* fol. 9ᵛa. 37–38). Fulgentius says that lust is the third stage of intoxication *(Mythologies* II.xii). Bachus pours the wine at Januarie's marriage feast, *MerchT* 1722. He has no power over Virginia's mouth, *PhysT* 58–59. Bacus can make "ernest out of game," *MancP* 99–100. Bacus sits beside Venus in her temple, *PF* 275. Bachus gives gifts to Autumn, *Bo* I, *Metr* 6.15.7. In the first age, men did not know how to mix the gifts of Bachus with honey, *Bo* II, *Metr* 5. Troilus curses Bacus, Ceres, and Cipris, *Tr* V.204–210, the gods of wine, food, and love. Procne tells Tereus, king of Thrace, that he is going on a pilgrimage to the temple of Bacus, *LGW* 2373–2378; in reality, she goes into the woods to rescue her sister Philomela. [Ceres: Cipride: Venus]

Bacus, the ME, OF, and medieval Latin variant, occurs medially, *PF* 275 and *LGW* 2376, *Bachus,* a variant of classical Latin *Bacchus,* occurs initially,

MerchT 1722 and *PhysT* 58, in the prose of the *Boece*, and medially, *MancP* 99 and *Tr* V.208.

Petrus Berchorius, *Ovidius Moralizatus*, ed. J. Engels, 42; Fulgentius, *Fulgentius the Mythographer*, trans. L. Whitbread, 77; *ibid., Mythographi Latini*, ed. T. Munckerus, 91; Ovid, *The Art of Love (Ars Amatoria)*, ed. and trans. J.H. Mozley, 2d ed., 28–29; *ibid., Met*, ed. and trans. F.J. Miller, I: 178–179; *OM*, ed. C. de Boer, II, deel 21: 13–15.

BAILLY. Harry Bailly is the owner and host of the Tabard Inn, where the Canterbury pilgrimage begins. John M. Manly has suggested that the Host is modeled on the real Henry Bailly of Southwark, an innkeeper in Chaucer's day. Henricus Bailly represented the borough of Southwark in Parliament, held at Westminster in 50 Edward III (1376–1377) and in 2 Richard II (1378–1379). He appears in the Subsidy Rolls in 4 Richard II (1380–1381) as Henricus Bailiff, Ostler, and his wife's name as Christian. Although Henricus Bailiff, Ostler, is not necessarily Harry Bailly, the possibility remains that Chaucer may have used him as a model for the Host.

Bailly's name appears once, when the Cook mentions it, *CoP* 4358. He owns the Tabard, the inn from which the pilgrims set out for Canterbury, *Gen Prol* 19–27, and he is their guide, governor, literary critic, and bully, along the way. **[Goodelief]**

J.M. Manly, *Some New Light on Chaucer*, 77–83; D.R. Pichaske and L. Swetland, "Chaucer on the Medieval Monarchy: Harry Bailly in the *Canterbury Tales*." *ChauR* 11 (1977–1978): 179–200.

BALLENUS. This name is applied to Apollonios of Tyana, born c. 4 B.C. or at the beginning of the Christian Era. He was a Neo-Pythagorean philosopher, and *The Secret of Creation* was attributed to him. In that work, the author's name is given as *Tunaya*, transliterated as *Tyana*. Philostratus wrote his *Life of Apollonios of Tyana* c. A.D. 216. Apollonios was supposed to have been a disciple of Hermes Trismegistus and was regarded as a magician during the medieval period. The sage Belinous (that is, Apollonios) was said to have discovered a book containing all the secrets of the universe under a statue of the great Hermes.

Ballenus appears with the magicians, *HF* III.1273. Langlois points out that the name occurs twice in *Renart le Contrefait*, 315–316, 25207–25208, meaning "magic" as well as "magician."

The name, possibly a variant of OF *Balenuz*, *RR* 14399, occurs in final rhyming position.

F.W.G. Campbell, *Apollonios of Tyana: A Study of his Life and Times*; *EI*, I: 620; Philostratus, *The Life of Apollonios of Tyana*, ed. and trans. F.C. Conybeare; *RR*, ed. E. Langlois, IV: 60, n. 289; *RR*, trans. C. Dahlberg, 246.

BALTHASAR. Belshazzar, grandson of Nebuchadnezzar, ruled Babylon (Daniel 1–4). As the king entertained at a feast, fingers of a hand appeared and wrote a message on the wall of the room. Daniel interpreted the message, which said that the king had been weighed in the balances and found wanting, signifying his fall. That night, Darius the Mede invaded the kingdom and ended Belshazzar's reign. The historical Bel-shar-usur was the oldest son of Nabu-na'id and seems to have acted as regent, 556–539 B.C. Belshazzar is called "son of Nebuchadnezzar," Daniel 5: 2.18. Machaut tells the story in *Confort d'Ami* 661–954.

The Monk's story of Balthasar illustrates the instability of power and the fickleness of Fortune, *MkT* 2183–2246. **[Daniel: Darius[1]: Nabogodonosor]**

The form, a variant of Latin *Balthazar*, occurs medially, *MkT* 2205, and in final rhyming position, *MkT* 2183.

Guillaume de Machaut, *Oeuvres*, ed. E. Hoepffner, III: 24–35.

BAPTIST JOHN (saint). John the Baptist, fl. first century A.D., was the son of Zachary, a priest of the course of Abia at the Temple, and Elizabeth, cousin of Mary. He was born six months before Jesus, but the date is uncertain (Luke 1: 1–45).

The Pardoner says that an inebriated Herod commanded that John the Baptist be beheaded, *PardT* 488–491. Neither Matthew 15 nor Mark 6 describes a drunk Herod. Innocent III, *De miseria condicionis humane (On the Misery of the Human Condition)* II.xviii, says that gluttony closed Paradise and beheaded the Baptist. **[Herodes[2]]**

Innocent III, *De miseria condicionis humane,* ed. and trans. R.E. Lewis, 22–23; *ibid., De miseria condicionis humane,* ed. and trans. M. Maccarrone, 52–53; *ibid., On the Misery of the Human Condition,* trans. M.M. Dietz, 46; Jacobus de Voragine, *GL,* trans. G. Ryan and H. Ripperger, 321–327; *ibid., LA,* ed. Th. Graesse, 566–575.

BARNABO VISCOUNTE: [VISCOUNTE]
BASIL: [BASILIE]

BASILIE (saint). Basil, A.D. 329–379, was born in Pontic. He became Bishop of Caesarea in 370 and died there (*NCE* II: 143–146).

The Parson quotes from Basil's *Homiliae in Psalmos*, Psalms 23.7 (*PG* 29: 298), *ParsT* 220–225.

The form of the name is the French variant.

Jacobus de Voragine, *GL,* trans. G. Ryan and H. Ripperger, 308–313; *ibid., LA,* ed. Th. Graesse, 121–126.

BASILIUS, fl. sixth century A.D., one of Boethius's accusers, had been falsely accused himself and forced to leave King Theodoric's service.

Boethius tells that Basilius, because he was in debt, was compelled to join his false accusers, *Bo* I, *Prosa* 4.111. [**Albyn: Boece: Conigaste: Cyprian: Decorat: Gaudenicus: Opilion: Trygwille**]

H.F. Stewart, *Boethius, An Essay*, 48.

BEAR: [BERE: CALISTOPEE: URSA]
BEAR DRIVER: [BOETES]

BELIAL was one of Satan's lieutenants, alluded to in II Corinthians 6:15. The term appears throughout the Bible with a connotation of evil, but especially in Judges 15:22, referring to certain devilish men: "*venerunt viri civitatis illius filii Belial, id est, absque iugo*—the men of that city came, sons of Belial, that is without bonds or restraints."

The Parson compares bad priests, *ParsT* 895–898, with the sons of Heli, who are called "sons of Belial," I Kings 2:12.

Belial denotes a worthless person, being a compound of two Hebrew words: *b'li* (without) and *ya'al* (usefulness). *Absque iugo*, which explains *Belial* in the passage from Judges, appears as *sans ioug* in the Old French translation. Skeat suggests that Chaucer has misread the words. [**Helie: Samuel**]

Skeat, V: 471.

BELLONA was the Roman goddess of war, whose temple was outside the gates of Rome (Livy, *Ab urbe condita libri* VIII.9.6; X.19.17). She was later identified with the Greek goddess of war, Enyo, called "sacker of cities," *Iliad* V.333.

Pallas Athena is called "the Bellona of Mars," *Anel* 5. Chaucer seems to have confused Pallas Athena with Bellona. He says his source for the poem is Statius, who keeps Bellona and Pallas distinct in the *Thebaid*. The two goddesses are, however, sometimes confused in several glosses on the poem. *Pallas est Enyo* appears in one gloss. Boccaccio observes that there are several Minervas, one of whom is Bellona, in *De genealogie deorum gentilium* V.48. The confusion also appears in *Ovide Moralisé* II.96–99, 108–112. [**Minerva: Pallas**]

Bellona, a proper name derived from Latin *bellum* meaning "war," appears medially, *Anel* 5.

Boccaccio, *De genealogia deorum gentilium,* ed. V. Romano, I: 282; P.M. Clogan, "Chaucer and the *Thebaid* Scholia." *SP* 61 (1964): 606; Homer, *Iliad,* ed. and trans. A.T. Murray, I: 218–219; Livy, *Ab urbe condita libri,* ed. and trans. B.O. Foster, III: 36–38, 428–431; R.A. Pratt, "The Importance of Manuscripts for the Study of Medieval Education, as Revealed by the Learning of Chaucer," *Progress in Medieval and Renaissance Studies* 20 (1949): 49; Statius, *Thebaid,* ed. and trans. J.H. Mozley, I: 190–193; B.L. Wittlieb, "Chaucer and the *Ovide Moralisé.*" *N&Q* 215 (1970): 202–204.

BELSHAZZAR: [BALTHASAR]
BENEDICT: [BENEDIGHT]

BENEDIGHT, BENEIT (saint). Benedict of Nursia, c. A.D. 480–c. 546, was the founder of Western monasticism. He founded abbeys at Subiaco and Monte Cassino, where he wrote the most celebrated monastic rule, the *Regula monachorum* or *Regula magistri*. First introduced at Monte Cassino, it subsequently became the rule for all Western monasteries. It prescribes a regimen of study, manual labor, and prayer. Benedict died at Monte Cassino. Gregory the Great, in Book II of his *Dialogues*, devotes the whole book to a life of St. Benedict.

The Monk, Dan Piers, finds that St. Benedict's rule is rather severe, *Gen Prol* 172–176. Gregory relates that the monks at Vicovaro, who were somewhat wayward, asked Benedict to be their abbot. When he imposed discipline, they tried to kill him with poisoned wine (*Dialogiae*, II.iii, *PL* 66: 125–204). The superstitious carpenter recites a charm called a "night-spell," using Benedict's name, *MillT* 3483–3486. The meaning of the charm is not at all clear. **[Maure]**

Benedight, the ME development of Latin *Benedictus*, occurs in final rhyming position, *MillT* 3483; *Beneit*, the French variant, occurs in final rhyming position, *Gen Prol* 173.

Benedict of Nursia, *The Rule of St. Benedict: The Abingdon Copy,* ed. J. Chamberlain; Gregory the Great, *The Dialogues, Book II: St. Benedict,* trans. M.L. Uhlfelder; Jacobus de Voragine, *LA,* ed. Th. Graesse, 204–213; *ibid., GL,* trans. G. Ryan and H. Ripperger, 195–204.

[BENOÎT DE SAINTE-MAURE, or SAINTE-MORE]. Chaucer does not mention Benoît, fl. twelfth century A.D., but it is clear that he knew his work. Benoît was a Norman cleric who seems to have been attached to the court of Henry II and Eleanor of Aquitaine. Eric Auerbach suggests that his great poem, *Le Roman de Troie (The Romance of Troy),* written in 1184, is dedicated to Eleanor (*riche dame de riche rei*) and that lines 971–972, which mention London and Poitiers, point to the Anglo-Norman court. Benoît mentions briefly the love affair between Troilus and Breseida, which Boccaccio develops in *Il Filostrato* as a love affair between Troilus and Criseyde. **[Boccaccio]**

E. Auerbach, *Literary Language and its Public in Late Latin Antiquity,* trans. Ralph Mannheim, 208–209; Benoît, *Roman de Troie,* ed. L. Constans; R.K. Gordon, *The Story of Troilus.*

BERE. The constellation Ursa Major or the Great Bear is referred to simply as the Bere, *HF* II: 1004. **[Calistopee: Ursa]**

The word appears in final rhyming position.

BERNABO: [VISCOUNTE]

BERNARD[1] (saint). Bernard of Clairvaux, c. A.D. 1090–1153, was born at Fontaines near Dijon, France. He became a member of the Benedictines in 1113, joining their monastery at Cîteaux, and in 1115 he was sent to be abbot of a new house in Valle d'Absinthe, which he named Clara Vallis or Clairvaux. He became embroiled in several controversies of his day, such as that engendered by the disastrous second crusade of Louis VII and that arising from the condemnation of Abelard. He also entered a dispute with the monks of Cluny, and in a letter to William of St. Thierry he condemned the monks' gluttony and the decorations of their churches. His most famous hymns are addressed to the Virgin Mary, to whom he had a special devotion. Dante celebrates this devotion in *Par* XXXIII.1–37.

Chaucer adapts St. Bernard's prayer from *Par* XXXIII for the *Invocacio ad Mariam* in the Prologue of *The Second Nun's Tale*. The Prioress's Prologue, *PrP* 453–487, is modeled on the *Invocacio*. The Parson says that he quotes from St. Bernard when he describes the sorrow for sin that accompanies penitence, *ParsT* 130. This quotation appears in one of the sources of the Parson's Tale, in the *Summa casum poenitentiae* by Raymund of Pennaforte, but R.M. Correale shows that it comes from Nicholas of Clairvaux, *Sermo in festo sancti Andrae* 8 (*PL* 184: 1052–1053). The Parson quotes from Pseudo-Bernard's *Sermo ad prelatos in concilio,* 5 (*PL* 184: 1098), *ParsT* 166; he quotes from *Feria IV Hebdomadae sanctae* ll at *ParsT* 256; and from the *Sermo super Cantica Canticorum,* 54 at *ParsT* 723. The references to Bernard in *ParsT* 253, 274, and 690 have not been identified.

The name appears medially in *SNT* 30 and in the prose of *The Parson's Tale.*

Bernard of Clairvaux, *Opera,* ed. Jean LeClercq, II: 107–108, V: 64; R.M. Correale, "Nicholas of Clairvaux and the Quotation from 'St. Bernard' in Chaucer's *The Parson's Tale,* 130–132." *AN&Q* 20 (1981): 2–3. Dante, *Divine Comedy,* ed. and trans. C.S. Singleton, III.1: 370–373; Jacobus de Voragine, *GL,* trans. G. Ryan and H. Ripperger, 465–477; *ibid., LA,* ed. Th. Graesse, 527–538; K.O. Petersen, *On the Sources of the Parson's Tale,* 10; G. Sanderlin, "Quotations from St. Bernard in the *Parson's Tale.*" *MLN* 54 (1939): 447–448.

BERNARD[2]. Bernard de Gordon, fl. c. 1285–1308, a Scottish physician in Montpellier, was a contemporary of Gilbert the Englishman. In his *Lilium Medicinae (The Lilies of Medicine)* he defines the illness of heroic love or "hereos," gives the symptoms of the disease, and prescribes its cure. He warns that "hereos," if not treated quickly, leads to mania and death. In this work, he also describes spectacles for the first time. Eyeglasses were invented in Tuscany between 1280 and 1285. Merton College Library owned a copy of *Lilium Medicinae* between 1360 and 1385.

Bernard appears in the Doctor's catalogue of authorities, *Gen Prol* 434. The name appears in initial position.

L.E. Demaître, *Doctor Bernard de Gordon: Professor and Practitioner*; F.M. Powicke, *The Medieval Books of Merton College*, 141; E. Rosen, "The Invention of Eyeglasses." *Journal of the History of Medicine and Allied Sciences*, 2 (1956): 13–46, 183–218; G. Sarton, *Introduction to the History of Science*, III: ii, 1066.

BERNARD[3]. Bernard the Monk, mentioned in *LGW G* 16, is probably a proverbial figure. Scholars suggest that Bernard of Clairvaux is meant here.

M.P. Hamilton, "Bernard the Monk: Postscript." *MLN* 62 (1947): 190–191; *Riverside Chaucer*, ed. L. Benson, 1061; R.M. Smith, "The Limited Vision of St. Bernard." *MLN* 61 (1946): 38–44.

BEVES is the hero of the romance, *Sir Beves of Hampton*. The motif of the story is one of exile and return. Beves's adventures during his exile make up the bulk of the work. The Middle English version, written c. 1300, was very popular in Chaucer's day. The work exists in several branches: the Anglo-Norman version, *Boeve de Hamtoune*, of the early thirteenth century, written in laisses; a fourteenth-century French prose version; the Middle English version, written in stanzas and couplets, closely following the Anglo-Norman text; and a sixteenth-century Welsh version. The Auchinleck manuscript is the most authoritative of the three English manuscripts.

Sir Thopas bears the flower of chivalry, surpassing Sir Beves, *Thop* 897–899. **[Thopas]**

The name appears medially, *Thop* 899.

Der Anglonormannische Boeve de Hamtone, ed. A. Stimming; *The Romance of Sir Beves of Hamtoun*, ed. E. Kölbing; J.E. Wells, *A Manual of the Writings in Middle English, 1050–1500*.

BIBLIS. Byblis was the daughter of Miletus, epomynous founder of the city of Ionia. Her mother was the nymph Cyane. Byblis had the misfortune to fall in love with her twin brother Caunus. He fled from her; she pursued him, weeping so continuously that the nymphs changed her into a fountain (*Met* IX.454–665; *OM* IX.1997–2530). Boccaccio mentions the story briefly in *Tes* VII.62.

Biblis appears in the temple of Venus as one of love's martyrs, *PF* 289. The name occurs in initial position.

Boccaccio, *Tutte le Opere*, ed. V. Branca, II: 475; Ovid, *Met*, ed. and trans. F.J. Miller, II: 34–51; *OM*, ed. C. de Boer, III, deel 30: 269–282.

BIG DIPPER: [CALISTOPEE: URSA]

BILIA: [BILYEA]

BILYEA. Bilia, fl. third century A.D., was the wife of Duilius, who defeated the Carthaginian fleet off Mylae in Sicily in 260 B.C. His victory was made possible by a new type of ship, the *corvus*, and Duilius celebrated the first naval triumph. Jerome tells that Bilia endured her husband's bad breath in silence, *Epistola adversus Jovinianum (Letter Against Jovinian)* I.46 *(PL* 23: 275).

Dorigen thinks Bilyea is an exemplary figure of wifely patience, *FranklT* 1455. **[Dorigen]**

The name appears in final rhyming position.

K. Hume, "The Pagan Setting of the *Franklin's Tale* and the Sources of Dorigen's Cosmology." *SN* 44 (1972): 289–294; *OCD* 367; J. Sledd, "Dorigen's Complaint." *MP* 45 (1947): 36–45.

BLANCHE: [BLAUNCHE]

BLAUNCHE. Blanche of Lancaster was the second daughter, and co-heiress with her sister Maude, of Henry, duke of Lancaster, one of the richest men in fourteenth-century England. Edward III applied to Pope Innocent V for a dispensation for her marriage to John of Gaunt, who was her third cousin. Blanche's age at her marriage has been disputed. If she was born in 1340, she was nineteen when she married John of Gaunt and twenty-eight when she died in 1368. If she was born in 1347, she was twelve when she married Gaunt and twenty-one years old when she died. Scholars believed that she died of the plague in 1369, but John N. Palmer has shown that the chronicles confuse the events of 1368 and 1369 and that Blanche died on September 12, 1368.

The portrait of "good, faire White," *BD* 831–1041, although idealized, is possibly a portrait of Blanche. However, similar portraits of ideal women appear in Machaut's *Le Jugement dou Roy de Behaigne* 302–383 and *Le Remede de Fortune* 52–352. Queen Alceste mentions Chaucer's poem on the death of Blanche the Duchess, *LGW F* 418, *LGW G* 406. Skeat (I: 59) and Anderson suggest that Blanche requested a translation of Guillaume de Deguilleville's *Le Pèlerinage de la Vie Humaine* from Chaucer, who obliged with his *ABC.* **[Alceste: Alcione]**

Blanche's name appears once, in the catalogue of Chaucer's works, *LGW F* 418, *LGW G* 406.

M. Anderson, "Blanche, Duchess of Lancaster." *MP* 45 (1947–1948): 152–159; Guillaume de Machaut, *Oeuvres,* ed. Hoepffner, I: 68–72, II: 3–13; G.L. Kittredge, "Guillaume de Machaut and the *Book of the Duchess.*" *PMLA* 30 (1915): 1–24; L.A. Loschiane, "The Birth of 'Blanche the Duchess': 1340 versus 1347." *ChauR* 13 (1978–1979): 128–132; J.N. Palmer, "The Historical Context of the *Book of the Duchess*: a Revision." *ChauR* 8 (1974–1975): 253–261; J.I. Wimsatt, "The Apotheosis of Blanche in the *Book of the Duchess.*" *JEGP* 66 (1967): 26–44.

[BOCCACCIO] Giovanni Boccaccio, c. 1313–1375, says that his father made him legitimate, probably in 1319 or 1320, *Amorosa Visione* 14.42–46. His father, Boccaccino da Certaldo, was a banker with the Bardi and came from the small town of Certaldo, twenty-three miles southwest of Florence. Nothing is known about his mother. The story of the seduction of a French woman by a Tuscan, *Filocolo* V.9 and *Ameto* XXIII, formerly believed to be Boccaccio's accounts of his conception and birth, is now discounted. Boccaccio was well taken care of and given a good education, as he tells throughout *De genealogia deorum gentilium (The Genealogy of the Pagan Gods)*. His father wanted him to be first a banker, then a lawyer, and Boccaccio studied canon law. But poetry claimed him. Between 1333 and 1339 he wrote *Il Filocolo, Caccia di Diana,* and *Il Filostrato.* In these years he loved a lady he called Fiammetta. In 1350 he met Petrarch, whom he had always revered. He began his *Vita di Dante (Life of Dante)* in 1351 and revised *Amorosa Visione* between 1355 and 1361. Between 1339 and 1341, he composed *Il Teseida di Nozze d'Emilia*; he added his own glosses to this poem and meant poem and glosses to be read as one unit. During the last twenty-five years of his life he worked on *De genealogia deorum gentilium*, which he referred to as his major work. Between 1349 and 1351, he composed his *Decameron,* following the incidence of the Black Death in Florence, never thinking that posterity would chose to remember him for those stories rather than for his Latin works. He composed *De claris mulieribus (Concerning Famous Women)* in 1361 and *De casibus virorum illustrium (The Fall of Illustrious Men)* between 1355 and 1373. Boccaccio never married, but he mourns the death of a daughter, Violante, in his *Eleventh Eclogue.* In this poem he says that he is a father of five children. Nothing is known of the mother, or mothers, of these children. Boccaccio died on December 21, 1375, in Certaldo, where he was born.

Chaucer never mentions Boccaccio by name, although he used his work more often than any other poet's. Critics have suggested that Chaucer mentions Boccaccio by other names: for example, "Lollius" may mean "loller," one who speaks with a thick tongue, in *Tr* I.394, V.1653, *HF* II.1468; "Corynne," *Anel* 21, has also been suggested as a pseudonym for Boccaccio, derived from Italian *corina,* "wry face," a synonym in Italian for *Boccaccio.* But these are conjectures. Other critics maintain that Chaucer means Lollius when he says Lollius. [**Corynne: Lollius**]

Chaucer's *Knight's Tale* (c. 1385) is based on Boccaccio's *Il Teseida delle Nozze d'Emilia*; *Troilus and Criseyde* (c. 1385) is based on *Il Filostrato.* The Adam, Hercules, Samson, and Zenobia tragedies in the *Monk's Tale* (c. 1384–1386) are indebted to *De casibus virorum illustrium* and *De claris mulieribus.*

G. Boccaccio, *L'Ameto,* trans. J. Serafini-Sauli; *ibid., CFW, trans. G. Guarino; ibid., De casibus virorum illustrium,* ed. P.G. Ricci and V. Zaccaria; *ibid., De claris*

mulieribus, ed. V. Zaccaria; *ibid., The Fates of Illustrious Men*, trans. and abr.
Louis B. Hall; *ibid., Il Filocolo*, ed. and trans. D.S. Cheney and T.G. Bergin; *ibid.,
De genealogia deorum gentilium libri*, ed. V. Romano; *ibid., Tutte le Opere di G.
Boccaccio*, ed. V. Branca; T.G. Bergin, *Boccaccio*; P. Boitani, *Chaucer and
Boccaccio*; R.A. Pratt, "Chaucer's Use of the Teseida." *PMLA* 62 (1947): 598–621;
B.A. Wise, *The Influence of Statius Upon Chaucer* (Baltimore, 1911; rpt. New
York, 1967), 6, 67–68; D. Wallace, *Chaucer and the Early Writings of Boccaccio.*

BOECE. Ancius Manlius Torquatus Severinus Boethius, c. A.D. 480–524,
came from a very old and very important family. His father was consul in
487, and Boethius himself became consul in 510 at the age of thirty.
Theodoric, the Ostrogothic king of Italy, gave him many honors, including
the coveted office of *magister officorum*, Master of the Offices. He married
Rusticiana, daughter of Symmachus, by whom he had two sons. He was
said to have translated the *Geometry* of Euclid, the *Musica* of Pythagoras,
the *Arithmetica* of Nichomachus, the *Mechanica* of Archimedes, the
Astronomica of Ptolemy, the theology of Plato, and the *Logic* of Aristotle,
with the *Commentary* of Porphyry. His rigorous pursuit of justice for the
poor aroused the hatred and jealousy of his enemies, who accused him of
high treason. Believing him guilty, Theodoric imprisoned Boethius in the
tower at Pavia; the Senate passed sentence without holding a trial. Boethius was brutally tortured, then clubbed to death in 524. He was buried
in the cathedral at Pavia; but in 721, his relics were transferred to the crypt
behind the altar of the Church of San Pietro in Ciel d'Oro. During the Middle
Ages he was regarded as a martyr for the faith and invoked as St. Severinus.
His works include, in addition to *De consolatione philosophiae*, written
while he was in prison, translations of Porphyry's *Isogage*, a commentary
on Cicero's *Topica (Topics)*, compilations from various authors, *De musica*
and *De arithmetica*, and several theological treatises, among them one
called *De Trinitate*. During the Middle Ages his edition of Euclid's theorems
without the proofs was very popular.

Dante places Boethius in the Heaven of the Sun among the *spiriti
sapienti, Par* X.121–129. The works of Boethius form the foundation of much
medieval philosophy and literature, permeating the thought of scholars
and poets. *De consolatione philosophiae* was translated into several vernaculars. King Alfred translated it (after 893) into Old English as one of the
books his people should know, adding his own glosses and changing the
form, for he translated the whole work as prose. He expanded the story of
Orpheus and Eurydice (*Bo* III, *Metr* 12), omitting the final allegorical
interpretation of Eurydice as the pit of hell and as the things of the earth.
He made the work more immediate to his readers, introducing the Saxon
hero Weland in place of Fabricius, *Bo* II, *Prosa* 7. A translation into
Provençal of the tenth century survives in a fragment of thirty-five stanzas;
a twelfth-century Anglo-Norman version of Simund de Freine (c. 1180) is
called the *Roman de philosophie*. Jean de Meun made his translation in the

late thirteenth century or early fourteenth century. There is a translation of Renaud de Louens (1336–1337) and several translations in French dialects. The form of *De consolatione philosophiae*, alternating verse and prose, appears in several important medieval works: *De nuptiis Mercurii et Philologiae (The Marriage of Mercury and Philology)*, by Martianus Capella; *De mundi universitate (On the Whole World)*, by Bernard Silvester, and *De planctu Naturae (The Complaint of Nature)* by Alain de Lille, all show heavy Boethian influence.

Commentaries appear as early as the ninth century in a work by Lupus of Ferrières. A commentary is attributed to Remigius of Auxerre, c. A.D. 904: *Incipit expositio in Libro Boetii de Consolatione Phylosophiae Remigii.* Gilbert of Poitiers's commentary on *De Trinitate (On the Trinity)* aroused Bernard of Clairvaux, and in 1147 a council at Paris examined Gilbert for heresy on the basis of this work. Bernard attempted to have him condemned, but Gilbert was acquitted of heresy.

Chaucer's translation of *De consolatione philosophiae* under the title *Boece* is dated after 1380, in the same period when he wrote *The Knight's Tale,* probably about 1382. He used a Latin text, a Latin commentary by Nicholas Trevet, and a French prose translation by Jean de Meun, *Li Livres de confort de philosophie.* Boethius's influence is most marked in *The Knight's Tale, Troilus and Criseyde, The Former Age, Fortune,* and *Truth.*

Specific borrowings include Arcite's lament, *KnT* 1251–1267 *(Bo* III, *Prosa 2);* Palamon's lament, *KnT* 1303–1314 *(Bo* I, *Metr* 5; IV. *Prosa* l); the passage on Destiny, *KnT* 1663–1673 *(Bo* IV, *Prosa* 6); Theseus's speech, *KnT* 2987–3074 *(Bo* II, *Metr* 8; III, *Prosa* 10; IV, *Prosa* 6, *Metr* 6). The old wife quotes Boethius on gentillesse, *WBT* 1168 *(Bo* III, *Prosa* 6, *Metr* 6). The Nun's Priest mentions Boece as a writer on free will, *NPT* 3240–3250 *(Bo* IV, *Prosa* 6; *Bo* V). The fox tells Chauntecleer that he has more feeling in music than Boece, *NPT* 3293–3294. The "other clerkys" who have written on sound include Boethius, *HF* II.760 *(De musica* I.3). The experiment of *HF* II.788–808 appears in *De musica* I.14. The dreamer quotes Boece on thoughts winged by Philosophy, *HF* II.972–978 *(Bo* IV, *Metr* 1.1–7).

The concept of Fortune and the role assigned to Fate as executor of the will of Providence in *Troilus and Criseyde* are essentially Boethian. Troilus laments that Fortune is his foe, *Tr* I.834–853 *(Bo* II, *Prosa* 2 and 3.75–79); Troilus's hymn to love, *Tr* III.1744–1771, is influenced by *Bo* II, *Metr* 8. The idea that men may sometimes be lords of Fortune, *Tr* IV.1587–1589, is a paraphrase from *Bo* II, *Prosa* 4. Fate is the executor of God, *Tr* V.1–3, influenced by *Bo* IV, *Prosa* 6.

Chaucer lists his *Boece* among his works, *ParsT* 1085; *LGW F* 425. The opening lines of the *Legend of Philomela, LGW* 2228–2230, follow *Bo* III, *Metr* 9, based on Plato's *Timaeus.* Chaucer wishes the scalle on Adam if he miscopies the *Boece, Adam* 1–2. Although *The Former Age* incorporates many Boethian concepts, it has been shown to be closer to Ovid than to

Boethius, especially *Metamorphoses* I. **[Albyn: Basileus: Cassiodore: Conigaste: Cyprian: Decorat: Erudice: Gaudenicus: Opilion: Orpheus: Symacus: Trygwille]**

Boece, the French variant, occurs once initially, *Adam* 2; twice in medial positions, *NPT* 3242, 3294; and four times in final rhyming position, *WBT* 1168, *HF* II.972, *LGW F* 425, *LGW G* 412.

Boethius, *The Theological Tractates and The Consolation of Philosophy*, ed. and
    trans. S.J. Tester; Dante, *Divine Comedy*, ed. and trans. C.S. Singleton, III.1:
    114–115; V.L. Dedeck-Héry, "Le Boece de Chaucer et les manuscrits français de
    la *Consolation* de Jean de Meun." *PMLA* 59 (1944): 18–57; *ibid.,* "Boethius's *De
    Consolatione* by Jean de Meun." *MS* 14 (1952): 165–275; P. Dronke, "Chaucer and
    Boethius's *De musica*." *N&Q* 211 (1966): 92; R.A. Dwyer, *Boethian Fictions*; M.
    Gibson, ed., *Boethius: His Life, Thought, and Influence*; M. Masi, ed., *Boethius and
    the Liberal Arts*; J. Norton-Smith, "Chaucer's 'Etas Primas.' *MAE* 32 (1963):
    117–124; J.J. O'Donnell, *Cassiodorus*; Gilbert of Poitiers, *The Commentaries on
    Boethius*, ed. N. Häring; A.V.C. Schmidt, "Chaucer and the Golden Age." *Essays
    in Criticism* 26 (1976): 99–115.

BOETES. Boötes, the constellation Artophylax, also known as the Bear Driver, lies in the northern hemisphere near Ursa Major, the Great Bear. The constellation, also known as the Haywain, the brightest star of which is Arcturus, is one of the oldest named, known as far back as Homer, *Odyssey* V.272.

Chaucer calls the constellation a star, *Bo* IV, *Metr* 5.5–7. The name *Boötes* was probably applied to the alpha or brightest star. **[Arctour: Calistopee: Ursa]**

R.A. Allen, *Star Names and their Meanings,* 92; Homer, *Odyssey,* ed. and trans. A.T.
    Murray, I: 188–189.

BOETHIUS: [BOECE]

BOLE, the zodiacal sign Taurus, is the night house of Venus.

Palamon, devoted to Venus, chooses Lycurge of Thrace as his second at the tournament Theseus has arranged to determine who shall have Emelie, *KnT* 2128–2129; Lycurge comes to the tournament in a chariot drawn by four white bulls, *KnT* 2139. The bull, as Taurus, is Venus's night house. On May 3, the sun is in the white bull, approximately 20 degrees in Taurus, when Palamon goes to visit Criseyde and to tell her that Troilus loves her, *Tr* II.50–56. Venus and Mars make love in her room painted with white bulls, *Mars* 85–86; that is, Venus is in her night house, Taurus. (See Glossary of astronomical terms in the Appendix.) The color probably refers to *Met* II.852, where Jupiter woos Europa in the form of a white bull, which became the constellation Taurus. **[Taur: Venus]**

R.A. Allen, *Star Names and their Meanings,* 378; Ovid, *Met,* ed. and trans. F.J. Miller,
    I: 118–119; *Riverside Chaucer,* ed. L. Benson, 1031.

BOOK OF DECREES: [GRATIAN]
BOOK OF THE LYON: [GUILLAUME DE MACHAUT]
BOOTES: [BOETES]
BOREAS: [EOLUS]
BRADWARDINE: [BRADWARDYN]

BRADWARDYN. Thomas de Bradwardine or de Braderwardina (1290?-1349), the name in public documents, was educated at Merton College, Oxford. He gained the highest reputation as a mathematician, astronomer, moral philosopher, and theologian. His famous treatise, *De causa Dei contra Pelagiani et de virtue causarem ad suos Mertonenses libri tres (Three Books Concerning the Cause of God Against the Pelagians and the Cause of Virtue Among the Mertonians)*, considers God's foreknowledge and man's free will and earned him the name Doctor Profundus. Bradwardine was elected Archbishop of Canterbury in July 1349 but died of the plague the same year.

The Nun's Priest links Bradwardine's name with Boethius, acknowledging his great reputation as a writer on God's foreknowledge, *NPT* 3242. [**Augustyn: Boece**]

The form, a contraction with a short vowel in the final syllable, appears in final rhyming position.

Thomas Bradwardine, *Tractatus de proportionibus,* ed. and trans. H. Lamar Crosby; E. Grant, "Bradwardine and Galileo: Equality of Velocities in the Void." *Archive for the History of Exact Sciences* 2 (1965): 344–364; Gordon Leff, *Bradwardine and the Pelagians*; Heiki A. Oberman, *Forerunners of the Reformation: the Shape of Late Medieval Thought,* trans. P.L. Nyhus, 151–164.

BRESEYDA, BRIXSEYDA. Briseis, a captive woman from Lyrnesus in Mysia, was given to Achilles to be his slave during the Trojan War. Agamemnon compelled Achilles to give her to him, whereupon Achilles remained in his tent and sulked over his loss, while Hector defeated the Greeks. Briseis tells her story in *Iliad* XIX.282–300; Ovid tells of Achilles's desertion in *Heroides* III.

The Man of Law says that Chaucer has narrated "the wo of Brixseyda," *MLI* 70–71, but there is no tale of Briseida in *The Legend of Good Women*. The story of her betrayal is a one-line reference, *HF* I.398. [**Achilles**]

Breseyda is derived from the accusative case, *Briseida,* feminine of *Briseis,* the Greek patronymic, meaning "daughter of Briseus," which occurs in Latin; it appears medially, *HF* I.398. *Brixseyda,* with intrusive -*x,* points to a variant pronunciation in -*x* for words where it represents -*s,* as in *Amphiorax.* It appears medially, *MLI* 71.

Homer, *Iliad,* ed. and trans. A.T. Murray, II: 356–359; Ovid, *Heroides,* ed. and trans. G. Showerman, 32–43; *Riverside Chaucer,* ed. L. Benson, 814; E.H. Wilkins, "Criseida." *MLN* 24 (1909): 65–67.

BRISEIS: [BRESEYDA]
BRIXSEYDE: [BRESEYDA]

BRUT(ES). Brutus, grandson of Aeneas, was the legendary founder of Britain, named after him, according to Geoffrey of Monmouth, *Historia Regum Britanniae (History of the Kings of Britain)* I.4–15. Jean le Maire de Belges, in *Illustrations de Gaul et singularités de Troie* (c. 1506), says that the Bretons are descended from Brutus, first king of Brittany, reflecting Geoffrey's claim.

Chaucer addresses the Envoy of his *Complaint to his Purse* to the "conqueror of Brutes Albyon." "Albion" is the ancient Celtic name for Britain; the conqueror is Henry Bolingbroke, who deposed Richard II and became Henry IV in 1400. The word *conquerour* was used by Henry in the proclamation read at his election to the crown; a petition from All Souls MS 182 addresses Henry as "le gracious conquerour d'Engleterre."

Brutes, the ME genitive case of *Brut*, occurs in medial position, *Purse*, 22.

Geoffrey of Monmouth, *Historia Regum Britanniae,* ed. J. Hammer, 25–34; *ibid., History of the Kings of Britain,* trans. L. Thorpe, 56–71; M.E. Giffin, *Studies in Chaucer and his Audience,* 89–106; M.D. Legge, "The Gracious Conqueror." *MLN* 68 (1953): 18–21; J. Seznec, *Survival of the Pagan Gods,* trans. B.F. Sessions, 24; Wace, *Le Roman de Brut,* ed. J.I. Arnold.

BRUTUS[1]: [BRUT]

BRUTUS[2]. Lucius Junius Brutus, founder of the Roman republic, was consul in 509 B.C. In that year he expelled the Tarquins after Sextus Tarquinius, son of Superbus, raped Lucretia (Cicero, *De officiis* III).

The illustrious Romans, Brutus and Cato, have not survived their fame, *Bo* II, *Metr* 7. Brutus swears to drive out the Tarquins after Lucrece's death, *LGW* 1862. Chaucer's sources are Livy, *Ab urbe condita liber* I.57–129, and Ovid, *Fasti* II.685–852, mentioned in *LGW* 1683. [**Colatyn: Lucrece: Tarquinius[1]: Tarquinius[2]**]

Cicero, *De officiis,* ed. and trans. W. Miller, 308–309; Livy, *Livy: Ab urbe condita libri,* ed. and trans. B.O. Foster, I: 198–209; Ovid, *Fasti,* ed. and trans. J.G. Frazer, 106–119.

BRUTUS[3]. Marcus Junius Brutus, c. 85–42 B.C., was Pompey's comrade during the civil war that brought Julius Caesar to power. Caesar pardoned him and made him governor of Cisalpine Gaul in 46 B.C. In 44, however, Brutus joined the conspiracy against Caesar because it seemed to him that Caesar was assuming tyrannical powers. He soon found himself involved in another civil war, this time against Antony and Octavian, and in 42 they defeated him at Philippi, where he committed suicide (Plutarch, *Life of Brutus*).

Porcia is the ideal wife because she could not live without Brutus, *FranklT* 1448–1450. False Brutus and others kill Caesar with bodkins, *MkT* 2705–2708. **[Porcia]**

Plutarch, *Parallel Lives,* ed. and trans. B. Perrin, VI: 125–246.

BRUTUS⁴ CASSIUS. This name appears in *MkT* 2697. It occurs in several medieval works, beginning with Chapter XIX of King Alfred's translation of *De consolatione philosophiae*, 2, *Metr* 7, through Lydgate's *Fall of Princes*. The form suggests that *et* had been omitted between *Brutus* and *Cassius* in the first manuscript, thus causing the error.

Riverside Chaucer, ed. L. Benson, 935; H.T. Silverstein, "Chaucer's 'Brutus Cassius.'" *MLN* 47 (1932): 148–159.

BUKTON. There are two Bukton men who were close to Chaucer, and his poem, *Lenvoy de Chaucer a Bukton* could have been addressed to either of them. Sir Peter Bukton (1350–1414) lived in Holderness in Yorkshire and was close to the House of Lancaster. He served in John of Gaunt's army in 1369 and later became Keeper of Knaresborough Castle, where he served as warden to Richard II. In 1399 Henry IV granted him the office of steward for life, and in 1400 he became constable of Knaresborough Castle. The other possibility, Sir Robert Bukton of Goosewold, Suffolk, served as equerry to Queen Anne, wife of Richard II. In 1390 he was appointed one of the king's justices in South Wales. He was a member of Parliament from Suffolk for several terms from 1390 to 1401. Like Chaucer, both Buktons were courtiers, serving either the king or the duke of Lancaster. Chaucer, Bukton, and Scogan all belonged to the same class. Haldeen Braddy and E.P. Kuhl support the identification of Sir Peter Bukton, while J.R. Hulbert and J.S.P. Tatlock support Sir Robert.

The *Envoy de Chaucer a Bukton* is dated after October 1396. Chaucer humorously warns Bukton against marriage, advising him to read Dame Alys of Bath's comments. **[Scogan]**

H. Braddy, "Sir Peter and the *Envoy to Bukton.*" *PQ* 14 (1935): 368–370; Chaucer: *The Minor Poems, Part One,* ed. G. Pace and A. David, 104; J.R. Hulbert, *Chaucer's Official Life*, 54–55; E.P. Kuhl, "Chaucer's 'My Maistre Bukton.'" *PMLA* 38 (1923): 115–132; J.S.P. Tatlock, *The Development and Chronology of Chaucer's Works*, 210–211.

BULL: [BOLE: TAUR]
BUSIRIS: [BUSIRUS]

BUSIRUS, BUSYRIDES. Busiris, son of Neptune, was king of Egypt. He sacrificed strangers to Jupiter in order to break the droughts. Hercules went to Egypt, allowed himself to be led to the altar, then broke the chains and slew Busiris and his men (*Met* X 183; *The Art of Love (Ars Amatoria)* I.647–652).

The Monk, in his tale of Hercules, *MkT* 2103–2104, says that horses ate Busirus's flesh, but that story is told of Diomedes, *Met* IX.194–196, not of Busiris. Busirus, who slays his guests, is in turn slain by a guest, *Bo* II, *Prosa* 6. Boethius appears to be the main source for the Monk's Tale of Hercules. R.L. Hoffman suggests that Chaucer's confusion of Busirus with Diomedes may have resulted from glosses on medieval manuscripts, such as those of the eleventh-century manuscript of Ovid's *Ibis* 401–402, where Busiris seems to have been confused with Diomedes.

Busirus is a misspelling for *Busiris, MkT* 2103, and appears in final rhyming position. *Busyrides* has been formed by analogy from other Greek patronymics and means "son of Busiris," but it is applied to Busirus himself, *Bo* II, *Prosa* 6.67. [**Ercules**]

R.L. Hoffman, *Ovid and the Canterbury Tales,* 186–189; Ovid, *The Art of Love (Ars Amatoria),* ed. and trans. J.H. Mozley, 56–57; *ibid., Met,* ed. and trans. F.J. Miller, II: 16–17.

BYBLIS: [BIBLIS]

CACUS, KACUS. Cacus, son of Vulcan, was a fire-breathing, half-human monster. He lived in a cave on the Aventine Hill and preyed on King Evander's subjects. He stole four bulls and many heifers of peerless beauty from Hercules as he drove the cattle of Geryon. Before Hercules could overtake him, the monster had entered his cave and had rolled a huge stone over the entrance. Since he could not remove the stone, Hercules opened up the top of the hill, reached in and caught Cacus, and squeezed him to death in his knotlike grip (*Aeneid* VIII.194–279). Ovid's account is slightly different. Hercules shoved aside the rock at the mouth of the cave, came face to face with Cacus, then clubbed him four times and killed him (*Fasti* I.543–586).

Theodulphus, the ninth-century bishop of Orleans, presents Cacus, the bad thief, opposed to Hercules as virtue in his poem, *De libris quos legere solebam et qualiter fabulae poetarum a philosophis mystice pertractentur* (*PL* 105: 331–332). Hercules and his labors were important to medieval writers because they saw in him a virtuous man who had conquered great obstacles. The incident with Cacus forms part of the tenth labor, *MkT* 2107, *Bo* IV, *Metr* 7.52–54. [**Ercules: Evander**]

Cacus appears medially, *MkT* 2107; *Kacus*, a spelling variant, occurs in *Bo* IV, *Metr* 7.52, 54.

Ovid, *Fasti*, ed. and trans. J.G. Frazer, 40–43; Virgil, *Aeneid,* ed. and trans. H.R. Fairclough, II: 72–79.

CADME, CADMUS was the son of Agenor, king of Tyre, and the brother of Europa. His father ordered him to set out in search of Europa after she disappeared riding the white bull. The Delphic Oracle instructed him to follow the sacred heifer and to build a city where she lay down. Thus he built Thebes, which suffered from Juno's hatred because Jupiter fell in love with several Theban princesses (*Met* III.1–130; *OM* III.1–204).

Arcite, a Theban prince, laments the woes of the house of Cadmus, *KnT* 1546–1550.

Cadme, the ME form, appears in medial position with elided final *-e*, *KnT* 1546; it is also found in Gower, *Confessio Amantis* I.339, in the story of Acteon, son of the Theban princess Autonoë. *Cadmus*, the Latin form, appears in medial position, *KnT* 1547. [**Agenor: Amphioun: Arcita: Europe**]

John Gower, *The Complete Works,* ed. G.C. Macaulay, I: 45; Ovid, *Met,* ed. and trans. F.J. Miller, I: 124–133; *OM,* ed. C. de Boer, I, deel 15: 299–303.

CAESAR: [CESAR]
CAIN: [CAYM]

CALCAS, CALKAS is Criseyde's father in *Troilus and Criseyde.* As Apollo's priest he is skilled in "calkulynge," *Tr* I.71; *Tr* IV.1398, and "calculating" gives some indication of his character. Susan Schibanoff points out that Calcas is one of the *redendenamen* or "speaking names" of medieval etymology, that is, a name that provides an interpretation of a character. [**Argyve[1]: Criseyde: Troilus**]

The name occurs 16 times in medial positions, *Tr* I.71, 87, 92; *Tr* IV.63, 64, 134, 333, 663, 761, 1466; *Tr* V.149, 508, 845, 846, 897, 1575; and twice in final rhyming position, *Tr* I.66; *Tr* IV.73.

S. Schibanoff, "Argus and Argive: Etymology and Characterization in Chaucer's Troilus." *Speculum* 51 (1976): 647–650.

CALKAS: [CALCAS]

CALIOPE, CALLYOPE. Calliope, eldest of the Muses, was the daughter of Zeus and Mnemosyne. The Muse of epic poetry, she was the mother of Orpheus and the keeper of the Castalian spring on Mount Parnassus, which was sacred to Apollo (*Met* V.662–663).

Calliope and her eight sisters sing Fame's praises in Fame's house, *HF* III.1399–1406. Even in the Underworld Orpheus sings the songs he learned from his mother's well, *Bo* III, *Metr* 12.23, a reference to the Castalian spring. The poet asks Calliope to lend her voice because he needs her now, *Tr* III.45–48. Fulgentius says that Calliope means "she of excellent voice," *optima vox* (*Mythologies* I.15). The invocation is influenced by Dante, *Purg* I.7–9. [**Cleo: Orpheus: Pierides**]

Caliope appears initially, *Tr* III.45, and in final rhyming position, *HF* III.1400.

Callyope appears as a gloss in *Bo* III, *Prosa* 12.23, to identify Orpheus's mother.

Dante, *Divine Comedy,* ed. and trans. C.S. Singleton, II.1: 2–3; Fulgentius, *Fulgentius the Mythographer,* trans. L. Whitbread, 55–57; Ovid, *Met,* ed. and trans. F.J. Miller, I: 284–285.

CALIPSA. Calypso was the nymph who detained Odysseus for eight years on her island of Ogygia (*Odyssey* V.14–168). Ovid mentions her charm in *Epistolae ex Ponto* IV.13–14.

Calipsa appears in company with Medea and Circe, famous sorceresses, *HF* III.1272. Gower says that Calipsa and Circe are queens of the island of Cilly, *Confessio Amantis,* VI.1427, and they know how to make the moon go into eclipse, *Confessio Amantis* VIII.2597–2600. **[Cerces]**

Calipsa, the ME variant, occurs in final rhyming position, *HF* III.1272.

John Gower, *The Complete Works,* ed., G.C. Macaulay III: 206, 456–457; Homer, *Odyssey,* ed. and trans. A.T. Murray, I: 170–189; Ovid, *Tristia and Epistolae ex Ponto,* ed. and trans. A.L. Wheeler, 464–465.

CALISTOPEE, CALYXTE. Callisto, daughter of Lycaon, was a nymph dedicated to Diana. Jupiter fell in love with her, and she bore him a son, Arcas. Diana dismissed her from her troupe, and Juno transformed her into a bear. One day, her son came upon her as he hunted in the forest; as he was about to shoot her, Jupiter changed him into a bear and placed mother and son among the stars. Callisto became Ursa Major (the Great Bear) and Arcas became Ursus Minor or Artophylax, the Little Bear (Met II.407–530; OM II.1365–1694).

The story of Diana and Callistopee is painted on the walls of Diana's oratory, *KnT* 2056–2061; Diana has changed her into a bear, and the loodesterre, or polestar, appears in her constellation. The polestar, however, appears in Ursus Minor. Chaucer's lines show a possible influence of Boccaccio, *De genealogia deorum gentilium (The Genealogy of the Pagan Gods),* V.49: here Callisto becomes Ursa Minor and Arcas becomes Ursus Major. Calyxte appears among love's martyrs, *PF* 286. **[Arctour: Boetes: Ursa]**

Calistopee occurs in final rhyming position, *KnT* 2056, expanded either to suit the meter or through confusion with *Calliope.* In Gower's version the name is also expanded, *Calistona, Confessio Amantis* V.6225–6358, influenced by Boccaccio's *Calistonem,* Latin accusative singular of *Calisto. Calyxte,* a pronunciation development of *-x* where it represents etymologically an *-s,* occurs medially, *PF* 286.

Boccaccio, *De genealogia deorum gentilium,* ed. V. Romano, I: 285; John Gower, *Confessio Amantis,* ed. G.C. Macaulay, III: 116–120; Ovid, *Met,* ed. and trans. F.J. Miller, I: 88–97; *OM,* ed. C. de Boer, I, deel 15: 201-208; *Riverside Chaucer,* ed. L. Benson, 814.

CALLISTO: [CALISTOPEE]
CALLYOPE: [CALIOPE]
CALYPSO: [CALIPSA]
CALYXTE: [CALISTOPEE]

CAMBALO, CAMBALUS is the younger son of King Cambyuskan in *The Squire's Tale*. His sister's lover is also called Cambalus. It is not clear that brother and lover are two separate people. [**Algarsyf: Cambyuskan: Canacee²: Elpheta**]

Cambalo occurs twice, *SqT* 31, 667, and *Cambalus* once, *SqT* 656, all in final rhyming position. Skeat (V: 370) suggests derivation from *Cambaluc*, Kublai's capital; Robinson (718) suggests *Kambala*, the name of Kublai's grandson. *Cembalo*, the medieval name for Balaklava, is closer to Chaucer's form.

N.E. Eliason, "Personal Names in the *Canterbury Tales*." *Names* 21 (1973): 137–152; *Riverside Chaucer*, ed. L. Benson, 891.

CAMBISES. Cambyses, son of Cyrus, was king of Persia and ruled 529–522 B.C. Herodotus says that Cambyses was a madman; his habitual anger was a symptom of his condition (*Histories* III.1–72). Seneca says that Cambyses *furiosus ac feliciter usus habuit*, "made successful use of his madness" (*Epistle* 86.1), and tells the story of how Cambyses slew his counselor's son in a fit of rage, *De ira* III.14.

Friar John illustrates his sermon of wrath with the story of how angry Cambyses slew his counselor's son, *SumT* 2043–2078. [**Cirus: Senec**]

Cambises, a spelling variant, occurs medially, *SumT* 2043.

Herodotus, *Histories*, ed. and trans. A.D. Godley, II: 3–7, 41–47; Seneca, *Ad Lucillum epistulae morales*, ed. and trans. R.M. Gummere, II: 310–311; *ibid., Moral Essays*, ed. and trans. J.W. Basore, I: 288–293.

CAMBYSES: [CAMBISES]

CAMBYUSKAN is the king of Sarre in Tartary and father of Algarsyf, Cambalus, and Canacee in *The Squire's Tale*. F.P. Magoun, Jr., identifies Sarre in the steppes of southern Russia as part of the western Mongol empire and suggests that Cambyuskan is not Genghis Khan (Chinggis Khan), who ruled 1162–1227. John M. Manly suggests that Chaucer may have used Marco Polo's account of his travels, from which he may have taken the name. [**Algarsyf: Cambalo: Canacee²: Elpheta**]

Cambyuskan occurs twice in medial positions, *SqT* 58, 345, and five times in final rhyming position, *SqT* 12, 28, 42, 266, 661.

F.P. Magoun, Jr., *A Chaucer Gazetteer*, 151; J.M. Manly, "Marco Polo and the *Squire's Tale*." *PMLA* 11 (1896): 349–362; *Riverside Chaucer*, ed. L. Benson, 891.

CAMPANEUS, CAPPANEUS. Capaneus was one of the seven chieftains who joined Adrastus in the war against Thebes. Jupiter killed him with a thunderbolt *(Thebaid* X.827–939; *Roman de Thèbes* 10086–10096).

The widow of Cappaneus meets Theseus at the temple of Clemence and tells him that Creon has forbidden the burial of the dead, including their husbands' bodies, *KnT* 931–947.

Campaneus appears in summaries of the Theban War, *Anel* 59, and *Cappaneus* appears in *Tr* V.1504. [**Adrastus: Amphiorax: Hemonydes: Parthonope: Polite: Tydeus**]

Campaneus occurs in final rhyming position, *Anel* 59, a variant of Boccaccio's *Campaneo*, *Tes* II.11.5. *Cappaneus* occurs medially, *Tr* V.1504, and in final rhyming position, *KnT* 932.

Boccaccio, *Tutte le Opere*, ed. V. Branca, II: 300; R.A. Pratt, "Chaucer's Use of the *Teseida." PMLA* 62 (1947): 605, n. 23; *Roman de Thèbes*, ed. L. Constans, I: 500; *Roman de Thèbes (The Story of Thebes)*, trans. J.S. Cole, 237; Statius, *Thebaid*, ed. and trans. J.H. Mozley, II: 378–389.

CANACE, CANACEE[1]. Canace was Aeolus's daughter. She fell in love with her brother Macareus and bore him a son. When Aeolus discovered this, he ordered the child exposed and abandoned; then he sent Canace a sword with which to commit suicide *(Heroides* XI).

The Man of Law says that Chaucer has never told the story of wicked Canacee, *MLI* 78–85. Gower tells the story in *Confessio Amantis* III.143–360. John H. Fisher suggests that those lines are Chaucer's answer to Gower's criticism of his bawdy tales. Canace appears in the ballad of faithful women, *LGW F* 265, *LGW G* 219. [**Gower**]

Canacee appears in final rhyming position, *MLI* 78; *Canace* appears in medial position, *LGW F* 265, *LGW G* 219. Both forms have three syllables.

J.H. Fisher, *John Gower*, 287–292; John Gower, *The Complete Works*, ed. G.C. Macaulay, II: 230–235; Ovid, *Her*, ed. and trans. G. Showerman, 132–141.

CANACEE[2] is the beautiful young daughter of King Cambyuskan and Queen Elpheta in *The Squire's Tale*. Near the end of the tale, the Squire proposes to tell how her brother Cambalus fought in tournaments "to win" Canacee. The story, however, remains unfinished. Chaucer may have been reminded of Ovid's story in *Heroides* XI, the story of incest mentioned in *MLI* 77–78, and may have decided against finishing the tale. [**Algarsyf: Cambalo: Cambyuskan: Elpheta: Gower**]

Chaucer may have borrowed the name from *Heroides* XI. J.D. North suggests derivation from the name of the star *Cauda Ceti*, found in Chaucer's time in the zodiacal sign Pisces. The name appears ten times in medial positions, *SqT* 178, 384, 410, 449, 475, 633, 635, 638, 651, 669; seven times in final rhyming position, *MLI* 78, *SqT* 33, 144, 277, 361, 432, 485. *Canacees*, the ME genitive case, appears medially only, *SqT* 247, 631.

J.D. North, "Kalenderes Enlumyned Ben They." *RES* 20 (1969): 259–261; Ovid, *Her*, ed. and trans. G. Showerman, 132–141.

CANCER, CANCRE, CANCRO. Cancer, the constellation the Crab, is the fourth sign of the zodiac and lies in the northern hemisphere between Leo and Gemini. Hera sent the Crab to help the Hydra when Hercules attacked its several heads. Although the Crab bit his toe, Hercules won the battle. As the moist and cold sign the Crab is the moon's house or mansion *(Confessio Amantis* VII.1060–1066), the exaltation or sign of maximum power of Jupiter, and the depression or sign of minimum power of Mars *(Tetrabiblos* I.19).

The moon has passed from the second degree of Taurus into Cancer in four days, *MerchT* 1885–1889. Phoebus, the sun, is in Gemini, not far from Cancer, his declination, that is, the sun's maximum northern latitude, which it entered on June 12, the summer solstice in Chaucer's time, *MerchT* 2222–2224, on the day that May meets Damian in the pear tree. Cancer is Jove's exaltation, *MerchT* 2224. The conjunction of the crescent moon with Saturn and Jupiter in Cancer, the moon's house, causes the downpour of the smoky rain and prevents Criseyde from going home, *Tr* III.624–626. This astrological conjunction actually occurred on or about May 13, 1385, and is one of the clues for dating the *Troilus.* When the sun enters Cancer and there is a drought (at the summer solstice on June 12), and the seeds do not sprout from the dry furrows, the sower must look for acorns under oak trees, *Bo* I, *Metr* 6. 1–4. According to Ptolemy, this northern declination or latitude is 23 degrees and 50 minutes in Cancer, *Astr* I.17.1–40. Skeat notes that in Ptolemy's time, the latitude of the sun was 23 degrees and 40 minutes and 23 degrees and 31 minutes in Chaucer's time. Cancer lies directly opposite Capricorn, *Astr* II.16. The zodiac is divided into two half circles, from the head or beginning of Capricorn to the head or beginning of Cancer, *Astr* II.16. The head of Cancer is the highest point of the zodiac, and the signs from its head or beginning to the end of Sagittarius are called the signs of right ascension, or "sovereign signs," or "western signs," *Astr* II.28 31–35. [**Ercules: Juno**]

Cancer, the English form, appears in medial position, *MerchT* 2224; *Cancre,* the French variant, appears in medial position, *MerchT* 1887, and in the *Boece.* Both forms appear in *A Treatise on the Astrolabe*, although *Cancer* is the preferred form there. *Cancro* occurs medially in *Tr* III.625.

John Gower, *The Complete Works,* ed. G.C. Macaulay, III: 261–262; Ptolemy, *Tetrabiblos*, ed. and trans. F.E. Robbins, 91; W.W. Skeat, ed., *A Treatise on the Astrolabe,* 9; *Riverside Chaucer*, ed. L. Benson,1099.

CANDACE is the Ethiopian queen of the Alexander romances. The name was the hereditary title of the queen-mother of Meroë, capital of ancient Nubia, sometimes called Ethiopia. Classical writers used *Candace* as a personal name for the queen of Ethiopia (Strabo, *Geography* 17.1.54). In the romance of Julius Valerius, *Res gestae Alexandri Macedonis* (c. A.D. 320–330), there is no love affair between Alexander and Candace. The French romances of the twelfth century develop a love affair between the queen and Alexander. Thomas of Kent, in his Anglo-Norman *Roman de Toute Chevalerie* (1174–1182), presents Candace in the antifeminist tradition, inserting several verses on the falsity of women, including Eve and Potiphar's wife. Froissart (c. 1337– c. 1400) celebrates Candace because she had the foresight to have a portrait made of Alexander, by which she recognized him when he visited her in disguise, *L'Espinette Amoureuse* 1798–1803.

Candace is one of love's martyrs, *PF* 288. Twelfth-century versions, such as the *Venjance Alixandre* (before 1181), present Candace as a love-sick queen, mourning the hero's death. The poet's lady is as fickle as Candace, Dalida, and Criseyde, *Against Woman Unconstant*, 16. Lists of women who have overcome men in one way or another are commonplaces in medieval antifeminist literature, such as Jankin's "Book of Wikked Wyves" in *The Wife of Bath's Tale*. In *Kyng Alisaundre* (before 1330), 7700–7710, Candace mentions Dalida in her list of perfidious women. [**Alisaundre: Dalida: Sampson**]

Candace appears medially, *PF* 288, and in final rhyming position, *Wom Unc* 16.

Five Versions of the Venjance Alixandre, ed. E. Billings Ham, 6–9; J. Froissart, *L'Espinette Amoureuse,* ed. A. Fournier, 98; *Kyng Alisaunder,* ed. G.V. Smithers, I: 417–419; R.M. Smith, "Five Notes on Chaucer and Froissart." *MLN* 66 (1951): 27–32; Strabo, *Geography,* ed. and trans. H.L. Jones, VIII: 136–141.

CANII: [CANYUS]
CANIUS: [CANYUS]

CANYUS. Julius Canius or Canus, fl. first century A.D., was a Roman noble accused by Caligula of knowing of a plot against him. Julius was condemned to death in A.D. 40. Seneca tells of Canius's stoicism in the face of death, *De tranquilitate animi* XIV.9.

Boethius, similarly accused of conspiracy, wishes he could answer like Canius: "If I hadde wyst it, thow haddest noght wyst it," *Bo* I, *Prosa* 4.178–185. [**Boece: Cesar³: Senec**]

Seneca, *Moral Essays,* ed. and trans. J.W. Basore, II: 268–271.

CAPANEUS: [CAMPANEUS]
CAPELLA, MARTIANUS: [MARCIAN]
CAPPANEUS: [CAMPANEUS]

CAPRICORN, CAPRICORNE, CAPRICORNUS is the constellation the Goat, which lies in the southern hemisphere near Sagittarius. The tenth sign of the zodiac, it is the day house of Saturn, the exaltation of Mars, and the depression of Jupiter (*Confessio Amantis* VII.1169–84; *Tetrabiblos* I.19).

The sun, Phoebus, is in Capricorn, the winter solstice, and bitter frosts destroy the green in every yard, *FranklT* 1248–1251. Capricorn is called the winter solstice or the tropic of winter, *Astr* I.17, because the sun enters the sign on December 13, the shortest day in the northern hemisphere in Chaucer's time. Today, the sun enters Capricorn on December 21. The circle of Capricorn is the widest circle of the three principal circles, *Astr* I.17, the others being the tropic of Cancer and the equator. The head or the beginning of Capricorn is the sun's most southern declination, that is, its southernmost point, *Astr* I.17. According to Ptolemy, the sun's southernmost latitude or declination is 23 degrees and 50 minutes in Capricorn, *Astr* I.17; Skeat notes that, in Ptolemy's time, the true value for both latitudes of the sun, north (Cancer) and south (Capricorn), was about 23 degrees and 40 minutes, but in Chaucer's time it was 23 degrees and 31 minutes. The signs found from the head or beginning of Capricorn to the end of Gemini are called tortuous signs, oblique signs, or obedient signs; that is, they obey the signs of right ascension or the western or sovereign signs: Capricorn obeys the sovereign (western) sign Sagittarius, *Astr* II.28.38–39. A sign is said to rise obliquely when a similar part of the equator rises with it. Every sign between the head or beginning of Capricorn and the end of Gemini rises in less than two equal hours, *Astr* II.28.25–26. The longitude and latitude of Venus are calculated by measuring its degree from Capricorn, *Astr* II.40.10–42.

Capricorn, the English variant, appears in *FranklT* 1248 and throughout the *Treatise on the Astrolabe. Capricorne,* the French variant, and *Capricornus,* the Latin variant, appear only in the *Treatise on the Astrolabe.*

John Gower, *The Complete Works,* ed. G.C. Macaulay, III: 264–265; Ptolemy, *Tetrabiblos,* ed. and trans. F.E. Robbins, 90–91; W.W. Skeat, ed., *A Treatise on the Astrolabe,* 9.

CASSANDRA, CASSANDRE. Cassandra was King Priam's daughter and Troilus's sister. Apollo fell in love with her and gave her the gift of prophecy, but she refused to return his love. Since he could not take back his gift, Apollo rendered it useless: no one would believe her prophecies. After the fall of Troy she was given as a concubine to Agamemnon, who took her home to Mycenae. She shared the horror of his homecoming, for Clytemnestra killed them both (*Aeneid* II.246–247, III.182–187).

The Man in Black says that Cassandra never had as much woe as he did the day his lady refused to accept him, *BD* 1236–1249. Cassandra is called Sibille, *Tr* V.1450, when she comes to Troilus to interpret his dream of the boar. The name *sibyl* was given by the Greeks and the Romans to female prophets, usually to those inspired by Apollo (*Aeneid* VI.77–101). **[Sibille: Troilus]**

Cassandra, the Latin and English form, appears medially, *BD* 1245. *Cassandre,* the French variant, appears three times initially: final -*e* is elided in *Tr* V.1451, 1456, but pronounced for the meter, *Tr* V.1534; it appears once medially, *Tr* III.410.

Virgil, *Aeneid,* ed. and trans. H.R. Fairclough, I: 310–311, 512–513.

CASSIDORE, CASSIDORIE. Flavius Cassiodorus Magnus Aurelius, c. A.D. 490–c.580/583, was born in Syllach, Calabria, into a family of Syrian origin. A description of Cassiodorus and of his family appears in the letter that introduces him to the aristocrats of Theodoric's court *(Epistola* I.4). The letter says that the family is of noble birth, healthy of body, and very tall. Cassiodorus became quaestor to Theodoric, the Ostrogothic king of Rome, in A.D. 507, consul in 514, and succeeded Boethius as *Magister officiorum* (Master of the Offices) in 527. In 537, after his retirement from public life, he issued his *Epistolae Theodoricianae variae (Various Letters Written for Theodoric),* letters written for both Ostrogothic kings, Theodoric and Athalaricus. His most influential work is a treatise on religious and secular education called *Institutiones.* After the collapse of the Ostrogothic kingdom in 540, Cassiodorus founded a monastery at Vivarium at Calabria, where the monks were to devote their time to sound learning and to the copying of manuscripts and books. His history of the Goths is summarized by Jordanes in his work *Getica* or *History of the Goths.*

All of Chaucer's references to Cassiodorus appear in *The Tale of Melibee,* translated from *Le Livre de Melibee et de Dame Prudence,* by Renaud de Louens (after 1336), which is an adaptation of the Latin work, *Liber consolationis et consilii* (c. 1246), by Albertanus of Brescia. The following references are to the letters written for Theodoric, *Epistolae Theodoricianae variae: Book* 10, *Letter* 18, p. 309, *Mel* 1196; *Book* I, *Letter* 17, p. 23, *Mel* 1348; *Book* I, *Letter* 4, p. 14, *Mel* 1438; *Book* I, *Letter* 30, p. 30, *Mel* 1528; *Book* 9, *Letter* 13, pp. 277–278, *Mel* 1564; *Book* I, *Letter* 4, p. 15, *Mel* 1642. **[Boece]**

The forms are the variants found in the French text.

Cassiodorus, *Institutiones,* ed. R.A.B. Mynors; *ibid., An Introduction to Divine and Human Readings,* trans. with introd. and notes by L.W. Jones; *ibid., Variae epistolae,* ed. Th. Momsen; J.J. O'Donnell, *Cassiodorus;* Renaud de Louens, *Le livre de Melibee et de Prudence,* ed. J. Burke Severs, *S&A,* 568–614.

CASSIODORUS: [CASSIDORE]

CASTOR was the twin brother of Pollux, sons of Jupiter and Leda and brothers of Helen. Together they form the constellation Gemini, the Twins, and are the third sign of the zodiac. Castor is also the name of the brightest star in the constellation, which lies in the northern hemisphere near Auriga, the Charioteer. Gemini is the night house of Mercury *(Confessio Amantis,* VII.1031–1050; *Tetrabiblos,* I.17).

The learned eagle tells the dreamer that Castor and Pollux have been "stellified," become stars, *HF* II.1000–1008. **[Gemini: Pollux]**

The name occurs initially, *HF* II.1006.

John Gower, *The Complete Works,* ed. G.C.Macaulay, III: 261; Ptolemy, *Tetrabiblos,* ed. and trans. F.E. Robbins, 83.

CATO: [CATON, CATOUN]

CATON[1], CATOUN[1]. Cato was the supposed author of *Disticha de moribus ad filium,* known also as *Ethica Catonis, Liber Catonianus,* and *Disticha Catonis,* written probably in the third or fourth century A.D. The work served as a Latin grammar as well as an introduction to ethics, its aim being to teach the four cardinal virtues. It was glossed by scholars from Remigius of Auxerre in the ninth century to Erasmus in the sixteenth. Twelfth- and thirteenth-century Latin satirical poets used Cato familiarly, as did Chaucer's contemporaries Deschamps, Langland, and Gower. The *Liber Catonianus* was an anthology, or *florilegium,* containing pieces by Cato, Avianus, Theodolus, Maximianus, Statius, and Claudian; Cato was thus one of the curriculum authors taught in the schools.

The Miller paraphrases *Distich* II.2; *MillT* 3163–3164; variations appear in *MillT* 3454, 3558. John the Carpenter is untaught and does not know Cato, *MillT* 3227. The Miller quotes from Cato, *MillT* 3229–3232; this quotation is not found in Cato but in glosses of *Facetus* 37. Alys of Bath paraphrases *Distich* III.23, *WBP* 781. The Merchant quotes *Distich* III.23, *MerchT* 1377. The Franklin's "Lerneth to suffre" is a paraphrase of *Distich* I.38, *FranklT* 773–777. Dame Prudence's exhortation on good counsel recalls *Distich* III.4, *Mel* 1181–1183; her remarks on examining advice resemble *Distich* III.15, *Mel* 1215–1216; on the value of true friends, Dame Prudence paraphrases *Distich* IV.13, *Mel* 1306; on the wisdom of suffering annoyances, she paraphrases *Distich* IV.39, *Mel* 1489; on the dangers of idleness, Dame Prudence recalls *Distich* I.2, *Mel* 1594; on stinginess and avarice, Dame Prudence quotes *Distich* IV.16, *Mel* 1602; on the dangers of waste, she recalls *Distich* III.21, *Mel* 1605. Pertelote quotes Cato on dreams, *Distich* III.3, *NPT* 2940. Chauntecleer replies that although Cato was doubtless a learned man, he gave an opinion that many others have reversed, *NPT* 2970–2981. *The Second Nun's Prologue,* 1–7, may be traced to glosses on *Distich* I.2. The narrator paraphrases *Distich* I.17, *CYT* 688–689; the gloss for this passage provides the identification (Manly-Rickert III: 522). The Manciple paraphrases *Distich* I.12, *MancT* 325–328. Robinson (770) identifies the "wise man" of *ParsT* 661 as "Dionysus Cato," *Distich* I.38; the *Riverside Chaucer* does not offer an identification.

Caton, one form of the French variant, appears in medial position, *NPT* 2976; *Catoun,* both French and Anglo-Norman variant, occurs four times in medial position, *MillT* 3227; *MerchT* 1377; *NPT* 2940; CYT 688; and once in final rhyming position, *NPT* 2971. Both forms appear in the prose tale of Melibee.

The Distichs of Cato: A Famous Medieval Textbook, ed. and trans. W.J. Chase; Max Förster, "Eine Nordenglische Cato-Version." *Englische Studien* 36 (1906): 1–55; R. Hazelton, "Chaucer and Cato." *Speculum* 35 (1960): 357–380; *ibid.,* "The Christianization of Cato." *MS* 19 (1957): 157–173; R.A. Pratt, "Karl Young's Work on the Learning of Chaucer." *A Memoir of Karl Young,* 54; *The Riverside Chaucer,* ed. L. Benson, 961.

CATON². Marcus Porcius Cato, 234–149 B.C., known as Cato Maior, became consul in 195 B.C. and censor in 184 B.C. As censor, he attacked the luxurious habits of the rich; he tried to reform the lax morals of the nobility by criticizing powerful offenders. He objected to Greek learning and culture, and he adopted the stance of the rustic Roman gentleman. He was the great-grandfather of Cato Uticensis (Plutarch, *Life of Cato Major*).

Lady Philosophy, using the *ubi sunt* theme, asks: "What is now Brutus or stierne Caton?" *Bo* II, *Metr* 7.19. **[Catoun²]**

Caton is the French variant of the family name *Cato.*

Plutarch, *Parallel Lives,* ed. and trans. B. Perrin, II: 302–385.

CATOUN². Marcus Porcius Cato, 95–46 B.C., was the great-grandson of Cato Maior. He was called "Uticensis" after the city of Utica, where he lived. During the civil war, he ruled Sicily for the Senate, but as he perceived that Caesar's victories were increasing, he withdrew to Libya with Scipio in order to live as far as possible from Caesar's tyranny. He saved Utica when Scipio was ready to massacre the citizens and, at their request, agreed to protect the city so that it would not fall into Caesar's hands. When he heard that Caesar had won the battle of Thapsus in 46 B.C., he gave a banquet for his friends and the magistrates of Utica, then spent the night reading Plato's *Phaedo,* after which he committed suicide. His daughter Porcia was Brutus's wife (Plutarch, *Life of Cato Minor*).

Lady Philosophy quotes the famous line from Lucan's *Pharsalia* I.128: *Uictrix causa deis placuit sed uicta Catoni,* "the victorious cause likide to the goddes, and the cause overcomen likide to Catoun," *Bo* IV, *Prosa* 6.233. **[Lucan: Marcia Catoun: Porcia]**

Catoun is the French as well as Anglo-Norman form.

Plutarch, *Parallel Lives,* ed. and trans. B. Perrin, VIII: 386–407.

CATOUN, MARCIA: [MARCIA CATOUN]

CATULLUS. Gaius Valerius Catullus, c. 84–c. 54 B.C., was born at Verona and died in Rome. He went to Rome about 62 B.C., and there he fell in love with a woman he calls Lesbia, who appears to have been Clodia, wife of Metellus Celer; Apuleius says that Lesbia was named Clodia. This love affair inspired much of his poetry.

Lady Philosophy reminds Boethius that many men who sit in the chair of dignity are wicked, as Catullus found in the consul Nonius, *Bo* III, *Prosa* 4.11. She says that Catullus called Nonius *postum* or *boch*, that is, an abcess. Boethius's *struma*, a "scrofulous tumor," refers to *Carmen* lii.2. **[Nonyus]**

Apuleius, *Apologia*, ed. and trans. H.E. Butler, 32–33; Catullus, *Carmina*, ed. R.A.B. Mynors; *ibid.*, *Catullus*, ed. and introd. D.F.S. Thomson; J.A.S. McPeek, "Did Chaucer Know Catullus?" *MLN* 46 (1931): 293–301.

CAYM. Cain was Adam's elder son, who slew his brother Abel when God accepted Abel's sacrifice and refused Cain's. God then made Cain a fugitive and a wanderer throughout the earth, and Cain felt his punishment was more than he could bear (Genesis 4:1–24).

The Parson tells of Cain's despair, *ParsT* 1015. **[Judas²]**
Caym is the ME and OF variant.

"Mactacio Abel," *The Wakefield Pageants in the Towneley Cycle*, ed. A.C. Cawley.

CECILE, CECILIE (saint). Cecilia became the patron saint of music and art, one of the celebrated saints of the Roman Catholic Church, although it is doubtful that she ever lived. She is mentioned neither by the Chronographer of 354, nor by Jerome, nor by Prudentius (*NCE* IV: 360). Her life is told in *Legenda Aurea* CLXIX.

The Second Nun tells a Life of St. Cecilia. G.H. Gerould suggests that Chaucer's source may have been a copy of the saint's life fuller than those available to modern scholars. Although Chaucer closely follows the *Life* in Jacobus de Voragine as far as verse 357, the rest of the story is so different that Gerould posits Chaucer used either a longer version or a different version.

Jacobus de Voragine begins the saint's life with etymologies of her name: *"Caecilia quasi coeli lilia cel caecis via vel a coelo et lya. Vel Caecilia quasi caecitate carens. Vel dicitur a coelo et leos, quod est populus."* Cecilia comes from *coeli lilia*, "lily of heaven," or from *caecis via*, "a way unto the blind," or from *coelum*, "heaven," and *lya*, "one who works." Or again, it is the same as *caecitate carens*, "free from blindness," or comes from *coelum*, "heaven," and *leos*, "people." The Second Nun begins her legend similarly, *SNP* 85–119. The name means "hevenes lilie, *SNP* 87; "wey to blynde," *SNP* 92; "hevene and Lia" mean "hoolynesse" and "bisynesse," *SNP* 94–98; "wantynge of blyndnesse," *SNP* 100; "hevene of peple," *SNP* 102–105.

Robinson (757) points out that these meanings are all wrong, but Russell Peck shows how appropriate they are to the tale itself. Susan Schibanoff suggests that *Cecile* is one of the *redendenamen* or "speaking names" of medieval etymology.

Queen Alceste lists the *Lyf of Seinte Cecile* among Chaucer's works, *LGW F* 426, *LGW G* 416. **[Almache: Ambrose: Maxime: Tiburce: Urban: Valerian]**

Cecile, Cecilie are variants of Latin *Caecilia. Cecile* occurs seven times initially, *SNP* 99, *SNT* 169, 379, 382, 407, 412, 493; eleven times in medial positions, *SNP* 92, 94; *SNT* 120, 176, 194, 222, 275, 284, 319, 422, 450; five times in final rhyming position, *SNP* 85; *SNT* 196, 218, 554; *LGW* 426. *Cecilie* appears twice medially, *SNP* 115; *SNT* 550, and once in final rhyming position, *SNP* 28. The rhymes show that both forms are pronounced alike.

G.H. Gerould, "The Second Nun's Prologue and Tale." *S&A,* 664–684; Jacobus de Voragine, *GL,* trans. Ryan and Ripperger, 689; *ibid., LA,* ed. Graesse, 771–777; R. Peck, "The Ideas of 'Entente' and Translation in Chaucer's *Second Nun's Tale." AnM* 8 (1967): 23–25; *Riverside Chaucer, ed.* L. Benson, 944; S. Schibanoff, "Argus and Argyve: Etymology and Characterization in Chaucer's *Troilus." Speculum* 51 (1976): 649–658.

CECILIA: [CECILE]

CECILIE: [CECILE]

CEDASUS. Scedasus lived in Leuctra, a village in Boeotia. He had two daughters, Hippo and Miletia, also called Theano and Eutupe, who were raped and killed by two Spartans. When Scedasus went to Sparta seeking satisfaction, he got none. He then killed himself. Plutarch tells the story in *Amatoriae narrationes* III, and Jerome gives a brief account, *Epistola adversus Jovinianum (Letter Against Jovinian),* I.41 (*PL* 23: 272–273).

Dorigen thinks the daughters of Cedasus are exemplary figures of maidenly virtue, *FranklT* 1428. **[Dorigen]**

Cedasus, the ME variant, is derived through OF rendering of Latin /sc/ as /c/ before *e* or *i.* It appears in medial position.

K. Hume, "The Pagan Setting of the *Franklin's Tale* and the Sources of Dorigen's Cosmology." *SN* 44 (1942): 289–294; Plutarch, *Moralia,* ed. and trans. H.N. Fowler, X: 10–17; J. Sledd, "Dorigen's Complaint." *MP* 45 (1947): 36–45.

CENOBIA, CENOBIE. Zenobia, fl. third century A.D., was the widow and successor of Odaenathus, king of Palmyra. She became one of the most powerful rulers in the Near East. After her husband's death, Zenobia reversed his policies of friendship to Rome and attacked parts of the Roman Empire, subduing Egypt and Syria. She cultivated Persians instead of Romans as allies after she defeated King Shapur of Persia. She took the name Augusta for herself and dressed her sons in the regalia of the Roman emperors. The emperor Aurelian decided to win back the conquered states of Egypt and Syria and attacked Zenobia in 272. She was captured as she attempted to flee to the Persians, and Aurelian forced her to walk in his triumphal march. She then lived in a villa near Tivoli until her death. Boccaccio emphasizes her manly qualities of courage in leading her soldiers in battle, her continence, and her victories in *De claris mulieribus* XCVIII, and in *De casibus virorum illustrium* VIII.6.

The Monk narrates a life of Cenobia, *MkT* 2247–2374, closely following Boccaccio's portraits. [**Aurelian: Claudius[1]: Galien: Hermanno: Odenake: Sapor: Thymalao**]

Cenobia and *Cenobie* are OF variants; *Cenobia* occurs initially, *MkT* 2247, and *Cenobie* appears medially with initial stress, *MkT* 2355.

Boccaccio, *CFW*, trans. G.A. Guarino, 226–230; *ibid., De casibus*, ed. P.G. Ricci and V. Zaccaria, 678–682; *ibid., De claris mulieribus*, ed. V. Zaccaria, 406–414; Trebellius Pollio, *Tyranni Triginta XXX*, and Flavius Vospiscus, *Divus Aurelianus* in *Scriptores historiae Augustae*, ed. and trans. D. Magie, III: 134–143, 244–263; A.C. Vaughan, *Zenobia of Palmyra*.

CENWULF: [KENULPHUS]

CERBERUS, the offspring of Typhon and Echidna, was the three-headed hound of the underworld. His capture was Hercules's twelfth and most difficult labor *(Met* VII.409–419).

Cerberus appears in the Monk's Tale of Hercules, *MkT* 2103, and in Lady Philosophy's rehearsal of the labors, *Bo* IV, *Metr* 7.36. Cerberus, the porter of hell, is abashed by Orpheus's song, *Bo* III, *Metr* 12.31–33. Pandarus swears by Cerberus in hell that if Troilus loved his sister, he should have her, *Tr* I.859–861. [**Ercules: Orpheus**]

Cerberus occurs in medial positions, *MkT* 2103; *Tr* I.859, and in the prose of the *Boece*.

Ovid, *Met*, ed. and trans. F.J. Miller, I: 370–373.

CERCES, CIRCES. Circe, daughter of Helios, was the famous enchantress who turned men into beasts. Hermes gave Odysseus the moly herb to chew as an antidote against her magic food, and he escaped her enchantment. Then he made her release the men turned into beasts in her court *(Odyssey* X.203–574; *Aeneid* VII.11–24; *Met* XIV.271–298). Medea and her aunt Circe were both unlucky in love. The Duenna points out that Circe's witchcraft could not hold Ulysses, *RR* 14404–14408.

Circes appears with Medea as an enchantress in Venus's temple, *KnT* 1944, and with Calipsa in Fame's house, *HF* III.1272. Cerces, the daughter of the Sun, enchanted Ulixes's men with drinks made from magic herbs, *Bo* IV,

Metr 3. Lady Philosophy explicates the story to show that the vices of the heart are stronger than the venom of Cerces. **[Calipsa: Medea: Ulixes]**

Cerces, a spelling variant, appears once, in *Bo* IV, *Metr* 3; *Circes,* Latin genitive singular of *Circe*, appears once in medial position, *HF* II.1273, three times in *Bo* IV, *Metr* 3, and once in final rhyming position, *KnT* 1944.

Homer, *Odyssey*, ed. and trans. A.T. Murray, I: 358–384; Ovid, *Met*, ed. and trans. F.J. Miller, II: 318–321; *RR*, ed. E. Langlois, IV: 60–61; *RR*, trans. C. Dahlberg, 246; Virgil, *Aeneid*, ed. and trans. H.R. Fairclough, II: 2–3.

CERES, the ancient Roman goddess of agriculture, took on the attributes of Greek Demeter, goddess of grains (wheat, oats, etc.), and was identified with her. Her daughter Proserpina was abducted by Pluto, also known as Hades, and taken to the underworld. The trio Ceres, Bacchus, and Venus appear together in classical and medieval literature and art.

Ceres appears in the temple of Venus, *PF* 276. Troilus curses Ceres, Venus, and Bacchus, *Tr* V.208. **[Bacus: Proserpina: Venus]**

Claudian, *De raptu Proserpinae,* ed. and trans. M. Platnauer.

CESAR[1]. The family name of the clan *Julia*, applied most generally to Julius Caesar. The Monk refers to Julius Caesar (c. 100–44 B.C.) once as "Cesar" in an apostrophe in his tragedy, *MkT* 2679. He says that his sources are Lucan, Suetonius, and Valerius. July is named after Julius Cesar, *Astr* I.10.9, who introduced the Julian calendar and named the seventh month after himself in 44 B.C. **[Julius: Lucan: Pompe: Socrates: Swetonius: Valerie[1]]**

Cesar is the medieval Latin and OF form.

Lucan, *Pharsalia*, ed. and trans. J.D. Duff; Suetonius, *De vita Caesarum*, ed. and trans. J.C. Rolfe, I: 2–119.

CESAR[2]. Octavius Caesar, 63 B.C.–A.D. 14, known later as Caesar Augustus, was the son of Julius Caesar's niece Atin, and Caesar adopted Octavius as his chief heir. Octavius was appointed pontifex in 46 B.C. at the age of seventeen. After his victory in the war of Mutina in 43 B.C., the army forced his appointment as Consul and the Senate recognized him as Caesar's adopted son under the name of Gaius Julius Caesar Octavius. He tried to win Antony over to his interests by agreeing to the marriage of his sister Octavia with Antony, but when Antony refused to leave Cleopatra, their rivalry broke out. Octavius defeated Antony at the Battle of Actium in 31 B.C. and became master of Egypt. Boccaccio also gives the repudiation of Octavia as the cause of the war between Antony and Octavian *(De claris mulieribus,* LXXXVIII). On January 16, 27 B.C., he received the title Augustus, and the month Sextilis was renamed Augustus after him in 8 B.C. When he died at Nola in A.D. 14, Caesar Augustus left a far-flung Roman Empire at peace; although Greek culture was being encouraged, and Roman traditions were given predominance in all parts of the empire, care was taken not to offend the traditions of the people of the provinces (Suetonius, *The Deified Augustus*).

Not only is Antony a rebel against Rome, but he falsely leaves Cesar's sister to take another wife, and because of these provocations, there is strife between Antony, Rome, and Cesar, *LGW* 592–595. Caesar shows no grace to Antony's wife, *LGW* 663. July and August are named after Julius Cesar and Augustus Cesar, *Astr* I.10. [**Antonius**[1]: **Cleopataras: Julius: Octavyan**]

Cesar, the medieval Latin and OF form, occurs twice in medial positions, *LGW* 595, 663, and once in final rhyming position, *LGW* 592.

Boccaccio, *CFW,* trans. G. Guarino, 194*; ibid., De claris mulieribus,* ed. V. Zaccaria, 142–146; Suetonius, *De vita Caesarum,* ed. and trans. J.C. Rolfe, I: 123–287.

CESAR[3]. Gaius Caesar, A.D. 12–41, was the son of Germanicus and Agrippina. The palace soldiers nicknamed him Caligula or Baby Boots because, at two years old, he was wearing military boots. He became emperor in A.D. 37, and his reign was marked by much brutality. He was assassinated in his palace on January 24, 41 A.D. (Suetonius, *Caius Caligula*).

Boethius remembers that Gaius Cesar accused Canius of concealing knowledge of treachery against him. Boethius has been accused of treason against Theodoric and hopes he will have the same chance to answer as Canius did: "If I had known it, you had not known it," *Bo* I, *Prosa* 4.81. [**Canyus: Germaynes**]

Suetonius, *De vita Caesarum,* ed. and trans. J.C. Rolfe, 404–487.

CESAR[4]. Cesar is used as the name of the ruler in *LGW F* 358–360, *LGW G* 333–336. Envy is the laundress of his court and does not leave his house. Chaucer cites Dante *(Inf* XIII.64) as the source for this line; Dante says that Envy is the meretrice or whore.

Dante, *Divine Comedy,* ed. and trans. C.S. Singleton, I.1: 132–133.

CESIPHUS. Sisyphus, son of Aeolus, was the reputed king of Corinth and the most cunning man in Greek mythology. He was placed in the underworld, condemned for fraud, beside Tityus and Ixion *(Met* IV.457–460; *OM* IV.3819–3830). His punishment was to roll a huge stone to the top of a hill; no sooner had he done so, the stone rolled down, and he had to push it up again.

The Man in Black says that he suffers more sorrow than Cesiphus "that lieth in hell," *BD* 588–590. Sisyphus, however, does not lie in hell, but pushes the stone up the hill. Tityus lies in hell while a vulture tears out his stomach. Sisyphus, Tityus, Tantalus, and Ixion all appear in the same passage, *Met* IV.457–460. Dame Nature describes the punishments of hell, where Sisyphus ceaselessly rolls the stone, *RR* 19295–19300. **[Ixion: Tantale: Ticius]**

Cesiphus, the ME variant determined by pronunciation, appears medially, *BD* 589.

Ovid, *Met*, ed. and trans. F.J. Miller, I: 210–213; *OM*, ed. C. de Boer, II, deel 2: 92; *RR*, ed. E. Langlois, IV: 263; *RR*, trans. C. Dahlberg, 318.

CEYS, SEYS. Ceyx was king of Trachis and a son of Lucifer, the morning star. On his way to consult Apollo's oracle at Delphi he encountered a series of disasters, among them the loss of his brother Onetor. On his way back from Delphi his ship ran into a storm, and he was drowned. His wife Alcyone mourned and grieved so continually that Juno, goddess of married women, took pity on her and sent her a vision of the dead Ceyx *(Met* XI.346–748; *OM* XI.2996–3787).

The Man of Law says that Chaucer has told the story of Ceys and Alcione, *MLI* 57. A full version appears in *BD* 44–269. Machaut tells the story in *La Fonteinne amoureuse*, 539–1034. It appears in Gower, *Confessio Amantis* IV.2928–3123. **[Alcione]**

Ceys, the French variant, appears once, medially, *MLI* 57; *Seys*, a spelling variant, appears six times in medial positions, *BD* 63, 75, 142, 220, 229, 1327.

John Gower, *The Complete Works*, ed. G.C. Macaulay, II: 380–385; Guillaume de Machaut, *Oeuvres*, ed. E. Hoepffner, III: 162–180; Ovid, *Met*, ed. and trans. F.J. Miller, II: 144–173; *OM*, ed. C. de Boer, IV, deel 37: 190–210.

CEYX: [CEYS]

CHARLEMAGNE: [CHARLES OLYVER]

CHARLES OLYVER means Charlemagne's Oliver and refers to Oliver, Roland's companion and friend in *La Chanson de Roland* (twelfth century). In the poem Oliver is always wise, while Roland is brave. Oliver and Roland courageously try to lead the French host in their attempt to fight their way out of the ambush into which the Saracens have trapped them in the Pass of Ronscevalles. The French host has been betrayed to the enemy by Roland's stepfather Ganelon.

The Monk says that Oliver de Mauny, a French nobleman who betrayed Don Pedro of Castille to his brother Don Enrique, cared not for honor like Charlemagne's Oliver, but was a "Genylon-Olyver," that is, a traitor, *MkT* 2387–2390. Froissart records the story in *Chronicles* I.245. **[Genylon-Olyver: Petro[1]: Rowland]**

Charles Olyver is the ME possessive case and occurs medially, *MkT* 2387.

La Chanson de Roland, ed. Cesare Segre; J. Froissart, *Chronicles,* ed. and trans. J. Jolliffe, 206–208; *The Song of Roland,* ed. S.J. Herrtage; *The Song of Roland,* trans. D. Sayers.

CHAUNTECLEER is the hero of *The Nun's Priest's Tale.* In one of Chaucer's sources, *Del Cok e del Gupil,* by Marie de France, the cock has no name, and his outstanding characteristic is his voice. Pierre de St. Cloud, author of Branch II of the *Roman de Renart,* named the cock Chantecler, as does the *clerc de Troyes,* author of *Renart le Contrefait.* **[Pertelote: Russell: Taur]**

Chauntecleer means "sing clear" in OF; it appears fifteen times in medial positions, *NPT* 2875, 2882, 2886, 3185, 3191, 3219, 3223, 3230, 3269, 3282, 3322, 3331, 3339, 3361, 3419; and four times in final rhyming position, *NPT* 2849, 3335, 3343, 3439. *Chauntecleres,* ME genitive case, appears in *NPT* 3354.

R.A. Pratt, "Three Old French Sources for the Nonnes Preestes Tale." *Speculum* 47 (1972): 422–444, 646–668; J.M. Steadman, "Chauntecleer and Medieval Natural History." *Isis* 50 (1959): 236–244.

CHAUNTE-PLEURE: [ANELIDA]

CHIRON the centaur was the son of Cronus (Saturn) and Phillyra. He was skilled in music and medicine and became the tutor of heroes. Achilles was his most outstanding pupil *(Met* VI.126; *Achilleid* I.104–197; *OM* VI.2949–3006).

"Eacides Chiron" appears as a harper, *HF* III.1204–1207. *Aeacides,* the Greek patronymic that appears in Latin, is applied to Achilles, grandson of Aeacus, throughout the *Achilleid* of Statius. Gower describes the education that Chiron gave Achilles but does not mention music, *Confessio Amantis* IV.1963–2013. **[Achilles: Eacides: Glascurion: Orion: Orpheus]**

John Gower, *The Complete Works,* ed. G.C. Macaulay, II: 354–355; Ovid, *Met,* ed. and trans. F.J. Miller, I: 296–297; *OM,* ed. C. de Boer, I, deel 15: 234–236; Statius, *Achilleid,* ed. and trans. J.H. Mozley, II: 516–523.

CHORUS: [EOLUS]
CHRIST: [CRIST]
CHRISTOPHER: [CRISTOPHER]
CHRYSIPPUS: [CRISIPPUS]
CHRYSOSTOM: [CRISOSTOM]

CIBELLA. Cybele was the Phrygian goddess of nature and fertility. Ovid calls her *deum Mater,* "mother of gods" *(Met* X.104, 686), and *deum genetrix,* "begetter of gods" *(Met* XIV.536). She wore a turreted crown and drove a lion car *(Met* X.696, 698–707). Cybele wearing her turreted crown is found in manuscripts of Remigius of Auxerre, *Commentum in Martianum Capellam* (after 1100).

Cibella made the daisy in honor of Alceste, queen of Thrace, *LGW F* 530–532, *LGW G* 518–520. Alceste wears a crown of white daisies as the queen of love, *LGW F* 212–225, *LGW G* 146–157. **[Alceste]**

Cibella, the ME variant of Latin *Cybele*, appears initially.

P.M. Clogan, "Chaucer's Cybele and the *Liber imaginum deorum.*" *PQ* 43(1964): 272–274; Ovid, *Met*, ed. and trans. F.J. Miller, II: 70–71; 114–115; 338–339; J. Seznec, *Survival of the Pagan Gods*, trans. B.F. Sessions, 167.

CICERO: [SCITHERO]

CILENIOS, CILENIUS is an epithet for Mercury (Hermes) after Mount Cyllene in Arcadia, where he was born. Ovid calls him *Cyllenius* (*Met* I.713; II.720).

Venus flees to Cilenios's tower to hide from Phebus, *Mars* 113. Venus is in two degrees of Gemini, the night house of Mercury, and Cilenius receives her as his dear friend, *Mars* 144. **[Mercurie: Venus]**

Cilenios, the byname of location used as a personal name, appears in a medial position, *Mars* 113, while *Cilenius,* a spelling variant of Latin *Cyllenius*, appears initially, *Mars* 144.

R.H. Allen, *Star Names and their Meanings*, 230–233; Ovid, *Met*, ed. and trans. F.J. Miller, I: 52–53; 110–111.

CINTHIA, CYNTHEA. Cynthia is the name given Diana (Artemis) after Cynthus, a mountain in Delos where she and Apollo were born. Ovid uses the name as a synonym for the goddess (*Met* II.465, VII.755, XV.537).

Criseyde swears by Cinthia, the moon, that she will return to Troilus on the tenth day, *Tr* IV.1608–1610. Cynthea as charioteer prepares to whirl out of the constellation Leo, lashing her horses on, *Tr* V.1018–1022, when Criseyde prepares for bed instead of returning to Troilus. **[Diane: Latona: Lucina: Proserpina]**

Cinthia, the byname of location used as a personal name, appears *Tr* IV.1608; *Cynthea,* a spelling variant, appears medially, *Tr* V.1018.

Ovid, *Met*, ed. and trans. F.J. Miller, I: 92–93; 394–395; II: 402–403.

CIPIOUN, SCIPIO, SCIPION, SCIPIOUN. Publius Cornelius Scipio Aemelianus Africanus Numantinus, c. 185–129 B.C., second son of Aemilius Paullus, who defeated Perseus, king of Macedonia, was adopted by P. Scipio, older son of Scipio Africanus Major, and became known as Scipio Minor. He was the hero of the Third Punic War and defeated Carthage in 148 B.C., thus earning the agnomen, or title of conquest, *Africanus* in his own right. In 133 B.C. he utterly destroyed the Spanish stronghold of Numantia, earning the additional agnomen *Numantinus*. For each victory, the Romans gave him a splendid triumph. Like Africanus Major, he cultivated a love for Greek philosophy and Greek civilization, forming a circle of the most famous writers of his day, which included Cicero and Terence. Scipio is one of the chief persons in Cicero's *De re publica*, of which the *Somnium Scipionis (The Dream of Scipio)* forms the end of the sixth book. In this dream, after conversing with Scipio Africanus about the afterlife, Scipio Minor gets a warning that he may suffer peril at the hands of his kindred. He died suddenly in 129 B.C. at the height of a political crisis, and his wife, Sempronia, sister of the Gracchi, was suspected of his murder (Polybius, *Histories*, XXXII.9–16).

Medieval writers knew the *Somnium Scipionis (The Dream of Scipio)* with commentary by Macrobius. It influenced much of medieval philosophy. Chaucer reads the *Somnium* in a Macrobius manuscript, *NPT* 3123–3124; *BD* 284–289. The Middle English title of the work appears in *PF* 31, "Tullyus of the Drem of Scipioun." Chaucer says his copy has seven chapters and gives a brief summary, *PF* 36–84. Scipioun appears in a catalogue of famous dreamers, *HF* II.514–517, and Scipio is among the celestial voyagers, *HF* II.914–919. **[Affrican: Macrobeus: Massynisse: Scithero: Tullius]**

Cipioun is derived from OF, which renders Latin /sc/ as /c/ or /s/ before *e* or *i*; it appears once, in final rhyming position, *NPT* 3123; S*cipioun* occurs three times medially, *PF* 36, 71, 97; three times in final rhyming position, *BD* 286; *PF* 31; *HF* II.514. *Scipio*, the Latin form, which means "staff" or "wand" and indicates a family of the clan *Cornelia*, appears once, in final rhyming position, *HF* II.916.

Macrobius, *Commentary on the Dream of Scipio*, trans.W.H. Stahl; *ibid., Saturnalia. In Somnium Scipionis Commentarius*, ed. J. Willis; Polybius, *Histories*, ed. F. Hulstch, trans. E.S. Shuckburgh, II: 452–477; H.H. Scullard, *Scipio Africanus: Soldier and Politician*, 11.

CIPRIDE, CIPRIS is an epithet of Venus. One myth states that she emerged from the sea near Cyprus, hence her epithet. The Cypriots were devoted to her worship, and her most important shrine was at Paphos (*Aeneid* I.415–417). Macrobius describes a male Aphroditos, found in Cyprus, with bearded face and female clothing, showing that love is both male and female (*Saturnalia* III.8.2).

"Faire blisful Cipris," *HF* II.518–519, echoes Dante's "la bella Cyprigna," *Par* VIII.2. Cipride lies between Bacus and Ceres, *PF* 274–279; Troilus asks Mars to help him, for love of Cipris, *Tr* III.724–725; Criseyde, after her fainting spell, thanks Cipride that she is yet alive, *Tr* IV.1211–1216; Troilus curses the gods, including Cipris, *Tr* V.206–210. **[Citherea: Dyone: Venus]**

Cipris, a byname of location used as a personal name, appears medially, *Tr* III.725, and in final rhyming position, *HF* II.518. *Cipride*, derived from Latin genitive singular, *Cypridis*, appears in final rhyming position only, *PF* 277; *Tr* IV.1216, V.208.

Dante, *Divine Comedy,* ed. and trans. C.S. Singleton, III.1: 82–83; Macrobius, *Saturnalia,* ed. J.J. Willis, 181; *ibid., Saturnalia,* trans. P.V. Davies, 214; Virgil, *Aeneid,* ed. and trans. H.R. Fairclough, I: 270–271.

CIRCE: [CERCES]

CIRUS. Cyrus the Great, son of Cambyses I, was the founder of the Persian Empire, and ruled 559–530 B.C. Seneca discusses Cyrus's anger in *De ira* III.xxi.

Friar John makes Cyrus an example of dangerous anger, *SumT* 2079–2088. Cirus defeats Croesus, *MkT* 2727–2730, *Bo* II, *Prosa* 2. [**Cambises: Cresus: Senec**]

Cirus, the ME variant, appears medially, *SumT* 2079; *MkT* 2928.

Seneca, *Moral Essays,* ed. and trans. J.W. Basore, I: 308–309.

CITHEREA, CITHERIA, CYTHEREA is another epithet of Venus. One version of her birth states that she first set foot on Cythera after emerging from the sea *(Heroides* VII.59–60).

Palamon prays to "blisful Citherea benigne," *KnT* 2215. Cytherea has a firebrand in her hand, *PF* 113–119, just as Venus has a firebrand at Januarie's wedding, *MerchT* 1726–1728. Venus throws a firebrand at the castle of jealousy, *RR* 15776–15778.

Citherea is also the name for the planet Venus. Dante refers to the planet as *Citerea, Purg.* xxvii.95. Chaucer refers to its position, *PF* 113–119, as north northwest. Robinson (793) points out that the planet may be so described when she is at or near her greatest distance from the equator. The meaning of the phrase is still the subject of various interpretations. Citheria is the "wel-nilly" or the "well-wishing" planet, *Tr* III.1254–1257, in a passage which blends mythology and astrology [**Palamon: Troilus: Venus**]

Citherea, the ME spelling variant, occurs medially, *KnT* 2215; *Citheria* appears medially, *Tr* III.1255; *Cytherea* occurs initially, *PF* 113.

Dante, *Divine Comedy,* ed. and trans. C.S. Singleton, II, I: 290–297; Ovid, *Her,* ed. and trans. G. Showerman, 86–87; *Riverside Chaucer,* ed. L. Benson, 996; *RR,* ed. E. Langlois, IV: 118; *RR,* trans. C. Dahlberg, 267.

CLARE (saint). Claire of Assisi, 1194–1253, was the founder of the Franciscan nuns, known popularly as the "poor clares." The order was noted for its strict observation of silence *(Legenda Aurea,* CCXXXVI).

The learned eagle swears by St. Clare immediately after the Dreamer has commented on the noise coming from Fame's house, *HF* II.1063–1067. This oath indicates a clear contrast between clamorous speech and silence.

Clare, the English variant of French *Claire,* means "light," and appears in final rhyming position, *HF* II.1063.

E. Gilliat-Smith, *St. Clare of Assisi: Her Life and Legislation*; Jacobus de Voragine, *LA*,
    ed. Th. Graesse, 949–950 (no English trans. in Ryan and Ripperger); M. Neville,
    "Chaucer and St. Clare." *JEGP* 55 (1956): 423–430; P. Robinson, *The Rule of St.
    Clare*; Thomas of Celano, *The Life of St. Clare,* trans. P. Robinson.

CLAUDIAN, CLAUDYAN. Claudius Claudianus, a Greek poet, fl. A.D.
395–404, was born in Alexandria. He became official poet to the young
emperor Honorius, for whose wedding he wrote an epithalamium. He also
wrote panegyrics on the emperor's great general Stilicho. The poem for
which he is best known is *De raptu Proserpinae.* Claudian remained a
popular writer for two hundred years after his death, as shown in the work
of several poets who borrowed from him; for example, Dracontius, who
lived in Carthage toward the end of the fifth century, wrote *De raptu
Helenae,* showing Claudian's influence. From the seventh to the eleventh
centuries, however, there is hardly a trace of his work in the literature.
Interest was rekindled in the twelfth century, when the centers of the
revival of classical learning were England and France. Excerpts from
Claudian were then found in the schoolboy's reading list, in a school reader
including the *Distichs* of Cato and the *Fables* of Avianus. Chaucer would
have read Claudian at school if he attended the Almonry School. The
headmaster of the Almonry bequeathed a number of books to the school,
among them the works of Arianus, Lucan, Juvenal, and Claudian. Chaucer
would not have known a separate edition of Claudian's poems but rather
would have become acquainted with him through excerpts found in the
Liber Catonianus, an anthology containing the *Distichs* of Cato, the *Fables*
of Avianus, pieces by Statius, Maximianus, and the *De raptu Proserpinae* by
Claudian. The version of *De raptu* in the *Liber Catonianus* was an edition of
the classical text with its two prefaces, to which medieval editors had
added a preface to the third book. This preface was taken from Claudian's
Panegyricus de Sexto Consulatu Honorii Augusti.
     The Merchant directs his listeners to Claudian for the story of
Proserpina's rape, *MerchT* 2225–2233. Claudian appears with Virgil and
Dante because he has revealed the torments of hell, *HF* I.445–450. He stands
on a pillar of sulfur, *HF* III.1507–1512, since sulfur is associated with the
volcanic Mount Etna in *De raptu Proserpinae* as the entrance to hell. The
"wery huntere" stanza, *PF* 99–105, is a translation of lines 3–17 of the
preface to the *Panegyricus,* and the tree list, *PF* 176–182, shows the
influence of *DRP* II.101–117. Chaucer uses *Signifer* as a name for the zodiac,
Tr V.1020, and Root gives the source as Claudian's *In Rufinum* 365. Pratt
points out that the line is nearer *DRP* I.101–102. Claudian is mentioned with
Valerian and Titus as poets who have written about women faithful in love,
LGW G 280. Chaucer probably had *Laus Serenae* in mind, a poem Claudian
wrote on the faithful and chaste wife of Stilicho, which also celebrates
other women famous for their fidelity, including Lucretia, Alcestis, and
Penelope, who are important in the *Legend.*

Claudian, the English variant of Latin *Claudianus,* appears in medial position, *HF* III.1507, and in final rhyming position, *HF* I.449; *Claudyan,* a spelling variant, occurs medially, *MerchT* 2232, and in final rhyming position, *LGW G* 280.

Claudian, *De raptu Proserpinae,* ed. and trans. M. Platnauer, in *Claudian: The Works* II: 300–301, 324–327; Geoffrey of Vitry, *Commentary on Claudian "De raptu Proserpinae,"* trans. by A.K. Clark and P.M. Giles; R.A. Pratt, "Chaucer's Claudian." *Speculum* 22 (1947): 419–429; E. Rickert, "Chaucer at School." *MP* 29 (1932): 257; R.K. Root, ed., *The Book of Troilus and Criseyde,* 547.

CLAUDIANUS: [CLAUDIAN]

CLAUDIUS[1]. Marcus Aurelius Claudius, called Gothicus, was Roman Emperor from A.D. 268 to 270. Chosen emperor after the assassination of Galienus, he was given the agnomen, or title of conquest, *Gothicus* for his defeat of the Goths at Doberus and Naissus. Although Zenobia recognized Claudius as emperor, she occupied Egypt in A.D. 269, thus defying him. Claudius died of the plague in 270, and his successor Aurelian defeated Zenobia in 271 (Boccaccio, *De claris mulieribus,* XCVIII).

The Monk remarks that Claudius, emperor of Rome, was not courageous enough to fight Cenobia, *MkT* 2335–2348. [**Aurelian: Cenobia**]

Claudius, the emperor's family name, appears in final rhyming position, *MkT* 2335.

Boccaccio, *CFW,* trans. G.A. Guarino, 226–230; *ibid., De casibus,* ed. P.G. Ricci and V. Zaccaria, 678–682; *ibid., De claris mulieribus,* ed. V. Zaccaria, 406–414; Trebellius Pollio, *Tyranni Triginta,* XXX, and Flavius Vospiscus, *Divus Aurelianus,* in *Scriptores historiae Augustae,* ed. and trans. D. Magie, III: 134–143, 244–263.

CLAUDIUS[2]. Marcus Claudius was a client of Appius the judge, who was seized with lust for Verginia, daughter of Verginius. He came before Appius, as prearranged, and claimed that Verginia was his slave, that Verginius had abducted and stolen her from him, and that Verginius now claimed her as his daughter. The plan was that, after Appius had awarded Verginia to Claudius, Claudius would give her to Appius (Livy, *Ab urbe condita liber* III.xliv-lviii). Livy calls the man Marcus Claudius. Gower narrates that "Claudius" was the other name of Apius and that Marcus Claudius was his brother (*Confessio Amantis* VII.5131–5306). Gower here shows some acquaintance with the system of Roman names; by "other name" he evidently means the family name, which was Claudius. Jean de Meun also calls him Claudius, *RR* 5651.

Claudius is the churl whom Apius bribes to carry out his plan for securing Virginia in *The Physician's Tale.* [**Apius: Virginia: Virginius**]

The name appears in final rhyming position, *PhysT* 153, 179, 269.

John Gower, *The Complete Works,* ed. G.C. Macaulay, III: 377–382; Livy, *Livy: Ab urbe condita libri,* ed. and trans. B.O. Foster, II: 142–167; *RR,* ed. E. Langlois, II: 263–265; *RR,* trans. C. Dahlberg, 114.

CLEMENCE. The goddess Clementia had an altar without a statue in the middle of Athens. Here Theseus met the widows of the men killed in battle whose bodies Creon had forbidden to be buried (*Thebaid* XII.481–585). Boccaccio places the temple outside the city (*Tes* II.17).

Theseus meets the widows at the temple, outside the city, where they have been waiting for a fortnight, *KnT* 912–930.

Clemence occurs in final rhyming position, *KnT* 912.

Boccaccio, *The Book of Theseus,* trans. B. McCoy, 56; *ibid., Tutte le opere,* ed. V. Branca, II: 302; *Roman de Thèbes,* ed. Constans, I: 481–506; *Roman de Thèbes (The Story of Thebes),* trans. J.S. Coley, 229–240; Statius, *Thebaid,* ed. and trans. J.H. Mozley, II: 480–489.

CLEMENCY: [CLEMENCE]
CLEMENTIA: [CLEMENCE]

CLEO. Clio, the second Muse, was the daughter of Jupiter and Mnemosyne and the Muse of history. She and her sisters were called "Pierides" because the seat of their worship was in Pieria.

Chaucer invokes Cleo to help him tell Troilus's story, *Tr* II.8–14. Since most of his sources purport to treat the Trojan War as history, Chaucer may have thought Clio the appropriate Muse to invoke. Statius likewise invokes Clio in *Thebaid* I.41. [**Caliope: Pierides**]

Cleo shows the influence of French pronunciation and appears in final rhyming position, *Tr* II.8.

Statius, *Thebaid,* ed. and trans. J.H. Mozley, I: 342–343.

CLEOPATARAS, CLEOPATRAS, CLEOPATRE. Cleopatra VII, 68–30 B.C., was the daughter of Ptolemy Auletes, king of Egypt. She was famous for her charm, her ruthless ambition, and her many lovers, the most noted being Julius Caesar and Mark Antony. Virgil depicts her story on Aeneas's shield, *Aeneid* VIII.675–713. Her name became synonymous with debauchery, lasciviousness, and cruelty. Beverly Taylor suggests that the atrocities of which the Romans accused her concealed their fear of her. Boccaccio follows Roman propaganda in *De claris mulieribus* LXXXVI.

Cleopatre is among love's martyrs, *PF* 291. She must make way for Alceste, paragon of wives, *LGW F* 259, *LGW G* 213. Chaucer presents Cleopataras as one of Cupid's saints, *LGW* 580–705. His conception of her character is so different from Boccaccio's that Pauline Aiken suggests Vincent of Beauvais, *Speculum historiale* V.53, as his source. Chaucer's Cleopatra is totally devoted to Antony and becomes his wife, contrary to historical fact. Robert W. Frank points out that Chaucer's is the first serious treatment of Cleopatra in English. Gower places her among lovers, *Confessio Amantis* VIII.2571–2577. Some scholars maintain that the treatment of Cleopatra in Chaucer's *Legend of Good Women* is ironic, since the queen's character is so totally at variance with that found in his sources. **[Antonius[1]: Cesar[2]: Julius: Octavyen]**

The form of the name varies to suit the needs of syllabic stress and rhyme: *Cleopataras,* the expanded form, occurs in final rhyming position, *LGW* 582, 601; *Cleopatras,* a contraction, appears medially, *LGW* 604; *Cleopatre,* with elided final *-e,* occurs in medial positions *PF* 291, *LGW F* 259, 566, *LGW G* 213, 542; *LGW* 669.

P. Aiken, "Chaucer's *Legend of Cleopatra* and the *Speculum Historiale.*" *Speculum* 13 (1938): 232–236; Boccaccio, *CFW*, trans. G. Guarino, 192–197; *ibid., De claris mulieribus,* ed. V. Zaccaria, 344–356; R.W. Frank, *Chaucer and the Legend of Good Women,* 37–46; R.M. Garrett, " 'Cleopatra the Martyr' and her Sisters." *JEGP* 22 (1923): 64–74; John Gower, *The Complete Works,* ed. G.C. Macaulay I: 456; B. Taylor, "The Medieval Cleopatra: The Classical and Medieval Tradition of Chaucer's *Legend of Good Women.*" *JMRS* 7 (1977): 249–269; W.K. Wimsatt, "Vincent of Beauvais in Chaucer's Cleopatra and Croesus." *Speculum* 12 (1937): 375–381.

CLEOPATRA: [CLEOPATARAS]
CLEOPATRE: [CLEOPATARAS]
CLIO: [CLEO]

CLITERMYSTRA. Clytemnestra was the wife of Agamemnon, high king of Mycenae. While her husband was fighting the Trojan War, Clytemnestra took his brother Aegistus as her lover. When her husband returned with Cassandra as his concubine, Clytemnestra and Aegistus murdered them both. Jerome cites her as an evil wife, *Epistola adversus Jovinianum (Letter Against Jovinian)* I.48 (*PL* 23: 280).

This story is in Jankyn's "Book of Wikked Wyves," *WBP* 737–739. **[Agamenon: Eriphylem: Phasipha]**

Clitermystra, a spelling variant influenced by pronunciation, appears in medial position, *WBP* 737.

R.A. Pratt, "Jankyn's Book of Wikked Wyves: Medieval Antimatrimonial Propaganda in the Universities." *AnM* 3 (1962): 5–27.

CLYTEMNESTRA: [CLITERMYSTRA]

COLATYN. Lucius Tarquinius Collatinus is regarded by Roman tradition as the founder of the republic and one of the first consuls of Rome for 509 B.C. During a lull in the siege of Ardea in 510 B.C., Collatinus boasted at supper of the beauty and virtue of his wife Lucretia, and to prove his words, took his cousin Tarquinius Superbus and other men to visit Lucretia in Collatia. Tarquinius was inflamed by her beauty and returned stealthily the following night. She welcomed him as a relative, and during the night he raped her at knifepoint. Lucretia sent for Collatinus and her father, told them what had happened, and then committed suicide. Legend tells that this was the cause of the expulsion of the Tarquins from Rome (*Fasti* II.685–852).

Colatyn, Lucretia's husband, says that his wife is thought good by all who know her, *LGW* 1706–1710. He takes Tarquinius to his house, and they watch Lucretia from a spot where she cannot see them, *LGW* 1712–1720. Then Colatyn makes himself known, and Lucretia receives them, *LGW* 1739–1744. The next night Tarquinius rides to Colatyn's house, *LGW* 1775–1778. Robinson (850) notes that Colatyn is not directly named in Ovid's account, while Shannon, on the basis of the word *Collatina*, discounts the use of Ovid, although Chaucer names him as one of his sources. Frazer notes variant readings for *Fasti* I.787, and points out that *Collatini* is the name in six of the best manuscripts. [**Brutus²: Lucrece: Tarquinius**]

Colatyn, the English contraction for Latin *Collatinus,* occurs twice in medial positions, *LGW* 1705, 1778; and twice in final rhyming position, *LGW* 1714, 1740. *Colatynes,* the ME genitive case, occurs in *LGW* 1713. *Colatinus* means in Latin "of Collatia," a town in Latium, and denotes that part of the Tarquin family native to Collatia.

Ovid, *Fasti*, ed. J.G. Frazer, I: 105; *ibid., Fasti*, ed. and trans. J.G. Frazer, 106–119; E.F. Shannon, *CPR,* 220–228.

COLLATINUS: [COLATYN]

COLLE TREGETOUR. This appears to be the name of a famous English magician who worked in Orleans during the fourteenth century. A French manual of conversation, composed about 1396, mentions an Englishman named Colin T, famous for magic. J.F. Royster points out that this book has been attributed to another Englishman, M.T. Coyfurelly, and suggests that Colin T. may stand for "Collin Tregetour." *Tregetour* means "magician," and Orleans was a town famous for the study of magic.

Colle Tregetour carries a windmill under a walnut shell, *HF* III.1277–1281. This impossible action seems to suggest that he is a magician.

Colle is the shortened form of *Nicholas.*

La Maniere de language, ed. P. Meyer; *Riverside Chaucer,* ed. L. Benson, 987; J.F. Royster, "Chaucer's 'Colle Tregetour.'" *SP* 23 (1926): 380–384.

CONIGASTE. Conigastus, fl. sixth century A.D., was addressed by Cassiodorus as *Cunigast, vir illustris,* "illustrious man," in a letter ordering him to administer justice to his poor neighbors (*Epistola* VIII.28).

Boethius has challenged Conigaste many times for fleecing the poor, *Bo* I, *Prosa* 4.56. **[Boece: Cassidore: Trygwille]**

Conigaste is a modification of French *Congaste* in Jean de Meun's *Li Livres de confort de philosophiae.*

Cassidorus, *Epistolae Theodoricianae variae,* ed. Th. Mommsen, 25; V.L. Dedeck-Héry, "Boethius' *De consolatione* by Jean de Meun." *MS* 14 (1952): 177.

CONIGASTUS: [CONIGASTE]
CONSTANCE: [CUSTANCE]
CONSTANTINUS: [CONSTANTYN]

CONSTANTYN. There is some uncertainty among scholars about the birthplace of Constantinus Africanus (c. 1015–1087). It is suggested either as Carthegenia (modern Tunis) or Sicily. He was perceived as African by his contemporaries, hence his agnomen or title of place, *Africanus,* quite unlike the title of conquest or achievement, the *Africanus* of the two Scipios, Major and Minor. The story of his life in *Chronica monasterii Cassinensis,* by Peter the Deacon, librarian at Monte Cassino in the early twelfth century, is based more on legend than on fact. Constantinus's translation of Arabic medical texts into Latin gave the West a number of important works. These formed the foundation of modern science and biology. He was a much cited authority from the twelfth until the sixteenth century, and his translations were widely circulated. Chief of these was the surgical part of *Kitab al-maliki (The Royal Book)* of Ali ibn al-Abbas, which Stephen of Antioch translated as *Regalis dispositio.* Other translations are his *De melancholia (On Melancholy)* and *De coitu (On Sexual Intercourse).* M. Bassan notes that comments on coitus as remedies for various afflictions are to be found in the works of Hippocrates, Galen, Rhazes, and ibn-Sina. Constantinus also translated Galen's *Pantegni,* a copy of which was owned by Merton College between 1360 and 1385. A printed edition of Constantinus's works appeared in Basel in 1536, *Constantini Africani post Hippocratem et Galenum ([Works of] Constantinus Africanus after Hippocrates and Galen).*

Constantyn is one of the Physician's authorities, *Gen Prol* 430–434. January eats and drinks before going to bed with May, as Constantyn, "the cursed monk," recommends, more than eight aphrodisiacs and three kinds of wine, as Paul Delany points out, *MerchT* 1809–1812. Constantinus discusses the advantages and disadvantages of coitus, prescribing remedies for sexual disorders, emphasizing the importance of nutrition for a healthy sex life, and places the function of coitus within the scheme for the perpetuation of the human species. **[Januarie: May]**

Constantyn, the ME contraction, occurs in final rhyming position, *Gen Prol,* 433, *MerchT* 1810.

M. Bassan, "Chaucer's 'Cursed Monk': Constantinus Africanus." *MS* 24 (1962): 127–140; Marie-Thérèse d'Alverny, "Translations and Translators." *Renais-*

sance and Renewal in the Twelfth Century, ed. R.L. Benson and G. Constable, 422–425; P. Delany, "Constantinus Africanus and Chaucer's *Merchant's Tale.*" *PQ* 46 (1967): 560–566; *ibid.,* "Constantinus Africanus' *De coitu*: A Translation." *ChauR* 4 (1971): 55–65; M.H. Green, "The *De genecia* Attributed to Constantine the African." *Speculum* 62 (1987): 299–323; F.M. Powicke, *The Medieval Books of Merton College,* 139; L. Thorndike, *HMES,* I: 742–759.

CORIBANTES. The Corybantes, attendants of the goddess Cybele, followed her with wild dances and music of the tambourine. They were sometimes identified with the Curetes, who guarded the child Jupiter, clashing their spears and shields together to drown out his cries. In this way they prevented his father Saturn from finding him (*Fasti* IV.199–219).

In expanding Jean de Meun's gloss on *Bo* IV, *Metr* 5.16–20, Chaucer adds that the people called Coribantes think that the moon is enchanted when it goes into eclipse, so they beat their basins of brass to release it from enchantment. Pliny attributes the custom to certain primitive peoples (*Natural History,* II.ix.54). Chaucer follows Trevet in attributing the custom to the Coribantes.

V.L. Dedeck-Héry, "Boethius' *De Consolatione* by Jean de Meun." *MS* 14 (1952): 247; Ovid, *Fasti,* ed. and trans. J.G. Frazer, 202–205; Pliny, *HN,* ed. and trans. H. Rackham, I: 203–205; *Riverside Chaucer,* ed. L. Benson, 1016.

CORINNA: [CORYNNE]
CORYBANTES: [CORIBANTES]

CORYNNE. This poet has not been identified. Lounsbury dismisses the possibility that she may be Korina, a contemporary of Pindar (518–438 B.C.), who wrote a work, *The Seven Against Thebes.* Edgar F. Shannon points out that early editors of Ovid, among them Hermolaus Barberus in 1454, labeled his *Amores* as *Corinna* and *Elegiae.* He suggests that Chaucer refers to Ovid under the name Corinna. Douglas Bush points out that Corinna appears in Lydgate's *Troy Book* in a catalogue of famous authors associated with the expression of grief. B.A. Wise suggests that *Corinna,* derived from *corina,* Italian for "wry face," alludes to Boccaccio, whose wry expression is mentioned in contemporary accounts.

The Poet says that Statius and Corynne are his sources for the story of Anelida, *Anel* 21. The name appears in final rhyming position.

D. Bush, "Chaucer's Corinne." *Speculum* 4 (1929): 106–107; T.R. Lounsbury, *Studies in Chaucer,* II: 403–404; E.F. Shannon, *CRP,* 15–20; B.A. Wise, *The Influence of Statius upon Chaucer,* 67–68.

CORVUS: [RAVEN]
CRAB: [CANCER]

CRASSUS. Marcus Licinius Crassus, c.112–53 B.C., came from an influential Roman family. In 59 B.C. he formed, with Caesar and Pompey, the first triumvirate. He was slain in the Parthian campaign in 53 B.C. His reputation for great wealth seemed to have been known among the Parthians, for they poured molten gold down his throat. This incident, taken from Florus's *Epitomia* III.11, emphasizes Crassus's avarice, and it appears in *Purg.* XX.116–117. John L. Lowes suggests *Li Hystore de Julius Cesar,* by Jehan de Tuim, as a source Chaucer may have known. Crassus is also a figure of avarice in Gower's *Confessio Amantis* V.2068–2224, in *The Tale of Virgil's Mirror.*

Crassus appears in a stanza on avarice, *Tr* III.1387–1393. **[Mida]**

Crassus, Latin for "coarse-grained," is the family name of the clan *Licinia;* it appears medially, *Tr* III.1391.

Dante, *Divine Comedy,* ed. and trans. C.S. Singleton, II, 1: 220–221; Florus, *Epitome of Roman History,* ed. and trans. E.S. Forster, 208–213; John Gower, *The Complete Works,* ed. G.C. Macaulay, III: 4–5; J.L. Lowes, "Chaucer and Dante." *MP* 14 (1917): 136.

CREON became king of Thebes during the war of the Seven Against Thebes, after Etiocles and Polynices, sons of Oedipus, killed each other during the battle. He refused burial for the bodies of the enemy, but Theseus intervened with an army, killed Creon, and allowed the dead warriors to be buried *(Thebaid* XII.773–781; *Roman de Thèbes,* 10003–10172).

Theseus rides out to fight Creon, his pennant embroidered with the figure of the Minotaur borne before him, *KnT* 979–980; he expects to slay Creon as he had killed the Minotaur. He fights and slays Creon, *KnT* 986–988, 1002. The incident also appears in *Tes* II.10–66. When Creon of Thebes sees how the royal families of Thebes have been decimated by the wars, he invites the nobility of the region to dwell in the city, *Anel* 64–70. Jason chooses the daughter of King Creon as his third wife, *LGW* 1660–1661. **[Jason: Theseus]**

Creon appears five times in medial positions, *KnT* 938, 961, 963, 1002; *Anel* 64; and once in final rhyming position, *LGW* 1661.

Boccaccio, *Tutte le Opere,* ed. V. Branca, II: 299–317; *Roman de Thèbes,* ed. Constans, I: 503–504; *Roman de Thèbes (The Story of Thebes),* trans. J.S. Coley, 235–239; Statius, *Thebaid,* ed. and trans. J.H. Mozley, II: 500–503.

CRESEYDE, CRESSEYDE, CRISEIDA, CRISEYDA, CRISEYDE, CRISEYDES, CRISSEYDE. Criseyde is Calcas's daughter in *Troilus and Criseyde.* Boccaccio's heroine, who provided the model for Chaucer's, is named variously in *Il Filostrato;* some manuscripts read *Cryseyda, Criseida;* others, *Criseyda.* E.H. Wilkins gives the name in its various forms in manuscripts of the fourteenth and fifteenth centuries, pointing out that *Criseida* and

Griseida appear in other works as well: in the Cueur d'amour espris (1457)
of René of Anjou, in the Comedieta de Ponza (shortly after 1434) of the
Marquis de Santillana, and in three Florentine manuscripts of Guido delle
Colonne, Historia destructionis Troiana. Boccaccio may have taken the
name from Ovid's Remedia amoris (The Remedies of Love) 469, and from
Tristia II.373, where it appears as Chryseis. In manuscripts of the Remedia
the name appears as Criseida, Chriseida, and once as Briseida. Besides
Boccaccio's Il Filostrato, Chaucer used a French translation, Le Roman de
Troyle et Criseide (before 1384), by Jean de Beauveau, seneschal of Anjou.
The form of the heroine's name in this title coincides with Boccaccio's and
Chaucer's spellings.

Creseyde occurs only in the F Prologue, medially in LGW F 332, 469, and
in final rhyming position, LGW F 441. Criseide occurs twice in medial
positions, LGW G 531, Wom Unc 16; Criseyda occurs once initially, Tr II.1424,
and once in final rhyming position, Tr I.169; Criseyde occurs thirty-five
times initially, Tr I.99, 392; Tr II.386, 449, 598, 649, 897, 1265, 1644; Tr III.85,
638, 799, 925, 981, 1163, 1177, 1198, 1372, 1548, 1564, 1715; Tr IV.207, 273,
479, 1194, 1527; Tr V.16, 57, 176, 504, 806, 848, 864, 1404, 1746; LGW G 459;
sixty-eight times in medial positions, where the final -e may be elided or not,
as the meter demands, Tr I.176, 273; Tr II.689, 884, 1453, 1562, 1590, 1606,
1678, 1724; Tr III.68, 95, 193, 507, 760, 883, 1068, 1070, 1126, 1209, 1238, 1275,
1350, 1448, 1492, 1670, 1740, 1820; Tr IV.15, 264, 281, 292, 307, 316, 457, 611,
682, 766, 807, 810, 825, 855, 868, 939, 1082, 1090, 1209, 1229, 1317; Tr V.5, 53,
228, 516, 595, 604, 843, 1187, 1247, 1252, 1254, 1260, 1315, 1573, 1587, 1661,
1683, 1720, 1774; fifty-two times in final rhyming position, Tr I.55, 459, 874,
1010; Tr II.877, 1235, 1417, 1550, 1603; Tr III.1054, 112, 1173, 1420, 1473; Tr
IV.138, 149, 177, 195, 212, 231, 347, 378, 666, 829, 875, 962, 1147, 1165, 1214,
1252, 1436, 1655; Tr V.216, 508, 523, 687, 735, 872, 934, 948, 1031, 1113, 1123,
1143, 1241, 1264, 1422, 1437, 1674, 1712, 1732, 1833. Crisseyde occurs only
in the G Prologue, once medially, LGW G 265, and once in final rhyming
position, LGW G 344; Criseydes, ME genitive case, occurs six times in medial
positions only, Tr III.1498, 1733; Tr IV.310, 472; Tr V.528, 775. [Argyve[1]:
Calcas: Diomedes: Pandarus: Troilus]

D. Aers, "Criseyde: Woman in Medieval Society." ChauR 13 (1979): 177–200; Benoît,
    Roman de Troie, ed. L. Constans, II: 287–328; Boccaccio, Tutte le Opere, ed. V.
    Branca, II: 17–228; E.T. Donaldson, "Briseus, Briseida, Criseyde, Cresseid,
    Cressid: Progress of a Heroine." Chaucerian Problems and Perspectives, ed. E.
    Vasta and Z.P. Thundy, 3–12; R.A. Pratt, "Chaucer and the Roman de Troyle et
    de Criseide." SP 53 (1956): 509–539; E.H. Wilkins, "Criseide." MLN 24 (1909):
    65–67.

CRESUS. Croesus (ruled 560–545 B.C.) was the last king of Lydia and was
famous for his wealth. Cyrus, king of Persia who defeated Croesus, ordered
his death by fire. As Croesus mounted the pyre, he called on Solon, the

great Athenian statesman, and Cyrus, impressed, spared his life (Herodotus, *Histories* I.29–90).

The rich Cresus, wretched in servitude, appears on the walls of Venus's oratory, *KnT* 1946–1949, illustrating that riches cannot rival Venus. The Monk narrates the story of Cresus's death to show how Fortune assails the thrones of the proud, *MkT* 2727–2766. Chaucer's immediate source may have been *RR* 6489–6622, which relates Croesus's dreams of Jupiter and Phoebus. Chauntecleer tells of Cresus's warning dream: he dreamed that he sat on a tree, which meant that he would be hanged, *NPT* 3138–3140. Cresus has an *avisioun* or warning dream that he would die on the gibbet, *HF* I.104–106. Lady Philosophy tells that when Cresus was led to the pyre to be burnt, after Cyrus had defeated him, the rain came down and saved him, *Bo* II, *Prosa* 2.58–63, illustrating the way Fortune works. **[Phanye]**

Cresus, the French variant, appears once initially, *HF* I.105; and five times in medial positions, *KnT* 1946; *MkT* 2727, 2728, 3759; *NPT* 3138.

Herodotus, *Histories*, ed. and trans. A.D. Godley, I: 33–117; *RR*, ed. E. Langlois, III: 7–12; *RR,* trans. C. Dahlberg, 126–128; W.K. Wimsatt, "Vincent of Beauvais in Chaucer's Cleopatra and Cresus." *Speculum* 12 (1937): 375–381.

CREUSA, one of Priam's daughters, was Aeneas's wife and the mother of Ascanius. She fled from Troy with Aeneas but was mysteriously lost on the way as they ran down to the ships *(Aeneid* II.730–743).

The story of Creusa is painted on the brass tablet in the temple of Venus, *HF* I.175–192. In the story of Dido, the loss of Creusa is given in one line, *LGW* 945. **[Ascanius: Dido: Eneas: Iulo]**

The name appears in medial positions, *HF* I.175, 183; *LGW* 945.

Virgil, *Aeneid*, ed. and trans. H.R. Fairclough, I.342–345.

CRISEIDA: [CRESEYDE]
CRISEYDA: [CRESEYDE]
CRISEYDE, CRISEYDES: [CRESEYDE]

CRISIPPUS. Jerome mentions this writer in his *Epistola adversus Jovinianum (Letter Against Jovinian)* I.48 (*PL* 23: 280). G.L. Hamilton suggests that Chaucer means the Stoic philosopher Crysippus, whom Cicero criticizes in *De divinatione.*

Alys of Bath says that one of Crisippus's works was bound up in Jankyn's "Book of Wikked Wyves," *WBP* 677. **[Alisoun[3]: Jankyn[2]: Jerome: Jovinian: Tertulan: Trotula]**

The name appears initially.

G.L. Hamilton, *ITC*, 109, note; R.A. Pratt, "Jankyn's Book of Wikked Wyves: Medieval Antimatrimonial Propaganda in the Universities." *AnM* 3 (1962): 5–27.

CRISOSTOM: [JOHN[6] CRISOSTOM]

CRIST, JHESU CRIST. The name *Crist* is mentioned 180 times through-out Chaucer's work. The name *Jhesu Crist* occurs 100 times, together making them the names mentioned with the greatest frequency of all proper names except *God.* The variant *Xhristus* appears initially, *ABC* 161.

Both forms are French variants.

CRISTOPHER (saint). Christopher was one of the very early saints, but it is now doubtful if he ever lived. A church in Bithynia was dedicated to him as early as A.D. 452. He was said to have been born in Zarasin in the land of Canaan. The hermit who converted him to Christianity bade him build a house beside a roaring river and to ferry across all who wished it. One night Christopher heard a child's voice asking to be ferried over. Picking up the child, he attempted to cross the river, but as he proceeded, the river grew more and more ferocious and the child grew heavier and heavier. When he reached the other side, he gently set the child down. Then the child explained that he was heavier than all the world because he had made the world out of nothing. Christopher became the patron saint of foresters and travelers (*Legenda Aurea* C).

The Knight's Yeoman wears a silver Cristopher medal, *Gen Prol* 115. The name means "Christ-bearer."

Jacobus de Voragine, *GL,* trans. G. Ryan and H. Ripperger, 377–382; *ibid., LA,* ed. Th. Graesse, 430–435; *The South-English Legendary,* ed. C. D'Evelyn and A.J. Mill, I: 340–348; "Vita Sancti Christophori," *Three Old English Prose Texts,* ed. S. Rypins, 108–114; Peggy C. Walwin, *St. Christopher Today and Yesterday;* H.C. Whaite, *St. Christopher in Mediaeval Wallpainting.*

CROESUS: [CRESUS]
CUPID: [CUPIDE]

CUPIDE, CUPIDES, CUPIDO. Cupid, son of Venus and Mars, is a Roman adaptation of the Greek god Eros. He is depicted winged, blindfolded, and armed with a bow and arrows. Ovid describes two kinds of arrows: blunt and tipped with lead, the kind that causes flight from the lover; sharp, golden, with a gleaming point, the other kind that kindles love (*Met* I.469–471). Isidore sees Cupid as a demon of fornication, who represents foolish and irrational love (*Etym* VIII.xi.80). Petrus Berchorius says that Cupid, son of Venus Voluptaria, is the god of carnality; he is painted winged because love flies away suddenly, and he is also blind (*De formis figurisque deorum*, fol.5ᵛa. 49–51, fol 6ʳa.13–14). Ovid refers to *caecus amor* (blind love) in *Fasti* II.762.

The Knight invokes Cupide, who is out of all charity, *KnT* 1623. Cupido appears in the temple of Venus, *KnT* 1963–1966, *HF* I.137. The Man of Law calls Chaucer's book of noble wives and lovers *The Seintes Legende of*

Cupide, MLI 61. The Learned Eagle calls Cupido, "blynde nevew of Jove," *HF* II.617. According to one tradition, Venus is the daughter of Jupiter and Dione, Cupid is then Jupiter's grandson. According to another tradition, Venus is the daughter of the mutilated Saturn, Jupiter's father; Cupid is then his nephew. ME *nevew* also means "relative." The Dreamer sees Cupide under a tree, beside a well, *PF* 211–212. The formel eagle says that she is not ready to serve Venus or Cupid, *PF* 651–652. Cupide is the god of love throughout *Troilus and Criseyde*.

Cupid of the *Prologue* to *The Legend of Good Women* is different from Cupid who accompanies Venus in the other poems. He is the mighty God of Love, clothed in silk embroidered with green boughs, and he wears a garland of rose petals, *LGW G* 160; a sun crowns his blond hair, *LGW F* 230–231. His face shines so brightly that the Dreamer, standing a furlong away, cannot look at his face. In one hand he carries two fiery darts; his wings are like an angel's, and he is not blind, but sees. Chaucer's source may have been *RR* 545–546, where Idleness is clothed in a green coat sewed with silk, and *RR* 847–872, where the God of Love is robed in flowers and is not blind. [**Alceste: Mars: Venus: Wille**]

Cupide, the ME variant, appears twice initially, *PF* 212; *Tr* III.186, and twice in medial positions, *KnT* 1623; *Scogan* 22, and five times in final rhyming position, *MLI* 61; *PF* 652; *Tr* III.1808, V.207, 582. *Cupides*, the ME genitive case, occurs once initially, *Tr* V.1590. *Cupido,* medieval Latin and OF variant, never appears initially, but three times in medial positions, *HF* II.668; *Tr* III.461; *LGW* 1140; and three times in final rhyming position, *KnT* 1963; *HF* I.137, *HF* II.617.

Petrus Berchorius, *Ovidius Moralizatus*, ed. J. Engels, 22, 24; D.S. Fansler, *Chaucer and the Roman de la Rose*, 62–72; Isidore, *Etymologiae*, ed. W.M. Lindsay, I; Ovid, *Fasti*, ed. and trans. J.G. Frazer, 112–113; *ibid., Met*, ed. and trans. F.J. Miller, I: 34–35; *RR*, ed. E. Langlois, 29, 44–45; *RR*, trans. C. Dahlberg, 38, 42.

CUSTANCE, CUSTANCES. Custance is the heroine of *The Man of Law's Tale*. Chaucer bases his characterization of Custance on Trevet's Constance in *Les Chroniques Ecrites pour Marie d'Angleterre, fille d'Edward I*, where she is the daughter of the Roman Emperor Constantin.

Custance is the type of heroine called "the accused queen," found in a certain genre of romance modeled on the saint's life. She is an example of perfect womanhood, first as maiden, then as wife, finally as suffering Christian.

The Syrian Sultan falls in love with Custance, and her father the Roman Emperor agrees to the marriage. The Sultan converts to Christianity, to the great dismay of his mother the Sultaness, who aranges to have the Sultan and all those courtiers who have converted with him slain at the wedding feast. Custance is then set adrift, and after three years lands on the coast of Northumbria, where she is rescued by the constable of King Alla's castle.

The constable's wife, Dame Hermengyld, converts to Christianity under Custance's guidance, and when she cures a blind man, her husband the constable also joins her faith. A young knight now falls in love with Custance, but she refuses him. Satan enters his heart, and he slays Dame Hermengyld, lays the knife near Custance, and departs. Custance is accused of the murder and brought before King Alla. The knight swears on the Evangelists that Custance has done the deed, and immediately a voice from heaven proclaims her innocence. The knight is slain and King Alla marries Custance. She bears a son while Alla is in Scotland and sends letters by messenger to tell the king the good news. The messenger stops at the court of Donegild, the king's mother, who drugs him and changes his letters. The new letters tell the king that Custance is an elf and that she has borne a fiendly creature. King Alla sends letters commanding that his wife and son be kept safe until his return. Once again the messenger stops at Donegild's court, and once again she drugs him and changes his letters. These new letters command that Custance and her son Maurice be set adrift. When Alla returns home and discovers what his mother has done, he kills her. Custance and Maurice drift for more than five years. They are rescued by the Roman Senator returning from the war of vengeance against the Syrians for Custance's dishonor. King Alla is finally reunited with Custance and Maurice when he comes to Rome to be cleansed of his sin, and they live happily. Chaucer follows Trevet closely, but he may have also known Gower's version, *Confessio Amantis* II.587–1612. [**Alla: Donegild: Hermengyld: Maurice**]

Custance, the French variant, appears six times initially, *MLT* 226, 264, 278, 570, 797, 906; thirty-three times in medial positions, *MLT* 208, 241, 245, 431, 438, 446, 536, 556, 566, 576, 583, 597, 608, 631, 651, 679, 689, 693, 719, 803, 817, 822, 900, 908, 953, 970, 978, 1033, 1107, 1125, 1129, 1145, 1147; and seventeen times in final rhyming position, *MLT* 151, 184, 249, 276, 369, 601, 612, 682, 912, 924, 945, 986, 1009, 1030, 1047, 1105, 1141. *Custances*, the ME genitive case, occurs once initially, *MLT* 1008, and once medially, *MLT* 684.

E. Clasby, "Chaucer's Constance: Womanly Virtue and the Heroic Life." *ChauR* 13 (1979): 221–233; S. Delany, "Womanliness in the *Man of Law's Tale*." *ChauR* 9 (1974): 63–72; John Gower, *The Complete Works,* ed. G.C. Macaulay, II: 146–173; M. Schlauch, *Chaucer's Constance and Accused Queens; ibid.,* "Trevet's Life of Constance." *S&A,* 165–181; P. Wynn, "The Conversion Story in Nicholas Trevet's 'Tale of Constance.'" *Viator* 13 (1980): 259–274.

CUTBERD (saint). Cuthbert, c. A.D. 635–687, became Bishop of Lindisfarne in 685. His name is connected with the famous Lindisfarne Gospels, Cotton Nero D.4, fol.8, in Latin glosses of the eighth century, written at Lindisfarne and placed as an offering to the saint. Bede tells how Cuthbert entertained angels without knowing who they were in *Vita metrica Sancti*

Cuthberti, episcopi Lindisfarnensis VIII *(PL* 94: 580).

John, the student from Strother in the north, asks the miller for hospitality in St. Cutberd's name, *RvT* 4127. **[John³]**

Cutberd is a variant of *Cudbert* and appears in final rhyming position. ME *Cudbert* is a development of OE *Cudbeorht.*

B. McKeehan, "The Book of the Nativity of St. Cuthbert." *PMLA* 48 (1933): 981–999; *Two Lives of Saint Cuthbert: A Life by an Anonymous Monk of Lindisfarne and Bede's Prose Life,* ed. B. Colgrave.

CUTHBERT: [CUTBERD]
CYBELE: [CIBELLA]
CYLLENIUS: [CILENIOS]
CYNTHIA: [CINTHIA]

CYPRIAN, fl. sixth century A.D., was an important noble at the court of Theodoric the Goth. Theodoric appointed him *Comes Sacrarium Largitionum* in a letter written by Cassiodorus for the king *(Epistola* V.40–41).

Boece says that he earned Cyprian's hatred when he withstood his false accusations against Albyn, a Roman consul, *Bo* I, *Prosa* 4.103. **[Albyn: Basilius: Boece: Conigaste: Decorat: Opilion: Trygwille]**

Flavius Cassiodorus, *Epistolae Theodoricianae variae,* ed. Th. Mommsen, 166–167.

CYPRIS: [CIPRIDE]
CYRUS: [CIRUS]
CYTHEREA: [CITHEREA]

DAEDALUS: [DEDALUS]

DALIDA, DALYDA. Delilah, a woman from the valley of Sorek, became Samson's lover. After many attempts, she persuaded him to tell her where his strength lay: in his hair. While he slept in her lap, she called a man to cut off his hair; then the Philistines captured him, blinded him, and put him to grind corn at a mill in Gaza. After a while his hair grew and his strength returned. Intending to humiliate him further, the Philistines placed him against a pillar in the temple to their god Dogon; but Samson brought down the temple with his great strength and died with the Philistines (Judges 16:1–31).

Dalida is a wicked woman in Jankyn's "Book of Wikked Wyves," *WBP* 721–723. She betrays Samson to the Philistines, *MkT* 2063–2078. In both stories she is called his "lemman" or "sweetheart." The Man in Black believes that Samson died for love of Dalida, *BD* 738–739. The Jealous Husband says that Samson was overcome when Dalida cut his hair, *RR* 9203–9206. Samson and Dalida appear in Gower's company of lovers, *Confessio Amantis* VIII.2703–2704. Chaucer says that his mistress is more fickle than Dalyda, Creseyde, or Candace, *Against Woman Unconstant*, 15–16. Dalyda appears in every medieval list of unfaithful women. [**Candace: Creseyde: Samson**]

Dalida, the Latin and OF variant, appears medially, *MkT* 2063; *BD* 738. *Dalyda,* a spelling variant, occurs medially in *Wom Unc* 16.

John Gower, *The Complete Works*, ed. G.C. Macaulay, III: 459; *RR*, ed. E. Langlois, III: 112; *RR*, trans. C. Dahlberg, 166.

DAMASCENUS: [DAMASCIEN]

DAMASCIEN. Johannes Damascenus, also called Johannes filius Mesue or Mesue the Younger, died c. 1015. A Christian, he studied in Baghdad and lived in Egypt. His work, *Liber Mesui* or *The Book of Mesue,* which survives only in Latin, was very popular during the medieval period. Merton College Library owned a copy between 1360 and 1385. His name was attached to two medical treatises, one written by Yuhanna ibn-Masawiah (d. 857), and the other by Yahya ibn-Sarafyun (fl. ninth century).

Damascien is one of the Physician's authorities, *Gen Prol* 433. **[Serapion]**

Damascien, the ME variant and contraction of Latin *Damascenus,* meaning "native of Damascus," appears in medial position.

M. Levey, "Ibn-Masawiah and his Treatise on Simple Aromatic Substances." *Journal of the History of Medicine* 16 (1961): 394–410; F.M. Powicke, *The Medieval Books of Merton College,* 139; G. Sarton, *Introduction to the History of Science,* I: 507.

DAMASIE. Pope Damasus I, c. 304–384 A.D., was pontiff A.D. 336–384. Jerome became his secretary in 377 and, at his suggestion, began the revision of the Latin scriptures. Damasus collected epigrams and inscriptions in honor of the Roman martyrs (*PL* 13: 109–424).

The Parson quotes a passage from Pope Damasie that all the sins of the world are nothing compared with the sin of simony, *ParsT* 788–789. Robinson (771) suggests Jerome's *Liber contra Joannem Hierosolymitanum* 8 (*PL* 23: 361); S. Wenzel notes that, while the quotation is attributed to Damasus in Peraldus, *Summa vitiorum* (1236), it actually appears in Gratian's *Decretal* 2.17.27.

Damasie, the French variant, suggests a possible French source for this portion of *The Parson's Tale,* perhaps the *Somme des vices et des vertus* of Frere Lorens, although K.O. Petersen has shown that the main source is a Latin tract, *Summa Casuum Poenitentiae,* by Raymund of Pennaforte.

Gratian, *Decretum,* ed. A. Friedrich, I: 438; K.O. Petersen, *On the Sources of the Parson's Tale;* E.K. Rand, *Founders of the Middle Ages,* 116; *Riverside Chaucer,* ed. L. Benson, 962; C.H. Turner, "Latin Lists of the Canonical Books I: The Roman Council under Damasus, A.D. 382." *Journal of Theological Studies* 1 (1899–1900): 554–560.

DAMASUS: [DAMASIE]
DAMIAN: [DAMYAN]

DAMYAN is the young squire in Januarie's household in *The Merchant's Tale.* He falls in love with May, Januarie's young wife. P.M. Griffith points out that Damyan is named after St. Damianus, the patron saint of physicians, particularly invoked to heal blindness. St. Damianus and his brother St. Cosimus were offered phallic *ex-voti* made of wax on their feast day and were regarded as patron saints of generative power. Damyan is aptly named because he acts as physician to Januarie, to whom sight is restored when Damyan and May make love in the pear tree. **[Januarie: May]**

Damyan, the English contraction of Latin *Damianus*, never appears initially. It occurs sixteen times in medial positions, *MerchT* 1869, 1875, 1900, 1936, 2002, 2009, 2019, 2093, 2120, 2150, 2152, 2210, 2326, 2352, 2361, 2394; and nine times in final rhyming position, *MerchT* 1772, 1789, 1866, 1898, 1923, 1933, 1979, 2097, 2207.

P.M. Griffith, "Chaucer's *Merchant's Tale*." *Explicator* 16, no. 13 (1957); R.A. Pratt, ed., *The Tales of Canterbury*, xxxvi.

DANAO. Danaus had fifty daughters and his brother Aegyptus had fifty sons. Danaus feared his brother's power and fled to Argos, but his nephews followed and asked for his daughters as their wives. Danaus consented but urged each daughter to kill her husband on the wedding night. One daughter, Hypermnestra, spared her husband Lynceus, who fled, leaving her behind. Danaus then imprisoned her (*Heroides* XIV; *OM* II.4587–4796).

Chaucer's version switches fathers and children, *LGW* 2562–2723. Danao has many sons but loves Lyno best in this version, which appears to be Chaucer's own. The *Ovide Moralisé*, which he may have used, assigns children and fathers correctly. **[Egiste: Lyno: Ypermestra]**

The form *Danao* may have been taken from Filippo Ceffi's Italian translation of the *Heroides* (c. 1320–1330). It appears once in a medial position, *LGW* 2600, and twice in final rhyming position, *LGW* 2563, 2568.

S.B. Meech, "Chaucer and an Italian Translation of the *Heroides*." *PMLA* 45 (1930): 110–128; Ovid, *Her*, ed. and trans. G. Showerman, 170–181; *OM*, ed. C. de Boer, I, deel 15: 268–273.

DANAUS: [DANAO]

DANE. Daphne, daughter of the river god Peneus, was pledged to the goddess Diana. Apollo fell in love with her, but she fled from him. Just as he overtook her, she appealed to her father, and he changed her into a laurel tree. Apollo made a wreath of its leaves, which became the reward for poets at festivals (*Met* I.452–567; *OM* I.2737–3064).

The story appears on the walls of Diana's oratory, *KnT* 2061–2064. Troilus invokes Phebus by his love for Dane, *Tr* III.726. **[Apollo: Diane: Penneus]**

Dane, the ME variant of OF *Dané* (Froissart's *L'Espinette amoureuse*, 1572) and the dative case of medieval Latin (Boccaccio, *De genealogia deorum gentilium* VII.xxix), occurs twice in a medial position, *KnT* 2063, *Tr* III.726, and once in final rhyming position, *KnT* 2064.

Boccaccio, *De genealogia deorum gentilium*, ed. V. Romano, I: 363; J. Froissart, *L'Espinette amoureuse*, ed. A. Fourrier, 90; Ovid, *Met*, ed. and trans. F.J. Miller, I: 34–43; *OM*, ed. C. de Boer, I, deel 15: 120–126; R.M. Smith, "Five Notes on Chaucer and Froissart." *MLN* 66 (1951): 27–32.

DANIEL, DANYEL. Daniel was the young prophet and reputed author of the book that bears his name. The stories about Daniel and his three friends, Shadrach, Meshach, and Abednego, were supposed to have taken place during the reign of Nebuchadnezzar, king of Babylon, in the sixth century B.C. Porphyry, the Neoplatonist and biographer of Plotinus, proved in the third century A.D. that the events described in the book of Daniel really took place in the second century B.C., during the time of Antiochus Epiphanes. Modern scholars agree with this assessment. *The Play of Daniel*, written in the twelfth century at Beauvais, was a magnificent liturgical drama and pageant.

The Man of Law asks rhetorically: "Who saved Daniel in the lion's cave?" *MLT* 475–476. The Monk narrates a tale of Daniel, *MkT* 2143–2166, in the story of Nabugodonosor; he says that the king commanded the castration of Daniel and his friends. This story appears in Vincent of Beauvais, *Speculum historiale* II.cxxi. Chauntecleer bids Pertelote look well to Daniel to see if he thought dreams were vanity, *NPT* 3127–3129. Machaut tells the stories of Daniel's visions, of his interpretations of Nabugodonosor's dreams, and of Belshazzar's feast in *Le Confort d'Ami*, 335–1282. The tree in Nabugodonosor's dream is the tree of Penitence, *ParsT* 1225–1230. No man may trust in his own perfection unless he be holier than Daniel, *ParsT* 954–955. [Balthazar: Darius[1]: Nabugodonosor]

Daniel appears once initially, *MkT* 2166, twice in medial positions, *MkT* 2154, 2209, and once in final rhyming position, *NPT* 3128. *Danyel*, a spelling variant, appears once, *MLT* 473. Both forms appear in the Parson's prose tale.

P. Aiken, "Vincent of Beauvais and Chaucer's *Monk's Tale*." *Speculum* 17 (1942): 60; P.M. Casey, "Porphyry and the Origin of the Book of Daniel." *Journal of Theological Studies*, n.s. 27 (1976): 15–33; Guillaume de Machaut, *Oeuvres*, ed. E. Hoepffner, III: 13–46; K. Young, *The Drama of the Medieval Church*, II: 290–301.

DANT, DANTE, DAUNTE. Dante Alighieri was born in Florence in May 1265. His family belonged to the Guelph Party (*Inf* X.46–50). His great-great-grandfather, Cacciaguida, was knighted by Conrad III (*Par* XV.139–141). In the *Vita nuova* Dante tells that at the age of nine he fell in love with Beatrice Portinari, who died in 1290. About 1298 he married Gemma di Manetto Donati, by whom he had three or four children. From May to September 1296 he was a member of the Council of a Hundred, which governed Florence; he served on another council in 1297. In 1300 he served as a prior of the city for two months, from June 15 to August 15. During this time the council banished from Florence the leaders of the Neri and the Bianchi, including Dante's friend Guido Cavalcanti, who belonged to the latter party. In October 1301 Dante was a member of an embassy sent by the Bianchi to Rome to protest the Neri's schemes, and during his absence, the Podesta pronounced a sentence of banishment against Dante, and all his goods were seized. From 1302 to 1316 Dante wandered from place to place. When, in 1316, an amnesty was declared under degrading conditions, Dante scornfully refused it. He settled finally in 1317 in Ravenna with two of his children at the invitation of Guido Novello da Polenta, and died on September 14, 1321, at the age of fifty-six. Besides the *Divine Comedy,* his works in Italian include the *Vita nuova, Convivio,* and a number of lyrical poems under the title *Rime* or *Canzoniere;* his Latin works are *De vulgari eloquentia, De monarchia,* various *Epistles,* and two *Eclogues.*

Although Chaucer mentions his name only six times, Dante's influence on his work is extensive. The Old Wife's speech on gentilesse, *WBT* 1125–1130, resembles *Convivio* IV.15, 19–38; Skeat suggests *Purg* VII.121. The Fiend tells the summoner that he will soon know hell from his own experience and will be able to hold a professorial chair on the subject better than Dante and Virgil, who have written on the subject, *FrT* 1516–1520. The Monk says that Dant is his source for the story of Ugolino of Pisa, *MkT* 2460–2462. The Dreamer advises his reader to read Virgil, Claudian, or Daunte for knowledge of hell, *HF* I.446–450. Chaucer says that Dante is the source for the idea that Envy is the laundress of Caesar's house, *LGW F* 358–361, *LGW G* 332–336. In *Inf* XIII.64, Dante says that Envy is a *meretrice* or "whore."

Chaucer uses Dante in other places where he does not mention his name. Special mention must be made of the invocations of *HF* II.518–528, influenced by *Inf* II.7; *HF* III.1091–1109, influenced by *Par* I.13–27. The *Invocacio ad Mariam* in *The Second Nun's Tale* is clearly based on several sources, including St. Bernard's prayer to the Virgin, *Par* XXXII.1–39.

Dant, WBT 1126, *FrT* 1520, *MkT* 2461, is contracted for the meter; *Dantes,* the ME genitive case, occurs in medial position, *WBT* 1127; *Daunte,* with silent final -*e,* appears in medial position, *HF* I.450. *Dante,* with final syllabic -*e,* occurs in final rhyming position, *LGW F* 360, *LGW G* 336.

Boccaccio, *Vita di Dante;* Dante Alighieri, *Divine Comedy,* ed. and trans. C.S. Singleton; *The Earliest Lives of Dante,* trans. J.R. Smith; J.L. Lowes, "Chaucer and Dante." *MP* 13 (1915–1916): 19–33; H. Schless, "Chaucer and Dante." *Critical Approaches to Medieval Literature,* 134–154; *ibid., Chaucer and Dante;* W.W. Skeat, V: 319; T. Spencer, "The Story of Ugolino in Dante and Chaucer." *Speculum* 9 (1934): 295–301; P. Toynbee, *Dante Alighieri: His Life and Works,* ed. C.S. Singleton, 26–108.

DANTE: [DANT]
DANYEL: [DANIEL]
DAPHNE: [DANE]

DARDANUS was King Priam's ancestor. The second of Troy's six gates was called Dardanus in his honor. Benoît names Dares Phrygius (*De excidio Troiae historia* IV) as the source of his description of the gates, *Roman de Troie* 3139–3159.

The Trojans return from battle through the gate Dardanus, and the crowd hails Troilus as he passes, *Tr* II.610–618.

The name appears medially, *Tr* II.618.

Benoît, *Roman de Troie*, ed. L. Constans, I: 159–160; Dares Phrygius, *De excidio*, ed.
    F. Meister, 5–6; Dares Phrygius and Dictys Cretensis, *The Trojan War*, trans.
    R.M. Frazer, 136–137.

DARES FRYGIUS. Homer says that Dares was a priest of Hephaestus at Troy, *Iliad*, V.9–11. During the medieval period there appeared a work, *De excidio Troiae historia*, or *The Fall of Troy, a History*, by one Dares Phrygius, purporting to be a true account of the Trojan War from an eyewitness. The work begins with the voyage of the Argonauts and ends with the destruction of Troy, frequently contradicting Homer. It is introduced by a letter, whose writer claims to be the Latin translator of a Greek original, presumed lost. Benoît de Sainte-Maure and Guido de Columnis acknowledge Dares as one of their sources for their versions of the Trojan War. The brief episode involving Troilus, Breseida, and Diomedes is developed in Benoît's *Roman de Troie* 13065–13782, and forms the basis for Boccaccio's *Il Filostrato* and Chaucer's *Troilus and Criseyde*.

The Man in Black says that Achilles and Antylegyus were slain in a temple, so says Dares Frygius, *BD* 1066–1070 (*De excidio Troiae historia* XXXIV). Dares stands on a pillar of iron with Homer, Dictys (Tytus), and other poets of the Trojan War, *HF* III.1464–1472. The narrator mentions Dares, Dictys, and Homer as writers of "Trojan gestes," *Tr* I.146, and directs the reader to Dares, *Tr* V.1771. R.K. Root suggests that when Chaucer says "Dares" he really refers to Joseph of Exeter, whose work is called *Frigii Daretiis Ylias*.

The whole name *Dares Frygius* appears in final rhyming position, *BD* 1070; *Frygius* preserves the Latin adjective *Phrygius*, a byname of location used as a personal name. *Dares* occurs medially, *HF* III.1467, *Tr* I.146, *Tr* V.1771.

Benoît, *Roman de Troie*, ed. L. Constans, II: 273–323; Dares Phrygius, *De excidio Troiae historia*, ed. F. Meister, 40–42; Dares Phrygius and Dictys Cretensis, *The Trojan War*, trans. R.M. Frazer, 160–161; Homer, *Iliad*, ed. and trans. A.T. Murray, I: 194–195; R.K. Root, "Chaucer's Dares." *MP* 15 (1917–1918): 1–22.

DARIUS[1], the Mede, invaded the Chaldean kingdom and overthrew Belshazzar (Daniel 5:3; 6:1–27). He is called *fil[ius] Asueri de semine Medorum*, "the son of Assuerus, of the seed of the Medes," Daniel 9:1. His historical identity has not been established.

The Monk tells how Darius overthrew Balthasar and occupied his kingdom, *MkT* 2231–2238. Machaut narrates this story in *Le Confort d'ami* 955–1130. **[Balthasar: Daniel]**

Darius appears in medial position, *MkT* 2237.

Guillaume de Machaut, *Oeuvres*, ed. E. Hoepffner, III: 355–341.

DARIUS², DARYUS. Darius III (c. 380–330 B.C.) became king of Persia in 336 B.C., when the vizier Bagos killed Artaxerxes III. Soon after he gained the throne, his kingdom was attacked by Alexander, who defeated him at Issus. Alexander went on to Egypt, but returned in 330 to inflict the final defeat at Gaugamela. Darius fled to his eastern provinces, where his soldiers slew him at Alexander's approach (Arrian, *Anabasis* III.xix-xxii).

Dame Alys says that her fourth husband's tomb was not as fine as the tomb Appelles made for Darius, *WBP* 495–499. Gautier de Châtillon describes a magnificent tomb made by Appelles for Satira, wife of Darius, *Alexandreis* IV.176–274, and the tomb Appelles made for Darius at Alexander's command, *Alexandreis* VII.379–430. The Monk tells of Alexander's defeat of Darius, *MkT* 2647–2694. **[Alisoun³: Appelles]**

Darius appears in medial position, *MkT* 2647; *Daryus*, a spelling variant, appears in final rhyming position, *WBP* 498.

Arrian, *Anabasis*, ed. and trans. E.I. Robson, I: 286–301; Gautier de Châtillon, *Alexandreis*, ed. F.A.W. Mueldner, 84–87, 163–165.

DAVID, DAVIT. David, the youngest son of Jesse, lived in Bethlehem in Judah. While still a young man, he fought and slew the Philistine champion Goliath. He became Israel's second king after Saul's death and ruled Israel for forty years (I and II Kings). The majority of the Psalms are attributed to him. He is one of the Nine Worthies in *The Parlement of the Thre Ages*, 442–453.

By God's grace, David, young and without armor, defeated Golias, *MLT* 932–938. The friar says that the brethren in some orders are full of great reverence when they pray for souls, saying the Psalm of David, *SumT* 1929–1934. Abigail, by good counsel, delivered her husband from David, *Mel* 1098–1100. Dame Prudence quotes Psalm 1:1 in *Mel* 1198; she quotes Psalm 126:1 in *Mel* 1304, and Psalm 20:4 in *Mel* 1735. The Manciple directs his listeners to David's Psalms on the wisdom of keeping silence, *MancT* 345. The Parson quotes the Psalms throughout his tale: Ps. 129:113 at *ParsT* 125; Ps. 75:6 at *ParsT* 193; Ps. 10:6 at *ParsT* 204; Ps. 107:34 at *ParsT* 220; Ps. 97:10 at *ParsT* 307; Ps. 32:5 at *ParsT* 309; Ps. 55:15 at *ParsT* 442; Ps. 4:5 at *ParsT* 540; Ps. 73:5 at *ParsT* 716. **[Abigayl: Custance: Golias]**

David appears medially, *MLT* 935; *MancT* 345, and throughout the *Tale of Melibee* and *The Parson's Tale*; *Davit* occurs in final rhyming position, *SumT* 1933.

N.D. Hillis, *David the Poet and King; The Parlement of the Thre Ages*, ed. M.Y. Offord, 20–21.

DE COITU: [CONSTANTYN]

DECORAT, fl. sixth century A.D., was an advocate at Rome. Cassiodorus's letter for Theodoric expresses regret at his death and promotes his brother, Honoratus, to the quaestorship, *Epistola* V.3–4.

Lady Philosophy calls Decorat an informer, *Bo* III, *Prosa* 4. 23–26. **[Albyn: Basilius: Boece: Cassidore: Conigaste: Gaudenicus: Opilion: Trygwille]**

Decorat, the contraction of Latin *Decoratus,* appears in Jean de Meun's translation *Li Livres de confort de philosophie.*

Flavius Cassiodorus, *Epistolae Theodoricianae Variae,* ed. Th. Mommsen, 144–145; V.L. Dedeck-Héry, "Boethius' *De Consolatione* by Jean de Meun." *MS* 14 (1952), 211.

DECORATUS: [DECORAT]

DEDALUS, DIDALUS. Daedalus is the famous engineer of mythological times. He was an Athenian, but he fled to Crete after he killed Perdix, his nephew and apprentice (*Met* VIII.236–250). In Crete he made a dancing ground for Ariadne, a wooden cow for Pasiphae, and the Labyrinth for Minos. After Minos discovered that Daedalus had made the cow for Pasiphae, he threatened his life, but Daedalus made wings for himself and his son Icarus, with which they flew away from Crete (*Met* VIII.188–195; *OM* VIII.1579–1709).

Not even Dedalus "with his playes slye" can distract the Man in Black from his sorrow, *BD* 570; the "playes slye" are Dedalus's inventions. The story of the flight from Crete is told briefly, *HF* II.919–924. The whirling house of wicker, painted red, green, white, and pale yellow, resembles a bird cage and is more intricately made than the *domus Dedaly, HF* III.1920; *domus Dedaly,* or "house of Daedalus," preserves the Latin genitive singular and provides the rhyme. W.O. Sypherd says that the phrase echoes a note on a passage in Aquinas: "*laborinthus dicebatur domus dedali,*" "the labyrinth is called the house of Daedalus." The description of the Labyrinth, "house of Didalus so entrelaced," *Bo* III, *Prosa* 12.156, is borrowed from Jean de Meun's translation: "*maison Dedalus si entrelaciee,*" *Li Livres de confort de philosophie.* Boethius does not mention Daedalus. **[Adriane: Minos: Phasipha: Ykarus]**

Dedalus, which means "cunningly wrought," appears in medial position, *BD* 570, and in final rhyming position, *HF* II.919; *Didalus,* a spelling variant, appears in the prose translation of Boethius.

V.L. Dedeck-Héry, "Boethius' *De consolatione* by Jean de Meun." *MS* 14 (1952): 231; F.P. Magoun, Jr., *A Chaucer Gazetteer,* 86–87; Ovid, *Met,* ed. and trans. F.J. Miller, I: 418–423; W.O. Sypherd, *Studies in Chaucer's Hous of Fame,* 138–139, n.3.

DEIPHEBE, DEIPHEBUS was the third son of Priam and Hecuba of Troy. He married Helen after Paris's death (*Heroides* XVI, 361–362; *Aeneid* VI.500–534; *Ephemeridos belli Troiani* I.10, IV.22, V.12).

The Dreamer sees Deiphebus in hell, *HF* I.444. Virgil says that Aeneas meets Deiphebus in the underworld, and Deiphebus tells the story of his betrayal by Helen, whom he married after Paris's death, and how he died when Odysseus and his companions came out of the Trojan horse. In *Troilus and Criseyde*, Deiphebus is Troilus's favorite brother. (Boccaccio describes briefly the affection between Troilo and Deifebo in *Il Filostrato* vii.77–83.) Pandarus arranges a rendezvous between Troilus and Criseyde at Deiphebus's house, where Troilus pretends to be ill, and Criseyde visits him there. Helen and Deiphebus also visit him; then they go down together into the garden to read a letter from Hector, *Tr* II.1394–1750. When they return, Troilus groans loudly, *Tr* III.204–207; then Helen and Deiphebus leave him, *Tr* III.218–226. [**Creseyde: Eleyne²: Pandar: Troilus**]

Deiphebe appears twice, with elided final -e: initially, *Tr* IV.1654, and medially, *Tr* V.1652. *Deiphebus* occurs seven times initially, *Tr* II.1422, 1442, 1486, 1549, 1693, 1702, *Tr* III.226; thirteen times in medial positions, *Tr* II.1398, 1402, 1408, 1425, 1496, 1514, 1540, 1542, 1558, 1569, 1601, 1675; *Tr* III.221; six times in final rhyming position, *HF* I.444; *Tr* II.1480, 1611, 1641; *Tr* III.204.

Boccaccio, *Tutte le opere*, ed. V. Branca, II: 207–209; Dictys Cretensis, *Ephemeridos belli Troiani libri*, ed. W. Eisenhut, 9–10, 98–101, 113–114; Dares Phrygius and Dictys Cretensis, *The Trojan War*, trans. R.M. Frazer, 28–29, 100–102, 113–114; E.H. Kelly, "Myth as Paradigm in *Troilus and Criseyde*." *PLL* 3 (1967), supplement 8–30; Ovid, *Her*, ed. and trans. G. Showerman, 222–223; M. Sundwall, "Deiphobus and Helen: A Tantalizing Hint." *MP* 73 (1975): 151–156; Virgil, *Aeneid*, ed. and trans. H.R. Fairclough, I: 540–543.

DEJANIRA: [DIANIRA]
DELILAH: [DALIDA]
DELPHICUS: [APPOLLO]
DELPHIN: [DELPHYN]
DELPHINUS: [DELPHYN]

DELPHYN. Delphinus, the Dolphin, is one of the smallest constellations and lies in the northern hemisphere. It represents the Dolphin that caught Arion as he leapt into the sea to escape the murderous captain of his ship *(Fasti* II.79–118).

The Learned Eagle points out the constellation to the frightened dreamer as they fly through the sky, *HF* II.1006. [**Arionis Harpe: Orion**]

Chaucer's *Delphyn* is a variant of Ovid's *Delphina* and occurs in final rhyming position.

R.H. Allen, *Star Names and their Meanings*, 198–199; Ovid, *Fasti*, ed. and trans J.G. Frazer, 62–65.

DEMETRIUS, 139–127 B.C., was a Spartan king, to whom the Parthian king sent, as an insult, a set of dice because he refused to behave as an adult. John of Salisbury tells the story to illustrate the uses and abuses of gambling. He adds the story of Chilo, who refused to conclude a treaty with the Corinthians because they all played chequers *(Policraticus* I.5).

The Pardoner includes this story in his homily on gambling, *PardT* 603–628. **[Athalus: Stilboun]**

The name appears in final rhyming position, *PardT* 621.

John of Salisbury, *Policraticus,* trans. J.B. Pike, 28–29.

DEMOCION(ES). Democion's daughter killed herself after her betrothed's death. Jerome tells her story in *Epistola adversus Jovinianum (Letter Against Jovinian)* I.41 *(PL* 23: 271).

Dorigen thinks that Democion's daughter is an exemplary figure of chastity, *FranklT* 1426. **[Dorigen]**

Demociones, ME genitive of *Democion,* itself a variant of Latin *Demotion,* appears medially.

K. Hume, "The Pagan Setting of the *Franklin's Tale* and the Sources of Dorigen's Cosmology." *SN* 44 (1972): 89–99.

DEMOPHON, DEMOPHOUN. Demophoön was the son of Theseus and Phedra. On his way home from Troy, he was shipwrecked on Rhodope, where Phyllis the queen repaired his ships and entertained him. He promised to marry her but forgot all about her once he was back in Athens *(Heroides* II). In despair Phyllis hanged herself, *RR* 13211–13214.

The Man of Law mentions this story as one of Chaucer's poems, *MLI* 65. The Dreamer tells the Man in Black that he will be as surely damned, if he kills himself, as Phyllis was for hanging herself for Demophoun, *BD* 725–728. The story is told in *HF* I.388–396; Phyllis, hanging for her Demophoun, appears in the catalogue of faithful women, *LGW F* 264, *LGW G* 218. There is no one falser than Demophon, except his father Theseus, *LGW* 2398–2400. The gods Thetis, Chorus, Triton, and Neptune cast Demophon up on the shore of Phyllis's kingdom, but he travels the same road as his father, Theseus. He deceives and betrays Phyllis just as Theseus betrayed Ariadne, *LGW* 2419–2496. Chaucer seems to have taken some details from Filippo Ceffi's translation of the *Heroides* for his own version. **[Adriane: Phillis: Theseus]**

Demophon occurs four times in medial positions, *HF* I.388; *LGW* 2405, 2427, 2486; four times in final rhyming position, *MLI* 65; *LGW* 2398, 2462, 2496; *Demophoun* appears three times in final rhyming position, *BD* 728; *LGW F* 264, *LGW G* 218.

S.B. Meech, "Chaucer and an Italian Translation of the *Heroides.*" *PMLA* 45 (1930): 111–112; Ovid, *Her,* ed. and trans. G. Showerman, 18–31; *RR,* ed. E. Langlois, IV: 10; *RR,* trans. C. Dahlberg, 228.

DEMOPHOON: [DEMOPHON]
DEMOTION: [DEMOCION(ES)]
DENIS: [DENYS]

DENYS (saint). Denis, fl. third century A.D., was bishop of Paris and became the patron saint of France. He died c. A.D. 250. He was also called Dionysius. Gregory of Tours tells that he was born in Italy and sent to preach Christianity to the Gauls. He was beheaded, and over his tomb was built a chapel and an abbey. In the ninth century he was identified with Pseudo-Denys the Areopagite, who claimed to have been one of Paul's disciples. In England forty-one churches were dedicated to him. In Abelard's time the monks of St. Denis still claimed that Dionysius the Areopagite was their founder.

The action of the *Shipman's Tale* is set in St. Denis, a village outside Paris. Don John the monk swears by St. Denis of France, *ShipT* 151. [**John**[5]: **Martyn**]

The form, an ME spelling variant, appears in medial position.

Peter Abelard, *The Story of Abelard's Adversities,* trans. J.T. Muckle; S.M. Crosby, *The Abbey of St. Denis, 475–1122,* I: 24–30; D.H. Farmer, *The Oxford Dictionary of Saints,* 105–106; Gregory of Tours, *The History of the Franks,* trans. L. Thorpe, 86–87; *The South-English Legendary,* ed. C. D'Evelyn and A.J. Mill, II: 434–439.

DEYSCORIDES. Dioscorides Pedanius of Anazarbus, fl. first century A.D., was a Greek physician during the reigns of the Roman emperors Claudius and Nero, A.D. 41–68. He says that he served in the Roman army. His work *Materia Medica* in five books describes six hundred varieties of plants and their medical properties. Illustrated by a Byzantine artist as early as A.D. 512, regarded as the chief work on pharmacology during the Middle Ages, it was also very much in use during the Renaissance.

Deyscorides appears among the Physician's authorities, *Gen Prol* 430.

The form, a pronunciation variant, occurs medially.

Dioscorides, *The Greek Herbal of Dioscorides,* ed. R.T. Gunther.

DIANA: [DIANE]

DIANE, DYANE. Diana is the Roman goddess identified with Artemis, the Greek goddess of the hunt. Like Artemis, she is Apollo's sister, goddess of the moon, of chastity, of hunting, and of childbirth. Any nymph in her train or priestess in her temple who strayed from her path was immediately punished. She was known as the Triple Goddess, or Trivia, in her three forms as Diana, Proserpina, and Hecate. Sometimes her aspect as Lucina took the place of Hecate *(Met* III.155–164; XV.196–198; *OM* III.337–570).

The triple goddess appears on the walls of Diane's oratory, *KnT*

2056–2086, as Diane, Lucina, and Proserpina. The description of the oratory is based on the anti-Diana passages in *Tes* VII.61, which describe Venus's temple, and *Tes* VII.79, 90. Emelye's rites, *KnT* 2272–2294, are paraphrased from *Tes* VII.71–92. Emelye prays to Diana as the goddess of the three forms, *KnT* 2313. The maiden Stymphalides is slain clinging to Diane's altar, *FranklT* 1387–1394; Jerome tells this story in his *Epistola adversus Jovinianum (Letter Against Jovinian)* I.41 (*PL* 23: 271). The Dreamer sees the many broken bows of maidens who have broken their vows to Dyane the chaste in Venus's temple, *PF* 281–287. Troilus invokes Diane, *Tr* III.731–732. Cassandra tells Troilus that the boar ravaged Calydonia because the Greeks there had neglected Diane's sacrifices, *Tr* V.1464–1470. **[Atthalante: Attheon: Calistopee: Cinthia: Emelie: Latona: Lucina: Lucrece: Proserpina: Stymphalides]**

Diane, the ME variant, occurs once initially, *Tr* V.1464; four times medially, *KnT* 2057, 2066, *PF* 81, *Tr* III.731; and once in final rhyming position, *KnT* 2063. *Dyane,* the OF variant, appears only in the *Knight's Tale,* once initially, *KnT* 2364; six times in medial positions, *KnT* 1912, 2051, 2066, 2072, 2296, 2346; and once in final rhyming position, *KnT* 1682. *Dianes,* the ME genitive case, occurs in medial position, *FranklT* 1390.

Boccaccio, *Tutte le opere,* ed. V. Branca, II: 475, 477–483; Ovid, *Met,* ed. and trans. F.J. Miller, I: 134–137; II: 378–379; *OM,* ed. C. de Boer, I, deel 15: 306–311; R.A. Pratt, "Chaucer's Use of the *Teseida.*" *PMLA* 62 (1947): 598–621.

DIANIRA, DIANIRE, DIANYRE, DYANIRA. Dejanira was the daughter of Oeneus of Calydon and Meleager's sister. Hercules won her in a contest against her other suitor, Achelous, a shape-shifter. As he took her home to Trachis, he came to the river Evenus, then in full flood. He paid the centaur Nessus a fee to carry Dejanira across. The centaur, however, ran off in the opposite direction when he reached the bank, intending to rape Dejanira. Hercules slew him with the shot of one arrow, which had been dipped in the poisoned blood of the Lernean Hydra. As he lay dying, Nessus told Dejanira to collect some of his blood; if she dyed Hercules's shirts with it, the shirts would become love charms to help her regain his love if she ever needed to. Later, when Hercules brought Iole to live with Dejanira, she sent him a shirt when he stopped at Cenaeum to offer sacrifice to Jupiter. The poison consumed his flesh, and he tore off his skin when he tried to remove it (*Heroides* IX; *Met* IX.1–272; *OM* IX.1–872). The story also appears in Boccaccio, *De claris mulieribus,* XXI and XXII. The Jealous Husband tells that Hercules overcame twelve dreadful monsters but was overcome when Dejanira sent him the poisoned shirt, *RR* 9195–9200. Gower tells the story of Hercules, Dejanira, and Nessus to illustrate Falssemblant, *Confessio Amantis* II.2145–2319; Machaut's version is *Le Confort d'ami,* 2683–2762.

The Man of Law says that Chaucer has told the "pleinte" of Dianire in a large book, *MLI* 60–66, but there is no story for her in *The Legend of Good*

Women. Jankyn reads the story to Dame Alys from his "Book of Wikked Wyves," *WBP* 724–726. The Monk tells the story as part of the Hercules legend, *MkT* 2120–2134. Hercules is false to Dyanira when he brings home Iole, *HF* I.402–404. [**Achaleous: Ercules: Nessus: Yole**]

Dianire, with elided final *-e*, occurs medially, *MLI* 66; *Dianyre*, with silent final *-e*, occurs finally, *WBP* 725; *Dianira*, in medial position with four syllables for the meter, *MkT* 2120. *Dyanira* occurs in final rhyming position, *HF* I.402. All variants are developments of Latin *Deianira*.

Boccaccio, *CFW*, trans. G. Guarino, 48; *ibid.*, *De claris mulieribus*, ed. V. Zaccaria, 98–106; John Gower, *The Complete Works*, ed. G.C. Macaulay, II: 188–193; Guillaume de Machaut, *Oeuvres*, ed. E. Hoepffner, III: 95–98; Ovid, *Her*, ed. and trans. G. Showerman, 108–121; *ibid.*, *Met*, ed. and trans. F.J. Miller, II: 2–23; *RR*, ed. E. Langlois, III: 112; *RR*, trans. C. Dahlberg, 166.

DICTYS: [DITE]
DIDALUS: [DEDALUS]

DIDO, DYDO. Dido was the legendary founder of Carthage and daughter of the king of Tyre, whom Virgil calls Belus. In Phoenicia she was known as Elissa, but she was called Dido (the Wanderer) in Carthage. Her brother Pygmalion murdered her husband Sychaeus, a priest of Hercules. Sychaeus's ghost appeared to Dido in a dream and warned her against Pygmalion. Escaping with a group to Libya, she founded Carthage. Here Aeneas met her when he landed at Carthage, his ships driven off course during a storm as he escaped from Troy. She entertained him lavishly and fell in love with him. But he felt his destiny was to found a new city, and he left her stealthily at night. When Dido discovered this, she killed herself on her funeral pyre with his sword (*Aeneid* I-IV; *Heroides* VII).

Ovid's account aroused sympathy for Dido during the Middle Ages. Beryl Smalley points out that John Ridewall, in his Commentary on Augustine's *De civitate Dei (The City of God)* I.2 (before 1333), says that Aeneas could not have met Dido since he lived three hundred years earlier. Ranulph Higden says that Dido built Carthage three score years and twelve (72 years) before the founding of Rome (*Polychronicon* II.xxvi, c. 1348–1352), adding that wise men deny that Aeneas saw Carthage. Higden's version says that Dido died on the pyre so as not to remarry. Dante, influenced by the Virgilian version, places Dido among the lustful (*Inf* V.61–62). Boccaccio's view is more complicated. He presents a chaste Dido who mounts the pyre rather than remarry as her councillors advise, *De claris mulieribus* XL, influenced by the chaste queen in Petrarch's *Trionfi* I.9–12; 154–159. But he also presents a Virgilian Dido, guilty of passion, in *Amorosa visione*, XXVIII.4–XXIX.30, and *Il Filocolo* II.18.12. Ovidian Dido, subjected to Amor, appears in *Il Filocolo* III, IV, V; in *RR* 13173–13210; in Machaut, *Jugement dou roy de Navarre*, 2095–2132.

Chaucer seems to have been touched with pity for Dido as Ovid presents her in *Heroides* VII. He mentions her story several times, and his presentation of Eneas emphasizes his falseness in love. The Man of Law says that Chaucer has told "the swerd of Dido for the false Enee," *MLI* 64. Dydo slew herself for the false Eneas, "which a fool she was," *BD* 731–734. The story is painted on a tablet of brass, *HF* I.241–444. Dido is one of love's martyrs, *PF* 289, and appears in the catalogue of faithful women, *LGW F* 264, *LGW G* 217. The full story appears *LGW* 924–1367. [**Anne¹: Ascanius: Eneas: Iulo: Yarbas**]

Dido occurs once initially, *HF* I.312; twenty-two times in medial positions, *MLI* 64; *PF* 289; *HF* I.241, 254, 287, 318, 432, 444; *LGW F* 263; *LGW G* 217; LGW 927, 993, 995, 1017, 1124, 1157, 1201, 1237, 1290, 1330, 1333, 1336; twice in final rhyming position, *LGW* 1004, 1309. *Dydo,* the OF variant, occurs once in medial position, *BD* 732, and once in final rhyming position, *LGW* 956.

E.B. Atwood, "Two Alterations of Virgil in Chaucer's Dido." *Speculum* 13 (1938): 454–457; Boccaccio, *L'Amorosa visione,* ed. V. Branca, 203–206; *ibid., CFW,* trans. G. Guarino, 86–92; *De claris mulieribus,* ed. V. Zaccaria, 168–182; *ibid., Il Filocolo,* ed. S. Battaglia, 83, 267, 302, 349, 378, 466; D.R. Bradley, "Fals Eneas and Sely Dido." *PQ* 39 (1960): 122–125; Dante, *Divine Comedy,* ed. and trans. C.S. Singleton, I.1: 50–53; Alan T. Gaylord, "Dido at Hunt, Chaucer at Work." *ChauR* 17 (1982–1983): 300–315; Guillaume de Machaut, *Oeuvres,* ed. E. Hoepffner, I: 209–210; Ranulf Higden, *Polychronicon,* ed. J.R. Lumby and C. Babington, II: 432–435; R. Hollander, *Boccaccio's Two Venuses,* 171–173; Ovid, *Her,* ed. and trans. G. Showerman, 82–99; Petrarch, *I Trionfo della Pudicizia,* ed. Ezio Chiorboli, 325–329; *ibid., The Triumphs of Petrarch,* trans. E.H. Wilkins, 39, 45; *RR,* ed. E. Langlois, IV: 9–10; *RR,* trans. C. Dahlberg, 228; B. Smalley, *English Friars and Antiquity,* 130–320; Virgil, *Aeneid,* ed. and trans. H.R. Fairclough, I: 264–275; 294–445.

DIOGENES, c. 400–c. 325 B.C., was the philosopher who founded the Cynic School of philosophy. He maintained that human needs were very simple and easy to satisfy, and to illustrate this idea he lived in extreme poverty. Jerome quotes Diogenes on poverty, *Epistola adversus Jovinianum (Letter Against Jovinian)* II.1 (*PL* 23: 300). Gower gives two accounts of Diogenes's poverty, by which he maintained his independence, *Confessio Amantis* III.1201–1316 and VII.2217–2320.

Diogenes says that real poverty is to be found where food is very scarce and thin, *Former Age* 33–37.

The name occurs in final rhyming position, *Former Age* 35.

John Gower, *The Complete Works,* ed. G.C. Macaulay, II: 259–262, III: 293–296.

DIOMEDE is the Greek warrior who wins Criseyde away from Troilus. In Benoît's version, *Roman de Troie* 13517–13617, Diomedes falls in love with Breseida, and Troilus engages him in battle *à se méfier de Breseida,* "taunting him about Breseida," *Roman de Troie* 20071–20103. In Guido, *Historia destructionis Troiae* XXIV.24–25, Troilus also taunts Diomedes for loving Breseida. Boccaccio develops a rivalry between Troilus and Diomede to develop the faithlessness of Breseida, *Il Filostrato*, VIII, and Chaucer's portrait of Diomede is drawn essentially from Boccaccio's characterization.

Diomede's courtship of Criseyde is an example of the workings of fickle Fortune, *Tr* IV.10–11. He is a forceful lover, and wins Criseyde away from Troilus. Criseyde gives him a brooch which was a gift from Troilus to seal their love. Diomede is referred to as "this Diomede" throughout the fifth book of *Troilus and Criseyde*. [**Criseyde: Troilus**]

The name never occurs initially. It appears sixteen times in medial positions, *Tr* V.37, 46, 92, 106, 771, 799, 844, 956, 1010, 1031, 1071, 1512, 1517, 1519, 1677, 1757; and thirteen times in final rhyming position, *Tr* IV, 11; *Tr* V.15, 86, 183, 841, 869, 1024, 1041, 1045, 1087, 1513, 1654, 1703.

Benoît, *Roman de Troie*, ed. L. Constans II: 306–313, III: 281–283; Boccaccio, *Tutte le opere*, ed. V. Branca, II: 216–225; Guido delle Colonne, *Guido de Columnis: HDT*, ed. N.E. Griffin, 197; *ibid., HDT*, trans. M.E. Meek, 189.

DIOMEDES, king of Thrace, owned horses which fed on human flesh. As his eighth labor, Hercules killed Diomedes and threw his body to the horses (*Met* IX.194–196; *OM* IX.1–872).

Lady Philosophy rehearses the labors of Hercules, *Bo* 4, *Metr* 7.28–62. Chaucer adds a gloss that the horses of Diomedes devoured him. [**Busirus: Ercules**]

Ovid, *Met*, ed. and trans. F.J. Miller, II: 16–17; *OM*, ed. C. de Boer, III, deel 30: 1–242.

DIONE: [DYONE]
DIOSCORIDES: [DEYSCORIDES]

DITE. Dictys Cretensis, the supposed author of *Ephemeridos belli Troiani (A Journal of the Trojan War),* said he accompanied Idomeneus the Cretan to the war. The work, however, dates probably from the fourth century of our era. There are two sets of manuscripts: one group is introduced by a preface, the other group by a letter in which the author claims to be the Latin translator of the original Greek of Dictys. Benoît de Sainte-Maure and Guido de Columnis used both Dictys and Dares for their versions of the Trojan War story. Dictys's *Journal* is longer than Dares's *History* and devotes much time to how the Greeks returned to their homeland.

The Tytus of *HF* III.1467 is probably Dictys, since his name is coupled with Dares. E.K. Rand suggests that Chaucer means Livy, but that is unlikely. Dite is one of the sources for the story of Troilus, *Tr* I.146, but clearly Chaucer never read *Ephemeridos belli Troiani*. He follows Benoît and Guido, who make several references to Dares and Dictys as their sources. The main source for Chaucer's *Troilus* is Boccaccio's *Il Filostrato* (1333–1339). **[Dares Frygius]**

Dite, a contraction, appears in final rhyming position, *Tr* I.146.

Dictys Cretensis, *Ephemeridos belli Troiani,* ed. W. Eisenhut; Dares Phrygius and Dictys Cretensis, *The Trojan War,* trans. R.M. Frazer; N.E. Griffin, "The Greek Dictys." *American Journal of Philology* 29 (1908): 329–335; Guido delle Colonne, *Guido de Columnis: HDT,* ed. N.E. Griffin, 1–17; *ibid., HDT,* trans. with introd. and notes by M.E. Meek; E.K. Rand, "Chaucer in Error." *Speculum* 1 (1926): 222–225.

DIVES was a rich man, at whose gate the beggar Lazarus sat, while Dives fared sumptuously every day. When he died, he opened his eyes in hell, while Lazarus went to Abraham's bosom when he died. The name occurs in the Latin Vulgate, Luke 16:19–31.

Dives and Lazarus lived differently and received different rewards, *SumT* 1873–1878. **[Lazar]**

Dives, Latin for "rich man," appears medially, *SumT* 1877.

Dives and Pauper, ed. P.H. Barnum.

DOG STAR: [SYRIUS]

DONEGILD is King Alla's mother in *The Man of Law's Tale.* In Trevet's *Les Chroniques,* King Alla's mother is called *Deumylde* or *Doumnilde,* meaning "sweet mildness," a name in direct contradistinction to her character and actions.

Donegild persecutes her daughter-in-law Custance, wife of her son Alla. Word is sent to Alla at the front that Custance has given birth to a beautiful son. On his way to King Alla's camp, the messenger stops at Donegild's court. She drugs him and substitutes another letter, telling the king that the child Custance has borne is a fiendly creature, contrary to the information in the Constable's original letter, which describes a beautiful child and a happy birth, *MLT* 729–784. On his way back to Custance from King Alla, the messenger again stops at Donegild's court; again she drugs him and substitutes a letter, this one banishing Custance and her child from the realm, contrary to King Alla's instructions that his wife and child be kept safe until his return, *MLT* 785–805. When King Alla comes home victorious and discovers his mother's evil actions, he slays her, *MLT* 890–896. **[Alla: Custance: Hermengyld: Maurice]**

Donegild, a Welsh name without connotations of good or evil, appears initially with two syllables, *MLT* 740, and four times in medial positions, with two syllables, *MLT* 695, 778, and with three syllables, *MLT* 805, 896.

M. Schlauch, ed., "Trivet's Life of Constance." *S&A*, 172–173.

DORIGEN is the faithful wife in *The Franklin's Tale.* Chaucer seems to have taken the main plot for his story from Boccaccio's *Il Filocolo* (1333–1339) and to have added elements from Geoffrey of Monmouth's *Historia Regum Britanniae* IV.15–16. In Geoffrey's *Historia* King Arvirargus loves his wife Genuissa above all else.

Dorigen and Arveragus agree to be friends and lovers in marriage, *FranklT* 729–760. She loves her husband as her heart's life and grieves when he is away in England seeking honor in arms, *FranklT* 814–821. To distract her, her friends encourage her to dance with them in a garden, where she meets Aurelius, who has loved her secretly for more than two years, *FranklT* 824–978. She rashly promises to be his love if he makes the hideous rocks in the harbor disappear, *FranklT* 979–1021. Aurelius hires a magician from Orleans, who performs the feat. Dorigen, in a quandary, thinks of all the famous women who have been faithful wives, such as Penelopee, and of those who have committed suicide rather than lose their honor, such as Hasdrubale's wife, and wonders if she will have to follow their example. She confides in her husband, however, and he insists that she keep her word. All ends well when Aurelius releases her from her promise. **[Alcebiades: Alceste: Aristoclides: Arthemesie: Arveragus: Aurelie: Bilyea: Cedasus: Democion(es): Diane: Habradate: Hasdrubal(es): Gaufride: Ladomya: Lucrece: Nicerate(s): Nichanore[1]: Penalopee: Phidoun: Porcia: Rodogone: Stymphalides: Valeria]**

Dorigen is a Celtic name, derived perhaps from *Dorguen* or *Droguen.* G.A. Lobineau points out that *Dorguen* or *Droguen* is late medieval spelling for the name of the wife of Alain I of Brittany, usually spelled *Ohurguen, Orgain,* or *Oreguen, Ohurgen.* Tatlock shows that *Droguen* is also the name of one of the prominent rocks among the *Rochers de Penmarch* off the coast of Brittany. The name never appears initially. It occurs ten times in medial positions, *FranklT* 815, 919, 936, 1457, 1469, 1488, 1500, 1542, 1551, 1598; twice in final rhyming position, *FranklT* 926, 1090.

G. Dempster, "Chaucer at Work on the Complaint in *The Franklin's Tale." MLN* 41 (1943): 6–16; Geoffrey of Monmouth, *Historia Regum Britanniae,* ed. J. Hammer, 80–83; *ibid., History of the Kings of Britain,* trans. L. Thorpe, 121–122; K. Hume, "The Pagan Setting of *The Franklin's Tale* and the Sources of Dorigen's Cosmology." *SN* 44 (1972): 289–294; A.T. Lee, "'A Woman Free and Fair': Chaucer's Portrayal of Dorigen in *The Franklin's Tale." ChauR* 19 (1984–1985): 169–178; G.A. Lobineau, *Histoire de Bretagne* I: 70; *Riverside Chaucer,* ed. L. Benson, 897; J. Sledd, "Dorigen's Complaint." *MP* 45 (1947): 36–45; J.S.P. Tatlock and P. Mackaye, *The Scene of The Franklin's Tale Visited,* 37–41.

DRACO: [DRAGOUN]

DRAGOUN. The alpha or brightest star in the constellation the Dragon lies in the Dragon's Tail. This Dragon, guardian of the golden apples of the Hesperides, was slain by Hercules when he went to gather the fruit in his eleventh labor (*Met* IX.187–190).

The slaying of the Dragoun is one of Hercules's labors, *MkT* 2101, *Bo* 4, *Metr* 7.34–35. Chaucer describes the "fortunat ascendent" as that sign in the house of a planet of friendly aspect, but not in the house of an evil planet, like Mars or the Dragoun's Tail, *Astr.* II.4. 30–35.

Dragoun, the ME variant, appears in final rhyming position, *MkT* 2101.

Ovid, *Met*, ed. and trans. F.J. Miller, II: 16–17.

DUNSTAN (saint), c. A.D. 909–988, was born in Glastonbury of noble parents. He became abbot of the Benedictine monastery at Glastonbury and served as Archbishop of Canterbury from 960–988. Throughout the medieval period, there was a tradition that St. Dunstan had devils as his servants, as instruments of God.

The fiend says that sometimes devils have been servants to man, as they were to Saint Dunstan, *FrT* 1502–1503.

Dunstan, Anglo-Saxon for "mountain stone," appears in final rhyming position, *FrT* 1502.

E.S. Duckett, *St. Dunstan of Canterbury*; Sister Mary Immaculate, "Fiends as 'servant unto man' in the *Friar's Tale*." *PQ* 21 (1942): 240–244; J.A. Robinson, *The Times of St. Dunstan*; *The South-English Legendary*, ed. C. D'Evelyn and A.J. Mill, I: 204–211.

DYANE: [DIANE]
DYANIRE: [DIANIRA]

DYONE. Dione, daughter of Oceanus and Tethys, was consort of Zeus and mother of Aphrodite Pandemos or "natural Venus" (*Iliad* V.370). In Roman mythology she was consort of Jupiter and mother of Venus Voluptaria or "carnal Venus " (*Aeneid* III.19–21).

The narrator praises Venus, Dione's daughter, Cupid, and the Nine Muses, for through them he has told the joy of Troilus's service, *Tr* III.1807–1820. [**Cupide: Pierides: Venus**]

Dyone, an ME spelling variant, appears in final rhyming position, *Tr* III.1807.

Homer, *Iliad*, ed. and trans. A.T. Murray, I: 222–223; Virgil, *Aeneid*, ed. and trans. H.R. Fairclough, I: 348–349.

EACIDES. Aeacides is the Greek patronymic, meaning "son of Aeacus," applied to Achilles, grandson of Aeacus throughout Statius's *Achilleid.*

Eacides serves as an adjective describing Chiron, Achilles's tutor, *HF* III.1204–1207. **[Achille: Chiron]**

Statius, *Achilleid,* ed. and trans. J.H. Mozley.

ECCLESIASTE: [JHESU SYRACH]
ECCLESIASTICUS: [JHESU SYRACH]
ECHO: [ECQUO]

ECLYMPASTEYR. This name does not appear in mythological dictionaries. Enclimpostair is a son of the god of sleep in Froissart's *Paradys d'Amours* 28 (before 1369).

Juno's messenger arrives at the cave of sleep and finds Morpheus and Eclympasteyr, *BD* 167. The poet says that Eclympasteyr is the heir of the god of sleep, *BD* 168, who sleeps and does no work, *BD* 169.

Eclympasteyr, Chaucer's variant of Froissart's *Enclimpostair,* appears in final rhyming position, *BD* 167. N.R. Cartier suggests that Froissart distorted known names to produce strange ones; in this case the final consonant of *Enclin* ("incline" or "lean") is assimilated to the initial bilabial plosive of *postere* (from French *postérieur,* "back" or "rear"). *Enclimpostair* is thus a compound meaning "supine" or "lazybones."

N.R. Cartier, "Froissart, Chaucer, and Enclimpostair." *RLC* 38 (1964): 18–34; G.L. Kittredge, "Chaucer and Froissart (with a discussion of the date of the *Méliador*)." *Englische Studien* 26 (1899): 321–336.

ECQUO, EKKO. When Juno discovered that Echo's incessant chatter was a ruse to detain her while Jupiter flirted, she deprived the nymph of her speech but did allow her to echo the last phrase of conversations. Afflicted thus, Echo met Narcissus and fell in love with him; he would not return her love, and she wasted away until only her voice remained *(Met* III.339–510).

The Clerk alludes to the incessant chatter, *ClT* 1189. Ekko died because she could not tell her woe, *FranklT* 951, and because Narcissus would not love her, *BD* 735–736. [**Narcisus**]

Ecquo, the OF variant, appears in medial position, *BD* 735; *Ekko,* the ME variant, appears in medial position, *ClT* 1189, and in final rhyming position, *FranklT* 951.

Ovid, *Met,* ed. and trans. F.J. Miller, I: 148–161.

ECTOR. Hector, eldest son of Priam and Hecuba of Troy, leader of the Trojans against the Greeks, was husband of Andromache and brother of Troilus and Paris. As the bravest of the Trojans, he led them unto the field. Achilles slew him to avenge Patroclus's death, then dragged the dead body around his friend's tomb. Subsequently, Priam went to Achilles and begged for his son's body; Achilles restored it, and Hector was buried at Troy *(Iliad* xxiv).

The medieval versions of the Troy story are *De excidio Troiae historia* of Dares Phrygius, of uncertain date but generally believed to have been written about the fourth century A.D.; *Ephemeridos belli Troiani* of Dictys Cretensis, dating from the fourth century A.D.; *Le Roman de Troie* (c. 1184), written by a Norman cleric, Benoît de Sainte-Maure; *Historia destructionis Troiae* by Guido delle Colonne (before 1287). Hector appears as one of the three pagan worthies in *The Parlement of the Thre Ages* (fourteenth century), 300–331. During the later Middle Ages poets began claiming descent from Trojan heroes for whole nations. Jean le Maire des Belges tells that the French and Germans were descended from Hector in *Illustrations de Gaule et singularités de Troie* (c. 1506).

The Knight compares the women's weeping at Arcita's funeral with the wailing of the Trojan women when Ector was brought home dead, *KnT* 2830–2833 (the lament for Hector occurs in Benoît's *Roman de Troie,* 16317–16502). Ector's death is foretold in the stars, *MLT* 198. Andromache dreams that Ector will die, *NPT* 3141–3148. Chauntecleer tells the story to illustrate the *visio,* the warning dream foretelling the future. R.A. Pratt suggests that Chaucer's immediate source for the dream is very likely *Renart le Contrefait* 31323–31340. Dares summarizes the dream in *De excidio Troiae historia* 24. Ector appears on the walls of the temple of glass, *BD* 325–331. The Man in Black says that he would have loved his lady even though he were as brave as Ector, *BD* 1065 (Hector's courage was a medieval commonplace). Chaucer's characterization of Ector in *Troilus and Criseyde* owes much to Boccaccio's conception in *Il Filostrato*

(1333–1339). After his death, Ector appears to Eneas as Troy burns, *LGW* 934. [**Achille: Andromacha: Ecuba: Guido: Julius: Pompe: Priam: Socrates: Turnus**]

Ector, the ME and OF variant, appears four times initially, *Tr* II.417; *Tr* IV.40, 176, 187; 27 times in medial positions, *KnT* 2832; *MLT* 198; *NPT* 3142, 3144; *BD* 328, 1065; *Tr* I.110, 113, 471; *Tr* II.153, 158, 171, 176, 183, 417, 740, 1450, 1481, 1627, 1698; *Tr* III.1775; *Tr* IV.33, 193, 214; *Tr* V.1549, 1804; *LGW* 934. *Ectores,* the ME genitive case, appears medially, *NPT* 3141. Latin initial *h* was not pronounced.

Benoît, *Roman de Troie,* ed. L. Constans, III: 79–89; C.D. Benson, "'O Nyce World': What Chaucer Really Found in Guido delle Colonne's History of Troy." *ChauR* 13 (1979): 308–315; Bernard Silvester, *Megacosmos,* ed. C.S. Barach and J. Wrobel, 16; Dares, *De excidio Troiae historia,* ed. F. Meister, 28–30; Dares Phrygius and Dictys Cretensis, *The Trojan War,* trans. R.M. Frazer, 152–153; Guido delle Colonne, *Guido de Columnis: HDT,* ed. N.E. Griffin; *ibid., HDT,* trans. M.E. Meek; Homer, *Iliad,* ed. and trans. A.T. Murray, II: 562–623; R.S. Loomis, "Verses on The Nine Worthies." *MP* 15 (1917): 19–27; *The Parlement of the Thre Ages,* ed. M.Y. Offord, 12–13; R.A. Pratt, "Three Old French Sources of the Nonnes Preestes Tale." *Speculum* 57 (1972): 411–444; 646–668; J.H. Roberts, "The Nine Worthies." *MP* 19 (1922): 297–305; Jean Seznec, *Survival of the Pagan Gods,* trans. B.F. Sessions, 24.

ECUBA. Hecuba, wife of Priam and queen of Troy, was mother of Cassandra, Deiphebus, Hector, Paris, and Troilus.

Ecuba is mentioned once, *Tr* V.12. [**Cassandra: Deiphebus: Ector: Paris: Poliyxena: Priam: Troilus**]

Chaucer's form is identical with Boccaccio's Italian, *Il Filostrato* VII.103, as well as with Benoît's Old French, *Roman de Troie* 5609. Latin initial *h* was not pronounced. The name appears medially, *Tr* V.12.

Benoît, *Roman de Troie,* ed. L. Constans, I: 288; Boccaccio, *Tutte le opere,* ed. V. Branca, II: 214.

EDIPPE, EDIPPUS. Oedipus, son of Laius, king of Thebes, was fated to kill his father and marry his mother. Warned by the Oracle at Delphi that his son would kill him, Laius had the infant Oedipus exposed on Mount Cithaeron, a spike driven through his ankles. A shepherd herding the flocks of King Polybus of Corinth found him and took him to the king, and the queen reared him as her son. When Oedipus became a young man, he consulted the Oracle, which told him he would kill his father and marry his mother. Horrified at such a fate, Oedipus ran away from home, thinking that Polybus and his wife were his parents. On the way to Thebes, he killed Laius in a chance encounter, not knowing who he was; after solving the riddle of the Sphinx, he was rewarded with the hand of the queen in marriage. In time, another plague ravaged Thebes, and Oedipus learned that the cause was to be found in the royal house. Then it was revealed that Oedipus had indeed killed his father and married his mother. His mother Iocasta, learning that Oedipus was her son and husband, hanged herself, and Oedipus blinded himself. The medieval sources are Statius's *Thebaid*, I.44–87, and the twelfth-century *Roman de Thèbes*, 1–518.

Criseyde and her friends read the story of Edippus, *Tr* II.99–102, in a volume with twelve "books," the number of books in Statius's *Thebaid*; Chaucer invented the scene, which does not appear in Boccaccio's *Il Filostrato* (1333–1339). Troilus complains that if Criseyde is taken from him he will see neither rain nor sunshine, but will live his sorrowful life in darkness, like Edippe, and die in distress, *Tr* IV.295–301. **[Ethiocles: Layus: Polymyte]**

Edippus, the French form in *Roman de Thèbes* 225, occurs medially, *Tr* II.102; *Edippe*, with elided final -e, occurs medially, *Tr* IV.300.

P.M. Clogan, "Chaucer and the *Thebaid* Scolia." *SP* 61 (1964): 599–615; *Roman de Thèbes*, ed. L. Constans, I: 1–28; *Roman de Thèbes (The Story of Thebes)*, trans. J.S. Coley, 1–13; Statius, *Thebaid*, ed. and trans. J.H. Mozley, I: 344–347.

EDWARD, called the Confessor, the last Anglo-Saxon king of England, reigned 1043–1066. Pope Alexander III canonized him in 1161. An earlier Edward, called Edward the Martyr, appears in English martyrology; born c. 962, he died in Dorset in 978 *(NCE* V: 181).

The Monk announces that his tale will be about Saint Edward, *MkP* 1970–1972, referring, most likely, to Edward the Confessor. **[Piers]**

The Anglo-Saxon Chronicle, ed. and trans by G.N. Garmonsway, 162–163, 193–195; W. Scholz, "The Canonization of Edward the Confessor." *Speculum* 36 (1961): 38–60; *The South-English Legendary,* ed. C.D. D'Evelyn and A.J. Mill, I: 110–118.

EGEUS. Aegeus, son of Pandion, was king of Athens and father of Theseus. After Androgeus, Prince of Crete, was slain in Athens, his father Minos exacted a tribute of youths and maidens to feed the Minotaur, which he kept in a labyrinth. Theseus accompanied the youths to Crete, slew the Minotaur with Ariadne's help, and set sail for home. But he forgot that he had promised his father to change the black funereal sails of the ship to white sails if he returned victorious. Aegeus, seeing the black sails and thinking his son dead, threw himself into the sea, which now bears his name *(Met* VII.402–450; VIII.169–182; *OM,* VIII.1083–1394).

In *The Knight's Tale* Egeus is still alive and appears after Arcite's death. He speaks the famous lines:

This world nys but a thurghfare ful of wo,

And we been pilgrymes, passynge to and fro *(KnT* 2847–2848).

After his funeral oration, *KnT* 2837–2852, he walks at the right side of the bier in the funeral procession, *KnT* 2905. Egeus must send his son, Theseus, as part of the tribute to Minos of Crete since the lot falls on him, *LGW* 1944–1947. [**Theseus**]

Egeus, the medieval Latin and OF form, occurs only in final rhyming positions, *KnT* 2838, 2905, *LGW* 1944.

Ovid, *Met*, ed. and trans. F.J. Miller, I: 370–375, 418–419; *OM*, ed. C. de Boer, III, deel 30: 134–192.

EGISTE, EGISTES, EGISTUS. Aegyptus had fifty sons and his brother Danaus had fifty daughters. He arranged marriages between his sons and nieces, but Danaus, fearing his brother's power, ordered his daughters to slay their husbands. When Hypermnestra disobeyed him, Danaus imprisoned her (*Heroides* XIV).

In *The Legend of Ypermystra*, Egistus is Ypermestra's father. Chaucer switches the parents and children. Egistus is false in love and has many daughters, but Ypermestra is his daughter dear. He agrees with his brother Danao to wed Ypermestra to Lyno, Danao's son, but Egistes commands her to slay Lyno. He calls her to his chamber on the wedding night and tells her that although he loves her, she shall die unless she does as he commands. He gives her a knife and commands her to slay Lyno because his dreams have told him that Lyno will cause his destruction. Ypermestra, however, spares Lyno's life, and they run away together. Ypermestra cannot run as fast as Lyno, and she is caught and imprisoned by her father. [**Danao: Lyno: Ypermestra**]

Egiste occurs as nominative in final rhyming position, *LGW* 2570, and as genitive in final rhyming position, *LGW* 2816, with unstressed final *-e*. *Egistes* occurs as dative, *LGW* 2600, and *Egistus*, nominative in initial position, *LGW* 2635. *Egiste* is a possible variant of *Egisto* in the Italian translation of the *Heroides* by Filippo Ceffi (c. 1320–1330); Chaucer may have also derived it from the Latin original.

S.B. Meech, "Chaucer and an Italian Translation of the *Heroides*." *PMLA* 45 (1930): 123–125; Ovid, *Her*, ed. and trans. G. Showerman, 170–181; *OM*, ed. C. de Boer, I, deel 15: 268–273.

EGLENTYNE is the Prioress's name. Chaucer's portrait of her is a composite of the ideal courtly heroine found in medieval romance, *Gen Prol* 118–162, especially in Jean de Meun's *Roman de la Rose*, 13341–13351, but overdone just enough to suggest that the Prioress might not be the aristocrat she pretends to be. She tells the story of the boy-martyr, which belongs to the type called a "Miracle of the Virgin." During Chaucer's time a nun named Madame Argentyn lived at the Benedictine Convent of St. Leonard at Stratford-atte-Bowe. She is mentioned in the will of Elizabeth of Hainault, sister of Queen Philippa, Edward III's wife. This convent was about two miles from Chaucer's house in Aldgate, and Chaucer mentions St. Leonard's shrine, *HF* I.115–118.

Eglentyne is a variant of *Aiglentine*, a name rich in romantic associations of courtly love as well as those of religious devotion. In *The Travels of Sir John Mandeville*, the author mentions three crowns of thorn used by the Roman soldiers when they tortured Jesus: one of hawthorn (when they arrested Jesus in the garden); one of eglentine or briar rose (when they brought him before Caiphas); and one of the sea reeds (when he was crowned before Pilate). *Eglentyne,* as the Prioress's name, appears once, in final rhyming position, *Gen Prol* 121. **[Leonard: Loy]**

R.T. Davies, "Chaucer's Madame Eglantine." *MLN* 67 (1952): 400–402; E.P. Kuhl, "Chaucer's Madame Eglantine." *MLN* 60 (1945): 325–326; J.L. Lowes, "Simple and Coy: A Note on Fourteenth-century Poetic Diction." *Anglia* 33 (1910): 440–451; *Mandeville's Travels*, ed. M.C. Seymour, 9–10; J.M. Manly, *Some New Light on Chaucer*, 206–212; C. Moorman, "The Prioress as Pearly Queen." *ChauR* 13 (1978): 25–33; *RR,* ed. E. Langlois, IV: 16, *RR,* trans. C. Dahlberg, 230.

EKKO: [ECQUO]

ELCANOR cannot be positively identified. It may refer to Helcanor/ Helcana, the heroine of the Old French prose romance *Cassidorus* (thirteenth century), who appears to her lover twelve times in dreams. The romance is a continuation of the prose redaction of the Old French *Les sept sages de Rome (The Seven Sages of Rome).*

Not even Elcanor has had a dream like this one of flying with an eagle, *HF* II.512–517.

The name appears in final rhyming position, *HF* II.516.

Le Roman de Cassidorus, ed. J. Palermo; *Les sept sages de Rome,* ed. G. Paris; *Riverside Chaucer,* ed. L. Benson, 982; J.S.P Tatlock, "Chaucer's 'Elcanor.' " *MLN* 36 (1921): 95–97.

ELEATICIS. These were philosophers of the Eleatic school of philosophy founded by Parmenides and Zeno, both of Elea.

Lady Philosophy commands the Muses to leave Boethius, who has been nourished in the studies of the Eleatics and the Academics in Greece, *Bo* I, *Prosa* I. **[Achademycis: Parmanydes: Plato: Zeno]**

Eleaticis is the Latin genitive case, found in Boethius's Latin text.

Boethius, *The Consolation of Philosophy*, ed. and trans. S.J. Tester, 134–135.

ELEYNE[1] (saint). Helena, (c. 250–330), wife of Constantinus Chlorus and mother of Constantine the Great, was reputed to have found the True Cross. Influenced by her son, she became a Christian and was subsequently given the title *Augusta*. About 324 she made a pilgrimage to Jerusalem, where she is said to have founded the Church of the Nativity and the Church of the Ascension on the Mount of Olives. Encouraged by dreams and visions, she made a second pilgrimage c. 326 to Jerusalem in search of the cross of the crucifixion. She enquired of the rabbinate for the place of the crucifixion, and when they would not tell her, she ordered them burnt. In fear, they sent her Judas, their leader, whom she had confined without food and water for six days when he also would not tell her. On the seventh day he agreed to do her bidding. Led to the place where it was hidden, Helena prayed, and there was a slight earthquake; then such a sweet perfume filled the air that Judas was converted on the spot. After digging to a depth of twenty feet, he discovered three crosses, which he brought to Helena. The cross that raised a man from the dead was considered the True Cross. Judas was baptized and became Bishop Cyriacus. He found, subsequently, the nails of the crucifixion, and Helena took these back to Rome. Constantine wore them in his bridle and in his helmet (*Legenda aurea* LXVIII). The story is the subject of one of Cynewulf's poems, *Elene*, written during the first half of the ninth century.

Harry Bailly swears, by the cross which St. Eleyne found, to do violence to the Pardoner, *PardT* 951–955. The medieval church celebrated the Feast of the Invention of the Cross on May 3, also considered a bad luck day. Palamon breaks out of prison on May 3, *KnT* 1462–1469. Pandarus falls in love on that day, *Tr* II.56, and on May 3 Chauntecleer is carried off by Daun Russell, *NPT* 3187–3197.

Eleyne, the ME variant, with initial stress and two syllables, appears medially, *PardT* 951.

A.S. Cook, "The Date of the Old English 'Elene.'" *Anglia* 15 (1893): 9–20; Cynewulf, *Elene*, ed. P.D.E. Gradon; Jacobus de Voragine, *GL,* trans. G. Ryan and H. Ripperger, 269–276; *ibid.*, *LA*, ed. Graesse, 303–311.

ELEYNE[2]. Helen, daughter of Jupiter and Leda, sister of Castor and Pollux, was Menelaus's wife and queen of Sparta. Considered the most beautiful woman in the world, she was abducted by Paris, youngest son of Priam of Troy, while he was her husband's guest. Paris took her to Troy, where she became his legal wife. This abduction caused the Trojan War (*Iliad* III.87–95).

The Man of Law says that Chaucer has described Eleyne's tears, *MLI* 70. Januarie will clutch May in his arms harder than Paris did Eleyne, *MerchT* 1752–1754. The story of Paris and Eleyne, both text and gloss from the *Roman de la Rose*, appears on the wall of the temple of glass, *BD* 331–334; Chaucer may have had in mind a manuscript with commentary and pictures. Eleyne is one of love's martyrs, *PF* 291; she appears among the lustful in *Inf* V.64. Attrides recovered the lost marriage of his brother by destroying Troy and winning Menelaus's wife back again, *Bo* IV, *Metr* 7.1–7. The Greeks besiege Troy to avenge the rape of Eleyne, *Tr* I.57–63. Criseyde is fairer than Eleyne, *Tr* I.442–455. Eleyne is included in the dinner party at Deiphebus's house and plays a small part in the plot of Book II of *Troilus and Criseyde*. Eleyne must hide her beauty before Alceste, the supreme example of conjugal love, *LGW F* 254, *LGW G* 208. (Helen's beauty is a medieval commonplace.) **[Deiphebus: Menelaus: Paris]**

Eleyne, the ME variant, appears twelve times medially, *MLI* 70, with elided final -*e*, *BD* 331, with initial stress and three syllables; with secondary stress and two syllables, *Tr* I.62, 455; *Tr* II.1447, 1576, 1625, 1687, 1703; *Tr* III.222, 410; *Tr* V.890; and six times in final rhyming position, *Tr* I.677; *Tr* II.1556, 1714; *Tr* V.890; *Eleyne*, with three syllables and final syllabic -*e*, occurs twice initially, *PF* 291, *Tr* II.1604; and three times medially, *Tr* II.1641; *Tr* III.204; *Tr* IV.1347.

Dante, *Divine Comedy*, ed. and trans. C.S. Singleton, I.1: 54; Dares Phrygius, *De excidio Troiae historia*, ed. F. Meister, 14–16; Dictys Cretensis, *Ephemeridos belli Troiani libri*, ed. W. Eisenhut, 9–10, 98–101, 113–114; Dares Phrygius and Dictys Cretensis, *The Trojan War*, trans. R.M. Frazer, 27–29, 142–143; Homer, *Iliad*, ed. and trans. A.T. Murray, I: 122–123; *Riverside Chaucer*, ed. L. Benson, 969; M. Sundwall, "Deiphobus and Helen: A Tantalizing Hint." *MP* 73 (1975): 151–156.

ELFETA: [ELPHETA]
ELI: [HELIE]

ELIACHIM was a priest of Bethulia, the city where Judith lived. When Holofernes attacked Judea with his army, Eliachim advised the people to seize the mountain passes and so prevent the Assyrians from approaching the city (Judith [The Latin Vulgate] 4: 5–7).

The Monk identifies Eliachim as a priest of Bethulia, *MkT* 2565–2566. **[Judith: Oloferne]**

The name occurs medially, *MkT* 2566.

ELIGIUS: [LOY]
ELIJAH: [ELYE]

ELISE. Elisha was an Israelite prophet in the days of Jereboam, son of Ahab, c. 800 B.C. As Elijah's disciple, he was anointed by the older prophet to take his place before Elijah was taken up to heaven in his chariot of fire (IV Kings 2:1–13). The Carmelites claim in *De origine fundatoribus et regulus monachorum et monacharum* (end of the fourteenth century) that Elijah and Elisha were friars and that Elijah was their founder.

Friar John tells sick Thomas that the friars' reputation for teaching and preaching began in the time of Elye and Elise, *SumT* 2116. **[Elye]**

Elise is a development of Latin *Heliseus*. Latin initial *h* was not pronounced. It occurs in final rhyming position.

R.A. Koch, "Elijah the Prophet, Founder of the Carmelite Order." *Speculum* 24 (1959): 547–560.

ELISHA: [ELISE]
ELOY: [LOY]

ELPHETA. Elfeta is one of the fixed stars of the constellation Scorpio. Early Arabian astronomers, however, applied the name to the constellation Ariadne's Crown and called it *al-fakkah,* because of the gaps in the crown, transliterated variously as *Alphaca, Alfeta, Alfecca. Na'ir al-fakkah* is the alpha or brightest star of the northern constellation Corona Borealis. J.M. Manly points out that the name occurs in *Liber Astronomicus qui Dicitur Albion,* c. 1326, ascribed to Richard de Wallingford (MS Harley 80, folio 51a). Elpheta is Cambyuskan's wife and mother of Algarsyf, Cambalo, and Canacee in *The Squire's Tale.* Chaucer may have found her name in a medieval list of stars. [**Algarsyf: Cambalo: Cambyuskan: Canacee**[2]]

Elpheta, derived from Arabic *al-fakkah,* meaning "the opened," from the verb *fakka,* "to open," "to breach," appears once, medially, *SqT* 29.

R.H. Allen, *Star Names and their Meanings,* 178; J.M. Manly, ed. *The Canterbury Tales,* 598.

ELYE. Elijah was a prophet in Israel during the reigns of Ahab and Ahaziah in the ninth century B.C. He prayed on Mount Carmel that God send rain to break the terrible drought (III Kings 18:42). Thus the Carmelites claim Elijah as their founder, *De origine fundatoribus et regulus monachorum et monacharum* (end of the fourteenth century). Elijah fasted on Mount Horeb before speaking with the Lord (III Kings 19:8), and he was swept up to heaven in a chariot of fire by a whirlwind (IV Kings 2:11).

Friar John mentions Elye's fast on Mount Horeb, *SumT* 1890–1893. Since the time of Elye and Elise, the friars have had a reputation for preaching and teaching, *SumT* 2116. Elye as celestial voyager appears in *HF* II.588. [**Elise**]

Elye, with final syllabic *-e,* is the ME variant of Latin *Helias;* Latin initial *h* was not pronounced; compare with Dante's Italian, *Elia, Inf* XXVI.35. The name occurs twice medially, *SumT* 1890, 2116, and once in final rhyming position, *HF* II.588.

Dante, *Divine Comedy,* ed. and trans. C.S. Singleton, I.1: 272–273; R.A. Koch, "Elijah the Prophet, Founder of the Carmelite Order." *Speculum* 24 (1959): 547–560.

ELYMAS: [LIMOTE]

EMELIE, EMELYA, EMELYE is an Amazon and sister of Ypolita, the Amazon queen in *The Knight's Tale.* Palamon and Arcite fall in love with her when they look out their prison window and see her walking in the garden. Emelye makes two solo appearances: in her May observances, *KnT* 1033–1055, and in her visit to Dyane's oratory before the tournament, *KnT*

2271–2366. She does not care for either knight and does not want marriage, but she asks Dyane that if her destiny is to marry one of them, the goddess send her the one who loves her most, *KnT* 2307–2310. But Theseus intends to give her as a prize to the knight who wins the tournament he arranges. Arcite, who has asked Mars for victory, wins the tournament but is killed when his horse, frightened by the fury sent by Saturn, stumbles and throws him. After some years, Emelye weds Palamon, who has asked Venus to give him Emelye, and thus her prayer is answered. [**Arcita: Diane: Palamon: Theseus: Ypolita**]

The forms are ME variants of Boccaccio's Italian, *Emilia*, in *Il Teseide delle nozze d'Emilia* (1339–1341). *Emelie* occurs once, in final rhyming position, *KnT* 2658. *Emelya* occurs twice: once in medial position, *KnT* 1880, and once in final rhyming position, *KnT* 1098. *Emelye* appears eighteen times in medial positions, *KnT* 972, 1035, 1046, 1061, 1068, 1427, 1486, 1686, 1737, 1749, 1820, 2243, 2282, 2332, 2361, 2817, 2941, 3103, *Anel* 38; twenty-seven times in final rhyming position, *KnT* 871, 1273, 1419, 1567, 1588, 1594, 1731, 1833, 2273, 2341, 2571, 2578, 2658, 2679, 2699, 2762, 2773, 2780, 2808, 2816, 2836, 2885, 2910, 2956, 2980, 3098, 3107.

Boccaccio, *Tutte le opere*, ed. V. Branca, II: 253–664.

EMELYA: [EMELIE]
EMELYE: [EMELIE]

EMETREUS, king of India, is Arcita's champion at the tournament in *The Knight's Tale*. Boccaccio says that Lycurgus comes to aid Arcita, *Tes* VI.14. Emetreus is Chaucer's invention. Like Arcita, Emetreus shows the influence of the planet Mars in his personality, *KnT* 2155–2186. [**Arcita: Lycurge**]

Emetreus is perhaps derived from *Demetreus*, the name of a Greco-Bactrian prince (third century B.C.) known during the Middle Ages as "King of the Indians." The name occurs three times in medial positions, *KnT* 2156, 2638, 2645.

Boccaccio, *Tutte le opere*, ed. V. Branca, II: 421; W.C. Curry, *Chaucer and the Mediaeval Sciences*, 130–134; H.B. Hinckley, "The Grete Emetreus the King of Inde." *MLN* 48 (1933): 148–149.

EMILY: [EMELIE]
ENCLIMPOSTAIR: [ECLYMPASTEYR]

ENEAS, ENEE, ENYAS. Aeneas, the Trojan prince, was the son of Anchises and Venus and leader of the Dardanians in the Trojan War. Virgil's *Aeneid* (30–19 B.C.) tells the story of his adventures after Troy fell until he settled in Italy and founded Rome. *Aeneid* I and IV describe the visit to Dido, queen of Carthage, while *Aeneid* II–III contain Aeneas's relation of his adventures to the queen. This section on Dido becomes Chaucer's chief interest: Dido is a betrayed queen, and Eneas is a perfidious and treacherous guest (*Heroides* VII). Chaucer's view of Eneas is influenced by both Virgil and Ovid, mentioned in *HF* I.378–380, his first detailed narration of the story, but more by the latter poet. *Heroides* VII, Dido's letter to Aeneas, shows Aeneas as a fickle lover. Chaucer may have known Boccaccio's version in *Amorosa visione* XXVIII–XXIX, but this source is not certain. He probably also used an Italian translation of the *Heroides* by Filippo Ceffi (c. 1320–1330), a work widely read during the period as shown by the thirty-six manuscripts from the fourteenth and fifteenth centuries. The Duenna tells the Lover the story in *RR* 13173–13210, showing how Eneas is ungrateful for all the help Dido gives him in refreshing his sailors and his company; she calls him *li traistres*, "the traitor." In these versions Aeneas's treachery and fickleness are emphasized. This view is radically different from Dante's; he calls Aeneas *de Romani il gentil seme*, "of Romans the noble seed," *Inf* XXVI.60.

Eneas is "fals," *MLI* 64, *BD* 731–734. The story from *Aeneid* I and IV appears in *HF* I.162–467. Virgil stands on a pillar of tinned iron, the metals of Mars and Jupiter, for holding up the fame of "pius Eneas," *HF* III.1481–1485. "Fals Eneas" appears in *LGW* 924–1367. Eneas and Antenor eventually betray Troy, *Tr* II.1473–1484; this part of the story appears in Benoît's *Roman de Troie* 24397–25713. [**Achate: Anchyses: Anne[1]: Ascanius: Creusa: Dido: Iulo: Turnus: Virgil**]

Eneas, the ME and French variant, occurs most often, once initially, *LGW* 1128; twenty-six times in medial positions, *HF* I.165, 175, 231, 240, 320, 434, 440, 452; *LGW* 927, 976, 1015, 1023, 1062, 1097, 1103, 1108, 1124, 1137, 1144, 1153, 1158, 1206, 1226, 1232, 1243, 1252, 1285; fourteen times in final rhyming position, *BD* 732; *HF* I.217, 253, 286, 293, 356, 427, 461; *HF* III.1485; *LGW* 983, 1027, 1047, 1057. *Enee*, also a French variant as in *RR* 13174, occurs once, in final rhyming position, *MLI* 64. *Enyas*, perhaps a pronunciation variant, occurs once, in medial position, *LGW* 940. *Eneydos*, ME variant for Latin *Aeneid*, occurs three times, *NPT* 3359, *HF* I.378, *LGW* 928.

Boccaccio, *L'Amoroso visione*, ed. V. Branca, 203–206; Dante, *Divine Comedy*, ed. and trans. C.S. Singleton, I.1: 274–275; *Eneas,* roman du XIIe siècle, ed. J.-J. Salverda de Grave; S.B. Meech, "Chaucer and the Italian Translation of the *Heroides.*" *PMLA* 45 (1930): 111–113; Ovid, *Her*, ed. and trans. G. Showerman, 82–99; *RR*, ed. E. Langlois IV: 9–10; *RR*, trans. C. Dahlberg, 228; Virgil, *Aeneid*, ed. and trans. H.R. Fairclough.

ENEYDOS: [VIRGILE]

ENNOK. Enoch was the son of Cain, his time given as the seventh generation of the human race. The world's first city was named after him

(*Etym*, VII.vi.11). The passage which says: "Enoch walked with God; and he was not, for God took him" (Genesis 5:24) is interpreted by Paul: "By faith Enoch was translated that he should not see death; and was not found, because God had translated him" (Hebrews 11:5). Thus it was thought that Enoch ascended into heaven. Enoch's ascent is described in *Ecloga Theoduli* 65–68, a ninth-century school text Chaucer probably knew.

The Dreamer wonders why the Eagle should take him into heaven since he is not Ennok, *HF* II.588. **[Elye: Ganymede: Romulus]**

Ennok appears medially, *HF* II.588.

Ecloga Theoduli, ed. J. Osternacher, 34; Isidore of Seville, *Etymologiae,* ed. W.M. Lindsay, I.

ENOCH: [ENNOK]
ENYAS: [ENEAS]

EOLUS. Aeolus was the ruler of the winds and the father of Alcyone and Athamas (*Met* IV.487, XI.431, 748). As a servant of Juno, he lived on Aeolia, an island near Thrace, where he kept the winds in a cave (*Aeneid* I.50–87). In medieval iconography Aeolus was represented blowing two trumpets, as in a miniature in a manuscript of *Fulgentius Metaforalis* (c. 1331), by John Ridewall (Panofsky, Plate XIII). There Aeolus blows two trumpets while working a pair of bellows with his feet. The trumpets and bellows are briefly described by Albericus Philosophus, *De deorum imaginibus libellus* XIII (1342). The trumpets of Fame appear in Gower's *Mirour de l'omme,* 22129–22152.

As Juno's servant, Eolus obeys her command to blow the Trojan ships off their course, *HF* I.198–206. Fame sends her messenger to fetch Eolus and his trumpets from Thrace, *HF* III.1572. The trumpets are named Sklaundre and Clere Laud, *HF* III.1575–1582. When blown, Sklaundre emits a black, blue, greenish, red smoke; the trumpet itself is black and "fouler than the devel." This foul smoke represents worldly praise, and the farther it spreads, the worse it becomes. When Eolus blows Clere Laud, a strong perfume like that of balsam in a basket of roses pervades the room, *HF* III.1678–1687. The pleasant odor represents popular recognition or honest praise. Sklaundre is made of brass, befitting the discord its filthy smoke creates, and Clere Laud is golden with a bright, clear sound. When one group of people, who had done good deeds, requests that their works' reputation be dead, Fame orders Eolus to blow Clere Laude and so send their fame throughout the world, *HF* III.1702–1726, giving them exactly the opposite of their request. Eolus has a servant, Triton, who carries the trumpets, *HF* III.1604. In Ovid (*Met* I.337–338), Triton blows a horn, and perhaps this detail gave Chaucer the idea of making Triton the bearer of Eolus's trumpets.

Eolus, the ME and OF development of Latin *Aeolus,* appears thirteen times in medial positions, *HF* I.203; *HF* III.1571, 1586, 1602, 1623, 1636, 1671, 1719, 1764, 1769, 1789, 1800, 2120; and once in final rhyming position, *HF* III.1861.

Seven names for the winds appear in *Boece,* Chaucer's translation of Boethius's *De consolatione philosophiae.* **Aquylon** is the OF name for the Latin *Aquilo,* the name for Boreas, the North Wind, and denotes the horrible wind that brings tempests, *Bo* I, *Metr* 6.11, *Bo* II, *Metr* 3.15. **Auster,** the Latin name for Greek *Notos,* the South Wind, stirs up the sea and makes it boil, *Bo* I, *Metr* 7.3. If the cloudy wind **Auster** blows heavily, the flowers on the thorns blow away, *Bo* II, *Metr* 3.11; the biting wind **Auster** torments the top of the mountain, and the loose sands refuse to bear the weight, *Bo* II, *Metr* 4.7. If **Boreas,** the North Wind, chases the clouds covering the sun, then Phebus shines with sudden light and smites the marveling eye, *Bo* I, *Metr* 3.12. **Boreas** blows away the autumn leaves, *Bo* I, *Metr* 5.24. **Chorus,** the swift wind, blows the clouds which hide the sun and the stars, *Bo* I, *Metr* 3.7. No one wonders when the blasts of **Chorus** stir up the seashore with floods, *Bo* IV, *Metr* 5.24. **Chorus** appears as a sea god, *LGW* 2422, a possible misreading of *Aeneid* V.823. Even the most stable man would be cast down by **Eurus,** the East Wind or the Southeast Wind, *Bo* II, *Metr* 4.4. **Eurus** blew Ulysses's ships to Circe's island, where his men lost their human shapes, *Bo* IV, *Metr* 3.1. Nero ruled all the peoples whom the violent wind, **Notus,** scorched: the people of the south, *Bo* II, *Metr* 6.25. The stars shine more brightly when **Notus** stops his ploughing blasts, *Bo* III, *Metr* 1.8. **Zephirus,** the West Wind with the sweet breath, appears in *Gen Prol* 5; debonair **Zephirus** brings the new spring leaves, *Bo* I, *Metr* 5.22. **Zephirus** the warm makes the wood flower in the first summer season, *Bo* II, *Metr* 3.10. **Zepherus** brings the tender green leaves, *Tr* IV.10. Zephyrus is Flora's mate and makes the flowers grow, *BD* 402. **Zepherus** and Flora give the flowers their sweet breath, *LGW F* 171. Ypermestre quakes like a branch shaken by **Zepherus,** *LGW* 2681. [Flora: Triton]

J.A.W. Bennett, *Chaucer's Book of Fama,* 158; J.H. Fisher, *John Gower,* 213–215; John Gower, *The Complete Works,* ed. G.C. Macaulay, I: 248; Ovid, *Met,* ed. and trans. F.J. Miller, I: 42–43, II: 150–151; E. Panofsky, *Studies in Iconology,* Plate XIII; J.S.P. Tatlock, *The Development and Chronology of Chaucer's Works,* 38–39; Virgil, *Aeneid,* ed. and trans. H.R. Fairclough, I: 244–247.

EPICURUS, son of Neocles and Chaerestrate, 341–271 B.C., was born in Samos and died in Athens. He founded the school of philosophy named after him, which held that the absence of pain, the result of perfect harmony between body and mind, was the only good. The goal of life was freedom from anxiety through the study of philosophy. Epicurus did not advocate sensuality and self-indulgent profligacy, as his later reputation suggests. Diogenes Laertius quotes several people who criticized Epicurus in his lifetime, adding that such people are all stark mad. Augustine (*City of God* XIV.2) expresses the medieval point of view that the Epicurean philosophers live by the flesh.

The Franklin is "Epicurus owene sone," *Gen Prol* 336–338, and believes that full delight is perfect happiness, showing a perfect misunderstanding of Epicurus's philosophy. Epicurus is meant but not named, *MerchT* 2021–2022, *Tr* III.1691–1692. Lady Philosophy, arguing against Epicurus's position, says that he claimed delight as the sovereign good, *Bo* III, *Prosa* 2.

Augustine, *Concerning the City of God,* trans. H. Bettenson, 548; Emerson Brown, Jr., "Epicurus and Voluptas in Late Antiquity: The Curious Testimony of Martianus Capella." *Traditio* 38 (1982): 75–106; Diogenes Laertius, *Lives of the Eminent Philosophers,* ed. and trans. R.D. Hicks, II: 528–677; Epicurus, *Letters, Principal Doctrines and Vatican Sayings,* trans. R.M. Greer; Lucretius, *De rerum natura* , ed. and trans. W.H.D. Rouse, 6–7; *OCD,* 390–392.

EPISTLES: [OVIDE]

ERCULES, HERCULES was one of the most famous heroes of antiquity. His Greek name, Heracles, means "Glory of Hera," but it seems ironic because Hera hated him from birth and was his implacable enemy throughout his life. Jealous of his mother Alcmene, Hera made his life miserable, forcing him to become a hero. No sooner was he placed in the cradle than Hera sent snakes to kill him, but the baby Heracles strangled them with his tiny fists. At eighteen he killed a mighty lion and afterward wore the skin as a cloak. After his marriage to Megara, Hera sent him a fit of madness, during which he slew his wife and children, believing them his enemies. He sought guidance from the Delphic Oracle, which bade him journey to Tiryns and serve Eurystheus the king for twelve years. Eurystheus set him the Twelve Labors as follows: (1) To kill the Nemean Lion, which then became the constellation Leo. (2) To kill the Lernean Hydra, a many-headed water-snake which infested the marshes of Lerna. Hera sent a crab to help the snake, but Heracles cut off its many heads, then dipped his arrows in its poisonous blood; the snake and the crab then became the constellations Hydra and Cancer. (3) To capture the Erymanthian boar in a net. (4) To capture the hind of Ceryneia alive. (5) To clear the Lake Stymphalus of the birds which infested the woods on its borders, which Heracles did with a brass rattle. (6) To clean the Augean stables, which Heracles did by diverting the river Alpheus from its course so that it flowed through the stables. (7) To capture the Cretan bull, which Heracles took back to Mycenae and let wander until it lay down near Marathon. (8) To slay the horses of Diomedes, which ate human flesh. Heracles slew their master and threw his body to the horses. (9) To obtain the girdle of the Amazon queen, Hyppolyte. There are two versions to this story: (a) Heracles took it from it from her dead body after he had slain her, or (b) he demanded it as the price of her freedom. (10) To bring back from the extreme west the oxen of Geryon; Heracles set up the Pillars of Hercules at the end of this journey. (11) To obtain the golden apples from the Garden of the Hesperides by slaying the dragon that guarded the tree. The dragon became the constellation Draco. (12) To capture Cerberus, the hound of the underworld, with the help of Hermes and Athena and to present it to Eurystheus (*Met* IX.1–272; *OM* IX.1–872).

The Middle Ages saw Hercules as a man who had overcome great obstacles; as a benefactor of humankind, he became an image of virtue. Theodulf, bishop of Orleans during the ninth century, in *De libris quos legere solebam et qualiter fabulae poetarum a philosophis mystice pertractentur* (*PL* 105:331–332), says that Hercules represents virtue. Jean le Maire des Belges claims that Hercules was an ancestor of the Burgundian royal house in *Illustrations de Gaule et singularités de Troie* (c. 1506); on his way to Spain, Hercules was said to have stopped in Burgundy, married Alise, a beautiful lady of noble birth, and thus became the progenitor of the royal house. Book Two of Raoul le Fevre's *Recueill des histoires de Troies* (1464) treats the labors of Hercules. Caxton published an English translation, *Recuyell of the Histories of Troy* in 1475, the first book published in English. Colucci Salutati interprets Hercules and his labors in Books Two and Three of his *De laboris Herculis* (1406). The constellations Cancer, Draco, Hydra, and Leo are all connected with the Hercules legend.

The strength of Hercules, a medieval commonplace or *topos*, appears in *KnT* 1943; *BD* 1057. His betrayal of Dejanira and subsequent death by poisoned shirt form part of the medieval antifeminist tradition, *RR* 9191–9202, and appear in *MLT* 200; *WBT* 725–726; *HF* I.402, III.1412–1413; *PF* 28. The death of Ercules is written in the stars, *MLT* 200. The Monk, *MkT* 2095–2142, and Lady Philosophy, *Bo* IV, *Metr* 7.28–62, recount Hercules's twelve labors. The sun is in the house of Ercules's Lion, *Tr* IV.32, the latter part of July and the first part of August. Ercules rescues Alceste from death, *LGW F* 513–516, *LGW G* 501–504. He helps Jason court Isiphile, *LGW* 1454–1546; Guido delle Colonne tells this story in *Historia destructionis Troiae* I–IV. [**Achaleous: Alceste: Busirus: Cacus: Cancer: Dianira: Dragoun: Idra: Leo: Socrates**]

Ercules, the ME variant of Italian *Ercule*, appears once initially, *HF* II.402; six times medially, *LGW F* 515, *LGW G* 503; *LGW* 1480, 1501, 1514, 1524; and six times in final rhyming position, *KnT* 1943, *MLT* 200, *BD* 1058, *LGW* 1454, 1519, 1544. *Hercules,* the Latin variant of Greek *Heracles*, never appears initially; it occurs three times in medial positions, *WBP* 725; *MkT* 2095; *Tr* IV.32; and three times in final rhyming position, *MkT* 2135, *HF* III.1413, *PF* 288. Both forms appear in the prose of Chaucer's *Boece*.

H.S. Bennett, *Chaucer and the Fifteenth Century*, 204–205; Guido delle Colonne, *Guido de Columnis: HDT*, ed. N.E. Griffin, 4–43; *ibid.*, *HDT*, trans. M.E. Meek, 1–32; *RR*, ed. E. Langlois, III: 111–112; *RR*, trans. C. Dahlberg, 166; Ovid, *Met*, ed. and trans. F.J. Miller, II: 2–23; *OM*, ed. C. de Boer, III, deel 30: 1–242; Jean Seznec, *Survival of the Pagan Gods*, trans. B.F. Sessions, 25.

ERINYES: [HERENUS]

ERIPHILEM. Eriphyle was the wife of Amphiaraus, an Argive seer. Her husband did not want to follow Polynices to the siege of Thebes and hid when the seven chieftains came to fetch him. Polynices bribed Eriphyle with a golden necklace, and she showed him where Amphiaraus was hidden. Amphiaraus went reluctantly, knowing he would be killed at the siege (*Thebaid* IV.187–213; *Roman de Thèbes*, 4711–4918).

Eriphylem is one of the evil wives in the medieval antifeminist tradition. Jankyn reads her story from Jerome, *Epistola adversus Jovinianum (Letter Against Jovinian)* I.48 (*PL* 23: 280), *WBP* 740–746. In Jankyn's version, Eriphilem betrays her husband for an "ouche" of gold, a jeweled ornament; Jerome mentions a necklace, *monile*. [**Amphiorax: Clitermystra: Phasipha: Polymyte**]

The form of the name is derived from Latin accusative singular *Eriphylam*. Interesting variants recorded in Manly-Rickert are: *Eriphilem, Exiphilon, Erphielen, Erphiden, Epiphelem*, all showing the accusative ending preserved in one form or another. *Eriphelem* appears medially, *WBP* 723.

Manly-Rickert, VI: 75; R.A. Pratt, "Jankyn's Book of Wikked Wyves." *AnM* 3 (1962): 5–27; *Roman de Thèbes*, ed. L. Constans, I: 230–241; *Roman de Thèbes (The Story of Thebes)*, trans. J.S. Coley, 111–115; Statius, *Thebaid*, ed. and trans. J.H. Mozley, I: 520–523.

ERIPHYLE: [ERIPHILEM]

ERRO, HERRO. Hero was a priestess of Venus's temple at Sestos. Her lover Leander swam the Hellespont every night from Abydos to visit her. One night he drowned during a terrible storm, and Hero threw herself into the sea (*Heroides* XVIII and XIX; *OM* IV.3150–3586). Machaut also tells the story in *Le Jugement dou roy de Navarre* 3221–3310.

The Man of Law lists this story in his catalogue of Chaucer's works, *MLI* 69, but there is no story of Hero in *The Legend of Good Women*. Herro must bow before Alceste, the paragon of conjugal love, *LGW F* 263, *LGW G* 217. [**Leandre**]

Erro is a Chaucerian variant of *Ero, Tes* VI.62.2, *MLT* 69, and occurs in final rhyming position; *Herro* occurs initially, *LGW F* 263, *LGW G* 217. Both variants would have been pronounced alike since Latin initial *h* was not pronounced.

Boccaccio, *Tutte le Opere*, ed. V. Branca, II: 440; Guillaume de Machaut, *Oeuvres*, ed. E. Hoepffner, I: 248–251; Ovid, *Her*, ed. and trans. G. Showerman, 244–275; *OM*, ed. C. de Boer, II, deel 21: 78–87.

ERUDICE. Eurydice was Orpheus's wife. Her name in Greek means "wide-judging" and was applied to princesses. While strolling with a group of Naiads through the grass after her wedding, Eurydice fell dead, bitten at the ankle by a snake. Orpheus mourned for her, then went down to Hades to seek her. He pleaded with Persephone to let her go or, if that was not possible, to accept them both. Touched by the music of his lyre, the Eumenides released Eurydice on condition that Orpheus not look backward until he had left the valley of Avernus, the entrance to the underworld. Just as they were nearing the margin of the upper world, Orpheus looked back, and Eurydice immediately slipped back to the underworld (*Met* X.1–85; *OM* X.1–195). Virgil's slightly different version appears in *Georgics* IV.453–529.

There are two references in the Chaucerian corpus: in the *Boece* and in the *Troilus*. Lady Philosophy's version, *Bo* III, *Metr* 12, ends the story thus: "Allas! whanne Orpheus and his wyf weren almost at the terms of the nyght . . . Orpheus lokede abakward on Erudyce his wife, and lost hire, and was deed." The moral Boethius attached to the fable, that the man who seeks to raise his mind to the clarity of the sovereign day loses all the excellence he has gained if he turns his eyes to the pit of hell, is the first in the development of allegorical interpretations of the story and inspired several commentaries during the medieval period on the meaning of Eurydice in the fable. John Block Friedman suggests that for Boethius Eurydice represents *temporalia*, the things of the earth; she is the concupiscent part of man, preventing him from reaching the light. The next commentary, written by Remigius of Auxerre about A.D. 904 and titled *Incipit expositio in libro Boetii de Consolatione phylosophiae Remigii*, uses both the Ovidian and the Virgilian accounts; here, Eurydice is an "insignificant thing." Giovanni del Virgilio states the contrary in an explanation of the *Metamorphoses* (c. 1325). For him, Eurydice appears as "profound thought." Fulgentius derives Eurydice from *eur dike* or "profound judgment" in *Mythologies* III.10 and associates her with tonic harmony. The Boethian view, however, prevailed throughout the period. The other reference appears in *Tr* IV.785–791. Criseyde assures Troilus that, although they may be parted on earth, they will be together in the Elysian Fields, like Orpheus and his wife, Erudice. **[Orpheus]**

Erudice, the OF variant in Jean de Meun's translation of Boethius, appears medially, *Tr* IV.791.

V.L. Dedeck-Héry, "Le *Boece* de Chaucer et les Manuscrits français de la *Consolatio* de Jean de Meun." *PMLA* 59 (1944): 18–25; *ibid.*, ed., "Boethius' *De consolatione* by Jean de Meun." *MS* 14 (1952): 232–233; John B. Friedman, "Eurydice,

Heurodis, and the Noon-Day Demon." *Speculum* 41 (1966): 22–29; *ibid., Orpheus in the Middle Ages,* 98–100, 231; Fausto Ghisalberti, ed., "Giovanni del Virgilio Espositore delle 'Metamorphosi.'" *Il Giornale Dantesco* 34 (1933): 89; Fulgentius, *Fulgentius the Mythographer,* trans. L. Whitbread, 96–98; Ovid, Met, ed. and trans. F.J. Miller, II: 64–71; *Sir Orfeo,* ed. A.J. Bliss; Virgil, *Georgics,* ed. and trans. H.R. Fairclough, II: 228–233.

ESCAPHILO. Ascalaphus, son of Orphne and Acheron, saw Proserpina when she plucked and ate the pomegranate while she was in the underworld. He informed the gods and, enraged, Proserpina changed him into an owl, the bird of ill omen and prophet of woe. Because six seeds from the fruit were found in her mouth, she was obliged to spend six months with Hades in the underworld (*Met* V.533–552; *OM* V.2251–2299).

The owl Escaphilo screeches near Troilus's apartments for two nights, causing him to feel that his death is near, *Tr* V.316–322.

Escaphilo, formed by metathesis, appears in final rhyming position, *Tr* V.319, which may account for the ending in -*o* instead of -*us.*

Ovid, *Met,* ed. and trans. F.J. Miller, I: 274–277; *OM,* ed. C. de Boer, II, deel 21: 236–237.

ESCULAPIUS. Aesculapius was the Latin god of medicine, son of Apollo and Coronis. The first temple, with a sanatorium, was erected to him in Rome in 293 B.C. During the medieval period, many works then current were attributed to him.

Esculapius appears in the Physician's catalogue of authorities, *Gen Prol* 429. The story of Apollo and Coronis is *The Manciple's Tale.*

The form of the name, medieval Latin and OF, is the development from *Aesculapius,* the classical Latin form of Greek *Asclepius.*

OCCD, 11.

ESON. Aeson, king of Thessaly, was Jason's father. His brother Pelias drove him from the throne, exiled his family, and ruled in his stead. When Jason appeared with only one sandal, Pelias recognized him as his brother's son and sent him in search of the Golden Fleece, hoping that he would die in the search and never return (*Met* VII.84, 162–293; Guido delle Colonne, *HDT* I–III).

Eson is Pelleus's brother; when he becomes too old to govern, he gives his kingdom to Pelleus, *LGW* 1396–1405. This different version of the story appears in *Ovide Moralisé* VII.1–193. Chaucer omits Medea's rejuvenation of Eson from his version. **[Guido: Jason: Medea: Pelleus]**

Guido delle Colonne, *Guido de Columnis: HDT,* ed. N.E. Griffin, 3–33; *ibid., HDT,* trans. M.E. Meek, 3–32; Ovid, *Met,* ed. and trans. F.J. Miller, I: 348–349, 352–363; *ibid., Her,* ed. and trans. G. Showerman, 142–159; *OM* ed. C. de Boer, III, deel 30: 15–19; *RR,* ed. E. Langlois, IV: 12–13; *RR,* trans. C. Dahlberg, 228–229.

ESPERUS, HESPERUS is the evening star, which pales when the sun rises and is then called *Lucifer,* derived from *lucem ferens,* "light bearing" (Cicero, *De natura deorum,* II.20, 53).

Boethius's description of Hesperus parallels Cicero's, *Bo* I, *Metr* 5.11–12. The moon commands the night, brought on by Esperus, the evening star, *Bo* II, *Metr* 8.7–8. Hesperus proclaims the late nights and Lucifer brings the clear day, *Bo* IV, *Metr* 6.15. **[Lucifer[1]]**

Both forms are pronounced alike; Latin initial *h* was not pronounced.

Cicero, *DND,* ed. and trans. H. Rackham, 174–175.

ESTER, HESTER. Esther is the heroine of The Book of Esther. When Queen Vashti refused to come when he called her, King Assuerus divorced her and chose Esther as his wife. Esther was very beautiful, and the king did not know that she was Jewish. Haman, the king's prime minister, persuaded him to issue an edict authorizing the death of all the Jews in the kingdom. Advised by her uncle Mordecai, Esther revealed her Jewish identity to the king, and he gave her leave to change the edict and thus save the Jews.

The medieval view of Esther emphasizes her beauty, her meekness, and her heroism. She represents a type of the Church in Jerome (c. 341–420), *Commentariorum in Sophoniam Prophetam,* I (*PL* 25: 1337); Isidore of Seville (c. 560–636), *Allegoria quaedam Sacrae Scripturae* (*PL* 83: 116, 147); and Rabanus Maurus (ninth century), *Expositio in librum Ester* III (*PL* 109: 646). Popular and devotional literature continued the association of Esther with a type of the Church. She is a *femme de bon conseil* or "a woman of good counsel," in *Liber consolationis et consilii (The Book of Consolation and Counsel),* by Albertanus Brixiensis (c. 1246), and in the adaptation by Renaud de Louens, *Le Livre de Mellibee et Prudence (The Book of Melibee and Prudence),* written after 1336.

Ester is a woman of good counsel, *MerchT* 1371–1374; *Mel* 1100. May is as meek as Ester, *MerchT* 1744–1745. The Man in Black laments Good Fair White, who was as debonaire and as witty as Ester, *BD* 985–990. Ester must lay down her meekness before Alceste, the paragon of conjugal love, *LGW* F 250, *LGW* G 204. **[Assuer: Mardochee]**

Ester, both ME and OF, appears initially, *LGW* F 250, *LGW* G 204, and medially, *MerchT* 1371. *Hester,* OF and Latin, occurs in *Mel* 1100 and medially, *BD* 988. Latin initial *h* was not pronounced; medial *h* in modern spellings is an addition.

K. Harty, "The Reputation of Queen Esther in the Middle Ages: *The Merchant's Tale* IV (E) 1742–1745." *Ball State University Forum* 19 (1978): 65–68.

ESTHER: [ESTER]
ESTORYAL MIROUR: [VINCENT OF BEAUVAIS]
ETEOCLES: [ETHIOCLES]

ETHIOCLES. Eteocles, son of Oedipus and brother of Polynices, refused to give up the Theban throne when his turn came to step down. Polynices attacked Thebes with the help of his father-in-law, Adrastus of Argos, and six other Greek chieftains. Statius's *Thebaid* (A.D. 91) and the twelfth-century *Roman de Thèbes* are the main sources for the story.

The war against Ethiocles appears in *Tr* V.1457–1512, when Cassandra interprets Troilus's dream of the boar. [**Adrastus: Amphiorax: Campaneus: Hemonydes: Ipomedon: Parthonope: Polymyte: Tydeus**]

Ethiocles, the OF variant, appears initially, *Tr* V.1507, and in final rhyming position, *Tr* V.1489. Intrusive *h* after *t* was not pronounced.

Statius, *Thebaid*, ed. and trans. J.H. Mozley; *Roman de Thèbes*, ed. L. Constans; *Roman de Thèbes (The Story of Thebes)*, trans. J.S. Coley.

EUCLID: [EUCLIDE]

EUCLIDE. Euclid, the Greek mathematician, fl. c. 300 B.C. under Ptolemy of Alexandria, 306–283 B.C. His most important work is *Stoicheia* or *Elements*, in thirteen books, composed of problems in geometry and the theory of numbers. Cassiodorus says that Boethius did a translation; of this, only the propositions of Books I–IV and the proofs of Book I, propositions 1–3, have survived. Three versions of *Elements* are attributed to Adelard of Bath, done c. 1126 or later; Gerard of Cremona translated the work from an Arabic source in the twelfth century.

Euclide is the great divider, *SumT* 2289. [**Boece: Gerard of Cremona**] The name occurs medially.

H.L.L. Busard, ed., *The First Latin Translation of Euclid's "Elements"*; M. Clagett, "The Medieval Latin Translations from the Arabic of the *Elements* of Euclid, with Special Emphasis on the Version of Adelard of Bath." *Isis* 44 (1953): 16–42; J.E. Murdoch, "*Euclides graeco-latinus*: A Hitherto Unknown Medieval Latin Translation of the Elements made Directly from the Greek." *Harvard Studies in Classical Philology* 71 (1967): 249–302.

EURIPIDES: [EURIPIDIS]

EURIPIDIS. Euripides, son of Mnesarchus, c. 480–406 B.C., wrote eighty-eight Greek plays, of which nineteen survive. Some of his plays seem to have been known in the early Middle Ages, since Boethius quotes from his *Andromacha.*

Lady Philosophy quotes from Euripides's *Andromacha* 319–320, *Bo* III, *Prosa* 6.2–3, and *Andromacha* 418–420, *Bo* III, *Prosa* 7.25.

Euripidis is the Latin genitive singular, which occurs in the Latin text.

Euripides, *The Plays of Euripides*, trans. R. Lattimore and D. Green in *The Complete Greek Tragedies*; G. Murray, *Euripides and his Age*; *OCD*, 418–421.

EUROPA: [EUROPE]

EUROPE. Europa was the daughter of Agenor, king of Tyre. Falling in love with her, Jupiter wooed her in the form of a white bull. When she playfully jumped on his back, he carried her off. The bull became the constellation Taurus (*Met* II.834–875, III.1–5; OM II.4937–5084).

Troilus appeals to Jove, who loved Europe in the form of a bull, *Tr* III.722–724. On the first of May the sun is in the breast of the beast that led "Agenore's daughter" away; that is, the sun is in Taurus, *LGW F* 114.

Europe, the ME variant with final syllabic -*e*, occurs in final rhyming position, *Tr* III.722.

Ovid, *Met*, ed. and trans. F.J. Miller, I: 118–125, *OM*, ed. C. de Boer, I, deel 15: 276–279.

EURUS: [EOLUS]
EURYDICE: [ERUDICE]

EVA, EVE is the first woman. There are two stories of the creation of Eve and Adam. The first tells that God created male and female together in His own image, and Eve is not named in this version (Genesis 1:27); the second tells that God created man out of the dust, placed him in Eden, then created woman out of Adam's rib while he slept. Adam called her Eve because she is the mother of all the living (Genesis 2:7–24, 3:20). The commandment to abstain from the fruit of the Tree of the Knowledge of Good and Evil was given to Adam (Genesis 2:17). The serpent persuaded Eve to disobey God and to eat the fruit; she then gave it to Adam, and he also ate it (Genesis 3:1–7).

The Biblical story is the basis for the medieval antifeminist view of Eve in particular and of woman in general. Medieval commentators present her with a dual nature. Isidore of Seville (c. 560–636) says that Eve represents life as well as calamity and woe, namely death (*Etymologiae* VII.vi.5–6). Augustine of Hippo (354–430) says that the creation of Eve symbolizes the creation of the Church (*City of God* XII.17).

Satan beguiled Eve and knows well how to make women sin, *MLT* 365–371. The story of the Fall shows Eve as the first wicked wife in Jankyn's book, *WBP* 713–718. God made Eve for Adam's comfort (Genesis 2:18), *MerchT* 1322–1329. The Second Nun calls herself "unworthy sone of Eve," *SNP* 62, evidence perhaps that the tale was not composed for her. Brown suggests that the phrase comes from the Office of Compline in the Hours of the Virgin, familiar to the Nun. The story of the Fall and its interpretation, *ParsT* 320–329, show that Eve stands for the delights of the flesh, *ParsT* 515–516. The antifeminist tradition is exemplified in Jankyn's "Book of Wikked Wyves," *WBP* 669–756. This anthology consisted of Ovid's *Ars Amatoria* (*The Art of Love*), the *Parables* of Solomon, Jerome's *Epistola adversus Jovinianum* (*Letter Against Jovinian*) of the late fourth century,

Theophrastus's *Aureolus liber de nuptiis* (*The Golden Book of Marriage*, of uncertain date and authorship), Walter Map's *Dissuasio Valerii ad Rufinum Philosophum ne Uxorem ducat* (*Valerius's Dissuasion of Rufus Not to Marry*, c. 1180–1183). The Parson says that the first sin is gluttony since Adam and Eve ate the fruit, *ParsT* 816–818 [**Adam¹: Caym**]

Eva appears twice in medial positions, *MLT* 368; *WBP* 715; *Eve* appears twice in final rhyming position, *MerchT* 1329; *SNP* 62, and in the prose of *ParsT* 20–329.

Augustine, *Concerning the City of God*, trans. H. Bettenson, 1057; C. Brown, "Chaucer and the 'Hours of the Blessed Virgin.' " *MLN* 30 (1950): 231–232; R.J. Dean, "Unnoticed Commentaries on the *Dissuasio Valerii* of Walter Map." *MRS* 2 (1950): 128–150; W.B. Gardner, "Chaucer's 'Unworthy Sone of Eve.'" *Texas University Studies in English* (1946–1947): 77–83; A.K. Hieatt, "Eve as Reason in a Tradition of Allegorical Interpretation of the Fall." *JWCI* 43(1980): 221–226; Isidore, *Etymologiae*, ed. W.M. Lindsay, I; J.A. Phillips, *Eve, The History of an Idea*; R.A. Pratt, "Jankyn's Book of Wikked Wyves." *AnM* 3 (1962): 5–27; *Riverside Chaucer*, ed. L. Benson, 944.

EVANDER, king of Arcadia, founded a colony on the spot where Rome later stood. He told Aeneas how Hercules slew the monster Cacus, which had been ravaging the countryside (*Aeneid*, VII.193–270). Ovid's version appears in *Fasti* I.543–586.

Cacus's death appeases Evander, *Bo* IV, *Metr* 7.52–54. [**Cacus: Ercules**]

Ovid, *Fasti,* ed. and trans. J.G. Frazer, 40–43; Virgil, *Aeneid,* ed. and trans. H.R. Fairclough, II: 72–79.

EVE: [EVA]

EZECHIAS, EZECHIE. Ezechias, son of Ahaz, was born in 745 B.C. He reigned as king of Judah from 720–691 B.C., ruling for twenty-nine years (Isaiah 38).

The Parson quotes the contrition of Ezechias, Isaiah 38:15, *ParsT* 135 and 983.

Ezechie, ME variant of Latin dative singular, appears in *ParsT* 135. *Ezechias,* the Latin nominative, appears in *ParsT* 983. The King James Bible gives the name as *Hezikiah.*

EZECHIEL was one of the major prophets of Israel, his prophecies recorded in the book bearing his name.

The Parson quotes the prophet Ezechiel 8:43, *ParsT* 141; God spoke by the mouth of Ezechiel, Ezechiel 8:24, *ParsT* 236.

Ezechiel is the form in the Latin Vulgate.

EZEKIEL: [EZECHIEL]

FABRICIUS. Gaius Fabricius Luscinus was Roman Consul in 282 B.C. and 278 B.C. and a general in 280 B.C. when Pyrrhus, king of Epirus, came to assist Tarentum against the besieging Romans. Pyrrhus found that he could not bribe Fabricius, and Fabricius's soldiers found that they could not offer to poison Pyrrhus for him. Virgil mentions his poverty (*Aeneid* VI.843–844), and Cicero repeatedly mentions Fabricius as an example of incorruptible Roman virtue (*De oratore* II.268).

Lady Philosophy introduces Fabricius in the *ubi sunt* formula, illustrating the fleeting quality of things, *Bo* II, *Metr* 7.18: "Where are the bones of Fabricius?"

Fabricius is the name of the clan, of which Gaius was the most famous member.

Cicero, *De oratore*, ed. and trans. E.W. Sutton, 400–401; *OCD*, 428; Virgil, *Aeneid*, ed. and trans. H.R. Fairclough, I: 564–566.

FATES: [ATROPOS: LACHESIS: PARCAS]
FISH: [FYSSH: PISCES]

FLEXIPPE is one of Criseyde's nieces. Boccaccio does not mention nieces in *Il Filostrato* (1333–1339); Chaucer has invented the garden scene in which they appear, *Tr* II.813–819. **[Antigone: Criseyde: Tharbe]**

Flexippe is perhaps derived from *Phlexippi*, genitive singular of *Phlexippus* (*Met* VIII.440) and appears initially, *Tr* II.816.

G.L. Hamilton, *ITC*, 94; Ovid, *Met*, ed. and trans. F.J. Miller, I: 436–437.

FLORA is the Roman goddess of flowers and gardens. Ovid says her name was formerly Chloris (*Fasti* V.183–198). Zephyrus carried her off, and she became his wife.

The Dreamer finds himself in a meadow where Flora and Zephyrus live, *BD* 400–404. Zephyrus and Flora give the flowers their sweet breath, *LGW F* 171–174. The long description of the work of Flora and Zephyrus, *RR* 8403–8454, is part of the evocation of the Golden Age. [Eolus]

Flora, derived from Latin *flos/floris*, occurs medially only, *BD* 402; *LGW F* 171.

Ovid, *Fasti*, ed. and trans. J.G. Frazer, 274–275; *RR*, ed. E. Langlois, III: 80–82; *RR*, trans. C. Dahlberg, 155–156.

FRANCIS PETRARCH: [FRAUNCEYS PETRAK]

FRAUNCEYS PETRAK. Francesco Petrarch, 1304–1374, was born in Arezzo, Italy. His father had been banished from Florence on the same day as Dante, January 27, 1302, and Petrarch says that when he was born they were "on the edge of poverty." In his *Epistle to Posterity* Petrarch says that when he was nine, his parents moved to Avignon, a city for which he had intense dislike and where he spent most of his youth. When he was thirty-four years old, he moved to Vaucluse ("Closed Valley"), where he says most of his works were conceived and executed. In a letter to Giovanni dell'Incisa (c. 1346) he describes his lust for books, which he calls a consuming desire or disease. He sent requests for books to his friends in Britain, France, and Spain, building up an extensive library. He discovered Cicero's *Letters to Atticus,* previously unknown, in the cathedral library of Verona in 1345; he helped Boccaccio commission the first Latin translation of Homer. Like another great bibliophile, Richard de Bury, he was a systematic book collector, gladly spending his money on books during his travels. He was fond of travel and frequently resided in five towns during his life: Milan, Pavia, Venice (to which he willed his library), Padua, and Arquà, where he died in 1374.

On April 6, 1327, Petrarch first met Laura de Sade (or de Sauze, or di Salso) in the church of Santa Clara at Avignon and fell in love. He calls this an overwhelming love affair and his only one. Yet he had two illegitimate children: a son, Giovanni, who caused him much distress and who died in his twenty-fourth year, and a daughter, Francesca, who married Francesco da Brossano and gave Petrarch two grandchildren. His letter to Donato Albanzani (1368) describes his grief at his grandson's death. He wrote a series of love poems to Laura, his *Rime* or *Canzoniere*, developing the sonnet form that bears his name. He recorded her death of the plague in his copy of Virgil in 1348. His major works include: *Africa* (inspired by Scipio Africanus), *Canzoniere, Sonetti, I Trionfi, De viris illustribus, De remediis utriusque Fortunae,* and *De vita solitaria.* In addition to his *Epistle to Posterity,* Petrarch's *Secret,* a dialogue between the poet and St. Augustine, is self-revelatory.

The Clerk says twice that he learned the story of Griselda from Petrak, *ClT* 26–38, 1147. There has been much conjecture about a possible meeting between Chaucer and Petrarch, but no reliable evidence. Chaucer is, perhaps, employing the topic of obligation to Petrarch in allusion to his source, *Epistolae Seniles* XVIII.3: *De obedientia ac fide uxoria mythologia,* his translation of Boccaccio's tenth story for the tenth day in the *Decameron.* The Monk says that the source for his story of Zenobia is Petrak, *MkT* 2325; the source, however, is Boccaccio, *De claris mulieribus,* XCVIII.

[Lollius]

The prevailing spelling in the manuscripts is *Petrak* or *Patrak,* the English contraction of Italian *Petracco,* the way Petrarch's father spelled his name. Francesco changed it to *Petrarca.* The name appears in medial positions, *ClT* 31, 1147; *MkT* 2325.

Boccaccio, *CFW,* trans. G. Guarino, 226–230; *ibid., Decameron,* trans. J. Payne, rev. and annotated C.S. Singleton, II: 780–794; *ibid., De claris mulieribus,* ed. V. Zaccaria, 406–414; G.L. Hamilton, "Chauceriana I: The Date of the *Clerk's Tale.*" *MLN* 23 (1908): 171–172; E.P. Kadish. "Petrarch's Griselda: An English Translation." *Mediaevalia* 3 (1977): 1–24; F. Petrarch, *Africa,* trans. and annotated by T.G. Bergin and A.S. Wilson; *ibid., De obedientia ac fide uxoria mythologia,* ed. B. Severs, *S&A,* 288–331; *ibid., Letters from Petrarch,* trans. M. Bishop; *ibid., Petrarch's Lyric Poems; ibid., Le Rime Sparse e Trionfi,* ed. E. Chiorboli; *ibid., Triumphs,* trans. E.H. Wilkins; E.H. Wilkins, *Petrarch's Eight Years in Milan; ibid., Petrarch's Later Years; ibid., Studies in the Life and Works of Petrarch.*

FRYDESWYDE (saint), fl. c. A.D. 680–735, became the patron saint of the town and University of Oxford. She was supposed to heal the sick.

The carpenter calls on St. Frydeswyde, *MillT* 3449, appropriate since the action of the story takes place in Oxford. **[John²]**

R.H. Cline, "Four Chaucer Saints." *MLN* 60 (1945): 480–482; E.W. Watson, *The Cathedral Church of Christ in Oxford.*

FURIES: [HERENUS]

FYSSH. The constellation Pisces, the twelfth sign of the zodiac, is the exaltation of the planet Venus and lies in the northern hemisphere (*Tetrabiblos,* I.19).

Cambyuskan's guests make merry because their lady (Venus) sits high in the Fyssh, *SqT* 272–274. The time is midday, and Venus, exalted in Pisces, is very powerful. **[Pisces: Venus]**

Fyssh, the English singular rendering of Latin singular *Piscis,* appears medially, *SqT* 273. *Fish* is also used as the English plural.

R.A. Allen, *Star Names and their Meanings,* 338; Ptolemy, *Tetrabiblos,* ed. and trans. F.E. Robbins, 91; C. Wood, *Chaucer and the Country of the Stars,* 100–101.

G

GABRIEL: [GABRIELLE]

GABRIELLE(S). Gabriel is the archangel of the Annunciation (Luke 1:26–38). He first appears in Daniel 8:16, 9:21.

The poet wonders wherefore and why the Holy Ghost sought Mary when Gabriel's voice came to her ear, *ABC* 113–115.

Gabrielles, the ME genitive case, is formed from OF *Gabrielle* and appears in medial position, *ABC* 115.

GADDESDEN: [GATESDEN]
GALATEA: [GALATHEE]

GALATHEE. Galatea was the beloved of Pamphilus in the medieval Latin comedy *Pamphilus de amore* (twelfth–thirteenth centuries), a dialogue in three acts. Pamphilus Mauritianus is sometimes named the author.

Aurelius loves Dorigen for more than two years, as secretly as Pamphilus loved Galathee, *FranklT* 1110. **[Arveragus: Aurelie: Dorigen: Pamphilles]**

Galathee, derived from French *Galatee,* appears in final rhyming position; *h* after *t* was not pronounced.

P. Dronke, "A Note on *Pamphilus.*" *JWCI* 42 (1979): 225–230; T.J. Garbaty, "*Pamphilus de Amore*: An Introduction and Translation." *ChauR* 2 (1967–1968): 108–134; *ibid.*,"The *Pamphilus* Tradition in Ruiz and Chaucer." *PQ* 46 (1967): 457–470.

GALAXIE, GALAXYE, the aggregate of stars, gas, and dust, of which there are several. The Earth's galaxy is the Milky Way, the center of which lies in Sagittarius in the southern hemisphere.

The Learned Eagle, as he flies by with the frightened Dreamer in his claws, points out the Galaxie, which some call the Milky Way or Watling Street, *HF* II.935–940. Scipio Africanus Minor dreams that his grandfather Scipio Africanus Major takes him up to heaven and shows him the Galaxie, *PF* 56.

F.P. Magoun, Jr., *A Chaucer Gazetteer*, 170–171.

GALEN: [GALYEN]

GALIEN. Publius Licinius Egnatius Gallienus was the son of Valerian and was elected Augustus in A.D. 253; he governed until A.D. 268. As general, he routed the barbarian Goths, who had begun to invade Italy by land and sea. He made Odaenathus, king of Palmyra, vice-regent for the Eastern Empire. When Zenobia became queen, however, she wanted to be an independent ruler. Gallienus sent Heraclianus against her, and she defeated him. Boccaccio says that Gallienus was effeminate in contrast to the manly Zenobia (*De claris mulieribus* XCVIII).

The Monk says that Emperor Galien had never been as courageous as Cenobia, *MkT* 2335–2342. [Cenobia: Odenake: Sapor]

Galien, the OF variant of Latin *Gallienus*, occurs in final rhyming position, *MkT* 2336.

Boccaccio, *Concerning Famous Women*, trans. Guarino, 226–230; *ibid., De claris mulieribus*, ed. V. Zaccaria, 406–414; Trebellius Pollio, *Tyranni Triginta XXX*, and Flavius Vospiscus, *Divus Aurelianus* in *Scriptores historiae Augustae*, ed. and trans. D. Magie, III: 135–143, 193–293.

GALLIENUS: [GALIEN]
GALLUS, SULPICIUS: [SIMPLICIUS GALLUS]

GALYEN. Galenos or Galen, A.D. 129–199, was born at Pergamum and went to Rome in 162. He became court physician in the court of Marcus Aurelius and grew famous as one of the most distinguished doctors in antiquity. The complete edition of his works fills twenty-two volumes on medicine, on anatomy, and on physiology. Merton College Library owned two copies of his works between 1360 and 1385.

Galyen is among the Doctor's authorities, *Gen Prol* 431. Not even Galyen, the famous physician, can cure the Man in Black, *BD* 571. Chaucer's lines:

Ne hele me may no phisicien
Noght Ypocras, ne Galyen;

directly echo *RR* 15959–15960:

Pas Ypocras ne Galien
Tout fussent bon fisicien.

The reference to Galien in *ParsT* 831 has not been traced.

Galyen, the ME variant of OF *Galien*, resembles Dante's *Galieno* (*Inf* IV.143) and appears in final rhyming position, *Gen Prol* 431; *BD* 571.

Dante, *Divine Comedy*, ed. and trans. C.S. Singleton, I, 1: 44–45; Galen, *On the Natural Faculties*, ed. and trans. A.J. Brock; F.M. Powicke, *The Medieval Books of Merton College*, 141; *RR*, ed. E. Langlois, IV: 126; *RR*, trans. C. Dahlberg, 271.

GANELON: [GENELLOUN]

GANYMEDE was the son of Troas, the eponymous founder of Troy. Jupiter fell in love with him and, changing himself into an eagle, swooped down on Ganymede. He carried him to Mount Olympus, where he made him his cupbearer (*Met* X.155–161).

As the Learned Eagle bears him away, the Dreamer asserts that he is not Ganymede, *HF* II.589–592. Ganymede is called the "goddys botiller," *HF* II.592. Chaucer could have taken the word from several sources: *boutiller* occurs in Jean de Condé's *La Messe de Oisiaus*, 453 (before 1345); Hebe is described as *bouteillière des cieulz*, "heaven's butler," in *Ovide Moralisé* IX.17–57. [**Jupiter**]

The name appears in final rhyming position, *HF* II.592.

Baudouin de Condé, *Dits et contes de Baudouin de Condé et de son fils Jean de Condé*, ed. A. Scheler, III: 15; Ovid, *Met*, ed. and trans. F.J. Miller, II: 74–75; *OM*, ed. C. de Boer, III, deel 30: 263; W.O. Sypherd, *Studies in Chaucer's Hous of Fame*, 54–56.

GATESDEN. John of Gaddesden, fl. fourteenth century, was regarded as an authority on women's diseases. His chief work, *Rosa medicinae*, known also as *Rosa anglica*, was a compilation of the works of previous doctors, most notably from Bernard de Gordon and Henri de Mondeville. Among the general medical lore of the period Gaddesden inserts advice on diet, cooking, the care of the teeth, the eradication of lice, and the making of beauty products. He died in 1361. Merton College Library owned two copies of *Rosa medicinae* between 1360 and 1385.

Gatesden appears among the Physician's authorities, *Gen Prol* 434. The byname of location appears in medial position. [**Bernard²**]

H.P. Cholmeley, *John Gaddesden and the* Rosa medicinae; R.W.T. Gunther, *Early Science at Oxford*, II: 11–20; F.M. Powicke, *The Medieval Books of Merton College*, 141.

GAUDENICUS, fl. sixth century A.D., was perhaps a patrician at Theodoric's court at Rome. Cassiodorus does not mention him.

Boethius says that Gaudenicus had been exiled for countless treacheries and frauds; now Theodoric listens to his accusations against Boethius, *Bo* I, *Prosa* 4.114. [**Albyn: Basilius: Boece: Conigaste: Cyprian: Opilion: Trygwille**]

GAUFRED. Geoffrey de Vinsauf (fl. twelfth–thirteenth centuries) is said to have been born in England of Norman parents; it is believed that he frequented the schools of England, Gaul, and Italy. It is thought that he received his surname *Vinsauf* (Safe Wine) because of a treatise on the conservation of wines attributed to him: *De vino et vitibus conservandis.* His two works, *Poetria nova* (*The New Poetry,* c. 1200–1202), dedicated to Innocent III, and *Documentum de modo et arte dictandi et versificandi* (*Documents on the Method and Art of Speaking and Versifying,* c. 1210) are handbooks on the art of rhetoric. They formed part of the curriculum of medieval schools and enjoyed great popularity.

The Nun's Priest hails Gaufred in an apostrophe, *NPT* 3347–3354, as he parodies *Poetria nova,* 368–430. In his vignette of the weeping hens, NPT 3355–3374, Chaucer borrows from *Poetria nova* 363–368. [**Richard**[1]]

Gaufred is the ME variant and contraction of Latin nominative *Gaufredus* and appears in medial position, *NPT* 3347. The *Incipit* to the *Poetria nova* reads *Incipit Poetria novella magistri Gaufredi Anglici de artificio loquendi.*

E. Faral, *Les arts poétiques,* 15–16, 197; Geoffrey of Vinsauf, *Poetria nova,* trans. M.F.
   Nims; M.C. Woods, ed., *An Early Commentary on the* Poetria nova *of Geoffrey
   of Vinsauf*; R.A. Pratt, "Three Old French Sources of the Nonnes Preestes Tale."
   Speculum 47 (1972): 662; K. Young, "Chaucer and Geoffrey of Vinsauf." *MP* 41
   (1943–1944): 172–182.

GAUFRIDE. Geoffrey of Monmouth, c. 1100–c. 1155, was born and brought up in Wales. He was appointed Archdeacon of Llandaff in 1140 and consecrated Bishop of Asaph in 1152. His *Historia regum Britanniae (History of the Kings of Britain)* was completed c. 1136. In manuscripts *E, D,* and *P* of this work, Geoffrey says that his work is a translation into Latin from the British tongue, *Historia regum Britanniae* I.1. It is, however, compiled from Celtic myths, legends, and borrowings from Nennius, *Historia Brittonum* (c. 800). The fourth book of this work, called *Prophetiae Merlini,* is derived mainly from the oral tradition of the Breton *conteurs.* Wace, a Norman poet, paraphrased Geoffrey's work about 1155 and called it *Le Roman de Brut,* and from this work Layamon made his *Brut* in English about 1205.

Chaucer borrowed material from *Historia regum Britanniae,* IV.12–16, VIII.10–12, for parts of *The Franklin's Tale. Englyssh Gaufride* stands on a pillar of iron, the metal of Mars, *HF* III.1470. [**Arveragus: Aurelius: Brut: Dorigen**]

Gaufride, a variant of Latin genitive singular *Gaufridi,* appears medially, *HF* III.1470.

R.A. Caldwell, "Wace's *Roman de Brut* and the Variant Version of Geoffrey of Monmouth's *Historia regum Britanniae.*" *Speculum* 31 (1956): 675–682; Geoffrey of Monmouth, *Historia regum Britanniae*, ed. A. Griscom, trans. R.E. Jones; *ibid., The History of the Kings of Britain,* trans. with introd. L. Thorpe; *ibid., A Variant Version of the* Historia regum Britanniae, ed. J. Hammer; Layamon, *Brut*, ed. G.L. Brook and R.F. Leslie.

GAWAIN: [GAWAYN]

GAWAYN. Gawain, the paragon of courtesy, was King Arthur's nephew, son of his sister Morgause (or Anna, in some versions). Chrétien says: *Devant toz les buens chevaliers/Doit estre Gauvains le premiers, Erec* 1691–1692, "Before all good knights, Gawain ought to be named first." Gawain was the *nonpareil* of Arthurian knights in the early stages of Arthurian romance, but his reputation was blackened in the later tradition, as in Chrétien's *Le Conte de Graal* (c. 1182). In the Middle English *Sir Gawain and the Green Knight* (late 14th century), he is still famous for courtesy and chastity.

Even Gawayn, for all his reputation, cannot surpass the strange knight's courtesy, *SqT* 95–96. **[Arthour: Launcelot]**

Gawayn, the ME variant of OF *Gauvin,* is derived from Welsh *Gwalltadvwyn*, and appears in medial position, *SqT* 95.

Chrétien de Troyes, *Erec und Enide*, ed. W. Foerster, 63; R.S. Loomis, *The Arthurian Tradition and Chrétien de Troyes,* 149; *Sir Gawain and the Green Knight: A New Critical Edition,* ed. T. Silverstein; B.J. Whiting, "Gawain: His Reputation, His Courtesy, and His Appearance in Chaucer's *Squire's Tale.*" *MS* 9 (1947): 189–234.

GEFFREY. The Learned Eagle addresses the Dreamer familiarly by his given name, HF II.729, the only place where the name appears in Chaucer's works.

The form is the ME variant influenced by pronunciation of the name now spelled *Geoffrey.*

GEMINI, GEMINIS, the constellation the Twins, is generally portrayed as Castor and Pollux, but also sometimes as a male and a female. The constellation lies in the northern hemisphere, partly in the Milky Way, near Orion. In the time of Hipparchus each constellation stood next to the sign bearing its name, but by Chaucer's time the constellation lay two-thirds into the sign bearing its name. Gemini, as a whole, produces an equable temperature (*Tetrabiblos* II.11); the foreparts of Gemini cause slenderness and the hindparts robustness (*Tetrabiblos* III.11). It is the night house of Mercury (*Tetrabiblos* I.17). The Twins are generally painted naked, wrestling with each other (*Confessio Amantis* VII.1031–1050).

The sun is in Gemini, a little from its declination or highest point, reached on June 13 in Chaucer's time, when May meets Damian in the pear tree, *MerchT* 2222. Venus flees to Cilenios's tower, that is, to Gemini, the night house of Mercury, *Mars* 113–114. Gemini is the third sign of the zodiac, *Astr* I.8.3. A man born under Gemini will have thin arms and armholes, *Astr* I.21.74–75. Gemini is the nadir (exactly opposite) of Sagittarius, *Astr* II.6.16. All the signs from the head or beginning of Capricorn to the end of Gemini rise above the horizon in less than two hours and are called tortuous, crooked, or oblique signs, *Astr* II.28.22–30. Gemini, an eastern sign, obeys Cancer, a western or "sovereign" sign, *Astr* II.28. 36. **[Cilenios: Damian: Januarie: May]**

Gemini, Latin nominative plural, appears four times in the *Astrolabe*; *Geminis*, Latin dative plural, appears medially, *MerchT* 2222, and three times in the *Astrolabe*.

John Gower, *The Complete Works*, ed. G.C. Macaulay, III: 261; Ptolemy, *Tetrabiblos*, ed. and trans. F.E. Robbins, 83, 203, 315–317; H.M. Smyser, "A View of Chaucer's Astronomy." *Speculum* 45 (1970): 362; C. Wood, *Chaucer and the Country of the Stars*, 149–151.

GENELLOUN, GENYLON. Ganelon was Roland's stepfather in the twelfth-century poem *La Chanson de Roland*. He betrayed the French to the Saracens, and his name became synonymous with treachery. Dante places him in the Antenora, the second division of Circle Nine of Hell, *Inf* XXXII.122.

Don Pedro is betrayed by a Genelloun-Olyver, that is, an Oliver who is like Ganelon, a friend who becomes a traitor, *MkT* 2378–2388. The merchant's wife swears to repay the monk and to give him pleasure, or she would be as false as Genylon, *ShipT* 190–194. The apostrophe on "newe Genylon," *NPT* 3226–3235, is a parody of the rhetorical ornament found in Geoffrey of Vinsauf's *Poetria nova, Ornata facilis*, 1095–1105. The Man in Black says that if he repented of his love, he would be as false as Genelloun, *BD* 1115–1121. **[Genylon-Olyver: Olyver: Rowland]**

Genelloun appears once initially, *MkT* 2389, and once in final rhyming position, *BD* 1121; *Genylon* occurs once medially, *ShipT* 194, and once in final rhyming position, *NPT* 3227.

La Chanson de Roland, ed. C. Segre; Dante, *The Divine Comedy*, ed. and trans. C.S. Singleton, I, 1: 346–347; E. Faral, *Les Arts poétiques*, 231; Geoffrey de Vinsauf, *Poetria nova*, trans. M.F. Nims, 56; *The Song of Roland*, ed. S.J. Herrtage; K. Young, "Chaucer and Geoffrey of Vinsauf." *MP* 41 (1943–1944): 177–180.

GENYLON-OLYVER, or Oliver who is like Ganelon, refers to Olivier de Mauny, nephew of Bertrand du Guesclin, the constable of France. Both de Mauny and du Guesclin were sent by the French king to support Henry the

Bastard in the Castilian civil war. After Don Pedro's murder in 1369 Henry established himself on the throne of Castile and gave Olivier de Mauny the estate of Crecte, worth two thousand florins a year. Froissart says that without the help of de Mauny and du Guesclin, Henry would never have won the throne of Castile (*Chronicles* I.245).

The Monk describes de Mauny as Genylon-Olyver, *MkT* 2389. Froissart does not mention treachery; Olivier was always on Henry's side throughout the war. **[Charles Olyver: Genylon: Petro[1]]**

La Chanson de Roland, ed. C. Segre; J. Froissart, *Chronicles*, ed. and trans. J. Jolliffe, 207–208; D.K. Fry, "The Ending of the *Monk's Tale*." *JEGP* 71 (1972): 355–368; *The Song of Roland*, ed. S.J. Herrtage.

GEOFFREY DE VINSAUF: [GAUFRED]
GEOFFREY OF MONMOUTH: [GAUFRIDE]

[GERARD OF CREMONA], 1114–1187, was the greatest of the early translators of Arabic works into Latin. He traveled to Toledo with the specific purpose of learning Arabic in order to translate Ptolemy's *Almagest* and other works not available in the Latin West into Latin. He was the most prolific of translators from Arabic into Latin, with the help of a Spanish Christian named Galippus. At Toledo Gerard found a wealth of Arabic works and worked diligently to translate them. He translated books in every field, and the catalogue of his translations is quite substantial, especially on astronomy, astrology, and alchemy. He translated a number of scientific writings of Aristotle, but the longest list is medical. As Haskins points out, most of Arabic science in general passed into the West at the hands of Gerard of Cremona.

Among his translations are the *Kitab al-Medjisti* or *The Book of Almagest* in 1175, which was widely circulated; al-Khwarizmi's *Hisab al-Djabr wa' l-Mukabala* with the Latin title *al-Goritmi de numero indorum* or *The Book of Addition and Subtraction*; Aristotle's *Meteorologica (Meteorology)*, *De caelo et mundo (On the Heavens)*, *Physica (Physics)*, and *Analytica Posteriora (Posterior Analytics)*; the *Toledan Tables*, also called the *Alfonsine Tables*, done for Alfonso the Wise of Castile c. 1272; Ibn-Sina's *Qanun*; the *Kitab al-tibb al Mansuri* (an encyclopedia of medicine) of Razis with the title *Liber almansoris*; and a medical compilation of Yahaya ibn-Sarafyun as *Practica sine breviarum*, which was very popular during the period. **[Argus[2]: Aristotile: Arsechiele: Avycen: Ptholome: Razis: Serapion]**

H.L.L. Busard, ed., *The Latin Translation of the Arabic Version of Euclid's Elements Commonly Ascribed to Gerard of Cremona;* Marie-Thérèse d'Alverny, "Translations and Translators," *Renaissance and Renewal in the Twelfth Century,* ed. R.L. Benson and G. Constable, 452–454; D.M. Dunlop, "The Work of Translation at Toledo." *Babel* 6 (1960): 55–59; *Encyclopedia of Islam*, II: 912–913; C.H. Haskins,

The Renaissance of the Twelfth Century, 286–290; Richard Lemay, "Gerard of Cremona." *DSB* 15 (1978): 176–192.

GERMANICUS: [GERMAYNES]

GERMAYNES. Germanicus, 15 B.C.–A.D. 19, was the son of Drusus and Antonia. His maternal uncle Tiberius adopted him in A.D. 4. Suetonius says that it was the general opinion that Germanicus possessed all the highest qualities of body and mind. In A.D. 19, while traveling in Syria, he suddenly fell ill, and he was convinced that Piso, governor of Syria, had poisoned him. He was thirty-four years old at his death (Suetonius, *Caius Caligula* i–iii).

Gaius Caesar, "Germanynes" son, accused Canius of secret knowledge of a conspiracy against him, and Canius replied that if he had known, Gaius would not have known, *Bo* I, *Prosa* 4.180–185. [**Canyus: Cesar³**]

Germaynes is the ME genitive case, *Bo* I, *Prosa* 4.181.

Suetonius, *De vita Caesarum*, ed. and trans. J.C. Rolfe, I: 404–407.

GERVEYS is the village smith in *The Miller's Tale*. He works very late at night in his shop, *MillT* 3760–3763, and Absolon borrows a "kultour" or plowshare from him to use on Nicholas, *MillT* 3782–3785. [**Absolon²**]

The name occurs once initially, *MillT* 3779; twice in medial positions, *MillT* 3765, 3775; and once in final rhyming position, *MillT* 3761.

GILBERTUS: [GILBERTYN]

GILBERTYN. Gilbertus Anglicus or Gilbert the Englishman, fl. A.D. 1250, was active at Montpellier. Of his many medical treatises, his most famous was the *Compendium medicinae,* containing detailed pathological descriptions of such diseases as leprosy and smallpox. He was the first physician to establish that smallpox is contagious and the first to write on the hygiene of travel. Merton College Library owned a copy of this work between 1360 and 1385.

The Doctor claims to know Gilbertyn's work, *Gen Prol* 434.

The name appears in final rhyming position, which perhaps has determined its form.

F.M. Powicke, *The Medieval Books of Merton College*, 140; G. Sarton, *Introduction to the History of Science,* II, 2: 520–521.

GILE, GYLE (saint). Giles is the English name for Aegidius, an Athenian who built a hermitage near Rome, where he died c. A.D. 720. There are no historical sources for his life, and his feast has been removed from the church calendar. During the Middle Ages St. Giles was regarded as the patron saint of blacksmiths and of outcasts such as lepers, cripples, and beggars (*Legenda aurea* CXXX). His most famous shrine in England is at Cripplegate, London.

"By Seint Gile" occurs as a rhyming tag, *CYT* 1185; "Be Seynt Gyle," also a rhyming tag, occurs *HF* III.1183.

F. Brittain, *Saint Giles*; A. Haskell, "The Saint Giles Oath in the Canon's Yeoman's Tale." *Essays on Chaucer's Saints*, 26–29; Jacobus de Voragine, *GL*, trans. G. Ryan and H. Ripperger, 516–519; *ibid.*, *LA*, ed. Th. Graesse, 582–584; *The South-English Legendary*, ed. C. D'Evelyn and A.J. Mill, II: 384–389.

GILES: [GILE]

GILLE is the name of the maid in the household of John and Alison in *The Miller's Tale*. She is also called a "wenche," *MillT* 3631. It was a familiar name for a lass. **[Robyn²]**

The name occurs medially, *MillT* 3556.

OED, IV: 163.

GLASCURION refers possibly to the Bard Geraint, who presided over an "Eisteddfodd" or music competition and festival in the ninth century. There are several bards named Geraint in Welsh musical history. One Geraint is the subject of a ballad in Percy's *Reliques* III: 43.1765; he harped in the queen's chamber "till the ladies waxed wood." Thomas Parry points out that many references to the Bard Geraint in the *Myvyrian Archaiology of Wales* are inventions of Edward Williams (1747–1826), written under the pen name Iolo.

The Dreamer sees the Bret Glascurion in Fame's house among the harpers, who include Chiron and Orion, *HF* III.1201–1208. **[Chiron: Orion]**

Glascurion is a compound of *Glas Geraint,* Geraint the Blue Bard, and appears in final rhyming position, *HF* III.1208.

T. Parry, *A History of Welsh Literature*, trans. H.I. Bell, 301–304, 381.

GLASGERION: [GLASCURION]
GODELIEF: [GOODELIEF]

GOLIAS. Goliath, the Philistine giant of Gath, challenged Israel to send out a champion to fight him. David volunteered and, armed only with a sling, defeated and killed Goliath (I Kings 17).

The Man of Law, in an apostrophe, calls Golias "unmesurable of length" and asks how David could make him so dead, except by God's grace, *MLT* 934–938. **[David]**

Golias, with initial stress, is the ME variant of *Goliath*; it appears in medial position, *MLT* 934.

GOLIATH: [GOLIAS]

GOODELIEF. Godelieve was the name of a Flemish saint. The hagiographers of the twelfth and thirteenth centuries emphasized her wifely obedience and submissiveness. In Chaucer's day the name was popular in Kent. The wife of Henricus Bailiff, a possible model for the Host, was named Christian, and Chaucer's intention in naming Harry Bailly's wife Goodelief is purely ironic, since she is the very opposite of her namesake.

Bailly wishes that his wife could have heard the Clerk's tale of Griselda, *ClT* 1212–1218, implying that Goodelief is not patient. At the end of *The Merchant's Tale*, Harry reveals that his wife is "as trewe as steel" but that she has a sharp tongue, *MerchT* 2419–2440. After Chaucer's *Tale of Melibee*, Bailly describes his wife as a hard mistress to his apprentices and gives more details about her. One day, he says, she will drive him to murder, *MkT* 1889–1923. **[Bailly]**

K. Malone, "Harry Bailly and Godelief." *ES* 31 (1950): 209–215; J.M. Manly, *Some New Light on Chaucer*, 77–83; E. Rickert, "Goode Lief, my Wyf." *MP* 25 (1927): 79–82.

GOWER. John Gower, c. 1330–1408, was Chaucer's contemporary and friend. He was an avid land purchaser, and by the end of 1369 two of his real estate transactions were involved in court action. He was known at the royal court, and his most famous poem, *Confessio Amantis*, was written at Richard II's request between 1382 and 1386, the same period as Chaucer's *Knight's Tale* and *Troilus and Criseyde*. His other works are *Speculum meditantis* or *Mirour de l'omme,* written in French and completed before 1377, and *Vox Clamantis,* written in Latin and completed between 1385 and 1399, when Chaucer was writing *The Legend of Good Women* and *The Canterbury Tales*. These three poems, each in a different language— English, French, and Latin—indicate that fourteenth-century poets, writers, intellectuals, and those who desired success at court had to be proficient in three languages. Chaucer appointed Gower as his attorney before he set out on his mission to Italy in 1378, a testimony to their friendship.

The Man of Law criticizes tales of incest such as stories of Canacee and Apollonius of Tyre, *MLI* 77–85, both of which tales appear in *Confessio Amantis* III.143–360 and VIII.271–2008. The first recension of *Confessio Amantis* contains a tribute to Chaucer, VIII.2941–2957, which is omitted in the second recension, persuading some scholars that this omission indicates a coolness between Chaucer and Gower. John Fisher shows that this is not the case. Chaucer dedicates *Troilus and Criseyde* to "moral Gower," *Tr* V.1856. Chaucer links "moral" and "virtue" to mean excellence of conduct; thus the dedication shows how much he valued Gower's friendship.

G.R. Coffman, "John Gower, Mentor for Royalty." *PMLA* 69 (1954): 953–964; J.H. Fisher, *John Gower: Moral Philosopher and Friend of Chaucer,* 1–69, 226; John Gower, *The Complete Works,* ed. G.C. Macaulay, II: 230–235, III: 393–440, 466.

[GRATIAN]. Chaucer does not mention this author of the *Decretum* when he refers to the book. Gratian appears to be unknown except as the author of the *Decretum,* composed in the first half of the twelfth century. This work includes about four thousand chapters and is divided into three parts.

Dame Prudence quotes from the *Book of Decrees,* Part 2, *Causa* i, Question l, chapter 25, *Mel* 1404. The reference is in Renaud de Louens's *Le Livre de Mellibee et Prudence,* 638, Chaucer's source for his *Tale of Melibee.* [Damasie]

J.B. Severs, *S&A,* 592; Gratian, *Decretum,* ed. A. Friedberg, in *Corpus iuris canonici* I.

GRAUNSON. Otes de Graunson, c. 1340–1397, was a noble from Savoy who spent much time in England. He swore allegiance to the English king and joined the household of John of Gaunt in 1374, where, it is certain, he met Chaucer. His estates in Savoy were confiscated in 1393, following his implication in a plot against the count of Savoy. He was killed in a duel in 1397 when he fought to prove his innocence of the charges made against him.

Chaucer calls Graunson "flour of hem that make in Fraunce," *Complaint of Venus* 82. This poem is composed from translations of three French balades by Graunson, who, even during his lifetime, enjoyed an outstanding reputation as a poet of courtly love.

The name appears in medial position, *Venus* 82.

H. Braddy, *Chaucer and the French Poet Graunson.*

GREAT BEAR: [CALISTOPEE: URSA]

GREGORIE (saint). Gregory the Great, c. A.D. 540–604, was born in Rome. He became one of the great fathers and one of the greatest prelates of the Roman Catholic Church. In A.D. 597, Gregory sent Augustine, a pupil of Felix of Messana, to convert the Anglo-Saxons to Christianity. Bede refers to Gregorie as "our own Apostle" because he was instrumental in converting the Anglo-Saxons, and gives the story of his life in *History of the English Church and People* II.1. He was canonized soon after his death in 604.

St. Gregorie says that when a man considers the number of his faults and sins, the pains and tribulations he suffers seem less, *Mel* 1497. This quotation is attributed to Gregory in all the French manuscripts but is missing from the Latin original of Albertanus Brixiensis. The Parson's quotation on penitence, *ParsT* 92, appears in *Moralia* IV.27.51–52 (*PL* 75:

662–664); on wretched felons, *ParsT* 214, appears in *Moralia* IX.66.100 (*PL* 75: 915); on remembrance of past sins, *ParsT* 238, appears in *Homiliae in Hiezech.* I.11.21 (*CC* 142: 178); on costly clothing, *ParsT* 414, 934, appears in *XL Homiliae in Evangelia*, II.40.3 (*PL* 76: 1305); on taking pride in the gifts of grace, *ParsT* 470, recalls *Moralia* XXXIII.12.25 (*PL* 76: 688). S. Wenzel notes that the quotation at *ParsT* 692 refers to the preceding sentence, not translated by Chaucer. The quotation on gluttony, *ParsT* 828, appears in *Moralia,* XXX.18.60 (*PL* 76: 556); those who continue in sin, *ParsT* 1069, appears in *Moralia,* XXXIV.19.36 (*PL* 76: 738*)*.

The form of the name is ME and OF, and occurs only in the prose works.

Bede, *Opera historica*, ed. and trans. J.E. King, I: 184–203; *ibid., A History of the English Church and People*, trans. L. Sherley-Price, 93–99; *The Earliest Life of Gregory the Great by an anonymous Monk of Whitby*, ed. B. Colgrave; G.R. Evans, *The Thought of Gregory the Great;* J.M. Petersen, *The Dialogues of Gregory the Great in their Late Antique Cultural Background; Riverside Chaucer*, ed. L. Benson, 961–962; J.B. Severs, *S&A,* 596.

GREGORY: [GREGORIE]

GRISEL. Chaucer calls himself *Grisel, Scogan* 35. He notes that Scogan gave up his lady at Michaelmas. For this sin against love, the God of Love may now punish all those who are hoary and round of shape, *i.e.*, Chaucer and Scogan, the least likely to succeed in love. But perhaps Scogan will think Old Grisel loves to make fun in rhymes, *Scogan* 29–35. **[Scogan]**

Grisel is the common name for an old graying man or horse, derived from OF *grisel*, meaning "grey." It appears medially, *Scogan* 35.

Riverside Chaucer, ed. L. Benson, 1087.

GRISELDE, GRISILD, GRISILDIS. Griselde is the heroine of *The Clerk's Tale*, which, the Clerk says, he has learned from a worthy clerk of Padua, Francis Petrak, *ClP* 21–38. The reference points to Petrarch's Latin tale, *De obedientia ac fide uxoria mythologia*; Chaucer also used an anonymous French translation, *Le Livre Griseldis*. The story is also the Tenth Tale on the Tenth Day of Boccaccio's *Decameron*. The Clerk states at the end of the tale that since Griselde was patient with a mortal man, we ought to be patient in all that God sends, *ClT* 1149–1155, realizing that his tale is a difficult one for his audience. It is also a difficult one for a modern audience. **[Fraunceys Petrak: Janicle: Walter]**

Griselde, with silent final -*e,* occurs seven times initially, *ClT* 274, 344, 953, 1029, 1030, 1062, 1177; eleven times in medial positions, *ClT* 232, 365; with final syllabic -*e,* 466, 470, 792; with elided final -*e,* 989, 1007, 1009, 1051; with final syllabic -*e,* 1143; with elided final -*e,* 1147. *Grisild* occurs once only, in final rhyming position, *ClT* 442. *Grisildis* occurs twice initially: once as nominative case, *ClT* 537, and once as accusative case, *ClT* 1182; twelve times in medial positions: once in the locative case, *ClT* 297; four times as nominative case, *ClT* 210, 335, 428, 537; once in accusative plural case, *ClT* 1165; twice as genitive case, *ClT* 576, *MerchT* 1224, and twice as dative case, *ClT* 752, 1187; and twice in final rhyming position in the dative case, *ClT* 752, 948.

Boccaccio, *Decameron*, trans. J. Payne, rev. and annotated C.S. Singleton, II: 780–794; E.P. Kadish, "Petrarch's Griselda: An English Translation." *Mediaevalia* 3 (1977): 1–24; N. Lavers, "Freud, *The Clerk's Tale*, and Literary Criticism." *CE* 26 (1964): 180–187; J. Sledd, "*The Clerk's Tale*: The Monsters and the Critics." *MP* 51 (1953–1954): 73–82; J.B. Severs, *S&A*, 288–331.

GUIDO, GUYDO. Guido de Columpnis, fl. thirteenth century, also known as Guido de Columnis or Guido delle Colonne, was a poet of the Sicilian school of poetry. He was born probably at Messina, where he became a judge. He died in 1287, the year he paraphrased Benoît de Sainte-Maure's *Roman de Troie* and called it *Historia destructionis Troiae*. It is written in Latin prose in thirty-one books, full of learned digressions and moral reflections not found in Benoît's poem. Guido does not mention Benoît but cites Dares and Dictys as his sources.

Guido "eek de Columpnis" stands on a pillar of iron, the metal of Mars, because he has written on the Trojan War, *HF* III.1469. Chaucer cites Guido as one of his sources for the story of Jason, *LGW* 1396, which takes up Book I of the *Historia*. Chaucer says that Guido tells nothing of Jason's adventures with Ysiphile, *LGW* 1464. Contrary to Chaucer, who shows distaste for Jason, Guido concentrates on Medea, whom he portrays as the paradigm of the wicked woman. **[Dares Frygius: Dite]**

Guido appears in medial position, *LGW* 1396; *Guydo,* a spelling variant, appears in medial position, *HF* III.1469, and in final rhyming position, *LGW* 1464.

C.D. Benson, *The History of Troy in Middle English Literature: Guido delle Colonne's Historia destructionis Troiae in Medieval England; ibid.,* "'O Nyce World': What Chaucer Really Found in Guido delle Colonne's History of Troy." *ChauR* 13 (1979): 308–315; G.A. Cesareo, *Le origine delle poesia lirica,* 149–157; Guido delle Colonne, *Guido de Columnis: HDT,* ed. N.E. Griffin; *ibid., HDT,* trans. with introd. and notes by M.E. Meek.

GUIDO DE COLUMNIS: [GUIDO]
GUIDO DE COLUMPNIS: [GUIDO]
GUIDO DELLE COLONNE: [GUIDO]

[GUILLAUME DE LORRIS.] Very little is known about this poet, fl. 1230, the author of the first part of *Le Roman de la Rose*. He was evidently from Lorris, a small town east of Orleans. The year of his birth is unknown, and the year of his death can only be inferred from Jean de Meun's section of the poem. Jean de Meun says that he was born about the time of Guillaume's death, the date of which is uncertain (c.1225–1240), and that he worked on the poem about forty years after Guillaume's death. Ernest Langlois proposes 1225–1240 as the period of Guillaume's death; Felix Lecoy suggests the years 1225–1230 as the time during which Guillaume worked on his poem. He invented the medieval dream vision of love, and this form enjoyed popularity down to the Renaissance. Unfinished, Guillaume's poem goes as far as line 4058. Courtly and refined, the poem leaves enough clues to justify Jean de Meun's more satirical and realistic treatment of its theme.

The narrator describes a dream he had when he was twenty years old, five years before he wrote his poem. In May, wandering in a meadow near a river, he comes to a walled garden. Outside the garden are images of Hate, Felony, Villainy, Covetousness, Avarice, Envy, Sorrow, Old Age, Pope-Holiness, and Poverty. Let into the garden by Idleness, an intimate acquaintance of Sir Mirth, the lord of the garden, the Dreamer finds Mirth and his companions dancing, while Gladness sings, sitting next to the God of Love. The dancers are Beauty, Richesse, Courtesy, Largess (Generosity), Franchise, and Youth. Sweet Looks keeps the two bows of the God of Love; in his right hand he holds five arrows that attract love and in his left hand five arrows that repel love. Walking about the garden, the Dreamer sees the perfect rosebud and stops to admire it. The God of Love wounds him with his five golden love arrows, and the Dreamer falls in love with the Rosebud. Now the God of Love takes charge, and the Dreamer swears an oath of vassalage to him, upon which he is given the ten commandments of love. Fair Welcome attaches himself to the Lover, and as they admire the Rose, the Dreamer/Lover tells Fair Welcome his desire. Suddenly Dangier, the Rose's guardian, rises from his hiding place and threatens them. In despair, they flee from the place. Reason, made in God's image, comes down from her tower, rebukes the Lover for his folly, and warns him that her daughter Shame guards and protects the Rose. The Lover, however, rejects Reason and joins Friend, who shows him how Dangier may be conquered. The Lover humbly apologizes to Dangier, who replies that he can love as long as he likes, but he may not come near the Rose. Seeing the Lover's distress, the God of Love sends Franchise and Pity to help him. Urging Dangier to have mercy, they cause him to relent. The Lover draws near to Fair Welcome and asks for permission to kiss the Rose, but Fair Welcome cannot comply because Chastity has forbidden it. When Venus appears with her blazing firebrand and persuades Fair Welcome to allow one kiss, Evil Tongue immediately spreads slander and arouses Jealousy, who castigates Fair Welcome for his friendship with the Lover. But Jealousy is adamant. Scolding Shame, she collects all the workmen she can find, and they build a strong tower around the Rose, garrisoned by Dangier, Shame,

Fear, and Evil Tongue. Jealousy imprisons Fair Welcome in the tower and sets an Old Woman to guard him. The Lover remains outside the walls, disconsolate and miserable. Here the poem breaks off.

The *Roman de la Rose* was enormously popular. Ernest Langlois found 215 manuscripts, and others are likely to exist. The Middle English translation, *The Romaunt of the Rose,* exists in three fragments: Fragments A and B (lines 1–5810) correspond to *RR* 1–5154; Fragment C (lines 5811–7696) corresponds to *RR* 10670–12360. Lines 5155–16678 of the original French have been omitted with no break in the manuscript. Fragment A is held to be fairly close to Chaucer's style; Fragments B and C are by separate authors. The Middle English *Romaunt* does not include the Discourse of Reason, *RR* 4229–7229; the Friend's Advice, *RR* 7281–10000; and the Old Woman's Sermon, *RR* 2740–14546, any of which may be called "heresy" against the God of Love's Law.

Chaucer never mentions Guillaume's name, but the *Roman de la Rose* pervades all his poetry. The dream poems and love visions—*The Book of the Duchess, The House of Fame,* and, most of all, *The Parliament of Foules*— owe much to the *Roman.* Chaucer's gardens are indebted to Guillaume's: Januarie's garden, *MerchT* 2029–2041, the garden where Aurelius courts Dorigen, *FranklT* 901–917, the garden of assignation in *ShipT* 89–207. Chauntecleer's domain, a rather drab yard, is the antithesis of such gardens, *NPT* 2847–2850.

In describing Januarie's garden, the Merchant says that it was such a fair garden that he who wrote the *Romance of the Rose* could not describe its beauty, *MerchT* 2031–2033. The Dreamer in *The Book of the Duchess* dreams that he lies in a room the walls of which are painted in beautiful colors, with the text and gloss of the *Romance of the Rose, BD* 332–334. Chaucer may have had in mind a particular manuscript with gloss and commentary. Since there were many illustrated manuscripts of the poem in Chaucer's day, he may have meant "illustrated" as well. The God of Love mentions Chaucer's translation of the *Romance of the Rose,* which is heresy against his law and causes folk to withdraw from him, *LGW F* 329–333, *LGW G* 255–257. The *Legend* is dated 1382–1394, and this passage indicates that by this date there already existed some criticism of the *Roman.* Christine de Pizan condemned the *Roman* in 1399 in *L'Epistre au dieu d'amours,* and this treatise may have been the cause of the celebrated *Querelle de la Rose* of 1400–1402. Queen Alceste suggests that as penance the narrator must now write of women who have loved truly. He must please the God of Love with a new work as much as he had offended him with his previous work, his translation of the *Roman* and his writing *Troilus and Criseyde, LGW F* 435–441, *LGW G* 425–431. The poet replies that true lovers ought to support him because he has written *Troilus and Criseyde* and has translated the *Rose, LGW F* 468–470, *LGW G* 458–460. **[Jean de Meun]**

P.-Y. Badel, *Le Roman de la Rose au XIVe siècle: Etude de la reception de l'oeuvre*; F.W. Bourdillon, *The Early Editions of the Roman de la Rose*; D.S. Fansler, *Chaucer and the Roman de la Rose*; John V. Fleming, *The Roman de la Rose: A Study in Allegory and Iconography*; Guillaume de Lorris and Jean de Meun, *Le Roman de la Rose*, ed. E. Langlois; *ibid., RR*, ed. F. Lecoy; *ibid., RR*, trans. C. Dahlberg; E. Langlois, *Les Manuscrits du* Roman de la Rose*: Description et Classement*; Maxwell Luria, *A Reader's Guide to the Roman de la Rose*; *Riverside Chaucer*, ed. L. Benson, 1103; R. Sutherland, *The Romaunt of the Rose and Le Roman de la Rose: A Parallel-Text Edition*; *ibid.,* "The *Romaunt of the Rose* and Source Manuscripts." *PMLA* 74 (1959): 178–183.

[GUILLAUME DE MACHAUT,] c. 1300–1377, was born in a little village of Machaut. In 1323 he entered the service of Jean de Luxembourg as secretary. In 1330 he became a canon at Verdun Cathedral; in 1332, a canon at Arras Cathedral; and in 1337, a canon at Rheims Cathedral. He was famous as composer and poet and wrote a mass for the coronation of Charles V in 1349. Much of his poetry shows the strong influence of the *Roman de la Rose* and the *Ovide Moralisé* besides the classical influence of Ovid. Among these are the *Dit dou Vergier, Le Jugement dou roy de Behaigne, Le Remede de Fortune,* written before 1342. In 1342 he wrote *Le Dit dou lion*; in 1349 he composed *Le Jugement dou roy de Navarre* in honor of Charles V. In 1356 Charles became prisoner of the king of France, and Guillaume wrote for him *Le Confort d'ami.* His epic poem, *La Prise d'Alexandrie* (1369) celebrates the exploits of Pierre de Lusignan, king of Cyprus and Jerusalem. In 1362, he wrote *Le Livre de la Fonteinne amoureuse*, also known as *Le Dit de la Fonteinne amoureuse.*

Chaucer does not mention Guillaume de Machaut although they were contemporaries and he used Guillaume's work extensively. Kittredge and Severs have shown the extent of Chaucer's indebtedness in his poem *The Book of the Duchess.* Machaut was one of the finest poets of his day, and Chaucer could not have escaped his influence. Chaucer says he translated *The Book of the Lion, ParsT* 1085, a reference, most likely, to Machaut's *Dit dou lion.* F.M. Dear suggests that this translation may have been made for Lionel, Duke of Clarence, in whose household Chaucer had been a page. The work has not survived.

F.M. Dear, "Chaucer's *Book of the Lion.*" *MAE* 7 (1938): 105–112; C. de Boer, "Guillaume de Machaut et *l'Ovide Moralisé.*" *OM*, I, deel 15: 28–43; M.J. Ehrhart, "Machaut's *Dit de la Fonteinne Amoureuse*, the Choice of Paris, and the Duties of Rulers." *PQ* 59 (1980): 119–139; Guillaume de Machaut, *The Judgment of the King of Bohemia*, ed. and trans. R.B. Palmer; *ibid., Oeuvres*, ed. E. Hoepffner; *ibid., La Prise d'Alexandrie*, ed. M.L. de Mas Latrie; G.L. Kittredge, "Guillaume de Machaut and *The Book of the Duchess.*" *PMLA* 30 (1915): 1–24; J.B. Severs, "The Sources of 'The Book of the Duchess.'" *MS* 15 (1963): 355–362; J.I. Wimsatt, "Guillaume de Machaut and Chaucer's Love Lyrics." *MAE* 47 (1978): 66–87; *ibid.,* "Guillaume de Machaut and Chaucer's *Troilus and Criseyde.*" *MAE* 44 (1976): 277–293; *ibid., The Marguerite Poems of Guillaume de Machaut.*

GUY: [GY]

GY is the hero of the romance, *Sir Guy of Warwick,* written before 1325 and a very popular work during the medieval period.

Sir Thopas, the flower of chivalry, surpasses even Sir Guy, *Thop* 899. **[Thopas]**

Gui de Warewic, ed. A. Ewert; *Guy of Warwick,* ed. J. Zupita; C. Strong, "Sir Thopas and Sir Guy." *MLN* 23 (1908): 73–77, 102–106.

GYLE: [GILE]

H

HABRADATE. Abradate was king of Susa (late fifth–early fourth century B.C.), husband of Panthea, and an ally of Cyrus the Great. When her husband was killed in a battle against the Egyptians (c. 401 B.C.), Panthea stabbed her bosom and mingled her blood with his before she died (Xenophon, *Cyropaedia* VII.1.29–32, VII.iii.3–14). Jerome tells the story in *Epistola adversus Jovinianum (Letter Against Jovinian)* I.45 (*PL* 23: 275).

Dorigen thinks that Habradate's wife is an exemplary figure of wifely fidelity, *FranklT* 1414–1418. **[Dorigen]**

The form is an inversion of Latin *Abradate*; Latin initial *h* was not pronounced.

G. Dempster, "Chaucer at Work on the Complaint in *The Franklin's Tale.*" *MLN* 52 (1937): 6–16; K. Hume, "The Pagan Setting of *The Franklin's Tale* and the Sources of Dorigen's Cosmology." *SN* 44 (1972): 289–294; Xenophon, *Cyropaedia*, ed. and trans. W. Miller, II: 218–221, 244–249.

HALI: [HALY]

HALY. Chaucer's Haly has not been positively identified. He may have been one of three men with the name Ali, transliterated as Haly. Haly Abbas, whose Arabic name is Ali ibn-'al-Abbas al-Majusi, was a Persian physician who died between A.D. 982 and 995. His chief work, *Kitab al-Maliki*, was translated into Latin, with the title *Liber regius (The Royal Book)*, by Stephen of Pisa in 1127 at Antioch. It appeared in Venice in 1492 and in Lyons in 1523. Constantinus Africanus translated the surgical section in the eleventh century. The second candidate for the identification is Hali filius Rodbon (Ali, son of Rodbon), whose Arabic name is Ali ibn-Ridwan ibn-'Ali ibn-Ja'far. He was born in Ghezeh c. A.D. 980. His commentary on Galen's

Tegni was famous during the Middle Ages. The last candidate is Abu-l-Hasan 'Ali ibn-Abu-l-Rijal, whose Latin name is Albohazen Haly. He was born in either Cordova or North Africa and flourished in Tunis about 1016–1040. His main work, *Al-Bari fi akham al-nujum*, called *The Distinguished Book on Horoscopes from the Constellations,* was translated from Arabic into Castilian by Judah ben Moses and from Castilian into Latin by Aegidius de Tebaldis of Parma and Peter of Riga under the Latin title *Praeclarissimus liber completus in Judiciis astrorum* and was printed in Venice in 1485. It was, however, well known before that date, and Merton College Library owned a copy between 1360 and 1385.

Haly is one of the Physician's authorities, *Gen Prol* 431.

The form is the English rendering of Arabic *'Ali* and occurs medially.

Ibn-Ridwan, *Medieval Islamic Medicine: Ibn-Ridwan's Treatise "On the Prevention of Bodily Ills in Egypt,"* trans. M.W. Dols, Arabic text ed. A.S. Gamal; D. Metlitzki, *The Matter of Araby in Medieval England,* 251, n. 9; G. Sarton, *An Introduction to the History of Science,* I: 715–716.

HANNIBAL: [HANYBAL]

HANYBAL. Hannibal, 247–182 B.C., was the son of the famous Carthagenian general Hamilcar Barca. He became even more famous than his father. From 218 to 203 B.C. he waged war against Rome, attacking the city again and again. He returned to Carthage in 203 when Scipio Africanus Major attacked that city and was defeated at Zama in 202 B.C. Polybius the historian praises Hannibal as one of the great generals of his time (Polybius, *Histories,* IX.19, XV.5–19).

The Man of Law compares the weeping at Custance's departure to that at Rome when Hanybal defeated it three times, *MLT* 290–294. **[Affrican]**

Hanybal, a spelling variant of Latin *Hannibal,* appears in final rhyming position, *MLT* 290.

Polybius, *Histories,* trans. E.S. Shuckburgh, II: 64, 140–152.

HASDRUBAL(ES). Hasdrubal was commander of the Carthaginian forces defeated by the Romans under Scipio Africanus Minor in 150 B.C. At the outbreak of the Third Punic War he was reinstated in his command and had several military successes, twice beating off the Romans, once at Nepheris and again in 148–146 B.C. when Scipio retreated at Carthage. When Scipio attacked again and proved invincible, Hasdrubal surrendered Carthage to him. Scipio burned the city. Hasdrubal's wife threw herself and their two sons into the burning streets. Later Hasdrubal was led in Scipio's triumph (Polybius, *Histories,* XXXVIII.1, XXXIX.4). Jerome tells the story in *Epistola adversus Jovinianum (Letter Against Jovinian)* I.43 (*PL* 23: 273).

Dorigen thinks that Hasdrubal's wife is an exemplary figure of wifely fidelity; distraught when the Romans capture the town, she skips into the fire, *FranklT* 1399–1404. The story is a little different in *NPT* 3362–3368; here Hasdrubal's wife wails loudly when he loses his life and then burns herself in the fire "with a steadfast heart."

Hasdrubales, the ME genitive case, appears in medial positions, *FranklT* 1399; *NPT* 3363.

K. Hume, "The Pagan Setting of *The Franklin's Tale* and the Sources of Dorigen's Cosmology." *SN* 44 (1972): 289–294; Polybius, *Histories*, trans. E.S. Shuckburgh, II: 513–515, 528–529.

HECTOR: [ECTOR]
HECUBA: [ECUBA]
HELEN: [ELEYNE²]
HELENA: [ELEYNE¹]

HELIE was a priest in Israel and lived at Shiloh during the period of the Judges. Hannah brought her son, Samuel, to him in fulfillment of a vow she made to God. Helie's sons cared nothing for the Lord's honor; they took uncooked meat from the people's sacrifices when the Law forbade eating such meats (I Kings 2).

Helie's sons are the sons of Belial; they seem to be angels of light but are really angels of darkness, *ParsT* 895–901. The Parson quotes I Kings 2:12: *filii Heli filii Belial,* "the sons of Helie are the sons of Belial." [**Belial: Samuel**]

Helie is the form in the Latin Vulgate. Latin initial *h* was not pronounced.

HELOISE: [HELOWYS]

HELOWYS. Heloise, 1101–1164, was the niece of Fulbert, a canon at the cathedral of Paris. Abelard says that he deliberately sought to be her tutor that he might seduce her. They were secretly married, but Fulbert hired three ruffians to harm him. They entered Abelard's room while he slept and castrated him. Abelard persuaded Heloise to become a nun at Argenteuil, and he became a monk at the abbey of St. Denis (*Historia calamitatum,* VI; *Epistolae* [*PL* 178: 181–378]). Jean de Meun translated the letters of Heloise and Abelard c. 1280, and used her arguments against marriage in the diatribe of the Jealous Husband, *RR* 8759–8832.

The letters of Heloise form part of Jankyn's anthology, *WBP* 677, which Dame Alys makes him throw into the fire.

Helowys, the ME variant, appears in final rhyming position.

Abelard, *Historia calamitatum,* ed. J. Monfrin; ibid., *The Story of Abelard's Adversities,* trans. J.T. Muckle; C. Charnier, *Héloïse dans l'histoire et dans la legende*; A. Hamilton, "Helowys and the Burning of Jankyn's Book." *MS* 34 (1972): 196–207; *The Letters of Abelard and Heloise,* trans. B. Radice; Jean de Meun, *Traduction de la première épître de Pierre Abelard (Historia calamitatum)*, ed. C. Charnier; *RR*, ed. E. Langlois, II: 94–97; *RR*, trans. C. Dahlberg, 160–161.

HEMONYDES. His name was Maeon, son of Haemon, and he was an augur, one of the fifty Thebans whom Eteocles sent to ambush Tydeus. When Tydeus and his men emerged from the ensuing slaughter, all the Thebans, except Maeon, had been killed. Tydeus sent him back to Eteocles with the news (*Thebaid* II.692–703). He is not mentioned in the *Roman de Thèbes* (before 1163).

Hemonydes appears in Cassandra's synopsis of the Theban siege, *Tr* V.1492. [**Adrastus: Amphiorax: Campaneus: Ethiocles: Parthonope: Polymyte: Tydeus**]

The name is the ME variant of the Greek patronymic *Haemonides,* meaning "son of Haemon."

Statius, *Thebaid,* ed. and trans. J.H. Mozley, I: 446–447.

HERCULES: [ERCULES]
HERDSMAN: [BOETES]
HEREMIANUS: [HERMANNO]

HERENUS, HERYNES. The Erinyes or the Furies, daughters of the Night, lived in the Underworld. They had snakes for hair and wore snakes around their waists, and their clothes dripped blood (*Met* IV.451–454, 481–484; *Aeneid* VI.554–557, 570–573). They guarded the infernal city of Dis and were the handmaidens of Proserpina, the queen of eternal lamentation (*Inf* IX.36–48). In Greek mythology they were given the propitiatory title, the *Eumenides,* "the kindly." Their names are Alecto, Megaera, and Tisiphone.

The three Furies weep for pity when Orpheus plays in the Underworld, *Bo* III, *Metr* 12.33–37. The poet invokes the Herynes, "Nyghtes doughtren thre," who complain endlessly in pain, *Tr* IV.22–24. Herenus, in *The Complaint of Pity,* has baffled commentators. The line, "Have mercy on me, thou Herenus quene," *Pity* 92, seems to suggest that Pity is the queen of the Erinyes; but the queen is Proserpina. Skeat (I: 461) suggests that only Pity can control the vindictiveness of vengeance, without proposing that Pity is Proserpina. John L. Lowes, on the other hand, suggests that Pity and Proserpina are the same person. Interpretation of Herenus in this line remains a problem. Juno and Imeneus do not attend the wedding of Tereus and Proigne, but the Furies, boding ill, do, *LGW* 2251–2252. [**Alete: Megera: Proserpina: Thesiphone**]

Herenus is a scribal variant of *Herynes,* the inversion of *Erinyes.* Latin initial *h* was not pronounced. *Herenus* appears in medial position, *Pity* 92. *Herynes* appears in medial position, *Tr* IV.22. Other variants are *Heremus, Herenius, Vertuous, Serenous.*

Dante, *Divine Comedy*, ed. and trans. C.S. Singleton, I, 1: 90–91; J.L. Lowes, "Chaucer and Dante." *MP* 14 (1917): 146–149; Ovid, *Met*, ed. and trans. F.J. Miller, II: 210–213; *Riverside Chaucer*, ed. L. Benson, 1078; Virgil, *Aeneid*, ed. and trans. H.R. Fairclough, I: 544–547.

HERMANNO. Heremianus, fl. third century A.D., was one of Zenobia's sons, whom she dressed in the regalia of the Roman emperors. Boccaccio gives this detail in *De casibus virorum illustrium* VIII.6.

The Monk says that Cenobia dressed her sons Hermanno and Thymalao in "kynges habit," *MkT* 2343–2346. **[Cenobia: Thymalao]**

Hermanno, the ME variant, appears in medial position, *MkT* 2345.

Boccaccio, *De casibus virorum illustrium*, ed. P.G. Ricci and V. Zaccaria, 678–682.

HERMENGYLD, HERMENGYLDES. Hermengyld is the constable's wife in *The Man of Law's Tale*. Chaucer may have borrowed the name from Trevet's *Les Chroniques Ecrites pour Marie d'Angleterre Fille d'Edward I* (early 14th century). In Gower's *Confessio Amantis* II.587–1612 the name is spelled *Hermyngheld, Hermyngeld*. The name was originally masculine. Hermangild was the oldest son of Leuvigild, the Visigothic king of Spain (late sixth century). He married Ingund, daughter of King Siebert, and converted to Catholicism under her influence. This infuriated his father, who belonged to the Arian branch of the church. Leuvigild attacked Hermangild's city several times, exiled him twice, and finally killed his son (Gregory of Tours, *The History of the Franks* IV.39; V.38; VI.18, 40, 43; VIII.28). In Trevet and Chaucer, Dame Hermengyld becomes a Christian.

Custance converts Dame Hermengyld, *MLT* 531–539. Hermengyld restores a blind man's sight, and her husband is converted to Christianity, *MLT* 561–567. The young knight, whose love Custance has refused, slays Dame Hermengyld, and Custance is accused of the murder, *MLT* 581–630. **[Alla: Custance: Donegild: Maurice]**

Hermengyld, a variant of Trevet's *Hermingyld*, appears in medial positions only, *MLT* 533, 535, 539, 562, 597, 600, 625, 627; *Hermengyldes*, the ME genitive case, appears once in medial position, *MLT* 595.

John Gower, *The Complete Works*, ed. G.C. Macaulay, II: 146–173; Gregory of Tours, *The History of the Franks*, trans. L. Thorpe, 233, 302–303, 348, 371–376, 456; M. Schlauch, "Trivet's Life of Constance." *S&A*, 169–171.

HERMES. Hermes Trismegistus ("Thrice Great Hermes") supposedly invented metals and alchemy. The body of his supposed work consists of fourteen tractates, collected into a single group c. A.D. 300. Medieval scholars considered him the father of philosophy; Albertus Magnus thought him a magician and composed a list of his works thought to be dangerous. The Middle English *Book of the Quinte Essence* calls Hermes "fadir of philosophris." Christine de Pizan uses Hermes as synonymous with "philosopher" throughout her *Epistle of Othea.*

Hermes is called "philosophres fader," *CYT* 1434. The Canon's Yeoman quotes from *Tractatus Aureus (The Golden Tract), CYT* 1345–1447. [Aristotile: Ballenus: Socrates]

Hermes occurs in final rhyming position, *CYT* 1434.

The Book of the Quinte Essence, ed. F.J. Furnivall, 16; Christine de Pizan, *The Epistle of Othea,* trans. S. Scrope, ed. C. Bühler; Hermes Trismegistus, *Corpus Hermeticum,* ed. A.D. Nock, trans. A.M.J. Festugière; *ibid., Hermetica; the Ancient Greek and Latin Writings which Contain Religious or Philosophic Writings* . . . , ed. and trans. W. Scott; L. Thorndike, *A History of Magic and Experimental Science,* II: 217.

HERMIONE: [HERMYON]

HERMYON. Hermione, the daughter of Helen and Menelaus, was married against her will to Pyrrhus, Achilles's son, although she had been previously betrothed to Orestes (*Heroides* VIII).

The Man of Law lists Hermyon's story among Chaucer's works, *MLI* 66, but there is no tale for her in *The Legend of Good Women* or anywhere else.

The shortened form appears in final rhyming position.

Ovid, *Her,* ed. and trans. G. Showerman, 98–107.

HERO: [ERRO]
HEROD: [HERODES[1,2]]

HERODES[1]. Called Herod the Great, he was king of Judaea from 37 B.C. to 4 B.C. He had several of his own family executed: his wife in 29 B.C. and her mother within a year; his two sons, Alexander and Aristobulus, in 7 B.C.; and his eldest son, Antipater, in 4 B.C. In that year he also had executed all the students who took part in a protest against his Romanization policies. Just before he died, there was a rumor that he had invited all the notable men to the temple in Jerusalem and had them executed, but this proved untrue. It is understandable that the story of the Slaughter of the Innocents should be told of Herod the Great (Matthew 2:1–18).

Absolon plays Herod on the high scaffold or stage in the hope of impressing Alison, *MillT* 3383–3384. The lines may possibly refer to the play *Herodes* or to a play about Herod, the Magi, and the Innocents. If the lines refer to Herod of the Passion plays, then Herod Antipas is meant (see next entry). [Absolon[2]: Herodes[2]]

Herodes, the ME form in accusative case, occurs medially, *MillT* 3384.

The Fleury Play of Herod, ed. T. Bailey; A.H.M. Jones, *The Herods of Judaea,* 1–155.

HERODES[2]. Herod Antipas became Tetrarch of Galilee upon the death of his father, Herod the Great, in 4 B.C. He married his niece, Herodias, who had been his brother's wife, a marriage that John the Baptist condemned. When Salome, his wife's daughter, danced at his birthday feast, Herod promised to give whatever she asked for. Her mother told her to ask for the Baptist's head. Herod was very sorry but could not take back his word. John was beheaded, and his head presented on a large dish to Salome, who then gave the head to Herodias (Matthew 14:1–11; Mark 6:17–28).

The Pardoner says that Herod, when drunk, commanded the slaying of John the Baptist, *PardT* 488–490. The Biblical accounts emphasize that Herod was sorry for Salome's request. The Prioress calls the Jews "cursed folk of Herodes all newe," *PrT* 574–575. The Prioress may be referring to the *Play of Herod*, which centers on Herod the Great and not on Herod Antipas (see above entry). [**Absolon²: Baptist John: Herodes¹**]

Herodes is nominative case in *PardT* 488 and genitive case in *PrT* 574.

The Fleury Play of Herod, ed. T. Bailey; A.H.M. Jones, *The Herods of Judaea,* 176–183.

HERSE: [HIERSE]
HERYNES: [HERENUS]
HESPERUS: [ESPERUS]
HESTER: [ESTER]
HEZEKIAH: [EZECHIAS]

HIERSE. Herse, Cecrop's daughter, was Mercury's beloved. Her sister Aglauros became jealous of her and incurred Athena's wrath (*Met* II.722–832; *OM* II.3777–3898, 4044–4076).

Troilus invokes Mercury's aid for Hierse's sake, *Tr* III.729–730. [**Aglawros: Mercurie**]

Hierse, the ME variant, occurs in medial position, *Tr* III.729.

Ovid, *Met,* ed. and trans. F.J. Miller, I: 110–119; *OM,* ed. C. de Boer, I, deel 15: 252–254, 257–258.

HIPPOCRATES: [YPOCRAS]
HIPPOLYTE: [IPOLITA]
HIPPOMEDON: [IPOMEDON]

HOGGE OF WARE. Hogge is the nickname of Roger the Cook, who accompanies the five guildsmen to Canterbury. [**Roger¹**]

Hogge appears in medial position, *CoT* 4336.

HOLOFERNES: [OLOFERNE]
HOMER: [OMER]

HORASTE is the fictitious lover, conjured up by Pandarus, of whom Troilus becomes jealous. This lover of Criseyde's does not appear in Boccaccio's *Il Filostrato* (1333–1339). Pandarus introduces this imaginary lover to extract oaths of fidelity from Criseyde, *Tr* III.792–805.

Horaste, a variant of *Orestes,* occurs in final rhyming position, *Tr* III.797, and medially, *Tr* III.806.

G.L. Kittredge, *Observations on the Language of Chaucer's Troilus,* 347.

HORN is the hero of the King Horn romances. The Anglo-Norman version is dated c. 1180; the Middle English *Horn Childe and Maiden Rimenhild,* in the southeast or Midland dialect, has been ascribed to the first half of the thirteenth century, c. 1225.

Sir Thopas surpasses the heroes of romance, even Horn, *Thop* 897–898. **[Thopas]**

King Horn, ed. J. Hall; D.M. Hill, "An Interpretation of *King Horn." Anglia* 75 (1957): 157–172; W.H. French, *Essays on* King Horn; W.H. Schofield, "The Story of Horn and Rimenhild." *PMLA* 18 (1903): 1–83.

HUBERD is the Friar on the pilgrimage, *Gen Prol* 208–269. Muscatine dismisses the suggestion that the Friar is named Huberd after St. Hubert, patron saint of hunters, and proposes an allusion to *Hubert l'escoufle,* the kite of Old French poems in the Renart tradition. The name Hubert had a dubious reputation in the medieval literary tradition, especially when associated with clerics and confessors.

Huberd, the ME development of French *Hubert,* appears in final rhyming position, *Gen Prol* 269.

C. Muscatine, "The Name of Chaucer's Friar." *MLN* 70 (1955): 169–172.

HUGELYN. Count Ugolino della Gherardesca, c. 1220–1289, was head of the Guelf party in Pisa. He betrayed his party to Ruggieri degli Ubaldini, the leader of the Ghibellines, who in turn revealed his treachery. Ugolino was imprisoned for eight months with his two sons and two grandsons, and all starved to death in the Tower of Famine in Pisa in March 1289. Dante places Ugolino and Ruggieri among the traitors in the second division of the Ninth Circle of hell, *Inf* XXXIII.1–90. Ugolino is frozen above Ruggieri in one hole, from which he gnaws on the archbishop's head.

The Monk's Tale of Ugolino follows Dante closely except for a few details. Chaucer gives Ugolini three little sons and omits the awful sight of Ugolino gnawing on Ruggieri's head, *MkT* 2407–2462. **[Roger[2]]**

Hugelyn, the ME variant and contraction of Italian *Ugolino,* appears in medial position, *MkT* 2407.

D.K. Fry, "The Ending of the *Monk's Tale." JEGP* 71 (1972): 355–368; T. Spencer, "The Story of Ugolino in Dante and Chaucer." *Speculum* 9 (1934): 295–301.

HUGH of Lincoln was an eight-year-old schoolboy whose body was found in a well near a Jew's house in 1255. The Jews were accused of his murder, and a fierce persecution was launched against them. G. Langmuir shows that John de Lexington, a canon of the cathedral of Lincoln, extorted a confession from a Jew named Koppin, which he then presented to the king. Koppin and eighteen others were executed. A cult grew up around "Little St. Hugh," but it was never officially sanctioned.

The Prioress invokes young Hugh of Lincoln at the end of her tale, *PrT* 684.

G. Langmuir, "The Knight's Tale of Young Hugh of Lincoln." *Speculum* 47 (1972): 459–482.

HUWE. Sir Huwe is used generically to indicate the sort of man who frequents "wenches," *FrT* 1356.

HYDRA: [IDRA]
HYMENAEUS: [IMENEUS]
HYPERMNESTRA: [YPERMESTRA]
HYPSIPYLE: [ISIPHILE]

I

IARBAS: [YARBAS]
IBN-RUSHD: [AVERROIS]
IBN-SINA: [AVYCEN]
ICARUS: [YKARUS]

IDRA, IDRE. The Hydra is the constellation the Water Snake with one hundred heads, lying in the southern hemisphere next to Corvus, The Raven (*Tetrabiblos*, I.9). The Hydra lived at Lerna and acted as sentinel to the border at the entry to the realm of the dead, while her brother, Cerberus, guarded the gates. Her fiery breath was her weapon, and when one head was cut off, two more sprang up in its place. In his second labor Hercules vanquished the Hydra. He killed her and dipped his arrows in her poisonous blood to make them deadly (*Met* IX.69, 192–193; *Aeneid* VI.576–577, VII.658).

The Water Snake does not appear as a constellation in Chaucer's works. It is called "the firy serpent venymus," *MkT* 2105, in the rehearsal of Hercules's labors. Chaucer seems to have misread *Aeneid* VI.288, where *flammisque* describes the Chimera. Lady Philosophy reminds Boethius that when one doubt is cut away, others spring up like the heads of Idra, the serpent that Hercules slew, *Bo* IV, *Prosa* 6.19–20. Hercules is celebrated for his labors, including the slaying of Idra the serpent, *Bo* IV, *Metr* 7.41–42. [Cancer: Draco: Ercules]

Idra is the ME variant, *Idre* the Italian variant, *Inf* IX.40. Latin initial *h* was not pronounced and it disappears in Italian.

Chaucer, *The Tales of Canterbury*, ed. R.A. Pratt, 214; Dante, *The Divine Comedy*, ed. and trans. C.S. Singleton, I, 1: 90–91; Ovid, *Met*, ed. and trans. F.J. Miller, II: 6–7, 16–17; Ptolemy, *Tetrabiblos*, ed. and trans. F.E. Robbins, 57.

IMENEUS, YMENEUS. Hymenaeus, son of Aphrodite and Bacchus, was the god of lawful sexual union (Martianus Capella, *The Marriage of Philology and Mercury* I.i).

Imeneus, Venus, and Bacchus are present at Januarie's wedding, *MerchT* 1730–1731. Chaucer mentions Martianus Capella's poem, *MerchT* 1732–35. Troilus thanks Imeneus for his happiness with Criseyde, *Tr* III.1258. The god's absence from the wedding of Progne and Tereus betokens disaster for the marriage, *LGW* 2250. [**Bachus: Januarie: Marcian: Proigne: Tereus: Venus**]

Imeneus, the ME variant, occurs in medial position, *Tr* III.1258; *Ymeneus*, a spelling variant, occurs initially, *MerchT* 1730, and medially, *LGW* 2250.

Martianus Capella, *De nuptiis Mercurii et Philologiae*, ed. A. Dick, 3; *ibid., The Marriage of Philology and Mercury*, trans. W.T. Stahl and R. Johnson, II: 3–4.

INNOCENT III, 1161–1216, was born at Gavignavo in Italy, and his father, the count of Segni, named him Lothario. When he became Pope in 1198, he took the name Innocent. He was one of the youngest popes in the history of the Roman Catholic Church. Before 1195, however, he had already written *De miseria condicionis humane (On the Misery of the Human Condition)*, also known as *De contemptu mundi (On Contempt for the World)*, a work in three books.

Most of the passages from *De miseria condicionis humane* occur in *The Man of Law's Tale*, constituting, in effect, Chaucer's translation. The Prologue, *MLP* 99–130, on the evils of poverty, paraphrases *De miseria condicionis humane, MCH* I.xv: *De miseria divitiis et pauperis* (ed. M. Maccarrone, 20–21). The section on sudden calamity, *MLT*, 421–424, comes from *MCH* I.xxii: *De inopinato dolore* (ed. Maccarrone, 29–30); on the unwisdom of too much wine, *MLT* 771–777, *MCH* II.xviii: *De ebrietate* (ed. Maccarrone, 53–54); on the evils that the desire for luxury causes men to commit, *MLT* 925–931, *MCH* II.xxi: *De luxuria* (ed. Maccarrone, 55); that no man is free from the sins of envy, pride, anger, passion, *MLT* 1132–1138, *MCH* I.xviii: *De miseria bonorum et malorum* (ed. Maccarrone, 25). Innocent says that the condition of the poor beggar is sorrowful and unhappy, *Mel* 1568 (*MCH* I.xv). Queen Alceste lists Chaucer's translation of Pope Innocent's *Wreched Engendrynge of Mankynde* among his works, *LGW G* 414–415.

The name appears once, in medial position, *LGW G* 415.

Innocent III, *De miseria condicionis humane*, ed. and trans. R.E. Lewis; *ibid., De miseria condicionis humane*, ed. and trans. M. Maccarrone; R.E. Lewis, "Chaucer's Artistic Use of Pope Innocent III's *De miseria humane condicionis* in the Man of Law's Prologue and Tale." *PMLA* 81 (1966): 485–492; *ibid.*, "Glosses to the *Man of Law's Tale* from Pope Innocent III's *De miseria humane conditionis*." *SP* 64 (1967): 1–16.

IOLE: [YOLE]

IPOLITA, YPOLITA. Hippolyte was the Amazon queen. Her country was never given an exact location but was thought to be near the Caspian or the Euxine Sea. The capture of her girdle was Hercules's sixth labor (*Met* IX.189). Theseus invaded the land of the Amazons, defeated the queen, and married her.

Ipolita is Theseus's wife in *The Knight's Tale* and has none of the characteristics of the warrior queen. Chaucer has condensed the greater part of Boccaccio's *Il Teseide* i and ii (1339–1341) and adds a "tempest at hir hoom comynge," *KnT* 884, which Boccaccio does not mention. Thomas Walsingham mentions a disturbance of water, "*maris commotio,*" when Anne of Bohemia landed at Calais, December 18, 1381, in his *Historia brevis Thomae Walsingham ab Edwardo primo ad Henricum quinto*. Perhaps Chaucer had this event in mind. **[Emelie: Theseus]**

The forms are variants of Boccaccio's *Ippolita*. *Ipolita* occurs once initially, *Anel* 36; *Ypolita* occurs once initially, *KnT* 2578; twice medially, *KnT* 977, 1685, and twice in final rhyming position, *KnT* 865, 881.

Boccaccio, *Tutte le opere*, ed. V. Branca, II: 253–326; J.L. Lowes, "The Tempest at Hir Hoom-comynge." *MLN* 19 (1904): 240–243; Ovid, *Met*, ed. and trans. F.J. Miller, II: 16; T. Walsingham, *Historia brevis Thomae Walsingham ab Edwardo primo ad Henricum quinto.*

IPOMEDON, YPOMEDOUN. Hippomedon was one of the Seven Chieftains who accompanied Adrastus to the war against Thebes. His death by drowning is told in *Thebaid* IX.522–539 (*Roman de Thèbes* 8601–9074).

The poet lists the names of the seven warriors who fought against Thebes, *Anel* 58. In her summary of the story, Cassandra describes Ypomedoun's death, *Tr* V.1502–1503. **[Adrastus: Amphiorax: Campaneus: Ethiocles: Hemonydes: Parthenope: Polymyte: Tydeus]**

Ipomedon, a variant of Boccaccio's *Ippomedone*, *Tes* II.11.2, occurs once medially, *Anel* 58; *Ypomedoun*, a variant of OF *Ypomedon*, also occurs once medially, *Tr* V.1502. Latin initial *h* was not pronounced.

Boccaccio, *Tutte le opere*, ed. V. Branca, II: 300; *Roman de Thèbes*, ed. L. Constans, I: 423–446; *Roman de Thèbes (The Story of Thebes)*, trans. J.S. Coley, 202–213; Statius, *Thebaid*, ed. and trans. J.H. Mozley, II: 290–293.

ISAAC: [YSAAC]
ISAIAH: [ISAYE]

ISAUDE, ISAWDE, YSOUDE. Yseult was an Irish princess, daughter of the king and queen of Ireland. King Mark of Cornwall fell in love with her hair, one strand of which he saw in the beak of a bird perched on his window, and sent his nephew Tristan to find the owner of the hair. Tristan reached Ireland and slew a dragon that was ravaging the countryside. Wounded in the fight, he was taken to the palace to be healed of his wounds by the queen and her daughter. The princess, Yseult, recognized him as the slayer (on a previous visit) of the Morholt, her uncle. As she admired his sword, she was able to match the piece taken from the Morholt's skull with the notch in Tristan's weapon. Although she had sworn vengeance on the Morholt's killer, when she saw Tristan's beauty as he lay in the bath, she could not carry out her vow. Her father commanded Yseult to accompany Tristan back to Cornwall to become Mark's bride, but on the voyage they accidentally drank the magic potion prepared by her mother for the wedding night and fell irrevocably in love. The first literary version of the story was composed c. 1150, possibly in Anglo-Norman; about 1160, the Welsh poet Thomas made it a tale of courtly love. A German version appeared about 1175 by Eilhart von Oberge and a French one about 1200 by Beroul. The version of Gottfried von Strassburg (fl. 1210) is based on Thomas's story.

Not even the beautiful Isawde can warn people against love, *HF* III.1793–1799. Isaude is love's martyr, *PF* 288–292. Ysoude must hide her beauty before Alceste's, *LGW F* 254–255, *LGW G* 208–209. **[Tristram]**

The forms are ME variants of OF *Yseut. Isaude* occurs once medially, *PF* 290; *Isawde* occurs once in final rhyming position, *HF* III.1796; *Ysoude* occurs twice medially, *LGW F* 254, *LGW G* 208.

Eilhart von Oberge, *Tristant*, trans. J.W. Thomas; Gottfried von Strassburg, *Tristan*, with the *Tristan* of Thomas, trans. A.T. Hatto; *Le Roman de Tristan par Thomas*, ed. J. Bédier.

ISAWDE: [ISAUDE]

ISAYE, YSAYE. Isaiah was a prophet in Israel, c. 740–700 B.C. Scholars think that the name may denote two distinct authors: one the prophet of Isaiah 1–55 and another the author of Isaiah 56–66, containing a number of separate poems of various dates.

The Parson quotes Ysaye on the fate of the rich in hell, *ParsT* 198–210; Isaiah 14:11. Christ's betrayal and death have fulfilled the words of Ysaye, *ParsT* 281, Isaiah 53:5. Isaye appears in a catalogue of dreamers, *HF* II.509–517. Here Chaucer refers to the visions either of Isaiah 1 or 6.

The forms are OF variants; *Isaye* appears once medially, *HF* II.509; *Ysaye* appears twice in the Parson's prose tale, *ParsT* 198, 281, pointing to the possible use of a French source, *La Somme des vices et des vertus* by Frere Lorens (1279), although Petersen discounts this.

K.O. Petersen, *On the Sources of* The Parson's Tale, 1–2.

ISCARIOT: [SCARIOT]
ISEULT: [ISAUDE]
ISIDORE: [YSIDRE]

ISIPHILE, YSIPHILE. Hypsipyle, daughter of King Toas, became queen of Lemnos. The women of the island had neglected the rites of Venus; in revenge the goddess caused their husbands to take concubines. The women avenged themselves by killing all the men on the island. Hypsipyle, however, saved her father by setting him adrift in a boat. When the Argonauts reached Lemnos, Hypsipyle entertained them royally and fell in love with Jason. Jason, however, betrayed her when he reached Colchis. There he promised to marry Medea and never returned to Lemnos (*Heroides* VI).

The Man of Law says that Chaucer has told the "pleinte of Isiphile," *MLI* 67. Jason has been false to Isiphile, *HF* I.400. She must bow before Alceste, the supreme example of wifely virtue, *LGW F* 266, *LGW G* 220. The full story appears in *LGW* 1467–1579. Chaucer lists his sources, *LGW* 1465, as Ovid, *Epistles (Heroides)* and Valerius Flaccus, *Argonauticon* (II.311–430). **[Jason: Ovide: Thoas: Valerius Flaccus]**

The forms are OF variants. *Isiphile* occurs once medially, *LGW* 1395, and twice in final rhyming position, *MLI* 67; *HF* I.400. *Ysiphile* occurs three times initially, *LGW F* 266, *LGW G* 220, *LGW* 1469, and once medially, *LGW* 1467.

Ovid, *Her*, ed. and trans. G. Showerman, 68–83; Valerius Flaccus, *Argonauticon*, ed. and trans. J.H. Mozley, 90–103.

ISIS: [YSIDIS]
ISOLDE: [ISAUDE]

ISOPE. Aesopus, fl. sixth century B.C., was a Thracian. He lived at Samos during the reign of Pharoah Amasis, c. 569–525 B.C. Herodotus says that he was a slave of Iadmon, a Samian (*Histories* II.134) and a contemporary of Sappho. Many fables are attributed to him.

Aesop's name is mentioned only once: Dame Prudence quotes him on the wisdom of not trusting new friends who were once enemies, *Mel* 1184. Neither Albertanus Brixiensis nor Chaucer himself is here quoting Aesop. The quotation is the last couplet from the tale "De bubonis et corvus" ("The Owl and the Crow"), Fable XI of the Italian fabulist Baldo, who flourished in the last half of the thirteenth century. At the beginning of his tales he had written *Incipit novus Esopus (Here begins the New Aesop)* and at the end, *Explicit novus Esopus (Here ends the New Aesop)*. The medieval collection bearing Aesop's name was composed mainly of the fables of Romulus, dated between A.D. 350 and 600 and based on the fables of Phaedrus (c. 15

B.C.–A.D. 50), a freedman of the Emperor Augustus. There are references to stories found also in Aesop, although the exact sources have not been identified. The fables of the Lion and the Bear, and the Lion, the Tiger, and the Fox, occur in *KnT* 1177–1180. J. Helterman points out that although Arcite knows the moral of the fables, he ignores their lessons. The Pear-Tree episode, without the elaborate incident concerning Pluto and Proserpina, *MerchT* 2149–2411, is based on an Aesopian fable.

The form is a pronunciation variant.

Albertanus Brixiensis, *Liber consolationis et consilii,* ed. Sundby, 49; Babrius and Phaedrus, *[The Fables of] Babrius and Phaedrus,* ed. and trans. B.E. Perry, LXXIII–XCVI; W. Caxton, *Caxton's Aesop,* ed. R.T. Lenaghan, 9–13; J. Helterman, "The Dehumanizing Metamorphoses of The Knight's Tale." *ELH* 38 (1971): 493–511; Herodotus, *Histories,* ed. and trans. A.D. Godley, I: 437; L. Hervieux, *Les fabulistes Latins,* V: 339–378; *Riverside Chaucer,* ed. L. Benson, 830; N.A. von Kriesler, "An Aesopic Allusion in *The Merchant's Tale.*" *ChauR* 6 (1971–1972): 30–37.

ISRAEL is the name the angel gave to Jacob after they had wrestled together (Genesis 32:28–29). The name was later given to the land of Canaan after the Israelites settled it.

The Monk says that Samson ruled Israel as a judge for twenty years, *MkT* 2055–2065; he also mentions that Nabugodonosor gelded the fairest children of the royal blood of Israel, *MkT* 2143–2153. At the end of *The Legend of Lucrece* the poet extols the steadfastness of women, saying that Christ himself pointed out that he had not found in Israel as great faith as he found in a woman, *LGW* 1879–1882. In Matthew 15:20–28 Jesus commends the Syro-Phoenician woman for her faith; in Matthew 8:10 Jesus says that he had not found as great faith in Israel as he found in the Roman centurion. The passage in *LGW* 1879–1882 seems to be a conflation of the two statements. **[Daniel: Jacob: Nabugodonosor]**

Israel occurs three times in medial positions only, *MkT* 2060, 2152; *LGW* 1880.

ITHACUS: [YTACUS]

IULO. Iulus is another name for Ascanius, son of Aeneas and Creusa (*Aeneid* I.267, 288). Virgil says that Iulus was Ascanius's *cognomen,* or family name, from whom the family of Julius Caesar was supposed to have descended.

Chaucer says that Iulo is another son of Eneas, *HF* I.177. **[Ascanius]**

Iulo, Latin ablative singular of *Iulus,* occurs in final rhyming position.

Virgil, *Aeneid,* ed. and trans. H.R. Fairclough, I: 258–259, 260–261.

IULUS: [IULO]
IVES: [YVE]

IXION, YXION, king of the Lapiths, was the son of Phlegyas. Jupiter invited him to eat at his table, but Ixion proved ungrateful and planned to seduce Juno. Jupiter, knowing his intentions, shaped a false Juno out of a cloud, with whom Ixion took his pleasure. Jupiter surprised him in the act, then bound him to a fiery wheel rolling ceaselessly about the sky (*Met* IV.461; *OM* IV.3821–3963; *RR* 19275–19280).

Yxion forgets his torment at the wheel when Orpheus plays in the Underworld, *Bo* III, *Metr* 12.37–38. Troilus turns on his bed in fury like Ixion turning in hell, *Tr* V.212. Chaucer omits the sharp-edged wheel with heavy spikes mentioned in the *Roman de la Rose*. [**Cesiphus: Tantale**]

Ovid, *Met,* ed. and trans. F.J. Miller, I: 210–211; *OM,* ed. C. de Boer, II, deel 21: 92–95; *RR,* ed. E. Langlois, IV: 262; *RR,* trans. C. Dahlberg, 318.

J

JACK: [JAKKE]

JACOB was the younger son of Isaac and Rebecca. At his mother's instigation, he cheated his brother Esau of his birthright. He obtained the blessing from blind Isaac by disguising himself as Esau. Because Esau swore to kill him, Rebecca sent Jacob away to her brother Laban. Jacob fell in love with Laban's daughter Rachel and served Laban seven years for her. But Laban substituted his older daughter Leah at the wedding service. Then Jacob served Laban an additional seven years for Rachel. Jacob received the name Israel after wrestling with the angel of the Lord at Peniel (Genesis 27–32).

Dame Alys, in her argument for remarriage, says that Jacob, a holy man, had more than two wives, *WBP* 56. Jerome notes that Jovinian, in his argument against virginity and chastity, says that holy men, Abraham and Jacob, have had more than one wife, *Epistola adversus Jovinianum (Letter Against Jovinian)*, I.5 (*PL* 23: 215–216). Januarie recalls that Rebecca gave Jacob good advice, *MerchT* 1362–1365. Rebecca is among *femmes de bon conseil*, "women of good counsel," in *Liber consolationis et consilii (The Book of Consolation and Counsel)* V, by Albertanus Brixiensis (1246). Dame Prudence reminds Melibee that Rebecca gave Jacob good counsel, *Mel* 1097. God blessed Laban because of Jacob's service, *ParsT* 443. [**Abraham: Alisoun³: Israel: Laban: Lia: Rachel: Rebecca**]

Albertanus Brixiensis, *Liber consolationis*, ed. T. Sundby, 17; Lea J. Henkin, "Jacob and the Hooly Jew." *MLN* 55 (1940): 254–259.

JACOBUS DE VORAGINE: [JACOBUS JANUENSIS]

JACOBUS JANUENSIS, also known as Jacobus de Voragine, was born c. 1128 or 1230 in Varaggio, not far from Genoa. He entered the Order of Preachers in 1244 and became Father Provincial of Lombardy in 1267. In 1288 he was elected archbishop of Genoa, but he refused the office. Again in 1292 he was elected, and this time he consented to take office. He died in 1298 and was buried in Genoa. He called his collection of saints' lives *Legenda sanctorum,* but by Caxton's time the title had become *Legenda aurea (The Golden Legend).* The stories tell of saints who have died heroic deaths. Caxton translated and printed the collection in 1483.

Chaucer gives the etymologies of St. Cecilia's name from Jacobus Januensis, *Legenda, SNT* 85–112, taken from *Legenda aurea* CLXIX. G.H. Gerould suggests that the differences between Chaucer's version and that of de Voragine may indicate that Chaucer had a fuller version or a different version of the saint's life. Chaucer may also have used the *Passio S. Caeciliae,* which exists in several texts. **[Cecile]**

G.H. Gerould, "The Second Nun's Prologue and Tale." *S&A,* 664–684; Jacobus de Voragine, *The Golden Legend,* trans. G. Ryan and H. Ripperger; *ibid., Legenda aurea,* ed. Th. Graesse; S.L. Reames, *The "Legenda Aurea": A Re-examination of its Paradoxical History.*

JAKKE[1]. Jack is a common name, and in Chaucer's time it was a popular name for a villager.

Alison chases Absolon from her window, calling him "Jakke fool," *MillT* 3708. The Friar uses the name to denote any village lad, *FrT* 1357.

Jakke, the ME variant, appears in medial position.

JAKKE[2]. Jack Straw was one of the leaders of the Peasants' Revolt of 1381. The revolt began in the counties of Kent, Sussex, Essex, and Bedford. Wat Tyler, a tiler of roofs, and the priest John Ball were the other leaders. On Monday before Corpus Christi, 1381, John Ball, Wat Tyler, Jack Straw, and sixty thousand people marched on London to speak with King Richard II and to gain their freedom from serfdom. At Canterbury they invaded the cathedral, damaged it, and wrecked the apartments of the archbishop. At Rochester they forced Sir John Newton to join them. Then they dispatched him to speak with the king on their behalf at the Tower. The king sent a reply that he would speak with the rebels on Thursday morning if they came down to the river Thames. On the Feast of Corpus Christi, the king met the rebels at Rotherhithe. But the Earl of Salisbury told the assembly that they were not properly dressed to speak to the king, and the king returned to the Tower. Thereupon the rebels set out for London, destroying several fine houses, and released the prisoners in the king's prison at Marshalsea. On Friday the king again met the rebels in a meadow at Mile End. In the meantime, Tyler, Straw, and Ball murdered the Archbishop of Canterbury, the Grand Prior of St. John, and a Dominican friar attached to the Duke of

Lancaster. The king agreed to the demands for freedom at Mile End and ordered thirty secretaries to draw up the letters that very day. Half the people returned home, but the other half remained to plunder and terrorize the London citizens. The King met the remaining rabble at Smithfield. Here Tyler tried to assault the king and was instantly killed. Later, Jack Straw and John Ball were found hiding in a ruin. They were executed and their heads, with Tyler's, were fixed on London Bridge. The peasants who had gone home were later punished (Froissart, *Chronicles* II.73–76).

The noise of the people and animals as they chase the fox is like that of Jack Straw and his company as they attacked the Flemish Quarter, *NPT* 3394–3397.

J. Froissart, *Chronicles*, ed. and trans. J. Jolliffe, 236–252; R.H. Hilton, *Bond Men Made Free; ibid., The English Peasantry in the Later Middle Ages.*

JAME (saint). James the Greater, fl. first century A.D., was the son of Zebedee and Salome and brother of John (Matthew 17:56). According to tradition, he preached Christianity in Spain and was put to death in A.D. 44 when he returned to Judaea. His most famous shrine is at Compostella, although the church has disputed the genuineness of the relics there. The shrine attracted many pilgrims during the Middle Ages, and in ecclesiastical art the saint is shown with the pilgrim's hat and scallop shell (*NCE* 7: 806). Jacobus de Voragine includes a Life of St. James in *Legenda aurea*, LXVII.

Alys of Bath has been to the shrine at Compostella, *Gen Prol* 466. "By seint Jame" appears as a rhyming tag, *RvT* 4264; *WBP* 312; *FrT* 1443; *ShipT* 355; *HF* II.885. The Clerk quotes from the Letter of St. James 1:13, *ClT* 1154; Dame Prudence quotes from James 1:5, *Mel* 1119; from James 1:4, *Mel* 1517. The quotation from James, *Mel* 1676, is from Seneca, *Letter* 94.46. Prudence quotes James 2:13, *Mel* 1869. The Parson quotes James 1:14, *ParsT* 348. **[Senec]**

Jame, the ME variant, occurs once medially, *Gen Prol* 466, and five times in final rhyming position as a rhyming tag.

S. Delany, "Doer of the Word: The Epistle of St. James as a Source for Chaucer's *Manciple's Tale.*" *ChauR* 17 (1982–1983): 250–254; Jacobus de Voragine, *GL*, trans. G. Ryan and H. Ripperger, 368–377; *ibid., LA*, ed. Th. Graesse, 295–303.

JAMES: [JAME]

JANEKYN is the blond young man who is apprenticed to Dame Alys's fourth husband. He accompanies Alys on her visits and shopping expeditions around the city, and these excursions make her husband intensely jealous, *WBP* 303–306. Alys lies brazenly to her husband, and she calls Janekyn and her niece to witness that her lies are truth, *WBP* 379–383. **[Alisoun³: Jankyn²]**

Janekyn is a variant of *Jankyn*, a diminution of the name *John*. It appears in final rhyming position, *WBP* 303, and in medial position, *WBP* 383.

JANICLE, JANICULA is Griselda's father in *The Clerk's Tale*. In Petrarch's Latin story, *De obedientia ac fide uxoria mythologia*, Griselda's father is Ianicole, and in the anonymous French translation *Le Livre Griseldis* he is called Janicole. He has no dramatic function in *The Clerk's Tale*; he is the recipient of all Griselda's love before she marries Walter, and he covers her with her old cloak when she returns to him in nothing but her smock. **[Griselde: Walter]**

The spelling varies according to the number of stresses in the line. *Janicula* occurs twice initially, *CIT* 208, 304; *Janicle* appears twice in medial positions, *CIT* 404 and 632.

J.B. Severs, "*The Clerk's Tale*." *S&A*, 296–331.

JANKYN[1], the diminutive of John, was used sometimes as the derisive name for a priest. When the good Parson upbraids Harry Bailly for swearing, Bailly calls him "Jankyn" and suspects him of being a Lollard, *MLT* 1172. **[Bailly]**

JANKYN[2] is a student from Oxford who has left the university and gone to Bath. There he boards with Alisoun, close woman friend of Dame Alys, *WBP* 525–559. Alys tells how she courts and marries Jankyn, *WBP* 543–631. He forbids her to visit her friends; he reads to her from his "Book of Wikked Wyves," a collection of antifeminist tracts bound together in one volume, which he calls "Valerie and Theophraste," *WBP* 641–671. This anthology includes Jerome's *Epistola adversus Jovinianum* (*Letter Against Jovinian,* late fourth century), Walter Map's *Dissuasio Valerii ad Rufinum philosophum ne uxorem ducat* (*Valerius's Dissuasion of Rufus Not to Marry,* c. 1180–1183), *Aureolus liber Theophrasti de nuptiis* (*Theophrastus's Golden Book on Marriage*), now lost, treatises by Tertullian, perhaps his *De exhortatione castitatis* (*On the Exhortation to Chastity*), *De monogamia* (*On Monogamy*), *De pudicitia* (*On Modesty*), Ovid's *Ars amatoria* (*The Art of Love*), *The Parables of Solomon,* the letters of Heloise and Abelard, and treatises on gynecology by the Salernian physician Trotula.

It is not quite clear from Alys's account that Jankyn the apprentice and Jankyn the student are two people. The name denoted the typical priest-lover and was coupled with Alison, a pun on *Aleison* from the Mass, as in the refrain from the popular lyric:

'Kyrie,' so 'kyrie,'
Iankyn syngyt merie,
    with 'aleyson.'

Chaucer's mating of Jankyn with Alison follows popular tradition **[Alisoun[3]: Crisippus: Janekyn: Jerome: Jovinian: Tertulan: Theofraste: Trotula: Valerie]**

Jankyn appears in medial positions only, *WBP* 548, 595, 628, 713.

R.A. Pratt, "Jankyn's Book of Wikked Wyves: Antimatrimonial Propaganda in the Universities." *AnM* 3 (1962): 5–27; R.H. Robbins, ed., *Secular Lyrics of the XIVth and XVth Centuries*, 21.

JANKYN[3] is the squire at the castle who carves meat at his lord's table and who solves the riddle of the fart, *SumT* 2243–2286. He divides the fart into twelve parts and wins a new robe for this feat, *SumT* 2287–2294.

Jankyn appears in medial positions only, *SumT* 2288, 2293.

JANUARIE is the old knight of Lombardy who commits the folly of marrying a young wife, May, in *The Merchant's Tale*. He says that he does not want a thirty-year-old wife, who would know too much of "Wade's Boat," *MerchT* 1421–1426. Januarie is a type of the *senex amans*, or "old lover." He marries May, who is not quite twenty, and she is unfaithful to him with Damian in the pear tree. **[Damyan: Justinus: May: Placebo: Pluto: Proserpina]**

Januarie never appears initially; the name appears thirty-four times in medial positions, *MerchT* 1393, 1478, 1566, 1579, 1586, 1724, 1750, 1788, 1801, 1821, 1859, 1886, 1895, 1920, 1946, 1956, 2008, 2013, 2023, 2042, 2054, 2056, 2065, 2069, 2102, 2107, 2118, 2134, 2156, 2186, 2214, 2218, 2355, 2412; and five times in final rhyming position, *MerchT* 1695, 1805, 1906, 2320, 2417.

E. Brown, Jr., "Chaucer and a Proper Name: Januarie in *The Merchant's Tale*." *Names* 31 (1982): 79–87; M.J. Donovan, "Chaucer's January and May: Counterparts in Claudian." *Chaucerian Problems and Perspectives*, ed. E. Vasta and Z.P. Thundy, 59–69.

JANUARY: [JANUARIE]

JANUS is exclusively a Latin deity, connected with the outer door of the house. He has two faces, one to look inward and the other to look outward. Ovid calls him the custodian of the universe, the opener and fastener of all things, looking inward and outward from the gate *(Fasti* I.117). Macrobius says that his two faces indicate wisdom, since Janus knows the past and foresees the future *(Saturnalia* I.7.20).

The time is January, *FranklT* 1252–1255, for Janus sits by the fire with double beard and drinks wine from his bugle horn. In the calendar of *Les Belles Heures of Jean, Duke of Berry*, folio 2, Janus is represented by two figures, one old, one young, and the old man drinks from a bugle horn. Pandarus invokes Janus, god of entry, as he enters Criseyde's palace, *Tr* II.77.

The name appears once initially, *FranklT* 1252, and once medially, *Tr* II.77.

Les Belles Heures of Jean, Duke of Berry, folio 2; Macrobius, *Saturnalia,* trans. P.V. Davies, 68.

JASON, JASOUN. Jason, son of Aeson, successfully brought the Golden Fleece of the Ram of Phrixus from Colchis to Thessaly. The story of the expedition was one of the favorites from late antiquity through the medieval period. Guido de Columnis, *Historia destructionis Troiae,* devotes Books I–III to the adventures of Jason and his men. Dante places Jason among the seducers, in Circle VIII of Hell, *Inf* XVIII.86–87. Jason appears in the *blazon des faulse amours, RR* 13173–13280. Machaut mentions his betrayal of Medea, *Le jugement dou roy de Navarre,* 2770–2804; in *Confessio Amantis* V.3247–4257 the Confessor tells the story of Jason and Medea to illustrate the sin of perjury among lovers, citing Ovid as a source (*Met* VII.1–403; *OM* VII.250–1506).

Jason is a false lover every time he is named, *MLI* 74; *SqT* 549–551; *BD* 330–334, 724–727; *HF* I.395–400; *LGW F* 266; *LGW G* 220. Jason is the "rote of false lovers," *LGW* 1368–1377, 1389–1393. He is extraordinarily beautiful, *LGW* 1548–1608, but a devourer of love, *LGW* 1580–1583, a bottomless well, *LGW* 1584–1585. Chaucer seems to have had a particular dislike for Jason. Most villains are false to one woman, but he is false to two. The narrator of the "Legend of Hypsiphile and Medea" challenges him to a duel: "Have at thee, Jasoun," *LGW* 1383. Jason swears to be true to Medea before the gods, but he is chief traitor in love, *LGW* 1629–1659. [**Ercules: Eson: Isiphile: Medea: Pelleus**]

Jason occurs five times initially, *SqT* 549; *LGW* 1451, 1589, 1611; thirty-one times in medial positions, *MLI* 74, *SqT* 548; *HF* I.400, 401; *LGW* 1383, 1394, 1402, 1410, 1415, 1419, 1440, 1454, 1472, 1480, 1499, 1501, 1513, 1524, 1544, 1548, 1559, 1570, 1576, 1585, 1601, 1603, 1620, 1636, 1651, 1654, 1667; and once in final rhyming position, *BD* 330; *Jasoun* occurs seven times, in final rhyming position only, *BD* 727; *LGW F* 266, *LGW G* 220; *LGW* 1368, 1420, 1580, 1663.

Dante, *The Divine Comedy,* ed. and trans. C.S. Singleton, I, 1: 188–189; John Gower, *The Complete Works,* ed. G.C. Macaulay, III: 35–62; Guido delle Colonne, *Guido de Columnis: HDT,* ed. N.E. Griffin, 3–33; *ibid., HDT,* trans. M.E. Meek, 1–32; Guillaume de Machaut, *Oeuvres,* ed. E. Hoepffner, I: 232–233; Ovid, *Met,* ed. and trans. F.J. Miller, I: 342–371; *OM,* ed. C. de Boer, III, deel 30: 21–50; *RR,* ed. E. Langlois, IV: 9–13; *RR,* trans. C. Dahlberg, 228–229; E.F. Shannon, *CRP,* 208.

[**JEAN DE MEUN.**] Jean de Meun or Jean Clopinel was born at Meung-sur-Loire, just outside Orleans. He says that he was born about the time of the death of Guillaume de Lorris, thought to be between 1225 and 1240, and that he worked on *Le Roman de la Rose* about forty years after Guillaume's death. His section of the poem was completed between 1276 and 1280. Jean also translated the Letters of Heloise and Abelard and used them in his section of the *Roman, RR* 8759–8832, in the Jealous Husband's arguments against marriage. He translated Boethius's *De consolatione philosophiae* into French as *Li Livres de confort de philosophie,* which Chaucer used for his translation into Middle English. He died about 1305.

Jean takes up Guillaume's poem at line 4059 in a radically different tone. Reason remonstrates with the Lover and explains the functions of Fortune, Friendship, and Wealth and, during her discourse, names the sexual organs, *RR* 6928–7184. This is one of the passages to which Christine de Pizan strenuously objects in her first letter to Jean de Montreuil (*La Querelle de la Rose* 48). Friend comforts the Lover; he describes how women have impoverished him; he longs for the Golden Age, which he describes; he advises the Lover on how to deceive Jealousy and the guards of the Castle where the Rose is imprisoned. He counsels the Lover that success in love depends on deceit and guile, and he discourses on the Jealous Husband. This episode includes quotations from Theophrastus's *Liber aureolus de nuptiis (The Golden Book of Marriage),* stories of Lucretia, Hercules and Dejanira, Samson and Delilah, quotations from Juvenal and from Walter Map's *Dissuasio Valerii ad Rufinum philosophum ne uxorem ducat (Valerius's Dissuasion of Rufus Not to Marry,* c. 1181–1183), *RR* 8245–9932. The God of Love and his barons arrive to help the Lover assault the Castle of Jealousy. The God of Love praises Guillaume's section of the poem and foretells Jean de Meun's birth and his continuation of the story, *RR* 10495–10678. The barons capture the Old Woman, Fair Welcome's guardian, give her a chaplet of flowers for him; she hurries to him and, when she has delivered the gift, discourses to him on love, *RR* 12541–14547, the bulk of which is antifeminist. This passage influenced Chaucer in his conception of the Wife of Bath; the section on table manners appears in Madame Eglentyne's portrait, *Gen Prol* 128–136. The section also includes stories about Dido, Phyllis, Paris and Oenone, Medea, Jason, Circe, lectures on the wiles of lovers, on cosmetics, influenced by Ovid's *Ars amatoria.* Love's barons again attack the Castle but fail to take it. He sends an embassy to Venus, but she is out hunting; as soon as she receives the message, however, she comes to the rescue, *RR* 15627–15890. Dame Nature, hearing the oath, laments the state of things and confesses to her priest, Genius, *RR* 15891–19434. Genius leaves Dame Nature at her forge and flies away to the God of Love. Vested by Love in a silk chasuble, Genius mounts a platform and preaches on the text, "Wax and multiply," giving examples from stories about Cadmus, the Fates (Atropos, Clotho, Lachesis), Jupiter's castration of Saturn, and he recaps the poem from the beginning, *RR* 19439–20703. Comforted by the sermon, Love's barons again assault the Castle. Venus arrives and, throwing one of her firebrands at the Castle, turns the battle in Love's favor as the Castle goes up in flames, *RR* 21228–21258. The inhabitants flee from the burning tower, and the Lover gains the Rose. The poem ends with a very explicit sexual embrace, *RR* 21259–21780.

Jean de Meun's section of the poem was the subject of a quarrel between Christine de Pizan, Jean Gerson, Jean de Montreuil, and the Brothers Col (Pierre and Gontier). The series of letters they exchanged, dated 1400–1402, form the basis for *La Querelle de la Rose (The Rose's Quarrel)*.

The description of Madame Eglentyne's table manners, *Gen Prol* 127–136, is influenced by *RR* 13408–13432. Much of Dame Alys's Prologue is indebted to the passage on the Jealous Husband and the Old Woman, as follows: *WBP* 1–3 correspond to *RR* 13006–13010; *WBP* 207–210 to *RR* 13269–13272; *WBP* 357–361 to *RR* 14393–14394; *WBP* 393 recalls *RR* 13838–13840; *WBP* 467–468 recall *RR* 13452–13463; *WBP* 469–479 recall *RR* 12924–12948; *WBP* 516–524 recall *RR* 13697–13708; *WBP* 534–542 correspond to *RR* 16347–16364; *WBP* 555–558 to *RR* 13522–13528; *WBP* 618 to *RR* 13336; *WBP* 624–626 to *RR* 8516–8600; *WBP* 662 recalls *RR* 9980. The Loathly Lady's speech to her new husband on poverty and gentillesse, *WBT* 1109–1123, 1133–1164, contains many ideas from *RR* 18607–18634, 18677–18695. [**Alisoun³: Eglentyne: Guillaume de Lorris**]

V.L. Dedeck-Héry, "Boethius' *De Consolatione* by Jean de Meun." *MS* 14 (1952): 165–275; *ibid.*, "Jean de Meun et Chaucer, traducteurs de la *Consolatione* de Boece." *PMLA* 52 (1937): 967–991; D.S. Fansler, *Chaucer and the Roman de la Rose*; J. Fleming, *The* Roman de la Rose: *A Study in Allegory and Iconography*; Guillaume de Lorris and Jean de Meun, *Le Roman de la Rose*, ed. F. Lecoy; *ibid.*, *Le Roman de la Rose*, ed. E. Langlois; *ibid.*, *The Romance of the Rose*, trans. C. Dahlberg; E. Hicks, *Le Débat sur le Roman de la Rose*; Jean de Meun, *Traduction de la première épître de Pierre Abelard*, éditée par C. Charnier (Paris: 1934); *La Querelle de la Rose: Letters and Documents*, ed. and trans. J.L. Baird and J.R. Kane; R. Sutherland, ed., *The Romaunt of the Rose and Le Roman de la Rose: A Parallel-Text Edition*; C.C. Willard, *Christine de Pizan: Her Life and Works*.

JEPTE. Jeptha was a judge in Israel in the eleventh century B.C. After the defeat of the Ammonites, Jeptha vowed to sacrifice to God the first thing he met on his return home. To his great distress, his daughter ran to meet him. When he told her of his vow, she begged for time to weep and bewail her death while still a virgin (Judges 11:1–40).

Virginia asks her father for leisure to bewail her death, just as Jepte gave his daughter permission to complain before he slew her, *PhysT* 238–244. Virginia blesses God that she will die a maid, while Jeptha's daughter is quite upset that she must die a virgin. The passage illustrates the Physician's ignorance of the Bible, *Gen Prol* 438, for he studies the Bible very little. [**Virginia: Virginius**]

The form is the medieval Latin variant and appears medially, *PhysT* 240.

R.L. Hoffman," Jeptha's Daughter and Chaucer's Virginia." *ChauR* 2 (1967): 20–31.

JEPTHA: [JEPTE]
JEREMIAH: [JEREMIE]

JEREMIE, JEREMYE. Jeremiah, the prophet of Israel, began to preach in 627 B.C. The Book of Jeremiah and the Book of Lamentations are attributed to him (*NCE* VII: 867).

The Pardoner quotes from Jeremiah 4:2, on swearing false oaths, *PardT* 635. The Parson begins his sermon with a text from Jeremiah 4:16, *ParsT* 75. Although the Parson names the prophet as his source, *ParsT* 189, he quotes I Kings 2:30. The passage on swearing false oaths, Jeremiah 4:2, appears in *ParsT* 592.

Jeremye, the English variant, appears in final rhyming position, *PardT* 635; *Jeremie/Jeremye* occur in the Parson's prose tale.

JEROME (saint), c. A.D. 341–430, was born in Stridon in Illyria, between Dalmatia and Pannonia, and died in Bethlehem. He studied under Aelius Donatus, the foremost teacher of his day, and later in Treves, one of the famous centers of learning in the fourth century. In A.D. 342 Pope Damasus urged Jerome to revise the Latin scriptures. While in Rome, Jerome founded the first convent there and presided over it as father confessor. He left Rome in 385 when it was thought that he wanted to be pope after Damasus died in 384. He continued his revision of the scriptures in Bethlehem, and his work formed the basis of the Latin Vulgate. He is one of the four Latin Doctors of the Church, the others being Augustine, Ambrose, and Gregory the Great. In his letters and treatises Jerome appears as an irritable cleric, gifted in the rhetoric of abuse, especially on the subject of heresy. His celebrated treatises are *Liber de viris illustribus ecclesiasticis* (*PL* 23: 602–726), which contains a life of Seneca; *Epistola adversus Jovinianum* (*PL* 23: 211–338); *Apologia adversus libros Rufini* (*PL* 23: 397–472); *Dialogos adversus Pelagianos* (*PL* 23: 495–590); a short letter on virginity, *Epistola ad Eustochium de virginitate* (*PL* 22: 397–398). Jacobus de Voragine gives a life of Jerome in *Legenda aurea* CXLVI.

The treatise *Epistola adversus Jovinianum,* or *The Letter Against Jovinian,* was an answer to Jovinian's advocacy of marriage for the clergy and his denigration of virginity. It forms part of Jankyn's "Book of Wikked Wyves," *WBP* 673–675. Alys calls Jerome a cardinal, *WBP* 674. The illuminator of *The Hours of Catherine of Cleves* paints Jerome in a cardinal's hat and robes (folio 118). Jerome is the author of a proverb linking the devil with idleness, *SNP* 6–7. Jehan de Vigny attributes the proverb to Jerome in the introduction to his French translation of *Legenda aurea.*

The Parson quotes Jerome seven times in his sermon, three of which appear in the probable source for the Tale. On the Judgment, *ParsT* 159, the *Summa casuum poenitentiae,* by Raymund de Pennaforte, has a marginal gloss that names Jerome as the source. The Parson remarks, "Jerome says . . .," *ParsT* 174, where Pennaforte has "Augustine ait. . . ." The quotation on lust, *ParsT* 345, comes from Jerome, *Epistola XXII ad Eustochium de virginitate* 7 (*PL* 23: 398). The quotation from Jerome, *ParsT* 657, has not been identified, and that in *ParsT* 933 comes from Cyprian, *De habitu virginum* XIII

(*PL* 4: 464). The quotation from Jerome on lust in marriage, *ParsT* 904, appears in *Epistola adversus Jovinianum (Letter Against Jovinian)* I.49 (*PL* 23: 293–294). The quotation on the virtues of fasting, *ParsT* 1047, has not been traced in Jerome's works. It is attributed to him in Pennaforte, *Summa casuum poenitentiae*. The God of Love mentions Jerome as a writer on chaste women, *LGW G* 281–287, a reference to *Epistola adversus Jovinianum*. [**Crisippus: Jovinian: Tertulan: Theofraste: Valerye[1]**]

Jerome occurs once in final rhyming position, *WBP* 674; in the prose of *The Parson's Tale* 159, 174, 657, 904, 1047; and twice in medial positions, *LGW G* 281, 284.

The Hours of Catherine of Cleves, introd. and commentary by J. Plummer; Jacobus de Voragine, *GL,* trans. G. Ryan and H. Ripperger, 587–592; *ibid., LA,* ed. Th. Graesse, 653–658; Jerome, *Select Letters of St. Jerome,* ed. and trans. F.A.W. Wright; J.N.D. Kelly, *Jerome;* K.O. Petersen, *On the Sources of the Parson's Tale,* 12–13; R.A. Pratt, "Saint Jerome in Jankyn's Book of Wikked Wyves." *Criticism* 5 (1963): 316–322; D.S. Silvia, Jr., "Glosses to the *Canterbury Tales* from St. Jerome's *Epistola adversus Jovinianum*." *SP* 62 (1965): 28–39; *Riverside Chaucer,* ed. L. Benson, 963.

JESUS CHRIST: [CRIST]
JESUS OF SYRACH: [JHESU SYRAK]
JHESU CRIST: [CRIST]

JHESU SYRAK. Jesus of Sirach, fl. 2nd century B.C., was a professional scribe who taught in a school for young men. His book, written in Hebrew c. 180 B.C., was translated by his grandson into Greek sometime after 132 B.C. Its Latin title is Ecclesiasticus, known in English as The Book of Jesus of Sirach (*NCE* XIII: 257).

Alys of Bath refers to Ecclesiasticus 25:25, *WBP* 651. Pluto mentions Jesus, and the gloss *filius Syrach* has been added, *MerchT* 2250, a reference to Ecclesiasticus, 9:1–13, 26:5–15. The quotations in *The Tale of Melibee* appear in Chaucer's sources, *Liber consolationis et consilii* by Albertanus Brixiensis (1246) and *Le livre de Melibée et de Dame Prudence* by Renaud de Louens (after 1336). The reference at *Mel* 995 is not from Jesus of Sirach but from Proverbs 17:22. The old wise man quotes from Ecclesiasticus 22:6, *Mel* 1045. Several characters quote Jesus of Syrach even when they credit Solomon. Melibee quotes Ecclesiasticus but cites Solomon in the following passages: Ecclesiasticus 32:6, *Mel* 1047; Ecclesiasticus 25:30, *Mel* 1059; Ecclesiasticus 32: 20–22, *Mel* 1060; Ecclesiasticus 19: 8, 9, *Mel* 1141; Ecclesiasticus 6:15, *Mel* 1159; Ecclesiasticus 6:14, *Mel* 1161. Dame Prudence cites Solomon, but Ecclesiasticus is her source: Ecclesiasticus 6:6, *Mel* 1167; Ecclesiasticus 8:17, *Mel* 1173; Ecclesiasticus 12:10, *Mel* 1186; Ecclesiasticus 60:28, *Mel* 1571; Ecclesiasticus 300:17, *Mel* 1572; Ecclesiasticus 33:27, *Mel* 1589; Ecclesiasticus 12:12, *Mel* 1639; Ecclesiasticus 3:27, *Mel* 1671; Ecclesiasticus 33: 19–20, *Mel* 1754. Melibee's adversaries claim they quote Solomon, but they too quote Ecclesiasticus 6:5, *Mel* 1740. The Nun's Priest quotes Ecclesiasticus 12:10, 11, 16, in *NPT* 3329–3330. **[Salomon]**

Albertanus Brixiensis, *Liber consolationis et consilii (The Book of Consolation and Counsel)*, ed. T. Sundby, 4, 10, 40; J.B. Severs, "The Tale of Melibeus." *S&A*, 568–614.

JOAB was commander-in-chief of David's army. He signaled the beginning and ending of battle by blowing a trumpet (II Kings 2:28, 18:16, 20:22).

At Januarie's wedding feast, every course is preceded by the kind of trumpeting that neither Joab nor Theodamas had ever heard, *MerchT* 1718–1721. The dreamer sees Joab in the great hall where many musicians have gathered in company with other trumpeters, Misenus and Theodamas, *HF* III.1245. **[Messenus: Theodamas]**

The name appears medially, *MerchT* 1719; *HF* III.1245.

JOB was the patriarch whose tribulations are recorded in The Book of Job. He is the archetype of patience in adversity.

Devils, with God's permission, may harm the body but not the soul, as in Job's case, *FrT* 1489–1491, a quotation from Job 1:12, 2:6. The proverbial patience of Job appears in *WBP* 436; *ClT* 932–938; *Mel* 998–1000.

The reference to Job at *ParsT* 134 is really to Proverbs 12:4; the Parson quotes Job 10:20–22, *ParsT* 176; Job 20:25, *ParsT* 191; Job 10:22, *ParsT* 211, 217, 223.

Jobes, the ME genitive case, occurs once, *WBP* 436.

JOCE (saint). Joce or Judocus, fl. seventh century A.D., was a Breton saint who became popular during the medieval period. He was known as Joce of Ponthieu because he built his hermitage at Ponthieu, where he died c. 668. Born a prince, he renounced the crown for the pilgrim's staff and was known as the patron saint of pilgrims. He was also invoked against fire, plague, animal diseases, and storms at sea (Réau, *IAC* III.2: 763).

Alys of Bath swears by St. Joce that she made her fourth husband "frye in his own grece," *WBP* 483–490. **[Alisoun³]**

The name appears in final rhyming position, *WBP* 483.

A.S. Haskell, "The Saint Joce Oath in the Wife of Bath's Prologue." *ChauR* 1 (1966): 85–87; Jacobus de Voragine, *LA*, ed. Th. Graesse, 859–886. (There is no English trans. in Ryan and Ripperger.)

JOHAN, JOHN¹. There are three writers in the New Testament with this name: John, the writer of the Fourth Gospel and the First Letter of John; John, the author of the two remaining letters that bear the name; and John, the writer of the Apocalypse or the Book of Revelation. The symbol for the

Gospel writer is the eagle.

The saint's name appears eight times in rhyming tags, *MLI* 18, *MLT* 1019; *WBP* 164; *SumT* 1800, 2252; *SqT* 596; *PardT* 752; *PF* 451. The reference in *BD* 1318 and the description of the "riche hill" and the "long castel" point to John of Gaunt, Earl of Richmond and Duke of Lancaster. The Prioress says that the "little clergeon," slain for his faith, will follow the celestial white Lamb, of whom St. John the Evangelist wrote from Patmos, *PrT* 579–585, referring to Revelation 14:3–4. The Parson says he quotes St. John the Evangelist when he quotes from Revelation 9:6, *ParsT* 216; he quotes I John 1:8, *ParsT* 349; I John 3:15, *ParsT* 564; Revelation 3:16, *ParsT* 687; Revelation 21:8, *ParsT* 840; Revelation 16:4, *ParsT* 993. The dreamer sees a female creature in Fame's hall, who has as many eyes as birds have feathers; she is like the four beasts full of eyes, which John describes in the Apocalypse, *HF* III.1381–1385, found in Revelation 4:6.

Johan, the shortened form of Latin *Johannes,* the Anglo-Norman form, appears once, *BD* 1318, and seems necessary to complete the number of stresses in the line. *John* appears medially, *SqT* 596; *Mars* 9, and in the Parson's prose tale.

A.N. McNeile, *An Introduction to the Study of the New Testament,* 263–265.

JOHN[2] is the old carpenter in *The Miller's Tale,* who lives in Oxford. Carpenters were numerous in medieval Oxford, as may be seen in the college account rolls. John is a rich man but takes in boarders, one of whom is Nicholas. John marries Alisoun, a very young woman, and Alisoun and Nicholas soon have an affair. [**Absolon[2]: Alisoun[2]: Nicholas[1]: Peter[2]**]

The name occurs five times in medial positions, *MillT* 3369, 3501, 3513, 3639, 3662, and once in final rhyming position, *MillT* 3577.

J.A.W. Bennett, *Chaucer at Oxford and at Cambridge,* 26; G. Cooper, "'Sely John' in the 'legend' of *The Miller's Tale.*" *JEGP* 79 (1980): 1–12.

JOHN[3] is the poor clerk at Soler Hall, Cambridge, in *The Reeve's Tale.* He comes from Strother, which means "a place overgrown with bushwood," a village far in the north. He swears by St. Cuthbert, the Northumbrian saint. John and Alayn take their corn to be ground at the village mill, but Symkyn the miller succeeds in stealing their meal. He lets their horse Bayard into a field of mares, and while John and Alayn try to capture the horse, he helps himself to their meal. Because it is too late to return to Cambridge, the students spend the night with the miller and his family, which includes his wife, his daughter Malyne, and a baby. During the night Alayn gets into Malyne's bed, while John, through the ruse of removing the baby's cradle, gets the miller's wife into his bed. By robbing Malyne of her maidenhead and by cuckolding Symkyn, they get even for the theft of their corn. [**Alayn: Malyne: Symkyn**]

The name appears twice initially, *RvT* 4013, 4020; twenty-one times in medial positions, *RvT* 4025, 4026, 4037, 4040, 4044, 4071, 4084, 4108, 4109, 4114, 4127, 4169, 4177, 4180, 4188, 4199, 4228, 4262, 4284, 4292, 4316; and six times in final rhyming position, *RvT* 4018, 4091, 4160, 4198, 4259, 4295.

JOHN[4] is the generic name for a priest. Harry Bailly wonders if the Monk's name is Daun John, *MkP* 1929; he addresses the Nun's Priest as "thou Sir John," *NPP* 2810–2815. It may also be his real name, for the poet addresses him as "this sweete preest, this goodly man, Sir John," *NPP* 2820.

JOHN[5]. Daun John, the monk in *The Shipman's Tale*, comes from the same village as his host, the merchant, with whom he claims "cosynage," or "cousinship." Daun John is thirty years old. When he visits the merchant, he is very generous to all the servants, and everyone welcomes him. The merchant's wife complains to Daun John that her husband is stingy and that she needs money. Daun John borrows from the merchant, gives the money to his wife, and is rewarded with a night in her arms. When the merchant asks for his money, Daun John says, quite truthfully, that he has returned the money to the merchant's wife. **[Denys]**

He is always called "Daun John." These names appear four times initially, *ShipT* 89, 187, 342, 349; eight times in medial positions, *ShipT* 43, 98, 255, 298, 312, 319, 322, 337; and ten times in final rhyming position, *ShipT* 58, 68, 158, 211, 282, 294, 308, 314, 387, 402.

R.M. Fisher, "'Cosyn' and 'Cosynage': Complicated Punning in Chaucer's *Shipman's Tale*." *N&Q* 210 (1965): 168–170; A.E. Singer, "Chaucer and Don Juan." *WVUPP* 13 (1961): 25–30.

JOHN[6] **CRISOSTOM** (saint), A.D. 347–407, was born at Antioch. He became one of the most prominent doctors of the Greek Church. When he died in 407, he was patriarch of Constantinople (*NCE* VII: 1041–1044).

The Parson's quotation from St. John Chrysostom, *ParsT* 108, comes from his *Sermo de Poenitentiae (Sermon on Penitence)*, an old Latin homily that does not appear in modern editions but appears in medieval and Renaissance editions of his work. R.M. Correale shows that the quotation appears in Raymund of Pennaforte's *Summa casuum Poenitentiae*, Chaucer's ultimate source, as a quotation from *Johannes Os Auream* (John the golden-mouthed).

The name appears once. *Chrysostom* means "the golden-tongued" in Greek.

Johannes Chrysostom, *Opera Omnia (PL* 47–62); B. Chrysostomus, *John Chrysostom and his Time,* trans. M. Gonzaga; R.M. Correale, "The Source of the Quotation from 'Crisostom' in *The Parson's Tale*." *N&Q* 225 (1980): 101–102.

JOHN THE BAPTIST: [BAPTIST JOHN]
JONAH: [JONAS]

JONAS was the son of Amathi. Although the Book of Jonah is named after him, modern Jewish and Christian scholars do not regard it as an historical narrative. The work is dated between the fourth and third centuries before our era. Jonas tried to escape from the errand the Lord had given him: to preach to the people of Nineveh. He took a ship to Tarshish instead, but the Lord sent a storm, and Jonas was thrown overboard. A great sea beast swallowed him, and after three days it cast him up on the beach at Nineveh (Jonas 1–4).

The Man of Law asks the rhetorical question, "Who kept Jonas in the fish's maw?" *MLT* 486–487.

Jonas, the form in the Latin Vulgate, appears medially, *MLT* 486.

Encyclopaedia Judaica, X: 169–176.

JONATHAN: [JONATHAS]

JONATHAS. Jonathan was the eldest son of Saul, king of Israel. The friendship between Jonathan and David became proverbial for the highest form of disinterested friendship (I Kings 17– 20).

Jonathas must hide his friendly manner before Alceste, *LGW F* 251, *LGW G* 205. **[Alceste: David]**

Jonathas, the medieval variant, appears in medial position, *LGW F* 251, *LGW G* 205.

JOSEPH[1], Jacob's favorite son, was sold into Egypt by his jealous brothers. There he was bought by Potiphar, Pharoah's minister, and lived in Potiphar's house. When Potiphar's wife found that she could not seduce him, she denounced him to her husband, and Joseph was imprisoned. In prison he interpreted the dreams of Pharoah's baker and butler, and the interpretations proved true. When the butler was restored to his place in Pharoah's palace, he recommended Joseph to Pharoah as an interpreter of dreams, and Joseph was released from prison. When he interpreted Pharoah's dreams, Pharoah made him his prime minister (Genesis 25–45).

Joseph is a dream interpreter, *NPT* 3130–3135; *BD* 275–282. God gave His blessing to Pharoah because of Joseph's service, *ParsT* 444. Joseph rebukes his lord's wife, *ParsT* 878–880. **[Jacob: Lia: Rachel]**

The name appears in medial positions, *NPT* 3130, *BD* 280.

K. Young, ed., "Joseph and his Brethren." *The Drama of the Medieval Church,* II: 266–274.

JOSEPH[2] (saint), fl. 1st century A.D., was the Virgin Mary's husband.

The angel told him that the child Mary was to bear should be called Jesus (Matthew 1:18–25).

The Parson recalls this incident, *ParsT* 285. [**Crist: Marie**[1]]

"The Annunciation," in *The Wakefield Mystery Plays*, ed. M. Rose, 175–185.

JOSEPHUS. Flavius Josephus, c. A.D. 37–c.100, belonged to a priestly, aristocratic family of the Hasmonean dynasty in Israel. As commander of the Jewish forces during the war with Rome in A.D. 66, he surrendered after Vespasian's forces surrounded his men. He saved his life by prophesying that Vespasian would become emperor. When this actually happened, Vespasian gave Josephus many honors, including Roman citizenship. He took the name Flavius, the family name of the Roman clan to which Vespasian belonged, as a gesture of gratitude to the imperial household for its kindness to him. The Jews of his day hated him because they regarded him as a traitor to their cause. His main works are *De bellum Judaicum (The Jewish War)* in seven books and *Antiquitates Judaica (Jewish Antiquities)* in twenty books, published c. A.D. 93/94 and written in Greek.

Josephus stands on a pillar of lead and iron and is of "secte Saturnyn," *HF* III.1429–1436. Lead is Saturn's metal, and iron is the metal of Mars, *HF* III.1445–1450. A.D. Miller explains that as Saturn is father of the planets, so the sect of the Jews is the father of all sects. Josephus bears up the fame of Jewry and stands with other historians, *HF* III.1437–1440. His pillar of lead and iron combines the influences of Saturn and Mars. [**Mars: Saturne**]

Josephus occurs medially, *HF* III.1433.

Encyclopaedia Judaica, X: 251–254; Flavius Josephus, *The Jewish War*, ed. and trans. H. St. John Thackeray, R. Marcus, A. Wikgren, and L.H. Feldman; A.D. Miller, "Chaucer's 'Secte Saturnyn.'" *MLN* 47 (1932): 99–102.

JOVE, JOVES, JOVIS. Jove, otherwise known as Jupiter, was the chief deity of the Roman pantheon. The name became a poetic alternative after Jupiter gained precedence during the Roman classical period.

Palamon addresses Venus as daughter of Jove, *KnT* 2222. The Dreamer sees the story of Troy depicted on a brass tablet in Venus's temple, how Jove kisses Venus and abates the tempest that jeopardizes Eneas's fleet, *HF* I.219–220. The dreamer wonders if Jove intends to "stellyfye" him as the eagle picks him up, *HF* II.584–587, but the great bird says that Jove has no such intention, *HF* II.595–599. Jove recognizes the dreamer's humility and virtue when he makes his head ache with study, *HF* II.630–640. Jove wants the eagle to bear the dreamer to the House of Fame as a recompense for his devotion to Cupid, *HF* II.661–671, *HF* III.2007–2010. Jove beats the air into thunder, *HF* II.1040–1041. Jove appears as a name for Jupiter throughout *Troilus and Criseyde*. [**Juno: Jupiter: Venus**]

Chaucer uses *Jove* or *Joves* where he needs one or two syllabic stresses and *Jupiter* when he needs three. *Jove* occurs three times initially as an apostrophe, *Tr* III.722, IV.1149, 1192; ten times in medial positions, *Tr* III.625, 1015, 1016, IV.335, 1079; V.207, 1544, 1853; *LGW F* 525, *LGW G* 513. *Joves*, originally OF nominative case, appears eleven times as ME nominative case, *Tr* II.1607, III.15, 2007, V.2, 1446, 1525; *HF* II.586, 597, 630, 661, 1041; twice as ME accusative case, *HF* I.219; *Tr* V.957; four times as ME genitive case, medially, *Tr* I.878, III.3, 150; IV.1337; *Jovis* appears once, as genitive case, *MerchT* 2224.

Jove is also another name for the planet Jupiter. Cancer is Jove's exaltation, *MerchT* 2222–2224. Jove in conjunction with Saturn and Cancer brings the smoky rain, *Tr* III.624–644.

Jovis, the Old and medieval Latin variant derived from Sanskrit *Djovis*, meaning "bright heaven," occurs as genitive case, *MerchT* 2224; *CCL* 232.

JOVINIAN, JOVINYAN, JOVYNYAN, fl. fourth century A.D., was a contemporary of Jerome. Although he was a monk, Jovinian published a treatise against asceticism and virginity in the priesthood and questioned the doctrine of the perpetual virginity of Mary. Pope Siricus condemned this treatise and excommunicated Jovinian in A.D. 390. Pammachius, one of Jerome's friends, sent Jerome a copy of the treatise and asked for a reply. Jerome obliged with the famous *Epistola adversus Jovinianum* (*Letter Against Jovinian*), in which he not only denounced Jovinian but also showed by numerous examples that chastity, virginity, and fidelity were prized among virtuous pagans as well as among Christians.

Alys of Bath says that this treatise was bound up with writings of an antifeminist nature, *WBP* 675. Friar John says that gluttons and lechers are like Jovinian, "fat as a whale and walkynge as a swan," *SumT* 1929–1930. Jerome describes Jovinian in similar terms, *Epistola*, I.40 (*PL* 23: 268). The Middle English title of this Work, *Jerome Agayns Jovynyan*, appears in *LGW G* 281. [**Crisippus: Helowys: Jerome: Tertulan: Theofraste: Trotula: Valerie**]

Jovinian occurs in final rhyming position, *WBP* 675; *Jovinyan*, a spelling variant, occurs also in final rhyming position, *SumT* 1929, and *Jovynyan*, also a spelling variant, in *LGW G* 281.

J.P. Brennan, Jr., "Reflections on a Gloss to the *Prioress's Tale* from Jerome's *Adversus Jovinianum.*" *SP* 70 (1973): 243–251; R.A. Pratt, "Chaucer's 'Natal Jove' and Seint Jerome . . . agayns Jovinian.'" *JEGP* 61 (1962): 244–248; D.S. Silvia, Jr., "Glosses to the *Canterbury Tales* from St. Jerome's *Epistola Adversus Jovinianum.*" *SP* 62 (1965): 28–39.

JUDAS was the disciple who betrayed Jesus to the Pharisees (Mark 14:10; Luke 12:3–4). His name, like Ganelon's and Synon's, became synonymous with treachery.

Judas is a thief, *FrT* 1351, a traitor, *CYT* 1003–1007; he is envious, *ParsT* 500–505, a flatterer, *ParsT* 615–618, and commits the sin of despair, *ParsT* 695–698, 1015–1018. **[Genelloun: Scariot: Synon]**

JUDITH is the heroine of the apocryphal Book of Judith. Nebuchadnezzar, king of Assyria, sent his general Holofernes to beseige the Jewish city of Bethulia. After holding out for a month, the city elders decided to open the gates and to surrender. Judith approached them and gained their permission to visit Holofernes in his camp. Impressed by her wisdom and attracted by her beauty, Holofernes invited her to a feast. He became very drunk. While he lay in a drunken sleep, Judith cut off his head, gave it to her maid to carry in a sack, and returned to Bethulia. The next morning the Assyrian army fled when the commanders discovered the slain Holofernes. Although the historicity of this story is in doubt, the events have been given probable dates, 362–352 B.C.

The Man of Law mentions Judith's courage in slaying Olofernus in his tent, *MLT* 939–942. Judith gave good counsel, *MerchT* 1366–1368; *Mel* 1097. The Monk tells how Judith slew Oloferne, *MkT* 2551–2574. **[Eliachim: Oloferne]**

Judith appears once initially, *MkT* 2571, and twice in medial positions, *MLT* 939, *MerchT* 1366.

JULIAN, JULYAN, called Julian the Hospitaller, was born of noble parents. He loved hunting, and one day, as he hunted the hart, the animal turned and told him that he would slay his parents. Julian left home and took service with the lord of a foreign country. He married a lady there, but once, while he was out, his parents came seeking him. His wife gave them her room to rest and to refresh themselves, then she went to church. When Julian returned, he saw a man and a woman in his bed. Thinking that they were his wife and a lover, he slew them both, locked the door, and went out again. As he approached the church, he saw his wife returning. In horror, he listened while she explained that the people he had slain were his parents. As penance, Julian and his wife wandered throughout the country until they came to a perilous river. There they built a hospice, and Julian ferried over any travelers who wanted to cross. One cold night he carried an old leper across the swollen river, and when he laid the leper in his bed, the leper became an angel, who told him that God had accepted his penance. After his death, travelers invoked him as the patron saint of hospitality (*Legenda aurea* XXX).

The Franklin, famous for his hospitality, is known as St. Julian in his county, *Gen Prol* 340. The garrulous eagle salutes St. Julian as he approaches Fame's house, *HF* II.1022–1023.

Julian appears in a medial position, *Gen Prol* 340, as does *Julyan*, a spelling variant, *HF* II.1022.

Jacobus de Voragine, *GL*, trans. G. Ryan and H. Ripperger, 128–133; *ibid.*, *LA*, ed. Th.
    Graesse, 142–143; *The South-English Legendary*, ed. C. D'Evelyn and A.J. Mill, I:
    32–37.

JULIUS. Gaius Julius Caesar was born c. 102 or 100 B.C. In 60 B.C., he
formed the first triumvirate with Pompey and Crassus, and in 59 B.C. was
elected Consul. Between 59 and 49 B.C., Caesar's successes in Gaul and
Britain increased his power in the Senate, but on January 1, 49 B.C., the
Senate voted that Caesar lay down his command. On January 10, 49 B.C.,
Caesar crossed the Rubicon into Italy and plunged Italy into civil war. He
defeated Pompey's forces in 47 B.C. and Pompey's sons in 45 B.C. In 48 B.C.
he was appointed dictator to hold elections. In 46 he was appointed
dictator for ten years, and in 44 he was made dictator for life, and the month
Quintilis was named Julius after him. Although he refused the title *Rex*, his
increasing powers offended many senators, and he was assassinated on
March 15, 44 B.C. in the Senate (Suetonius, *The Deified Julius*). *Pharsalia* III
is Lucan's lament that Caesar had no triumph. He is one of the Nine
Worthies in *The Parlement of the Thre Ages*, 405–420.

The death of Julius is painted on the walls of Mars's oratory, *KnT* 2031,
and foretold in the stars, *MLT* 199. The Man of Law says, erroneously, that
Lucan describes Julius's triumph, *MLT* 400–401. The Monk tells the story of
Julius, *MkT* 2670–2726, and gives his sources as Lucan, Suetonius, Valerius,
MkT 2719–2721, but he also uses Vincent of Beauvais, *Speculum historiale*
VI.35–42, as Pauline Aiken shows. Lucan, historian of the Roman civil war
caused by Julius, stands on a pillar of iron, Mars's metal, *HF* III.1497–1502.
Chaucer says that Julius took two days from February and added two days
to July, *Astr* I.10. When Caesar revised the calendar, he adapted the
Egyptian solar calendar to Roman use and inserted a day between February
23 and 24 in the leap year or bissextile year. [**Cesar**[1]: **Lucan: Pompe:**
Socrates: Swetonius: Valerie]

Julius, "descendant of Iulus" since the family claimed descent from
Aeneas's son, is the name of the Roman clan to which Caesar belonged. The
name never occurs initially. It appears seven times in medial positions, *MLT*
199; *MkT* 2673, 2692, 2700, 2703, 2711; *HF* III.1502, and three times in final
rhyming position, *KnT* 2031; *MLT* 400; *MkT* 2695.

P. Aiken, "Vincent of Beauvais and Chaucer's *Monk's Tale.*" *Speculum* 27 (1942):
    56–58; Lucan, *Pharsalia*, ed. and trans. J.D. Duff; *The Parlement of the Thre Ages*,
    ed. M.Y. Offord, 18–19; Suetonius, *De vita Caesarum*, ed. and trans. J.C. Rolfe,
    I: 2–119.

JUNO, the Roman goddess, was Saturn's daughter. She closely re-
sembled the Greek Hera, whose functions she assumed at a very early date.
As the goddess of married women and of childbirth, she was also known as
Lucina (*Fasti* II.436). She hated the house of Thebes because Jupiter openly

courted the Theban princesses Europa and Semele (*Thebaid* I.256–260; this passage appears in manuscripts B and C of the Old French *Roman de Thèbes*, II: 86–87, not the manuscript Constans prints as the main poem). She hated the Trojan house because Paris, the Trojan prince-shepherd, did not give her the golden apple inscribed "To the Fairest." At the wedding of Peleus and Thetis, the goddess Eris, or Strife, threw down the golden apple. To settle the dispute that arose among Juno, Venus, and Athena as to whom the apple should be given, the three took the apple to Paris and asked him to decide. He chose Venus, who offered him the most beautiful woman in the world, not telling him that she was Helen of Mycenae. Because Paris passed her over, Juno hated the Trojans (*Aeneid* I.26–27; *Heroides* V.33–40).

Jealous Juno has almost destroyed the house of Thebes, *KnT* 1329, 1543, 1555, 1559; *Anel* 51. As goddess of married women, she helps Alcyone, *BD* 108–110, 121–152. Her traditional shrewishness is evident in the expletives that accompany her name: "cruel Juno," *HF* I.198; "olde wrath of Juno," *Anel* 51, "Juno thrugh thy crueltee," *KnT* 1543. She pursues Eneas out of spite and hates the Trojans, *HF* I.198–218, an inference to the Judgment of Paris. In spite of Juno's wrath, Eneas carries out his mission, *HF* I.461–463. Juno is "blisful Juno" and "hevenes quene," *Tr* IV 1116, 1594. Juno's absence from Proigne's wedding, *LGW* 2249, bodes disaster. [**Alcione: Jupiter: Philomene: Proigne: Tereus**]

Juno occurs once initially, *BD* 187; fourteen times in medial positions, *KnT* 1329, 1543, 1555; *BD* 109, 129, 132, 136; *Anel* 51; *Tr* IV.1116, 1538, 1594; V 601; *HF* I.1461; *LGW* 2249; and four times in final rhyming position, *KnT* 1559; *BD* 243, 267; *HF* I.198.

Ovid, *Fasti*, ed. and trans. J.G. Frazer, 88–89; *ibid., Her*, ed. and trans. G. Showerman, 60–61; Statius, *Thebaid*, ed. and trans. J.H. Mozley, I: 358–361; Virgil, *Aeneid*, ed. and trans. H.R. Fairclough, I: 242–243.

JUPITER, JUPITERES, JUPPITER. Jupiter, Saturn's son and Juno's husband, was the chief god of the Roman pantheon. He was the god of light, fire, and air (*Etym* VIII.xi.69). Because of his affairs with Alcmena, Europa, Io, Semele, and Ganymede, Isidore calls him extremely lewd (*Etym* VIII.xi.34).

Jupiter tries to stop the argument between Venus and Mars, *KnT* 2442. Arcite prays that Jupiter guide his soul and keep part of it, *KnT* 2786–2792. Theseus calls Jupiter prince and cause of all things, *KnT* 3035–3037, and thanks him for his grace, *KnT* 3067–3069. Cresus dreams that Jupiter washed him, *MkT* 2743; his daughter interprets Jupiter as snow and rain, *MkT* 2752. Jupiter is the heathen god whom Cecile refuses to worship, *SNT* 364–413. Jupiter's metal is tin, *CYT* 828. Venus appeals to Jupiter to save her son, Eneas, *HF* I.215, and Jupiter takes care of him, *HF* I.465. The dreamer reasons that he is not Ganymede to be taken up to heaven, *HF* II.588–592. The learned eagle lives with Jupiter, god of thunder, *HF* II.605–611. He says that Jupiter pities the poet, who serves Cupid and Venus without reward, *HF* II.612–626. Jupiter slays Phaeton when the sun's chariot goes out of control, *HF* II.944–949. Pandarus swears by Jupiter, who makes the thunder ring, *Tr* II.233. Criseyde beseeches Jupiter to reward with bad luck those who brought the treaty in which she is exchanged for Antenor, *Tr* IV.666–672. She prays that Jupiter grant to herself and Troilus the grace to meet again after ten nights, *Tr* IV.1681–1687. Dido prays to die if it be Jupiter's will, *LGW* 1338. Jupiter is "Jupiter the likerous" because of his many love affairs, *The Former Age* 57.

Jupiter is also the sixth and largest planet, counting away from the sun (see Ptolemaic map). The beneficent planet, it governs touch, the lungs, the arteries, and semen (*Tetrabiblos* III.12). Gower points out that the planet "Jupiter the delicat" causes peace; those born under it are meek and patient, fortunate in business and lusty in love. Clerks call it the planet of "delices," *Confessio Amantis* VII.909–923. Jupiter aids those born under him in greater decorum, restraint, and modesty (*Tetrabiblos* III.14).

Ypermestre is born under Jupiter and thinks that happiness consists of truth, good conscience, dread of shame, and true wifehood, *LGW* 2584–2589. The first inequal hour and the ninth hour of the day belong to Jupiter, *Astr* II.12. 24. [**Almena: Calistopee: Europe: Ganymede: Jove: Juno: Pheton: Ypermestra**]

Jupiter, derived from Sanskrit *Dyaus-pater*, "sky-father," occurs once initially, *HF* II.642; nine times in medial positions, *HF* I.215, 464; II.955; *Tr* II.233; IV.669, 1683; *LGW* 1806, 2585; *Form Age* 57; and throughout the *Astrolabe*. *Jupiteres*, the ME genitive case, occurs once, in medial position, *HF* I.199. *Juppiter* occurs in medial positions, *KnT* 2442, 2786, 2792, 3035, 3069, 3934, 3942; *SNT* 364, 413; *CYT* 828.

John Gower, *The Complete Works,* ed. G.C.Macaulay, III: 257–258; Isidore, *Etymologiae,* ed. W.M. Lindsay, I; Ptolemy, *Tetrabiblos,* ed. and trans. F.E. Robbins, 319, 373; B. Witlieb, "Jupiter and Nimrod in *The Former Age.*" *Chaucer Newsletter* 2 (1980): 12–13.

JUPPITER: [JUPITER]

JUSTINUS, JUSTYN is Januarie's brother in *The Merchant's Tale.* His name indicates his character, for Justinus is a just man and warns Januarie against marriage to a very young woman. He is the opposite of his brother Placebo, who seeks to please Januarie and agrees with his plan to marry May. Justinus attempts to show Januarie that his fantasies about marriage are ephemeral by quoting from the philosophers, but Januarie says that Seneca is not worth a straw. [**Damyan: Januarie: May: Placebo**]

The name occurs only in medial positions. *Justinus*, the Latin form, appears in *MerchT* 1477, 1519, 1655; *Justyn*, the English contraction, in *MerchT* 1689.

JUVENAL. Decimus Junius Juvenalis, fl. first–second century A.D., was born at Aquinum c. A.D. 60 or 70. His *Sixteen Satires* are fierce attacks on vices, abuses, and follies of Roman life in his time.

The "olde wyfe" quotes Juvenal, *WBT* 1192–1194, sentiments found in *Satire* X.21–22. The narrator quotes from *Satire* X.2–4 in *Tr* IV.198–199: "Folk little know what is fitting for them to desire so that they are not disappointed in their desire."

Juvenal appears initially in *WBT* 1192 and in an apostrophe, *Tr* IV.197.

Juvenal, *Satires*, ed. and trans. G.G. Ramsay, 192–193, 194–195.

KACUS: [CACUS]

KENELM. Cynhelm, d. A.D. 812 or 821, was the son of Cenwulf, king of Mercia. He was buried in Winchcombe Abbey, where his father had established a monastery of monks in 798. In the eleventh century he was regarded as a martyr, and a legend grew up that his ambitious sister Cwendryth, an abbess, instigated his tutor to murder him. The legend states that Kenelm was seven years old when he was murdered, but Kenelm signed several charters between 803 and 811.

Chauntecleer tells Dame Pertelote the story of Kenelm, who saw his murder in a vision. His nurse interprets it that he will die and counsels Kenelm to be careful because treason was about; but since he was only seven years old, he took little heed, *NPT* 3110–3121. **[Chauntecleer: Kenulphus]**

Kenelm, the ME variant of OE *Cynhelm* which suggests that medial *h* was not pronounced and therefore dropped out of the spelling, occurs in medial positions, *NPT* 3110, 3112.

W. Levinson, *England and the Continent in the Eighth Century,* 249–259; *The South-English Legendary,* ed. C. D'Evelyn and A.J. Mill, I: 279–291.

KENULPHUS. Cenwulf ruled Mercia A.D. 796–821. In 798, he endowed a monastery of monks in Winchcombe Abbey, where he was later buried beside his son Kenelm.

Kenulphus is Kenelm's father, *NPT* 3110–3121. **[Kenelm]**

Latin *Kenulphus* instead of OE *Cenwulf* seems necessary for the meter and appears in medial position, *NPT* 3111.

W. Levinson, *England and the Continent in the Eighth Century,* 249–259.

KHWARIZMI, AL- : [ARGUS³]

L

LABAN was Jacob's uncle and father of Rachel and Leah. When Esau sought to kill Jacob because he had robbed him of his father's blessing, Jacob went to Laban to escape Esau's vengeance. He worked for Laban for seven years, hoping to marry Rachel at the end of that time, but Laban substituted Leah under the wedding veil. So Jacob worked for Laban another seven years, after which he married Rachel. Laban became rich during the fourteen years of Jacob's service (Genesis 19–30).

God gave his blessing to Laban because of Jacob, *ParsT* 440–444. **[Jacob: Lia: Rachel: Rebekke]**

LACHESIS was the second of the three Fates or Parcae, daughters of Night. She apportioned out the length of human life by spinning the wool from Clotho's distaff (Hesiod, *Theogony* 214–222; *Etym* VIII.11.93).

Troilus will die because Lachesis will no longer weave the thread of his life, *Tr* V.3–7. **[Atropos: Parcas]**

Lachesis means "the allotting one," *Tristia* V.x.45–46, and appears in medial position, *Tr* V.7.

Hesiod, *The Homeric Hymns and Homerica*, ed. and trans. H.G. Evelyn-White, 94–95; Isidore, *Etymologiae*, ed. W.M. Lindsay, I; Ovid, *Tristia*, ed. and trans. A.L. Wheeler, 248–249.

LADOMYA, LAODOMYA, LAUDOMIA. Laodomia was the wife of Protesilaus, who was killed when the Greeks landed at Troy, even before the main battles began (*Iliad* II.695–699). Laodomia killed herself when he did not return (*Heroides* XIII). Jerome mentions her among faithful wives, *Epistola adversus Jovinianum (Letter Against Jovinian)* I.45 (*PL* 23: 275).

The Man of Law lists a story of Ladomya among Chaucer's works, *MLI* 71, but no story exists. Dorigen thinks Ladomya is exemplary of wifely virtue, *FranklT* 1445; Laudomia appears in the catalogue of love's martyrs, *LGW F* 263, *LGW G* 217. **[Dorigen: Protheselaus]**

The forms appear to be scribal variants, all with four syllables. *Ladomya* occurs in final rhyming position, *MLI* 71; *Laodomya* appears in medial position, *FranklT* 1445; and *Laudomia* occurs medially, *LGW F* 263, *LGW G* 217.

G. Dempster, "Chaucer at Work on The Complaint in *The Franklin's Tale*." *MLN* 52 (1937): 6–16; Homer, *Iliad*, ed. and trans. A.T. Murray, I: 102–103; K. Hume, "The Pagan Setting of *The Franklin's Tale* and the Sources of Dorigen's Cosmology." *SN* 44 (1972): 289–294; Ovid, *Her*, ed. and trans. G. Showerman, 158–171.

LAIUS: [LAYUS]

LAMEADOUN, LAMEDON. Laomedon, king of Troy, was Priam's father. He engaged Apollo and Neptune to build the walls of Troy but refused to pay them when the work was finished (*Met* XI.194–220).

Lamedon's story is pictured in the windows of the Dreamer's room, *BD* 326–331. Phebus and Neptune are angry with the Trojans because of Lameadoun's fraud, *Tr* IV.120–126, and Troy will be burnt. **[Phebus: Neptune]**

Chaucer varies the form to suit the rhyme: *Lamedon*, *BD* 329; *Lameadoun*, *Tr* IV.124.

Ovid, *Met*, ed. and trans. F.J. Miller, II: 132–135.

LAMECH: [LAMEK]

LAMEK, LAMEKES, LAMETH. Lamech was Cain's descendant. He had two wives, Ada and Sella. Ada's sons were Jabel, the ancestor of shepherds, and Jubal, the inventor of music. Sella's son was Tubalcain, the maker of brass and iron (Genesis 4:16–24).

Alys of Bath says that Lamek was a bigamist, *WBP* 52–54. Lameth was the first to love two women, *SqT* 549–551. Medieval exegetes called Lamech a bigamist: Peter Comestor, *Historia scholastica, Liber Genesis* (*PL* 198: 1078–1079), and Peter Riga, *Aurora* 485–526. The Man in Black says that he is not as skilled in making songs as Lamek's son, Tubal, *BD* 1160–1163. *Tubal* is a scribal variant for *Jubal* in manuscripts of the Vulgate and appears in Isidore, *Etymologiae* III.16, and in some manuscripts of Peter Riga's *Aurora,* which Chaucer names as his source, *BD* 1169. Lamek is false in love, the first man to love two women, and that is bigamy, *Anel* 148–154. He was the first to live in a tent, *Anel* 154. There is some confusion here with Jabel, the founder of those who live in tents, Genesis 4: 20. Chaucer's source may have been Trevet's *Les Cronicles*, fol. 3ʳ: *Cist Jubal le fitz lamec contreva primes tentes*, "This Jubal, son of Lamech, contrived the first tents." [**Peter**[1] **Riga: Tubal**]

All the forms appear medially, *Lamek, SqT* 550; *Lameth, WBP* 54; *Anel* 150; *Lamekes,* the ME genitive case, *BD* 1162.

R.A. Pratt, "Chaucer and *Les Cronicles* of Nicholas Trevet." *SLL,* 306; E. Reiss, "The Story of Lamech and Its Place in Medieval Drama." *JMRS* 2 (1972): 35–48; Peter of Riga, *Aurora,* ed. P.E. Beichner, I: 46–47; K. Young, "Chaucer and Peter Riga." *Speculum* 12 (1937): 300–301.

LAMETH: [LAMEK]

LAMUEL. Lemuel, king of Massa, ruled a North Arabian tribe. He was one of Ishmael's sons mentioned in Genesis 25:14. The Israelites highly esteemed his people's wisdom, and the words of Lemuel's mother on the evils of wine appear in Proverbs 31.

The Pardoner is at pains to establish the correct name, *PardT* 583–586. [**Samuel**]

Lamuel occurs in final rhyming position, *PardT* 584, and medially, *PardT* 585.

LANCELOT: [LAUNCELOT]
LAODAMIA: [LADOMYA]
LAODAMYA: [LADOMYA]
LAPIDAIRE: [MARBODE]
LATINUS: [LATYNE]

LATONA was the mother of Apollo and Diana by Jupiter. Diana was sometines addressed as *Latonia*, "Latona's daughter" (*Met* I.696, VIII.394). Isidore explains that Diana is sometimes called *Latonia* because she was Latona's daughter (*Etym* VIII.xi.59).

Troilus addresses the moon (Diana) as "Latona the clere," *Tr* V.655. [**Diane**]

Isidore, *Etymologiae*, ed. W.M. Lindsay, I; Ovid, *Met*, ed. and trans. F.J. Miller, I: 50–51, 434–435.

LATUMYUS. Chaucer substitutes this name for Pacuvius, who had a tree in his garden on which his three wives hanged themselves. When Pacuvius complained to Arrius, weeping, the latter begged him for a cutting to plant in his garden, hoping for the same results. Cicero tells this story, without names, in *De oratore*, II.xix; Walter Map rehearses it in his *Dissuasio Valerii ad Rufinum philosophum ne uxorem ducat*, IV.iii. (c. 1180–1183).

Jankyn reads this story to Alys from his "Book of wikked wyves," *WBP* 757–766. [**Alisoun**[3]**: Arrius**]

The name occurs in final rhyming position, *WBP* 757.

Cicero, *De oratore*, ed. and trans. E.W. Sutton and H. Rackham, 408–409; Walter Map, *De nugis curialium,* ed. and trans. M.R. James, rev. C.N.L. Brooke and R.A.B. Mynors, 302–303.

LATYNE. Latinus, king of Latium, promised his daughter Lavinia to Aeneas although she was already betrothed to Turnus. He made this betrothal part of the treaty he signed with the Trojans when they arrived in Italy (*Aeneid* VII.45–285; XII).

King Latyne with his treaty is engraved on the walls of the temple of glass, *HF* I.453. **[Eneas: Laveyne: Turnus]**

Latyne, ME contraction of Latin *Latinus*, appears in medial position.

Virgil, *Aeneid*, ed. and trans. H.R. Fairclough, II: 4–23; 298–365.

LAUDOMIA: [LADOMYA]

LAUNCELOT. Lancelot, son of King Ban of Benoic or Brittany, was brought up by the Lady of the Lake, and thus called Lancelot du Lac. In Chrétien's *Erec et Enide* (late 1150s), 1694, Lancelot is third in the hierarchy of knights, Gawain the first and Erec the second. He appears as Queen Guenevere's lover in *Le Chevalier de la charrette* (c. 1172), and in the prose romance *Le Livre de Lancelot du Lac* (1215–1222) he is called *la flor des cheualiers del monde,* "the flower of the world's knights." He plays a very important role in Malory's *Le Morte Darthur* (c. 1468–1470). Francesca da Rimini tells Dante that he and Paolo were reading the story of Lancelot's adulterous affair with Guenevere when they fell in love, *Inf* V.127–137. Because of his love for the queen, Lancelot fails in the Grail quest, and Arthur's kingdom is destroyed.

No one could describe the dances and the subtle looks at Cambyuskan's feast but Launcelot, and he is dead, *SqT* 283–287. The Nun's Priest says that his story is as true as the book of Launcelot de Lake, *NPT* 3210–3214. **[Arthour]**

Chrétien de Troyes, *Erec und Enide*, ed. W. Foerster, 63; *ibid.*, *Lancelot or The Knight of the Cart* (*Le chevalier de la charrette*), trans. W.W. Kibler; *"Lancelot do lac,"* the Non-Cyclic Old French Prose Romance, ed. E. Kennedy; N.J. Lacy, ed., *The Arthurian Encyclopedia*; Sir Thomas Malory, *Works,* ed. E. Vinaver; J. Weston, *The Legend of Sir Launcelot du Lac.*

LAVEYNE, LAVINA, LAVYNE. Lavinia, princess of Latium, was first betrothed to Turnus, king of the Rituli. She was later given to Aeneas, and Turnus declared war on Latium (*Aeneid* VII.45–285, XII).

Lavyne's story is painted on the glass of the dreamer's room, *BD* 331; Eneas marries Lavina, *HF* I.458. Lavyne/Laveyne must bow before Alceste, *LGW F* 257, *LGW G* 211. After Eneas deserts Dido, he weds Lavyne, *LGW* 1325–1331. **[Dido: Eneas: Latyne: Turnus]**

Laveyne appears once initially, *LGW G* 211 with elided final -*e; Lavina* appears once in medial position, *HF* I.458 with three syllables; *Lavyne* appears once initially, *LGW F* 257 with elided final -*e*, and twice in final rhyming position, *BD* 331; *LGW* 1331, with final syllabic -*e*.

Virgil, *Aeneid,* ed. and trans. H.R. Fairclough, II.4–23; 298–365.

LAYUS. King Laius of Thebes was warned by the Delphic Oracle that his son would kill him. When Oedipus was born to his wife Jocasta, Laius ordered the baby killed by driving a spike through his ankles and by exposure on Mount Cithaeron. A shepherd found the baby and took him to the king and queen of Corinth. When Oedipus inquired of the Delphic Oracle about his parentage, he was told that he would kill his father and marry his mother. Thinking that the people who had reared him were his parents, he fled from home. On the way to Thebes, he met a litter with an old man, whose servants refused to let him pass. During the fight that ensued, Oedipus killed the old man. Later, after he had married the queen, Jocasta, he learned that the old man had been his father, Laius (*Roman de Thèbes* 1–517; *The Story of Thebes* 1–517).

Pandarus finds Criseyde reading the story of Thebes, and how King Layus died because of his son Edippus, *Tr* II.100–102. **[Edippe]**

Layus, the ME spelling variant, occurs in medial position, *Tr* II.101.

Roman de Thèbes, ed. L. Constans, I: 1–28; *Roman de Thèbes (The Story of Thebes),* trans. J.S. Coley, 1–13; Statius, *Thebaid,* ed. and trans. J.H. Mozley, I: 344–347.

LAZAR. Lazarus was the poor man who sat begging at the gate of Dives's house. When the two men died, Lazarus went to Abraham's bosom, while the rich man went to hell (Luke 16:19–31). The name was also a popular term to denote lepers.

The Friar knows the innkeepers better than the "lazars," *Gen Prol* 242. Dives and Lazar lived differently and had different rewards, *SumT* 1877–1878. **[Dives]**

The abbreviated form, *Lazar,* occurs initially, *SumT* 1877, and medially with initial stress, *Gen Prol* 242, 245.

Dives and Pauper, ed. P.H. Barnum.

LAZARUS of Bethany was the brother of Martha and Mary. When he died, Jesus raised him from the dead (John 12:1-44).

Melibeus remembers that Jesus wept at Lazarus's death, *Mel* 985–986. *Lazarus* occurs only once.

Hilarius, "The Raising of Lazarus." *The Drama of the Medieval Church,* ed. K. Young, II: 212–218.

LEAH: [LIA]
LEANDER: [LEANDRE]

LEANDRE. Leander of Abydos fell in love with Hero, priestess of Venus at Sestos. Guided by the light from her window, he swam the Hellespont every night to be with her. During a storm the wind blew out the light, and Leander drowned. Hero, in despair, threw herself into the Hellespont (*Heroides* XVIII, XIX; *OM* IV.3150–3586; Machaut, *Le Jugement dou roy de Navarre*, 3221–3310).

The Man of Law says that Chaucer has narrated the story of the drowned Leandre and his Hero, *MLI* 69, but there is no story extant in his corpus. **[Erro]**

Leandre, the OF variant, appears medially.

Guillaume de Machaut, *Oeuvres*, ed. E. Hoepffner, I: 248–251; Ovid, *Her*, ed. and trans. G. Showerman, 244–275; *OM*, ed. C. de Boer, II, deel 21: 78–87.

LEGNANO: [LYNYAN]
LEMUEL: [LAMUEL]

LENNE. Nicholas of Lynne in Norfolk, fl. fourteenth century, was a Carmelite lecturer in theology. He is not to be confused with Nicholas the Franciscan friar, who is remembered as philosopher, cosmographer, and astronomer. In 1386 John of Gaunt requested a calendar from Nicholas of Lynne, who composed one for the years 1387 to 1462, arranged for the latitude and longitude of Oxford and set with elaborate astronomical tables.

Chaucer says that he has used the *Kalendarium* of Nicholas of Lynne in his *Treatise on the Astrolabe* and that he intends to give the tables used to find the altitude meridian after the calendars of Frere J. Somer and N. Lenne, *Astr Prol* 80–85. Besides this brief mention, there is evidence that Chaucer used the *Kalendarium* in *The Canterbury Tales.* Sigmund Eisner points out that the astronomical periphrasis of *MLI* 1–14, where Bailly calculates that it is ten o'clock on April 18 on the Julian calendar, is indebted to the *Kalendarium.* The phrase "the ark of his artificial day" is explained correctly in *Astr* II.7.1–22, but Bailly makes an error, for he is "nat depe ystert in loore," *MLI* 4. Chauntecleer, on the third of May, gives the sun's position in an astronomical periphrasis, *NPT* 3187–3199, which, Eisner points out, uses Nicholas of Lynne's shadow scale. The astronomical periphrasis at *ParsP* 1–11 is also indebted to the shadow scale of Nicholas of Lynne. Here the narrator makes an error: he says that Libra is the moon's exaltation, but Libra is Saturn's exaltation or point of greatest influence. The lines mean that Libra is just a few degrees above the horizon, 3 degrees in ascension. **[Somer]**

The Kalendarium of Nicholas of Lynne, ed. S. Eisner, trans. G. MacEoin and S. Eisner, 29–55; J.D. North, "Kalenderes Enlumyned Ben They." *RES* 20 (1969): 129–154, 257–283, 418–444; H.M. Smyser, "A View of Chaucer's Astronomy." *Speculum* 45 (1970): 359–373; C. Wood, *Chaucer and the Country of the Stars*, 275–280.

LEO, LEON, LEOUN, LYOUN. Leo the Lion is the fifth sign of the zodiac and both day house and night house of the sun (*Tetrabiblos* I.17). The hot and dry sign, it lies in the northern hemisphere between Cancer and Virgo (*Confessio Amantis* VII.1067–1072).

Saturn is particularly destructive when he enters Leo, *KnT* 2461–2462. The sun has left the "angle meridional" or the tenth mansion, and the Lion is ascending with his Aldiran; that is, the time is very much past noon, *SqT* 263–267. The Lion begins to rise at noon and is fully risen at about a quarter to three. Aurelius asks Phebus to request Lucina, his sister the moon, to hold the waters over the rocks when the next opposition takes place and the sun is in Leo, *FranklT* 1055–1061. Since the sun controls the moon and both move at the same rate, the resulting flood tide could last as long as two years. Ector decides to fight the Greeks on the day when Phebus is in the breast of Hercules's Lion, *Tr* IV.29–35; thus the sign is identified as the Nemean Lion. The time is either the latter part of July or the beginning of August. Skeat (II: 485) suggests that since the sun is in the breast of Leo or near Regulus, the brightest star of the sign, the time is the first week of August. Criseyde promises to return before the moon passes out of Aries, beyond Leo, *Tr* IV.1592. The moon passes out of Leo as Criseyde prepares for bed instead of returning to Troy, *Tr* V.1019. Leo is the fifth sign of the zodiac, *Astr* I.8.3; it lies directly opposite Aquarius, *Astr* II.6.17, and is the sovereign or western sign that Taurus obeys, *Astr* II.28.7. [**Aldiran: Ercules: Saturn**]

Leo, the Latin variant, appears in the prose of the *Astrolabe*; *Leon* appears once medially, *SqT* 265; *Leoun* occurs twice medially, *Tr* IV.1592, V.1019, and in the prose of the *Astrolabe*; once in final rhyming position, *FranklT* 1058; *Lyoun* occurs once in final rhyming position, *Tr* IV.32. *Leon, Leoun, Lyoun* are variants of OF *Lion* and Anglo-Norman *Leun*.

John Gower, *The Complete Works,* ed. G.C. Macaulay, III: 262; Ptolemy, *Tetrabiblos,* ed. and trans. F.E. Robbins, 79; M. Stokes, "The Moon in Leo in Book V of *Troilus and Criseyde.*" *ChauR* 17 (1982–1983): 116–129.

LEON: [LEO]

LEONARD (saint). Leonard de Nolac, fl. sixth century A.D., was the hermit and abbot of Limousin. Jacobus de Voragine says that he was born c. A.D. 50 and spent his youth at the court of King Clovis, his godfather. The king was so fond of him that he set free any prisoner the young man visited. As he became more and more known for holiness, the king wanted to give him a bishopric, but Leonard refused, preferring a life of solitude. After his death, his cult spread to Belgium, Italy, Germany, and England. He is the patron saint of prisoners (*Legenda aurea* CLV). There was a Benedictine convent of St. Leonard's about two miles from Chaucer's house in Aldgate.

The poet compares himself to a pilgrim traveling wearily the two miles to St. Leonard's shrine, *HF* I.115–118.

The name appears in final rhyming position, *HF* I.117.

Jacobus de Voragine, *GL*, trans. G. Ryan and H. Ripperger, 657–661; *ibid., LA*, ed. Th. Graesse, 687–691; H.M. Smyser, "Chaucer's Two-Mile Pilgrimage." *MLN* 56 (1941): 205–207; *The South-English Legendary,* ed. C. D'Evelyn and A.J. Mill, II: 476–483.

LEOUN, BOOK OF THE: [GUILLAUME DE MACHAUT]
LEWIS: [LOWYS]

LIA. Leah, Laban's elder daughter with weak eyes, was stealthily married to Jacob in place of Rachel, whom he loved. Not until the next morning did Jacob know that Laban had deceived him (Genesis 29:13–35).

The Second Nun defines *Cecile* as a "conjoynynge of heaven and Lia," explaining that Lia represents the saint's busyness, *SNP* 94–98. Jacobus de Voragine says that the saint is called *Lya* because of her hard work, *LA* CLXIX. Leah represents the active life, *Purg* XXVII.97–108. **[Cecile: Jacob: Jacobus Januensis: Rachel]**

Lia is the form in the Latin Vulgate, and appears twice medially, *SNT* 96, 98.

Dante, *Divine Comedy,* ed. and trans. C.S. Singleton, II, 1: 296–297; Jacobus de Voragine, *GL*, trans. G. Ryan and H. Ripperger, 689; *ibid., LA*, ed. Th. Graesse, 771.

LIBEAUS DESCONUS: [LYBEUX]

LIBRA, the constellation the Balance, the seventh sign of the zodiac and the day house of Venus, is the exaltation or sign of maximum power of Saturn and the depression or sign of minimum power of the sun (*Tetrabiblos* I.17, 19) and the hot and moist sign (*Confessio Amantis* VII.1111–1120). It lies in the southern hemisphere between Scorpio in the south and Virgo in the north. Libra, which the sun enters on September 21 in modern times, is the autumn or fall equinox as Aries is the spring equinox.

The narrator makes an error when he says that Libra is the moon's exaltation, or sign in which the moon is most powerful, *ParsP* 1–11. Sigmund Eisner points out that the narrator means that Libra is just a few degrees above the horizon, 3 degrees in its ascent. Libra is the seventh sign of the zodiac, *Astr* I.8.4. The heads or beginnings of Aries and Libra turn on their circles of the equinox, *Astr* I.17.14–16; Aries is the spring equinox and Libra is the autumn equinox. When the sun is in the head or beginning of Libra, days and nights are of equal length, *Astr* I.17.22–23. All the signs moving within the heads or beginnings of Aries and Libra are said to move northward, *Astr* I.17.26–28. Libra lies directly opposite Aries, *Astr* II.6.14–15.

The beginning of Libra in its equinox is as far from the south of the horizon as is the zenith from the arctic pole, *Astr* II.22.1–3. To calculate altitude, the altitude of the sun must be measured when the sun is in the head of Libra or Aries, *Astr* II.25.13–16. To calculate latitude, find the altitude of the sun at noon at the time of the equinox, which can only be done on two days of the year, March 12 and September 12 in Chaucer's day. If it is too long to wait until the sun is in Aries (spring equinox) or Libra (autumn equinox), observe its midday altitude and allow for its declination or celestial latitude (point in the celestial sphere), *Astr* II.25.34–39. All the signs from the beginning of Libra to the end of Pisces are called southern signs because they lie in the southern hemisphere, *Astr* II.28.37. The sun never rises due east unless it is at the beginning of Aries or Libra, in the spring or autumn equinox, *Astr* II.31.3–6. [**Aries: Lenne: Venus**]

The name appears once medially, *ParsP* 11, and in the prose of the *Astrolabe*.

Chaucer, *A Treatise on the Astrolabe*, ed. W.W. Skeat; John Gower, *The Complete Works*, ed. G.C. Macaulay, III: 263; Ptolemy, *Tetrabiblos*, ed. and trans. F.E. Robbins, 80–81, 88–91; C. Wood, *Chaucer and the Country of the Stars*, 275–287.

LIGNACO: [LYNYAN]

LIGURGE(S) is Phyllis's father in "The Legend of Phillis." He does not play a significant part in the story. [**Demophon: Phillis**]

The form, the ME genitive case, appears initially, *LGW* 2425.

LIMOTE. Skeat (III: 273) suggests that this name identifies Elymas the sorcerer, whom Paul the Apostle encountered at Paphos. Sergius Paulus, the Roman deputy, invited Paul and Barnabas to preach to him, but Elymas tried to prevent it. Paul denounced him, and Elymas was immediately struck blind. Then Sergius Paulus believed in the new faith (Acts 13:6–12).

Limote appears with witches and sorcerers in the hall of Fame's house, *HF* III.1274.

The name appears once, initially.

LITTLE BEAR: [ARCTOUR]
LITTLE DIPPER: [ARCTOUR]
LIVILLA: [LYVIA]

LIVIUS, LIVYUS. Titus Livius, 59 B.C.–A.D. 17, was born at Padua. Little is known of his life. Augustus was interested in his work and seems to have respected him despite his republican sentiments (Tacitus, *Annales* IV.34). Suetonius records that he encouraged Claudius in his historical studies. His great work, *Ab urbe condita libri,* originally consisted of 142 books, set out in decades of 10 books, of which 35 are extant. Livy used the annalistic tradition, setting out events year by year, a method adopted by Tacitus.

Plutarch and Lucan used his work; Dante, Chaucer, and Jean de Meun seem to have known Livy. The same books known to us were available during the medieval period. Nicholas Trevet (c. 1265–c.1334) wrote a commentary on Livy's great work.

The Physician identifies Livius as his source, *PhysT* 1, just as Jean de Meun does for his version, *RR* 5589–5658. Chaucer names Livius as his source for Lucretia's story, *BD* 1084; *LGW* 1683; it is more likely that he used *RR* 8608–8616, where the Jealous Husband commends her suicide and regrets that no Lucretia lives in Rome today. Shannon points out that Chaucer's version resembles Ovid, *Fasti* II.721–783.

Livius appears in final rhyming position, *PhysT* 1, *BD* 1084; *Lyvius,* a spelling variant, appears in final rhyming position, *LGW* 1683.

R.J. Dean, "The Earliest Medieval Commentary on Livy." *Medievalia et Humanistica* 3 (1945): 86–98, 4 (1946): 110; Henry L. Harder, "Livy in Gower's and Chaucer's Lucrece Stories." *PMPA* 2 (1977): 1–7; Livy, *Livy* [*Ab urbe condita libri*], ed. and trans. B.O. Foster *et al.*; *RR*, ed. E. Langlois, III: 89; *RR*, trans. C. Dahlberg, 114; E.F. Shannon, *CRP*, 224; Suetonius, *De vita Caesarum,* ed. and trans. J.C. Rolfe, II: 75; Tacitus, *Annals of Imperial Rome,* trans. M. Grant, 170.

LIVY: [LIVIUS]
LIVYUS: [LIVIUS]

LOLLIUS. Scholars have advanced many candidates for this name. Lillian Hornstein asserts that Lollius was the pseudonym of Petrarch's classicist friend, Lelus Petri Stephani de Toseltes. Boyd A. Wise proposes that Lollius is another name for Boccaccio. H.J. Epstein advocates Bassus Lollius, whose epigrams are dated A.D. 19. G.L. Kittredge and R.A. Pratt maintain that Chaucer means Lollius when he says Lollius, and they show that Lollius of Horace's *Epistles* I.ii.1–2 was thought to be a writer on the Trojan War. John of Salisbury also misread Horace's lines in *Policraticus* VII.9.

Lollius, with other writers on war—Homer, Dares, Titus Livius, and Guido—stands on a pillar of iron, metal of Mars, *HF* III.1465–1472. Chaucer names Lollius as his source for the story of Troilus, *Tr* I.393–399. **[Dares Frygius: Guido: Livius: Omer]**

Lollius appears only in final rhyming position, *HF* III.1468; *Tr* I.394; *Tr* V.1653.

H.J. Epstein, "The Identity of Chaucer's Lollius." *MLQ* 34 (1942): 391–400; D.K. Fry, "Chaucer's Zanzis and a Possible Source for *Troilus and Criseyde* IV.407–413." *ELN* 9 (1971): 81–85; L.H. Hornstein, "Petrarch's Laelius, Chaucer's Lollius?" *PMLA* 63 (1948): 64–84; G.L. Kittredge, "Chaucer's Lollius." *Harvard Studies in Classical Philology* 28 (1917): 47–133; R.A. Pratt, "A Note on Chaucer's Lollius." *MLN* 65 (1950): 183–187; B.A. Wise, *The Influence of Statius upon Chaucer*, 6.

LONGINUS: [LONGIUS]

LONGIUS. Longinus, fl. first century A.D., a Roman centurion, pierced the side of Jesus with his sword as he hung on the cross, according to tradition. He subsequently became blind and was converted to Christianity, for which he suffered martyrdom (*Legenda aurea* XLVII).

Longius pierced Christ's heart and made his blood run down, *ABC* 163. The shortened form, *Longius*, appears medially.

Jacobus de Voragine, *GL*, trans. G. Ryan and H. Ripperger, 191; *ibid., LA*, ed. Th. Graesse, 202–203.

LOOTH. Lot was the son of Abraham's brother Amram. He accompanied his uncle to the land of Canaan and settled in Jordan near Sodom and Gomorrah. After the Lord destroyed the two cities, however, Lot lived in a cave with his two daughters. On two successive nights his daughters gave him wine and slept with him. They said to each other that in this way they would preserve their father's posterity. Each daughter subsequently bore Lot a son (Genesis 19:30–38).

In his denunciation of drunkenness, the Pardoner says that Lot lay with his two daughters, so drunk he was, *PardT* 485–487. R.A. Pratt suggests Trevet's *Les Cronicles*, fol. 5ʳ, for the detail of Lot's drunkenness.

Looth, a variant of ME Loth, appears medially, *PardT* 485.

R.A. Pratt, "Chaucer and *Les Cronicles* of Nicholas Trevet." *SLL*, 305.

LORRIS, GUILLAUME DE: [GUILLAUME DE LORRIS]
LOT: [LOOTH]

LOWYS. Chaucer says that he has written *A Treatise on the Astrolabe* for "lyte Lowys, my sone," *Astr Prologue* I.1. G.L. Kittredge offers a conjecture that the "sone" is more likely a "godson," perhaps Lewis Clifford, son of Chaucer's close friend, Sir Lewis Clifford. Little Lewis died in 1391, the date Chaucer gives for carrying out his experiments with the instrument, and Kittredge suggests that his death accounts for the unfinished state of the treatise. John M. Manly suggests that Lewis is the name of Chaucer's younger son, the older being Thomas Chaucer.

The name appears in *The Prologue to the Astrolabe*.

M.M. Crow and C.C. Olson, eds., *Chaucer Life Records*, 544; G.L. Kittredge, "Lewis Chaucer or Lewis Clifford." *MP* 14 (1916–1917): 513–518; J.M. Manly, "Litel Lowis my Sone." *TLS*, June 7, 1929: 430.

LOY (saint). Loy or Eloy is the English name for St. Eligius, c. 588–660, who became bishop of Noyon. As goldsmith to Clothaire II, Dagobert I, and Clovis II of France, he was famous for his gold chalices, for his courtesy and refinement. He incurred King Dagobert's displeasure for refusing to swear. While he was a courtier, under his fine clothes and adornments he wore a hair shirt. After embracing the religious life, he became known for his acts of mercy and concern for the poor, and he was invoked as patron saint of the poor and of poorhouses after his death. He was also adviser and confessor to several Benedictine convents. St. Godebertha, St. Gertrude, and St. Aurea were the three abbesses with whom he was especially connected (*PL* 87: 481–594).

Madame Eglentyne, a Benedictine abbess, swears by St. Loy, *Gen Prol* 120. The saint is invoked as patron saint of blacksmiths and carriers, *FrT* 1564. [**Eglentyne**]

Loy, formed by aphesis or loss of the initial unstressed syllable from OF *Eloi* and derived from Latin *Eligius,* appears in final rhyming position, *Gen Prol* 120; *FrT* 1564.

B. Foster, "Chaucer's Seint Loy: An Anglo-Norman Pun?" *N&Q* 213 (1968): 244–245; A.S. Haskell, "The St. Loy Oath Reconsidered." *Essays on Chaucer's Saints,* 32–38; Jacobus de Voragine, *LA* 952–953 (no English translation in G. Ryan and H. Ripperger's translation); J.L. Lowes, "The Prioress's Oath." *Romanic Review* 5 (1914): 368–385; Paul Parsy, *Saint Eloi (590–659).*

LUC (saint). Luke, is traditionally regarded as the author of the third Gospel and The Acts of the Apostles. Paul calls him "Luke the Physician," Colossians 4:14. His symbol is the ox.

Chaucer reminds Harry Bailly that the evangelists differ in their stories about the pain of Jesus Christ, yet their stories are all true, and he names the four evangelists, *Mel* 943–952. The Parson quotes from Luke 15:7, 24, *ParsT* 700–701, and Luke 23, *ParsT* 702.

Luc, possibly derived from Latin *Lucanus,* appears in medial position, *Mel* 951.

C.K. Barrett, *Luke the Historian in Recent Study; The South-English Legendary,* ed. C. D'Evelyn and A.J. Mill, II: 439–443.

LUCAN. Marcus Annaeus Lucanus, A.D. 39–65, was born in Cordova, Spain. He was grandson of Seneca the Elder and a nephew of Seneca the philosopher. His most famous poem, *Pharsalia,* deals with the civil wars of Julius Caesar and Pompey and has been called the greatest Latin epic after the *Aeneid.*

The Man of Law compares the procession that conveys Custance to her house with the triumph of Julius, of which Lucan boasts, *MLT* 401. Lucan says that Caesar had no triumph, *Pharsalia* III.71–79. Robinson (694) suggests that Chaucer may have used *Li Hystoire de Julius Cesar,* by Jehan de Tuim, for this detail. The Monk recommends Lucan's *Pharsalia* for the story of Julius Caesar, *MkT* 2719–2720. Lucan stands on a pillar of iron, the metal of Mars, *HF* III.1499, bearing up the fame of Julius and Pompey. Lady

Philosophy quotes *Pharsalia* I.128, *Bo* IV, *Prosa* 6.231–233. Chaucer sends his poem to kiss the steps of Virgil, Omer, Ovide, Lucan, and Stace, *Tr* V.1786–1792, in a stanza influenced perhaps by Boccaccio's *Envoy*, *Il Filostrato* II.376–378. [**Catoun²: Omer: Ovide: Stace: Swetonius: Virgil**]

Lucan appears once initially, *MkT* 2719; twice in medial positions, *MLT* 401, *Tr* V.1792; and once in final rhyming position, *HF* III.1499.

Jehan de Tuim, *Li Hystoire de Julius Cesar*, ed. F. Settegast; Lucan, *Pharsalia*, ed. and trans. J.D. Duff; *Riverside Chaucer*, ed. L. Benson, 860.

LUCIA, LUCYE. Lucilla gave her husband a dose of poison, mistaking it for a love potion. Walter Map tells the story in *Dissuasio Valerii ad Rufinum ne uxorem ducat,* IV.3 (c. 1180–1183).

Jankyn reads the story to Alys from "Valerie and Theofraste," *WBP* 752–756. [**Alisoun²: Jankyn²: Valerie**]

Lucia appears initially, *WBP* 752, and *Lucye* occurs in final rhyming position, *WBP* 747.

W. Map, *De nugis curialium: Courtiers Trifles*, ed. and trans. M.R. James, rev. C.N.L. Brook and R.A.B. Mynors, 304–305.

LUCIFER¹, LUCYFER, is the name of the morning star. Cicero says that *Lucifer* is the Latin translation of Greek *phosphorus*, a name for Venus (*De natura deorum* II.20, 53). Ovid refers to Venus as Lucifer (*Heroides* XVIII.112).

Hesperus rises as the evening star but pales when the sun rises and is then called Lucifer, *Bo* I, *Metr* 5.11–16. Lucifer is the day star, *Bo* III, *Metr* 1.9–12. Lucifer brings the day, *Bo* IV, *Metr* 6.15–18, and is the day's messenger, *Tr* III.1417–1418. [**Hesperus: Venus**]

Lucifer is derived from *lucem ferens*, "light-bearing." *Lucyfer* is a spelling variant.

Cicero, *DND*, ed. and trans. H. Rackham, 174–175; Ovid, *Her*, ed. and trans. G. Showerman, 250–251.

LUCIFER². Lucifer, later identified with Satan, was originally called "son of the morning," Isaiah 14:12. Dante places Lucifer as a three-headed monster in the very pit of hell, frozen from mid-breast firm in the ice, *Inf* XXXIV.23–60.

The Monk gives a brief stanza on the tragedy of Lucifer, now Sathanas, *MkT* 1999–2006. The Parson preaches that the sale of sacred things is the most horrible sin after pride, the sin of Lucifer, *ParsT* 785–790. [**Satan**]

Lucifer appears in medial position, *MkT* 1999, and in an apostrophe, *MkT* 2004.

Dante, *Divine Comedy*, ed. and trans. C.S. Singleton, I, 1: 362–365; J.B. Russell, *Lucifer: The Devil in the Middle Ages*.

LUCILLA: [LUCIA]

LUCINA, LUCYNA is an epithet of Diana and Juno, both goddesses of childbirth. Isidore says that Diana is called Lucina because she is bright (*Etym* VIII.xi.57).

Chaucer applies the name exclusively to Diana. A woman in labor appeals to Lucina, *KnT* 2085. Aurelius asks for help from Apollo's sister, "Lucina the sheene," *FranklT* 1045, empress of the sea. Criseyde swears by "Lucina the sheene" to return to Troilus by the tenth day, *Tr* IV.1591. **[Cinthia: Diane: Latona: Proserpina]**

Both *Lucina* and the spelling variant *Lucyna* appear medially, *KnT* 2085; *FranklT* 1045; *Tr* IV.1591.

Isidore, *Etymologiae,* ed. W.M. Lindsay, I.

LUCRECE, LUCRESSE. Lucretia, fl. late sixth century B.C., daughter of the consul Lucretius, was the wife of Tarquinius Collatinus, an officer in the Roman army. During a break in the fighting during the siege of Ardea, the officers were entertained at a feast. Collatinus boasted of his wife's fidelity and beauty and suggested that they all ride off to Collatia to prove the truth of his boast. When he reached his house, Collatinus found his wife Lucretia spinning with her maids. Sextus Tarquinius, Collatinus's cousin, immediately caught fire with lust for Lucretia. He later returned to the house, and Lucretia welcomed him as a relative. She prepared a meal for him, but after the meal Tarquinius pulled his sword and threatened her with death unless she yielded to his lust. After he had threatened her several times, she at length gave way. When day came, she sent for her father and her husband and told them what had happened. They forgave her, but Lucretia stabbed herself and fell dead at their feet (*Fasti* II.685–852; Livy, *Ab urbe condita liber* I.57–59). The virtue of Lucretia is a medieval commonplace. Augustine emphasizes the inappropriateness of her suicide, *The City of God* I.18, in a comparison of Christian and pagan virtue. Jealous Husband tells the story and says that there are no more Lucretias in Rome, *RR* 8608–8642. Gower uses the story to illustrate unchastity, *Confessio Amantis* VII.4754–5130.

Lucretia is exemplary of wifely virtue, *MLI* 63; *FranklT* 1405; *BD* 1087; *Anel* 82. Lucresse is a virtuous wife, but Alceste surpasses her, *LGW F* 257, *LGW G* 211. The full story appears in *LGW* 1680–1885. **[Augustin: Brutus[2]: Colatyn: Livius: Tarquinius[2]]**

Lucrece is the French variant of Latin *Lucretia,* feminine of *Lucretius,* the name of a Roman clan. It occurs only in final rhyming position, *BD* 1082. *Lucresse,* a pronunciation variant, never appears initially; it appears four times in medial positions, *MLI* 63; *FranklT* 1405; *LGW F* 257, *LGW G* 211; *LGW* 1691; and four times in final rhyming position, *Anel* 82; *LGW* 1686, 1786, 1872.

Augustine, *Concerning the City of God*, trans. H. Bettenson, 28–30; Ian Donaldson, *The Rapes of Lucretia: A Myth and its Transformations*; John Gower, *The Complete Works*, ed. G.C. Macaulay, III: 367–377; H.H. Harder, "Livy in Gower's and Chaucer's Lucrece Stories." *PMPA* 2 (1977): 1–7; Livy, *Livy* [*Ab urbe condita libri*], ed. and trans. B.O. Foster, I: 198–209; Ovid, *Fasti*, ed. and trans. J.G. Fraser, 106–119; *RR*, ed. E. Langlois, III: 89–90; *RR*, trans. C. Dahlberg, 158.

LUCRESSE: [LUCRECE]
LUCRETIA: [LUCRECE]
LUCYE: [LUCIA]
LUCYNA: [LUCINA]
LUKE: [LUC]
LYBEUS: [LYBEUX]

LYBEUX. Sir Lybeus is the hero of the romance, *Libeaus Desconus*, or *The Fair Unknown*. He is Sir Gawain's son, named Gingelein, and the romance appears in the *Gawain* cycle, written about 1350.

Sir Thopas, the flower of chivalry, surpasses Sir Lybeux, *Thop* 900.

Lybeux is one of those names that developed *-x* in place of *-s* as a variant pronunciation in Middle English. Others are *Amphiorax*, *Brixseyda*, *Calyxte*. The name appears medially.

Libeaus Desconus, ed. M. Mills; *Riverside Chaucer*, ed. L. Benson, 814; W. Schofield, *Studies in Libeaus Desconus.*

LYCURGUS: [LIGURGE]

LYGURGE is Palamon's champion in *The Knight's Tale*. In Boccaccio's *Il Teseida delle nozze d'Emilia* VI.14, Lycurgus is Arcite's champion. Chaucer probably had in mind Ovid's mention of Lycurgus of Thrace (*Met* IV.22). W.C. Curry sees Lygurge as a man influenced by Saturn, accompanying Palamon, who is under Saturn's protection as Venus's knight. [**Arcita: Emetreus: Palamon**]

The form, the ME variant, occurs once initially, *KnT* 2129, and once in medial position, *KnT* 2644.

Boccaccio, *Tutte le opere*, ed. V. Branca, II: 421; W.C. Curry, *Chaucer and the Mediaeval Sciences*, 134–137; Ovid, *Met*, ed. and trans. F.J. Miller, I: 180–181.

LYNCEUS: [LYNO]
LYNNE: [LENNE]

LYNO. Lynceus was one of the fifty sons of Aegyptus who married their cousins, the fifty daughters of Danaus. Danaus commanded his daughters to slay their husbands because he did not trust Aegyptus. All obeyed except Hypermnestra, who married Lynceus. She helped him to escape, and Danaus imprisoned her. (*Heroides* XIV; *OM* II.4587–4796).

Chaucer switches the sons and daughters; Lyno becomes Danao's son and marries Ypermestra, Egiste's daughter. She saves his life by warning him about her father's command, and he flees, leaving her behind, *LGW* 2562–2723. **[Danao: Egiste: Ypermestra]**

Lyno is ablative singular of nominative *Linus*. It appears in Filippo Ceffi's Italian translation of *Heroides* (c. 1320–1330), which Chaucer may have known. It occurs four times in medial positions, *LGW* 608, 2676, 2711, 2716, and twice in final rhyming position, *LGW* 2569, 2604.

S.B. Meech, "Chaucer and an Italian translation of the *Heroides*." *PMLA* 45 (1930): 123; Ovid, *Her*, ed. and trans. G. Showerman, 170–181; *OM*, ed. C. de Boer, I, deel 15: 268–273.

LYNYAN. Giovanni da Legnano, fl. fourteenth century A.D., was born in Milan. He became professor of canon law at Bologna University about 1350, where he developed a reputation as one of its most renowned professors. He was famous for a variety of works, most of them dedicated to princes of the church. He dedicated *De bello* (c. 1360) to Cardinal Albornoz; for Urban V, he prepared *De pace* (1364), and *De pluralitate beneficiorum* (1365) as well as several treatises for Gregory XI. He defended Urban VI after the outbreak of the Great Western Schism and achieved an international reputation. When he died in 1383, he was at the height of his fame. After 1378, the English court took Urban's side, and its members, therefore, would be concerned with the views of his chief apologist, John of Legnano. As a member of Richard II's court, Chaucer would have been familiar with these events, especially since he was in Italy when the Schism broke out. Legnano wrote works on ethics, theology, and astronomy in addition to his works on law.

The Clerk says that Petrarch illumined the poetry of Italy as Lynyan did philosophy, law, and the arts, *ClT* 33–35.

Lynyan, the ME variant derived by pronunciation of the Italian word, occurs once, in medial position, *ClT* 34.

J.P. McCall, "Chaucer and John of Legnano." *Speculum* 40 (1965): 484–489.

LYRA: [ARIONIS HARPE]
LYRE: [ARIONIS HARPE]

LYVIA. Livilla, c. 13 B.C.–A.D. 31, was the daughter of Antonia and Drusus, son of Tiberius Claudius Nero. She married Drusus, son of the emperor Tiberius, and in A.D. 23 murdered him at the instigation of Sejanus, captain of the Imperial Guard. When Sejanus asked Tiberius for permission to marry Livilla in A.D. 25, Tiberius refused. Eight years later, Tiberius learned that Livilla had poisoned Drusus, and he ordered her execution (Suetonius, *Tiberius* LXII; *The Deified Claudius* I; Tacitus, *Annals* IV.iii-ix).

Walter Map says that Livilla killed her husband because she hated him very much, *Dissuasio Valerii ad Rufinum philosophum ne uxorem ducat*, IV.3 (c. 1180–1183).

Lyvia is a wicked wife who kills her husband, *WBP* 747–749. [**Alisoun³: Jankyn²: Valerie**]

Chaucer uses the shortened form, probably for metrical reasons. It appears once initially, *WBP* 750, and once in medial position, *WBP* 747. Skeat (V: 311) points out that the name is *Luna*, sometimes *Lima*, in manuscripts of Map's *Dissuasio*. Either form could be confused with *Livia*.

W. Map, *De nugis curialium: Courtiers' Trifles,* ed. and trans. M.R. James, rev. C.N.L. Brooke and R.A.B. Mynors, 304–305; Suetonius, *De vita Caesarum*, ed. and trans. J.C. Rolfe, I: 380–381, II: 6–7; Tacitus, *Annals*, ed. and trans. J. Jackson, III: 6–19.

M

MABELY was probably one popular form of address to an old woman. It is a variant of *Mabel.*

The fiend addresses the old woman who curses the summoner as "Mabely," *FrT* 1626.

ODECN, 89.

MACHABEE. Judas Maccabee, fl. second century A.D., was the famous Jewish general who led the revolt against Antiochus IV Epiphanes, king of Syria. Antiochus sent his generals Nicanor and Timotheus against the Jews in 161 B.C., but Judas Maccabee defeated them decisively. These triumphs are celebrated in the book of Maccabees. Maccabee is one of the Nine Worthies in Caxton's preface to the 1485 edition of *Le Morte d'Arthur* and in *The Parlement of the Thre Ages* 454–461.

Dame Prudence quotes I Mac 2:18, 19: victory lies in God's might, *Mel* 1658–1662. The Monk refers his listeners to II Maccabees 9 for Antiochus's story, *MkT* 2579. [**Alexander: Arthour: David: Ector: Julius**]

G. Cary, *The Medieval Alexander,* 246–268, 340–344; R.S. Loomis, "Verses on the Nine Worthies." *MP* 15 (1917): 19–27; Sir Thomas Malory, *Le Morte d'Arthur,* ed. J. Cowen, I: 3; *The Parlement of the Thre Ages,* ed. M.Y. Offord, 20–21; J.H. Roberts, "The Nine Worthies." *MP* 19 (1922): 297–305.

MACHAUT: [GUILLAUME DE MACHAUT]

MACROBEUS, MACROBYE. Ambrosius Theodosius Macrobius, fl. c. A.D. 399–422, appears to have been a North African. In the Preface to Book I, 11–12, of *Saturnalia,* Macrobius says that he was born in a foreign country and indicates that Latin is not his native tongue. If so, he belongs to a group of North African writers with a similar background, including Apuleius, Fronto, Fulgentius, Maritanus Capella, and Suetonius. Two of his works, *Saturnalia* and *Commentarius in somnium Scipionis*, are dedicated to his son Eustachius. *Saturnalia* is a dialogue among twelve friends at a banquet on the night of a pagan feast and follows Platonic tradition; the *Commentarius* is a Neoplatonic commentary on Cicero's *Somnium Scipionis*, which formed part of *De re publica* VI. The *Saturnalia* influenced Isidore of Seville, Bede, and John of Salisbury.

According to Macrobeus, dreams warn of the future and are called *avisiouns*, *NPT* 3122–3126. In *Commentarius in Somnium Scipionis* I.iii.2, Macrobius discusses five kinds of dreams: (1) the *somnium* or enigmatic dream, (2) the *visio* or prophetic dream, (3) the oracular dream, (4) the *insomnium* or nightmare, and (5) the *visum* or apparition in a dream. The first three are prophetic in that they point to future events. Not even Macrobeus can interpret the poet's dream, *BD* 284–290. Affrican will reward the poet for reading in his old torn book, of which Macrobye wrote not a little, *PF* 109–112. The syntax of these references confuse the authorship of the commentary and the text. Chaucer's copy has seven chapters, *PF* 29–84, and this number suggests a combined edition of Cicero and Macrobius. [**Affrican: Cipioun: Scithero: Suetonius**]

Macrobeus occurs once initially, *NPT* 3123, and once in final rhyming position, *BD* 284; *Macrobye*, three syllables, occurs in medial position, *PF* 111.

C.R. Dahlberg, "Macrobius and the Unity of the *Roman de la Rose.*" *SP* 58 (1961): 573–582; Macrobius, *Macrobius's Commentary on the Dream of Scipio,* trans. W.H. Stahl; *ibid., Saturnalia,* trans. P.V. Davies; *ibid., Saturnalia. In somnium Scipionis commentarius,* ed. J. Willis, I: 3, II: 3–11; J. Winny, *Chaucer's Dream Poems.*

MACROBIUS: [MACROBEUS]
MACROBYE: [MACROBEUS]

MADRIAN. There is no decisive opinion about this saint. D.M. Norris posits a "corruption" of Italian *Madre*; G.L. Frost thinks that a confection called "Conserve of Madrian" is meant; J.R. Byers suggests that Bailly means St. Hadrian or St. Adrian. A.S. Haskell shows that Adrian is the saint meant here. His wife Natalia supported him in his martyrdom in much the same way that Bailly's wife Goodelief urges him to beat his apprentices. Adrian was the patron saint of brewers, and Harry Bailly owns a tavern.

Harry Bailly swears by this saint, *MkP* 1892.

The name appears in final rhyming position.

J.R. Byers, "Harry Bailly's St. Madrian." *ELN* 4 (1966): 6–9; G.L. Frost, "That Precious Corpus Madrian." *MLN* 57 (1942): 177–179; A.S. Haskell, "The Host's Precious

Corpus Madrian." *JEGP* 67 (1968): 430–440; D.M. Norris, "Harry Bailly's 'Corpus Madrian.'" *MLN* 48 (1933): 146–148.

MAEON: [HEMONYDES]
MAGDALEN: [MAGDELENE]

MAGDALENE, MAGDALEYNE, MAUDELEYNE (saint). Mary of Magdala in Galilee, fl. first century A.D., was one of the women whom Jesus healed of evil spirits (Luke 8:2). On the third day after the crucifixion she came to the garden where Jesus was buried, and an angel told her that Jesus had arisen. Jesus appeared first to Mary Magdalene (Mark 16:1–11). Mary Magdalene is identified with Martha's sister in the *South-English Legendary* and the *Legenda aurea.*

In his homily on envy the Parson says that Judas was envious when Mary Magdalene poured her precious ointment on Jesus's head, *ParsT* 500–503. The account in John 12:1–6 tells that Mary, sister of Martha and Lazarus, anointed Jesus. Other accounts in the Gospels do not mention the woman's name (Matthew 26:6–13, Mark 14:3–9). The Parson says that resentment comes because of pride as when Simon the Pharisee resented the Magdalene for weeping at Jesus's feet, *ParsT* 503–504. Luke's account of the incident says that "a woman who was a sinner" anointed Jesus's feet with precious ointment (Luke 7:37–39). Mary Magdalene is identified with the *peccatrix* (sinner) in Gregory's *XL Homiliae in evangelica* XXX and XXXIII (*PL* 16: 1189, 1238–1246). Mary's ointment is the sweet odor of Holy Church, *ParsT* 947–1000. Alceste reminds the God of Love that Chaucer has translated "Orygenes upon the Maudeleyne," *LGW F* 428, *LGW G* 418. She refers to *De Maria Magdalena,* a popular medieval Latin homily attributed to Origen, the earliest manuscripts of which date from the thirteenth century. J.P. McCall points out that *Homelia Origenis de Maria Magdalena* follows the medieval Latin tradition and not the Greek tradition, to which Origen belonged. It enjoyed wide circulation between the thirteenth and sixteenth centuries. McCall lists some 162 manuscripts in Latin, French, Italian, Portuguese, Provençal, Castilian, Dutch, Czech, and English. R. Woolf suggests that Chaucer may have been asked to translate the work for a noble lady. McCall points out that there is some resemblance between the sorrowing Magdalene and Alcyone in *The Book of the Duchess* and between the Magdalene and the women of *The Legend of Good Women.* **[Origenes]**

Maudeleyne is the ME development of OE and Latin *Magdalene.* OE /ag/ becomes ME /au/, as in OE *lagu* > ME *lawe. Magdalene* appears in the *Parson's Tale; Maudeleyne* occurs in final rhyming position, *Gen Prol* 410, as the name of the Shipman's barge, and in *LGW F* 428, *LGW G* 418.

J.E. Cross, "Mary Magdalene in the Old English Martyrology: the Earliest Extant 'Narrat Josephus' variant of her Legend." *Speculum* 53 (1978): 16–25; H.M. Garth, *Saint Mary Magdalene in Medieval Literature*; Jacobus de Voragine, *GL,*

trans. G. Ryan and H. Ripperger, 355–364; *ibid., LA,* ed. Th. Graesse, 407–417;
M. Jennings, "The Art of the Pseudo-Origen Homily *De Maria Magdalena.*"
Medievalia et Humanistica, New Series, no. 5 (1954): 139–152; J.P. McCall,
"Chaucer and the Pseudo-Origen *De Maria Magdalena*: A Preliminary Study."
Speculum 46 (1971): 491–509; D.A. Mycoff, *A Critical Edition of the Legend of Mary
Magdalena from Caxton's "Golden Legende" of 1483*; *The South-English Legen-
dary,* ed. C. D'Evelyn and A.J. Mill, I: 302–315; R. Woolf, "English Imitations of the
Homelia Origenis *De Maria Magdalena.*" *Chaucer and Middle English Studies in
Honor of Rossell Hope Robbins,* ed. B. Rowland, 384–391.

MAGUS: [SYMON MAGUS]

MAHOUN, MAKOMETE, MAKOMETES. Muhammad, c. A.D. 570–632,
son of Abdullah, founded Islam. For over twenty years, between 612 and
632, he claimed to have received revelations from the angel Gabriel, which
he recited to his followers. The Qur'an (or The Recitation) is thus regarded
by Muslims as the Speech of God. When the Meccans rejected his teaching
and threatened his life, Muhammad fled to Medina in 622. The year of the
flight (*hejira*) became the first year of the Islamic calendar (*EI* III: 641–657).

In the eleventh century there appeared the *Vita Mahumeti* (*Life of
Muhammad*), a poem of 1142 lines, sometimes attributed to Hildebert of
Tours, sometimes to Embrico, Treasurer of Mainz, 1090–1112. Muhammad
is here portrayed as a *magus* or magician. Ten of the fourteen manuscripts
date from the twelfth and early thirteenth centuries. Walter of Compiègne
wrote his *Otia de Machomete,* a poem of 1090 lines, between 1137 and 1155.
In his *Gesta Dei per Francos III* (*PL* 156: 689–693), completed before 1112,
Guibert of Nogent included a chapter on Muhammad's life. In 1258 Alexandre du Pont published his poem, *Roman de Mahomet,* which tells the
story of Muhammad and Bahira Sergius, the Nestorian monk who was said
to have converted Muhammad to his heresy. In 1143, Peter the Venerable
of Cluny commissioned Robert of Ketton, for a high fee, to make the first
Latin translation from Arabic of the Qur'an, and the work was completed
at Toledo. Peter wrote to Bernard of Clairvaux that he could not decide
whether the "Muhammadan" error was heresy and its followers heretics or
whether they were to be called pagans (*Epistola Petri Cluniacensis ad
Bernardum Claraevallis, Letter of Peter of Cluny to Bernard of Clairvaux*).

Dante depicts Muhammad among the schismatics; terribly mutilated,
he warns against heresy and schism, *Inf* XXVIII.26–63. Langland relates that
Muhammad was a renegade cardinal and a false Christian, *Piers Plowman*
B. XV.389–414. Muhammad as cardinal appears in the life inserted by Jean
le Clerc of Troyes in his *Roman de Renart le contrefait,* written in the first half
of the fourteenth century. Muhammad appears as heretic and as renegade
cardinal in Ranulph Higden, *Polychronicon* V.xiv. In the *Chansons de geste*
Makomete is one of the several gods of the Saracens, in direct contradiction
to the monotheism of Islam.

Mahoun is the prophet of the Syrians, *MLT* 211–224, 330–336, 337–340. Chaucer also uses the common nouns *mawmet* and *mawmetry*, derived from the Italian form of the name *Maometto* and from OF *mahumet*, meaning "idol" and "idolatry." The Sultaness refers to "the hooly lawes of our Alkoran," *MLT* 332; *alcoran* means "the Koran," the Arabic article is attached to its noun.

The form of the name varies. *Mahoun*, the OF variant, occurs twice medially, *MLT* 224, 340; *Makomete*, derived from medieval Latin *Machometus*, occurs in final rhyming position, *MLT* 333; *Makometes*, the ME genitive case, occurs in medial position, *MLT* 336.

Alexandre du Pont, *Roman de Mahomet en vers du XIIIe siècle;* Dante, *Divine Comedy*, ed. and trans. C.S. Singleton, I, 1: 300–301; R. Higden, *Polychronicon*, ed. J.R. Lumby and C. Babington, VI: 14–51; J. Kritzeck, *Peter the Venerable and Islam*, 212–214; W. Langland, *Piers Plowman*, ed. A.V.C. Schmidt, 190; D. Metlitzki, *The Matter of Araby in Medieval England*, 200–201; R.W. Southern, *Western Views of Islam in the Middle Ages*, 29–30, n. 26.

MAKOMET: [MAHOUN]
MALKIN: [MALKYN]

MALKYN[1](ES). Malkin, a name found generally among working-class women, was also used in proverbial expressions (Whiting 90).

Harry Bailly quotes one of these proverbs, *MLI* 27–31. Martin Stevens suggests that, since the proverb appears after the *Reeve's Tale*, the Host has Malyne, the miller's daughter, in mind. **[Bailly: Malyne]**

Malkynes, the ME genitive case, appears medially, *MLT* 30.

M. Stevens, "Malkyn in the Man of Law's Headlink." *Leeds Studies in English* 1 (1967): 1–5; B.J. Whiting, *Chaucer's Use of Proverbs*, 90.

MALKYN[2] is the widow's maid in *The Nun's Priest's Tale*. She pursues Russell the Fox with the distaff in her hand, *NPT* 3384. **[Chauntecleer: Pertelote: Russell]**

MALYNE is the name of Symkyn's daughter in *The Reeve's Tale*. She reveals to Aleyne that the flour her father stole from him is hidden behind the mill. N.D. Hinton suggests that in thus "maligning" her father she lives up to her name. **[Alayn: Malkyn[1]: Symkyn]**

Malyne, a form of Malkyn, is a pet name for *Mathilda* (Skeat V: 126). Skeat points out that the name generally means "dish cloth" or "oven mop" and is usually the nickname for a promiscuous woman. It appears once, medially, *RvT* 4236.

N.D. Hinton, "Two Names in *The Reeve's Tale*." *Names* 9 (1961): 117–120.

[MARBODE], fl. 1067–1101. Chaucer does not mention Marbode of Rennes, author of *De lapidibus*, a very popular work during the medieval period. Chaucer shows that he had knowledge of this work in an Anglo-Norman translation when he refers to *Lapidaire, HF* III.1350–1352. Marbode of Rennes was born in Angers, France, where he became master of the cathedral school c. 1067 and chancellor of the diocese of Angers c. 1069. In 1096 he became archbishop of Rennes in Britanny. His work, *De lapidibus* (*On Stones*), written in hexameters, is based on Isidore of Seville and Solinus and describes some sixty stones, their real and symbolic qualities. It was translated into Provençal, Italian, French, Irish, Danish, Hebrew, Spanish, and Anglo-Norman.

Chaucer also seems to have been indebted to Marbode's work for the name *Thopas,* derived from the stone *topazius,* which had chivalric and courtly associations. **[Thopas]**

J. Evans, *Anglo-Norman Lapidaries,* xv–xviii; Marbode of Rennes, *Marbode of Rennes' De lapidibus,* ed. J.M. Riddle, trans. C.W. King; F.J.E. Raby, *A History of Christian Latin Poetry,* 273–277.

MARCIA. Marsyas, a Phrygian flute player in Cybele's train, found a flute discarded by Pallas Athena because it distorted her lips when she played it. Marsyas challenged Apollo to a contest, to which Apollo agreed on condition that each play his instrument upside down as well as in its usual position. Since his instrument was the lyre, Apollo won the contest, then skinned Marsyas alive for his presumption. He hung the skin on a plane tree near the source of the river that now bears his name (*Met* VI.382–400; *OM* VI.1921–1980).

Marcia, who lost her skin through Apollo's envy, stands with musicians in Fame's house, *HF* III.1229–1232. Here Chaucer follows a tradition in which Marsyas is feminine. *Marse* appears in an interpolation of forty lines in several manuscripts of the *Roman de la Rose*, between lines 10830 and 10831, indicating a female. *Marsie,* which could be mistaken for a female name, occurs in *OM* VI.1921–1980. **[Apollo: Phebus]**

The name appears in medial position, *HF* III.1229.

A. David, "How Marcia Lost her Skin: A Note on Chaucer's Mythology." *The Learned and the Lewed,* 19–29; Ovid, *Met,* ed. and trans. F.J. Miller, I: 314–317; *OM,* ed. C. de Boer, II, deel 21: 330–332; *RR,* ed. E. Langlois, III: 305–307.

MARCIA CATOUN. Marcia, daughter of Marcius Philippus, was the wife of Cato Uticensis, for whom she bore three children, one of whom was Porcia, who became Brutus's wife. Cato divorced her so that he could marry her to his friend Quintus Hortensius, who wanted her to bear him children and so cement his friendship with Cato. He died several years later, and Marcia begged Cato to make her his wife again. They were remarried but remained wedded in name only (Lucan, *Pharsalia* II.326–349).

Dante gives the story allegorical interpretation: Marcia is a symbol of the noble soul returning to God at the beginnng of old age (*Convivio* IV.xxviii.14–19).

Marcia is a faithful wife, *LGW F* 252, *LGW G* 206. T.R. Lounsbury suggests that Chaucer means Marcia, daughter of Cato Uticensis, who appears in Jerome's *Epistola adversus Jovinianum (Letter Against Jovinian)* I.46 (*PL* 23: 275). [**Catoun²**]

Marcia, feminine of *Marcius,* the name of the Roman clan to which the family belonged, appears in final rhyming position.

Dante, *Il Convivio,* ed. M. Simonelli, 217–218; T.R. Lounsbury, *Studies in Chaucer,* II: 294; Lucan, *Pharsalia,* ed. and trans. J.D. Duff, 80–83.

MARCIAN. Martianus Mineus Felix Capella, fl. fifth century A.D., was the author of *De nuptiis Mercurii et Philologiae.* He appears to have been North African; *Afer Carthaginiensis* (African of Carthage) is added to his name in the manuscripts. Scholars now believe that the book was written after Alaric's sack of Rome, A.D. 410, but before 439. *De nuptiis* is written in Latin prose, interspersed with verses. In nine books it tells of Mercury's marriage with the learned virgin Philologia. The bride ascends to heaven accompanied by the Nine Muses and the Seven Liberal Arts as bridesmaids: Grammar, Logic, Rhetoric, Geometry, Arithmetic, Astronomy, and Music. The last seven books are devoted to these last, forming an encyclopedia of the liberal arts. A key element in the history of European intellectual development, the work preserves, with Boethius, Cassiodorus, and Isidore, the classical learning available in the Middle Ages. Two commentaries on *De nuptiis* appear in the ninth century: one by Remigius of Auxerre, *Commentum in Martianum,* and the other by John Scott Eriugena, *Annotationes in Marcianum.*

The wedding of Philology and Mercury was not more splendid than that of January and May, *MerchT* 1732–1735. The frightened dreamer thinks of Marcian's descriptions of the heavens, *HF* II.985–990, a reference to Book VIII, "De astronomia." [**Mercurie**]

Marcian, the English contraction of Latin *Martianus* and derived from *Marcius,* the name of a Roman clan, appears in final rhyming position, *MerchT* 1732; *HF* II.985.

De nuptiis Philologiae et Mercurii, in *Martianus Capella,* ed. A. Dick; M.L.W. Laistner, "Martianus Capella and his Ninth Century Commentators." *Bulletin of the John Rylands Library* 9 (1925): 130–138; C.E. Lutz, "The Commentary of Remigius of Auxerre on Martianus Capella." *MS* 19 (1957): 137–156; W.H. Stahl, "The *Quadrivium* of Martianus Capella: Its Place in the Intellectual History of Western Europe." *Arts libéraux et philosophie au moyen âge* (1969): 959–967; *The Wedding of Philology and Mercury. Martianus Capella and the Seven Liberal Arts,* trans. W.H. Stahl and R. Johnson.

MARCIEN: [MARS]

MARDOCHEE. Mordecai was Esther's uncle and her guardian, whom she obeyed in everything. When Haman persuaded King Assuerus, Esther's husband, to proclaim an edict against the Jews in his kingdom, Mordecai advised Esther how to save her people. The king hanged Haman and gave his estates to Mordecai (Esther 2–8).

Because of the advice Esther gave the king, Mordecai was advanced at court, *MerchT* 1371–1374. **[Ester]**

The form is a variant of Latin *Mardochaeus* and occurs in final rhyming position, *MerchT* 1373.

MARIE[1] (saint). Mary, the mother of Jesus, fl. first century A.D., the daughter of Joachim and Anna, was cousin of Elizabeth, John the Baptist's mother. The Apochryphal Gospels give the names of her parents and episodes of her early life. The Annunciation, the Visitation to Elizabeth, Jesus's birth, and Mary's Purification are recorded in the Gospels of Matthew and Luke. The *Legenda aurea* contains all these episodes and adds the Assumption into heaven. The cult of the Virgin flowered in the twelfth century, and cathedrals were built in her honor. Bernard of Clairvaux was especially devoted to her.

Custance and the Second Nun invoke Marie as daughter of St. Anne, *MLT* 641; *SNP* 70. Marie is invoked as mother and maid, *MLT* 841; *SNP* 36, *Astr Prol* 103. She is Christ's mother, *MLT* 950; *SumT* 1762; *PrT* 537–538, 550, 556, 597, 620, 654–655, 677–678, 690; *ParsT* 557, 1088. She is called God's mother, *SumT* 2202; *CYT* 1243. The pilgrims and the characters in the stories they tell swear by Marie, *FrT* 1604; *MerchT* 2418, *PardT* 685; *ShipT* 402; *Thop* 784; *CYT* 1062. The Learned Eagle swears by Marie, *HF* II.573. The Prioress and the Second Nun invoke the Virgin at the beginning of their tales. The Prioress's Invocation is composed of passages from the Office of the Blessed Virgin and of paraphrases of Dante's *Par* XXXIII.16–20. The Second Nun's Invocation is composed of passages from several sources, the main one that of St. Bernard's address to the Virgin, *Par* XXXIII. Chaucer borrows passages from each to compose these Invocations. The Virgin is compared with the burning bush that Moses saw, *PrT* 468, *ABC* 89–94. Medieval exegesis held that the miracle of the bush that burned and was not consumed prefigured the Virgin. The *ABC,* a prayer to Mary, is a free translation of a prayer from Guillaume de Deguilleville, *Le pelèrinage de vie humaine* (1320–1355). The Ave Marie mentioned in *ABC* 104 is the short familiar prayer to the Virgin. **[Anne**[2]**: Joseph: Moises: Zacharie]**

Marie, the French form as well as a pronunciation variant, appears three times initially, *MLT* 641; *ShipT* 402; *CYT* 1062; five times in medial positions, *MLT* 920; *MerchT* 1337; *MerchT* 1899; *PardT* 685; *Thop* 784; and five times in final rhyming position, *MLT* 841; *FrT* 1604; *MerchT* 2418; *PrT* 690; *HF* II.573.

"The Gospel of the Pseudo-Matthew and the Protoevangelicon." *Lost Books of the Bible*; Guillaume de Deguilleville, *The Pilgrimage of the Life of Man*; *"The Lyf of Oure Lady": The ME Translation of Thomas of Hales' "Vita Sanctae Marie,"* ed. S.M. Horall; Jacobus de Voragine, *GL*, trans. G. Ryan and H. Ripperger, 304–308, 519–530; *ibid., LA*, ed. Th. Graesse, 158–167, 585–593; E.L. Mascall and H.S. Box, *The Blessed Virgin Mary*; R.W. Tryon, "Miracles of Our Lady in Middle English Poetry." *PMLA* 38 (1923): 308–388; K. Young, ed., "The Plays of the Blessed Virgin Mary." *The Drama of the Medieval Church*, II: 225–257.

MARIE[2] (saint). Mary the Egyptian, fl. A.D. 344–421, led a life of pleasure as a prostitute in Alexandria. She was converted when she made a pilgrimage to Palestine, and she then lived a devout life in a cave in the desert for forty-seven years (*Legenda aurea* LVI).

The Man of Law compares Custance's preservation to that of Mary the Egyptian, *MLT* 498–504.

Marie, the French form and a pronunciation variant, appears medially, *MLT* 500.

Jacobus de Voragine, *GL*, trans. G. Ryan and H. Ripperger, 228–230; *ibid., LA*, ed. Th. Graesse, 248–249; *The South-English Legendary*, ed. C. D'Evelyn and A.J. Mill, I: 136–148.

MARK (saint), the Evangelist, fl. first century A.D., is the author of the Gospel that bears his name. Scholars now believe that his account was the first one written. His symbol is the winged lion, and his most famous shrine is the Church of St. Mark in Venice.

Alys of Bath compares wives to barley bread and virgins to pure white flour, *WBP* 145–146. She says that Mark tells how Jesus refreshed many with barley bread. Mark says only that the loaves were five but does not say what they were made of, Mark 6:36; John says that there were five barley loaves. The narrator reminds Harry Bailly that, although Mark tells about the passion of Christ, he does not describe the same things as Matthew, Luke, and John, and their stories are true, *Thop* 943–952. **[Jerome]**

The name appears medially, *WBP* 145, *Thop* 952.

Jacobus de Voragine, *GL*, trans. G. Ryan and H. Ripperger, 238–244; *ibid., LA*, ed. Graesse, 265–271; K.M. Wilson, "Chaucer and St. Jerome: The Use of 'Barley' in the *Wife of Bath's Prologue*." *ChauR* 19 (1984–1985): 245–251.

MARS, MARTE. Mars, son of Jupiter and Juno, was the most important god in the Roman pantheon because he was father of Romulus, Rome's founder. As the god of war, red, the color of blood, was his color, and the wolf, the symbol of Rome, his animal. Mars and Venus fell in love, and the Sun told Vulcan, her husband, of their amours. Vulcan forged a fine golden net, which was almost invisible, and he installed it above Venus's bed.

Locked in each other's arms, Venus and Mars were caught in the net. Vulcan opened the doors and called the gods to see their embarrassment. The gods laughed, and the story became the talk of heaven (*Met* IV.173–189; *OM* IV.1268–1371; *Confessio Amantis*, V.635–746).

Mars is Theseus's patron throughout *The Knight's Tale*. The red image of Mars appears on his banner, *KnT* 975. He builds an oratory to Mars, Arcite's patron, *KnT* 975, a description of which comes largely from *Tes* VII.29–37 and from *Thebaid* VII.34–73, a temple decorated with pictures of war and death. The statue of Mars stands on a cart, and over his head are two figures from geomancy, Puella and Rubeus; at his feet a red-eyed wolf eats a man. Jean Seznec has published illustrations from several manuscripts in which Mars stands in a heavy peasant's cart, accompanied by a wolf. The archaic form *Mavors* emphasizes the connection between Mars and *mors* (death) and is a blend of *Mars* and *vorans* (devouring) in Petrus Berchorius, *De formis figurisque deorum*, fol.4ʳb.18–19 and in Isidore's *Etymologiae* VIII.xi.50–51. Iron is Mars's metal, so Mars is called iron in alchemy, *CYT* 827; *HF* III.1446. Arcita is devoted to Mars in *Anelida and Arcite*. Anelida sacrifices to Mars, *Anel* 351–357. Mars is the god of war throughout *Troilus and Criseyde*. To look on Troilus is to see Mars, *Tr* II.624–630. Troilus asks Mars to help him, for love of Cipris, *Tr* III.724–725; he refers to the story of the love affair between Venus and Mars. Mars is Theseus's patron, *LGW* 2063, 2109.

Mars is also the fifth planet counting away from the earth, and the third planet counting toward the earth from Saturn (see Ptolemaic map). It is the planet of battles; conquerors, fierce and desirous of war, are born under this sign (*Confessio Amantis* VII.889–906).

The "infortune of Mars" is the evil caused by the planet, *KnT* 2021, graphically depicted on the walls of the temple. The planet's position is unfavorable at the time of Custance's wedding, *MLT* 295–308: the conjunction of Mars and Luna is the sign Scorpio, as well as the eighth house, the house of death. Aries, the house or mansion of Mars, compounds its evil, *MLT* 302, because it is "tortuous"; that is, it ascends most obliquely of the eastern signs. In Dame Alys's case, the influence of Mars has nullified the good influence of Venus; her heart is Martian, and Mars gave her her sturdiness, *WBP* 610–619. On March 15, Cambyuskan's birthday, the sun is in Aries, Mars's mansion, also called the face of Mars, *SqT* 50. At Ypermestra's birth red Mars is so feeble that there is no malice in it; thus it influences Ypermestra so that she cannot hold the knife to murder Lyno, *LGW* 2589–2595. The third and tenth hours of Saturday belong to Mars, *Astr* II.12.24, 28.

The *Complaint of Mars* may be compared with several types of poems: the moralized Ovid, the astrological poem, the aubade, the Valentine poem, the lover's complaint, and the courtly-love poem. It is built on the Venus and Mars myth. [**Arcita: Emetreus: Theseus: Venus**]

In *The Knight's Tale Mars* occurs once initially, *KnT* 2669; twenty-three times in medial positions, *KnT* 975, 1559, 1682, 1708, 1747, 1907, 1969, 1972, 1974, 1982, 2035, 2041, 2050, 2248, 2367, 2369, 2372, 2431, 2434, 2441, 2473, 2480, 2815; and once in final rhyming position, *KnT* 2159. In the rest of the tales, *Mars* occurs initially, *CYT* 827; medially *MLT* 301, 305; *WBP* 612, 613. In *Anelida and Arcite*, *Mars* appears once initially, *Anel* 50; three times in medial positions, *Anel* 1, 31, 355; in *Troilus and Criseyde*, eight times in medial positions, *Tr* II.593, 630; III.22, 716, 724; IV.25; V.306, 1853. In *The Legend of Good Women*, five times in medial positions, *LGW* 535, 2063, 2109, 2589, 2593. In *The Complaint of Mars*, once initially, *Mars* 148; ten times in medial positions, *Mars* 25, 45, 53, 75, 77, 78, 90, 92, 106, 123.

Marte, the Italian variant, with final syllabic -*e*, occurs only in final rhyming position, *KnT* 2021, 2581; *Tr* II.435, 988; *LGW* 2244. *Martes*, ME genitive case, and derived from Italian *Marte,* occurs only in medial positions, *KnT* 2024; *WBP* 619; *SqT* 50; *Tr* III.437; *HF* III.1446.

Petrus Berchorius, *Ovidius moralizatus,* ed. J. Engels, 15; Boccaccio, *Tutte le opere,* ed. V. Branca, II: 453–458; W.C. Curry, *Chaucer and the Mediaeval Sciences,* 91–118; John Gower, *The Complete Works,* ed. G.C. Macaulay, II: 419–422, III: 257; Isidore, *Etymologiae,* ed. W.M. Lindsay, I; *OM,* ed. C. de Boer, II, deel 21: 39–41; J. Parr and N.A. Holtz, "The Astronomy and Astrology in Chaucer's *The Complaint of Mars.*" *ChauR* 15 (1981): 255–266; J. Seznec, *The Survival of the Pagan Gods,* trans. B.F. Sessions, 190–194; G. Stillwell, "Convention and Individuality in Chaucer's *Complaint of Mars.*" *PQ* 35 (1956): 69–89; M. Storm, "The Mythological Tradition in Chaucer's *Complaint of Mars.*" *PQ* 57 (1978): 323–335.

MARSYAS: [MARCIA]
MARTE: [MARS]
MARTIANUS CAPELLA: [MARCIAN]
MARTIN: [MARTYN]

MARTYN (saint). Martin of Tours, c. A.D. 316–397, was born in Pannonia (Hungary). While he was in the Roman army, his regiment was sent to Amiens in Gaul. One winter's day, he met a naked man in the street, who begged for alms. Taking his sword, he cut his mantle in two and gave half to the beggar. That night he dreamed that Christ appeared to him, wearing the half cloak. Martin was eighteen at the time and a catechumen. Becoming a disciple of Hilary of Poitiers, he lived as a solitary monk at Ligugé, where others joined him to create the first monastery in Gaul. In 372 he was made bishop of Tours and served for twenty-five years. During this time he became famous as a wonder-worker in healing lepers (Sulpicius Severus, *De vita beati Martini, PL* 20: 159–222).

Daun John swears by St. Martyn, *ShipT* 149.

The form is a spelling variant and occurs in final rhyming position.

C. Donaldson, *Martin of Tours: Parish Priest, Mystic, and Exorcist; The Early South-English Legendary,* ed. C. Horstmann, 449–451; D.H. Farmer, *The Oxford Dictionary of Saints,* 265–266; Jacobus de Voragine, *GL,* trans. G. Ryan and H. Ripperger, 663–674; *ibid., LA,* ed. Th. Graesse, 741–750; W. Levinson, *England and the Continent in the Eighth Century,* 259–265.

MARY: [MARIE[1,2]]
MASINISSA: [MASSYNISSE]

MASSYNISSE. Masinissa, c. 240–148 B.C., king of Numidia, fought with the Carthagenians against the Romans until Scipio Africanus the Elder won him over with friendship and the restoration of his hereditary domains. Africanus Major owed his victory at Zama in 202 B.C. to the decisive action of Masinissa's cavalry. Polybis says that he was "the best man of all the kings of his time and the most completely fortunate" (*Histories* XV.3–5, 12; XXXVII.10). Cicero describes the friendship between Masinissa and Scipio Africanus in his *Somnium Scipionis (Dream of Scipio), De re publica* VI.ix–x.

The Dreamer recalls that he has read in *Tullyus of the Drem of Scipioun* of the close friendship between Scipio and Massynisse, *PF* 36–42. [**Affrican: Cipioun**]

Massynisse, a spelling variant, occurs in final rhyming position, *PF* 37.

Cicero, *De re publica,* ed. and trans. C.W. Keyes, 260–263; Polybius, *Histories,* ed. F. Hultsch, trans. E. Shuckburgh, II: 138–147, 511–512; H.H. Scullard, *Scipio Africanus,* 1–160.

MATHEW (saint), fl. first century A.D., is the reputed author of the Gospel that bears his name. Jesus called him from the toll house or "receipt of custom," for he was a tax collector (Matthew 9:9; 10:3). He is called Levi, son of Alphaeus, Mark 2:13; Luke 5:27–29. His symbol is a man because his genealogies emphasize the human family of Jesus. Jacobus de Voragine gives a life of St. Matthew, *Legenda aurea,* CXL.

The Pardoner refers to Matthew 5:34 on swearing, *PardT* 633–634. Chaucer the pilgrim points out that there are different ways to tell the same story, as the evangelists have done, *Thop* 943–952. The Parson quotes Matthew 19:5, *ParsT* 842; Matthew 5:28 at *ParsT* 845; Matthew 5:14–16, *ParsT* 1036–1037.

The name occurs medially, *PardT* 634; *Thop* 951.

Jacobus de Voragine, *GL,* trans. G. Ryan and H. Ripperger, 561–566; *ibid., LA,* ed. Th. Graesse, 622–628.

MATTHEW: [MATHEW]

MAURE (saint). Maurus of Subiaco, fl. sixth century A.D., was one of Benedict's pupils at Monte Cassino and became his trusted companion

(Gregory, *Dialogues* II [*PL* 66: 142, 144–150]). Because he was the patron saint of charcoal burners and because of his name, which means "black," he is sometimes painted as a black man.

The Monk disregards the rule of St. Maure and St. Benedight because it is somewhat strict, *Gen Prol* 173–176. **[Benedight: Gregorie]**

Maure, the French variant, occurs medially, *Gen Prol* 173.

Gregory the Great, *The Dialogues of Gregory the Great, Book II: Saint Benedict,* trans. M.L. Uhlfelder; L. Réau, *IAC,* III, 2: 932.

MAURICE, MAURICES, MAURICIUS. Maurice is Custance's son in *The Man of Law's Tale.* Chaucer follows Trevet, who names his heroine's son *Morys.* **[Alla: Custance: Donegild: Hermengyld]**

Maurice is OF from Latin *Mauritius,* of which *Mauricius* is a variant. *Maurice* appears once medially, *MLT* 1063, and once in final rhyming position, *MLT* 1086; *Mauricius* appears once, initially, *MLT* 723. *Maurices,* the ME genitive case, appears once, initially, *MLT* 1127.

M. Schlauch, ed., "Trivet's Life of Constance." *S&A,* 173.

MAURUS: [MAURE]

MAXIME, MAXIMUS is the officer and registrar of Rome whom Almachius sends to force Cecile and her company to sacrifice to Jupiter (*Legenda aurea* CLXIX).

Maximus is Almachius's registrar, and he arrests Tiburtius and Valerian in *The Second Nun's Tale.* Cecile baptizes him secretly, *SNT* 379–385. He helps to convert many to Christianity, and Almachius beats him with a leaden whip until he dies, *SNT* 393–406. **[Almache: Cecile: Tiburce: Urban: Valerian]**

Maxime, derived from Latin ablative case, occurs once, with elided final *-e,* in medial position, *SNT* 377. *Maximus,* Latin for "greatest," appears three times in medial position, *SNT* 368, 372, 400.

Jacobus de Voragine, *GL,* trans. G. Ryan and H. Ripperger, 694–695; *ibid., LA,* ed. Th. Graesse, 775–777.

MAXIMUS: [MAXIME]

MAY, MAYUS is the name of the twenty-year-old young woman chosen by sixty-year-old Januarie to be his wife in *The Merchant's Tale.* She is beautiful but of lower social class than Januarie. After a particularly wretched wedding night, May casts her eye on Januarie's squire Damyan, who burns in Venus's fire with love for her. When Januarie becomes blind, May makes a tryst with Damyan to meet in the pear tree in the garden. As Damyan makes love to May in the tree, Pluto, god of the Underworld, gives

Januarie back his sight, and he sees them in the act. Proserpina, Pluto's wife, gives May her answer, and May tells Januarie that she wrestled with Damyan so as to cure him of his blindness. For the connection between the month of May and lechery, see the illuminations for May in the calendar of *The Belles Heures of Jean, Duke of Berry.* Instead of Castor and Pollux, the traditional figures of Gemini, this Book of Hours shows a nude couple embracing, a shield barely covering their genitalia. May is also the month favorable to physicians, and May tells Januarie that her action has restored his sight. **[Damyan: Gemini: Januarie: Mercurie[1]: Pluto: Proserpina]**

The epithet "fresshe" occurs seventeen times of the twenty-six times the name is mentioned, emphasizing the incongruity between May and Januarie. *Mayus*, the ME variant of Latin *Maius*, occurs once initially, *MerchT* 1742, and three times in medial positions, *MerchT* 1693, 1888, 2157. May occurs eleven times in medial positions, *MerchT* 1782, 1822, 1851, 1932, 1995, 2050, 2116, 2137, 2185, 2218, 2328; and fifteen times in final rhyming position, *MerchT* 1748, 1774, 1859, 1871, 1882, 1886, 1895, 1914, 1955, 1977, 2002, 2054, 2092, 2100, 2321.

The Belles Heures of Jean, Duke of Berry, introd. by M. Meiss, fol. 6; E. Brown, Jr., "Why Is May called 'Mayus'?" *ChauR* 2 (1967): 273–277.

MAYUS: [MAY]

MEDEA, daughter of Aeetes, king of Colchis, and niece of Circe, was famous for her powers of healing and witchcraft. She fell passionately in love with Jason when he came to Colchis seeking the Golden Fleece of Phrixus's Ram, and she helped him perform the impossible tasks her father set for him. He took her with him when he sailed with the Fleece and married her in Greece. Later, however, he decided to marry Glauce, Creon's daughter, for political reasons, and Medea took her revenge by killing their two children and by poisoning the bride (*Met* VII.1–403; *Heroides* XII; *OM* VII.250–1506).

The enchantments of Medea appear on the wall of Venus's oratory, *KnT* 1944. The poet points out that none of Medea's enchantments could hold Jason, *RR* 14404–14405. The Man of Law says that Chaucer has told of Queen's Medea's cruelty; she hanged her children by the neck because Jason was false, *MLI* 72–74. Medea strangles her children in *RR* 13259. Medea appears with characters from the *Roman de la Rose* in the stained-glass windows of the Dreamer's room, *BD* 321–330. The Dreamer tells the Man in Black that, if he slays himself, he will be as surely damned as Medea, who slew her children for Jason, *BD* 725–726. Medea is a betrayed woman, *HF* I.401; she stands among the sorcerers, *HF* III.1271–1272. She is one of love's martyrs, *LGW* 1580–1679. Gower also makes Medea a more positive figure, *Confessio Amantis* V.3247–4237, and cites Ovid as his source, possibly *Heroides* XII. Machaut tells of Jason's treachery to Medea, *Le*

Jugement dou roy de Navarre 2770–2804. Chaucer omits the slaying of the children and Medea's killing of Glauce (sometimes called Creusa in classical sources). At the end of the story, Medea laments that she liked Jason's yellow hair, fair speech, and infinite graciousness better than her own honesty, *LGW* 1672–1675. **[Eson: Jason: Oetes]**

Medea appears once initially, *LGW* 1599; seven times in medial positions, *KnT* 1949; *BD* 330, 726; *LGW* 1395, 1629, 1652, 1663; and three times in final rhyming position, *MLI* 72; *HF* I.401; *HF* III.1271.

John Gower, *The Complete Works*, ed. G.C. Macaulay, III: 35–62; Guillaume de Machaut, *Oeuvres*, ed. E. Hoepffner, I: 232–233; Ovid, *Her*, ed. and trans. G. Showerman, 142–159; *ibid.*, *Met*, ed. and trans. F.J. Miller, I: 342–371; *OM*, ed. C. de Boer, III, deel 30: 21–50; *RR*, ed. E. Langlois, IV: 60; *RR*, trans. C. Dahlberg, 228–229; R.K. Root, "Chaucer's Legend of Medea." *PMLA* 24 (1909): 124–154.

MEGAERA: [MEGERA]

MEGERA. Megaera was one of the Furies or Erinyes, her sisters being Allecto and Tisiphone. Daughters of the Night, they lived in the Underworld, where Proserpina was their mistress (*Met* IV.451–454, 481–484; *Aeneid* VI.554–556, 570–572; *RR* 19835–19837).

The poet invokes the Erinyes and asks Megera, Alete, and Thesiphone to help him, *Tr* IV.22–24. **[Alete: Herenus: Proserpina: Thesiphone]**

Megera, the French variant, appears initially, *Tr* IV.24.

Ovid, *Met*, ed. and trans. F.J. Miller, I: 210–213; Virgil, *Aeneid*, ed. and trans. H.R. Fairclough, I: 544–547; *RR*, ed. E. Langlois, V: 18; *RR*, trans. C. Dahlberg, 326.

MELEAGER: [MELEAGRE]

MELEAGRE. Meleager was the son of Althaea, wife of King Oeneus of Calydon. When Oeneus organized the hunt to kill the boar sent by Diana to ravage the country, he invited famous hunters from around the kingdom. Atalanta came from Arcadia to join the hunt, and Meleager fell in love with her. When he killed the boar, he presented her with its pelt, since hers was the first arrow to draw blood. The other hunters were enraged at Meleager's action (*Met* VIII.324–444; *OM* VIII.2002–2332).

The story of Meleagre and the boar hunt is painted on the walls of Diane's temple, *KnT* 2071, because Atthalante had sworn to follow the goddess. Cassandra tells the story when she interprets Troilus's dream, *Tr* V.1457–1519. Diomede is Meleagre's descendant and is thus identified with the boar of Troilus's dream. **[Atthalante]**

Meleagre, the OF variant, appears medially only; once with elided final -e, *KnT* 2071; and three times with final syllabic -e, *Tr* V.1474, 1482, 1515.

Ovid, *Met*, ed. and trans. F.J Miller, I: 428–437; *OM*, ed. C. de Boer, III, deel 30: 157–165.

MELIBEE, MELIBEUS is the hero of Chaucer's second tale, *The Tale of Melibeus*. A translation of the French tale, *Le Livre de Mellibee et de Prudence,* by Renaud de Louens (after 1336), it is also an adaptation of the *Liber consolationis et consilii (The Book of Consolation and Counsel),* by Albertanus of Brescia (c. 1246). After his enemies attack his wife Prudence and his daughter Sophia, Melibee wants to avenge himself, but Dame Prudence, by quoting the scriptures, the ancient philosophers, and the folk wisdom of proverbs dissuades him, and he is reconciled to his enemies. **[Prudence: Sophie]**

In both Latin and French sources the hero's name is Melibeus and Mellibee, meaning "a man that drynketh hony," *Mel* 1410. *Melibee* occurs thirty-two times, *Mel* 1019, 1054, 1111, 1410, 1426, 1444, 1451, 1518, 1540, 1671, 1681, 1697, 1711, 1724, 1742, 1745, 1768, 1769, 1773, 1784, 1789, 1791, 1801, 1805, 1806, 1808, 1809, 1827, 1830, 1832, 1834, 1870; and once in final rhyming position, *MkP* 1887. *Melibeus* appears thirteen times, *Mel* 967, 973, 986, 1001, 1003, 1008, 1026, 1049, 1051, 1232, 1261, 1279, 1333. *Melibees,* the ME genitive case, appears once, *Mel* 1787.

Albertanus Brixiensis, *Liber consolationis et consilii,* ed. T. Sundby; Renaud de Louens, *Le Livre de Mellibee et de Prudence,* ed. J.B. Severs. *S&A,* 568–614; L.J. Matthews, "The Date of Chaucer's *Melibee* and the Stages of the Tale's Incorporation in *The Canterbury Tales.*" *ChauR* 20 (1985–1986): 221–234; D. Palomo, "What Chaucer Really Did to *Le Livre de Mellibee.*" *PQ* 53 (1974): 304–320.

MENELAUS, son of Atreus, was Agamemnon's brother, Helen's husband, and king of Sparta. After Paris kidnapped his wife Menelaus sought revenge, and the Greeks sailed for Troy. In the *Iliad* Agamemnon assumes a greater role than the betrayed husband, Menelaus, because he is the high king of Mycenae, while Menelaus is king of a lesser city.

Lady Philosophy says that Agamenon, son of Atreus, purged the marriage chambers of his brother by destroying Troy. Chaucer adds a gloss identifying Menelaus as Agamemnon's brother, *Bo* IV, *Metr* 7.6–7. **[Agamenon: Helen: Paris]**

The name appears only in this instance.

Homer, *Iliad,* ed. and trans. A.T. Murray.

MERCURIE, MERCURIUS, MERCURYE. Mercury, son of Jupiter and Maia (one of the Pleiades), was born on Mount Cylennius, hence his byname of location, Cylennius. At an early stage of development, his myth took over the aspects of the myth of Hermes, the Greek messenger of the gods. He was Jupiter's winged messenger, the god of cunning, wit, and eloquence, and became the guide of souls, a function of Hermes Psychopompos (*Met* I and II). Isidore says that Mercury devised deception (*Etym* VIII.ix.33) and that the magic wand with two snakes entwined, or *caduceus*, represents the power of language (*Etym* VIII.xi.48). Petrus Berchorius adds that the wand signifies eloquence (*De formis figurisque deorum*, fol. 6ᵣa, 46–55, fol. 6ᵣb, 9–16). Mercury was famous for his feat of putting the hundred-eyed Argus to sleep. Jupiter loved Io, whom he changed into a white heifer to save her from Juno's anger. Juno set Argus with his hundred eyes to guard Io and to report to her any visits from Jupiter. Jupiter, however, commanded Mercury to slay Argus, quite a project since the hundred eyes were never closed all at the same time. Taking his sleep-producing wand and his reed pipe, Mercury approached Argus. He put him to sleep with the aid of the music and the wand, then slew him (*Met* I.668–721).

The winged Mercurie appears to Arcite and bids him be merry, *KnT* 1384–1386; he carries his "slepy yerd," *KnT* 1387, which, Berchorius says, induces sleep. He is arrayed as when he put Argus to sleep, *KnT* 1388. The poet Marcian (Martianus), who has written about the wedding of Mercurie and Philology, must hold his peace, for both his pen and his tongue are too meager to describe the marriage of Januarie and May, *MerchT* 1732–1735. To excuse Eneas, the book says that Mercurie commands him to leave Dido and go to Italy, *HF* I.427–432, *LGW* 1295–1300. Mercurie helps Ulixes escape Circe's enchantments, *Bo* IV, *Metr* 3.16–23. Boethius does not mention Mercury by name but writes: *Sed licet variis malis / Numen Arcadia alitis*, which Chaucer expands to: "But al be it so that the godhede of Mercurie, that is cleped the bridd of Arcadye, hath had merci on duc Ulixes." Troilus invokes Mercurie who loved Hierse, *Tr* III.729. Mercurye acts as psychopompos or soul-guide to Troilus, *Tr* V.321, 1826–1827. Mercury provides an abode of refuge for the fleeing Venus, *Mars* 113–121.

Mercurie, Mercury is the second planet, counting away from the earth (see Ptolemaic map). It is exalted (or has its greatest power) in Virgo, and Pisces is the sign in which it is weakest or has its depression (*Tetrabiblos* I.19). It is thus the very opposite of Venus, whose exaltation is Pisces and whose depression is Virgo. Mercury controls speech and thought (*Tetrabiblos* III.12). Those born under Mercury are studious and love ease and rest (*Confessio Amantis* VII.755–770). Mercury is quicksilver in alchemy.

The children of Mercury are "contrarius" to the children of Venus, *WBP* 697–698. Mercury's children love wisdom and science, *WBP* 699. The illustration in Christine de Pizan's *Epître d'Othée*, British Library Ms. Harley 4431, fol. 102ᵣ, shows a group of monks discoursing, while Mercury presides in the stars above them (Seznec, plate 23). Pisces is Mercury's depression but Venus's exaltation, *WBP* 703–704. The sun is in Mercury when Apollo whirls his chariot up to the mansion of Mercurius, *SqT* 671–672. The sixth inequal hour of Saturday belongs to Mercury, *Astr* II.12.25–26. [**Aglawros: Argus[1]: Cillenios: Gemini: Hierse: Marcian: Mars: Venus**]

Mercurie is quicksilver in alchemy, *CYT* 772, 774, 827, 1431, and is also called the Dragon, *CYT* 1438.

Mercurie, the ME variant, appears twice initially, *WBP* 699; *Tr* III.729; six times in medial positions, *WBP* 697, 703, 705; *CYT* 1438; *HF* I.429; *LGW* 1297; and twice in final rhyming position, *KnT* 1385, *MerchT* 1734. *Mercurius,* the Latin form, appears once medially, *SqT* 672, and in the *Treatise on the Astrolabe*; *Mercurye,* a spelling variant, appears twice medially, *Tr* V.321, 1827.

Petrus Berchorius, *Ovidius moralizatus,* ed. J. Engels, 25–26; Isidore, *Etymologiae,* ed. W.M. Lindsay, I; John Gower, *The Complete Works,* ed. G.C. Macaulay, III: 253–254; Ovid, *Met,* ed. and trans. F.J. Miller, I: 2–121; Ptolemy, *Tetrabiblos,* ed. and trans. F.E. Robbins, 91, 321; J. Seznec, *Survival of the Pagan Gods,* trans. B.F. Sessions, 74.

MERCURY: [MERCURIE]

MESSENUS. Misenus, son of Aeolus, was Hector's comrade in the Trojan War. During the war he blew his trumpet to signal the charge in battle. After Hector's death, he followed Aeneas to Italy. While Aeneas consulted the Cumean Sybil in the cave of Avernus, Misenus challenged Triton, Neptune's son, to a musical contest and lost. Triton then drowned him for his presumption (*Aeneid* II.239; VI.162–176).

Messenus, of whom Virgil speaks, appears with other trumpeters of battle charges, Joab and Theodamas, *HF* III.1243–1244. **[Joab: Theodamas: Triton]**

The name appears in final rhyming position, *HF* III.1243.

Virgil, *Aeneid,* ed. and trans. H.R. Fairclough, I: 310; 516–519.

METAMORPHOSIOS: [OVIDE]

METELLIUS. Valerius Maximus (fl. first century A.D.) tells the story of Metellius, whose wife was fined her dowry for drinking wine, *Factorum dictorumque memorabilium liber* VI.3.9.

Alys of Bath says that not even Metellius, who killed his wife with a staff because she drank wine, could have kept her from wine, *WBP* 460–463. R.A. Pratt suggests that Chaucer may have taken this very different version of the story from John of Wales, *Communoloquium sive summa collationum,* written in the second half of the thirteenth century. **[Valerie[1]]**

The name appears medially, *WBP* 460.

R.A. Pratt, "Chaucer and the Hand That Fed Him." *Speculum* 41 (1966): 621–642; Valerius Maximus, *Factorum dictorumque memorabilium libri,* ed. J. Kappy, I: 616–617.

MEUN: [JEAN DE MEUN]
MICAH: [MICHIAS]

MICHIAS. Micah was a prophet in Israel during the reigns of Jothan, Ahaz, and Hezekiah, and the reputed author of the prophecies in the Bible that bear his name.

The Parson quotes Michias 7:6, *ParsT* 201.

The form is a variant of Latin *Michaeas.*

MIDA, MYDA. Midas, son of Gordius and the goddess Cybele, a non-historical figure, was king of Phrygia. In a musical contest Tmolus gave the crown to Apollo, but Midas thought that Pan deserved it. Apollo thereupon punished him with a pair of ass's ears, which Midas successfully concealed in his purple turban. Eventually, his barber discovered his secret and longed to tell someone, but dared not. He finally dug a hole in the ground and whispered his secret into it. Reeds grew out of the hole and, when the wind rustled through them, they whispered, "Midas has ass ears" (*Met* XI.85–193; *OM* XI.303–770).

Alys of Bath substitutes Myda's wife for his barber, a version she has undoubtedly learned from Jankyn, *WBT* 951–980. In Machaut, *La Fonteinne amoureuse* 1689–1702, Midas's barbers discover the ass ears. Mida is called "full of coveteise," *Tr* III.1389, and is linked with Crassus, who had molten gold poured down his throat. Gower tells the story of Midas, whose golden touch turned all to gold, to illustrate avarice, *Confessio Amantis* V.153–362. Hugh Capet recalls the fates of Midas and Crassus, two examples of avarice, *Purg* XX.106. **[Crassus]**

Mida, the Italian form, appears medially, *Tr* III.1389; *Myda*, a spelling variant, appears medially, *WBP* 951, 953.

J.B. Allen and P. Gallagher, "Alisoun Through the Looking Glass: or Every Man his Own Midas." *ChauR* 4 (1970): 99–105; Dante, *Divine Comedy*, ed. and trans. C.S. Singleton, II, 1: 218–219; John Gower, *The Complete Works*, ed. G.C. Macaulay, II: 406–412; Guillaume de Machaut, *Oeuvres*, ed. E. Hoepffner, III: 203; J.L. Lowes, "Chaucer and Dante." *MP* 14 (1916–1917): 705–735; Ovid, *Met*, ed. and trans. F.J. Miller, II: 126–133; *OM*, ed. C. de Boer, IV, deel 37: 124–136; L. Patterson, "'For the Wyves love of Bath': Feminine Rhetoric and Poetic Resolution in the *Roman de la Rose* and the *Canterbury Tales*." *Speculum* 58 (1983): 656–695.

MIDAS: [MIDA]
MILKY WAY: [GALAXIE]

MINERVA, MYNERVA, MYNERVE. Minerva was the Roman goddess of commerce, industry, and schools. At a very early stage of the development of her myth, she took on the attributes of the Greek goddess Pallas Athena and became the goddess of war, wisdom, weaving, and embroidery. The owl, Athena's bird, was also transferred to Minerva, whom Virgil represents as goddess of war and handicrafts (*Aeneid* VII.805–806; *Met* II.563, 752–756).

Like Virgil, Chaucer uses the names Minerva and Pallas interchangeably. The wisdom of Minerva/Pallas was a medieval commonplace and appears in *BD* 1072. Pandarus swears by Minerva, patron of Troy, *Tr* II.232. Troilus appeals to "Minerva, the white," *Tr* II.1062, when he sits down to write his letter to Criseyde. The phrase seems to have no significance, except perhaps for the rhyme. "Antigone the white" appears in *Tr* II.887, also at the end of the line. The wooden horse, by which many Trojans will die, is offered to Minerva, *LGW* 930–933. **[Pallas]**

Minerva appears once, medially, *Tr* II.1002; *Mynerva,* a spelling variant, appears once, in final rhyming position, *BD* 1072; *Mynerve,* also a spelling variant and three syllables, with final syllabic -*e*, appears twice, *Tr* II.232; *LGW* 932.

Ovid, *Met,* ed. and trans. F.J. Miller, I: 98–99; 112–113; Virgil, *Aeneid,* ed. and trans. H.R. Fairclough, II: 58–59.

MINOS, MYNOS. Minos was the royal title of the kings of Crete. The first Minos, son of Jupiter and Europa, was brother of Rhadamanthys and Sarpedon and became judge of the Underworld (*Met* IX.440–442; *Aeneid* VI.431–433; *Inf* V.4, 17). The second Minos, grandson of Jupiter, was Pasiphae's husband and father of Androgeus, Ariadne, and Phaedra. When Minos beseiged Alcathoe, Scylla, the king's daughter, fell in love with him. To win his love, she cut off her father's purple lock, on which the safety of the kingdom depended. Minos won the battle but recoiled from Scylla because she betrayed her father (*Met* VIII.6–151; *OM* VIII.1–352). After his son Androgeus was killed at Athens, Minos attacked the city. Winning this war, he imposed a tribute of seven Athenian youths and seven Athenian girls, who were sent every ninth year to feed the Minotaur (a beast half man, half bull), which was kept in the labyrinth. Theseus joined the group of youths in the third tribute. With Ariadne's help, he slew the Minotaur (*Met* VIII.152–183; *OM* VIII.1083–1394; Machaut, *Le Jugement dou roy de Navarre,* 2707–2768).

When Troilus thinks that Criseyde is dead, he pulls out his sword to send his soul to wherever the judgment of Minos sees fit, *Tr* IV.1184–1188. This "juge infernal, Mynos, of Crete kyng" also appears in *LGW* 1886–1938. Chaucer has combined the two kings into one, influenced perhaps by glosses on the *Metamorphoses* or from Boccaccio's *De genealogia deorum gentilium* XI.26. **[Adriane: Androgeus: Mynotaur: Nysus: Phasipha: Silla]**

Minos appears once medially, *Tr* IV.1188; *Mynos,* the OF variant, appears once initially, *LGW* 1894, and thirteen times medially, LGW 1886, 1900, 1906, 1911, 1915, 1922, 1924, 1928, 1936, 1938, 1949, 1964, 2042.

Boccaccio, *De genealogia deorum gentilium,* ed. V. Romano, II: 563–565; Dante, *The Divine Comedy,* ed. and trans. C.S. Singleton, I, 1: 46–47; Guillaume de Machaut, *Oeuvres,* ed. E. Hoepffner, I: 230–232; S.B. Meech, Chaucer and the *Ovide Moralisé*—a Further Study." *PMLA* 46 (1931): 185; Ovid, *Met,* ed. and trans. F.J. Miller, I: 416–419, II: 34–35; *OM,* ed. C. de Boer, III, deel 30: 109–117, 134–142; Virgil, *Aeneid,* ed. and trans. H.R. Fairclough, I: 536–537.

MINOTAUR: [MYNOTAUR]

MIRRA. Myrrha was the daughter of Cinyras, king of Cyprus, and great-granddaughter of Pygmalion. Her mother boasted that Myrrha was more beautiful than Venus herself, and for such presumption, Venus caused Myrrha to fall in love with her father. With her nurse's help, she managed to take her mother's place in her father's bed and conceived Adonis. When Cinyras discovered this deed, he chased his daughter out of his palace and pursued her with his sword. As she fled, she prayed the gods to deliver her, and she became the myrrh tree. Her tears became myrrh that the tree distilled, hence her name (*Met* X.298–518; *OM* X.1080–1959; *RR* 21121–21214).

The tears of Troilus and Criseyde are compared with Mirra's tears, *Tr* IV.1139. **[Adoon: Pigmalion: Venus]**

The form appears medially.

Ovid, *Met,* ed. and trans. F.J. Miller, II: 84–101; *OM,* ed. C. de Boer, IV, deel 37: 37–58; *RR,* ed. E. Langlois, V: 73–75; *RR,* trans. C. Dahlberg, 345–346.

MISENUS: [MESSENUS]
MNESTHEUS: [MONESTEO]

MOISES, MOYSES. Moses, son of Amram and Jochebed, exposed in the bullrushes on the order of Pharoah, was saved by the Pharoah's daughter and brought up as an Egyptian prince. The Lord called him to lead the Israelites out of Egypt, and after many plagues and disasters Pharoah agreed to allow the Hebrews to leave the country. Moses led them into the Sinai desert, where he received the commandments from the Lord (Exodus 2–20). Scholars calculate that he lived during the first half of the thirteenth century before our era (*EJ* XIII: 371). During the medieval period Moses was regarded as somewhat of a magician; Peter Comestor wrote that he possessed two rings: one conferred remembrance and the other oblivion (*Historia scholastica* 114; *PL* 198: 1144). R.A. Pratt points out that Trevet, *Les Cronicles* fols. 8ʳ–8ᵛ, says that Moses gave his wife two rings carved with great quaintness, one called Memory and the other Forgetfulness.

Moses fasted for forty days and nights before he spoke with the Lord on Mount Sinai, *SumT* 1885. The magic rings of Moses and Solomon appear in *SqT* 247–251. The Virgin is the burning bush that Moses saw, *PrT* 467–473, *ABC* 89–96. The Parson quotes Moses from Deuteronomy, 32:24, 33, *ParsT* 195. The quotation from *ParsT* 354 has not been identified. **[Marie[1]]**

Moises, the OF variant, occurs once, medially, *ABC* 89; *Moyses*, a spelling variant, appears five times in medial positions, *SumT* 1885; *SqT* 250; *PrT* 1658; *ABC* 93; *ParsT* 195, 354.

R.A. Pratt, "Chaucer and *Les Cronicles* of Nicholas Trevet." *SLL*, 307.

MONESTEO. Mnestheus was one of Aeneas's crew (*Aeneid* IV.288, V.114–123). Boccaccio says that he was one of the Trojans taken prisoner when the Greeks captured Antenor (*Il Filostrato* IV.3).

In spite of Monestheo's valiant effort, Antenor is taken prisoner, *Tr* IV.50–56. **[Antenor: Phebuseo: Polite: Polydamas: Polymestore: Ripheo: Santippe: Sarpedon]**

The form, a variant of Boccaccio's *Menesteo*, with stress on the penultimate syllable, appears in final rhyming position, *Tr* IV.51.

Boccaccio, *Tutte le opere*, ed. V. Branca, II: 110; Virgil, *Aeneid*, ed. and trans. H.R. Fairclough, I: 414–415; 452–455.

MORDECAI: [MARDOCHEE]

MORPHEUS, one of the sons of the god Somnus, was the god of dreams. He lived in a cave in a hollow mountain, from the bottom of which flowed the stream Lethe, the river of forgetfulness. His couch was ebony, his coverlet the color of smoke (*Met* XI.592–636).

Juno sends her messenger to wake Morpheus and to command him to enter the drowned body of Ceys, in which guise Morpheus was to appear before Alcyone and tell her the truth concerning her husband's death, *BD* 136–211. The narrator, who suffers from insomnia, asks Morpheus to send him sleep, in return for which he will give the god a feather bed made of imported black satin trimmed with gold and pillows covered with pillow cases of fine Rennes linen, *BD* 242–269. **[Alcione: Ceys: Juno]**

The name appears once initially, *BD* 167, and three times in final rhyming position, *BD* 136, 242, 265.

Ovid, *Met*, ed. and trans. F.J. Miller, II: 162–165.

MOSES: [MOISES]
MOYSES: [MOISES]
MUHAMMAD: [MAHOUN]
MYDA: [MIDA]
MYNERVA: [MINERVA]
MYNERVE: [MINERVA]
MYNOS: [MINOS]

MYNOTAUR. The Minotaur was said to be the son of Pasiphae, queen of Crete, and a bull. Daedalus constructed a wooden cow for Pasiphae, which she entered to mate with the bull. The result was the Minotaur, half man, half bull. Minos lodged it in the labyrinth, which Daedalus also constructed. After his son was killed in Athens, Minos demanded that the Athenians send a tribute of seven youths and seven maidens to be eaten by the Minotaur. The third tribute brought Theseus to Crete, and with Ariadne's help, he entered the labyrinth, slew the monster, and returned safely to the light (*Met* VIII.155–182).

The figure of the Minotaur is embroidered on Theseus's pennant, *KnT* 978–980. Theseus discusses his lack of weapons with which to slay the Mynotaur with Ariadne, *LGW* 2102–2122; she gives him a reel of thread or a clue when he enters the Mynotaur's dwelling, *LGW* 2140–2143. Theseus is led to his death when he goes to the Mynotaur, *LGW* 2144–2145. **[Adriane: Dedalus: Minos: Phasipha: Phedra: Theseus]**

Mynotaur, a spelling variant, means "bull of Minos"; it appears medially only, *KnT* 980; *LGW* 2104, 2141, 2145.

R.H. Green, "Classical Fable and English Poetry." *Critical Approaches to Medieval Literature*, 113, 131–133; Ovid, *Met*, ed. and trans. F.J. Miller, I: 416–419.

MYRRHA: [MIRRA]

N

NABAL was a rich man who owned large flocks of sheep and goats in Carmel. He refused to provision David's men, and David set out to raid Nabal's farm. Nabal's wife, Abigail, met David with several asses laden with food and thus pacified David into calling off the raid. When Nabal learned what Abigail had done, his heart turned to stone, and he died ten days later. Abigail subsequently married David (I Kings 25).

Nabal is Abigail's husband, to whom she gave good advice, *MerchT* 1369; *Mel* 1098–1100. Nabal means "fool" in Hebrew, and in the Biblical account his wife is more interested in saving their lives than in giving good advice. [**Abigayl: David**]

The name occurs medially, *MerchT* 1369.

NABUGODONOSOR. Nebuchadnezzar III, fl. 605–562 B.C., was the Chaldean king of Babylon. He dreamed that a great tree grew in the middle of the earth. Its branches reached to heaven, and the tree filled the whole earth. Laden with fruit, the tree provided food for birds and beasts. Then a holy being came from heaven and commanded that the tree be cut down but that the roots be left in the earth, bound with bands of iron and brass. The tree that filled the earth was now as low as the grass. Daniel interpreted the dream as a warning of coming calamity for the Babylonian kingdom. Nebuchadnezzar later went mad, ate grass, and lived with the beasts, but subsequently recovered (Daniel 1–4). Gower tells the story to illustrate pride, *Confessio Amantis* I.2786–3066.

The Monk narrates Nabugodonosor's story to define tragedy, *MkT* 2143–2182. The Parson says that penitence is the tree the king sees in his dream, *ParsT* 125. Not even King Nabugodonosor has had as wonderful a dream as the poet's dream, *HF* II.515. [**Balthasar: Daniel: Darius**[1]]

Nabugodonosor, the ME variant found also in Gower, appears once initially, *MkT* 2562, and twice in final rhyming position, *MkT* 2145; *HF* II 515.

John Gower, *The Complete Works,* ed. G.C. Macaulay, II: 111–119.

NARCISSUS: [NARCISUS]

NARCISUS. Narcissus was the beautiful son of the river god Cephisus and the nymph Liriope. He refused the love of both youths and maidens, including the love of the nymph Echo, who followed him, pitifully trying to tell him of her love. One of the scorned youths prayed that Narcissus would love and never gain his desire. The goddess Nemesis heard the prayer and caused Narcissus to love his own reflection, which he saw in a pool. He sat by the pool, hoping in vain to embrace his reflection, until he wasted away and was changed into the flower that bears his name (*Met* III.339–510; *OM* III.1292–1846). Gower tells the story to illustrate "surquidry" or haughty pride, *Confessio Amantis* I.2275–2358.

The story of Narcisus appears on the walls of Venus's temple, *KnT* 1941. Aurelius thinks that he must die like Echo, who could not tell her woe to Narcisus, *FranklT* 951–952. Echo died because Narcissus would not love her, *BD* 735–736. **[Aurelius: Ecquo]**

Narcisus, the French variant, occurs twice medially, *KnT* 1941; *FranklT* 952, and once in final rhyming position, *BD* 735.

F. Goldin, *The Mirror of Narcissus in the Courtly Love Lyric*; John Gower, *The Complete Works,* ed. G.C. Macaulay, II: 97–99; Ovid, *Met,* ed. and trans. F.J. Miller, I: 148–161; *OM,* ed. C. de Boer, I, deel 15: 327–338; *Three Ovidian Tales of Love,* ed. R.J. Cormier; L. Vinge, *The Narcissus Theme in Western European Literature up to the Early Nineteenth Century.*

NASO is the *cognomen* or family name of Publius Ovidius Naso, 43 B.C.–A.D. 17.

The name appears three times in medial positions, for metrical reasons, *LGW* 724, 928, 2220. The poet's clan name, *Ovidius,* in its OF variant, *Ovide,* appears more frequently. **[Ovide]**

NEBUCHADNEZZAR: [NABUGODONOSOR]

NEMBROT. Nimrod, son of Chus and great-grandson of Noah, was a mighty hunter. His city was Babel, where the great tower was built (Genesis 10:8–10; 9:9). In medieval tradition, Nimrod was a man of pride who wanted to work great wonders and so built the tower higher than heaven (*Cursor mundi* 2195–2304).

Nembrot was the first tyrant to build high towers, *Form Age* 56–59.

Nembrot, a variant of the ME *Nembrothe* in the *Cursor mundi,* occurs medially in *Form Age* 58.

Cursor mundi, ed. R. Morris, I: 136–138; J. Norton-Smith, "Chaucer's *Etas Primas.*"
MAE 32 (1963): 117–124; A.V.C. Schmidt, "Chaucer and the Golden Age." *Essays in Criticism* 26 (1976): 99–115.

NEOT: [NOTE]

NEPTUNE, NEPTUNUS. Neptune, the Roman sea god, was identified with the Greek Poseidon, lord of the sea, of earthquakes, and of horses. Neptune and Apollo helped King Lamedon build the walls of Troy; then the king refused to pay them as he had agreed and thus earned their hatred (*Met* XI.199–215).

Neptunus is the god of the sea, *FranklT* 1047; *Tr* II.443. Phebus and Neptunus are angry with Troy because King Lameadoun did not pay them their wages, *Tr* IV.120–124. Neptune has compassion on Demophon and tosses him, almost dead, on the beach of Rhodopeya, *LGW* 2421–2438. **[Demophon: Phebus]**

Neptune, the English variant, with silent final -*e,* occurs once, in medial position, *LGW* 2421. *Neptunus*, the Latin form, occurs three times in medial positions, *FranklT* 1047; *Tr* II.443, IV.120.

Ovid, *Met*, ed. and trans. F.J. Miller, II: 134–135.

NERO, NEROUN. Nero, the Roman emperor, ruled A.D. 54–68. In A.D. 59 he had his mother murdered, and in 65 he ordered his teacher Seneca to commit suicide (Suetonius, *Nero*). The story in *RR* 6345–6488, which illustrates the destructiveness of Fortune, cites Suetonius as the source.

Nero's death is painted on the walls of Mars's temple, *KnT* 2032. The Monk tells the story, *MkT* 3369–3373. As the fox carries off Chauntecleer, the hens in the farmyard cry out, just as the senators' wives cried for their husbands when Nero burned Rome, *NPT* 3369–3373. Lady Philosophy describes the great harm and destructiveness done by Nero, *Bo* II, *Metr* 6.1–32; she points out his love of luxury, *Bo* III, *Metr* 4.1–13. Nero forced Seneca to give him his wealth, then he banished him; later, he commanded him to choose the manner of his death, *Bo* III, *Prosa* 5.47–49, 53–60. **[Senec: Swetonius]**

Nero, the English variant, appears seven times medially, *KnT* 2032; *MkT* 2403, 2504, 2511, 2510; *NPT* 3370, 3373. *Neroun*, a variant of French *Neron,* occurs once, in final rhyming position, *MkT* 2537.

RR, ed. E. Langlois, III: 1–6; *RR,* trans. C. Dahlberg, 125–126; Suetonius, *De vita Caesarum,* ed. and trans. J.C. Rolfe, II: 86–151.

NEROUN: [NERO]

NESSUS was a centaur. He met Hercules on the banks of the flooded river Evenus, as he prepared to cross with Dejanira. Nessus ferried her across, then tried to rape her. Hercules shot him with one of the arrows dipped in the blood of the Lernean Hydra. As he lay dying, Nessus advised Dejanira to collect some of his blood and to use it as a means of regaining Hercules's love, if she ever needed to. Dejanira followed his advice after Hercules brought Iole home to live with them. She sent him a shirt smeared with the blood as he prepared to sacrifice to Jupiter. When Hercules put the shirt on, the poison burned into his flesh. In his agony, Hercules commanded a pyre to be built, the fire lit; then he climbed onto it. Jupiter caught him up and placed him among the constellations (*Met* IX.98–272; *OM* IX.347–452, 487–872). The Confessor tells the story of Nessus, Hercules, and Dejanira to illustrate the work of Faussemblant, *Confessio Amantis* II.2145–2307.

The Monk says that some blame Nessus for Hercules's death and excuse Dejanira, *MkT* 2119–2128. **[Dianira: Ercules: Yole]**

The name occurs medially, *MkT* 2128.

John Gower, *The Complete Works*, ed. G.C. Macaulay, II: 188–192; Ovid, *Met*, ed. and trans. F.J. Miller, II: 8–23; *OM*, ed. C. de Boer, III, deel 30: 229–242.

NICANOR: [NICHANORE[1,2]]

NICERATE(S). Niceratus, fl. fifth century B.C., was the son of Nicias, the famous Athenian who became *strategos* or general after Pericles's death in 429 B.C. Niceratus was put to death during the reign of the Thirty Tyrants, 404–403 B.C. (Diodorus Siculus XIV.5). Jerome says that his wife committed suicide after his death, *Epistola adversus Jovinianum (Letter Against Jovinian)* I.44 (*PL* 23: 274). C.H. Oldfather points out that Jerome knew Diodorus Siculus's work (*The Library of History*, I.vii).

Dorigen thinks that Nicerate's wife is exemplary of wifely fidelity, *FranklT* 1437. **[Dorigen]**

Nicerates, the ME genitive case, occurs medially.

Diodorus Siculus, *The Library of History*, ed. and trans. C.H. Oldfather, VI: 20–23; K. Hume, "The Pagan Setting of *The Franklin's Tale* and the Sources of Dorigen's Cosmology." *SN* 44 (1972): 289–294.

NICERATUS: [NICERATES]

NICHANORE[1]. Nicanor of Stagira, c. 360–317 B.C., was the son of Parmenion. He was one of Alexander's officers (Arrian, *Anabasis*, I.14; III.25; Diodorus Siculus, *The Library of History* XVII.57). Jerome mentions a Theban maiden who killed herself for love of him, *Epistola adversus Jovinianum (Letter Against Jovinian)* I.41 (*PL* 23: 272).

The Theban maiden appears in Dorigen's list of virtuous women, *FranklT* 1432. **[Dorigen]**

The name occurs in final rhyming position.

Arrian, *Anabasis of Alexander*, ed. and trans. E.I. Robson, I: 60–62, 308–311; Diodorus Siculus, *The Library of History,* ed. and trans. C.B. Welles, VIII: 280–281; K. Hume, "The Pagan Setting of *The Franklin's Tale* and the Sources of Dorigen's Cosmology." *SN* 44 (1972): 289–294.

NICHANORE[2] was one of the generals sent to quell the Jewish revolt in Judea, 167–165 B.C. Judas Maccabee routed the Roman army he commanded (II Maccabees 8).

The Monk mentions Nichanore's defeat in his story of Antiochus, *MkT* 2591–2593. [**Anthiochus: Judas Machabee: Thymothee[1]**]

The name occurs medially, *MkT* 2591.

NICHOLAS[1], NICHOLAY. Nicholas is the student who boards with John the carpenter and his wife Alison in *The Miller's Tale.* He hangs herbs in his room to sweeten the air, and he is expert at "derne love." He is also an astrologer and has his "augrym stones" or arithmetic counters neatly spaced on shelves above his bed. His scheme to spend a night with Alison is successful but includes some painful surprises. [**Absolon[2]: Alison[1]: John[1]: Nicholas[2]**]

Nicholas occurs twenty times medially, *MillT* 3288, 3303, 3396, 3401, 3403, 3409, 3420, 3424, 3444, 3472, 3492, 3499, 3513, 3538, 3721, 3798, 3806, 3810, 3832, 3853, and fourteen times in final rhyming position, *MillT* 3199, 3272, 3285, 3298, 3386, 3397, 3413, 3426, 3462, 3487, 3526, 3653, 3742, *RvT* 3856. *Nicholay* appears once in medial position, *MillT* 3477; and four times in final rhyming position, *MillT* 3437, 3579, 3648, 3824.

P.E. Beichner, "Chaucer's 'Hende Nicholas.'" *MS* 14 (1952): 151–153; K.B. Harder, "Chaucer's Use of the Mystery Plays in *The Miller's Tale.*" *MLQ* 17 (1956): 193–198; A.S. Haskell, "Hende Old St. Nicholas in *The Miller's Tale.*" *Essays on Chaucer's Saints*, 38–45.

NICHOLAS[2]. No historical evidence of St. Nicholas's life exists. Legend says that he died on December 6, A.D. 345 or 352. He was supposed to have been bishop of Myra or Lycia sometime during the fourth century and became patron saint of students. He was sometimes reputed to have been holy from infancy, feeding from his mother's breast only once on Wednesdays and Fridays. In Germany, the legend that he provided dowries for poor girls was combined with local folklore, and St. Nicholas became bringer of secret presents for children on the eve of his feast day (*NCE* X: 454; *Legenda aurea* III).

The holiness of the schoolboy martyr reminds the Prioress of the holiness of the infant St. Nicholas, *PrT* 513–515.

A.D. DeGroot, *Saint Nicholas: A Psychoanalytic Study of his History and Myth*; A.S. Haskell, "St. Nicholas and the Prioress's Calendar," and "St. Nicholas and the Prioress's 'cursed Jewes.'" *Essays on Chaucer's Saints,* 46–57; Jacobus de

Voragine, *GL,* trans. G. Ryan and H. Ripperger, 16–24; *ibid., LA,* ed. Th. Graesse, 22–29; *The South-English Legendary,* ed. C. D'Evelyn and A.J. Mill, II: 550–566. K. Young, ed., "The Miracle Plays of St. Nicholas." *The Drama of the Medieval Church,* II: 307–360.

NICHOLAS OF LYNNE: [LENNE]
NICHOLAY: [NICHOLAS[1]]
NIMROD: [NEMBROT]
NINUS: [NYNUS]
NIOBE: [NYOBE]
NISUS: [NYSUS]
NOAH: [NOE]

NOE. Noah, son of Lamech, was father of Shem, Ham, and Japheth. In order to save Noah from the flood with which He intended to drown the world, God gave him specific instructions about building the ark and ordered him to take every clean beast by sevens, the male and the female, into the ark. After the flood subsided Noah and his family disembarked and became progenitors of a new human race (Genesis 5–10). Noah's wife is mentioned in the Biblical story, when she enters the ark with her husband (Genesis 7:7, 13) and when she leaves the ark after the flood (Genesis 8:16, 18). Like her daughters-in-law, she has no name. In the medieval dramas of the flood she is known as *uxor Noe* or "Noah's Wife," and she is given a shrewish character.

Nicholas tells John the carpenter that Noe had so much trouble before he could get his wife to enter the ship that he would have preferred her to go in a ship by herself, *MillT* 3539–3543. Nicholas promises to save the carpenter's wife from the coming flood, *MillT* 3558–3560. He tells the carpenter that, after the flood, the three of them will be lords all their lives like Noe and his wife, *MillT* 3581–3582. When Absolon strikes Nicholas on the buttocks with the hot iron, Nicholas's cries bring out the neighbors, but the carpenter thinks that the flood has come, and he cuts the ropes of his tub, which crashes to the ground. Nicholas and Alison tell the neighbors that John is foolish enough to be afraid of Noe's flood, *MillT* 3832–3837. **[Absolon[2]: Alison[2]: Nicholas[1]: Nowelis]**

Noe, both the ME and medieval Latin variant, appears three times medially, *MillT* 3539, 3560, 3582, and once in final rhyming position, *MillT* 3534. *Noes,* the ME genitive case, appears in the penultimate position, *MillT* 3518; *Noees,* tri-syllabic, occurs initially, *MillT* 3616.

R.J. Daniels, "Uxor Noah: Raven or Dove?" *ChauR* 14 (1979–1980): 23–32; "Processus Noe cum filiis." *The Wakefield Pageants in the Towneley Cycle,* ed. A.C. Cawley, 14–28.

NONIUS: [NONYUS]

NONYUS. Nonius was a protegé of one of the triumvirs during the years 55 or 54 B.C. Catullus mentions him in *Carmen* 52 as *struma*, "tumor," which was quite possibly his surname.

Lady Philosophy remarks that when wicked men are placed in high positions, their villainy becomes more evident as shown in Nonyus, *Bo* III, *Prosa* 4.10–16. Boethius calls Nonyus *struma* after Catullus. Chaucer translates it "postum" or "boch," adding a gloss that Nonyus "had a congregation of vices in his breast." Jean de Meun adds a definition: "*Postume, c'est à dire boce.*"

Nonyus is a spelling variant of Latin *Nonius*.

V.L. Dedeck-Héry, "Boethius' *De Consolatione* by Jean de Meun." *Speculum* 14 (1952): 211; C.J. Fordyce, *Catullus: A Commentary*, 221.

NOTE. St. Neot, who died c. 877, lived as a hermit near Bodmin Moor, where he established a small monastery. He had shrines at Glastonbury in Cornwall, where he had founded his monastery, and in Cambridgeshire, founded c. 1086.

Gerveys swears by St. Note, *MillT* 3771.

Skeat (V: 111) notes that in some manuscripts the name appears as *Noet*, derived from OE *Neot* and ME *Neet*. *Note* seems to be a variant of these and appears medially.

D.H. Farmer, *The Oxford Dictionary of Saints*, 289–290; A. MacDonald, "Absolon and Neot." *Neophilologus* 48 (1964): 235–237; M.P. Richards, "*The Miller's Tale*: "By Saint Note.'" *ChauR* 9 (1975): 212–215.

NOTUS: [EOLUS]

NOWELIS, a word derived from English "Nowell," or Christmas, is used by John the carpenter to designate Noah. Skeat (V: 111–112) suggests that the carpenter has confused Noë with Noël or Nowell, a sign of his illiteracy.

The carpenter, on hearing Nicholas's cries for water, thinks: "Alas, now comes Nowelis flood," *MillT* 3818. Alison and Nicholas tell the neighbors that John was much afraid of "Nowelis" flood through fantasy, *MillT* 3831–3834.

NYNUS. Ninus, fl. ninth century B.C., was king of Assyria and husband of Semiramis. Together they waged war over the greater part of Asia, and when Ninus died Semiramis succeeded him. At the time of the story of Pyramus and Thisbe, Ninus has already died (*Met* IV.88–901; *OM* VIII.229–1149).

Pyramus and Thisbe agree to steal away at night and to meet at Nynus's tomb, *LGW* 785. [**Piramus: Semyrame: Tesbee**]

Nynus is the OF variant.

Ovid, *Met*, ed. and trans. F.J. Miller, I: 184–185; *OM*, ed. C. de Boer, II, deel 21: 18–36.

NYOBE. Niobe, Tantalus's daughter and wife of Amphion of Thebes, boasted that she was just as much a goddess as Latona, Apollo's mother. She had seven sons and seven daughters, while the goddess had only two, Apollo and Diana. Thereupon Latona's children slew all of Niobe's children. Niobe was inconsolable and wept continually. Jupiter changed her into a statue that weeps in summer (*Met* VI.146–312; *OM* VI.973–1378). Dante makes Niobe a symbol of defeated pride and places her in Circle One of Purgatory, where she weeps over her dead children, *Purg* XII.37–39.

Pandarus compares Troilus to the weeping Nyobe, whose marble statue they have both seen, *Tr* I.699–700. Troilus replies that he wants no examples from old books, for he knows nothing of Queen Nyobe, *Tr* I.759.

Nyobe, the OF variant, occurs once medially, *Tr* I.699, and once in final rhyming position, *Tr* I.759.

Dante, *The Divine Comedy*, ed. and trans. C.S. Singleton, II.1: 122–123; Ovid, *Met*, ed. and trans. F.J. Miller, I: 298–309; *OM*, ed. C. de Boer, II, deel 21: 311–319.

NYSUS. Nisus was king of Megera, whose capital Alcathoe was beseiged by Minos of Crete as he sailed to Athens to avenge his son's death. In spite of his great skill, Minos could not take the city. Nisus's daughter Scylla fell in love with Minos as she watched from the walls. To win his love, Scylla cut off her father's purple lock, on which the safety of the kingdom depended, and gave it to Minos, but Minos recoiled in horror from the gift. He sailed from Alcathoe, forbidding Scylla ever to set foot on Crete. She leaped into the water to swim after the ship, but her father, changed into an osprey, approached her to tear her to pieces. To her great horror, she found she had been changed into a bird, and she was called *Ciris* (lark) because she had cut her father's lock of hair (*Met* VIII.11–151; *OM* VIII.1–352).

Phebus is rising in the east, and Nysus's daughter sings with fresh intent when Troilus sends for Pandarus, *Tr* V.1107–1111. S.B. Meech suggests that Chaucer may have learned that *ciris* means "lark" from the gloss on the name in a manuscript of the *Metamorphoses* or from the *Ovide Moralisé*. The story is told at some length, *LGW* 1909–1920. **[Minos: Silla]**

Nysus, the OF variant, appears three times medially, *Tr* V.1110; *LGW* 1904, 1908.

S.B. Meech, "Chaucer and the *Ovide Moralisé*—A Further Study." *PMLA* 46 (1931): 188–189; Ovid, *Met*, ed. and trans. F.J. Miller, I: 406–417; *OM*, ed. C. de Boer, III, deel 30: 109–117.

OCTAVIA: [CESAR²]
OCTAVIUS: [OCTAVYEN]

OCTAVYEN. Gaius Octavius, 63 B.C.–A.D. 14, was given the added names Julius Caesar when his uncle Julius Caesar adopted him into the clan. His mother, Atia, was Julius Caesar's niece, and Caesar made Octavius his chief heir. After Caesar's murder in 44 B.C., the Senate recognized him as Caesar's adopted son under the name Gaius Julius Caesar Octavius. When he won the war of Mutina in 43 B.C., he tried to win Antony over to his interests by agreeing to his sister's marriage with Antony, but when the latter refused to leave Cleopatra, their rivalry broke out. Octavius defeated Antony at the Battle of Actium in 31 B.C. and became master of Egypt. He was given the title Augustus in 27 B.C. The emperor appears to have been popular during the Middle Ages. Three Middle English *Octavyan* romances are extant: one South-English version and two North-English versions, all dated c. 1350.

The Dreamer asks one of the kennel men leading the hounds, "Who hunts in the forest?" The man replies, "The Emperor Octavyen," *BD* 365–369. Skeat (I: 472–473) identifies the emperor with Edward III because Chaucer refers to the emperor as "this king," apparently meaning "the reigning king," *BD* 1314. [**Cesar²**]

Octavyen, the ME variant of Latin *Octavius*, the name of Augustus's paternal clan, appears in final rhyming position, *BD* 368.

Octavian, ed. G. Sarrazin; *Octavian*, ed. F. Sparran.

ODAENATHUS: [ODENAKE]

ODENAKE. Odaenathus Septimus, fl. third century A.D., king of Palmyra, was Zenobia's husband. From A.D. 262–267 he led the Roman army in the east and was rewarded with the title *Imperator.* He was murdered with his eldest son in 267, and some ancient historians blame Zenobia for his death (Trebellius Pollio, *Tyranni Triginta* XXX). Boccaccio says that Odaenathus and his son were killed by Meronius, a maternal cousin (*De claris mulieribus* XCVIII).

Cenobia marries Odenake, and they live in joy and happiness, *MkT* 2271–2278. Cenobia forces Odenake to be celibate during her pregnancies, *MkT* 2285–2294. They have two sons, and together Cenobia and Odenake reign over many kingdoms in the east, *MkT* 2295–2316. Cenobia reigns alone after Odenake's death, *MkT* 2327–2330. **[Aurelian: Cenobia: Hermanno: Thymalao]**

Odenake, the OF variant and a contraction of Latin *Odaenathus,* appears four times medially, *MkT* 2272, 2291, 2295, 2327. *Odenakes,* the ME genitive case, appears once, medially, *MkT* 2318.

Boccaccio, *CFW,* trans. G. Guarino, 226–230; *ibid., De claris mulieribus,* ed. V. Zaccaria, 406–414; *ibid., Scriptores historiae Augustae,* ed. and trans. D. Magie, III: 135–143.

OEDIPUS: [EDIPPE]

OENONE, a nymph and shepherdess, married the Trojan prince Paris while he was a shepherd in Phrygia. He deserted her after Venus promised him the most beautiful woman in the world (*Heroides* V; *RR* 13215–13218).

Paris, false to Oënone, appears in the *blazon de faulse amours, HF* I.399. Pandarus relates a summary of her letter, from *Heroides* V, *Tr* I.652–665, in which she says that Phebus, god of medicine, could not cure himself of love for King Amete's daughter. **[Amete: Paris: Venus]**

The name appears in final rhyming position, *HF* I.399; *Tr* I.654.

M. Arn, "Three Ovidian Women in Chaucer's *Troilus:* Medea, Helen, Oënone." *ChauR* 15 (1980): 1–10; Ovid, *Her,* ed. and trans. G. Showerman, 56–69; *RR,* ed. E. Langlois, IV:11, *RR,* trans. C. Dahlberg, 228.

OETES. Aeetes, son of Helios, was king of Colchis, Circe's brother, and Medea's father. He owned the Golden Fleece of the Ram of Phrixus, on which the life of his kingdom depended and which Jason came seeking with the Argonauts (*Met* VII.7–10). Guido de Columnis blames Aeetes for seating Medea next to Jason at the palace banquet and thus helping to ignite the passion between them (*HDT* II.255–269). Aeetes's role is more important in Guido's version than in Ovid's.

Oëtes, king of Colchis and Medea's father, owns the Golden Fleece, *LGW* 1438, 1593. Jason woos his daughter and takes her away with him after she helps him to win the Fleece. **[Jason: Medea]**

Oëtes, the medieval Latin variant, occurs twice, medially.

Guido delle Colonne, *Guido de Columnis: HDT*, ed. N.E. Griffin, 7–8, 14–22; *ibid., HDT*, trans. M.E. Meek, 4–5, 16–17; Ovid, *Met*, ed. and trans. F.J. Miller, l: 342–343.

OLIPHANT is a giant who threatens Sir Thopas and throws stones after him when he enters the fairy queen's domain, *Thop* 807–832. **[Thopas]**

Oliphant, "elephant" in Middle English, occurs in final rhyming position, *Thop* 808.

OLIVER: [OLYVER]

OLOFERNE, OLOFERNUS. Holofernes was the Assyrian general of Nebuchadnezzar's armies. He attacked the Jewish city of Bethulia and besieged it for a month. Just when surrender seemed imminent, he received a visit from a beautiful widow, Judith, and entertained her at a feast. When he was drunk, she slew him, cut off his head, and gave it to her maid to put in a sack (Judith 1–16). Judith appears among *femmes de bon conseil,* "women of good counsel," in *Liber consolationis et consilii (The Book of Consolation and Counsel)* V by Albertanus of Brescia (1246).

The Man of Law asks: "Who gave Judith courage to slay Olofernus in his tent and deliver God's people?" *MLT* 939–942. Judith's counsel saves her country from Oloferne, *MerchT* 1368, *Mel* 1099. The story of Olofernus appears among the Monk's tragedies, *MkT* 2551–2574. **[Abigayl: Judith: Rebekke]**

Oloferne, the ME and OF variant, appears once medially, with final syllabic -*e*, *MkT* 2556, and once in final rhyming position, with final syllabic -*e*, *MkT* 2567. *Olofernus,* a variant of Latin *Holofernus,* appears twice, medially, *MLT* 940; *MerchT* 1368, and once in *Mel* 1099. Latin initial *h* was not pronounced.

Albertanus Brixiensis, *Liber consolationis et consilii*, ed. T. Sundby, 16–17; Renaud de Louens, *Le Livre de Mellibee et de Prudence*, ed. J.B. Severs, *S&A*, 576.

OLOFERNUS: [OLOFERNE]

OLYVER. Oliver was Roland's comrade-in-arms and his prospective brother-in-law. Of the two knights, Oliver was the more prudent, while Roland was the more courageous. They both died as a result of the Saracen ambush at the pass of Roncevalles, betrayed by Ganelon, Roland's stepfather. This incident is the subject of the twelfth-century *chanson de geste, La Chanson de Roland.*

The Man in Black says that if he repented of his love he would be worse than Ganelon, who betrayed Roland and Oliver, *BD* 1115–1123. **[Charles Olyver: Genyllon-Olyver: Rowland]**

The name appears in final rhyming position, *BD* 1123.

La Chanson de Roland, ed. C. Segre; *The Song of Roland*, ed. S.J. Herrtage; *The Song of Roland*, trans. D. Sayers.

OMER. According to legend, Homer was born either at Chios or at Smyrna. Herodotus dates him four hundred years before his own time, *i.e.*, c. 850–700 B.C. (*Histories* 11.53), and modern scholars have accepted this date. He is the author of the *Iliad*, a poem on the Trojan War, and the *Odyssey*, a poem of Odysseus's wanderings before he returned to Ithaca. The fidelity with which Homer endowed Odysseus's wife Penelope became legendary. Jerome mentions her in his *Epistola adversus Jovinianum* (*Letter Against Jovinian*) I.45 (*PL* 23: 275). The medieval versions of the Troy story are *De excidio Troiae historia*, by Dares Phrygius, of uncertain date but generally believed to have been written about the fourth century of our era; *Ephemeridos belli Troiani*, by Dictys Cretensis, also dating from the fourth century; *Le Roman de Troie* (c. 1184), by Benoît de Sainte-Maure, and the *Historia destructionis Troiae*, by Guido de Columnis (before 1287).

Dorigen asks herself, "What does Omer say of good Penelope?" *FranklT* 1443–1444. Omer stands on a pillar of iron, Mars's metal, as one of the poets of the Trojan War, *HF* III.1466–1474, with other writers on the same subject—Dares, Guido, Dictys. The narrator detects a little envy among the poets; one says that Omer told lies about the war and favored the Greeks, *HF* II.1475–1479. Dares implies that Homer lied and swears he tells the truth, *De excidio*, l. Benoît echoes the accusation against Homer, *Roman de Troie*, 45–70, 110–116. "Omer with the honey mouth" appears in *Bo* V, *Metr* 2.1–6, and he is one of the writers of the "Troian gestes," *Tr* I.146, V.1792. [**Dares Frygius: Dite: Guido: Lollius: Penalopee: Ulixes**]

Omer, the OF variant, appears four times medially, *FranklT* 1443; *HF* III.1477; *Tr* I.146, V.1792; and once in final rhyming position, *HF* III.1466.

Benoît, *Le Roman de Troie*, ed. L. Constans; Dares Phrygius, *De excidio Troiae historia*, ed. F. Meister, 2–3; Dares Phrygius and Dictys Cretensis, *The Trojan War*, trans. R.M. Frazer, 133; Dictys, *Ephemeridos belli Troiani*, ed. W. Eisenhut; Guido delle Colonne, *Guido de Columnis: HDT*, ed. N.E. Griffin; *ibid., HDT*, trans. M.E. Meek; Herodotus, *Histories*, ed. and trans. A.D. Godley, I: 340–341; Homer, *Iliad*, ed. and trans. A.T. Murray; *ibid., Odyssey*, ed. and trans. A.T. Murray.

OPILIO: [OPILION]

OPILION. Opilio, fl. sixth century A.D., was Cyprian's brother and one of Boethius's accusers. Cassiodorus writes to him for the Emperor Athalaricus, informing him that he has been made one of the counts of the sacred Largesses, or *comes sacrarium largitionum* (*Epistola* VIII.16).

Opilion is among Boethius's accusers, *Bo* I, *Prosa* 4.114 [**Boece: Cyprian: Gaudenicus**]

The form is OF, found in Jean de Meun's translation, *Li Livres de confort de philosophie*, I, *Prose* 4.60–61.

Cassiodorus, *Epistolae Theodoricianae variae*, ed. Th. Mommsen, 246–247; V.L. Dedeck-Héry, "Boethius' *De consolatione* by Jean de Meun." *MS* 14 (1952): 178.

ORIGEN: [ORIGENES]

ORIGENES, ORYGENES. Origines Adamantius was born c. A.D. 186 in Alexandria. His father Leonides was martyred in 202, when Origen was not quite seventeen, during a persecution against Christians and Jews under Septimius Severus. After his father's death Origen's devotion increased so that he sought martyrdom himself, but it escaped him. He was a brilliant scholar, and by the time he was eighteen Demetrius, bishop of Alexandria, made him head of the Catechetical School, a post he held until 231. Both boys and girls came to the school and, to avoid temptation, Origen took Jesus's saying in Matthew 19:12 literally and castrated himself. Because of this action, Demetrius later denied him the priesthood, and Origen eventually left Alexandria. He settled in Caesarea, where a friendly bishop ordained him. There he established a school surpassing in renown that at Alexandria. During the Decian persecution between 250 and 251, Origen was repeatedly tortured, and his death in 255 perhaps resulted from his sufferings (Eusebius, *Ecclesiastical History* VI). Influenced by the Platonic allegories of Philo Judaeus, also of Alexandria, Origen became the father of allegorical interpretation of certain books of the Bible. He wrote commentaries on Matthew, John, Isaiah, Ezekiel and, most famous of all, on the Canticle of Canticles, which interprets the Beloved as the Church and the Bridegroom as Christ. A thirteenth-century work entitled *Homilia Origenis de Maria Magdalena* was attributed to Origen, but it is in the Latin tradition, not the Greek tradition, to which Origen belonged.

Alceste reminds the God of Love that Chaucer has translated *Orygenes upon the Maudeleyne, LGW F* 428, *LGW G* 418. **[Magdalena]**

Origenes, the ME variant of Greek and Latin *Origenes*, appears initially, *LGW F* 428; *Orygenes*, a spelling variant, appears initially, *LGW G* 418.

Eusebius, *Ecclesiastical History,* ed. and trans. J.E.L. Oulton, II: 9–85; M. Jennings, "The Art of the Pseudo-Origen Homily *De Maria Magdalena.*" *Medievalia et Humanistica,* new series 5 (1974): 139–152; J.P. McCall, "Chaucer and the Pseudo-Origen *de Maria Magdalena.*" *Speculum* 46 (1971): 491–509; Origen, *The Song of Songs: Commentary and Homilies,* trans. R.P. Lawson.

ORION. Arion was a semi-mythical poet, born at Methymnan, Lesbos, where he is said to have been a pupil of Alcman, the Greek lyric poet of the second half of the seventh century B.C. As court poet to Periander, tyrant of Corinth, Arion was well paid for his services. While he was returning to Lesbos by ship, the captain and his crew threatened his life if he did not give up his gold. He asked permission to sing one last song before his death, which was granted. As he finished his song, he leapt into the sea, but a dolphin caught him on its back, and in this way he reached Lesbos. His dolphin and lyre were placed in the heavens (*Fasti* II.79–118). Gower presents Arion as a figure of harmony (*Confessio Amantis, Prologue,* 1054–1075).

The eagle points out the constellations Arion's Harp and the Dolphin to the terrified poet-dreamer, *HF* II.1005. Orion stands with other musicians in Fame's house, *HF* III.1203–1205. [**Arionis Harpe: Delphyn**]

The genitive singular, *Arionis Harpe*, *HF* II.1005, shows that Chaucer knew that the name was Arion. *Orion*, possibly a scribal error, occurs in final rhyming position, *HF* III.1205.

John Gower, *The Complete Works*, ed. G.C. Macaulay, II: 33–34; Ovid, *Fasti*, ed. and trans. J.G. Frazer, 62–65.

ORPHEUS was the son of Calliope, the Muse of epic poetry, and Oeagrus, king of Phrygia. Apollo gave him his lyre, and the Muses taught him to play it. He became such a marvelous musician that he charmed trees, birds, and beasts. He married the nymph Eurydice and disaster struck immediately. As she wandered through the grass with her friends on her wedding day a snake bit her and she died. Orpheus, inconsolable, went down to the Underworld to fetch her back. With the music of his lyre he charmed Cerberus, the three-headed dog of the Underworld, then Hades and his wife Persephone. Finally, in agreement with the Erinyes, Hades and Persephone allowed Eurydice to return to earth on condition that Orpheus not look back at her until they had left the valley of Avernus, the entrance to the Underworld. Just as they neared the light, Orpheus looked back, and Eurydice was lost forever (*Met* X.1–63; *OM* X.1–195). Virgil says that Eurydice stepped on a snake while she fled the advances of Aristaeus, but the end of the story is the same (*Georgics* IV.454–529).

Ovid's story is the main source for medieval writers, while Boethius's interpretation of the myth in *De consolatione philosophiae* III, *Metr* 12, prevailed for most medieval commentators. Chaucer translates the interpretation thus: "This fable apertenith to yow alle, whosoevere desireth or seketh to lede his thought into the sovereyn day (*that is to seyn, into cleernesse of soveryn good*)," *Bo* III, *Metr* 12. Other traditions interpret the figures of both Orpheus and Eurydice allegorically. Isidore (c. 560–636), in discussing rhythm, the third division of music, says that Mercury invented music and that Orpheus handed it down to posterity (*Etym* III.10). Fulgentius (fifth to sixth centuries) interprets the myth as an allegory of the art of music and derives Orpheus from *Orea fone*, or "matchless voice" (*Mythologiae* III.10). As a musician, Orpheus appears at the wedding feast of Mercury and Philology in Martianus Capella's *De nuptiis Mercurii et Philologiae IX (The Wedding of Mercury and Philology IX)*, written between 410 and 439. A different approach to the story is found in the Middle English poem *Sir Orfeo* (beginning of the fourteenth century), where Orpheus and Dame Heurodis return to their kingdom and live happily ever after.

Neither Orpheus nor Amphioun ever made such melody as the instruments at Januarie's wedding feast, *MerchT* 1715–1716. Not even Orpheus, the god of melody, can cure the Man in Black of his sorrow, *BD* 567–569. The poet hears Orpheus play the harp skilfully at Fame's court, *HF* III.1201–1203. Criseyde comforts Troilus with the thought that while they may be separated during their lifetimes, they will be united in the Elysian Fields, like Orpheus and Erudice, *Tr* IV.785–791. The story is told in *Bo* III, *Metr* 12. **[Caliope: Erudice]**

The name occurs initially, *HF* III.1203; three times in medial positions, *MerchT* 1716; *BD* 569; *Tr* IV.791; and in *Bo* III, *Metr* 12.4, 17, 46, 55, 58.

J.B. Friedman, *Orpheus in the Middle Ages*; Fulgentius, *Fulgentius the Mythographer*, trans. L.G. Whitbread, 96–98; Isidore, *Etymologiae*, ed. W.M. Lindsay, I; Martianus Capella, *Martianus Capella: De nuptiis Mercurii et Philologiae*, ed. A. Dick, 480; *ibid.*, *Martianus Capella and the Seven Liberal Arts*, trans. W.H. Stahl, II.351–352; Ovid, *Met*, ed. and trans. F.J. Miller, II: 64–71; *OM*, ed. C. de Boer, IV, deel 37: 11–16; *Sir Orfeo*, ed. A.J. Bliss; Virgil, *Georgics*, ed. and trans. H.R. Fairclough, I: 228–233.

OSEWOLD. The Reeve on the pilgrimage to Canterbury is named after the Northumbrian saint who died in 642. He also comes from the north, as the dialect of his tale confirms. His portrait appears in *Gen Prol* 587–623. When he objects to the Miller's intention to tell a story about a carpenter and wife, the Miller replies, "Leve brother Osewold,/Who hath no wyf, he is no cokewold," *MillP* 3151–3152. Osewold's self-revelation appears in *RvP* 3864–3898.

The name appears twice medially, *RvT* 3860, 3909, and once in final rhyming position, *MillP* 3151.

W.C. Curry, *Chaucer and the Mediaeval Sciences*, 71–79; J.E. Grennen, "The Calculating Reeve and his *Camera obscura*." *JMRS* 14 (1984): 245–259.

OSWALD: [OSEWOLD]
OTES DE GRAUNSON: [GRAUNSON]
OVID: [OVIDE]

OVIDE, OVYDE. Publius Ovidius Naso, 43 B.C.–A.D. 17 or 18, was born at Sulmo and died in exile at Tomi. He tells the story of his life in *Tristia* 4.10. He studied rhetoric in Rome because his father wanted him to be a lawyer, but after holding a few minor posts, he abandoned law for poetry. Married three times, he had one daughter. With the publication of *Ars amatoria (The Art of Love)* in c. 1 B.C. he became popular and famous. In A.D. 8 Augustus banished him to Tomi for reasons not quite clear. Ovid says that he was exiled because of a poem (*carmen,* possibly *Ars amatoria)* and because of an error or indiscretion. Repeated appeals to Augustus and, later, Tiberius, brought no relief, and he died in exile. The following are his works in approximate (but uncertain) order:

1. *Amores* (*The Loves*), in three books, consisting of love elegies influenced by Propertius.
2. *Heroides*, or *Epistulae heroidum* (*The Heroines*, or *Heroines's Letters*), letters from certain famous women to false lovers or absent husbands.
3. *Medicamine faciei femineae* (*Face Cosmetics for Women*), a poem on cosmetics.
4. *Ars amatoria* (*The Art of Love*), books 1 and 2 written for men, book 3 added for women at their request.
5. *Remedia amoris* (*The Remedies of Love*), a pretended recantation of the previous work.
6. *Metamorphoses* (*The Metamorphoses*), in fifteen books, each episode describing or alluding to a change of shape, generally from human form to that of beasts or plants.
7. *Fasti* (*Feasts*), a calendar of Roman festivals.
8. *Tristia* (*Sorrow*), five books of poems giving the story of his life, describing his exile and defending *Ars amatoria*.
9. *Epistulae ex Ponto* (*Letters from Pontus*), four books of poems from various periods of his life.
10. *Medea* (a play), *Ibis*, and *Nux* said to be spurious works.

     The twelfth-century writer Arnulf of Orleans prefixed to his glosses on the *Metamorphoses* the first "life" of the poet with the following order of his works: *Heroides, Sine titulo (Amores), Ars amatoria, Remedia amoris, Fasti, Tristia, Metamorphoses, Epistolae Ex Ponte, Ibis*. Arnulf assigned *Metamorphoses* to moral philosophy, thus bringing it into the culture of the time. The introduction to each of Ovid's works during the medieval period carried an *accessus*, or an additional introduction, positing that the work had a moral aim, showing that the commentator thus hoped to escape the church's censure. Medieval commentators gave three reasons for the poet's exile: *quod ipse concubuit cum Livia, quod vidit Augustum condormientem puero, quod ipse composuit librum de arte amatoria,* "that he slept with Livia, that he saw Augustus sleeping with a boy, that he composed the book on the art of love." (For the medieval view of Ovid's life, see Fausto Ghisalberti, "Mediaeval Biographies of Ovid," *JWCI* 9 [1946]: 10–59.)

     The early Middle Ages were devoted to Virgil because Christian writers interpreted his *Eclogue* VI as prophecy concerning the birth of Christ; they rejected Ovid mainly because of the forthright erotic nature of his work. By the twelfth century, however, his *Fasti* and *Epistulae ex Ponto* were in the school curriculum, and *Heroides* and *Metamorphoses* were presented with moral aims. The process of moralizing Ovid had begun as early as the fifth century when Fulgentius (c. A.D. 467–532) presented his fables-with-moral, *Mythologiarum libri tres*. Theodulphus, the ninth-century bishop of Orleans (d. 821), proposed that truth was hidden by the false covering in Ovid's work and produced his *Theodulfi Carmina: de libris quos legere solebam, et qualiter fabulae poetarum a philosophis mystice petractentur* (*PL* 105: 331–332). Theodulf interpreted the gods and heroes as allegorical figures, *e.g.*, Hercules was Virtue, Proteus was Truth. By the eleventh and twelfth centuries library catalogues showed regular increases in copies of Ovid, as well as of Horace and other classical writers.

Excerpts from Ovid appear in *florilegia,* anthologies of passages from classical authors. One *florilegium,* composed of fourteen books, devoted five of them to Ovid (*Survival of the Pagan Gods* 91). In the twelfth century Ovid's name was listed for school study, and in the thirteenth century John of Garland's *Integumenta* on the *Metamorphoses* appeared. The thirteenth and fourteenth centuries have been called *Aetas Ovidiana,* the Age of Ovid, because Ovidian sentiments and meters dominate the literature of the period. In the early fourteenth century, between 1316 and 1328, came the *Ovide Moralisé* by an anonymous writer, done at the request of Queen Jeanne, probably Philip V's wife, Jeanne of Bourgogne (d. 1329), and sometimes attributed to Philippe de Vitry, bishop of Meaux. At the same time, several Ovidian works appeared: Robert Holcott's *Moralia super Ovidii* Metamorphoses *(The Morals of Ovid's Metamorphoses);* Petrus Berchorius's *Ovidius moralizatus (The Moralized Ovid),* of which book fifteen, called *De formis figurisque deorum,* gives allegorical interpretations of the gods; Thomas Waleys's *Metamorphosis Ovidiana moraliter explanata (Ovid's* Metamorphoses *Explained with Morals);* Giovanni dei Bonsogni's *Allegorie ed esposizioni delle* Metamorphosi *(Allegories and Expositions of the* Metamorphoses*).* The allegories interpret Jupiter as Christ, the triple goddess Diana as the Trinity, Juno as the Virgin, and so on. About 1331 John Ridewall composed his *Fulgentius metaforalis,* based not only on Ovid but also on the Bible and the church fathers. Here Juno is Memoria, Neptune is Intelligencia, Pluto Providence. The late fourteenth-century *Libellus de imaginibus deorum* of Albericus Philosophus is a recension of the earlier thirteenth-century *Mythographus tertius Vaticanus (The Third Vatican Mythographer),* identified with Albericus of London. Derived chiefly from Fulgentius, these two works have little Ovidian material.

It is not surprising, then, to find that Ovid's influence is the greatest of any single influence on Chaucer's work, providing plots as well as *exempla* and commonplaces. The Man of Law says that Chaucer has written more love stories in English than Ovid has in his *Epistles, MLI* 46–55, referring to *Epistulae heroidum.* Ovid's *Ars amatoria* is bound with others in Jankyn's anthology, *WBP* 680. Alys refers to Ovid for her tale of Midas, *WBT* 952–982. The Merchant invokes "noble Ovide," who says that love will find a way as it did with Piramus and Tesbee, *MerchT* 2125–2128. Dame Prudence quotes from Ovid's *Remedia amoris,* 127–130, *Mel* 976–977; from *Remedia amoris* 421–422, *Mel* 1325; from *Amores* 1.8.104, *Mel* 1414–1415. The Man in Black is in such despair that not all the remedies of Ovid can cure him, *BD* 568, having in mind *Remedia amoris.* The narrator refers his audience to the "Epistle of Ovyde" for Dido's story, *HF* I.379–380, found in *Heroides* VII. Ovyde, as "Venus clerk," stands on a copper pillar, *HF* III.1486–1492. Chaucer directs his "litel bok" to kiss the footsteps of the great poets, Virgile, Ovyde, Omer, Lucan, and Stace, *Tr* V.1786–1792. The God of Love asks the poet: "What says 'the Epistle of Ovyde' about faithful wives?" *LGW G* 305, referring to *Epistulae heroidum.* The poet refers the reader to Ovyde for Dido's letter to Eneas, *LGW* 1367 (*Heroides* VII). Ovyde, in his *Epistles,* tells Ysiphile's story, *LGW* 1465 (*Heroides* VI). The poet asserts that Ovyde has given Medea's letter to Jason in verse, *LGW* 1678–1679 (*Heroides* XII). Ovyde is one of the sources for Lucresse's story, *LGW* 1683 (*Fasti* II.685–952).

Chaucer refers to the *Heroides* as *Epistles*, *MLI* 53–55; *HF* I.379; *LGW* 1465, showing that he knew the full title, *Epistulae heroidum* or *Letters from Heroines*. Most of the names mentioned in the *Balade, LGW F* 249–269, *LGW G* 202–223, are taken from the *Heroides*. The story of Jason, Ypsipyle, and Medea, *HF* I.400 and developed in *LGW* 1368–1679, is based on *Heroides* VI and XII. Ariadne's story, *HF* I.405–426 and *LGW* 1886–2227, is based on *Met* VIII.169–182 and *Heroides* X; that of Phyllis and Demophoon, *HF* I.388–396 and *LGW* 2394–2561, is based on *Heroides* II; that of Ypermestra, *LGW* 2562–2723, from *Heroides* XIV. Stories mentioned in *HF* I.397–404 are based on *Heroides* III, V, IX.

Chaucer mentions *Metamorphoses* only once, *MLI* 93, but he uses it extensively throughout his work. The description of Mercury, *KnT* 1385–1390, comes from *Met* I.671–721; the story of King Midas, *WBT* 952–982, comes from *Met* XI.174–193; the reference to Echo and Narcissus, *FranklT* 1951–1952, comes from *Met* III.407. The source of the Manciple's Tale is *Met* II.534–632; the story of Ceys and Alcyone, *BD* 60–770, comes from *Met* XI.410–768; the reference to Niobe, *Tr* I.699, although a well-known story, may have been influenced by *Met* VI. Some of the stories in *The Legend of Good Women* are taken from the *Metamorphoses*: Pyramus and Thisbe, *Met* IV.55–166; Ariadne, *Met* VII and VIII; Philomela, *Met* VI.424–605.

Metamorphosios, *MLI* 93, is a variant of *Metamorphoseos*, the genitive of *Metamorphosis*. Early manuscripts and editions of Ovid's work contain the erroneous genitive form instead of the plural *Metamorphoseon*, as in the eleventh-century manuscript known as Codex Marcianus Florentinus 225 in the Bibliotheca Laurentiana and the manuscript of Guido de Columnis, *Liber de Casu Trojae* of the Harvard Library, in addition to several others. [**Naso: Philippe de Vitry**]

Ovide, the French variant of Latin *Ovidius*, the writer's clan name, appears twice medially, *MLI* 54; *Tr* V.1792; twice in final rhyming position, *HF* I.379, *HF* III.1487. *Ovyde*, a spelling variant, appears once initially, *WBP* 952; six times in medial positions, *WBP* 982; *MerchT* 2125; *LGW* 1367, 1465, 1678, 1683; and twice in final rhyming position, *BD* 568; *LGW G* 305. *Ovydes*, the ME genitive case, appears once initially, *WBP* 680.

F.M. Fyler, *Chaucer and Ovid*; F. Ghisalberti, "Medieval Biographies of Ovid." *JWCI* 9 (1946): 10–59; R.L. Hoffman, *Ovid and* The Canterbury Tales; Ovid, *The Art of Love and Other Poems*, ed. and trans. J.H. Mozley; *ibid., Fasti*, ed. and trans. J.G. Frazer; *ibid., Heroides and Amores*, ed. and trans. G. Showerman; *ibid., Metamorphoses*, ed. and trans. F.J. Miller; *OCD* 763–765; J. Seznec, *Survival of the Pagan Gods*, trans. B.F. Sessions, 90–95; E.F. Shannon, *Chaucer and the Roman Poets*, 308–312; Beryl Smalley, *English Friars and Antiquity in the Early Fourteenth Century*.

P

PALAMON, PALAMOUN, is Arcita's cousin and *felawe* (sworn brother) in *The Knight's Tale*. He is devoted to Venus and thinks that Emelye is the goddess when he sees her in the garden from his prison window, *KnT* 1074–1102. After seven years' imprisonment, Palamon breaks out of prison on the third of May, *KnT* 1451–1487. He meets Arcita, who is out observing May in the forest, and challenges him to a duel on the next day, *KnT* 1574–1622. As they fight up to their ankles in blood, Theseus intervenes and orders their executions because they have flouted his edict, *KnT* 1674–1747, but Ypolita and Emelye beg for their lives, and Theseus commands Palamon and Arcita to appear at a tournament the next year, *KnT* 1742–1880. Since Palamon is Venus's knight, Theseus builds him an oratory to the goddess on the east gate of the stadium, *KnT* 1918–1966. Palamon worships Venus in her oratory and asks not for victory but for possession of Emelye, *KnT* 2221–2267. Several years after Arcita's death he finally marries her. In Boccaccio's *Il Teseide delle nozze d'Emilia*, the name is *Palaemon*. Alceste reminds the God of Love that the poet has told all the love of Palamon and Arcita, *LGW G* 419–421, *LGW G* 407–409. **[Arcita: Emelie: Lycurge: Venus]**

Palamon never appears in initial position. It occurs twenty-nine times medially, *KnT* 1031, 1063, 1092, 1115, 1123, 1128, 1234, 1334, 1450, 1455, 1574, 1590, 1620, 1636, 1714, 2094, 2210, 2212, 2314, 2471, 2639, 2763, 2797, 2909, 3077, 3090, 3098; *LGW F* 420, *LGW G* 408. *Palamon* also occurs fourteen times in final rhyming position, *KnT* 1014, 1275, 1452, 1698, 2117, 2128, 2261, 2271, 2584, 2783, 2794, 2817, 2882, 2976. *Palamoun* occurs three times in medial positions, *KnT* 2633, 2647, 2742; sixteen times in final rhyming position, *KnT* 1070, 1341, 1348, 1467, 1479, 1516, 1627, 1655, 1734, 1791, 1870, 2629, 2643, 2652, 2858, 2882.

Boccaccio, *Tutte le opere*, ed. V. Branca, II: 253–664; H.N. Fairchild, "Active Arcite, Contemplative Palamon." *JEGP* 26 (1927): 285–293.

PALAMOUN: [PALAMON]

PALINURUS was Aeneas's pilot. As they sailed toward Italy, the god of sleep overpowered Palinurus during the night and hurled him into the sea (*Aeneid* V.814–871). Aeneas later met him in the Underworld, where he told him how he had died (*Aeneid* VI.337–383).

The story of Eneas's meeting with Palinurus is painted on the brass tablet in the temple of Venus, *HF* I.443. **[Eneas]**

The name occurs in final rhyming position.

Virgil, *Aeneid*, ed. and trans. H.R. Fairclough, I: 500–505, 528–533.

PALLAS is one of Athena's epithets. She was originally the Minoan-Mycenaean snake goddess, and the exact meaning of *Pallas* is unknown. Isidore suggests that she is named after an island in Thrace or after a giant she killed (*Etym* VIII.xi.57). She is the goddess of wisdom because she sprang fully grown and fully armed out of Zeus's head. The Palladium, an ancient wooden statue of the armed Pallas, was the Luck of Troy, sent by Jupiter from heaven to Ilus, the descendant of Dardanus who founded Troy. As long as the statue was preserved, Troy was impregnable (*Fasti* VI.417–436). After the theft of the statue, Troy was easily attacked and destroyed. Pallas is represented helmeted, with a snake peeping out from under her shield, a detail indicative of her Minoan origin. She wears a goatskin or *aegis* thrown over her shoulders and bosom. The owl is her bird. The Roman goddess Minerva took over some of Pallas Athena's attributes as goddess of war, wisdom, and handicrafts.

Virginia is as wise as Pallas, *PhysT* 49–50. Pallas is confused with Bellona, Mars's sister, *Anel* 5. Her Palladium protects Troy, *Tr* I.152–154. Criseyde goes to the temple to celebrate the feast of the Palladion, and Troilus sees her for the first time, *Tr* I.155–172. Criseyde asks for Pallas's help, *Tr* II.425. Pallas was angry with Aglawros when she became jealous of Hierse, *Tr* III.729–730. Troilus leaves his shield to Pallas after his death, *Tr* V.307–308. Criseyde swears by "Pallas with hire heres clere," *Tr* V.999. "Heres clere" seems to be Chaucer's rendering of Latin *flavius*, the customary adjective for Minerva; *flavae Minervae* occurs in *Met* II.749, *Met* VIII.275, "of golden Minerva." **[Aglawros: Bellona: Minerva]**

The name never occurs initially. It appears five times in medial position, *PhysT* 49; *Anel* 5; *Tr* III.730, V.308, 999; and twice in final rhyming position, *Tr* II.425, V.977.

Isidore, *Etymologiae*, ed. W.M. Lindsay, I; Ovid, *Fasti*, ed. and trans. J.G. Frazer, 350–353.

PAMPHILLES, PAMPHILUS. Pamphilus is the hero of the medieval Latin comedy in three acts, *Pamphilus de amore,* a story about Pamphilus's love for Galatea. Pamphilus Mauritianus, a poet of the late twelfth or early thirteenth century, is sometimes named as the author.

Aurelius loves Dorigen as secretly as Pamphilus loved Galathee, *FranklT* 1110. The quotation on wealth attributed to Pamphilles, *Mel* 1556, occurs in *Pamphilus de amore* 53–54. Dame Prudence says she quotes Pamphilles, *Mel* 1558, but she quotes Ovid, *Tristia* I.9.5–6. The quotation from Pamphilles at *Mel* 1561 refers to Petrus Alfonsi, *Disciplina clericalis* IV. Severs points out that this quotation is lacking in the Latin version of the tale (*S&A* 600). The passage is not an exact translation of Petrus Alfonsi's story in the edition cited below.

Pamphilles appears only in the *Melibee*, *Mel* 1556, 1558, 1561; *Pamphilus* appears medially, *FranklT* 1110.

Albertanus Brixiensis, *Liber consolationis et consilii*, ed. T. Sundby, 54, 71, 98; Peter Dronke, "A Note on *Pamphilus*." *JWCI* 42 (1979): 225–230; T.J. Garbaty, "*Pamphilus, De amore:* An Introduction and Translation." *ChauR* 2 (1967–1968): 108–134; *ibid.*, "The *Pamphilus* Tradition in Ruiz and Chaucer." *PQ* 46 (1967): 457–470; Gustave Cohen, ed., *La "Comédie" Latine en France au XIIe siècle*, II: 194–223; *Seven Medieval Latin Comedies*, trans. A.G. Elliott, 1–25; Petrus Alfonsi, *Disciplina clericalis*, ed. and trans. E. Hermes, trans. into English P.R. Quarrie, 114; Renaud de Louens, *Le Livre de Mellibee et Prudence*, ed. J.B. Severs, *S&A*, 568–614.

PAN, Mercury's son, was god of flocks and shepherds. He invented the musical pipe of seven reeds and called it the syrinx after the nymph he loved. To elude him, Syrinx jumped into a pond and was changed into a reed (*Met* I.689–712). Isidore calls Pan the god of nature (*Etym* VIII.xi.81), and Petrus Berchorius says that Pan, since antiquity, was called the god of nature (*De formis figurisque deorum* fol.8ᵛb, 1–2).

The Man in Black is more anguished than Pan, the "god of kynde," or the god of nature, *BD* 511–513.

Petrus Berchorius, *Ovidius moralizatus XV*, ed. J. Engels, 40; Isidore, *Etymologiae*, ed. W.M. Lindsay, I; Ovid, *Met*, ed. and trans. F.J. Miller, I: 50–53.

PANDAR, PANDARE, PANDARES, PANDARUS is Criseyde's uncle and Troilus's best friend in *Troilus and Criseyde*. Troilus appeals to him to act as a go-between, and he promises to help Troilus win Criseyde's love. Because of the part he plays in the poem, Pandarus foresees the development of his name as "male bawd" when he says: "I am becomen/Betwixen game and ernest, swich a meene/As maken women unto men to comen," *Tr* III.252–255. His name and his function appear in Boccaccio's *Il Filostrato*, Chaucer's source for the poem. **[Creseyde: Troilus]**

Pandar, the English contraction, occurs twenty-nine times in medial positions only, *Tr* I.582, 736, 868, 876, 1030, 1037, 1045, 1070; *Tr* II.490, 1093, 1226, 1252, 1492, 1561, 1676; *Tr* III.115, 512, 548; *Tr* III.1094; *Tr* IV.353, 368, 376, 452, 641, 822, 1085; *Tr* V.281, 1111, 1709. *Pandare* appears eleven times initially with elided final -*e*, *Tr* II.67; *Tr* III.1555, 1656; *Tr* IV.582, 638; *Tr* V.323, 484, 1128, 1160, 1170, 1275; *Pandare*, trisyllabic, appears four times initially with final syllabic *-e*, *Tr* II.1275, 1415; *Tr* IV.344, 806. *Pandare* appears fifteen times medially with elided final *-e*, *Tr* I.829, 939, 1009, 1015; *Tr* II.974, 1051, 1260, 1285, 1344, 1352, 1479, 1547; *Tr* III.68; *Tr* IV.366, 828; twice medially with final silent *-e*, *Tr* II.1207; *Tr* III.629; *Pandare*, trisyllabic, appears three times medially with final syllabic *-e*, *Tr* I.658; *Tr* IV.872; *Tr* V.521. *Pandare*, with final syllabic *-e*, appears fourteen times in final rhyming position and rhymes mostly with *care* and *fare*, *Tr* I.548, 588, 610, 624; *Tr* II.1679; *Tr* III.603, 1105, 1644; *Tr* IV.461, 578; *Tr* V.280, 505, 1120, 1147. *Pandares*, the ME genitive case, occurs three times in medial positions, *Tr* I.725; *Tr* II.1341, 1529. *Pandarus*, the Latin form, never occurs initially; it appears ninety-two times in medial positions, mostly the second word and the first stressed syllable in the line: *Tr* I.727, 761, 778, 841, 1023, 1051, 1058; *Tr* II.57, 58, 106, 208, 220, 254, 505, 937, 939, 953, 989, 1109, 1142, 1180, 1193, 1296, 1308, 1313, 1318, 1329, 1355, 1399, 1406, 1431, 1531, 1588, 1600, 1612, 1625, 1640, 1681, 1688, 1710, 1723, 1727; *Tr* III.59, 148, 183, 208, 227, 235, 346, 358, 484, 654, 680, 694, 708, 736, 747, 762, 841, 932, 960, 974, 1077, 1135, 1188, 1571, 1582, 1592, 1616, 1664, 1678, 1738; *Tr* IV.379, 445, 498, 521, 849, 913, 946, 1086; *Tr* V.295, 498, 554, 557, 1121, 1157, 1244, 1245, 1253, 1268, 1668, 1723. It occurs twenty times in final rhyming position: *Tr* I.618, 771, 822; *Tr* II.93, 120, 155, 169, 190, 429, 1046, 1185, 1459, 1625; *Tr* III.1585, 1662; *Tr* IV.463; *Tr* V.430, 477, 682, 1291. In Boccaccio's *Il Filostrato* the name is *Pandaro*.

Boccaccio, *Tutte le opere*, ed. V. Branca, II: 17–228; R.G. Cook, "Chaucer's Pandarus and the Medieval Ideal of Friendship." *JEGP* 69 (1970): 407–424; S.K. Slocum, "How Old is Chaucer's Pandarus?" *PQ* 58 (1979): 16–25.

PANDION, PANDYON. Pandion, legendary king of Athens, was father of Procne and Philomela. Procne married Tereus, king of Thrace; but Tereus was seized with violent lust for Philomela. He went to Athens to fetch her for a visit with her sister and found Pandion unwilling to part with his daughter. Tereus persuaded him, and Pandion let her go with heavy foreboding. As she left, he wept (*Met* VI.438–510; *OM* VI.2217–3684).

In Chaucer's version, Pandion has no forebodings. He weeps because he would not let her go, but Philomena persuades him to give his permission, *LGW* 2279–2286. Pandion feasts Tereus well and gives him great gifts as he departs, *LGW* 2299–2308. It appears that Chaucer follows Chrétien's version, *La Muance de la Hupé et l'aronde et de rossignol*, inserted in *Ovide Moralisé* VI. [**Philomene: Proigne: Tereus**]

Pandion occurs once in medial position, *LGW* 2279; *Pandyon*, a spelling variant, appears once medially, *LGW* 2295. *Pandiones*, the ME genitive case, appears once, medially, *LGW* 2247.

J.L. Lowes, "Chaucer and the *Ovide Moralisé*." *PMLA* 33 (1918): 302–325; Ovid, *Met*, ed. and trans. F.J. Miller, I: 318–323; Chrétien de Troyes, *La Muance de la hupé et l'aronde et de rossignol* in *OM*, ed. C. de Boer, II, deel 21: 336–366.

PAPINIANUS: [PAPYNIAN]

PAPYNIAN. Aemilius Papinianus, fl. third century A.D., became *praefectus praetorio*, prefect of magistrates, in A.D. 203. He was one of the most brilliant jurists of his day. Caracalla ordered his execution in 212 because Papinianus, one of Geta's supporters, expressed disapproval when the emperor ordered his brother's murder (Spartianus, *Antoninus Caracalla* IV.i).

Lady Philosophy says that among great men executed by powerful rulers stands Papynian, *Bo* III, *Prosa* 5.49–52.

Papynian, the English contraction of Latin *Papinianus*, is the French variant in Jean de Meun's *Li Livres de confort de philosophie*.

V.L. Dedeck-Héry, "Boethius' *De consolatione* by Jean de Meun." *MS* 14 (1952): 213; *Scriptores historiae Augustae*, ed. and trans. D. Magie, II: 11.

PARCAE: [PARCAS]

PARCAS. *Parcae* is the Latin name for the Three Fates, daughters of Night: Clotho, Lachesis, and Atropos were their Greek names; Nona, Decuma, and Morta their Latin names. Clotho held the distaff with the thread of life; Lachesis allotted the span of life; and Atropos cut the thread short at death (Hesiod, *Theogony,* 217–222; Isidore, *Etym* VIII.11.93.)

The narrator invokes the "angry Parcas, sustren thre" to help him tell the fatal destiny of Troilus, *Tr* V.3–7. The Fates are called the "fatal sustren," *Tr* III.733 and *LGW* 2630.

Parcas, Latin accusative plural of *Parcae*, appears medially, *Tr* V.3.

Hesiod, *The Homeric Hymns and Homerica*, ed. and trans. H.G. Evelyn-White, 94–95; Isidore, *Etymologiae*, ed. W.M. Lindsay, I.

PARIS, PARYS, also called Alexandros, was one of the younger sons of Priam and Hecuba of Troy. Exposed on the hills of Phrygia because of a prophecy that he would bring about Troy's destruction, he was found and brought up by shepherds. He married the nymph Oënone but deserted her when Venus offered him the most beautiful woman in the world. The three goddesses Juno, Minerva, and Venus approached him one day with a golden apple and asked him to choose which one was fairest. Juno offered him greatness, Athena success as a warrior, and Venus the most beautiful woman in the world, who happened to be Helen, wife of Menelaus, king of Sparta. With Venus's help Paris abducted Helen, and thus began the Trojan War, which lasted ten years and ended with Troy's destruction (*Heroides* V; *Iliad*; *RR* 13215–13222).

Januarie will clutch May in his arms harder than Paris did Eleyne, *MerchT* 1753–1754. Paris is a false lover, *SqT* 543–557; *HF* I.399, because he deserted Oënone. The story of Paris and Eleyne appears on the walls of the dreamer's room, *BD* 326–331, as it appears in the *Roman de la Rose*. Chaucer refers only slightly to the Judgment of Paris, *HF* I.199–201: Juno hates all the Trojan people, presumably because Paris bypassed her and gave the golden apple to Venus. Paris appears in the *blazon de faulse amours*, the list of false lovers, *HF* I.399. Paris and Eleyne are among love's martyrs in Venus's temple, *PF* 288–294. The Greeks intend to avenge Paris's rape of Helen, *Tr* I.57–63. Pandarus recalls Oënone's letter to Paris, *Tr* I.652–665. Deiphebus acknowledges that Eleyne can lead Paris wherever she wills, *Tr* II.1445–1449. Pandarus reminds Troilus that if Criseyde goes to the Greek camp and does not return, he can surely get another love, just as his brother Paris has done, *Tr* IV.596–609, referring to Paris's changing his loves, Oënone for Helen. [**Eleyna: Juno: Minerva: Oënone: Venus**]

Paris occurs seven times in medial positions, *BD* 331; *HF* I.399; *PF* 290; *Tr* I.63, 653; *Tr* II.1449; *Tr* IV.608. *Parys*, a spelling variant, occurs twice in medial positions, *MerchT* 1754; *SqT* 548.

Homer, *Iliad*, ed. and trans. A.T. Murray; Ovid, *Her*, ed. and trans. G. Showerman, 56–69; *RR*, ed. E. Langlois, IV.11; *RR*, trans. C. Dahlberg, 228.

PARMANYDES. Parmenides of Elea, said to be 65 years old in 450 B.C., founded the Eleatic School of Philosophy and was the first to declare that the earth was round (Diogenes Laertius IX.3). His most famous pupil was Zeno of Elea.

Lady Philosophy quotes Parmanydes that the divine substance turns the world and the movable circle of things, while the divine substance keeps itself without moving, *Bo* III, *Prosa* 12.189–199. Boethius quotes Parmenides in Greek, then explains in Latin: "*rerum orbem mobilem rotat, dum se immobilem ipsa conservat,*" "it turns the moving circle of the universe while it keeps itself unmoved." [**Eleatics: Plato: Zeno**]

Parmanydes is the ME variant of Greek *Parmenides*, which also appears in Latin.

Diogenes Laertius, *Lives of the Eminent Philosophers,* ed. and trans. R.D. Hicks, II: 428–433; *OCD*, 782.

PARMENIDES: [PARMANYDES]
PARTHENOPAEUS: [PARTHONOPE]

PARTHONOPE. Parthenopaeus was the son of Atalanta of Tegea and Meleager, the hunters of the Calydonian boar. He was still very young when he joined Adrastus in the war against Thebes. He died of wounds received in the battle (*Thebaid* IX.852–907; *Roman de Thèbes* 9165–9396).

Parthonope's death appears in summaries of the Theban war, *Anel* 58; *Tr* V.1503. [**Adrastus: Amphiorax: Atthalante: Campaneus: Ethiocles: Hemonydes: Meleagre: Polymyte: Tydeus**]

The name occurs medially, *Anel* 58; *Tr* V.1503.

Roman de Thèbes, ed. L. Constans, I: 451–463; *Roman de Thèbes (The Story of Thebes)*, trans. J.S. Coley, 213–220; Statius, *Thebaid*, ed. and trans. J.H. Mozley, II: 315–319.

PASIPHAE: [PHASIPHA]

PAUL, PAULUS, POUL (saint). Paul the Apostle c. A.D. 3–c.65, was born in Tarsus in Cilicia. He was a Jew of Roman citizenship with a classical Greek education. As a great persecutor of Christians, he presided over the stoning of Stephen, the first martyr, but he was converted when he saw a vision on the road to Damascus (Acts of the Apostles 8–9, 13; Letter to the Galatians 1:15–16). His letters to the early churches form much of Christian doctrine. He was arrested in Caesarea in 59 and deported to Rome, where he spent the next five years in prison. He was executed c. 65. His surviving letters were collected and published toward the end of the first century, some thirty years after his death. The collection consisted of two letters to the Corinthians, two to the Thessalonians, one each to Philemon, the Romans, the Colossians, the Philippians, and the Galatians.

Dame Alys quotes from Paul's First Letter to the Corinthians on virginity, marriage, and husbands, *WBP* 73–76; from I Corinthians 7:7–25 in *WBP* 77–9, 100–104, 129–138, 146–160. Paul's words on the marital debt are discussed in *ParsT* 940. The Friar says that he could describe hell, using the text of Christ, Paul, and John, *FrT* 1645–1652. Friar John says that he studies the works of Peter and Paul, *SumT* 1816–1819. The Pardoner quotes Paul on gluttony, I Corinthians 7:13, *PardT* 517–523. Dame Prudence says that the sorrowful man must weep, as Paul wrote to the Romans, *Mel* 989; she quotes Paul on rendering evil for good, *Mel* 1292, both from Romans 12:15–17. Men fear to do evil when the judge is severe, Romans 13:4, *Mel* 1440. The Nun's Priest advises his listeners to take the moral, Romans 16:4, *NPT* 3438–3443. The Parson refuses to tell fables since Paul warns against them, I Timothy 1:4, *ParsT* 30–34. Fear of the day of doom ought to move men to contrition, Romans 14:10, *ParsT* 162–163. The Parson discourses on the beginning of sins, Romans 5:12, *ParsT* 322; on the war of the flesh against the spirit, Galatians 5:17, *ParsT* 342; on the penance that St. Paul did by water and by land, II Corinthians 9:25–27, and Romans 7:24, *ParsT* 342–344. The Parson speaks on the supremacy of the name of Jesus and quotes Philippians 2:10, *ParsT* 598; St. Paul says that those who curse *(maledici)* forfeit the kingdom of God, I Corinthians 6:10, *ParsT* 619. The Parson condemns chiding because St. Paul says that the servant of God must not chide, II Timothy 11:24, *ParsT* 629–630. In the same section on chiding, the Parson quotes Paul that wives must submit to husbands, Colossians 3:18, *ParsT* 634. St. Paul forbids indecent behavior and ribaldry, Ephesians 5:14, *ParsT* 651; he says that worldly remorse leads to death, II Corinthians 7:10, *ParsT* 725, that covetousness is the root of all harms, and Chaucer's gloss cites I Timothy 6:10, *ParsT* 739. Paul says that the avaricious man is in the thraldom of idolatry, Ephesians 5:5, *ParsT* 748. The Parson quotes Paul on gluttony, Philippians 3:18–19, *ParsT* 819–820; on lechery, Galatians 5:19–21, *ParsT* 867. St. Paul says that Christ shall destroy the adulterer, I Corinthians 3:17, *ParsT* 879; that Satan transformed himself into an angel of light, II Corinthians 9:14, *ParsT* 895; that a man should love his wife as Christ loved the Church, Ephesians 5:25, *ParsT* 929; that Jesus Christ is more pleased with the clothing of mercy, cheerfulness, and patience than with hair shirts, Colossians 3:12, *ParsT* 1054.

St. Paul is called simply "the Apostle" in several places. Alys of Bath refers to him thus, *WBP* 47, 94, 160, 340–345. The Pardoner also quotes the Apostle, *PardT* 529–534. Dame Prudence quotes the Apostle on avarice, I Timothy 7:10, *Mel* 1130, 1840; on the judgments of the Lord God Almighty, *Mel* 1405; that the joy of God is everlasting, II Corinthians 4:17, *Mel* 1510; on the joy of a good conscience, II Corinthians 1:12, *Mel* 1634.

Paul is the most common spelling of the Apostle's name in the prose works, *The Tale of Melibee* and the *Parson's Tale*. It appears twice, in *Mel* 989, 1292, 1440; and seventeen times in *ParsT* 322, 342, 343, 598, 619, 630, 634, 651, 725, 939, 748, 819, 867, 879, 895, 929, 1054. *Paul* occurs twice medially, *PardT* 521; *NPT* 3441. *Paulus* occurs once in the penultimate position, *PardT* 523. *Poul*, possibly a scribal variant, appears initially, *WBP* 73, and in the penultimate position, *FrT* 1647.

F.W. Beare, *St. Paul and His Letters*; E.T. Donaldson, *Speaking of Chaucer,* 168–173.

PAULINUS: [PAULYN]

PAULUS. Lucius Aemilius Paullus, fl. second century B.C., was given the *agnomen* or title of conquest *Macedonicus* after he defeated the last king of Macedonia, Perseus III, in 168 B.C. at Pydna. His son Cornelius, who is known as Scipio Africanus Minor, was present at that battle (Livy, *Ab urbe condita liber* XLIV.1–3).

Lady Philosophy, speaking in Fortune's voice about mutability, tells Boethius how Paulus wept after he had captured Perseus III, *Bo* 2, *Prosa* 2.63–66. **[Boece]**

Paulus is the family name of the Aemilia clan.

Livy, *Livy: Ab urbe condita libri,* ed. and trans. A.C. Schlesinger, III: 234–235.

PAULYN. Decius Paulinus, fl. fifth century A.D., was consul in 498. Cassiodorus writes to Coelianus and Agapitus that Theodoric has ordered the speedy prosecution of Paulinus *(Epistola* I.xxiii).

Boethius says that he snatched "the richesses" of Paulinus "out of the jowes of hem that gapeden," *Bo* I, *Prosa* 4. 92–97. **[Boece]**

Paulyn is both ME and OF.

Flavius Cassiodorus, *Epistolae Theodoricianae variae,* ed. Th. Mommsen, 27; V.L. Dedeck-Héry, "Boethius' *De consolatione* by Jean de Meun." *MS* 14 (1952): 178.

PEDRO: [PETRO]
PELIAS: [PELLEUS]

PELLEUS. Pelias, Jason's uncle, usurped the throne of Iolchos in Thessaly from old Aeson, his half-brother. He sent Jason in search of the Golden Fleece of the Ram of Phrixus, hoping to rid himself of the heir and thus rule the kingdom (*HDT*). Jason, aided by Medea, successfully brought back the Fleece to Iolchos. Medea then restored his old father Aeson to youth. Impressed by this feat, Pelias's daughters requested the same restoration for their father. But Medea omitted part of the charm and substituted different herbs in the cauldron, from which experiment Pelias died (*Met* VII.179–349).

Chaucer begins the Legend of Hypsipyle with the story of Pelias's usurpation of the Iolchian throne, *LGW* 1396–1450. He cites Guido, *HDT* 1–111; *LGW* 1390, and *Argonauticon* by Valerius Flaccus, *LGW* 1457, as his sources for Jason's story.

Pelleus, the ME variant, occurs three times medially, *LGW* 1400, 1409, 1439, and once in final rhyming position, *LGW* 1397.

Guido delle Colonne, *Guido de Columnis: HDT*, ed. N.E. Griffin, 3–33; *ibid.*, *HDT*, trans. M.E. Meek, 1–32; Valerius Flaccus, *Argonauticon*, ed. and trans. J.H. Mozley.

PENALOPEE, PENELOPE, PENELOPEE, wife of Odysseus, remained steadfastly faithful to him for the ten years he was at Troy. This fidelity became one of the commonplaces of classical and medieval literature. Jerome names her in this connection, *Epistola adversus Jovinianum (Letter Against Jovinian)*, I.45 (*PL* 23: 275), and Gower mentions her as one of four loyal wives, *Confessio Amantis* VIII.2621–2631. The others are Lucrece, Alceste, Alcyone.

Penelope is exemplary of wifely fidelity, *MLI* 75; *FranklT* 1443; *BD* 1081; *Anel* 82; *Tr* V.1772–1778; *LGW F* 252–253, *LGW G* 206–207. **[Dorigen: Ulixes]**

Penalopee, with a long final vowel, occurs once initially, *LGW F* 252; and once in final rhyming position, *FranklT* 1443. *Penelope* occurs once initially, *LGW G* 206; and once medially, *Anel* 82. *Penelopee*, with a long final vowel, occurs twice medially, *MLI* 75; *BD* 1081. *Penelopeës*, the ME genitive case with five syllables, occurs once, *Tr* V.1778.

John Gower, *The Complete Works*, ed. G.C. Macaulay, III: 457; K. Hume, "The Pagan Setting of *The Franklin's Tale* and the Sources of Dorigen's Cosmology." *SN* 44 (1972): 289–294.

PENEUS: [PENNEUS]

PENNEUS. Peneus, the river god, had a daughter, Daphne, whom Apollo loved. As she fled from Apollo, Daphne appealed to her father, and Peneus changed her into a laurel tree (*Met* I.452–576; *OM* I.2737–3064).

This story is painted on the walls of Diane's oratory, *KnT* 2060–2064. **[Dane]**

Penneus, the ME variant, occurs medially, *KnT* 2064.

Ovid, *Met*, ed. and trans. F.J. Miller, I: 34–43; *OM*, ed. C. de Boer, I, deel 15: 120–126.

PERCEVAL: [PERCYVELL]

PERCYVELL. Sir Perceval is the hero of the Grail legend. In Chrétien de Troyes's *Le Conte de Graal,* several versions of the legend come together. Perceval was reared in the Waste Forest by his mother after his father's death. He did not know his name because he was always called *biaus filz,* "fine son," or *biaus sire,* "fine sir." After meeting several of Arthur's knights, he decided to seek out the king, and his mother gave her reluctant consent. She told him that his father was the most renowned warrior of the islands in the sea and that he died of grief when his two older sons were slain. After many adventures, Perceval came to the Grail Castle, where the Fisher King lay suffering from an unhealed wound. Perceval failed to ask the question, "Whom does one serve with the Grail?" and the Fisher King remained unhealed of his wound. Because of his utter naiveté, he was given the name Perceval—"pure fool." The most famous version of the romance is the twelfth-century *Parzival* by Wolfram von Eschenbach, inspired by Chrétien's poem. The Middle English romance *Sir Perceval of Galles* was written, c.1350–1400, in the North of England, in the sixteen-line tail-rhyme stanza form, each stanza linked to its preceding and following stanzas. The unique copy is that of the fifteenth-century Thornton manuscript.

Sir Thopas drinks water from the well as did Sir Perceval, *Thop* 915–916. In *Sir Perceval of Galles,* this incident appears twice: at the beginning where the poet describes Perceval's ancestry and upbringing and near the end when Perceval drinks water from the well while searching for his mother. [Thopas]

Percyvell, the northern ME variant, appears in final rhyming position, *Thop* 916.

Chrétien de Troyes, *Perceval; or, The Story of the Grail,* trans. R.H. Cline; *ibid., Le Roman de Perceval, ou Le Conte du Graal,* ed. H. de Briel; R.H. Griffith, *Sir Perceval of Galles: A Study of the Sources of the Legend The Romance of Perceval in Prose,* trans. Dell Skuls; *Sir Perceval of Galles,* ed. J. Campion and F. Holthausen, 70–71; J.E. Wells, *A Manual of Writings in Middle English, 1050–1500,* ed. A. Hartung, 72.

PERKIN: [PERKYN REVELOUR]

PERKYN REVELOUR is the main character in the Cook's unfinished tale. His name indicates his main activities: dancing and wenching, *CoT* 4365–4422. [Roger[2]]

Perkyn is the diminutive of Peter; *Revelour,* a kind of surname, means "reveler." *Perkyn* appears twice in medial positions, *CoT* 4371, 4387.

PEROTHEUS. Pirithous, king of the Lapiths, was Theseus's close friend since childhood. Ovid calls them *felix concordia,* "a happy concord" (*Met*

VIII.304). Pirithous invited the centaurs to his wedding with Hippodamia, but the centaurs attempted to carry off the bride, and a great battle broke out between the Lapiths and their guests (*Met* XII.210–535). Pirithous and Theseus themselves attempted to carry off Persephone, queen of the Underworld, but Pluto intercepted them and chained them until Hercules rescued them. Virgil says that Theseus remained in the Underworld forever, while Pirithous was allowed to leave (*Aeneid* VI.617–618). Gower tells the story of the battle between the Lapiths and the centaurs to illustrate the evils of drunken lust, *Confessio Amantis* VI.485–536.

Perotheus visits Theseus, his *felawe* since childhood, *KnT* 1189–1195. When one of them died, the other sought him in hell, *KnT* 1196–1201. This version of the story appears in *RR* 8148–8154. Theseus frees Arcita because Perotheus entreats him, *KnT* 1202–1208. [**Arcita: Theseus**]

Perotheus, a variant of Latin *Pirithous* and Italian *Perithoo* from *Tes* VIII, occurs twice in medial positions, *KnT* 1202, 1205, and twice in final rhyming position, *KnT* 1191, 1227.

Boccaccio, *Tutte le opere*, ed. V. Branca, II: 500–539; John Gower, *The Complete Works*, ed. G.C. Macaulay, III: 180–181; Ovid, *Met*, ed. and trans. F.J. Miller, I: 426–427, II: 194–219; *RR*, ed. E. Langlois, III: 70–71; *RR*, trans. C. Dahlberg, 151; Virgil, *Aeneid*, ed. and trans. H.R. Fairclough, I: 548–549.

PERTELOTE is Chauntecleer's favorite hen and his severest critic in *The Nun's Priest's Tale*. She misinterprets his dream of the fox and advises Chauntecleer to take a laxative when he needs to be shrewd and alert to the fox's flattery. In Pierre de Saint Cloud's *Roman de Renart*, the name of the Cock's wife is Pinte. R.A. Pratt suggests that, in his creation of Pertelote's character, Chaucer may have been influenced by the *clerc de Troyes's* creation in *Le Roman de Renart le Contrefait*. [**Chauntecleer: Renard**]

Pertelote, formed by the reduplication of sounds, never occurs initially. It appears eight times in medial positions, *NPT* 2888, 3105, 3122, 3158, 3177, 3200, 3268, 3362; and once in final rhyming position, *NPT* 2870.

R.A. Pratt, "Three Old French Sources of the Nonnes Preestes Tale." *Speculum* 47 (1972): 422–444, 646–668.

PETER ALPHONSO: [PIERS ALFONCE]

[**PETER**[1] **RIGA**], c. 1140–1209, was born at Rheims. His poem, *Aurora*, a versification of certain books of the Bible, was written between 1170 and 1200. It was one of the most widely read and most accessible of medieval writings.

The Man in Black says that, although he wrote many songs, he could not make songs as well as Tubal, Lamech's son, who invented the first songs; he adds that the Greeks say Pythagoras invented the art, *Aurora* says so, *BD* 1157–1170, a reference to *Liber Genesis* 477–484. [**Absolon**[1]**: Pictagoras: Tubal**]

Chaucer does not mention Peter Riga's name but the name of his work, *Aurora.*

Peter Riga, *Aurora*, ed. P.E. Beichner.

PETER², PETRE (saint). Peter the Apostle (died c. A.D. 64) was the son of Jonas. A fisherman with his brother Andrew when Jesus called them, Peter subsequently became chief of the disciples (Matthew 4:18–22; Mark 1:16–20). Tradition says he was the first bishop of Rome. He was executed there about A.D. 64. Two letters in the New Testament are attributed to him.

The Pardoner boasts that he has a piece of the sail from Peter's boat, *Gen Prol* 696–698. St. Peter's sister is invoked in the carpenter's night spell, *MillT* 3483–3486. Friar John tells Thomas's wife that he is diligent in preaching and in studying the works of St. Peter and St. Paul, *SumT* 1816–1819. Dame Prudence quotes St. Peter that Christ is an example of patience, I Peter 2:21–23, *Mel* 1501–1503. The pilgrims swear by St. Peter, *WBP* 446; *FrT* 1332; *CYT* 665, and so does the merchant's wife in *ShipT* 1404. The Parson gives the second cause why men should disdain sin from II Peter 2:19, *ParsT* 141. To explain the meaning of Jesus's name, the Parson quotes from Acts 4:12, *ParsT* 287 and 597. The Parson tells how Simon Magus tried to buy the gift of the Holy Spirit from Peter, Acts 8:17–24, *ParsT* 781–783. Women should be subject to their husbands as Peter says, I Peter 3:1, *ParsT* 930. On how to make a good confession, the Parson quotes I Peter 5:6, *ParsT* 988. St. Peter himself wept bitterly after he denied Jesus, *ParsT* 994. The frightened dreamer swears by St. Peter, *HF* II.1034–1042, and so does the learned eagle, *HF* III.2000.

Peter occurs four times initially, as an oath, *WBP* 446; *FrT* 1332; *CYT* 665; *HF* II.103; twice in medial positions, *Gen Prol* 697; *ShipT* 1404. In the Parson's prose tale, the name appears seven times, *ParsT* 141, 287, 597, 781, 930, 988, 994. *Petre* occurs once as an oath, HF III.2000. *Petres*, the ME genitive case, occurs twice medially, *MillT* 3486, *SumT* 1819.

Jacobus de Voragine, GL, trans. G. Ryan and H. Ripperger, 330–331; ibid., LA, ed. Th. Graesse, 368–379; C.H. Turner, "St. Peter in the New Testament." Theology 13 (1926): 66–78.

PETRARCH: [FRAUNCEYS PETRAK]

PETRO¹. Pedro IV, King of Castile and Leon from 1350 to 1369, was known as Pedro the Cruel. His illegitimate brother, known as Henry the Bastard, instigated an insurrection against him, and Pedro sought aid from Edward, Prince of Wales, who was in Bordeaux at the time. Froissart says that the prince's advisers cautioned against aiding Pedro and gave as reasons the Pope's excommunication, his reputation for great pride, cruelty, and wickedness. It was generally rumored that Pedro murdered his young wife, the duke of Bourbon's daughter. The Prince of Wales, however, decided to help Pedro regain his throne. In 1365 Henry the Bastard appealed to the French king for help, and Charles sent him Bertrand du Guesclin, who helped establish the Bastard on the throne. In 1367 the Prince of Wales defeated Henry and Bertrand at Navarretta near Roncevalles. In 1369 Pedro again faced Henry and du Guesclin; this time he was defeated and captured, and his brother later killed Pedro with his own hand. Bertrand du Guesclin was made Constable of Spain; Charles made him Constable of France and Lord of Boucicault (Froissart I, 232–245).

The Monk tells Pedro's story in two stanzas, *MkT* 2375–2390. Chaucer may have learned of the manner of Pedro's death from several sources. In 1371, John of Gaunt married Constance of Castile, Pedro's daughter, and styled himself "King of Castile." Chaucer's wife Philippa was assigned to her household, and he may have learned the story from her. H.L. Savage suggests Fernando de Castro, a Spaniard at the English court, as a source. Haldeen Braddy thinks that Sir Guichard d'Angle, who had served with the Black Prince in the Castilian civil war, is a more likely source than de Castro. The fact that Philippa Chaucer served John of Gaunt's wife may account for Chaucer's laudatory stanzas on Don Pedro. A. Brusendorff suggests that a *ballade* on du Guesclin, attributed to Eustache Deschamps, may have given Chaucer further information; he points out certain verbal resemblances between Chaucer's story and the *ballade*. [**Charles Olyver: Genylon-Olyver**]

Petro occurs medially, *MkT* 2375.

H. Braddy, "The Two Petros in *The Monk's Tale*." *PMLA* 50 (1935): 69–80; A. Brusendorff, *The Chaucer Tradition*, 489; J. Froissart, *Chronicles*, ed. and trans. J. Jolliffe, 188–208; D.K. Fry, "The Ending of *The Monk's Tale*." *JEGP* 71 (1972): 355–368; P.E. Russell, *The English Intervention in Spain and Portugal in the Time of Edward III and Richard II*; H.L. Savage, "Chaucer and the 'Pitous deeth' of Petro, 'Glorie of Spayne.'" *Speculum* 24 (1949): 357–375; B.F. Taggie, "John of Gaunt, Geoffrey Chaucer, and 'O Noble, O Worthy Petro of Spayne.'" *FCS* 10 (1984): 195–228.

PETRO². Pedro, king of Cyprus (fl. fourteenth century), was known as Pierre de Lusignan. Like Don Pedro of Castile, he had a reputation for cruelty, and it was said that his cruelty to Marie de Giblet led to his assassination in 1369. Haldeen Braddy suggests that, although Chaucer may have heard the story from his acquaintances, Machaut's poem, *La Prise d'Alexandrie* (1369), may have provided additional information, since Machaut presents Pierre de Lusignan in a favorable light. Pierre made a great impression on Machaut when he visited Paris for Charles V's coronation. He also visited London and Paris in 1363 and 1364 to solicit aid for his crusade to the Holy Land. He conquered Alexandria in 1365 (Froissart I: 217–223).

The Monk tells a brief story of Petro, *MkT* 2391–2398.
The name appears medially, *MkT* 2391.

H. Braddy, "The Two Petros in *The Monk's Tale.*" *PMLA* 50 (1935): 78–80; J. Froissart, *Chronicles*, ed. and trans. J. Jolliffe, 183–185; D.K. Fry, "The Ending of *The Monk's Tale.*" *JEGP* 71 (1972): 355–368; Guillaume de Machaut, *La Prise d'Alexandrie*, ed. M.L. de Mas Latrie.

PETRUS ALPHONSUS: [PIERS² ALFONCE]
PHAEDRA: [PHEDRA]
PHAETON: [PHETON]
PHANIE: [PHANYE]

PHANYE. Phanie was the daughter of Croesus, King of Lydia. She interpreted his dreams about his death (*RR* 6489–6593).

Phanye interprets her father's dream of Jupiter and Phebus: Croesus would be hanged, the rain would wet his body and the sun dry it, *MkT* 2751–2758. **[Cresus]**

Phanye is derived from Greek *pheinein,* "to show," an appropriate name for a dream interpreter. It occurs once, in final rhyming position, *MkT* 2758.

RR, ed. E. Langlois, III; 7–11; *RR*, trans. C. Dahlberg, 126–127.

PHARAO, PHAROO. Pharaoh is the hereditary title of the ancient Egyptian kings. The pharaoh who appears in Chaucer's work is Amenhotep IV, also known as Akhenaten, the heretic pharaoh who ruled during the eighteenth dynasty, 1375–1358 B.C. He is believed to be the pharaoh whose dreams Joseph interpreted (Genesis 40, 41).

Joseph interpreted Pharao's dreams, which foretold coming events, *NPT* 3132–3135. God blesses those who repent as he blessed Pharao because of Joseph, *ParsT* 441–442. Not even Joseph, who interpreted Pharao's dream, can interpret the poet's dream, *BD* 277–283. The dream of the eagle is more wonderful than Pharoo's dream, *HF* II.515–516. **[Joseph]**

Pharao reflects Dante's spelling in *De monarchia* II.iv.2. It occurs in final rhyming position, *NPT* 3133, *BD* 282, and in the prose of *ParsT* 443. *Pharoo*, with a long final vowel, occurs initially, *HF* II.516.

Dante, *De monarchia*, ed. P.G. Ricci, 182.

PHARAOH: [PHARAO]

PHASIPHA. Pasiphae, daughter of the Sun, was King Minos's wife and queen of Crete. Because her husband refused to sacrifice a beautiful white bull he had promised Poseidon, the god caused Pasiphae to fall in love with the animal. Daedalus made a wooden cow into which the queen entered when she wanted to enjoy her passion. The Minotaur, half man, half bull, was the result (*Met* VIII.130–137, IX.736–740; *OM* VIII.617–956).

Phasipha is an evil wife in Jankyn's book of wikked wives, *WBP* 733–736. **[Clitermystra: Eriphilem: Jankyn²: Minos: Mynotaur]**
Phasipha, the medieval spelling variant, occurs in a medial position, *WBP* 733; *ph* is the medieval rendering of aspirated /p/.

Ovid, *Met*, ed. and trans. F.J. Miller, I: 414–415; II: 56–57; *OM*, ed. C. de Boer, III, deel 30: 123–132; R.A. Pratt, "Jankyn's Book of Wikked Wyves: Medieval Antimatrimonial Propaganda in the Universities." *AnM* 3 (1962): 5–27; B.L. Witlieb, "Chaucer and the *Ovide Moralisé.*" *N&Q* 215 (1970): 206.

PHEBUS. Phoebus, another name for Apollo, is an epithet from his maternal grandmother, Phoibe, "the bright one." Isidore says that Phoebus is Apollo as a youth and that the sun is painted as a youth because it rises daily and is born with new light. As early as the fifth century B.C., Apollo was equated with Helios, the Sun god, and this assimilation prevailed into Hellenistic, Roman, and medieval times. Isidore combines the three aspects of the god, seer, and physician (Etym VIII.xi.53–54).

Aurelius prays to Phebus, *FranklT* 1036–1061. *The Manciple's Tale* is the story of Phebus and the Crow (*Met* II.531–632). Phebus, also called Apollo Delphicus, tells Calcas that Troy will be destroyed, *Tr* I.64–70. Troilus reminds Phebus of his love for Daphne and asks the god's help in his love, *Tr* III.726–728. Calcas recalls that Phebus and Neptune built the walls of Troy and that Lameadoun defrauded them of their wages, *Tr* IV.120–126. Eneas mistakes Venus for Phebus's sister, Diana, *LGW* 986.

When Phebus rises, Arcita prepares to celebrate May, *KnT* 1491–1500. Phebus is 45 degrees in the sky when the shadow of the tree is the same length as the tree, and Bailly proclaims that it is ten o'clock, *MLI* 7–15. Phebus is in Gemini, not far from Cancer, his declination, that is, his maximum northern latitude, obtained when he enters Cancer at the summer solstice, *MerchT* 2220–2224. Phebus is near his exaltation in Aries, also called the night house of Mars, *SqT* 48–51, on Cambyuskan's birthday. Phebus has left the meridian angle, and gentle Leo with his Aldiran, one of the stars in his forepaws, is ascending, *SqT* 263–267, when Cambyuskan rises from his birthday feast. It is then very much past noon. Phebus grows old and takes on a dull hue, for he is now in Capricorn in the south when the magician arrives from Orleans to make the rocks disappear from the coast, *FranklT* 1245–1248. Phebus dyed Virginia's hair like the streams of his burned heat, *PhysT* 37–38; she is therefore a blond. Cresus dreams that Phebus brings him a fair towel to dry him, *MkT* 2745–2746; this means that the sun will dry the body of the hanged Cresus, *MkT* 2753–2756. Phebus is called Apollo Delphicus, *Tr* I.70.

In his translation of *De consolatione philosophiae*, Chaucer follows Boethius in using *Phebus* as a synonym for the sun.

Phebus spreads his bright beams in the white bull on the third of May, *Tr* II.50–63; the sun is in Taurus on this day, a bad-luck day in the medieval calendar. Criseyde swears that Phebus will fall from his sphere before she forgets Troilus, *Tr* III.1495. Troilus knows that dawn has come because Pirois and three swift steeds pull the sun's chariot across the sky, *Tr* III.1702–1708. The other horses of Helios's chariot are Eous, Aethon, and Phlegon (*Met* II.153–154). Phebus is in the breast of Hercules's lion when Hector decides to fight the Greeks, *Tr* IV.29–35; the time is either the latter part of July or the early part of August. Criseyde promises to return before Lucina, Phebus's sister, passes out of Aries beyond Leo, *Tr* IV.1590–1593. Phebus has three times melted the snow since Troilus first loved Criseyde, *Tr* V.8–14. Phebus begins to rise with his rosy cart, *Tr* V.278–280. Venus follows Phebus as he sets (the moon leaving Leo), *Tr* V.1016–1017.

Phebus the sun appears in the astrological allegory *The Complaint of Mars*. The bird's song tells how Mars departed from Venus in the morning, when Phebus, with fiery red torches, chases away lovers, *Mars* 22–28. Lying in Venus's room, Mars feels dread when Phebus comes within the palace gates, *Mars* 78–84. In her room painted with white bulls, Venus sees the light and knows that Phebus has come to burn her with his heat, *Mars* 85–88 (Mars and Venus are in her night house Taurus). Mars bids Venus flee lest Phebus see her, *Mars* 104–105, and for fear of Phebus's light, Venus flees to Cilenios's tower, *Mars* 113–114 (Venus is now in 2 degrees of Gemini, the night house of Mercury). Mars blames Phebus for the pain of separation from Venus, *Mars* 134–140. [**Aldiran: Apollo: Aries: Cilenios: Dane: Diane: Latona: Leo: Mars**]

Phebus, the ME and OF variant of Greek and Latin *Phoebus,* occurs six times initially, *MerchT* 2220; SqT 48, 263; *FranklT* 1245; *MancT* 249; *Tr* I.659; forty-three times in medial positions, *KnT* 1493; *MLJ* 11; *FranklT* 1036, 1041, 1055, 1065, 1078; *PhysT* 37; *MkT* 2745, 2753; *MancT* 105, 125, 130, 139, 156, 196, 200, 203, 238, 242, 244, 249, 262; *MarsT* 27, 81, 105, 114, 140; *Tr* I.70; *Tr* II.54, 726; *Tr* III.1495, 1755; *Tr* IV.31, 120, 1591; *Tr* V.8, 278, 1017, 1107; *LGW* 773, 986, 1206. The name never appears in final rhyming position.

J. Hawkes, *Man and the Sun*; Isidore, *Etymologiae*, ed. W.M. Lindsay, I; Ovid, *Met*, ed. and trans. F.J. Miller, I: 70–71, 96–105.

PHEBUSEO is the name of the Trojan hero who fights to save Antenor from capture by the Greeks, *Tr* IV.50–54. He is not mentioned in Boccaccio's *Il Filostrato,* and Chaucer apparently invented the name.

Phebuseo, with stress on the penultimate syllable, is derived from *Phebus,* which it so much resembles, and occurs in final rhyming position, *Tr* IV.54.

PHEDRA. Phaedra was Ariadne's younger sister and the daughter of Minos and Pasiphae of Crete. She became Theseus's second wife and fell in love with his son Hippolytus, bringing destruction to them both (*Heroides* IV).

Theseus abandons Adriane for her sister Phedra, *HF* I.405–420; the story is repeated in *LGW* 2169–2178, where Theseus abandons Adriane because her sister is fairer than she is. This development of the story is not found in Ovid. S.B. Meech suggests Filippo Ceffi's Italian translation of *Heroides* X. Chaucer may have also used Machaut's *Le Jugement dou roy de Navarre*. [**Adriane: Androgeus: Ipolita: Minos: Mynotaur: Phasipha: Theseus**]

Phedra, the OF variant, appears initially, *LGW* 1985, and three times in medial positions, *HF* I.419; *LGW* 1970, 1978.

Guillaume de Machaut, *Oeuvres*, ed. E. Hoepffner, I: 230–232; S.B. Meech, "Chaucer and an Italian translation of the *Heroides*." *PMLA* 45 (1930): 117–118; Ovid, *Her*, ed. and trans. G. Showerman, 44–57; 120–133.

PHETON. Phaeton was the son of Helios, the Sun god, in Greek mythology; in Roman mythology his father was Phoebus. The Sun god promised Phaeton that he would grant whatever he asked, and he requested to be allowed to drive the Sun's chariot for one day. Phoebus granted the request. Phaeton found, however, that he could not control the horses; as they left their course, the chariot scorched the earth and the crops, and the heat caused the death of all the animals. Jupiter stopped Phaeton with a thunderbolt, and he fell into the river Eridanus (*Met* II.19–328; *OM* II.1–63).

The Learned Eagle tells the frightened poet that the Milky Way was formed when Pheton lost control of the horses as they sped across the heavens and burned the earth and the atmosphere, *HF* II.940–959. Troilus thinks that Pheton still drives his father's chariot, because the sun seems to have taken a longer route, *Tr* V.659–665.

Pheton, the ME and OF variant, appears medially, *HF* II.942; *Tr* V.664.

J.A. Dane, "Chaucer's Eagle's Ovid's Phaeton: A Study in Literary Reception." *JMRS* 11 (1981): 71–82; Ovid, *Met*, ed. and trans. F.J. Miller, I: 60–83; *OM*, ed. C. de Boer, I, deel 15: 174–186.

PHIDON was a prominent Athenian, fl. fifth century B.C., slain during the reign of the Thirty Tyrants, c. September 404–May 403 B.C. During this period the tyrants executed, without trial, several prominent men of democratic and oligarchical views (Diodorus Siculus, *The Library of History* XIV, 5–6). Jerome tells the story of Phidon's daughters, who were forced to dance naked over their father's blood before the tyrants; they then drowned themselves in a cistern to preserve their virginity, *Epistola adversus Jovinianum (Letter Against Jovinian)*, I.41 (*PL* 23: 271).

Dorigen thinks that Phidon's daughters are exemplary figures of maidenly virtue, *FranklT* 1369. **[Dorigen]**

The name occurs medially.

G. Dempster, "Chaucer at Work on the Complaint in *The Franklin's Tale*." *MLN* 52 (1937): 6–16; Diodorus Siculus, *The Library of History*, ed. and trans. C.H. Oldfather, VI: 20–25; K. Hume, "The Pagan Setting of *The Franklin's Tale* and the Sources of Dorigen's Cosmology." *SN* 44 (1972): 289–294.

PHILIPP(ES). Philip II of Macedonia, c. 382–336 B.C., was the younger son of King Amyntas and father of Alexander the Great. Between 359 and 336, he made Macedonia the supreme Greek state.

Alexander is Philipp's son, *MkT* 2656. **[Alexander]**

The name occurs once, initially, in the genitive case, *Philippes*.

OCD, 815.

[PHILIPPE DE VITRY.] This bishop of Meaux, 1291–1361, is sometimes identified as the author of the *Ovide Moralisé*, written during the first years of the fourteenth century. The other author to whom the work is attributed is Chrétien Legouais. Chaucer mentions neither the authors nor the work, but it is clear that he knew the *Ovide Moralisé*, which tells the stories found in Ovid's *Metamorphoses*, with allegorical and Christian interpretations for them. Ceres, for example, represents the Church seeking the souls of the faithful. **[Ovide]**

J.L. Lowes, "Chaucer and the *Ovide Moralisé*." *PMLA* 33 (1918): 302–335; S.B. Meech, "Chaucer and the *Ovide Moralisé*—A Further Study." *PMLA* 46 (1931): 182–204; A.J. Minnis, "A Note on Chaucer and the *Ovide Moralisé*." *MAE* 48 (1979): 254–257; Ovid, *Her*, ed. and trans. G. Showerman; *ibid., Met*, ed. and trans. F.J. Miller; *Ovide Moralisé*, ed. C. de Boer; B.L. Witlieb, "Chaucer and the *Ovide Moralisé*." *N&Q* 215 (1970): 202–207.

PHILLIS. Phyllis, daughter of Lycurgus of Thrace, ruled the kingdom after her father's death. She welcomed Demophoön to Rhodope when he was shipwrecked on the beach. Demophoön accepted the young queen's hospitality, married her, then left for Athens, promising to return. He did not keep his promise, and Phyllis committed suicide. She contemplated several ways to die: to drown herself, to use the knife, or to hang herself, but had not decided by the end of the letter (*Heroides* II).

Chaucer tells the story, *LGW* 2394–2561. Indebted mainly to Ovid, he also possibly used *RR* 13211–13214, where Phyllis hangs herself. Phillis hangs herself on a tree, *MLI* 65, with a cord, *LGW* 2485. She is love's martyr, *BD* 727–728; *HF* I.388–397. Chaucer may have been influenced by an Italian translation of the *Heroides* for his portrait of Phyllis. **[Demophon]**

The name appears in medial positions only, *MLI* 65; *BD* 728; *HF* I.390; *LGW F* 264, *LGW G* 217; *LGW* 2424, 2452, 2465, 2469, 2482, 2494, 2497.

S.B. Meech, "Chaucer and an Italian Translation of the *Heroides.*" *PMLA* 45 (1930): 110–128; Ovid, *Her*, ed. and trans. G. Showerman, 18–31; *RR,* ed. E. Langlois, IV: 10; *RR,* trans. C. Dahlberg, 228.

PHILOCTETES: [PHILOTETES]
PHILOMELA: [PHILOMENE]

PHILOMENE. Philomela was the daughter of Pandion, king of Athens, and Procne's sister. Procne, married to Tereus of Thrace, longed to see her sister, and Tereus went to Athens to fetch Philomela. Upon returning to Thrace, he took Philomela into the woods, raped her, cut out her tongue, and shut her up in a house in the woods. Philomela, however, wove her story into a tapestry of purple on a white background and sent it to Procne by a messenger. Telling Tereus that she was going to celebrate the Bacchic rites in the woods, Procne left home, rescued her sister, and took her back with her. To avenge herself on Tereus, she killed her son Itys, cut him up and cooked him, and served the dish to Tereus. When he discovered that he had eaten his son, he pursued the sisters, but Philomela was changed into a nightingale and Procne into a swallow (*Met* VI.424–674; *OM* VI.2217–3684).

Proigne the swallow begins her wailing, for Tereus has taken her sister, *Tr* II.64–70, a reference to Philomela. Criseyde hears a nightingale singing a lay of love in the moonlight, *Tr* II.918–922. Philomene is the nightingale, the nocturnal songbird. Criseyde is compared to the newly startled nightingale, *Tr* III.1233–1239. Chaucer follows Ovid closely for most of the story in *LGW* 2228–2392 and may have also used a version by Chrétien de Troyes, *Philomene,* inserted in the *Ovide Moralisé* VI.217–3684. J.L. Lowes shows that the *LGW* is a composite of both Ovid and Chrétien. Chaucer omits the barbarous vengeance and the transformations. The nightingale appears throughout his work without further mention of Philomela. The Squire sleeps no more than does the nightingale, *Gen Prol* 98. Nicholas sings in a quavering voice like a nightingale, *MillT* 3377. Alys says that she used to sing like a nightingale, *WBP* 458. Sir Thopas is merrier than the nightingale, *Thop* 834. The foolish priest who fleeces his clients is gladder than the nightingale in May; he takes the silver, which the Canon has turned into gold, to be weighed by a goldsmith, *CYT* 1341–1344. No nightingale can sing more sweetly than Phoebus's crow, *MancT* 136–138, but Phoebus

takes away his power to sing, *MancT* 291–295. [**Pandion: Proigne: Tereus**]
Philomene, the French name for *Philomela*, appears three times in medial positions only, *LGW* 2274, 2284, 2339.

J.L. Lowes, "Chaucer and the *Ovide Moralisé*." *PMLA* 33 (1918): 302–325; Ovid, *Met*, ed. and trans. F.J. Miller, I: 316–335; *OM*, ed. C. de Boer, II, deel 21: 337–366; W. Pfeffer, *The Change of Philomel: The Nightingale in Medieval Literature*; *Rossignol*, ed. and trans. J.L. Baird and J.R. Kane; *Three Ovidian Tales of Love*, ed. and trans. R. Cormier.

PHILOSTRATE is the name Arcita takes when he returns to Athens in disguise in *The Knight's Tale*. In Boccaccio's *Il Teseida delle nozze d'Emilia* (1339–1341), Arcita takes the name *Penteo, Tes* IV.12. Chaucer has borrowed the pseudonym for Arcita from the title of another Boccaccio poem, *Il Filostrato* (1333–1339), which means "conquered by love." [**Arcita**]

The name occurs three times, twice medially, *KnT* 1428, 1558, and once in final rhyming position, *KnT* 1728.

Boccaccio, *Tutte le opere*, ed. V. Branca, II: 25–228, 356.

PHILOTETES was Jason's companion and pilot of the *Argo*, which sailed in search of the Golden Fleece (*HDT* I). He is not mentioned in Valerius Flaccus's *Argonauticon*.

Philotetes is the ship's pilot when the Argonauts sail from Thessaly, *LGW* 1459–1461. [**Argus²: Jason: Medea: Ram**]

The form is medieval Latin, possibly a variant of *Philoctetes*, and appears initially, *LGW* 1459.

Guido delle Colonne, *Guido de Columnis: HDT*, ed. N.E. Griffin, 10–11; *ibid., HDT*, trans. M.E. Meek, 8–9.

PHITONISSA. The priestess of Apollo was called Pythia. The witch of Endor is called *mulier Pythonem habens*, "a woman having the python," I Kings 28:7, indicating that she had some aspects of the pagan priestess. Isidore, in his discussion of magicians, says that the woman who called up Samuel was Pythonissa (*Etym* VIII.ix.7, 21).

The fiend explains to the summoner that sometimes devils arise with dead bodies and speak as reasonably and as fairly as Samuel did to the Phitonissa, *FrT* 1506–1511; aware of biblical exegesis, he adds that some say it was not Samuel. [**Samuel**]

Phitonissa is the medieval variant of *Pythonissa; ph* is the medieval rendering of aspirated /p/. The name appears once medially, *FrT* 1510.

Isidore, *Etymologiae*, ed. W.M. Lindsay, I.

PHOEBUS: [PHEBUS]

PHYLLIS: [PHILLIS]

PICTAGORAS, PITHAGORES. Pythagoras, c. 582–500 B.C., was the son of a gem engraver, Mnesarchus of Samos. He emigrated to Kroton c. 531 B.C. and there founded an order, later known as the Pythagoreans, devoted to Apollo the Giver of Life, a cult forbidding the use of fire or of animal victims. Pythagoras believed in metempsychosis or the transmigration of souls (*Met* XV.60–487; *OM* XV.211–1228). He requested his disciples to refrain from meat and the flesh of animals, mullets, eggs or egg-sprung animals, and beans. He is credited with the discovery of the principal intervals of the musical scale and with the interpretation of the world as a whole through number. His three treatises are *On Education, On Statesmanship,* and *On Nature.* One story of his death involves the commandment against eating beans. His enemies set fire to his house, and as Pythagoras fled, he found himself in a field of beans. Rather than trample them, he allowed his pursuers to slay him (Diogenes Laertius VIII.I).

The Man in Black says that if he knew all the problems or "jeupardyes" of chess that Pithagoras knew, he would have played the game against Fortune better, *BD* 665–669. He says that Tubal made the first songs, but the Greeks say Pictagoras did so, *BD* 1160–1170, Aurora says so, a reference to Peter Riga's *Aurora, Liber Genesis* 481–484. Isidore makes this statement in *Etymologiae* III.16, and it appears in Peter Comestor's *Historia scholastica* XVII.xxv (*PL* 198: 1078–1079). Boethius reminds Lady Philosophy that she has always told him of Pictagoras's comment that men shall serve God and not gods, *Bo* I, *Prosa* 4. 258–262 **[Boece: Peter¹ Riga]**

Pictagoras occurs in final rhyming position, *BD* 1167, and in *Bo* I, *Prosa* 4.260. *Pithagores* appears in final rhyming position, *BD* 667.

H. Baker, "Pythagoras of Croton." *Persephone's Cave,* 151–187; *ibid.,* "Pythagoras of Samos." *Sewanee Review* 80 (1972): 1–38; Diogenes Laertius, *Lives of the Eminent Philosophers,* ed. and trans. R.D. Hicks, II: 320–367; Isidore, *Etymologiae,* ed. W.M. Lindsay, I; Ovid., *Met,* ed. and trans. F.J. Miller, II: 368–399; *OM,* ed. C. deBoer, V, deel 43: 196–222; Peter Riga, *Aurora,* ed. P.E. Beichner, I: 45–46; O. Strunk, *Source Readings in Music History,* 94, 98, 180–181; K. Young, "Chaucer and Peter Riga." *Speculum* 12 (1937): 299–303.

PIERIDES is the patronymic of the nine daughters of King Pieros of Emathia. They challenged the Muses to a contest of song, which they lost, and the Muses, in revenge, changed the presumptuous maidens into magpies (*Met* V.294–678; *OM* V.1763–1832). The Muses themselves are also called Pierides because their most ancient seat of worship was in Pieria. They were said to be the daughters of Jupiter and Mnemosyne, but their father was also said to be Pieros of Macedonia. *Pierides* is then either their byname of location or their patronymic.

The Man of Law says that on no account does he want to be compared with the Muses called Pierides and gives *Metamorphoses* as his source, *MLI* 90–95. The word, however, does not occur in *Metamorphoses*; the daughters of King Pieros are called by their byname of location, *Emathides* (*Met* V.669). Virgil uses *Pierides* throughout his *Eclogae,* and it is possible that Chaucer may have come across the word there. The narrator praises Venus, Cupid, and the Nine Sisters because through them he has told the story of Troilus's service, *Tr* III.1807–1920.

Pierides appears in final rhyming position, *MLI* 92.

K. Harty, "Chaucer's Man of Law and the 'Muses that Men Clepe Pierides.'" *SSF* 18 (1981): 75–77; Ovid, *Met*, ed. and trans. F.J. Miller, I: 258–285; *OM*, ed. C. de Boer, II, deel 21: 226–227.

PIERS[1]. Daun Piers is the monk who makes the pilgrimage to Canterbury, *Gen Prol* 165–207. He is a monastic outrider and loves hunting. Although Bailly does not know his name at first, *MkP* 1928–1930, and asks if his name is "Daun Albon," "Daun John," or "Daun Thomas," all traditional names for monks, he discovers that it is Piers by the time the monk has finished his tale, *NPP* 1792.

Piers is the Anglo-Norman form of French *Pierre*.

P.E. Beichner, "Daun Piers, Monk and Business Administrator." *Speculum* 34 (1959): 611–619; O.F. Emerson, "Some of Chaucer's Lines on the Monk." *MP* I (1903): 105–115; J.V. Fleming, "Daun Piers and Dom Pier: Waterless Fish and Unholy Hunters." *ChauR* 15 (1981): 287–294; R.B. White, "Chaucer's Daun Piers and the Rule of St. Benedict: The Failure of an Ideal." *JEGP* 70 (1971): 13–30.

PIERS[2] ALFONCE. Pedro Alphonso, b. 1062 in Aragon, known also as Petrus Alfonsi in Italian, was named Moshe Sephardi. He became a Christian on June 29, 1106, and took the name of his godfather, Alfonso VII of Castile, to whom he was physician. He is the author of *Contra Judaeos*, a polemical treatise against Judaism and Islam, and of *Dialogus Petri Cognomento Alphonsi, ex Judaeo Christiani et Moysi Judaei,* which influenced the polemics of Peter of Cornwall (1197–1221). An adaptation of his astronomical tables for October 19, 1116, based on the tables of al-Khwarizmi, appears in a version generally attributed to Adelard of Bath in the twelfth-century manuscript, *Corpus Christi* 283. Leaving Spain soon after his conversion, he later became physician to Henry I of England about 1110. His *Disciplina clericalis (A Discipline for Scholars),* a collection in Latin of thirty-four Arabic and Sanskrit tales, was meant to serve as a rule for clerics. As early as the twelfth century, the work was rendered into French.

The references to Piers Alfonce appear only in *The Tale of Melibee* and correspond to similar passages in *Le Livre de Mellibee et de Prudence (The Book of Melibee and Prudence)* by Renaud de Louens (after 1336) and the

Liber consolationis et consilii (The Book of Consolation and Counsel) by Albertanus of Brescia (1246). On the wisdom of repaying good or evil slowly, *Mel* 1053 (*S&A* 573; Sundby 11–12), see *Disciplina clericalis* XXIV. On not making friends of old enemies, *Mel* 1189 (*S&A* 581; Sundby 50), see *Disciplina clericalis* IV.4; on doing nothing of which one may later repent, *Mel* 1218 (*S&A* 582; Sundby 59), see *Disciplina clericalis* IV.4; on not keeping company with people one does not know, *Mel* 1309–1311 (*S&A* 587; Sundby 69–70), see *Disciplina clericalis* XVII.2. Instead of Pamphilles, Dame Prudence quotes Petrus Alfonsi, *Disciplina clericalis* iv, *Mel* 1561. On the indignity of asking alms from former enemies, *Mel* 1566 (*S&A* 600; Sundby 99), see *Disciplina clericalis* ii.2.

Chaucer uses *Piers*, the Anglo-Norman variant of French *Pierre*, four times, *Mel* 1053, 1218, 1309, 1566, and the English variant, *Peter*, once, *Mel* 1189.

Albertanus Brixiensis, *Liber consolationis et consilii*, ed. T. Sundby; D. Metlitzki, *The Matter of Araby in Medieval England*, 19–26; Petrus Alfonsi, *The Disciplina Clericalis*, ed. and trans. E. Hermes, 109, 115–116, 135, 146; Renaud de Louens, *Le Livre de Mellibee et Prudence*, ed. J.B. Severs, *S&A*, 615–644; B. Septimus, "Petrus Alfonsi on the Cult at Mecca." *Speculum* 56 (1981): 517–533.

PIGMALION. Pygmalion, king of Cyprus, was also a sculptor. Disgusted with the priestesses of Venus, who practiced sacred prostitution, he carved for himself an ivory statue, more beautiful than any real woman. At a festival honoring the goddess, he prayed for a wife as beautiful as the creature he had left at home. Pitying him, Venus breathed life into the statue, and when Pygmalion returned home, his new wife welcomed him. He became the father of Cinyras and grandfather of Myrrha and Adonis (*Met* X.243–297; *OM* X.929–1079; *RR* 20817–21198).

Nature boasts that not even Pigmalion could imitate her when she created Virginia, *PhysT* 14. [**Adoon: Mirra: Virginia**]

Pigmalion, a spelling variant of *Pygmalion*, appears initially, *PhysT* 14.

Ovid, *Met*, ed. and trans. F.J. Miller, II: 80–85; *OM*, ed. C. de Boer, IV, deel 37: 33–37; *RR*, ed. E. Langlois, V: 59–73; *RR*, trans. C. Dahlberg, 340–346.

PILATE(S). Pontius Pilate, fl. first century A.D., was the prefect of Judaea from A.D. 26–36 who condemned Jesus to death. In medieval drama, he appears in plays of the Trial, Flagellation, and Passion of Christ.

The drunken Miller cries out "in Pilate's voice" that he can tell a tale equally as good as the Knight's, *MillT* 3124. "Pilates voys" was a high voice, something like a counter-tenor falsetto, which medieval actors used for the role in the cycle drama.

Pilates, the ME genitive case, appears medially.

The Chester Mystery Cycle, ed. R.M. Lumiansky and D. Mills, 284–324; L. Ellinwood, "A Further Note on 'Pilates voys.'" *Speculum* 8 (1933): 526–528; *The South-English Legendary*, ed. C. D'Evelyn and A.J. Mill, II: 697–706.

PIRAMUS. Pyramus was the most beautiful youth in the East and lived in Babylon. He fell in love with his neighbor Thisbe, but their parents refused consent to their marriage. They planned to escape together; first, they would meet at King Ninus's tomb, near which grew a mulberry tree. Thisbe arrived first but, frightened by a lioness, she fled into the tomb, leaving her cloak behind. The lioness tore the cloak with her bloody jaws, then went off. When Pyramus arrived and saw the bloody cloak, he presumed that Thisbe had been slain. He drew his sword and killed himself, and as his blood spurted upwards, it changed the white fruit of the mulberry tree to deep purple. Arriving soon afterwards, Thisbe found Pyramus dead and slew herself with his sword (*Met* IV.55–166; *OM* IV.229–1169). The story is also told in an Anglo-Norman poem of the twelfth or thirteenth century, *Pyrame et Tisbé,* in an Old French poem, *Piramus et Tisbé* (c. 1170), and in Machaut's *Jugement dou roy de Navarre,* 3171–3212.

The Merchant remarks that love will find a way as in the story of Piramus and Tesbee, *MerchT* 2125–2128. Piramus is among love's martyrs in Venus's temple, *PF* 289. Chaucer tells the story, omitting the mulberry tree, *LGW* 706–923. **[Nynus: Semyrame: Tesbee]**

Piramus, the ME and OF variant, occurs eight times medially, *MerchT* 2128; *LGW* 777, 794, 823, 868, 880, 907, 916; and five times in final rhyming position, *PF* 289; *LGW* 724, 855, 880, 918.

E. Faral, "Le Poème de *Piramus et Tisbé* et quelques romans français du XIIe siècle." *Recherches sur les sources latines des contes et romans courtois. . . ,* 5–36; *ibid.,* "'*Pyrame et Thisbé.*' Texte normand du XIIe siècle." *Romania* 41 (1912): 294–305; Guillaume de Machaut, *Oeuvres,* ed. E. Hoepffner, I: 246–247; S.B. Meech, "Chaucer and the *Ovide Moralisé*—A Further Study." *PMLA* 46 (1931): 182–204; Ovid, *Met,* ed. and trans. F.J. Miller, I: 182–191; *OM,* ed. C. de Boer, II, deel 21: 18–37; *Piramus et Thisbé,* ed. C. de Boer; *Pyrame et Thisbé,* ed. C. de Boer; J.W. Spisak, "Chaucer's *Pyramus and Thisbe.*" *ChauR* 18 (1983–1984): 204–210; *Three Ovidian Tales of Love,* ed. R. Cormier.

PIRITHOUS: [PEROTHEUS]
PIROIS: [PHEBUS]

PIRRUS. Pyrrhus was another name for Neoptolemus, son of Achilles and Deidamia. When the Greeks took Troy, Pyrrhus slew Priam at the palace altar (*Aeneid* II.469–505, 526–558).

The Man of Law says that there was never such tender weeping for pity when Pirrus broke down the wall of Troy as there was for Custance's departure for Syria, *MLT* 288–294. The ladies of Ilion did not make a greater lamentation when Pirrus caught Priam by the beard and slew him as the hens make when the fox grabs Chauntecleer, *NPT* 3355–3361. The story of how Pirrus slew Priam and Polytes is painted on the brass tablet, *HF*

I.159–161. **[Polite: Priam]**

Pirrus, a spelling variant, occurs twice medially, *MLT* 288; *NPT* 357; and once in final rhyming position, *HF* I.161.

Virgil, *Aeneid,* ed. and trans. H.R. Fairclough, I: 324–331.

PISCES, PISCIS, the constellation the Fish, is the twelfth sign of the zodiac, the exaltation or sign of maximum power of Venus, the depression or sign of minimum power of Mercury, and the night house of Jupiter. One fish lies in the northern hemisphere south of Andromeda and the other lies in the southern hemisphere near Aquarius. The whole constellation is called a southern sign (*Tetrabiblos* I.17, 19). It is the cold and moist sign (*Confessio Amantis* VII.1215–1219).

Alys of Bath accounts for the differences between those born under Venus and Mercury in the differences in their constellations: Venus is exalted in Pisces, but Mercury is desolate in that sign, *WBP* 701–705. Piscis is the twelfth sign of the zodiac, *Astr* I.8.5, and lies directly opposite Virgo, *Astr* II.6.18. All the signs from the head or beginning of Libra to the end of Piscis are called signs of the south, *Astr* II.28.37. Piscis, an eastern sign, obeys the sovereign or western sign Libra, *Astr* II.28.37. The sign is used for calculating the degree of a planet, *Astr* II.40.51–59. **[Fyssh: Mercurie: Venus]**

Pisces, Latin plural, occurs in medial position, *WBP* 704; *Piscis,* Latin singular, appears only in the *Astrolabe.*

John Gower, *The Complete Works,* ed. G.C. Macaulay, III: 266; Ptolemy, *Tetrabiblos,* ed. and trans. F.E. Robbins, 81, 91.

PITHAGORES: [PICTAGORAS]

PLACEBO is the name of Januarie's second brother in *The Merchant's Tale.* He agrees with Januarie in everything he says about marriage and encourages him in his folly. Januarie is sixty years old. Afraid that in the next world he will be punished for his fornications, he intends to marry in order to make his sexual appetite lawful. Placebo agrees with his arguments in favor of his marriage to May. Placebo means "I will please" and occurs at the beginning of the Office of the Dead. The Summoner uses the phrase "to sing Placebo," meaning "to flatter," when he warns against flatterers, *SumT* 2075. The Parson is more specific: "Flattereres been the develes chapelleyns, that syngen evere Placebo," *ParsT* 617.

Placebo occurs twice initially, *MerchT* 1478, 1617; twice medially, *MerchT* 1520, 1571; and once in final rhyming position, *MerchT* 1476.

D.W. Robertson, Jr., *A Preface to Chaucer,* 111.

PLATO, PLATON. Plato, c. 427–348 B.C., was the son of Ariston, who traced his descent from Codrus, the last king of Athens. His mother was Perictone, the sixth descendant of the great Athenian lawgiver Solon. Given the name Aristocles after his grandfather, he was nevertheless called Plato because of his broad wrestler's face. In his youth he wrote poetry and plays but gave them up when he met Socrates. After 399 B.C., the year of Socrates's execution, Plato traveled to Megera, Egypt, and returned to Athens in 389 to form his Academy. He is the author of about twenty-five dialogues, conversations between Socrates and his disciples, the most famous being *Ion, Protagoras, Apology, Crito, Symposium, Phaedo, Republic, Timaeus, Meno,* and *Laws.* He died in 347 (Diogenes Laertius III).

The *Timaeus* was the best known of Plato's dialogues during the Middle Ages. Although Aristippus, archdeacon of Catania, had translated the *Phaedo* and the *Meno* before 1162, neither of these translations appear to have been widely known. Medieval scholars knew the *Timaeus* in the fourth-century translation with commentary by Calcidius, on which medieval Platonism is based. Its influence may be seen in the works of Martianus Capella (*De nuptiis Mercurii et Philologie*), Boethius (*De consolatione philosophiae*), Macrobius (*Commentarius in Somnium Scipionis,* based largely on Porphyry's commentary on the *Timaeus*), Alain de Lille (*De planctu Naturae*), Abelard (*Introductio ad theologiam* and *Theologia christiana*), Bernard Silvester (*De mundi universitate* and *Cosmographia*).

Chaucer quotes from *Timaeus* 29B: "the wordes moote be cosyn to the dede," *Gen Prol* 741–742, *MancT* 207–210, *Bo* III, *Prosa* 12.205–207. The story of the disciple who asked Plato the name of the secret stone, *CYT* 1448–1471, is told of Solomon in *Tabula Chemica of Senior Zadith* in Zetner's *Theatrum chemicum* V.224 (1622). Plato is quoted at *HF* II.757–765, an idea found in *Bo* III, *Prosa* 11. 43–47. Plato is the authority for the doctrine that the air is the habitation of certain citizens and beasts, *HF* II.929–932. Augustine cites Plato on the subject in *De civitatis Dei (The City of God)* VII.15–16, where "beasts" refer to the demons of the air. Skeat (III: 264) suggests that "beasts" refers to the signs of the zodiac and "citizen" to aerial powers, as in Alain de Lille, *Anticlaudianus* IV.271–278. The zodiac is the circle of beasts, *Astr* I.21.49–62.

Boethius was much indebted to Plato in *De consolatione philosophiae.* Lady Philosophy laments the long time that she has been striving against foolishness, long before Plato's time, *Bo* I, *Prosa* 3.23–28, and that Plato confirms her teaching that the commonwealth would be happier if the rulers studied wisdom, *Bo* I, *Prosa* 4.26–30. This notion appears in *Republic* V.473C–D, VI.485B–E. She reminds Boethius that her disciple Plato says, *In Thymeo,* that people should ask God's help in little things, *Bo* III, *Prosa* 9.189–194, *Timaeus* 27C. Scholars have pointed out that *Metrum* 9 of *Book* III is an abridgement of the first part of the *Timaeus.* Lady Philosophy gives Plato's doctrine that men record things that they have forgotten, that is, the doctrine of the recollection of the former life, *Bo* III, *Metr* 11.43–47, as found in *Phaedo* 72–76, *Meno* 81–86. Plato says that only wise men do what they desire, *Bo* IV, *Prosa* 2.260–268. Boethius quotes Plato that God is eternal and the world perpetual, *Bo* V, *Prosa* 6.59–67. In *Timaeus* 37D Plato says that the father made the universe, a movable image of eternity. There is an apparent reference to the *Symposium*, *LGW F* 521–526, *LGW G* 511–514, where Chaucer mentions Agaton, the poet in whose honor the banquet in the *Symposium* is held. [**Agaton: Boece: Senior**]

The name never occurs initially. *Plato* appears 5 times in medial positions, *Gen Prol* 741; *CYT* 1453, 1456, 1463; *MancT* 207; and three times in final rhyming position, *CYT* 1448, 1460; *HF* II.931, and throughout the prose of *Boece*. *Platon*, the French variant, occurs once, in final rhyming position, *HF* II.759.

Alan of Lille, *Anticlaudianus*, trans. and commentary J.J. Sheridan, 127–128; *ibid.*, *The Plaint of Nature*, trans. and commentary J.J. Sheridan; Alanus de Insulis, *Anticlaudianus*, ed. R. Bossaut, 115; *ibid.*, *De planctu Naturae*, ed. N.M. Häring; *Studi Medievali*, 3 serie, 19.2 (1978): 797–879; Calcidius, *Calcidius on Matter, His Doctrines and Sources . . . by J.C.M. van Winden*; Diogenes Laertius, *Lives of the Eminent Philosophers*, ed. and trans. R.D. Hicks, I: 272–373; M.T. Gibson, "The Study of the *Timaeus* in the Eleventh and Twelfth Centuries." *Pensamiento* 25 (1969): 183–194; R. Klibansky, *The Continuity of the Platonic Tradition during the Middle Ages*; Macrobius, *Saturnalia. In somnium Scipionis commentarius*, ed. J. Willis; *ibid.*, *Macrobius's Commentary on the Dream of Scipio*, trans. W.H. Stahl; Martianus Capella, *De nuptiis Mercurii et Philologiae. Martianus Capella*, ed. A. Dick; *ibid.*, *The Wedding of Mercury and Philology. Martianus Capella and the Seven Liberal Arts*, trans. W.H. Stahl, R. Johnson and E.L. Burg; *OCD*, 839–842; Plato, *Meno*, ed. and trans. W.R.M. Lamb, 300–325; *ibid.*, *Phaedo*, ed. and trans. H.N. Fowler, 248–269; *ibid.*, *Republic*, ed. and trans. P. Shorey, I: 506–509; II: 4–9; *ibid.*, *Symposium*, ed. and trans. W.R.M. Lamb; *ibid.*, *Timaeus*, ed. and trans. R.G. Bury, 48–49, 74–75; P.G. Ruggiers, "Platonic Forms in Chaucer." *ChauR* 17 (1983): 366–381; W. Wetherbee, *Platonism and Poetry in the Twelfth Century*.

PLEYNDAMOUR is the name of one of the heroes with whom Sir Thopas is compared, *Thop* 900. Skeat (V: 199) points out that Playn de Amours occurs in Malory's *Morte d'Arthur* IX.7 as the name of one of the three brothers whom La Cote Mal Taillé meets. Laura H. Loomis notes that no existing manuscript of *Tristan* records this name, so that it is only conjecture that Malory found the name in an expanded French prose *Tristan*. [**Thopas**]

The name, derived from *plein d'amour*, "full of love," appears in final rhyming position.

L.H. Loomis, *S&A*, 487.

PLEYNTE OF KYNDE: [ALEYN²]
PLOUGH: [URSA]

PLUTO is one of the names of Hades, king of the Underworld. He carried off Proserpina, Ceres's daughter, to be his queen, after he failed to persuade several goddesses to marry him. This rape is the subject of Claudian's poem *De raptu Proserpinae.*

Diane's statue is painted with eyes cast down to Pluto's lower realm, *KnT* 2082. Emelye prays to Dyane as queen of Pluto's realm, *KnT* 2299. Diana and Proserpina are two aspects of the triple goddess: Diana is the goddess as virgin, Proserpina is the goddess as queen of the afterworld. Pluto, at Saturn's request, sends a fury from hell, who startles Arcite's horse, *KnT* 2685. Pluto and Proserpina dance with their company near the well in Januarie's garden, *MerchT* 2038–2041. Pluto is called "kyng of fayerye," *MerchT* 2227, a borrowing from *Sir Orfeo,* where Pluto is similarly portrayed. Pluto lectures his wife on women's sins, *MerchT* 2225–2263, and promises to restore Januarie's sight, *MerchT* 2258–2263. M.J. Donovan suggests that Pluto is Januarie's counterpart, a type of *senex amans* or old lover. Aurelius prays to Phebus Apollo that he entreat Lucina his sister to sink the rocks into Pluto's realm, her own dark region, *FranklT* 1075, a blending of Lucina, goddess of childbirth and an aspect of Diana with Proserpina, goddess of the underworld. Claudian stands on a pillar of sulfur because he has told Pluto's story, *HF* III.1507–1512. Pluto abducted Proserpina while she gathered flowers near Mount Etna, a sulfurous, volcanic mountain. Pandarus swears by Pluto, *Tr* III.590–593. [**Claudian: Diana: Proserpina**]

Pluto appears once initially, *MerchT* 2227; eleven times in medial positions, *KnT* 2082, 2229, 2685; *MerchT* 2038, 2311, 2354; *FranklT* 1075; *Tr* III.592; *Tr* IV.790; *HF* III.1511. It never appears finally.

Claudian, *De raptu Proserpinae,* ed. and trans. M. Platnauer, II: 292–377; M.J. Donovan, "Chaucer's January and May: Counterparts in Claudian." *Chaucerian Problems and Perspectives,* ed. E. Vasta and Z. Thundy, 59–69; J.B. Friedman, *Orpheus in the Middle Ages.*

POLIPHEMUS. Polyphemus, a one-eyed cyclops and son of Poseidon, lived in a cave in Sicily and dined on human flesh. Ulysses, driven by a storm to Sicily, took refuge in Polyphemus's cave. When the cyclops discovered the men, he began eating them two by two. But Ulysses blinded the monster in his one eye, lashed his men to the cyclops's sheep, and when the cave was opened, they made their escape. Aeneas found one of the survivors, Achaemenides, on Sicily as he sailed to Italy, from whom he learned the story (*Odyssey* IX.160–542; *Met,* XIV.154–222; *Aeneid* II.613–691). Dictys Cretensis also tells the story in *Ephemeridos belli Troiani,* VI.5, 6.

Lady Philosophy reminds Boethius of the sufferings of famous men to show him that all fortune that seems sharp corrects and exercises the good man, *Bo* IV, *Metr* 7.18–27, and she tells him the story of Ulysses and Poliphemus. Chaucer adds a gloss to explain further Lady Philosophy's words. **[Ulixes]**

The spelling *Poliphemus* reflects Jean de Meun's translation in *Li Livres de confort de philosophie.* The name appears only in *Bo* IV, *Metr* 7.20, 22, 25.

V.L. Dedeck-Héry, "Boethius' *De consolatione* by Jean de Meun." *MS* 14 (1952): 256; Dictys Cretensis, *Ephemeridos belli Troiani*, ed. W. Eisenhut, 123–125; Dares Phrygius and Dictys Cretensis, *The Trojan War,* trans. R.M. Frazer, 122–124; D.K. Fry, "Polyphemus in Iceland." *Acta* 4 (1977): 65–86; Homer, *Odyssey,* ed. and trans. A.T. Murray, I: 314–341; Ovid, *Met,* ed. and trans. F.J. Miller, II: 310–317; Virgil, *Aeneid*, ed. and trans. H.R. Fairclough, I: 388–395.

POLIPHETE is the Trojan hero who, Pandarus tells Criseyde, is about to bring legal proceedings against her. Chaucer has invented this episode; there is no Poliphete in Boccaccio's *Il Filostrato* (1333–1339) or in Benoît's *Roman de Troie* (1184). Virgil mentions a Trojan priest, Polyboetes (*Aeneid* VI.484). **[Creseyde: Pandar: Troilus]**

Poliphete, which means "many entertainments," or "many feasts," may denote a frivolous person and occurs once in medial position, *Tr* II.1619, and twice in final rhyming position, *Tr* II.1467, 1616.

Virgil, *Aeneid*, ed. and trans. H.R. Fairclough, I: 538–539.

POLITE, POLYTES. Polytes was one of Priam's sons, whom Pyrrhus killed when the Greeks captured Troy (*Aeneid* II.526–558).

Pyrrhus's slaughter of Priam and his son Polytes appears in the Troy story, *HF* I.158–161. Antenor is taken prisoner in spite of the valiant efforts of the Trojan princes, including Polytes, *Tr* IV.50–56. The story of Antenor's capture appears in Boccaccio's *Il Filostrato* (1333–1339) IV.2–3. **[Monesteo: Pirrus: Polydamas: Polymestore: Rupheo: Santippe: Sarpedon]**

Polite, Boccaccio's form, appears once initially, *Tr* IV.53; *Polytes*, a spelling variant of Boccaccio's form, appears once medially, *HF* I.160.

Boccaccio, *Tutte le opere*, ed. V. Branca, II: 110; Virgil, *Aeneid,* ed. and trans. H.R. Fairclough, I: 328–331.

POLIXENA, POLIXENE. Polyxena was one of King Priam's daughters. According to medieval recensions of the Troy story, Achilles fell in love with her and proposed marriage. He arranged to meet Paris and Hecuba in the temple of Apollo Thymbraeus to discuss the proposal, but instead he was ambushed and killed (Benoît, *Roman de Troie* 21838–22334; Dares, *De excidio Troiae historia* 24; Dictys, *Ephemeridos belli Troiani* IV.10–11).

Achilles died for love of Polixena, *BD* 1067–1071. Criseyde is more beautiful than Polixena, *Tr* I.455. Troilus promises Pandarus Polixene if he would help him in his love suit to Criseyde, *Tr* III.409. Polixene is among love's martyrs, *LGW F* 258, *LGW G* 212. Achilles's ghost claimed her, and she was sacrificed at his tomb (*HDT* XXX). **[Achilles: Antylegyus: Dares**

Frygius: Dite]

Polixena appears once in final rhyming position, *BD* 1071. *Polixene*, a spelling variant, appears twice with final silent -e, *LGW F* 258, *LGW G* 212, and twice in final rhyming position, with final syllabic -e, *Tr* I.455; *Tr* III.409.

Benoît, *Roman de Troie*, ed. L. Constans, III: 373–399; Dares Phrygius, *De excidio Troiae historia*, ed. F. Meister, 40–42; Dictys Cretensis, *Ephemeridos belli Troiani*, ed. W. Eisenhut, 88–90; Dares Phrygius and Dictys Cretensis, *The Trojan War*, trans. R.M. Frazer, 93–94, 160–161; Guido delle Colonne, *Guido de Columnis: HDT*, ed. N.E. Griffin, 207–208; *ibid., HDT*, trans. M.E. Meek, 177–182, 198–203.

POLLUX is the Latin name for the Greek hero Polydeuces, twin brother of Castor, brothers of Helen. It is also the name of the beta or second brightest star in the constellation Gemini, in the head of the figure Pollux; it lies in the northern hemisphere (*Tetrabiblos* I.9).

The Learned Eagle, with the Dreamer in his claws, flies by the zodiacal sign, *HF* I.1006. **[Castor: Gemini: Mercurie]**

The name appears medially.

Ptolemy, *Tetrabiblos*, ed. and trans. F.E. Robbins, 49.

POLYDAMAS was Antenor's son and one of the Trojan heroes. Chaucer follows Boccaccio's *Il Filostrato* (1333–1339) IV.3 by giving, in one stanza, the names of those heroes who tried to prevent Antenor's capture, among them Polydamas, *Tr* IV.50–56. **[Antenor: Monesteo: Polite: Polymestore: Rupheo: Santippe: Sarpedon]**

The name appears medially, *Tr* IV.51.

Boccaccio, *Tutte le opere*, ed. V. Branca, II: 110.

POLYHYMNIA: [POLYMYA]

POLYMESTORE, king of Thracian Chersonesus, was one of the valiant Trojans who defended the city against the Greeks in Boccaccio's *Il Filostrato* (1333–1339) IV.3.

Polymestore is among the heroes who try to prevent Antenor's capture by the Greeks, *Tr* IV.50–56. **[Antenor: Monesteo: Polydamas: Rupheo: Santippe: Sarpedon]**

The name occurs in final rhyming position, *Tr* IV.52.

Boccaccio, *Tutte le opere*, ed. V. Branca, II: 110.

POLYMNESTORE: [POLYMESTORE]

POLYMYA. Polyhymnia, daughter of Zeus and Mnesmosyne, lived with her eight sisters on Mount Helicon. She was the Muse of mime, rhetoric, and song. Fulgentius makes her the Muse of memory, her mother's attribute, *Mythologies* I.15.

Chaucer invokes Polymya, who "singest with vois memorial in the shade," *Anel* 15–21, a stanza inspired by Boccaccio, *Tes* XI.62–63, and by Dante, *Par* XXIII.56–58.

The form, a variant of medieval Latin *Polymia* from classical Latin *Polyhymnia* or "many hymns," appears in final rhyming position, *Anel* 15.

Boccaccio, *Tutte le opere*, ed. V. Branca, II: 624–625; Dante, *The Divine Comedy*, ed. and trans. C.S. Singleton, III.1: 260–261; Fulgentius, *Fulgentius the Mythographer*, trans. L.G. Whitbread, 56–57.

POLYMYTE, POLYMYTES. Polynices was one of Oedipus's sons. His brother Eteocles refused to yield up the throne when his year of power was up, and Polynices gathered an army and launched a siege against Thebes. This war is the subject of Statius's *Thebaid.*

Diomedes's father Tydeus was slain in Polymytes's war, *Tr* V.932–938. Cassandra gives a summary of the story of the siege, *Tr* V.1485–1509, and says that Polymytes was Tydeus's "felawe," a term indicating a contract of fellowship and close friendship. In *Thebaid* I.468–480, King Adrastus persuades Tydeus and Polynices to swear an oath of fellowship after he has stopped their fight. [**Adrastus: Amphiorax: Campaneus: Hemonydes: Ipomedon: Parthenope: Tydeus**]

Polymyte, the ME development of Latin accusative singular *Polymytem*, appears once, in medial position, *Tr* V.1507; *Polymytes* appears once initially, *Tr* V.938, and once in final rhyming position, *Tr* V.1488.

Le Roman de Thèbes, ed. L. Constans; *Roman de Thèbes (The Story of Thebes)*, trans. J.S. Coley; Statius, *Thebaid*, ed. and trans. J.H. Mozley.

POLYPHEMUS: [POLIPHEMUS]
POLYTES: [POLITE]
POLYXENA: [POLIXENA]

POMPE, POMPEI, POMPEUS, POMPEYE. Gnaeus Pompeius, 106–48 B.C., was one of the generals who formed the first triumvirate with Caesar and Crassus. In 54 B.C. he became estranged from Caesar, and in 49 B.C. Caesar engaged Pompey in the first civil war. Defeated at Pharsalus, Pompey fled to Egypt, where he was murdered. Lucan records these wars in his *Pharsalia.*

The death of Pompei is written in the stars, *MLT* 197–199. The Monk says that Pompeus was Caesar's father-in-law, *MkT* 2680. Pompey had married Caesar's daughter, Julia, so that Caesar was Pompey's father-in-law. Suetonius states that Caesar had asked Pompey for his daughter in marriage, but does not add that Pompey refused the match (*The Deified Julius* XXVII). Medieval writers interpreted the passage to mean that Caesar had married Pompey's daughter. Ranulph Higden calls Pompey *socerum* or "father-in-law" to Caesar, *Polychronicon* III.xli. Julius fights in Thessaly against Pompeus and slays his men, *MkT* 2678–2686. One of Pompeus's men slays him and brings his head to Julius, *MkT* 2687–2692. Pompeye, conqueror of the orient, is brought low by Fortune, *MkT* 2693–2394. Lucan stands on a pillar of iron, Mars's metal, because he has written on the civil wars between Caesar and Pompe in *Pharsalia, HF* III.1497–1502. [**Cesar²: Julius**]

Pompe, a pronunciation variant, appears once in final rhyming position, *HF* III.1502; *Pompei,* derived from Latin *Pompeius,* occurs once, in a medial position, *MLT* 199; the expanded form *Pompeus,* also derived from the name of the clan to which the family belonged, *Pompeius,* appears three times in medial positions, *MkT* 2680, 2684, 2688; *Pompeye,* trisyllabic with final syllabic -*e,* appears once, in medial position, *MkT* 2693.

R. Higden, *Polychronicon,* ed. J.R. Lumby and C. Babington, IV: 188–189; Lucan, *Pharsalia,* ed. and trans. J.D. Duff; Suetonius, *De vita Caesarum,* ed. and trans. J.C. Rolfe, I: 36–37.

POMPEIUS: [POMPE]
POMPEY: [POMPE]

PORCIA, wife of Marcus Brutus, fl. first century B.C., was the daughter of Marcus Porcius Cato Uticensis. While Brutus was in the East fighting against Caesar and Antony, she committed suicide by inhaling the fumes of a live charcoal rather than suffer from a disease she had contracted (Plutarch, *Life of Brutus*). Valerius Maximus (*Factorum dictorumque memorabilium* IV.vi.5: *De amore conjugali*) perpetuated the later tradition that she died in 42 B.C. after she learned of Brutus's death. Jerome says that she did not wish to live without him, *Epistola adversus Jovinianum (Letter Against Jovinian)* I.47 and 49 (*PL* 23: 276, 282).

Porcia is one of Dorigen's exemplary wives, *FranklT* 1448–1450. [**Brutus²: Catoun²: Dorigen**]

Porcia, the Latin feminine form of *Porcius,* the name of the clan to which the family belonged, occurs medially, *FranklT* 1448.

K. Hume, "The Pagan Setting of the *Franklin's Tale* and the Sources of Dorigen's Cosmology." *SN* 44 (1972): 289–294; Plutarch, *Parallel Lives,* ed. and trans. B. Perrin, VI: 125–245; Valerius Maximus, *Factorum dictorumque memorabilium libri novem,* ed. J. Kappy, I: 473.

PORTIA: [PORCIA]

PRIAM, PRIAMUS. Priam, son of Laomedon, was king of Troy, husband of Hecuba, and father of Hector, Troilus, Paris, Deiphebus, Cassandra, and Polyxena. When the Greeks took Troy, Neoptolemeus (Pyrrhus) killed Priam as he clung to the altar of Jupiter in his own palace (*Aeneid* II.506–538).

The Nun's Priest says that the ladies of Ilion did not make a greater lamentation when Pyrrhus caught Priam by the beard and slew him than the hens make when the fox grabs Chauntecleer, *NPT* 3355–3361. The story of Ector and King Priam is painted on the glass windows of the Dreamer's room, *BD* 328. The story of how Pirrus slew Priam is painted on the brass tablet, *HF* I.159–161. Troilus is King Priam's son, *Tr* I.2. Priam sends a safe-conduct to bring the Greek ambassadors to Troy, *Tr* IV.139–140. Priam holds a parliament to hear the ambassadors, *Tr* IV.142, and is persuaded to exchange Criseyde for Antenor, *Tr* IV.194–195. Pandarus tells Criseyde that although Priam may have good intentions toward Troilus, Troilus should not test them by visiting Criseyde, *Tr* IV.918–921. Troilus, in a soliloquy, bids his father Priam farewell, *Tr* IV.1205–1211. Pandarus neglects to visit Troilus because he spends the whole day with King Priam, *Tr* V.281–284. Priam tries to comfort his son Troilus after Criseyde's departure, *Tr* V.1226–1232. When Ilion fell, King Priam was destroyed, *LGW* 936–939. **[Ecuba: Ector: Paris: Pirrus: Polites]**

Priam, the English contraction, occurs twice initially, *Tr* IV.142; *Tr* V.1226; nine times in medial positions, *NPT* 3358; *Tr* III.791; *Tr* IV.57, 139, 194, 921, 1206; *Tr* V.284; *HF* I.159; *Priamus,* the Latin form, occurs twice in medial positions, *Tr* IV.1393; *LGW* 939; and once in final rhyming position, *BD* 28.

Virgil, *Aeneid,* ed. and trans. H.R. Fairclough, I: 328–333.

PRIAPUS, son of Venus and Bacchus, was the god of gardens. His symbol is the phallus. He was represented as a misshapen little man with enormous genitals. When the nymph Lotis, with whom he was in love, refused him, he determined to take her by force. While she slept one night, Pirapus approached her stealthily, but just as he was about to grasp her, Silenus's ass brayed, and the nymphs and gods awoke. They laughed when they saw Priapus's condition (*Fasti* I.415–440).

Priapus cannot devise a more beautiful garden than Januarie's, *MerchT* 2034–2037. The Dreamer finds himself in Venus's temple where he sees Pirapus as he was when the ass brayed, *PF* 253–259. **[Januarie: May]** The name occurs medially, *MerchT* 2034; *PF* 253.

E. Brown, Jr., "Hortus Inconclusus: The Significance of Priapus and Pyramus and Thisbe in *The Merchant's Tale.*" *ChauR* 4 (1970): 31–40; *ibid.,* "Priapus and *The Parlement of Foulys.*" *SP* 72 (1975): 258–274; Ovid, *Fasti,* ed. and trans. J.G. Frazer, 30–33.

PROCNE: [PROIGNE]

PROIGNE. Procne was the elder daughter of King Pandion of Athens. She married Tereus, king of Thrace, and went to live in his country. After five years away from home, Procne longed to see her sister Philomela, and Tereus went to Athens to fetch her. Mad lust seized him for Philomela and, upon returning to Thrace, he took her into the woods, raped her, cut out her tongue, and left her shut up in a house in the woods. He arrived home and told Procne that Philomela was already dead when he arrived in Athens. Philomela, however, wove her story in a tapestry in purple on a white background and sent it to her sister by messenger. When the feast of Bacchus came around, which only women celebrated, Procne went into the woods and rescued her sister. Returning home, she exacted cruel vengeance on Tereus. She cut up their little son, cooked him, and served him to Tereus. When he learned that he had eaten his son, Tereus pursued the sisters, but Procne was changed into a swallow and Philomela became a nightingale (*Met* VI.424–674; *OM* VI.2217–3684).

The swallow Proigne sings a sorrowful lay, how Tereus has taken her sister, *Tr* II.64–65. Proigne pretends to go on a pilgrimage to Bacchus's shrine but rescues Philomela from the castle in which she is imprisoned, *LGW* 2342–2382. Chaucer omits the awful vengeance from his version of the story. There are only two other references to the swallow. Alison's song is as loud and as eager as the swallow's as she sits on a barn, *MillT* 3257–3258; the swallow, murderer of small bees, appears among the birds in Nature's park, *PF* 253. [**Bacus: Pandion: Philomene: Tereus**]

Proigne, a variant of OF *Progne,* appears medially only, *Tr* II.64; *LGW* 2248, 2275, 2346, 2348, 2373, 2380.

J.L. Lowes, "Chaucer and the *Ovide Moralisé*." *PMLA* 33 (1918): 302–325; Ovid, *Met,* ed. and trans. F.J. Miller, I: 316–335; *OM,* ed. C. de Boer, II, deel 21: 337–366.

PROSERPINA, PROSERPYNA, PROSERPYNE. Proserpina is the Latin name for the Greek goddess Persephone. Pluto, king of the Underworld, complained to Jupiter that he alone had no wife. Jupiter promised him Proserpina, his daughter by Ceres, the goddess of grain and of harvests, and with the collusion of Venus, Jupiter and Pluto planned the abduction. As Proserpina gathered violets and lilies in the valley of Henna in Sicily, Pluto appeared suddenly and carried her off to his kingdom. Her mother Ceres, not to be consoled, sought Proserpina throughout the world, neglected her sacred tasks of giving grains to the world, and all the crops died. Finally, Ceres appealed to Jupiter, who told her that her daughter was now Pluto's queen. Proserpina was restored to her mother, but because she had eaten the pomegranate, of which seven seeds were found in her mouth, Jupiter decreed that she should spend half the year in the upper world and the other half in the lower (*Met* V.346–571; *OM* V.1833–1998; Claudian, *De raptu Proserpinae*; Guillaume de Machaut, *Le Confort d'ami,* 2353–2516). As queen of the Underworld, Proserpina is one of the aspects of the triple goddess, *Trivia.* Remigius of Auxerre gives her three names as Lucina in the sky, Diana on earth, and Proserpina in hell (*Commentum in Martianum Capellam* VII.369.I). As queen of the Underworld, Proserpina is mistress of the Erinyes or the Three Furies—Allecto, Megaera, and Tisiphone, *Inf* IX.36–48.

Proserpina, Pluto's wife, is queen of "fayerye," *MerchT* 2028–2029, a borrowing of her portrait in the poem, *Sir Orfeo.* Proserpina arms May with an answer to her husband's accusations when Pluto restores Januarie's sight, *MerchT* 2264–2319. Proserpina is "quene of the derk peyne," *HF* III.1511–1512. Troilus expects to go to her dark realm in pain when he dies, *Tr* IV.473–476. [**Alete: Claudian: Diane: Herenus: Megera: Pluto: Thesiphone**]

Proserpina appears once, initially, *MerchT* 2039; *Proserpyna*, a spelling variant, occurs once, in final rhyming position, *MerchT* 2229; *Proserpyne*, with final syllabic -e, appears once, medially, *MerchT* 2264; and twice in final rhyming position, with final syllabic -e, *HF* III.1511; *Tr* IV.473, both times rhyming with *pyne.*

Claudian, *De raptu Proserpinae*, ed. and trans. M. Platnauer, II: 292–377; Dante, *The Divine Comedy*, ed. and trans. C.S. Singleton, I.1: 90–91; Guillaume de Machaut, *Oeuvres*, ed. E. Hoepffner, III: 83–89; Ovid, *Met*, ed. and trans. F.J. Miller, I: 262–277; *OM*, ed. C. de Boer, II, deel 21: 227–231; Remigius Autissiodorensis, *Commentum in Martianum Capellam*, ed. C. Lutz, II: 185.

PROSERPYNA: [PROSERPINA]
PROSERPYNE: [PROSERPINA]
PROTESILAUS: [PROTHESELAUS]

PROTHESELAUS. Protesilaus was commander of the contingent of troops from Phylace during the Trojan War. He was killed when the Greeks landed at Troy (*Iliad* II.695–699). Homer says that Protesilaus left his marriage "half-completed," and Ovid develops this aspect in *Heroides* XIII. Chaucer's sources also include Jerome, *Epistola adversus Jovinianum (Letter Against Jovinian)* I.45 (*PL* 23: 275).

Laodomya, wife of Protheselaus, refused to live another day after he was killed, *FranklT* 1445–1446. [**Dorigen: Ladomya**]

Protheselaus occurs in final rhyming position, *FranklT* 1446; intrusive *h* after *t* was not pronounced.

G. Dempster, "Chaucer at Work on the Complaint in the *Franklin's Tale*." *MLN* 52 (1937): 6–16; Homer, *Iliad*, ed. and trans. A.T. Murray, I: 102–103; K. Hume, "The Pagan Setting of *The Franklin's Tale* and the Sources of Dorigen's Cosmology." *SN* 44 (1972): 289–294; Ovid, *Her*, ed. and trans. G. Showerman, 158–171; J. Sledd, "Dorigen 's Complaint." *MP* 45 (1947): 36–45.

PRUDENCE is Melibee's wife in *The Tale of Melibeus.* Chaucer found the name in his sources, *Le Livre de Mellibee et de Prudence* by Renaud de Louens (after 1336) and *Liber consolationis et consilii* by Albertanus of Brescia (1246). Prudence's character is defined by her name; she finds the right answers to all Melibee's questions and dissuades him from seeking vengeance on his enemies. [**Melibee: Sophie**]

Prudence is the English and French variants of Latin *Prudentia*, "prudence."

Albertanus Brixiensis, *Liber consolationis et consilii*, ed. T. Sundby; Renaud de
  Louens, *Le Livre de Mellibee et de Prudence*, ed. J.B. Severs. *S&A*, 560–614; J.B.
  Severs, "The Source of Chaucer's *Melibeus*." *PMLA* 50 (1935): 92–99.

PSEUSTIS. This is the name of a character in the poem *Ecloga Theoduli*,
a tenth-century poem whose author is otherwise unknown. Pseustis plays
a flute and comes from Athens; he represents paganism and debates
Alethia, who claims descent from David and plays a harp. The poem formed
part of the *Auctores octo morales* (*Eight Moral Authors*) used as a primary
school text from the Middle Ages until the middle of the sixteenth century;
it served as a book of instruction in grammar as well as a moral and religious
tract. Bernard of Utrecht wrote a commentary on the poem at the end of the
eleventh century, and Bernard Silvester also wrote a commentary about
1150. Wynkyn de Worde published an edition in 1515. Pseustis presents
examples from mythology in his argument with Alethia, who counters with
examples from Christian sources, and Pseustis loses the debate.

Pseustis appears with other flute players, Atiteris and Marcia, *HF*
III.1227–1230. **[Atiteris: Marcia]**

Pseustis, which means "liar," appears in final rhyming position, *HF*
III.1228.

Ecloga Theoduli, ed. J. Osternacher, 31–55; B.N. Quinn, "Ps. Theodolus." *Catalogus
  translationum et commentariorum: Medieval and Renaissance Translations and
  Commentaries*, ed. P.O. Kristellar, II: 383–397.

PTHOLOME, PTHOLOMEE, THOLOME. Claudius Ptolemaeus (Ptolemy), fl. A.D. 139–161, invented the science of trigonometry and improved
the method of fixing geographical positions by referring to their latitudes
and longitudes. His most famous work, *Mathematica syntaxis*, or *The System
of Mathematics*, a work in thirteen books written c. A.D. 151 and known as
Almageste, a title derived from the Arabic name, *al-Kitab-al-Midjisti* (*The
Greatest Book*), is a manual of the entire astronomy of the time, including
the work of his predecessors, particularly Hipparchus, which has been
lost. Ptolemy deals mainly with the stars, the sun, the moon, and the
planets, and omits the comets, which he does not consider part of astronomy. He is also the first to portray the heavens as a geometrically conceived universe. *Mathematica syntaxis* was first translated from Greek into
Arabic in 827, in the reign of the Abassid Caliph Ma'mum (813–833), but the
translator is unknown. The first translator from Arabic into Latin was
Gerard of Cremona, who completed the work at Toledo in 1175. An earlier
translation from Greek into Latin was done in Sicily about 1160, also by an
anonymous translator, but only Gerard's work passed into general circulation. Ptolemy's other works were also translated. The Latin rendering of

Centiloquium, an abridgement of *Quadripartitum* (a short title meaning "The Four Books") done in 1136, is generally assigned to John of Seville. Plato of Tivoli translated *Quadripartitum* in 1138. *Quadripartitum* is the Latin translation of *Tetrabiblos*, "four books," the short title for *Mathematical Treatise in Four Books*. J.D. North suggests that the *Tetrabiblos* was Chaucer's principal source for astronomical and astrological information; the work was very well known and widely consulted during Chaucer's time.

Nicholas has *Almageste* among his books, *MillT* 3208. Dame Alys quotes two proverbs attributed to Ptolemy, *WBP* 181–182, 324–327; for these Karl Young cites a Latin *Almagestum* in a fourteenth-century manuscript, which Chaucer may have known. The proverbs are ascribed to Ptolemy in the preface to Gerard of Cremona's translation of 1175 (published in Venice in 1515). Ptolemy and Euclid are masters of dividing, *SumT* 2289. Lady Philosophy says that, according to Tholome, only a fourth part of the world is inhabited by living creatures, *Bo* II, *Prosa* 7.31–34. According to Ptolemy, the summer solstice or northern latitude of the sun is 23 degrees and 50 minutes in the head or beginning of Cancer, the tropic of summer, *Astr* I.17.8–10. Skeat (III: 354) points out that in Ptolemy's time the true value was 23 degrees 40 minutes, but in Chaucer's time it was 23 degrees 31 minutes. The references here are to *Almagest* I.13. [**Gerard of Cremona: Nicholas**[1]]

Ptholome, the ME variant of Latin (from Greek) *Ptolemaeus*, occurs once, in final rhyming position, *WBP* 324; *Ptholomee*, with long final vowel, appears twice in final rhyming position, *WBP* 182; *SumT* 2289; *Tholome*, a variant of Jean de Meun's *Tholomee*, occurs in *Bo* II, *Prosa* 7.34.

V.L. Dedeck-Héry, "Boethius' *De consolatione* by Jean de Meun." *MS* 14 (1952): 201; *EI*, I: 1100; C.H. Haskins, *Studies in the History of Mediaeval Science*, 68–69; J.D. North, "Kalenderes Enlumyned Ben They." *RES*, new series, 20 (1969): 134; A. Pannekoek, *A History of Astronomy*, 158; Ptolemy, *Tetrabiblos*, ed. and trans. F.E. Robbins; K. Young, "Chaucer's Aphorisms from Ptolemy." *SP* 34 (1937): 1–7.

PTOLEMY: [PTHOLOME]

[**PUBLILIUS SYRUS.**] This name does not appear in Chaucer's work. Many of the *sententiae* or sentences attributed to Seneca in the *Tale of Melibee* are really from the *Sententiae* of Publilius Syrus. He was a slave from Antioch in the first century B.C. and received his freedom because of his intellectual gifts. He was also a famous mime, and the dramatic passages from his mimes were collected into a book, which Seneca, Petronius, and Aulus Gellius greatly admired. During the medieval period some of his *Sententiae* were collected in an anthology called *De Moribus*, which included aphorisms from Seneca, Ausonius, and Lactantius, and attributed, wrongly, to Martin of Braga (d. A.D. 579). Many of Chaucer's references to Seneca are either directly to Publilius Syrus or to this anthology. [**Senec**] from *Sententiae* 594. The quotation attributed to Seneca at *Mel* 1127 is from *Sententiae* 281. The proverb at *Mel* 1135 is from *Sententiae* 32; "the book," *Mel* 1183, is from *Sententiae* 91. Many quotations attributed to Seneca in this tale are from Publilius Syrus. The quotation at *Mel* 1185 is from *Sententiae* 389. At *Mel* 1187 Dame Prudence quotes *Sententiae* 281 instead of Seneca. *Mel* 1320 is from *Sententiae* 607; *Mel* 1324 is from *Sententiae* 255. The attribution to Tullius, *Mel* 1347, is from *Sententiae* 125. The anonymous quotation at *Mel* 1439 is from *Sententiae* 528. Instead of Seneca at *Mel* 1449, *Sententiae* 320; *Mel* 1450 is from *Sententiae* 189; *Mel* 1455 is from *Sententiae* 172. The anonymous quotations at *Mel* 1463 and 1466 are from *Sententiae* 645 and 487. Instead of Seneca, *Mel* 1488, the quotation is from *Sententiae* 483; the anonymous author in *Mel* 1777 is Publilius Syrus, *Sententiae* 489. The quotations attributed to Seneca, *Mel* 1859 and 1866, are from *Sententiae* 64 and *Sententiae* 366 respectively.

OCD, 747–748; Publilius Syrus, *Publilii Syri mimi, similesque sententiae, selectae e poetis antiquis, Latinis*, ed. J.F. Kremsiev; *ibid.*, *Publilii Syrii Sententiae*, ed. E. Woelfflin; *ibid.*, *The Moral Sayings of Publilius Syrus*, trans. D. Lyman.

PYGMALION: [PIGMALION]
PYRAMUS: [PIRAMUS]
PYRRHUS: [PIRRUS]
PYTHAGORAS: [PICTAGORAS]
PYTHONESSA: [PHITONISSA]

QUIRINUS: [QUYRYNE]

QUYRYNE. Quirinus, a god of Sabine origin, was later taken over by the Romans. Romulus had stolen women from the Sabines to be wives for his men when he founded Rome on the Palatine Hill. As time passed, forty years according to legend, Romulus assumed the identity of Quirinus, whose name became another name for Romulus. Quirinus is called a son of Mars in *Aeneid* I.274–275; *Met* XV.863. Dante uses Quirinus as a name for Romulus, *Par* VIII.131–132.

The narrator calls on Mars, father of Quirinus, to help him tell Troilus's story, *Tr* IV.25. **[Romulus]**

Dante, *The Divine Comedy*, ed. and trans. C.S. Singleton, III, 1: 90–91; Ovid, *Met,* ed. and trans. F.J. Miller, II: 426–427; Virgil, *Aeneid*, ed. and trans. H.R. Fairclough, I: 260–261.

R

RACHEL was Laban's daughter, for whom Jacob worked fourteen years to win as his bride. Laban had agreed to Jacob's marriage to Rachel if Jacob gave him seven years' labor, but substituted his elder daughter Leah under the wedding veil. Determined to have Rachel, Jacob agreed to work for Laban another seven years. Rachel bore him Joseph and Benjamin, his favorite sons (Genesis 27–32).

The Prioress, comparing the weeping mother of the murdered schoolboy to Rachel, who weeps for her children, *PrT* 625–627, refers to Jeremiah 31:15. Rachel's weeping is interpreted in Matthew 2:18 as a prophetic reference to the lamentation of the mothers whose children Herod the Great slew. The First Nocturne of Matins on the Feast of the Holy Innocents uses Jeremiah's words about Rachel. [**Eglentyne: Jacob: Laban: Lia: Rebekke: Sarra**]

The name occurs medially, *PrT* 627.

R.J. Schoeck, "Chaucer's Prioress: Mercy and Tender Heart." *The Bridge, a Yearbook of Judaeo-Christian Studies*, ed. J.M. Oesterreicher, 2 (1956): 239–255.

RAM is the English translation of *Aries*, the first sign of the zodiac, and refers to the winged ram of Phrixus. Phrixus and Helle were the children of Athamas of Thebes by his first wife. His second wife Ino hated them and planned to murder them, but they escaped on the back of their winged ram with the Golden Fleece. As they flew over the straits between Asia and Europe, Helle grew giddy and fell off into the sea, which was named the "Hellespont" after her. Phrixus reached Colchis safely, sacrificed the ram to Jupiter, and gave its Golden Fleece to Aeetes, king of Colchis. To retrieve the Fleece, Jason and his Argonauts sailed to Colchis (*Argonauticon* I; *Fasti* III.849–876; *OM* IV.2786–2928).

The young sun is halfway through his course in the Ram on the night the Pilgrims assemble at the Tabard Inn, *Gen Prol* 7–8. Because the sun begins its annual course in Aries, its exaltation or sign of maximum power, it is called "young" in this reference. The Squire says that Canacee awakes as fresh and bright as the young sun when he is in 4 degrees in the Ram, *SqT* 384–387. **[Aries: Canacee²: Valerius Flaccus]**

The name appears medially, *Gen Prol* 8; *SqT* 386.

H. Cummings, "Chaucer's *Prologue* 1–7." *MLN* 37 (1922): 86–90; J.E. Hawkins, "Chaucer and the *Pervigilium Veneris*." *MLN* 49 (1934): 80–83; Ovid, *Fasti*, ed. and trans. J.G. Frazer, 182–185; *OM*, ed. C. de Boer, II, deel 21: 70–73; J.A. Rea, "An Old French Analogue to *General Prologue* 1–18." *PQ* 46 (1967): 128–130; R. Tuve, "Spring in Chaucer and Before Him." *MLN* 52 (1937): 9–16; Valerius Flaccus, *Argonauticon*, ed. and trans. J.H. Mozley, 24–25.

RAPHAEL, one of the three archangels of Heaven, seems to have been of Chaldean origin. He is one of the chief figures of the Book of Tobias (*EJ* XIII: 1549–1550)

The Parson quotes from the Book of Tobias 6.17, where the angel Raphael talks with Thobie about lechery, *ParsT* 906–910. **[Thobie²]**

RAUF is a popular name, generally found among villagers. The modern form is Ralph, with intrusive /l/.

The false summoner encourages the "wenches" of his retinue to spy on the populace and to tell him who lay with the men of the town, with the aristocrats like Sir Robert or the villagers like Rauf, *FrT* 1355–1358.

RAVEN is the constellation Corvus, sacred to Apollo, who adopted its form to escape the monster Typhon. It lies in the southern hemisphere near Libra (*Met* V.329; *OM* V.1812–1821). The Raven's feathers were once white, when he was Apollo's favorite bird. At that time, Apollo loved Coronis of Thessaly. When the Raven discovered that Coronis had other lovers, he complained of her unchastity to Apollo, who immediately strung his bow and killed Coronis with his arrow. As she died, she revealed to him that she was pregnant, and remorse assailed Apollo. In his rage he changed the Raven's white feathers to black (*Met* II.531–632; *Confessio Amantis* III.768–835).

The Manciple tells the tale of Phebus, the Crow, and Coronis, *MancT* 105–362. The Learned Eagle tells Geoffrey that the gods "stellefye" birds, such as the Raven, *HF* II.1004. **[Apollo: Phebus]**

The name appears in medial position.

John Gower, *The Complete Works,* ed. G.C. Macaulay, II: 246–248; Ovid, *Met.,* ed. and trans. F.J. Miller, I: 96–105, 260–261; *OM*, ed. C. de Boer, II, deel 21: 227.

RAZIS. Abu Bakr Muhammad ibn-Zakaruya al-Razi, A.D. 865–925, known in Latin as Rhazes, was born in Ray near Teheran, Persia. He was physician, physicist, alchemist, and the greatest clinician of Islam and the Middle Ages. His most important work, an encyclopedia of medicine called *Kitab al-tibb al-Mansuri (Al-Mansur's Book of Health)*, was dedicated to the sultan of Khorasan, al-Mansur. It was translated into Latin as *Liber medicinalis Almansoris* by Gerard of Cremona in the late twelfth century. Michael Scot used it in his own work, *Physiognomica (Physiognomy)*, in the early thirteenth century. Al-Razi also wrote a famous monograph on smallpox and measles entitled *Kitab al-jadari wal-Lasaba* in Arabic or *De variolis et morbiliis* in Latin, sometimes called *La Peste* and *De pestilentia (On the pestilence)*. It is the oldest description of smallpox. He wrote commentaries on Aristotle's *Categories*; *On Interpretation,* a treatise on Aristotle's *Analytica priora*; a short treatise on metaphysics using commentaries on Aristotle's *Physica (Physics)*; as well as treatises on gynecology, obstetrics, and ophthalmic surgery. Between 1360 and 1385 Merton College owned a copy of the *Liber medicinalis Almansoris*. **[Gerard of Cremona]**

Razis, which means in Arabic "the man from Ray," is a byname of location used as a proper name; it appears in the Physician's catalogue of authorities, *Gen Prol* 432.

A.J. Arberry, "Rhazes on the Philosophic Life." *Asiatic Review* 45 (1949): 703–713; G. Heym, "Al-Razi and Alchemy." *Ambix* 1 (1938): 184–191; F.E. Peters, *Aristoteles Arabus,* 11, 14, 63–64; F.M. Powicke, *The Medieval Books of Merton College,* 138; Rhazes (al-Razi), *A Treatise on the Smallpox and Measles,* trans. W.A. Greenhill; G. Sarton, *Introduction to the History of Science,* I: 609; L. Thorndike, "Latin Manuscripts of Works by Rasis at the Bibliothèque Nationale, Paris." *Bulletin of the History of Medicine* 32 (1958): 54–67.

REBECCA: [REBEKKA]

REBEKKA, REBEKKE. Rebecca was Bethuel's daughter and Laban's sister. She married Isaac and became the mother of Esau and Jacob. She advised Jacob to dress in animal skins and to pretend to be Esau and thus obtain blind old Isaac's blessing. When Esau discovered this trick, he swore to kill Jacob, but Rebecca helped him flee to Laban's farm (Genesis 24). Dante places her in the Celestial Rose as exemplary of wifely obedience (*Par* XXXII.10). The medieval marriage service cited Rebecca for her *sapiens* (wisdom) and Sara for her fidelity.

Rebekke is one of Januarie's *femmes de bon conseil* or women of good counsel, *MerchT* 1362–1365, because she advised Jacob to wear animal skins and thus receive the blessing. The priest bids May take Sarra and Rebekke as her models, *MerchT* 1704–1705; ironically, she does, for she deceives Januarie. The story of Rebekka and Jacob is told in *Mel* 1098. The Friar puns on the name "rebekke," *FrT* 1573–1580, when he compares the old woman to the musical instrument. **[Jacob: Rachel: Sarra: Ysaac]**

Rebekka occurs in *Mel* 1098; *Rebekke,* a spelling variant with final syllabic -*e,* occurs in final rhyming position, *MerchT* 1363, 1704.

Dante, *The Divine Comedy*, ed. and trans. C.S. Singleton, III, 1: 355–359.

REGULUS. Marcus Atilius Regulus, fl. third century B.C., defeated the Carthagenians during his consulship in 256 B.C. and captured Tunis. In 255, however, he was defeated and captured by Xantippus. Cicero uses the story to illustrate political and moral expediency (*De officiis* III.xxvi.99–115).

Lady Philosophy tells how Regulus suffered reversals of Fortune, *Bo* II, *Prosa* 6.70–78.

Regulus is the family name of the Roman clan *Atilia.*

Cicero, *De officiis*, ed. and trans. Walter Miller, 374–397.

REMEDIA AMORIS: [OVIDE]
REMEDIES OF LOVE: [OVIDE]

RENARD is the hero of the medieval cycle of beast fables, *Roman de Renart.* Pierre de St. Cloud was the first French writer to tell stories about Renard the Fox, Ysengrin the Wolf, and Hersint his wife in his *Roman de Renart* (1180–1185). His possible antecedents were Aesop's *Fables* and Nivard's Latin poem *Ysengrimus* (c. 1150). The *Roman* is divided into Branches: Branch Va—including *Renard and Chauntecleer*—by Pierre de St. Cloud, and the others by several writers.

Just as Renard, the son of a fox, behaves like a fox, Jason's son Demophon behaves like Jason: they are both false in love, *LGW* 2448–2449. **[Russell]**

The name does not appear in *The Nun's Priest's Tale,* where it might be expected, but only here, medially, *LGW* 2448.

E. Colledge, *Renard the Fox and other Netherlands Secular Literature*, 45–164; *The History of Renard the Fox from the edition printed by Caxton in 1481,* trans. W. Caxton, ed. D.B. Sands; *Renard the Fox,* trans. P. Terry; *Le Roman de Renard* (Branches I, II, III, IV, V, VIII, X, XV), ed. J. Dufournet; K. Varty, *Reynard the Fox: A Study of the Fox in Medieval English Art.*

RHAZES: [RAZIS]
RHEA SILVIA: [ROMULUS]
RHODOGONE: [RODOGONE]

RICHARD[1]. Richard I, Coeur de Lion, 1157–1199, was the third son of Henry I and Eleanor of Aquitaine. Geoffrey of Vinsauf published his *Poetria nova (New Poetry)* soon after Richard's death, lamenting the king's death in lines 368–430.

The Nun's Priest apostrophizes Geoffrey, who chided Friday, the day on which Richard was slain, *NPT* 3347–3354. The fox seizes Chauntecleer on a Friday, which is also Venus's day.

The name appears once, medially, *NPT* 3348.

E. Faral, *Les Arts poétiques du XIIe et XIIIe siècle*, 208–210; Geoffrey de Vinsauf, *Poetria nova*, trans. M.F. Nims, 29–31; John Gillingham, *Richard the Lionheart*; H.S. Howser, *Richard the First in England*.

RICHARD². Richard II, 1367–1400, was the younger son of Edward, the Black Prince, grandson of Edward III, and nephew of John of Gaunt. He was deposed by Henry Bolingbroke in 1399 and imprisoned in the Tower of London. His subsequent death has been laid to Bolingbroke's charge.

Chaucer addresses the Envoy of the Balade, *Lak of Stedfastness*, to King Richard, admonishing him to cherish his folk and to hate extortion. The dedication of the Envoy has enabled scholars to date the poem between 1386 and 1390.

L.D. Duls, *Richard II in the Early Chronicles*; G. Mathew, *The Court of Richard II*.

RIGA: [PETER¹ RIGA]

RIPHEUS: [RUPHEO]

ROBERT. Sir Robert is used generically as a name for a nobleman who frequents "wenches." *FrT* 1356.

ROBIN: [ROBYN]

ROBYN¹ is the name of the Miller on the pilgrimage to Canterbury. The Host calls him by name, *MillT* 3129. His portrait appears in *Gen Prol* 545–566. **[Robyn²: Symkyn]**

The form is the diminutive of *Robert*.

W.C. Curry, *Chaucer and the Mediaeval Sciences*, 79–90; C.A. Owen, "One Robyn or Two." *MLN* 67 (1952): 336–338; R.A. Pratt, "Was Robin the Miller's Youth Misspent?" *MLN* 59 (1944): 47–49.

ROBYN² is also the name of the carpenter's apprentice in *The Miller's Tale*. There are some similarities between Robin the Miller and Robin the Apprentice: both are exceedingly strong; both can break down doors with their heads. R.A. Pratt has suggested that the Miller tells a tale from his own youthful experiences, when he worked for Oswald the Reeve. C. Owen points out that the carpenter in the Tale is too old to be identified with Oswald.

Robyn, the diminutive of *Robert,* occurs twice, medially, *MillT* 3466, 3555.

C.A. Owen, "One Robin or Two." *MLN* 67 (1952): 336–338; R.A. Pratt, "Was Robin the Miller's Youth Misspent?" *MLN* 59 (1944): 47–49.

ROBYN³. Jolly Robin is the common name for a country fellow.

Pandarus quotes a proverb about Jolly Robyn who "pleyed" in the "haselwode," *Tr* V.1174–1176, a proverb which may refer anachronistically to Robin Hood. Chaucer substitutes an English proverb for original Italian in *Il Filostrato* VII.10.

Boccaccio, *Tutte le opere,* ed. V. Branca, II: 188–189; *Riverside Chaucer,* ed. L. Benson, 1054.

RODOGONE. Rhodogune was one of Darius's daughters. She killed her nurse for suggesting that she remarry after her husband's death. Jerome tells her story in *Epistola adversus Jovinianum (Letter Against Jovinian)* I.45 (*PL* 23: 275).

Rodogone is one of Dorigen's examples of virtuous wives, *FranklT* 1456. **[Dorigen]**

The name appears in medial position.

G. Dempster, "Chaucer at Work on the Complaint in *The Franklin's Tale.*" *MLN* 52 (1937): 6–16; K. Hume, "The Pagan Setting of *The Franklin's Tale* and the Sources of Dorigen's Cosmology." *SN* 44 (1972): 289–294; J. Sledd, "Dorigen's Complaint." *MP* 45 (1947): 36–45.

ROGER¹ of Ware or Hogge of Ware is the Cook on the pilgrimage. He seems to have been a historical person. E.D. Lyon points out that Roger, knight of Ware, was a plaintiff in a plea of debt in 1384–1385, and Edith Rickert shows that Roger Ware sold wood to the king's household (3 Henry IV).

The Cook's portrait appears in *Gen Prol* 379–387; his tale of Perkyn Revelour is unfinished. **[Hogge of Ware: Perkyn Revelour]**

The name appears three times medially, *CoT* 4345, 4353, 4356.

E.D. Lyon, "Roger of Ware, Cook." *MLN* 52 (1937): 491–494; E. Rickert, "'Chaucer's 'Hodge of Ware.'" *TLS,* October 20, 1932, 761.

ROGER². Ruggieri degli Ubaldini was archbishop of Pisa and a member of the Ghibelline party in the years 1278–1295. Count Ugolino della Gherardesca betrayed the Guelphs to him, and he betrayed Ugolino, who was imprisoned with his sons in the Tower of Famine, where they starved to death. Dante places Ruggieri and Ugolino in Antenora among traitors, in the second division of the Ninth Circle of Hell, where Ugolino gnaws on Ruggieri's head (*Inf* XXXIII.1–90).

The Monk tells the story, *MkT* 2407–2462. Chaucer omits the cannibalism of Dante's version. **[Hugelyn]**

Roger, the English variant of Italian *Ruggieri,* appears in medial position, *MkT* 2416.

Dante, *The Divine Comedy,* ed. and trans. C.S. Singleton, I, 1: 348–355; D.K. Fry, "The Ending of *The Monk's Tale.*" *JEGP* 71 (1972): 355–368; T.H. Spencer, "The Story of Ugolino in Dante and Chaucer." *Speculum* 9 (1934): 295–301.

ROLAND: [ROWLAND]
ROMAN DE LA ROSE: [GUILLAUME DE LORRIS]
ROMAN DE LA ROSE: [JEAN DE MEUN]
ROMANCE OF THE ROSE: [GUILLAUME DE LORRIS]
ROMANCE OF THE ROSE: [JEAN DE MEUN]

ROMULUS, a Roman hero, was said to be the son of Mars. His mother was Rhea Silvia, a Vestal virgin and daughter of King Numitor. Amulius usurped the throne from Numitor, and when Rhea Silvia bore the twins, Amulius ordered them thrown into the Tiber. A she-wolf, the animal of Mars, rescued them and succoured them until one of the royal herdsmen found them and brought them up. They grew to be mighty warriors and founded the city of Rome on the Palatine Hill (*Fasti* II.491–501). After ruling for forty years, Romulus disappeared in a storm and became the god Quirinus. Macrobius states that Romulus was assured a place in the heavens because he practiced all the virtues (*Commentarius in somnium Scipionis,* II.xvii.7–8).

The mother of Romulus appears among love's martyrs, *PF* 292; in this line Chaucer suggests that he has forgotten her name. E.T. Donaldson suggests that Chaucer may have seen her name in the *Pervigilium Veneris* (*The Vigil of Venus*), a poem of unknown authorship, written not earlier than the second century A.D. The Dreamer thinks that he is not Romulus as the eagle snatches him up, *HF* II.589. **[Mars: Quyryne]**

The name appears once medially, *HF* II.589, and once in final rhyming position, *PF* 292.

E.T. Donaldson, "Venus and the Mother of Romulus: *The Parliament of Fowls* and the *Pervigilium Veneris.*" *ChauR* 14 (1979–1980): 313–318; Macrobius, *Commentary on the Dream of Scipio,* trans. W.H. Stahl, 244–245; *ibid., In somnium Scipionis,* ed. J. Willis, 152; Ovid, *Fasti,* ed. and trans. J.G. Frazer, 92–93.

RONYAN, RONYON, a supposed saint, has evoked much comment. Harry Bailly swears by this saint as he comments on the pitiful qualities in *The Physician's Tale, PardI* 310. Some scholars have tried to show that St. Ninian is meant; that the word means "testicle" and balances the "coillons" at the end of *The Pardoner's Tale.* The Pardoner echoes Bailly and swears by St. Ronyan when he agrees to tell a tale, *PardI* 320. Chaucer may also have meant St. Ronan, a Celtic saint who came to pre-Christian Brittany at the end of the first century. The holly in the saint's legend was very likely used as an agent of birth control and is appropriate to the Pardoner.

Ronyan appears in final rhyming position, *PardI* 310; *Ronyon* also appears in final rhyming position, *PardI* 320.

E.P. Hamp, "St. Ninian/Ronyan Again." *Celtica* 3 (1956): 290–294; A.S. Haskell, "The Pardoner's St. Ronyan." *Essays on Chaucer's Saints*, 17–25; J. Sledd, "*Canterbury Tales,* C, 310, 320: 'By Seint Ronyan.'" *MS* 13 (1951): 226–233.

ROSARIE: [ARNALD OF THE NEWE TOUN]

ROSEMOUNDE. Chaucer addresses a poem to this lady, whose identity is unknown. Edith Rickert suggests Lady Alice de Bryenne, betrothed to Richard II while they were both children. Rossell H. Robbins suggests Princess Isabella of Valois, the seven-year-old bride of Richard II. He posits that one of the dresses in her trousseau, embroidered with pearl roses, may have inspired the name Rosemound. The lady addressed in the poem seems to have been very young. There is no way of knowing her identity for certain.

Rosemounde, a variant of *Rosa mundi,* rose of the world, appears in final rhyming position, *Rosemounde* 15.

Chaucer, *The Minor Poems, Part One,* ed. G. Pace and A. David, 161–162; E. Rickert, "A Leaf from a Fourteenth-Century Letter Book." *MP* 25 (1927): 249–255; R.H. Robbins, "Chaucer's 'To Rosemounde.'" *Studies in the Literary Imagination* 4 (1971): 73–81.

ROWLAND. Roland, nephew of Charlemagne, is the hero of the twelfth-century *chanson de geste, La Chanson de Roland.* Genelon, his stepfather, betrayed the French to the Saracens, who wiped out the battalion.

The Man in Black says that he would be worse than Ganelon, who purchased the treason of Roland and Oliver, if he forgets his lady, *BD* 1123–1124. **[Charles Olyver: Genelloun-Olyver]**

The name appears medially, *BD* 1123.

La Chanson de Roland, ed. C. Segre; *The Song of Roland,* ed. S.J. Herrtage.

RUFUS of Ephesus, fl. first century A.D. under Trajan, emperor A.D. 98–117. He was the greatest Greek anatomist and physician of the Roman Empire after Galen. He made detailed researches on monkeys and pigs and wrote the first descriptions of the eye. His treatise on the pulse is the first attempt to base pathology on anatomy and physiology.

Rufus is one of the Physician's authorities, *Gen Prol* 430.

The phrase, "eek Rufus," occurring in final rhyming position, *Gen Prol* 430, suggests that it is added for the rhyme.

G. Sarton, *Introduction to the History of Science*, I: 281–282; L. Thorndike, *History of Magic and Experimental Science*, II: 277.

RUGGIERI DEGLI UBALDINI: [ROGER²]

RUPHEO. Ripheus was one of Aeneas's comrades in the Trojan War, *Aeneid* II.339–343. Boccaccio's Rifeo is one of the Trojan heroes taken prisoner by the Greeks, *Il Filostrato* (1333–1339) IV.3.

Antenor is taken prisoner despite the efforts of Ripheo and other brave Trojans, *Tr* IV.50–56. [**Antenor: Polite: Polydamas: Polymestore: Santippe: Sarpedon**]

Rupheo, a variant of Boccaccio's *Rifeo*, with primary stress on the penultimate syllable, appears once, in final rhyming position, *Tr* IV.53.

Boccaccio, *Tutte le opere,* ed. V. Branca, II: 110; Virgil, *Aeneid*, ed. and trans. H.R. Fairclough, I: 316–317.

RUSSELL is the fox in *The Nun's Priest's Tale*. He flatters Chauntecleer and persuades him to close his eyes and sing. Then he grabs him by the throat and runs off with him. Chauntecleer persuades the fox to open his mouth to talk to the farmhands behind them and so saves his life. [**Chauntecleer: Renard**]

The name occurs once, *NPT* 3334, derived from OF *russel*, "reddish."

SAGITTARIE, SAGITTARIUS, the constellation the Archer or the Centaur, is the ninth sign of the zodiac and the day house of Jupiter (*Tetrabiblos* I.17). It is the hot and dry sign (*Confessio Amantis* VII.1141–1168). A large constellation in the southern hemisphere near Scorpius, it is called a sign of the south. It is the largest portion of the Milky Way, our galaxy.

Sagittarius is one of the twelve signs of the zodiac, *Astr* I.8.4. It lies directly opposite Gemini, *Astr* II.6.16. The signs from the head or beginning of Cancer to the end of Sagittarius are called "sovereign" or western signs and take more than two hours to rise above the horizon, *Astr* II.28.35. Capricorn obeys the sign Sagittarius, *Astr* II.28.38. **[Jupiter]**

Sagittarie, the ME variant of Latin *Sagittarius*, occurs only in *The Treatise on the Astrolabe*.

Chaucer, *A Treatise on the Astrolabe*, ed. W.W. Skeat, 38–39; John Gower, *The Complete Works*, ed. G.C. Macaulay, III: 264; Ptolemy, *Tetrabiblos,* ed. and trans. F.E. Robbins, 81.

SAGITTARIUS: [SAGITTARIE]

SALOMON. Solomon, the second son of David and Bathsheba, reigned as king of Israel during the tenth century B.C. and became legendary for his wisdom and for his many wives: seven hundred wives and three hundred concubines (II Kings 11:3). During the Middle Ages collections of aphorisms known as the "Sayings of Solomon" were circulated.

Salomon appears as a fool of love, *KnT* 1937–1942; *MerchT* 2291–2302. Nicholas quotes Salomon, *MillT* 3526–3530, but the reference is to Jesus of Syrach, Ecclesiasticus 32:19. Dame Alys wishes she could be sexually refreshed half as many times as Salomon, *WBP* 35–40. He is a misogynist in Jankin's book of wikked wives, *WBP* 679; the Book of Proverbs is bound up in that anthology. Solomon's famous saying, "Everything hath time," appears in *FrT* 147; *ClT* 6; *MerchT* 1972; *Tr* II.989, III.855. The quotations in *MillT* 3526–3530 and *MerchT* 1478–1486 are not from Solomon but from Jesus of Syrach. Solomon is the wise man of *MerchT* 2242–2248; *CYT* 960–961; *MancT* 314–315, and a magician, *SqT* 247–252. W.A. Clouston recounts the legends from Jewish and Muslim sources about Solomon's magic ring on which was engraved the Most Great Name and points out that Solomon's ring plays a part in many Eastern romances.

Dame Prudence quotes Proverbs 25:20 at *Mel* 997; the quotation at *Mel* 1003 is not from Salomon but is attributed to Pseudo-Bede *Liber Proverbium* (see also *MillT* 3530). *Mel* 1047 is from Jesus of Syrach's Ecclesiasticus 32:6; Melibee quotes Salomon's Ecclesiastes 7:28 at *Mel* 1057; from Jesus of Syrach's Ecclesiasticus 25:30 at *Mel* 1059. Dame Prudence answers this quotation, *Mel* 1075–1078, but quotes Ecclesiasticus 25:16, and adds a quotation from Proverbs 21:19 at *Mel* 1087. Melibee quotes Proverbs 24:24 at *Mel* 1113. Dame Prudence quotes Proverbs 27:9, *Mel* 1158. The quotation at *Mel* 1167 is not from Salomon but from Jesus of Syrach's Ecclesiasticus 6:6. Dame Prudence quotes Proverbs 11:14 at *Mel* 1171; from Jesus of Syrach's Ecclesiasticus 8:20, not from Salomon, *Mel* 1173; from Proverbs 29:5, *Mel* 1178. Dame Prudence quotes Jesus of Syrach's Ecclesiasticus 12:10, not from Salomon, *Mel* 1186; she quotes Salomon, Proverbs 31:4 at *Mel* 1194; Proverbs 28:14 at *Mel* 1317; Proverbs 20:3 at *Mel* 1485; Proverbs 19:11 at *Mel* 1512; Proverbs 15:18 at *Mel* 1514; Proverbs 19:19 at *Mel* 1539. Melibee quotes Proverbs 26:17 at *Mel* 1542 and Ecclesiastes 10:19 at *Mel* 1550. Instead of Salomon, Dame Prudence quotes Jesus of Syrach's Ecclesiasticus 40:28 at *Mel* 1571; Ecclesiasticus 30:17 at *Mel* 1572; she quotes Proverbs 28:20 at *Mel* 1578, Jesus of Syrach's Ecclesiasticus 33:27, not Salomon, at *Mel* 1589, but Proverbs 28:19 at *Mel* 1590; Proverbs 15:16 at *Mel* 1628; Proverbs 22:1 at *Mel* 1638; Jesus of Syrach's Ecclesiasticus 41:12, not Salomon at *Mel* 1639; Solomon's Ecclesiastes 5:11 at *Mel* 1653, Jesus of Syrach's Ecclesiasticus 3:27, not Salomon, at *Mel* 1671; from Proverbs 28:14, *Mel* 1696. Melibee quotes Proverbs 28:23 at *Mel* 1704. Dame Prudence quotes Ecclesiastes 7:4–6 at *Mel* 1707; Proverbs 16:7 at *Mel* 1719. The wicked adversaries quote Jesus of Syrach's Ecclesiasticus 6:5, not Salomon, at *Mel* 1740. Dame Prudence quotes Jesus of Syrach's Ecclesiasticus 33:19–20 at *Mel* 1754. The Parson quotes Proverbs 16:6 at *ParsT* 119; Proverbs 11:22 at *ParsT* 155; Proverbs 11:7 at *ParsT* 227; Proverbs 25:18 at *ParsT* 566; Proverbs 28:15 at *ParsT* 568; Proverbs 8:17 at *ParsT* 709; he quotes from Jesus of Syrach's Ecclesiasticus 26:10, not from Solomon, *ParsT* 854. **[David: Jhesu Syrak]**

Salomon, the ME and OF variant, never occurs initially but does occur seven times in medial positions, *MillT* 3529; *CoT* 4330; *ClT* 6; *MerchT* 1487,

2242; *MancT* 314, 344; and eight times in final rhyming position, *KnT* 1942; *WBP* 35, 679; *MerchT* 1483, 2277, 2292; *SqT* 250; *CYT* 961.

W.A. Clouston, *On the Magical Elements in Chaucer's Squire's Tale, with Analogues*; *EJ* XV: 96.

SAMPSON, SAMSOUN. Samson, the man most famous for his strength, was one of the judges of Israel. He revealed to Delilah that his strength lay in his uncut hair, and she betrayed his secret to the Philistines. She stealthily cut his hair while he lay asleep in her lap; then the Philistines captured him, blinded him, and made him their slave. His strength returned as his hair grew. One day the Philistines called him to entertain them at a great feast in honor of their god, and Samson pulled down the hall, killing himself and his enemies (Judges 12–16).

Saturn says that he caused Samson's death, *KnT* 2466. The death of Samson is written in the stars, *MLT* 197–201. Samson's story is bound into Jankyn's anthology, *WBP* 721–723. The Monk's story, *MkT* 2015–2094, emphasizes the folly of revealing secrets to wives, as in *RR* 16541–16700. The Monk gives *Judicum* as his source, *MkT* 2046. *Judicum* is the Latin genitive plural from the full title *Liber Judicum (The Book of Judges)*. It is evident, however, that Chaucer follows Boccaccio's story in *De casibus virorum illustrium* I.17. J.E. Grennen suggests *Enseignements* by Geoffrey de la Tour-Landry as another possible source. Samson never drank wine, *PardT* 554–555; *MkT* 2055. The strength of Samson is a medieval commonplace, *ParsT* 955. Samson is an example of the folly of suicide; he died for Dalida, *BD* 738–741. **[Dalida]**

Sampson never appears initially. It occurs five times in medial positions, *MLT* 201; *WBP* 721; *MkT* 2031, 2055, 2090; and once in final rhyming position, *BD* 738. *Sampsoun* appears once initially, *MkT* 2023; five times in medial positions, *KnT* 2466; *PardT* 555; *MkT* 2015, 2052, 2075; and twice in final rhyming position, *PardT* 554, 572. Both forms are OF variants.

Boccaccio, *De casibus virorum illustrium*, ed. P.G. Ricci and V. Zaccaria, 84–90; J.E. Grennen, "'Sampsoun' in *The Canterbury Tales:* Chaucer Adapting a Source." *NM* 47 (1966): 117–222.

SAMSON: [SAMPSON]

SAMUEL was the Israelite prophet and judge who lived in the eleventh century B.C. Born in Ramah, Samuel was dedicated by his mother to a Nazarite life in the sanctuary of Shiloh. His career is closely interwoven with that of Saul, the first king of Israel (I and II Kings). After Samuel had died, Saul visited the Witch of Endor and commanded her to call up Samuel's ghost, from whom he then asked advice (I Kings 28: 3–35).

The fiend assures the cursed summoner that sometimes the devils assume the shape of the dead and speak reasonably and fairly as the

Phitonissa did to Samuel, although some people say that she did not speak with Samuel, *FrT* 1506–1512. The Pardoner preaches on the evils of wine and refers his listeners to Lamuel; he emphasizes that he means Lamuel, not Samuel, *PardT* 584–585. **[Phitonissa]**

The name appears once in medial position, *PardT* 585, and once in final rhyming position, *FrT* 1510.

SANTIAGO: [JAME]

SANTIPPE. Santippo was a Trojan soldier, taken prisoner with Antenor in Boccaccio's *Il Filostrato* (1333–1339) IV.3.

Antenor is taken prisoner despite the brave fighting of Santippe and other Trojan heroes, *Tr* IV.52. **[Antenor: Monesteo: Polite: Polydamas: Polymestore: Rupheo: Sarpedon]**

The name appears once, initially, *Tr* IV.52.

Boccaccio, *Tutte le opere*, ed. V. Branca, II: 110.

SAPOR. Shapur, the hereditary name of the Sassanid kings of Persia, is applied to the most famous one, Shapur I, who reigned A.D. 241–272. He continually attacked the eastern provinces of the Roman Empire and captured the emperor Valerian in 260. Odaenatus and Zenobia defeated Shapur and forced him to withdraw from Roman territory (Boccaccio, *De claris mulieribus* XCVIII).

The Monk gives Petrarch as his source for the story of Cenobia's defeat of Sapor, *MkT* 2319–2326; Chaucer, however, is following Boccaccio. **[Cenobia: Odenake]**

Sapor, the Latin variant that appears in Boccaccio's work, occurs in medial position, *MkT* 2320.

Boccaccio, *CFW*, trans. G. Guarino, 226–230; *ibid., De claris mulieribus*, ed. V. Zaccaria, 678–682; Trebellius Pollio, *Tyranni Triginta*, XXX; *Scriptores historiae Augustae*, ed. and trans. D. Magie, III: 135–143.

SARAH: [SARRA]

SARPEDON was a son of Zeus by Laodamia. As king of the Lycians, he was the best warrior among the Trojans' allies. Patroclus killed Sarpedon against Zeus's wishes, who then sent Sleep and Death to carry him back to Lycia (*Iliad* XVI.477–683). Virgil says that Sarpedon was killed before Troy (*Aeneid* I.99–101). Boccaccio mentions Sarpedon in a list of Trojan heroes taken prisoner with Antenor, *Il Filostrato* (1333–1339) IV.3.

Antenor is taken prisoner despite the valiant efforts of Sarpedon and other heroes, *Tr* IV.52. Troilus spends some time with him after Criseyde's departure for the Greek camp, *Tr* V.400–501. **[Antenor: Moneteso: Polite: Polydamas: Polymestore: Rupheo: Santippe]**

Sarpedon occurs medially seven times, *Tr* IV.52, V.403, 434, 435, 479, 489, V.500, and once in final rhyming position, *Tr* V.431.

Boccaccio, *Tutte le opere*, ed. V. Branca, II: 110; Homer, *Iliad*, ed. and trans. A.T. Murray, II: 198–215; Virgil, *Aeneid*, ed. and trans. H.R. Fairclough, I: 248–249.

SARRA. Sarah was Abraham's wife and Isaac's mother (Genesis 9:1–7). Biblical scholars of the Middle Ages made Sarah an example of wifely obedience, basing their interpretation on I Peter 3:6. Dante places her in the Celestial Rose (*Par* XXXII.10). The medieval marriage service cited Sarah for her fidelity and Rebecca for her wisdom.

The priest exhorts May to be like Sarra and Rebekke, *MerchT* 1704–1705, part of the medieval marriage service. Sarah, unlike Rebecca, does not deceive her husband, but she is cruel to Hagar, his lawful concubine. **[Abraham: Rachel: Rebekke: Ysaac]**

The form, a pronunciation variant, occurs medially, *MerchT* 1704.

Dante, *The Divine Comedy*, ed. and trans. C.S. Singleton, III, 1: 355–359.

SATAN, SATHANAS. Satan is the name Lucifer acquired after he fell from heaven (Isaiah 14:12–15; Job 1:6).

Absolon vows his soul to Sathanas in hope of revenge for the misplaced kiss, *MillT* 3750. Satan knows how to manage women, *MLT* 365–367. Satan tempts the young knight with hot love for Custance, *MLT* 582–602. Custance has no champion except he who bound Satan, *MLT* 631–635. Satan bound appears in Revelation 20:12, *Inf* XXXIV.28–29, *Ovide Moralisé* XII.4293–4300. Sathanas appears as a yeoman to the summoner in *The Friar's Tale*. The Summoner retorts by giving a picture of friars under the tail of Sathanas, *SumT* 1685–1691. The Prioress says that Sathanas made his nest in the hearts of the Jews and encouraged them to take action against the schoolboy, *PrT* 558–564. The Monk's first tragedy tells of Lucifer's fall and how he became Sathanas, *MkT* 1999–2006. The Parson quotes St. Paul that Sathanas can transform himself into an angel of light, *ParsT* 894–895, and quotes II Corinthians 11:14. The poet dares not say that marriage is the chain of Satanas, but he dares to say that were Satan unbound, he would never be bound again, *Bukton* 9–16. **[Lucifer²]**

The name in Hebrew means "adversary." *Satan*, the English variant, occurs once, initially, *MLT* 582; twice in medial positions, *MLT* 365, 634; *Sathanas*, the medieval Latin variant, appears six times in medial positions, *MLT* 598; *SumT* 1686, 1687, 1689; *MkT* 200; *Bukton* 10; and four times in final rhyming position, *MillT* 3750; *FrT* 1526, 1685; *PrT* 558, and *ParsT* 895.

Dante, *The Divine Comedy*, ed. and trans. C.S. Singleton, I, 1: 362–363; F.C. Jennings, *Satan, His Person, Work, Place and Destiny;* B.G. Koonce, "Satan the Fowler." *MS* 21 (1959): 176–184; T.H. Spencer, "Chaucer's Hell: a Study of Medieval Convention." *Speculum* 2 (1927): 177–200; B.L. Witlieb, "Chaucer and the *Ovide Moralisé.*" *N&Q* 215 (1970): 206.

SATURN: [SATURNE]

SATURNE, SATURNUS. Saturn was the oldest of the Roman gods, identified with the Greek Kronos, father of all the gods. In a fight for supremacy, Jupiter defeated and castrated Saturn and threw his genitals into the sea. From their foam emerged Venus (*Met* IV.535–537, XIV.585). This version of Venus's birth appears in Isidore, *Etym* VIII.xi.77, and in Petrus Berchorius's *De formis figurisque deorum*, fol. l^v.b.7–9. Saturn's chilly character is associated with the qualities of the planet.

Pale Saturnus the cold, who causes all sorts of disasters, appears in *KnT* 2438–2452. He asks Pluto to send up a fury from the Underworld, *KnT* 2684–2685, and it frightens Arcite's horse, which throws his rider. Criseyde vows that, if she be false, may Saturne's daughter Juno make her as mad as Athamas, *Tr* IV.1534–1540.

Saturn is the seventh planet, counting away from the earth, farthest from the light and warmth of the sun; hence it is called the cold planet (see Ptolemaic map). It is the maleficent planet (*Tetrabiblos* I.5). Those born under Saturn are malicious and cruel; all his works are grievous to men's health (*Confessio Amantis* VII.935–946).

Saturne is the planet under whose influence men are imprisoned, *KnT* 1088, 1328. Saturne finds a way to please both Mars and Venus, *KnT* 2437–2452. He lists the disasters his planet causes, *KnT* 2453–2478. Lead is Saturnus's metal, *CYT* 828. Josephus stands on a pillar of lead and iron, *HF* III.1430–1450; lead is Saturn's metal and iron is Mars's metal, and Josephus has written about the Jewish wars. Josephus is of "secte Saturnyn," *HF* III.1432–1433, because as Saturn is the father of all the planets so Judaism is the father of all sects, since all sects trace themselves to the sect of the Jews. Chaucer and Jean de Meun identify the old cold planet with Saturnus, *Bo* IV, *Metr* 1.11–12. Saturne, in conjunction with Jupiter and Cancer, causes the downpour of the smoky rain that prevents Criseyde from returning home, *Tr* III.624–630. Troilus prays Venus to soften any evil influence of Mars and Saturne that may have been present in his horoscope, *Tr* III.716. Ypermestra dies in prison because of bad aspects of Saturne, *LGW* 2596–2599. The first and eighth inequal hour of Saturday belongs to Saturn, *Astr* II.4.30–35, *Astr* II.12.22–23. **[Dragoun: Josephus: Venus]**

Saturne occurs twice, initially, *KnT* 2450; *Tr* III.625; six times in final rhyming position, *KnT* 1328, 2453, 2685; *Tr* III.716; *HF* III.1449, *LGW* 2597, and in the *Treatise on the Astrolabe. Saturnes,* the ME genitive case, occurs initially, *Tr* IV.1538; *Saturnus,* the Latin variant, appears twice initially, *KnT* 2668; *CYT* 828; and once medially, *KnT* 2443.

Petrus Berchorius, *Ovidius Moralizatus,* ed. J. Engels, 4–5; John Gower, *The Complete Works,* ed. G.C. Macaulay, III: 258; Isidore, *Etymologiae,* ed. W.M. Lindsay, I; D.B. Loomis, "Saturn in Chaucer's *Knight's Tale.*" *Anglia* 14 (1968): 149–161; A. Miller, "Chaucer's 'Secte Saturnyn.'" *MLN* 47 (1932): 99–102; Ovid, *Met,* ed.

and trans. F.J. Miller, I: 216–217, II: 340–343; Ptolemy, *Tetrabiblos*, ed. and trans. F.E. Robbins, 39.

SCARIOT. Judas Iscariot was the disciple who betrayed Jesus (Mark 14:43–46; Luke 22:1–6). His name became synonymous with treachery.

The Nun's Priest calls Russell the fox a "newe Scariot" in an apostrophe on treachery, *NPT* 3226–3236. The first of several, this apostrophe is a parody of the apostrophes in Geoffrey de Vinsauf's *Poetria nova* 264–450. References to Judas's betrayal appear in Old French fables of the adventures of Renard. In *Renart le Contrefait*, Branch VII 35485–35486, Hubert the Kite gives Renard the example of Judas as a picture of repentance. The York cycle drama includes a play called "The Remorse of Judas." **[Gaufred: Judas]**

Scariot is formed by aphesis, through loss of the initial unstressed vowel. Its initial *I* has been elided with the final syllabic *-e* of the preceding *newe*, *NPT* 3226.

E. Faral, *Les arts poétiques*, 205–211; Geoffrey de Vinsauf, *Poetria nova*, trans. M.F. Nims, 25–32; R.A. Pratt, "Three Old French Sources of the Nonnes Preestes Tale." *Speculum* 47 (1972): 653; *The York Plays*, ed. R. Beadle.

SCEDASUS: [CEDASUS]
SCIPIO: [CIPIOUN]
SCIPION: [CIPIOUN]
SCIPIOUN: [CIPIOUN]

SCITHERO. Marcus Tullius Cicero, 106–43 B.C., was one of the greatest Roman orators and statesmen. His speeches as a lawyer show every kind of rhetorical device and a variety of literary styles. The most important of his works, which greatly influenced medieval writers, especially Jerome, Ambrose, and Augustine, are *De oratore (On Oratory)*, *De re publica (On Public Matters,* of which Book Six is the famous *In somnium Scipionis [On Scipio's Dream])*, *De officiis (On Offices)*, *De senectute (On Old Age)*, and *De amicitia (On Friendship)*, and several volumes of letters to his friends. One work, *Rhetorica ad herennium*, written by one Cornificius (fl. 86–82 B.C.), was attributed to Cicero during the medieval period and greatly influenced the rhetoricians of the period, Geoffrey de Vinsauf and Matthew of Vendome, whose works Chaucer knew and used frequently.

Chaucer's references to "colours of rhetoric" and "figures," *ClT* 16; *FranklT* 722, are terms appropriated from *Rhetorica ad herennium*. The Franklin says that he has not slept on Parnassus nor learned Marcus Tullius Scithero, *FranklT* 721–722. **[Tullius]**

The peculiar spelling *Cithero*, a variant of *Cicero*, the family name, has been found in manuscripts dated before and during the fourteenth century and may account for Chaucer's *Scithero*. It is also found in Walter Map's

Dissuassio Valerii ad Rufinus philosophum ne uxorem ducat (1181–1183).
The name appears in final rhyming position, *FranklT* 722.

E. Faral, *Les Arts poétiques*, 48; R.A. Pratt, "The Importance of Manuscripts for the
    Study of Medieval Education, as Revealed by the Learning of Chaucer." *PMRS,
    Bulletin* 20 (1940): 20, 48.

SCOGAN is generally believed to be Henry Scogan, c. 1361–1407. He
inherited the manor of Haviles when his older brother John Scogan died.
He was part of the royal household in the 1390s as tutor to the sons of Henry
IV. He refers to Chaucer as his master in his only work, *Moral balade*, where
he quotes entire Chaucer's poem *Gentilesse.*

In *Lenvoy de Chaucer a Scogan* Chaucer humorously accuses Scogan of
causing the recent deluge of rain. Since he has decided to forswear his lady
at Michaelmas, Scogan has caused Venus to weep such tears. **[Bukton:
Grisel]**

Scogan appears once initially, *Scog* 43; six times in medial position, *Scog*
13, 20, 21, 25, 36, 47.

R.F. Green, *Poets and Prince Pleasers,* 75–79; M.N. Hallmundsson, "Chaucer's Circle:
    Henry Scogan and his Friends." *Medievalia et Humanistica,* new series 10
    (1981): 129–139; G.L. Kittredge, "Henry Scogan." *Harvard Studies and Notes* 1
    (1892): 109–117; R. Lenaghan, "Chaucer's *Envoy to Scogan*: The Uses of Literary
    Conventions." *ChauR* 10 (1975–1976): 46–61.

SCORPIO, SCORPIOUN, SCORPIUS, the constellation the Scorpion, is
the eighth sign of the zodiac, the day house of Mars, the depression of the
Moon (*Tetrabiblos* I.18, 19), and the moist and cold sign (*Confessio Amantis*
VII.1121–1140). It lies in the southern hemisphere near Libra, partly in the
Milky Way.

Pheton, unable to control his father's horses, let go the reins when he
passed Scorpion, *HF* II.944–959. It is one of the signs of the zodiac, *Astr* I.8.4.
At 9 P.M. Scorpius is in 10 degrees of its ascent, *Astr* II.3.56–58. The sign lies
directly opposite Taurus, *Astr* II.6.16. It is the "sovereign" or western sign
that Aquarius obeys, *Astr* II.28.38. **[Pheton]**

Scorpio and *Scorpius*, both Latin variants, occur in the *Treatise on the
Astrolabe; Scorpioun*, the OF variant, appears in final rhyming position, *HF*
II.948.

John Gower, *The Complete Works*, ed. G.C. Macaulay, III: 263–264; Ptolemy, *Tetra-
    biblos*, ed. and trans. F.E. Robbins, 87, 89.

SCYLLA: [SILLA]
SEA GOAT: [CAPRICORN]
SEA SERPENT: [IDRA]
SEMIRAMIS: [SEMYRAME]

SEMYRAME, SEMYRAMIS, SEMYRAMUS. Semiramis, fl. late eighth–early ninth century B.C., whose Assyrian name was Sammuramat, was the wife of Ninus, king of Assyria, and after he died she ruled from 810 to 805 B.C. Her life story is a mixture of legend and fact, since she won a reputation in war as a skillful campaigner and conqueror of Ethiopia, wore trousers to hide her sex from her soldiers, and took many lovers. She also built and fortified Babylon (Orosius I.iv.4.7–8). The reputation for arms and good administration was overshadowed during the medieval period by one for licentiousness. Irene Samuel shows that Semiramis's sexuality was mentioned in the ancient sources, but that ancient historians did not make it of first importance in her life. Orosius brought her sexuality to the fore, downplaying her other qualities. Dante places Semiramis among the lustful, *Inf* V.58–60, and Boccaccio says that she stained all her accomplishments when she gave herself to many men, *De claris mulieribus* II. Chaucer follows these sources in the treatment of Semiramis.

The Man of Law calls the Sultan's mother, who kills her son, "Virago, thou Semyrame the secounde," *MLT* 358–359. Semiramis did not kill her son; on the contrary, Boccaccio says that she was his lover and that she usurped the throne from him. Since Semyramis wore trousers and led the troops, the word "virago" coupled with her name implies the meaning of "mannish." Semiramis is among those who died for love, *PF* 288. She built and fortified Babylon, the city of Pyramus and Thisbe, *LGW* 706–709. **[Nynus: Piramus: Tesbee]**

Semyrame, the ME variant, occurs in medial position, *MLT* 359; *Semyramis* occurs initially, *PF* 288; and *Semyramus* occurs in final rhyming position, *LGW* 707.

Boccaccio, *CFW,* trans. G. Guarino, 4–7; *ibid., De claris mulieribus,* ed. V. Zaccaria, 33–38; Dante, *The Divine Comedy,* ed. and trans. C.S. Singleton, I, 1: 50–51; Paulus Orosius, *Seven Books of History Against the Pagans,* trans. I.W. Raymond, 49–50; J. Parr, "Chaucer's Semiramis." *ChauR* 5 (1970): 57–61; *Riverside Chaucer,* ed. L. Benson, 860; I. Samuel, "Semiramis: The History of a Legend in the Middle Ages." *Medievalia et Humanistica,* Fasc. III (1944): 32–44.

SENEC, SENECA, SENEK, SENEKKE. Lucius Annaeus Seneca, 4 B.C.–A.D. 65, was born in Cordova, Spain, and died at Campania. By A.D. 37, the time of Caligula's accession to the imperial throne, Seneca had become an orator of the first class. He was banished by the Empress Messalina to Corsica in 41 on a charge of adultery but was recalled by Agrippina to be tutor to her son Nero in 49. Nero made Seneca a minister in 54, and Seneca found himself confronted with the emperor's brutality and madness. He composed Nero's speech explaining the death of Agrippina, whom Nero had put to death. However, when he found he could not check the emperor's excesses, he retired to Campania in 64, having by then amassed a considerable fortune. He was named in the Pisonian conspiracy in 65, and Nero commanded him to take his own life. He opened his veins while lying in a hot bath.

Seneca's reputation reached its pinnacle during the Middle Ages. His dialogues, letters, and essays became basic texts of medieval rhetoric with Cicero's writings. His moral essays persuaded medieval scholars that he was almost Christian, and there grew a tradition of a correspondence between Seneca and St. Paul. Seneca's *Letters to Lucilius* were known by the twelfth century in the whole of France, a large part of Germany, in Austria, and in England. Manuscripts were imported into England from France following the Norman Conquest in 1066. Many Benedictine and Cluniac houses had manuscripts of the *Letters* in France as well as in England. The *Letters* were quoted by Bernard of Clairvaux, William of St. Thierry, Abelard, William of Malmesbury, and Otto of Freising. Albertanus of Brescia knew Seneca's *Letters* in the Q manuscript; he quotes frequently from the *Letters* throughout his work *Liber consolationis et consilii* (*The Book of Consolation and Counsel*), written in 1246.

There is no proof that Chaucer knew Seneca at firsthand. Many of the quotations from Seneca are in his sources, and when they are not, it is likely that he learned of them from anthologies and *florilegia*. One such anthology was *De moribus,* a collection of works by Seneca, Publilius Syrus, Ausonius, and Lactantius and attributed, wrongly, to Martin of Braga (d. A.D. 579). Modern scholars refer to its author as the pseudo-Seneca. Martin of Braga's work, *Formula vitae honestae,* written after 570 and taken directly from Seneca, was also attributed to Seneca by A.D. 1100 under the name *De quattuor virtutibus cardinalibus* (Barlow 5–7). Seneca's aphorism on the loss of time, *MLT* 27–28; *Tr* IV.1283, was current in the preaching of Chaucer's time. S. Wenzel points out that in Bromyard's *Predicantium* there are two passages expressing the same idea and written in the margin next to each passage is the word "senc."

The old wife advises her knight to read Seneca, *WBT* 1168; she quotes Seneca on poverty, *Epistle* XVII.3–5, *WBT* 1184. The friar tells the story of the angry governor, identified as Piso in Seneca's *De ira* I.18, *SumT* 2019. The story about Cambyses, *SumT* 2043–2073, comes from *De ira* 3:14, *Epistle* 86.1; and the story about Cyrus, *SumT* 2079–2088, comes from *De ira* 3:21. Januarie quotes Seneca, *MerchT* 1375–1376, a reference from Albertanus Brixiensis, *Liber consolationis* 18. The passage from Seneca, *MerchT* 1523–1525, is influenced in a general way by *De beneficiis* I.14–15 (Robinson 714). The Pardoner quotes Seneca on drunkenness, *Epistle* LXXXIII.18, *PardT* 492–497. The quotations in *The Tale of Melibee* appear in the sources *Liber consolationis et consilii* by Albertanus Brixiensis (1246) and *Le Livre de Mellibee et de Prudence* by Renaud de Louens (after 1336). Dame Prudence quotes Seneca, *Epistle* LXXIV.30, *Mel* 984. Instead of Seneca, she quotes Publilius Syrus, *Sententiae* 281, *Mel* 1127. She quotes from pseudo-Seneca, *De moribus, Sententiae* 16 (*PL* 72: 29), not from Seneca, *Mel* 1147; from Publilius Syrus *Sententiae* 389, *Mel* 1185; Dame Prudence says she quotes Seneca, *Mel* 1226, but the quotation cannot be identified; she quotes from Publilius Syrus, *Sententiae* 607, not Seneca, *Mel* 1320; from Publilius Syrus, *Sententiae* 255, not Seneca, *Mel* 1324; from Publilius Syrus, *Sententiae* 172, *Mel* 1455; from Publilius Syrus, *Sententiae* 483, *Mel* 1488; from pseudo-Seneca, *De moribus* VI (*PL* 72: 32), *Mel* 1531. Melibee quotes pseudo-Seneca, *De moribus* IV (*PL* 72: 31), not Seneca, *Mel* 1775–1776; Dame Prudence quotes Seneca, *De clementia,* I.24.1, *Mel* 1857, and Publilius Syrus, *Sententiae* 64, not Seneca, *Mel* 1859; from Publilius Syrus, *Sententiae* 366, not Seneca, *Mel* 1866. Nero slays his "maister deere," *MkT* 2495–2518; Seneca dies in his bath after he has failed to lead Nero from vice and dies rather than suffer torment. The reference at *MancT* 345 has not been traced. The quotation in *ParsT* 144–145 has not been traced. The Parson quotes from *De Clementia* I.3.3, I.19.2, in *ParsT* 466–468. The quotation in *ParsT* 759–763 is from *Epistle* XLVII. Seneca had tried to hand over his wealth to Nero, but Nero banished him, *Bo* III, *Prosa* 5.47–49; he subsequently commanded Seneca to choose the manner of his death, *Bo* III, *Prosa* 5.53–60. [**Cambises: Cirus: Nero: Papynian: Publilius Syrus**]

Senec occurs twice medially, *MLI* 25; *WBT* 1184; *Seneca* occurs once initially, *PardT* 492; *Senek,* an ME spelling variant of *Senec,* appears once initially, *MerchT* 1523, and four times medially, *WBT* 1168; *SumT* 2018; *MerchT* 1376, 1567; *Senekke,* trisyllabic ME spelling variant of Latin *Seneca,* occurs in final rhyming position, *MancT* 345. The three forms *Senec, Senek, Seneca* appear throughout the *Melibee, The Parson's Tale,* and the *Boece.*

C.W. Barlow, "Epistulae Senecae ad Paulinum et Pauli ad Senecam (quae vocantur)." *Papers and Monographs of the American Academy in Rome* 4 (1938); M.T. Griffin, *Seneca;* Martin of Braga, *Opera Omnia,* ed. C.W. Barlow; Publilius Syrus, *The Moral Sayings of Publilius Syrus,* trans. D. Lyman; *ibid., Publilii Syrii Sententiae,* ed. E. Woelfflin; L.D. Reynolds, *The Medieval Tradition of Seneca's Letters,* 100–124; Seneca, *Epistulae morales,* ed. and trans. R.M. Gummere, I: 110–111; II: 132–133, 268–269, 310–311; *ibid., Moral Essays,* ed. and trans. J.W. Basore, I: 152–157, 288–293, 308–309, 364–366, 408–409, 420; III: 42–49; S. Wenzel, "Chaucer and the Language of Contemporary Preaching." *SP* 73 (1976): 138–161.

SENECA: [SENEC]
SENEK: [SENEC]
SENEKKE: [SENEC]

SENIOR. Muhammad ibn-Umail al-Tamimi, fl. A.D. 900–960, was called al-Sadik. In English al-Sadik becomes "Zadith" and *ibn-Umail* is translated as "son of Hamuel." He wrote three treatises on alchemy, the most famous of which is *Kitab al-ma' al-waraqi wal-ard an-najmiyah,* or *The Book of the Silvery Water and the Starry Earth.* Ibn-Umail wrote it as a commentary on an alchemical poem, *Risalah ash-Shams ila 'l-hilal,* translated in Latin as *Epistola solis ad lunam crescentem* (*The Letter of the Sun to the Waxing Moon,* no date given) and attributed to "Senior Calid filius Hahmil" in medieval manuscripts. This attribution indicates some confusion between ibn-Umail and Khalid ibn-Yazid, referred to in the Latin text of "the Book Senior" as "Calid filius Seid," or, more correctly, "Calid filius Isid." The Latin work was published in volume V of Zetner's *Theatrum chemicum* in 1622.

The Canon's Yeoman tells the story of one of Plato's disciples as found in Senior's book, *CYT* 1448–1471. J. Ruska points out that the Arabic text mentions neither Solomon nor Plato, but Qalimus, who discourses on chalk and lime (Greek *titanos*). In *Tabula chemica,* chapter *Tincture operatio,* the story is told about Solomon, not Plato. E.H. Duncan shows that Chaucer uses an edition of *Epistola solis* in which *Dixit Senior, i.e.,* Plato ("Senior, that is Plato, says"), is written in the margin of one fourteenth-century manuscript.

Senior, the Latin translation of the Arabic title, *Sheik,* appears medially, *CYT* 1450.

E.H. Duncan, "The Literature of Alchemy and Chaucer's Canon's Yeoman's Tale: Framework, Theme, and Characters." *Speculum* 43 (1968): 653–654; D. Metlitzki, *MAME,* 85–87, 275; Muhammad ibn-Umail, "Three Arabic Treatises on Alchemy," ed. Muhammad Turab 'Ali, trans. H.E. Stapleton and M. Hidayat Husain. *Memoirs of the Asiatic Society of Bengal* 12 (1933): 147–197; J. Ruska, "Chaucer und sein Buch Senior." *Anglia* 61 (1937): 136–137.

SEPTEM TRYONES. Septemtriones are the Seven Plough Oxen or the seven stars in the constellations Ursa Minor and Ursa Major. Ptolemy describes the people of the North as those who have the Bears over their heads (*Tetrabiblos* II.2).

Nero ruled all the people who lived under the cold stars of Septem Tryones, *Bo* II, *Metr* 6. Chaucer's gloss explains that this means the people of the North. [**Arcturus: Boötes**]

Ptolemy, *Tetrabiblos,* ed. and trans. F.E. Robbins, 123.

SEPTEMTRIONES: [SEPTEM TRYONES]

SERAPION is a name held by three medical writers. Serapion of Alexandria, who flourished in the first half of the second century B.C., was the founder of the empirical school of medicine. He based all his data on experiment and on reliable clinical cases. The second Serapion was Yahya ibn-Sarafyun, called "Serapion the Elder," of the second half of the ninth century, a Christian physician who wrote two medical compilations in Syriac. One of these was translated into Latin by Gerard of Cremona as *Practica sive breviarium* before 1187. Its last book, which dealt with antidotes, was very popular during the period. The third Serapion, called "Serapion the Younger," possibly a Christian, wrote in Arabic. His treatise, translated into Latin as *Liber de simplici medicina (The Book of Simple Medicine)* or *Liber aggregatus (The Aggregate of Medicine),* was derived from Byzantine and Muslim sources and enjoyed much popularity. Between 1360 and 1385 Merton College Library owned a copy.

Serapion is one of the Physician's authorities, *Gen Prol* 432. Chaucer does not say which Serapion is meant.

G. Sarton, *Introduction to the History of Science*, I: 186–187, 608, II, 1: 229.

SEYS: [CEYS]
SHAPUR: [SAPOR]

SIBILLE, SIBYLE. Sibyl was the name the Greeks and Romans gave to Apollo's prophetesses. The Cumaean Sibyl, who led Aeneas into the Cave of Avernus and later into the Underworld, was Apollo's priestess and prophetess (*Aeneid* VI.42–155).

The story of Eneas's descent, led by Sibyle, is painted on the brass tablet in Venus's temple, *HF* I.439–442. Cassandra, Apollo's priestess and seer, is called Sibille, *Tr* V.1450, when she comes to interpret Troilus's dream. **[Cassandra]**

Sibille, the ME variant, occurs medially, *Tr* V.1450; *Sibyle* occurs in final rhyming position, *HF* I.439.

Virgil, *Aeneid,* ed. and trans. H.R. Fairclough, I: 508–517.

SIBYL: [SIBILLE]
SICHAEUS: [SYTHEO]

SIGNIFER is another name for the Sign-Bearer, or the zodiacal belt, which carries the twelve signs. Claudian uses the word, *De raptu Proserpinae* I.101–102, which Chaucer may have known as *Liber Catonianus*, a medieval schoolbook.

Criseyde prepares for bed instead of returning to Troy as Cinthia whirls out of the Lion and all the candles of Signifer are bright, *Tr* V.1016–1022.

The name appears in a medial position, *Tr* V.1020.

Claudian, *De raptu Proserpinae,* ed. and trans. M. Platnauer, II: 300–301; R.A. Pratt, "Chaucer's Claudian." *Speculum* 22 (1947): 421.

SILLA. Scylla was the daughter of Nisus of Megera. She fell in love with King Minos as he besieged her city, Alcathoe, and in order to help him win, she cut off her father's purple lock on which his life and the fate of the kingdom depended, and gave it to Minos. He captured the city, but Scylla's action horrified him. He sailed away and forbade her to set foot on Crete. As she leaped from the battlements to escape her father and to follow Minos's ships, she was changed into the lark or the *ciris* (*Met* VIII.11–151; *OM* VIII.1–352).

Silla is among those who have died for love, *PF* 292. The story appears in *LGW* 1909–1920. [**Minos: Nysus**]

Silla, the Italian variant, occurs initially, *PF* 292.

Ovid, *Met,* ed. and trans. F.J. Miller, I: 406–417; *OM,* ed. C. de Boer, III, deel 30: 109–117.

SIMKIN: [SYMKYN]

SIMON the Pharisee invited Jesus to dinner. As they sat at the table, a sinful woman brought a pot of precious ointment and stood behind Jesus, weeping. Then she washed his feet with her tears, wiped them with her hair, and anointed them with the ointment. Simon thought to himself that if Jesus were a prophet he would know that the woman who touched him was a sinner. Jesus rebuked Simon and pointed out that because the woman loved greatly, much was forgiven her (Luke 27:36–50). Mary Magdalene is identified with the sinful woman in Gregory's *XL Homiliae in evangelica* XVXV and XXXIII (*PL* 76: 1189 and 1238–1246), written c. A.D. 584.

In his homily on envy, the Parson says that sometimes people grumble because of pride, like Simon the Pharisee, who grumbled against the Magdalene when she wept at Jesus's feet for her sins, *ParsT* 504–507. [**Magdalene**]

SIMON MAGUS: [SYMON MAGUS]

SIMPLICIUS GALLUS. Sulpicius Gallus was a Roman who left his wife beause she looked out the door bareheaded. Valerius Maximus tells the story in *Factorum dictorumque memorabilius liber* VI.3.10, written in the first century A.D. R.A. Pratt suggests that it more likely, however, that Chaucer knew the version in John of Wales's *Communiloquium sive summa collationum* (second half of the thirteenth century).

Alys of Bath tells the story as she heard it from Jankyn, *WBP* 642–646. [**Valerie**]

The whole name occurs medially, *WBP* 643.

Simplicius appears to be the ME variant of *Sulpicius.* Manly-Rickert does not record any variants.

R.A. Pratt, "Chaucer and the Hand that Fed Him." *Speculum* 41 (1966): 621; Valerius Maximus, *Factorum dictorumque memorabilium libri novem,* ed. J. Kappy, I: 617.

SINON: [SYNOUN]
SIRACH: [JHESUS SYRACH]
SIRIUS: [SYRIUS]
SISYPHUS: [CESIPHUS]

SOCRATES, 469–399 B.C., was the son of Sophronius, a stonemason, and his wife Phaenarete. Although his father had been reasonably wealthy, Socrates was later reduced to poverty. He was the first person to apply serious critical and philosophical methods to the examination of the conduct of life and to question the assumptions upon which people based their general conduct. His method of questioning his fellow citizens and of forcing them to answer their own questions aroused the anger and suspicions of the older generation, and in 399 B.C. he was charged before the judges with two crimes: denying the gods of the state and corrupting the youth of the city. The latter charge may have been prompted by Alcibiades's arrogance and pranks in Athens's most sacred places. Socrates was found guilty and sentenced to exile. He refused to comply and was condemned to death. Thirty days after his conviction, he drank the hemlock (Diogenes Laertius II.5). Plato's *Apology* gives an account of the trial; his *Phaedo* relates Socrates's last conversation and his composure in the face of death.

The Middle Ages saw the growth of the tradition that Socrates's wife Xantippe was a shrew. One story appears in Jerome's *Epistola adversus Jovinianum* (*Letter Against Jovinian*) I.48 (*PL* 23: 278). The confessor tells how Socrates endured the torments of his wicked wife, *Confessio Amantis* III.640–713. Socrates's name was also synonymous with "philosopher." Throughout the *Epistle of Othea* (1399), Christine de Pizan attributes many philosophical sayings to him not found in classical sources. In marked contrast to the antifeminist portrayal of Xantippe, Christine's portrait in *The Book of the City of Ladies* II.21.1 shows Socrates and Xantippe in loving relationship.

The death of Socrates is written in the stars, *MLT* 197–203. Alys of Bath recounts a story about Xantippe, which Jankyn read from his book of wikked wyves, *WBP* 727–732. The dreamer exhorts the Man in Black to remember how Socrates was steadfast against anything Fortune could do, *BD* 717–719. The story of Socrates's life and death appear in *RR* 5831–5838, which Chaucer knew. Lady Philosophy says that while Plato lived, Socrates won the victory of "unryghtful deth," *Bo* I, *Prosa* 3.26–28. Chaucer glosses "the heritage of Socrates" as Socrates's doctrine of "felicitee," which the Epicureans and the Stoics seized, *Bo* I, *Prosa* 3.29–34. Socrates, like Anaxagoras and Zeno, suffered because he was brought up in the ways of Lady Philosophy, *Bo* I, *Prosa* 3.53–59 Lady Philosophy follows Socrates's judgment that it is not lawful to conceal the truth, *Bo* I, *Prosa* 4.157–162. A stanza on Socrates begins with an apostrophe to the philosopher, whom Fortune could not torment, *Fortune* 17–24. [**Anaxagore: Xantippa: Zeno**]

Socrates occurs twice in medial positions, *WBP* 728; *Fortune* 17; twice in final rhyming position, *MLT* 201; *BD* 717; and in the prose of the *Boece.*

John Gower, *The Complete Works*, ed. G.C. Macaulay, II: 243–245; Diogenes Laertius, *Lives of the Eminent Philosophers*, ed. and trans. R.D. Hicks, I: 148–177; Christine de Pizan, *The Book of the City of Ladies*, trans. E.J. Richards, 130–131; Plato, *Apology* and *Phaedo*, ed. and trans. H.N. Fowler.

SOLOMON: [SALOMON]

SOMER. Friar John Somer, fl. 1383, was a Minorite of the Franciscan Order at Bridgewater. The provincial Master of the Order encouraged him to write a calendar with astronomical tables for Joan, Princess of Wales, Richard II's mother. This calendar is dated 1380; there are many copies with varying dates, two of which are in the Vatican Collection: the manuscript belonging to the queen of Sweden, dated 1384, and that of Alexander Peteu, dated 1372, ascribed to John Semur.

Chaucer says that he intends to add a third part to his *Treatise on the Astrolabe*, using the tables of longitudes, latitudes, and declinations of the sun after the calendars of Frere J. Somer and Frere N. Lenne, *Astr Prol* 80–85. **[Lenne]**

R.T. Gunther, *Early Science in Oxford*, II: 60–63; Nicholas of Lynne, *The Kalendarium of Nicholas of Lynne*, ed. and trans. G. MacEoin and S. Eisner, 8–9.

SOPHIE is the daughter of Melibee and Prudence in *The Tale of Melibee*. In neither the Latin original nor the French version is the daughter named. Melibee's three enemies wound Sophie in five places: her feet, her hands, her ears, her nose, and her mouth, *Mel* 972. The three enemies are the world, the flesh, and the devil, and Sophie is wounded in her five senses, *Mel* 1421–1425. Sophie represents the soul. **[Melibee: Prudence]**

Sophie, the English variant of Greek *Sophia*, "wisdom," occurs once, at the beginning of the tale, *Mel* 967.

SORANAS. Barea Soranus was proconsul in Asia sometime before A.D. 63. He angered Nero by his fairness and energy and refused to punish Pergamum for employing force to prevent the Caesarian infantry from looting Asian statues and paintings. In A.D. 66 Publius Egnatius Celer, one of his former clients, accused him of plotting in Asia. Tacitus says that Egnatius Celer affected the pose of a Stoic, and so his accusations were convincing. Soranus and his daughter Servilla were condemned to death (*Annals* XVI.xxi–xxxii).

Lady Philosophy reminds Boethius of famous men like Soranas who have been betrayed by friends, *Bo* I, *Prosa* 3.53–59.

Tacitus, *Annals*, ed. and trans. J. Jackson, IV: 366–385.

STACE. Publius Paninius Statius, c. A.D. 45–96, was born in Naples and won prizes for poetry as a young man. His chief works, *Thebaid* and *Achilleid*, were much admired during the medieval period, and a romance based on his *Thebaid*, the *Roman de Thèbes*, by an anonymous writer, appeared in the twelfth century. Two Anglo-Norman romances of Hue de Rotelande owe inspiration to the *Roman de Thèbes*: *Ipomedon* (c. 1186) and its sequel, *Prothesilaus* (c. 1190). Lydgate follows with the *Siege of Thebes*

(1420–1422). Dante presents Statius as a Christian, drawn to Christianity through reading Virgil's *Eclogue* IV.55–57, and baptized before be wrote the *Thebaid*, *Purg* XXI-XXII. Dante makes Statius a native of Toulouse, *Tolosano*, *Purg* XXI.89, a possible confusion with Lucius Statius, a rhetorician of Toulouse. Boccaccio perpetuates the error in *Amorosa Visione*, V.34: *Stazio di Toloza.*

The Knight directs his audience to Stace of Thebes for details of Emelye's ceremonies in Diane's temple, *KnT* 2294–2295. Skeat (V:87) contends that the passage is influenced by *Tes* VII.72–76, for nothing of the kind appears in Statius. *Anel* 22–42 is a paraphrase of *Thebaid* XII.519–521. "The Tholosan that highte Stace" stands on a pillar of iron painted with tigers' blood, *HF* III.1456–1463. In *Thebaid* VII.564–628 Tisiphone arouses the tigers of Bacchus, and the tigers kill three Greeks. Aconteus kills the tigers near the walls of Thebes, and the infuriated Thebans renew the war with greater force. Iron is Mars's metal, and Mars has an iron temple, *Thebaid* XII.519–521. Paul Clogan suggests that Chaucer may have known the glosses of Lactantius Placidus on the lines about iron in the *Thebaid*. Chaucer directs his little book to kiss the steps of the great epic poets, including Stace, *Tr* V.1791–1792.

Stace, the French variant, occurs twice in medial positions, *KnT* 2294, *Anel* 21; twice in final rhyming position, *HF* III.1460; *Tr* V.1792.

P.M. Clogan, "Chaucer and the *Thebaid* Scholia." *SP* 61 (1964): 599–615; *ibid.,* "Chaucer's Use of the *Thebaid*." *EM* 18 (1967): 9–31; S. Haller, "*The Knight's Tale* and the Epic Tradition." *ChauR* 1 (1966): 67–84; Statius, *Thebaid and Achilleid,* ed. and trans. J.H. Mozley; *ibid., The Medieval Achilleid of Statius,* ed. P. Clogan; B.A. Wise, *The Influence of Statius upon Chaucer.*

STATIUS: [STACE]

STILBOUN. In his exemplum on gambling, the Pardoner tells the story of the Spartan Stilboun, who went to Corinth and found the leaders playing dice and checkers, "at hazard," *PardT* 599–628. In his *Sententiae* Publilius Syrus gives the name as Chilon of Sparta; John of Salisbury tells how Chilo refuses to conclude a treaty with the Corinthians because they all played checkers, *Policraticus* I.5. [**Demetrius**]

Stilboun, apparently a Chaucerian variant of Latin *Chilon,* appears initially, with initial primary stress, *PardT* 603.

John of Salisbury, *Policraticus,* trans. J.B. Pike, 28–29; Publilius Syrus, *Sententiae,* ed. E. Woelfflin, 151.

STRODE. Ralph Strode, fl. 1350–1400, was educated at Merton College, Oxford, where he became a fellow before 1360. There he was a colleague of Wycliffe, whose doctrine of necessity and predestination he later opposed. His two surviving treatises, *Consequentiae* and *Obligationes,* were published in 1477 and 1507 respectively, and together in Venice in 1493. He enjoyed the high reputation of a Thomist philosopher and a slight reputation as a poet of love. On November 25, 1373, Strode was elected Common Pleader or Common Sarjeant of the City of London. In 1375 he was granted the mansion over Aldgate, including the gardens, and although the grant was extended for life in 1377, he relinquished his office in 1382. In 1386 he was appointed standing counsel for the City of London for seven years.

Chaucer dedicates *Troilus and Criseyde* to "philosophical Strode" and to "moral Gower," *Tr* V.1856–1862. **[Gower]**

The name occurs in final rhyming position, *Tr* V.1857.

Riverside Chaucer, ed. L. Benson, 1058; L. Stephen and S. Lee, eds., *Dictionary of National Biography* XIX: 57–59; R. Strode, *Consequentiae et obligationes cum commentiis; ibid., An Edition and Translation of the* Tractatus de consequentiis *by Ralph Strode*, by W.K. Seaton.

STYMPHALIDES. Stymphalis was a virgin whom the tyrant Aristoclides of Orchomenos wooed. When her father was slain, Stymphalis fled to Diana's temple, where she clung to the altar until she was stabbed to death. Jerome tells her story, *Epistola adversus Jovinianum (Letter Against Jovinian)* I.41 *(PL* 23: 272).

Dorigen remembers that Stymphalides, desired by the tyrant Aristoclides, took sanctuary in Diane's temple and clung to the altar while being stabbed to death, *FranklT* 1387–1394. **[Aristoclides: Dorigen]**

The form is the Greek patronymic meaning "son of Stymphalis" and seems to have been formed by analogy to *Aristoclides* or "son of Aristocles." It occurs in final rhyming position, *FranklT* 1388, and its placement may have determined its form. Interesting variants *Simphalides* and *Nymphalides* preserve the Greek patronymic ending even when the scribe is unfamiliar with the name.

G. Dempster, "Chaucer at Work on the Complaint in *The Franklin's Tale.*" *MLN* 52 (1937): 6–16; K. Hume, "The Pagan Setting of *The Franklin's Tale* and the Sources of Dorigen's Cosmology." *SN* 44 (1972): 289–294; Manly-Rickert, VI: 646.

STYMPHALIS: [STYMPHALIDES]
SUETONIUS: [SWETONIUS]
SUSANAH: [SUSANNA]

SUSANNA, SUSANNE. Susannah was the virtuous wife of Joachim. Two lustful elders, whose advances she repulsed, accused her of adultery (Daniel 13). Machaut tells this story in *Le Confort d'ami*, 73–426. "Susannah and the Elders" is a favorite subject in medieval illuminations in Books of Hours.

Custance prays to God who saved Susanne from false blame, *MLT* 639–641. False witnesses caused Susanna great pain and sorrow, *ParsT* 797.

Susanna occurs in *ParsT* 797; *Susanne*, the French variant, occurs in final rhyming position, *MLT* 639.

Guillaume de Machaut, *Oeuvres*, ed. E. Hoepffner, III: 3–16; A.L. Kellogg, "Susannah and *The Merchant's Tale*." *Speculum* 35 (1960): 275–279; *Susannah*, ed. A. Miskimin.

SWETONIUS, SWETOUN. Gaius Suetonius Tranquillus, c. A.D. 70–c. 160, was the son of Suetonius Laetus. It appears that he was born in Hippo Regius, Algeria; a monument to him has been unearthed there. His principal surviving work, *De vita Caesarum*, was written while he was one of the imperial secretaries under Trajan.

The Monk says that Swetonius is the source for his tale of Nero, *MkT* 2463–2465. Chaucer has, however, used Boccaccio's *De casibus virorum illustrium* VII.4, and Boethius's *De consolatione philosophiae* II, *Metr* 6.1–32; *Bo* III, *Metr* 4.1–12. The Monk recommends Swetoun for the facts about Julius, *MkT* 2720. **[Julius: Neroun]**

Swetonius occurs in final rhyming position, *MkT* 2465; *Swetoun*, the shortened form, occurs in medial position, *MkT* 2720. Both forms are derived through pronunciation of Latin *Suetonius*, the family's clan name.

Suetonius, *De vita Caesarum*, ed. and trans. J.C. Rolfe; A. Wallace-Hadrill, *Suetonius: The Scholar and his Caesars.*

SYCHAEUS: [SYTHEO]

SYMACUS. Symmachus, fl. sixth century A.D., was Boethius's father-in-law. In a letter to Coelianus and Agapitus, Cassiodorus informs them that Theodoric orders Festus and Symmachus to prosecute Paulus and encourages the speedy rendering of justice (*Epistola* I.xxiii). In a letter to Symmachus, Cassiodorus conveys Theodoric's commendation for his spending of his own money to decorate Rome with new buildings (*Epistola* IV.li). Symmachus subsequently fell into disfavor with the king, and he was executed some time after Boethius's death in 525.

Lady Philosophy says that Symachus is a man "maked al of sapience and of vertu," *Bo* II, *Prosa* 4.25–29. **[Boece]**

The form is a spelling variant.

Flavius Cassiodorus, *Epistolae Theodoricianae varie*, ed. Th. Mommsen, 27, 138–139.

SYMKYN, the diminutive of Symond, is the name of the miller in *The Reeve's Tale*. The details of his appearance and character are very much like those of Robin the Miller on the pilgrimage, and W.C. Curry suggests that the two millers are in reality the same person. Robin the Miller, however, does not have a camus nose, the hereditary characteristic of Symkyn's family. J.M. Steadman points out that the name involves a Latin pun, for the Latin adjective *simus* means "flat-nosed" or "camus-nosed." It is thus fitting that a snub-nosed person be called Symond. [**Robyn**[1]: **Symond**]

Symkyn occurs six times in medial positions, *RvT* 3945, 3947, 3955, 4024, 4034, 4291; twice in final rhyming position, *RvT* 3941, 3959.

W.C. Curry, *Chaucer and the Mediaeval Sciences*, 79–90; J.M. Steadman, "Simkin's Camus Nose: A Latin Pun in *The Reeve's Tale*?" *MLN* 75 (1960): 4–8.

SYMMACHUS: [SYMACUS]

SYMON MAGUS was a sorcerer who had bewitched the citizens of Samaria. He was converted to Christianity when Philip the Apostle preached in that city. When he later tried to buy the power of the Holy Spirit, Philip denounced him (Acts 8:9–13). He thus gave his name to the sin of buying or selling spiritual blessings—simony.

Sick Thomas swears by St. Simon, *SumT* 2094, a reference that seems to indicate St. Simon, who is usually coupled with St. Jude. Ann Haskell suggests that Simon Magus is meant here. Simony is called after Symon Magus, who wanted to buy the gift of God for temporal goods, *ParsT* 782–783. Symon stands with other sorcerers in the hall of Fame's house, *HF* III.1274.

Symon Magus occurs in final rhyming position, *HF* III.1274; *Symoun* occurs in final rhyming position, *SumT* 2094.

A.S. Haskell, "St. Simon in *The Summoner's Tale*." *ChauR* 5 (1971): 218–224.

SYMOND is the given name of the miller in *The Reeve's Tale*. It occurs once initially, *RvT* 4026, and three times in medial positions, *RvT* 4022, 4127, 4288. [**Symkyn**]

SYMOUN: [SYMON MAGUS]

SYNON, SYNOUN is a name synonymous with treachery. Aeneas tells Dido the story of the Trojan horse and Sinon's part in the episode, *Aeneid* II.1–355. Sinon persuaded the Trojans to haul into Troy the great wooden horse left on the beach when the Greeks apparently sailed away; the horse, he said, was an offering to Pallas Athena. At night Sinon opened the horse, the bravest Greeks jumped out, and Troy was taken. Virgil develops the story from two brief mentions in *Odyssey* IV.271–274 and VIII.499–500. He shows that the Greeks won Troy through guile and treachery, not through force of arms. Dante places Sinon in Bolgia Ten of Circle Eight of Hell among the falsifiers, *il falso Sinon greco da Troiae, Inf* XXX.98. The story is told in Dictys Cretensis, *Ephemeridos belli Troiani* V.11–12 and Dares, *De excidio Troiae historia*, 40.

The courtiers at King Cambyuskan's court stare at the bronze horse as if it were "the Greeks hors Synon," *SqT* 209. Chaucer uses the group genitive, meaning "the Greek horse of Sinon." Sinon's story is painted on the walls of Venus's temple, *HF* I.151–156. The fox is classed with traitors including Sinon, and he is the "false dissymulour," *NPT* 3228, an echo of Dante. The Legend of Dido begins with a brief summary of Sinon's treachery, *LGW* 930–933. **[Genylon]**

Synon, a spelling variant of Latin *Sinon*, occurs in final rhyming position, *SqT* 209; *NPT* 3229; *HF* I.152. *Synoun* occurs in final rhyming position, *LGW* 931.

Dares Phrygius, *De excidio Troiae historia*, ed. F. Meister, 48–49; Dares Phrygius and Dictys Cretensis, *The Trojan War*, trans. R.M. Frazer, 112–113, 165; Dictys Cretensis, *Ephemeridos belli Troiani*, ed. W. Eisenhut, 111–114; Homer, *Odyssey*, ed. and trans. A.T. Murray, I: 126–127, 294–295; Virgil, *Aeneid*, ed. and trans. H.R. Fairclough, I: 57–267, 302–313.

SYRAK: [JHESUS SYRAK]

SYRIUS. Sirius is the alpha or brightest star of the constellation *Canis Major*, the Greater Dog, known also as Orion's Dog. It lies in a descending line from Orion's belt, and is the brightest star in the heavens, best seen in winter and in summer. It thus rules the extremes of heat and cold, and the scorching heat of Sirius the dog star was thought to account for the "dog days" of summer.

Boethius remarks that the seeds sown when Arcturus was high in the sky grow to high ears when Sirius scorches them, *Bo* I, *Metr* 5.26–28. **[Alhabor]**

R.H. Allen, *Star Names and their Meanings*, 117–129.

SYTHEO. Sychaeus was Dido's Phoenician husband. Pigmalion, her brother, envied Sychaeus's wealth and arranged to have him murdered. Sychaeus's ghost warned Dido to flee, and she went to Africa where she founded Carthage (*Aeneid* I.340–360).

Sytheo is Dido' s deceased husband, *LGW* 1005. **[Dido]**

The form, a variant of Italian *Sicheo*, occurs in final rhyming position, *LGW* 1005.

Virgil, *Aeneid*, ed. and trans. H.R. Fairclough, I: 264–267.

T

TANTALE, TANTALUS was king of Phrygia and father of Pelops and Niobe. He cut his son into little pieces and offered them to the gods to test their divinity. The gods recognized Pelops and restored him to life, but his right shoulder was missing because Ceres, mourning for Proserpina, had absentmindedly eaten it. Jupiter replaced it with an ivory shoulder (*Met* VI.404–411). To punish Tantalus, Jupiter hung him on a tree laden with fruit he could not reach; a pool of water lay nearby but receded whenever he attempted to drink (*Met* IV.457–460; *OM* IV.3819–3830). Tantalus, Ticius, and Sisyphus appear together in *RR* 19281–19286 and in Machaut's *Le Confort d'ami* 2517–2534 as inhabitants of the Underworld.

The Man in Black says that he has more sorrow than Tantale, since his love has died, *BD* 709. Tantalus despises the water he has been trying to drink when he hears Orpheus play in the Underworld, *Bo* III, *Metr* 12.38–40. Pandarus swears to Criseyde that all shall be well when she comes to dinner, or he would rather be in hell with Pluto and Tantalus, *Tr* III.589–593.
[Cesiphus; Nyobe; Ticius]

Tantale, the French variant, appears in final rhyming position, *BD* 709; *Tantalus,* the Latin variant, appears in *Bo* III, *Metr* 12.38, and in medial position, *Tr* III.593.

Guillaume de Machaut, *Oeuvres,* ed. E. Hoepffner, III: 89–90; Ovid, *Met,* ed. and trans. F.J. Miller, I.206–207, 210–211; *OM,* ed. C. de Boer, II, deel 21: 92; *RR,* ed. E. Langlois, IV.262–263; *RR,* trans. C. Dahlberg, 318.

TARQUINIUS, TARQUYN, TARQUYNY. Sextus Tarquinius, son of Tarquinius Superbus, was the cousin of Lucretia's husband, Collatinus. During a lull of the siege of Ardea, Collatinus boasted of his wife's beauty and virtue and took a group of officers, including Tarquinius, to check on

Lucretia. They found her working among her maids. Tarquinius was seized with violent lust for Lucretia and returned later to her house. She received him as a guest and a relative and offered refreshments. Tarquinius, however, threatened her with death if she did not yield to him, then he raped her. The next day Lucretia called her husband and father, told them what had happened, and stabbed herself to death. Tarquinius's deed caused an insurrection in Rome, and the people drove out his family (Livy, *Ab urbe condita liber* I.57–59; *Fasti* II.685–852).

Lucrece slew herself after the shame of Tarquyn's rape, *FranklT* 1405–1408. The full story appears in *LGW* 1680–1885, where Chaucer gives Ovid and Livy as his sources. He also knew it from *RR* 8608–8660. [**Colatyn: Lucrece: Tarquinius Superbus**]

Tarquinius, the Latin variant, occurs four times initially, *LGW* 1711, 1714, 1745, 1819; once in medial position, *LGW* 1698; twice in final rhyming position, *LGW* 1682, 1789. *Tarquyn,* the shortened English form, appears twice in medial position, *FranklT* 1407, *LGW* 1863. *Tarquyny* occurs once in medial position, *LGW* 1837.

Livy, *Ab urbe condita libri,* ed. and trans. B.O. Foster, I: 198–209; Ovid, *Fasti,* ed. and trans. J.G. Frazer, 106–119; *RR,* ed. E. Langlois, III: 89–90; *RR,* trans. C. Dahlberg, 158–159.

TARQUINIUS COLLATINUS: [COLATYN]

TARQUINIUS SUPERBUS was Rome's last king and ruled 534–510 B.C. His son Sextus raped Lucretia, wife of his nephew Tarquinius Collatinus, a deed that led to an insurrection, during which the people drove the Tarquins from Rome (Livy, *Ab urbe condita liber* I.57–59; Ovid, *Fasti* II.685–852).

The narrator says that he will tell of the exiling of kings and of the last king of Rome, as told by Ovid and Titus Livy, *LGW* 1680–1683. [**Colatyn: Lucrece: Tarquinius**]

The name appears in final rhyming position, *LGW* 1682. *Tarquinius* is the adjective of *Tarquinii,* the Etruscan town from which the Tarquins came.

Livy, *Ab urbe condita libri,* ed. and trans. B.O. Foster, I: 198–209; Ovid, *Fasti,* ed. and trans. J.G. Frazer, 106–119.

TARQUYN: [TARQUINIUS]
TARQUYNY: [TARQUINIUS]

TAUR, TAURUS, TAWR. Taurus, the constellation the Bull, is the second sign of the zodiac and lies in the northern hemisphere between Aries and Gemini, near Orion, partly in the Milky Way. It is the night house of Venus, the exaltation of the Moon (*Tetrabiblos* I.19), the dry and cold sign. Taurus controls the neck and throat of those born under its sign (*Confessio Amantis* VII.1015–1030).

Alys of Bath says that Taurus was in the ascendant (rising in the east) when she was born, *WBP* 609–613. W.C. Curry shows how its position affects her appearance. The moon passes from the second degree of Taurus into Cancer when Januarie weds May, *MerchT* 1885–1889; that is, the moon is in her zodiacal house or mansion, at her most powerful influence. Chauntecleer rises and crows when the sun is 21 degrees in the sign of Taurus, *NPT* 3187–3197. Standish Henning shows how Taurus controls Chauntecleer's throat, hence his destiny. The sun is in Taurus on the third of May when Pandarus visits Criseyde as Troilus's emissary, *Tr* II.50–63. Adriane's crown lies in the sign of Taurus, *LGW* 2223–2224. Skeat (III: 340) explains that when the sun is in Taurus, that is, during April-May, the crown is clearly seen in the midnight sky. Mars and Venus make love in Venus's chamber, which is painted with white bulls, *Mars* 85–88; that is, Venus is in her night house, Taurus. Taurus is the second sign of the zodiac, *Astr* I.8.3. Taurus controls the neck and throat of those born under the sign, *Astr* I.21.74. It lies directly opposite Scorpio, *Astr* II.6.16, and obeys the "sovereign" or western sign Leo, *Astr* II.28–37. [**Alisoun³: Bole: Chauntecleer: Venus**]

Taur, the contraction of Latin *Taurus*, appears once medially, *WBP* 613; *Taurus* occurs medially, *NPT* 3194; *Tawr*, a spelling variant of *Taur*, appears medially, *MerchT* 1887.

W.C. Curry, *Chaucer and the Mediaeval Sciences*, 91–118; John Gower, *The Complete Works*, ed. G.C. Macaulay, III: 260–261; S. Henning, "Chauntecleer and Taurus." *ELN* 3 (1965): 1–4; Ptolemy, *Tetrabiblios*, ed. and trans. F.E. Robbins, 88–89.

TELEPHUS: [THELOPUS]

TEREUS, one of Mars's descendants, was king of Thrace. When his wife Procne desired to see her sister, Tereus went to Athens to fetch Philomela. Seized by a violent lust for Philomela, he took her to the Thracian woods and raped her, cut out her tongue when she threatened to tell of his deed, and shut her up in a house. Philomela wove her story in a tapestry and sent it to her sister, who first rescued her sister, then avenged herself on Tereus. She cut up and cooked their son Itys and fed him to his father. After Tereus had eaten, she told him what his dinner consisted of, and as he rushed upon her with his sword, he was changed into a hoopoë, while Procne became a swallow and Philomela a nightingale (*Met* VI.424–674; *OM* VI.2217–3684).

The swallow sings her sorrowful lay, how Tereus has taken her sister, *Tr* II.64–70. The full story appears in *LGW* 2228–2393, and the poet traces Tereus's cruelty to his ancestor Mars. He omits Procne's terrible vengeance. [**Pandion: Philomene: Proigne**]

Tereus appears eight times in medial positions, *Tr* II.69; *LGW* 2234, 2243, 2270, 2289, 2342. 2363, 2389; and once in final rhyming position, *LGW* 2315.

Ovid, *Met*, ed. and trans. F.J. Miller, I.316–335; *OM*, ed. C. de Boer, II, deel 21: 337–370.

TERMAGANT: [TERMAGAUNT]

TERMAGAUNT. Medieval Christians believed that Termagant was part of the Muslim pantheon of gods. He appears as a god of the Saracens throughout *La Chanson de Roland* (63, 2589, 2696, 2712, 3267, etc.) and as part of the Saracen trinity of Appolyn, Mahound, and Termagant in the ME romance, *Sir Guy of Warwick* 3701.

Sir Oliphant swears by Termagaunt, *Thop* 810. **[Thopas]**

La Chanson de Roland, ed. C. Segre, 116, 475, 490, 492, 573, etc.; *Sir Guy of Warwick*, ed. Jupita, 213.

TERTULAN. Quintus Septimus Florens Tertullian, c. A.D. 160–c. 240, was born probably at Carthage, the son of a centurion in the service of the proconsul of Africa. He became an advocate in the Roman Law Courts and is usually identified with the jurist Tertullian. Converted to Christianity c. 195, he became an instructor to catechumen at Carthage. He gradually became attracted to the Montanist heresy, and c. 212 or 213 he broke with the church. There is no evidence that he returned before he died. Married, he confessed that he committed adultery repeatedly. He is still regarded as the greatest Christian writer in the West before Augustine, and thirty-one authentic treatises are extant. Whether he became a priest is still a matter of dispute. His tract, *De monogamia,* written c. 217 for the Montanists, stigmatizes all second marriages as adultery. In direct contrast with this tract and in opposition to it is *Ad uxorem*, written earlier, c. 200, addressed to his wife. Here he asserts that second marriage is no sin (*NCE* XIII:1019–1022).

Jankyn's anthology contains one of Tertullian's tracts, *WBP* 676, most likely *De monogamia*, which is against second marriages. **[Alisoun³: Jankyn²]**

Tertullian, *Apology, De spectaculis*, ed. and trans. T.R. Glover.

TERTULLIAN: [TERTULAN]

TESBEE, THISBEE, THYSBE, TISBE, TYSBE. Thisbe, a young Babylonian maiden, fell in love with her neighbor Pyramus. Their parents refused consent to their marriage, and they planned to leave Babylon together, meeting first at King Ninus's tomb. Thisbe arrived first, but a bloody lioness scared her, and she fled into the tomb, leaving her cloak behind. The lioness tore the cloak with her bloody jaws, then went off. Pyramus arrived later and, seeing the bloody cloak, presumed that Thisbe had been slain and killed himself. When Thisbe emerged from the tomb, she found Pyramus dead, and she slew herself with his sword (*Met* IV.55–166; *OM* IV.229–1169; Machaut, *Le Jugement dou roy de Navarre*, 3171–3212). The story is also told in an Anglo-Norman poem of the twelfth or thirteenth century, *Pyrame et Tisbé,* and in an Old French poem, *Piramus et Tisbé* (c. 1170).

The Man of Law lists the story of "babilan Tesbee" among Chaucer's works, *MLI* 63. The story of Piramus and Tesbee shows that love will find a way, *MerchT* 2125–2128. Thisbe is among love's martyrs in Venus's temple, *PF* 289, and in the catalogue of faithful women, *LGW F* 261, *LGW G* 215. The full story appears in *LGW* 706–923. [Nynus: Piramus: Semyrame]

Tesbee appears once medially, *MerchT* 2128, and once in final rhyming position, *MLI* 63. *Thesbe* appears once in final rhyming position, *LGW* 751. *Thisbe* appears twice medially, *PF* 289; *LGW* 870, once in final rhyming position, *LGW* 849. *Thysbe* appears once in final rhyming position, *LGW* 777. *Tisbe* occurs eight times in medial positions, *LGW F* 26, *LGW* 793, 809, 853, 877, 881, 884, 916, and twice in final rhyming position, *LGW* 835, 907. *Tysbee* occurs twice initially, *LGW* 725, 887, once medially, *LGW G* 215. The forms are all spelling variants; intrusive *h* was not pronounced.

E. Faral, "Le Poème de *Piramus et Tisbé* et quelques romans français du XIIe siècle." *Recherches sur les sources latines des contes et romans courtois du moyen âge,* 5–36; Guillaume de Machaut, *Oeuvres,* ed. E. Hoepffner, I: 246–247; Ovid, *Met,* ed. and trans. F.J. Miller, I: 182–191; *OM,* ed. C. de Boer, II, deel 21: 18–37; *Pyramus et Tisbé,* ed. C. de Boer; J.W. Spisak, "Chaucer's *Pyramus and Thisbe.*" *ChauR* 18 (1983–1984): 204–210; *Three Ovidian Tales of Love,* ed. R. Cormier.

TEUTA was the warrior queen of Illyria. The Illyrians were pirates, and their adventures provoked Rome. Teuta became queen in 231 B.C. and refused to give Rome satisfaction for the murder of some Roman merchants in 329 B.C., an incident that had occurred before her reign. She even insulted the Roman ambassadors who had come to her court (Polybius, *Histories* 2. 3–12). Jerome mentions her chastity, her strong rule over the Illyrians, and her insults to the Romans, *Epistola adversus Jovinianum* (*Letter Against Jovinian*) I.41 (*PL* 23: 274).

Dorigen remarks that Teuta's chastity is a mirror to wives, *FranklT* 1453–1454. [Dorigen]

The name occurs in medial position, *FranklT* 1453.

Polybius, *Histories,* ed. and trans. W.P. Paton, I: 248–271.

THARBE is one of Criseyde's nieces, with whom she walks in the garden while Antigone sings a song of love, *Tr* II.813–825. She accompanies Criseyde to dinner at Deiphebus's house, *Tr* II.1562–1563.

G.L. Hamilton suggests that Chaucer found the name "rex Thabor" in the *Historia destructionis Troiae* and made it feminine. **[Antigone: Creseyde: Flexippe]**

The name appears medially, *Tr* II.816, 1563.

G.L. Hamilton, *The Indebtedness of Chaucer's* Troilus and Criseyde *to Guido delle Colonne's* Historia destructionis Troiae, 94.

THELOPUS. Telephus was a son of Hercules and king of Mysia. The Greeks landed at Mysia on their way to Troy and, in the battle that ensued, Achilles wounded Telephus with his spear. When his wound would not heal, he consulted the Delphic Oracle, which counseled Telephus that the wounder would be the healer, so he followed Achilles to Troy. Here Achilles and the sons of Aesculapius healed his wound with rust from the spear (Dictys, *Ephemeridos belli Troiani,* II.1–12). Dante mentions the healing spear, *Inf* XXXI.4–6.

The magic sword reminds the people at Cambyuskan's court of Achilles's spear, which wounded and healed Thelopus the king, *SqT* 236–240. **[Achilles]**

Thelopus, the ME variant of medieval Latin *Thelephus* in Guido's *Historia* XIII, occurs medially, *SqT* 238. Intrusive *h* after *t* was not pronounced.

Dante, *The Divine Comedy,* ed. and trans. C.S. Singleton, I, 1: 325–326; Dictys Cretensis, *Ephemeridos belli Troiani,* ed. W. Eisenhut, 20–29; Dares Phrygius and Dictys Cretensis, *The Trojan War,* trans. R.M. Frazer, 37–44; Guido delle Colonne, *Guido de Columnis: HDT,* ed. N.E. Griffin, 110–112; *ibid., HDT,* trans. M.E. Meek, 107–114.

THEODAMAS was a Theban augur with the army who encouraged the troops with an invocation followed by blasts from the trumpets (*Thebaid* VIII.279–343).

The courses of Januarie's wedding feast are preceded by the music of trumpets, *MerchT* 1720–1721; the trumpets of Joab and Theodamas were not half as clear. The Dreamer hears the trumpet of Theodamas, *HF* III.1246. Chaucer has made Theodamas a trumpeter.

The name occurs once initially, *HF* III.1246, and once in medial position, *MerchT* 1720.

Statius, *Thebaid,* ed. and trans. J.H. Mozley, II: 214–219.

THEODORA is a princess for whose sake Algarsyf suffers great peril in *The Squire's Tale.* She is saved by the magic horse, *SqT* 663–666.

Theodora, meaning "the gift of God," occurs once, medially, *SqT* 664.

THEODORIC was the Ostrogothic king of Italy, reigned A.D. 493–526, and was an adherent to the Arian doctrines of Christianity. He was an able administrator and a tolerant ruler, and he took an interest in the arts although he could not write. Flavius Cassiodorus, quaestor and consul in Theodoric's government, acted as his secretary and wrote letters in the king's name. Theodoric gave Boethius great favors, but when he was accused of treason, the king believed the accusations and threw Boethius into prison. The Senate then passed sentence without trial, and Boethius was cruelly tortured and clubbed to death.

Boethius does not mention the king by name in his *De consolatione philosophiae*. Chaucer translates a gloss added by Jean de Meun to his French translation, explaining that Boethius had countermanded one of Theodoric's ordinances on the sale of corn during a difficult year, *Bo* I, *Prosa* 4.72–84. Theodoric's name appears in another gloss, which explains that Boethius had refused to serve as a colleague with Decoratus, even if his refusal displeased Theodoric, *Bo* III, *Prosa* 4.23–26. This gloss does not appear in Jean de Meun's translation. [**Boece: Cassidore: Decorat**]

V.L. Dedeck-Héry, "Boethius' *De consolatione* by Jean de Meun." *MS* 14 (1952): 177–178; T. Hodgkin, *Theodoric the Goth*; J.J. O'Donnell, *Cassiodorus*.

THEOFRASTE. Theophrastus was the supposed author of the *Liber aureolus de nuptiis* (*The Golden Book of Marriage*), an antifeminist work that was bound in an anthology with Jerome's *Epistola adversus Jovinianum* (*Letter Against Jovinian*) I.47 (*PL* 23: 276–278) and Walter Map's *Dissuasio Valerii ad Rufinum philosophum ne uxorem ducat* (*The Advice of Valerius to Rufinus Not to Marry*, 1180–1183). The *Liber aureolus* is now lost but survives in Jerome's *Epistola*, I.41. There is no evidence that Theophrastus (d. 287 B.C.) wrote this tract.

Jankyn calls his favorite book "Valerye and Theofraste," which indicates that it was an anthology, *WBP* 669–680. The Merchant, in his ironic reverie about marriage, tells how a wife should joyfully serve her husband, but some clerks, including Theofraste, say that this does not happen, *MerchT* 1293–1295. The Merchant invites his listeners to defy Theofraste and listen to him, *MerchT* 1310. [**Crisippus: Helowys: Jankyn²: Jerome: Jovinian: Tertulan: Trotula: Valerie**]

Theofraste, the French variant, occurs three times medially, *MerchT* 1294, 1295, 1310, and once in final rhyming position, *WBP* 671.

Jerome, *The Principal Works of St. Jerome*, trans. W.H. Freemantle, 383–385; R.A. Pratt, "Jankyn's Book of Wikked Wyves: Antimatrimonial Propaganda in the Universities." *AnM* 3 (1962): 5–27.

THEOPHRASTUS: [THEOFRASTE]

THESEUS was the son of Aethra, daughter of King Pittheus of Troezen, and King Aegeus of Athens. On his way from Troezen to Athens, Theseus encountered various strong men and tyrants, enemies of travelers, and conquered them by a combination of cunning and strength (*Met* VII.430–452). Soon after his arrival in Athens, he joined the young Athenians who were selected as tribute to Minos of Crete. In Crete the king's daughter Ariadne gave Theseus a ball of thread, which he let out as he went through the Labyrinth toward the Minotaur. After he had killed the monster, he followed the thread back to the light. He promised to marry Ariadne, and she sailed away with him. But he abandoned her on the island of Naxos (*Met* VIII.169–182; *OM* VIII.1083–1394). With his close friend Pirithous, king of the Lapiths, he attempted to carry off Proserpina, queen of the Underworld, but failed, and Pluto kept him there forever (*Aeneid* VI.392–397, 617–618). The story of the Minotaur appears in Machaut, *Le Jugement dou roy de Navarre* 2707–2804.

Two characterizations of Theseus appear in Chaucer's works. Theseus is a philosopher in the Boethian tradition in *The Knight's Tale*, based on Boccaccio's Teseo in *Il Teseida delle nozze d'Emilia* (1339–1341). His speech, *KnT* 2987–3074, is a summary of ideas from *Bo* II, *Metr, Bo* III, *Prosa* 10; *Bo* IV. *Prosa* 6, *Metr* 6. In *The Legend of Ariadne, LGW* 1886–2227, Theseus is twenty-three years old, unscrupulous, and cruel. No one is falser in love than Demophon, except his father Theseus, *LGW* 2399–2400. Chaucer's source for this characterization is *Heroides* X. [**Adriane: Egeus: Mars: Minos: Mynotaur: Phedra**]

Theseus never occurs initially. It appears fifty-one times in medial positions, *KnT* 878, 907, 963, 998, 1022, 1206, 1210, 1434, 1439, 1448, 1484, 1498, 1562, 1662, 1684, 1690, 1874, 1883, 1900, 1913, 2093, 2190, 2199, 2523, 2528, 2577, 2621, 2654, 2695, 2700, 2731, 2818, 2853, 2870, 2889, 2975, 2980, 2982; *Anel* 22; *LGW* 1890, 1960, 1968, 2007, 2028, 2074, 2137, 2144, 2190, 2443, 2459, 2464; seventeen times in final rhyming position, *KnT* 860, 1001, 1192, 1213, 1228, 1585, 1673, 2089, 2837, 2906; *Anel* 45; *HF* I.405; *LGW* 1945, 1952, 2026, 2400, 2464.

Guillaume de Machaut, *Oeuvres*, ed. E. Hoepffner, I: 230–233; Ovid, *Heroides*, ed. and trans. G. Showerman, 120–133; *ibid., Met*, ed. and trans. F.J. Miller, I: 372–375, 418–419; *OM*, ed. C. de Boer, III, deel 30: 134–142.

THESIPHONE. Tisiphone, a daughter of the Night and sister of Allecto and Megaera, was the guardian of the gates to the Underworld (*Aeneid* VI.554–556; 570–572). Her locks were snakes that hissed when they were disturbed, and her arms were wreathed with serpents (*Met* IV.473–476, 491–492). She and her sisters were handmaidens to Proserpina, queen of the Underworld (*Inf* IX.344–345).

Thesiphone is the "goddesse of torment . . . sorwynge evere in payne," *Tr* I.6–7. The Erinyes, also called the Furies, "compleignen evere in pyne," *Tr* IV.22–24. Dante makes the Furies the handmaidens of the queen of eternal lamentation (*Inf* IX.43–44). Fulgentius derives Tisiphone from *tuton phone*, that is, the voice of these same Furies, since the second stage of fury is to burst forth into words (*Mythologies* I.7). The three Furies are mentioned in *RR* 19835–19837. **[Alete: Herenus: Megera: Proserpina]**

Thesiphone, the French variant, occurs once initially, *Tr* I.6, and once in final rhyming position, *Tr* IV.24.

Dante, *The Divine Comedy,* ed. and trans. C.S. Singleton, I, 1: 90–91; Fulgentius, *Fulgentius the Mythographer,* trans. L.G. Whitbread, 52; Ovid, *Met,* ed. and trans. F.J. Miller, I: 210–213; *RR,* ed. E. Langlois, V: 18; *RR,* trans. C. Dahlberg, 326.

THETIS, daughter of Nereus, an old sea god, was Achilles's mother. Since it was foretold that she would bear a son greater than his father, Jupiter and Poseidon decided to marry her to a mortal (*Met* IX.221–228, 256–265).

Thetis and the sea gods rescue Demophon from drowning and cast him up on the beach in Thrace, *LGW* 2421–2426. Chaucer's source for this line is apparently *Aeneid* V.823. **[Achilles: Demophon: Phillis]**

Thetis occurs once in medial position, *LGW* 2422.

Ovid, *Met,* ed. and trans. F.J. Miller, II: 18–21; Virgil, *Aeneid,* ed. and trans. H.R. Fairclough, I: 500–501.

THIMALAUS: [THYMALAO]
THIODAMAS: [THEODAMAAS]
THISBE: [TESBEE]
THISBEE: [TESBEE]

THOAS was king of Lemnos and father of Hypsipyle. When the Lemnian women, enraged by jealousy, killed all the men on the island, Hypsipyle saved her father's life and helped him escape by boat (*Heroides* VI.139–140; *Argonauticon* II.311–430).

Ysiphele, daughter of Thoas, is queen of Lemnos when Jason and his companions arrive, *LGW* 1465–1468. **[Isiphile: Jason]**

Thoas appears once, in medial position, *LGW* 1468.

Ovid, *Heroides,* ed. and trans. G. Showerman, 68–83; Valerius Flaccus, *Argonauticon,* ed. and trans. J.H. Mozley, 90–105.

THOBIE[1]. Tobias, the elder, was an honest man of the tribe of Naphthali and was exiled to Assyria. The book of Tobias, one of the Apocryphal books, is included in the Septuagint and the Vulgate.

Dame Prudence quotes Tobias, *Mel* 1118, from Tobias 4:19.

Thobie is the French variant; intrusive *h* after *t* was not pronounced.

EJ XV:1183–1187.

THOBIE[2], the younger, was Tobias's son.

The Parson, in his homily on lechery, reminds his audience that married people commit adultery when they think that, because they are married, they may indulge in fleshly delights. The angel Raphael reminded Tobias that the fiend has power over such people, *ParsT* 905–906. In Tobias 4:16–18 the angel says that the fiend has power over those who put God out of their hearts. **[Raphael: Thobie[1]]**

Thobie is the French variant.

THOLOME[1]: [PTHOLOME]

THOLOME[2]. Ptolemy was the title of the Macedonian dynasty, which ruled Egypt from the death of Alexander to the Battle of Actium, 31 B.C. Ptolemy XIII, 63–47 B.C., was Cleopatra's brother, whom she married in 51, then exiled. Caesar defeated him, and he drowned in the Nile. Caesar then made Ptolemy XIV, c. 59–44 B.C., another of Cleopatra's brothers, husband and joint ruler with her in 47. She later ordered his murder; Josephus says she poisoned him. This second brother is the one usually associated with Cleopatra and mentioned by Boccaccio (*De claris mulieribus* LXXXXVI).

Cleopatra rules Egypt after the death of Ptolemy the king, *LGW* 580–582. **[Cleopataras]**

Tholome, the OF variant pronounced like its Greek form, appears once, medially, *LGW* 580.

E. Bevan, *A History of Egypt under the Ptolemaic Dynasty*, 359–384; Boccaccio, *CFW*, trans. G. Guarino, 192; *ibid., De claris mulieribus*, ed. V. Zaccaria, 344–356; Josephus, *Jewish Antiquities*, ed and trans. R. Marcus and A. Wikgren, VIII: 42–43; *OCD*, 897.

THOMAS[1] (saint). Thomas the Apostle was one of the twelve disciples of Jesus (Matthew 10:2). Jacobus de Voragine gives his life story, *Legenda aurea* V. Christian tradition says that he was martyred in India, c. A.D. 46 (*NCE* XIV: 101).

The Merchant swears by St. Thomas of India, *MerchT* 1229–1231.

A.S. Haskell, "Attributes of Anger in the Summoner's Tale (St. Thomas of India)." *Essays on Chaucer's Saints*, 58–63; Jacobus de Voragine, *GL*, trans. G. Ryan and H. Ripperger, 39–46; *ibid., LA*, ed. Th. Graesse, 32–39; *The South-English Legendary*, ed. C. D'Evelyn and A.J. Mill, II: 571–586.

THOMAS[2] is the sick man whom the greedy friar visits in *The Summoner's Tale.* When the friar asks for a donation at the end of the sermon, Thomas gives him a big surprise.

The name occurs six times initially, *SumT* 1772, 1942, 1961, 1970, 1974, 1978; eleven times in medial positions, *SumT* 1770, 1815, 1918, 1954, 1966, 1992, 2000, 2089, 2107, 2112, 2119. It never appears in final rhyming position.

THOMAS[3] is also a generic name for a priest. Harry Bailly wonders if the Monk's name is Daun Thomas, *MkP* 1930.

THOMAS[4] (saint). Thomas à Becket, c. 1118–1170, was born of Norman parentage. He was Henry II's chancellor until 1162, when the king made him archbishop of Canterbury. Thomas, in trying to prevent Henry's seizure of church property, entered a ten-year struggle with the king and endured six years of exile. He returned to England while Henry was in France, at Bar in Normandy, and he excommunicated members of the de Broc family to whom Henry had given church property. When the news reached the king, he was furious and railed that beggars who had eaten at his table had turned against him. Four of his knights, who had suffered from Becket's policies, rode off to England. They were Reginald Fitzurse, Hugh de Moreville, William de Tracy, and Richard le Breton. In England they were joined by the de Brocs and their men. On December 29, 1170, they burst into the cathedral and murdered Thomas before the high altar. Henry, in the grip of remorse, flagellated himself before Thomas's tomb every year as part of his penance, and the archbishop was canonized three years after his death.

The Pilgrims travel to St. Thomas's shrine at Canterbury, *Gen Prol* 826. The Oxford Alison swears by St. Thomas, *MillT* 3291, and the carpenter also, *MillT* 3425, 3461. "Thomas of Kent" and "By seint Thomas" appear as rhyming tags, *MillT* 3291, 3425, 3461. Oxford had a parish of St. Thomas, an annual gathering for mass on St. Thomas's Day, a St. Thomas Hall, and a fraternity of St. Thomas. Thus Oxford's people, scholars, and workers might have had special devotions to St. Thomas. The oaths on St. Thomas's name of Alys of Bath, *WBP* 666, and the Eagle, *HF* III.1131, occur as rhyming tags.

Thomas occurs twice medially, *MillT* 3296; *HF* III.1131; and three times in final rhyming position, *Gen Prol* 826, *MillT* 3425, 3461.

J.A.W. Bennett, *Chaucer at Oxford and at Cambridge*, 15; Garnier de Pont-Sainte-Maxence, *Vie de Saint Thomas le martyr de Cantorbire*, trans. J. Shirley; E. Hibbert, *The Plantagenet Prelude*; Jacobus de Voragine, *GL*, trans. G. Ryan and H. Ripperger, 68–71; *ibid.*, *LA*, ed. Th. Graesse, 66–69; *The South-English Legendary*, ed. C. D'Evelyn and A.J. Mill, II: 610–692; B. Smalley, *The Becket Conflict and the Schools*.

THOPAS is the hero of *The Tale of Sir Thopas*, Chaucer's parody of the romances current in his day. He is named for the semiprecious stone topaz, which, in medieval lapidaries, was linked to all the virtues, including chastity. It was prized among the nobility in Chaucer's day. Sir Thopas is to other splendid knights of renowned romances as the topaz is to other gems. [Beves: Gy: Horn: Lybeux: Oliphant: Percyvell: Pleyndamour: Termagaunt: Ypotis]

Thopas occurs seven times in medial positions, *Thop* 724, 750, 772, 778, 827, 836, 891; and twice in final rhyming position, *Thop* 717, 830.

J. Conley, "The Peculiar Name *Sir Thopas*." *SP* 73 (1976): 42–61; A.T. Gaylord, "The Moment of Sir Thopas: Towards a New Look at Chaucer's Language." *ChauR* 16

(1981–1982): 311–329; A.S. Haskell, "Sir Thopas: The Puppet's Puppet." *ChauR* 9 (1974–1975): 253–261.

THYMALAO. Thimolaus, fl. third century A.D., was one of the sons of Zenobia and Odaenathus of Palmyra. His brother was called Heremianus. Boccaccio says that Zenobia dressed her sons in the regalia and insignia of the Roman emperors, *De casibus virorum illustrium liber* VIII.6.

The Monk mentions this detail, *MkT* 2343–2346. **[Cenobia: Hermanno]**

Since *Thymalao* occurs in final rhyming position, *MkT* 2345, its placement may have determined its form.

Boccaccio, *De casibus*, ed. P.G. Ricci and V. Zaccaria, 678–682.

THYMEO: [PLATO]

THYMOTHEE[1]. Timotheus, fl. second century B.C., was one of the Seleucid generals sent by Antiochus Epiphanes to quell the revolt of the Judaean Jews in 161 B.C. Judah Maccabee routed the Seleucid army, a defeat that led to the death of Antiochus (II Maccabee 8, 9).

The Monk mentions the general Thymothee in his story of Antiochus's fall, *MkT* 2591–2593. **[Anthiochus: Machabee: Nichanore[2]]**

Thymothee occurs in final rhyming position, *MkT* 2591.

THYMOTHEE[2]. Timothy, fl. first century A.D., one of Paul's disciples, was born in Lystra, Lyconia. When Paul visited Lystra in A.D. 80, he found that the local Christians thought well of Timothy, and he took him as a co-worker. He became Paul's constant companion and was the co-writer of the Letters to the Thessalonians, the second Letter to the Corinthians, the Letters to the Philippians, Colossians, and Philemon. Paul addressed two epistles to him, which show fatherly concern. Tradition says Timothy was martyred in A.D. 97 during Nerva's reign (*NCE* XIV: 167).

The Parson refuses to tell a story or a fable since St. Paul, when he wrote to Timothy, reproves those who waive truth and tell fables, *ParsT* 31–34. In I Timothy 1:4, Paul says that some people need to be warned against occupying their minds with strange doctrines and with legends; in I Timothy 4:4, Paul says that when people grow tired of truth, they turn their attention to fables instead. At the beginning of his homily on avarice, the Parson quotes St. Paul that "the root of all harms is covetousness," *ParsT* 739; here a gloss refers *ad Thimotheum sexto* from I Timothy 6:10. This quotation occurs also in *Mel* 1130, 1840, and it is the text of the Pardoner's sermon, *PardT* 334. Neither Paul nor Timothy is named in these latter references. **[Paul]**

F.W. Beare, *St. Paul and his Letters.*

THYSBE: [TESBEE]

TIBURCE, Valerian's brother and Cecile's brother-in-law, is martyred for his faith (*Legenda aurea* LXIX).

Tiburce is converted through Valerian's teaching and becomes a Christian. He suffers martyrdom with his brother, *SNT* 242–409. **[Almache: Cecile: Maxime: Urban: Valerian]**

Tiburce apparently means "the man from Tibur," a famous resort for rich Romans at this time. Both names, *Valerian* and *Tiburce*, indicate that the brothers are from noble Roman families. *Tiburce* occurs twice initially, *SNT* 260, 302; nine times in medial positions, *SNT* 242, 265, 289, 307, 333, 348, 349, 354, 408. It never appears in final rhyming position. *Tiburces*, the ME genitive case, occurs medially, *SNT* 277.

Jacobus de Voragine, *GL*, trans. G. Ryan and H. Ripperger, 689–695; *ibid., LA*, ed. Th. Graesse, 771–777.

TICIUS, TYCIUS. Tityus was one of the giant sons of the Earth. He tried to assault Latona, mother of Apollo and Diana, and as punishment, Jupiter chained him on his back to the pit of Tartarus, where a vulture tore eternally at his liver (*Met* IV.456–460; *OM* IV.3819–3830; *Aeneid* VI.595–600). The story is mentioned briefly in *RR* 19305–19309. In Machaut's *Le Confort d'ami*, 2517–2534, Ticius forgets his evil adventure when he hears Orpheus's harp and the sound of his song.

The vulture is so charmed by Orpheus's song that he pauses in his eating of the stomach or the liver of Ticius, *Bo* III, *Metr* 12.41–43. Pandarus says that Troilus suffers woe as sharp as that of Tycius, whose stomach the vultures eat, *Tr* I.787–788. **[Cesiphus: Tantale]**

Ticius, the OF variant, appears medially, *Tr* I.786, and *Tycius,* a spelling variant, appears in *Bo* III, *Metr* 12.42.

Guillaume de Machaut, *Oeuvres,* ed. E. Hoepffner, III: 89–90; Ovid, *Met,* ed. and trans. F.J. Miller, I: 710–711; *OM,* ed. C. de Boer, II, deel 21: 92; *RR*, ed. E. Langlois, IV: 263–264; *RR*, trans. C. Dahlberg, 318; Virgil, *Aeneid,* ed. and trans. H.R. Fairclough, I: 546–547.

TIMAEUS: [PLATO]
TIMOTHEUS: [THYMOTHEE[2]]
TIRESIAS: [TYRESIE]
TISBE: [TESBEE]
TISIPHONE: [THESIPHONE]

TITAN is the sun in Ovid (*Met* I.10) and Virgil (*Aeneid* IV.19, VI.724–725). Dante (*Purg* IX.1) confuses Titan, the sun, with Tithonous, Aurora's mortal lover, mentioned in *Aeneid* IV.584–585.

Troilus chides Titan, the sun, *Tr* III.1463–1470, because he has allowed the dawn to rise too soon. Chaucer indicates here the confusion between Titan and Tithonous.

The name occurs medially, *Tr* III.1464.

Chaucer, *The Book of Troilus and Criseyde*, ed. R.K. Root, 490; Dante, *The Divine Comedy*, ed. and trans. C.S. Singleton, I, 1: 86–87; Ovid, *Met*, ed. and trans. F.J. Miller, I.2–3; Virgil, *Aeneid*, ed. and trans. H.R. Fairclough, I: 404–405, 434–435, 556–557.

TITYUS: [TICIUS]

TOAS. Thoas was king of Aetolia and one of the Greeks' allies in the Trojan War (*HDT* VIII). The Trojans captured him and later exchanged him for Antenor from the Greeks. He does not appear in Boccaccio's *Il Filocolo* (1333–1339). Chaucer uses Benoît, *Roman de Troie* 12803–13120, in addition to Guido.

The Trojans exchange Toas and Criseyde for Antenor, *Tr* IV.138.
[Antenor: Creseyde]
The name appears medially.

Benoît, *Roman de Troie,* ed. L. Constans, II: 258–276; C. David Benson, "King Thoas and the Ominous Letter in Chaucer's *Troilus*." *PQ* 58 (1979): 364–367; Guido delle Colonne, *Guido de Columnis: HDT*, ed. N.E. Griffin, 88.

TOBIAS: [THOBIE]
TOBIT: [THOBIE]
TREGETOUR: [COLLE TREGETOUR]
TRIGUILLA: [TRYGWILLE]
TRISTAN: [TRISTRAM]

TRISTRAM. Tristan was the son of Blanchefleur of Cornwall and Rivalen of Lyonesse. He was born in Brittany four days after his mother learned of her husband's death, and because she had borne him in sadness, she called him *Tristan,* "child of sadness." While serving his uncle, King Mark, Tristan slew the Morholt of Ireland in battle and left the tip of his sword in the Morholt's side. Upon his return to Cornwall, King Mark sent him in quest of the damsel with hair of gold. Again the quest took him to Ireland, where he slew a terrible dragon that was ravaging the countryside, during which battle he was gravely wounded. Only the queen and her daughter Iseult could cure him of the wounds suffered in that battle. As he lay in the bath, Iseult matched his sword with the piece taken from the Morholt's side. She rushed toward him and raised the sword to kill him, but when she saw how beautiful he was, she could not. Her father betrothed her to King Mark, and she set out for Cornwall with Tristan as her escort. On the ship, they accidentally drank the magic potion, which Iseult's mother had prepared for the wedding night, and fell irrevocably in love.

The first literary version of the story was composed c. 1150, possibly in Anglo-Norman. The Welsh poet Thomas made it a story of courtly love about 1160. A German version appeared about 1175, written by Eilhart von

Oberge, and a French one by Beroul appeared in 1200. The most famous version is by Gottfried von Strassburg (fl. 1210).

Tristram is among love's martyrs, *PF* 288–292. The poet calls himself a second Tristram, *Rosemounde* 20. **[Isaude: Rosemounde]**

Tristram, the English variant, occurs once, initially, *PF* 290; and once medially, *Rosemounde* 20.

Eilhart von Oberge, *Tristant,* trans. J.W. Thomas; Gottfried von Strassburg, *Tristan,* with the *Tristan* of Thomas, trans. A.T. Hatto; *The Romance of Tristan by Beroul,* ed. A. Ewert; *Le Roman de Tristan par Thomas,* ed. J. Bédier; *Le Roman de Tristan en prose,* ed. R.L. Curtis; *The Romance of Tristan and Ysolt by Thomas of Britain,* trans. R.S. Loomis; *Tristan, receuil de ce qui reste des poèmes relatifs à ses aventures,* ed. F. Michel.

TRITON, a sea god, was Poseidon's son in Greek mythology and Neptune's son in Roman mythology. Neptune commands the winds at sea as Aeolus commands them on land (*Aeneid* I.132–141). Triton, Neptune's son, blows a sea conch; Misenus, Aeolus's son, blows a battle trumpet for Hector and, later, for Aeneas. Misenus challenged Triton to a musical contest and lost, whereupon Triton drowned him (*Aeneid* VI.162–176).

Triton carries Eolus's trumpets as they go up to Fame's house, *HF* III.1595–1604. Virgil seems to have connected Aeolus and Triton in some slight way in the *Aeneid.* When Demophon's ship is wrecked, Neptune, Thetis, Chorus, and Triton pity him and wash him up on the beach of Rhodope, where Phillis is the queen, *LGW* 2417–2424. **[Demophon: Eolus: Messenus: Neptune: Phillis: Thetis]**

The name occurs twice medially, *HF* III.1604; *LGW* 2422, and once in final rhyming position, *HF* III.1596.

Virgil, *Aeneid,* ed. and trans. H.R. Fairclough, I: 250–251, 516–519.

TROILUS, son of King Priam and Queen Hecuba of Troy, was one of the chief warriors in the Trojan War. Dares mentions him as a brave warrior, *De excidio Troiae historia,* 12, but there is no love affair between him and Briseis. Benoît de Sainte-Maure invents the love affair about Briselda's betrayal of Troilus in *Roman de Troie,* 13261–13865, composed in the second half of the twelfth century. Guido delle Colonne uses Benoît in his *Historia destructionis Troiae* VIII, XVIIII–XXI (1287); although he does not mention Benoît's name, he uses his portrait of a faithless Briseida. Boccaccio changed the heroine's name to Criseida in his *Il Filostrato* (c. 1338) and invented the whole process of Troilo's falling in love and his wooing, as well as developed the consummation and faithlessness he found in his sources— Dares, Guido, and Benoît. He created Pandaro, a young cousin of Criseida, to act as friend and go-between.

Chaucer's contribution to Boccaccio's story is the psychological development of the characters, which propels the plot as the story unfolds.

The end is in the beginning, the inevitable result of psychological traits. He makes Pandarus, Criseyde's uncle, slightly older than the lovers; he creates the details of Troilus's wooing, the scene in Deiphebus's house (*Tr* II.1394–III.231) and the supper at Pandarus's house, which leads to the lovers' union (*Tr* III.509–1309). In addition to Benoît, Guido, Boccaccio, and perhaps Dares, Chaucer uses *Le Roman de Troyle et de Criseide*, a French translation done in the early 1380s by Jean de Beauveau, Seneschal of Anjou. [**Calcas: Criseyde: Diomede: Pandarus**]

Troilus means "little Troy." Of its two hundred and fifty-three times of occurrence, it never appears initially. It occurs two hundred and fifty times in *Troilus and Criseyde*, two hundred and seven times in medial positions, *Tr* I.1, 30, 35, 55, 183, 215, 268, 288, 309, 396, 498, 519, 568, 621, 624, 722, 737, 749, 776, 834, 866, 871, 936, 1009, 1014, 1056, 1072, 1086; *Tr* II.6, 32, 73, 181, 184, 196, 319, 624, 683, 685, 687, 693, 701, 933, 942, 950, 972, 1058, 1248, 1305, 1312, 1322, 1339, 1394, 1404, 1411, 1494, 1527, 1537, 1548, 1572, 1629, 1666, 1684, 1692, 1752; *Tr* III.48, 65, 78, 128, 194, 201, 219, 228, 230, 238, 345, 425, 488, 693, 515, 533, 569, 577, 600, 700, 706, 713, 742, 781, 786, 839, 920, 953, 981, 1054, 1065, 1101, 1127, 1170, 1184, 1202, 1205, 1245, 1352, 1421, 1443, 1498, 1521, 1529, 1549, 1588, 1590, 1639, 1669, 1702, 1717, 1815, 1819; *Tr* IV.8, 15, 28, 148, 219, 228, 270, 350, 360, 365, 432, 519, 540, 610, 631, 674, 676, 699, 714, 778, 854, 875, 880, 896, 946, 1088, 1121, 1148, 1150, 1156, 1213, 1227, 1253, 1373, 1422, 1476, 1537, 1552, 1653, 1690; *Tr* V.6, 22, 27, 64, 74, 91, 196, 280, 282, 287, 289, 293, 295, 330, 414, 433, 502, 508, 513, 520, 529, 621, 627, 697, 715, 734, 753, 768, 827, 835, 865, 1041, 1046, 1072, 1100, 1111, 1120, 1121, 1135, 1143, 1182, 1312, 1432, 1437, 1566, 1632, 1642, 1647, 1747, 1752, 1801, 1828; and forty-one times in final rhyming position, *Tr* I.309, 396. 621, 657, 773, 820; *Tr* II.157, 171, 192, 198, 612, 668, 1014, 1317, 1457, 1627, 1639; *Tr* III.50, 206, 507, 806, 1583, 1660; *Tr* IV.372, 766, 806, 1200, 1597; *Tr* V.197, 323, 407, 428, 449, 953, 1039, 1053, 1163, 1289, 1564, 1655, 1744. *Troilus* also occurs in medial positions, *Adam* 2; *LGW G* 265, and in final rhyming position, *PF* 291.

Benoît, *Roman de Troie*, ed. L. Constans, II: 287–328; Boccaccio, *Tutte le opere*, ed. V. Branca, II: 17–228; Chaucer, *The Book of Troilus and Criseyde*, ed. R.K. Root; A. Coville, *La Vie intellectuelle dans les Domaines d'Anjou-Provence de 1380 à 1435*; H.M. Cummings, *The Indebtedness of Chaucer's Work to the Italian Works of Boccaccio*; Dares, *De excidio Troiae historia*, ed. F. Meister, 15; *ibid., The Trojan War*, trans. R.M. Frazer, 143; R.K. Gordon, *The Story of Troilus*; Guido delle Colonne, *Guido de Columnis: HDT*, ed. N.E. Griffin, 85, 163–166, 169–173; *ibid., HDT*, trans. M.E. Meek, 84, 156–168; L. Moland and C. d'Héricault, *Nouvelles françaises en prose du XIVe siècle*; R.A. Pratt, "Chaucer and the *Roman de Troyle et de Criseide*." *SP* 53 (1956): 509–539; K. Young, *The Origin and Development of the Story of Troilus and Criseyde*.

TROPHEE. This name has not been identified. Glosses in the margins of the Ellesmere and Hengwrt manuscripts carry the notation: *ille vates*

Chaldeorum Tropheus, "Tropheus was a Chaldean priest." The name thus appears to have been unknown to fifteenth-century scribes. F. Tupper suggests that Trophee is another name for Guido de Columnis, who describes the West Gates of the world, *Historia destructionis Troiae* I. G.L. Kittredge suggests that "tropaea" or "tropea," the common noun for "pillar," came to be thought the name of an author or a book.

The Monk refers his listeners to Trophee, who has written that Hercules set pillars at both ends of the world, *MkT* 2116–2118. **[Ercules]**

Trophee occurs in final rhyming position, *MkT* 2117.

D.K. Fry, "Chaucer's *Zanzis* and a Possible Source for *Troilus and Criseyde* IV.407–413." *ELN* 9 (1971): 81–85; Guido delle Colonne: *Guido de Columnis: HDT,* ed. N.E. Griffin, 3; G.L. Kittredge, "The Pillars of Hercules and Chaucer's 'Trophee.'" *Putnam Anniversary Volume,* 545–566; F. Tupper, "Chaucer and Trophee." *MLN* 31 (1916): 11–14.

TROTULA di Ruggiero, fl. twelfth century A.D., was a physician at the Salerno medical school. She was also the wife of one of the physicians at the school and mother of two sons. She collaborated with her husband in writing the *Encyclopaedia regimen sanitatis* and is credited with the authorship of a treatise on gynecology and obstetrics, *Trotulae curandarum aegritudinum mulierorium ante et post partum,* also known as *De passionibus mulierum,* in sixty chapters. This treatise is referred to simply as *Trotula.* K.C. Hurd-Mead states that Trotula's identity as a female doctor and specialist in women's diseases was never questioned during the fifteenth and sixteenth centuries. Scholars and physicians accepted her reputation as the most noted woman physician of the Middle Ages. Hurd-Mead sees no necessity to claim that Trotula was a man who chose the name as a *nom de plume.* Her work was continuously copied as late as the sixteenth century. P. Meyer gives the dates of three such manuscripts: 1544, 1547, 1566.

Dame Alys says that Trotula's treatise was bound up in Jankyn's anthology, *WBP* 677. **[Jankyn²]**

The name occurs medially, *WBP* 677.

L.Y. Baird-Lange, "Trotula's Fourteenth-Century Reputation, Jankyn's Book, and Chaucer's Trot." *Studies in the Age of Chaucer* (1984): 245–256; K.C. Hurd-Mead, "Trotula." *Isis* 14 (1930): 349–367; P. Meyer, "Les Manuscrits Français de Cambridge." *Romania* 32 (1903): 88–91; B. Rowland, "Exhuming Trotula, *sapiens matrona* of Salerno." *Florilegium* 1 (1979): 42–57; Trotula of Salerno, *The Diseases of Women by Trotula of Salerno,* trans. E. Mason-Hohl.

TRYGWILLE. Boethius says that Trigguilla and Conigastus used their positions with the emperor to oppress the poor and that he (Boethius) upbraided them both for their evil ways, *Bo* I, *Prosa* 4.57–61. Cassiodorus does not mention him. **[Albyn: Basilius: Boece: Conigaste: Cyprian: Decorat: Opilion]**

The form is a variant of Jean de Meun's *Triguille* in *Li Livres de confort de philosophie.*

V.L. Dedeck-Héry, "Boethius' *De consolatione* by Jean de Meun." *MS* 14 (1952): 177.

TUBAL. Lamech's son by his wife Adah was Jubal, "the father of all such as handle the harp and the organ," Genesis 4:21–22. During the Middle Ages Jubal was sometimes called Tubal. The son of Lamech and Sellah was called Tubalcain, and he instructed his descendants in the art of fashioning brass and iron. Isidore names Tubal as the inventor of music before the flood and adds that the Greeks say Pythagoras was the inventor, *Etym* III.16. Jacob of Liège says that he wrote reasonably well on plain song, *Speculum musicae* VII. Both Peter Comestor, *Historia scholastica, Genesis* 28 (*PL* 198: 1079), and Peter Riga, *Aurora, Liber Genesis* 477–484, continue the tradition that Tubal invented music, but the Greeks say it was Pythagoras.

The Man in Black says that, although he wrote many songs, he could not make songs as well as Tubal, Lamech's son, who invented the first songs; he adds that the Greeks say Pythagoras invented the art; *Aurora* says so, *BD* 1157–1170, a reference to Peter Riga's *Aurora.* P.E. Beichner points out that Tubal is a variant reading in some manuscripts of Peter Riga's *Aurora.* [**Absolon**[1]: **Peter**[1] **Riga: Pictagoras**]

The name occurs in final rhyming position, *BD* 1162.

P.E. Beichner, *The Medieval Representative of Music, Jubal or Tubalcain?*; Isidore, *Etymologiae,* ed. W.M. Lindsay, I; Peter Riga, *Aurora,* ed. P.E. Beichner, I: 45–46; O. Strunk, *Source Readings in Music History,* 94, 98, 180–181; K. Young, "Chaucer and Peter Riga." *Speculum* 12 (1937): 299–303.

TULLIUS[1], TULLYUS, TULYUS. Tullius is the name of the Roman clan to which Marcus Tullius Cicero belonged. It was a medieval and Renaissance convention to refer to him familiarly as Tully or Tullius. The references to Tullius in *The Tale of Melibee* also appear in *Le Livre de Mellibee et de Prudence,* by Renaud de Louens (after 1336), and in *Liber consolationis et consilii,* by Albertanus of Brescia (1246). The quotations from Tullius in this tale are mostly from Cicero's *De officiis.* Dame Prudence quotes *De senectute,* VI.17, *Mel* 1165; the quotation from "the book," *Mel* 1176, is from Cicero's *Tusculan Disputations,* III.30.73; Dame Prudence quotes *De amicitia* XXV.91 at *Mel* 1176; *De officiis* I.26.91 at *Mel* 1180; *De officiis* II.7.23 at *Mel* 1192; *De officiis* II.5.18 at *Mel* 1201; from *De officiis* I.9 at *Mel* 1221. Instead of Tullius, Dame Prudence quotes Seneca, *De clementia* I.19.6 at *Mel* 1339; she quotes Tullius, *De officiis* I.21.73 at *Mel* 1344. Instead of Tullius, she quotes Publilius Syrus, *Sententiae* 125 at *Mel* 1347. She quotes Tullius, *De officiis* II.5.16–17 at *Mel* 1355; *De officiis* III.5.21 at *Mel* 1585; *De officiis* II.15.55 at *Mel* 1621; *De officiis* I.25.88 at *Mel* 1860. The poet has been reading "Tullyus on the Drem of Scipioun" before he falls asleep, *PF* 29–35. Lady Philosophy quotes Tullius, *Somnium Scipionis* in *De re publica* VI.20.22, *Bo*

II, *Prosa* 7.59–66. She refers to Cicero's *De divinatione* by name, *Bo* V, *Prosa* 4.3–5, where he discusses God's providence in Book II.8.20. **[Cipioun: Macrobeus: Scithero]**

The forms are spelling variants.

Albertanus Brixiensis, *Liber consolationis et consilii,* ed. T. Sundby; Cicero, *De amicitia,* ed. and trans. W.A. Falconer, 198–199; *ibid., De officiis,* ed. and trans. W. Miller, 74–75, 92–93, 182–185, 190–191, 224–227, 288–289; *ibid., De senectute,* ed. and trans. W.A. Falconer, 26–27; Renaud de Louens, *Le Livre de Mellibee et de Prudence,* ed. J.B. Severs, *S&A,* 560–614; Seneca, *Moral Essays,* ed. and trans. J.W. Basore, I: 412–413.

TULLIUS[2] HOSTILLIUS. Tullus Hostilius is traditionally regarded as the third king of Rome, 673–642 B.C. The Hostilius clan defended Rome against the Sabines and were regarded as founders of the Curia Hostilia (*De casibus virorum illustrium* III.2). Valerius Maximus tells the story of Hostilius's rise from poverty to riches in his chapter *De humili loco natis, Factorum dictorumque memorabilium Liber* III.iv.1.

The Old Wife quotes Valerius's story of Tullius Hostillius, *WBT* 1165–1167. It is doubtful that Chaucer knew Valerius Maximus at firsthand. R.A. Pratt suggests that he found the story in the *Communiloquium* III.iii.3 of John of Wales (second half of the thirteenth century), which shows similar language. Chaucer refers to the generosity of Tullius Hostillius, *Lenvoy de Chaucer a Scogan.* **[Valerie]**

Tullius, derived perhaps by analogy from *Tullius Cicero,* is the family name and appears in Valerius Maximus; *Hostillius* is the clan name. The two names appear in final rhyming position.

Boccaccio, *De casibus,* ed. P.G. Ricci and V. Zaccaria, 200–202; *OCD,* 1099; R.A. Pratt, "Chaucer and the Hand That Fed Him." *Speculum* 41 (1966): 619–642; Valerius Maximus, *Factorum dictorumque memorabilium libri novem,* ed. J. Kappy, I: 373–374.

TULLYUS: [TULLIUS]
TULYUS: [TULLIUS]

TURNUS, king of the Rituli, was betrothed to Lavinia, King Latium's daughter, and fiercely opposed the settlement the king made with the Trojans. He attacked Aeneas, who slew him and married Lavinia (*Aeneid* VII, XII).

Turnus, with hardy, fierce heart, is painted on the wall of Venus's temple, *KnT* 1945. The strife of Turnus is written in the stars, *MLT* 201; the story of how Eneas robbed Turnus of his life is painted on the walls of the temple of glass, *HF* I.457. Turnus's dream of the Fury, *Aeneid* VII.413–434, appears in *HF* II.516. **[Eneas: Gemini: Laveyne]**

Turnus appears four times, in medial positions only, *KnT* 1945; *MLT* 201; *HF* I.457; *HF* II.516.

Virgil, *Aeneid*, ed. and trans. H.R. Fairclough, II: 2–59, 298–365.

TYCIUS: [TICIUS]

TYDEUS, king of Calydon, was a descendent of Meleagre, who had hunted the boar with Atalanta. As brother-in-law to Adrastus, he joined in the war against Thebes. Before they reached the city, fifty Thebans ambushed them, but Tydeus and his men slew all the Thebans except Maeon, whom they sent back to the city to give Eteocles the news (*Thebaid* II.682–703; *Roman de Thèbes* 1479–1794).

Tydeus is slain at Thebes, *Anel* 57. Diomede is his son, *Tr* V.88, 803, 932. Tydeus appears in Cassandra's summary of the Theban War, *Tr* V.1480–1515. **[Adrastus: Amphiorax: Campaneus: Ethiocles: Hemonydes: Parthonope: Polymyte]**

The name appears once initially, *Tr* V.1514; seven times in medial positions, *Tr* V.88, 932, 1485, 1493, 1501, 1514, 1746; and three times in final rhyming position, *Anel* 57; *Tr.* V.803, 1408.

Roman de Thèbes, ed. L. Constans, I: 75–91; *Roman de Thèbes (The Story of Thebes)*, trans. J.S. Coley, 35–42; Statius, *Thebaid*, ed. and trans. J.H. Mozley, I: 444–447.

TYRESIE. Tyresias was a legendary Theban seer. One day he saw two snakes mating, and he struck them apart with his staff. Because he had disturbed nature, the gods turned him into a woman, and he remained female for seven years. During the eighth year he saw two snakes coupling and did the same thing. Immediately, he became a man. Jupiter and Juno asked him to settle a dispute between them about who got more pleasure from sexual intercourse, and Tyresias said the woman did. Juno struck him blind for his insolence, but Jupiter gave him the gift of prophecy as compensation (*Met* III.316–338; *OM* III.999–1106; *Confessio Amantis* III.363–380, 746–767).

Lady Philosophy says that if God's foreknowledge is uncertain, if the things he foresees will either happen or not happen, how is such foreknowledge better than the ridiculous prophecy of Tyresie: "All that I say, either it shall be or it shall not be" *Bo* V, *Prosa* 3.132–136. This quotation is from Horace, *Satire* ii.5.59–60.

Tyresie is the French variant of Latin and Greek *Tyresias.*

John Gower, *The Complete Works*, ed. G.C. Macaulay, II: 235–236, 246; Horace, *Satires*, ed. and trans. H.R. Fairclough, 202–203; Ovid, *Met*, ed. and trans. F.J. Miller, I: 146–149; *OM*, ed. C. de Boer, I, deel 15: 320–323.

TYRO APPOLLONIUS. *Apollonius of Tyre* is a Greek romance, written between the fifth and sixth centuries of the Christian era. It tells how King Antiochus rapes his beautiful daughter, then sets a riddle for all subsequent suitors to solve. Prince Apollonius of Tyre solves the riddle, and the king sets a price on his head. He escapes and embarks on a series of adventures (*Confessio Amantis* VIII.271–2008).

The Man of Law says that Chaucer has not written stories like that of Tyro Apollonius, *MLI* 81–88, and gives a brief summary of the plot. [**Antiochus: Gower**]

Tyro is the Latin ablative of *Tyrus*, the place name used as a personal name. *Tyro Appollonius* appears in final rhyming position, *MLI* 81.

John Gower, *The Complete Works*, ed. G.C. Macaulay, III: 393–440; J.H. Fisher, *John Gower*, 29, 289; *Riverside Chaucer*, ed. L. Benson, 856.

TYTUS: [DITE]

U

UGOLINO: [HUGELYN]

ULIXES. Ulysses of Ithaca, son of Laertes, was Penelope's husband and one of the great heroes of the Trojan War. He was noted for his intelligence and guile, for his capacity to think quickly, and for his ability to find solutions. He could always extricate himself from tight spots, even if it meant lying to Athena. Virgil says that it was Ulysses's stratagem to capture the city of Troy by building a wooden horse in which a battalion of troops could hide themselves, to have Synon lie to the Trojan guards at the gates, and to encourage them to pull the horse into the city. At night, while the city slept, the troops descended from the horse, the last battle began, and Troy was captured (*Aeneid* II.108–623). After the war Ulysses wandered for ten years before he finally reached Ithaca. Homer's *Odyssey* tells of his adventures.

Lady Philosophy recounts Ulixes's visit to Cerce's island, *Bo* IV, *Metr* 3.1–47. She says that Cerces changed the men into different animals: a boar, a lion, a tiger, a wolf. Homer says that the men were changed into pigs (*Odyssey* X.203–574), and Ovid agrees (*Met* XIV.271–298). Only the moly herb, given him by Hermes, protected Ulysses from Circe's enchantments. Then he forced Circe to restore his men to their human form. Lady Philosophy adds that the venom of vice is stronger than Circe's venom, for it changes hearts but not bodies. Jean de Meun says that Circe could not hold Ulixes easily, *RR* 14406–14408. Gower tells the story to illustrate witchcraft, *Confessio Amantis* VI.1415–1473. Lady Philosophy tells how Ulysses smote and blinded the one-eyed man-eating cyclops, Polyphemus, *Bo* IV, *Metr* 7.18–27. She calls Ulysses *Ytakus*, and Chaucer glosses this

Ulixes, following Jean de Meun's translation. [**Cerces: Penelope: Poliphemuss: Ytakus**]

Ulixes is the OF, ME, and Latin form of Greek *Odysseus*.

V.L. Dedeck-Héry, "Boethius' *De consolatione* by Jean de Meun." *MS* 14 (1952): 256; John Gower, *The Complete Works,* ed. G.C. Macaulay, III: 205–207; Homer, *Odyssey*, ed. and trans. A.T. Murray, I: 358–385; Ovid, *Met*, ed. and trans. F.J. Miller, II: 318–321; *RR*, ed. E. Langlois, IV: 60–61; *RR*, trans. C. Dahlberg, 246; Virgil, *Aeneid*, ed. and trans. H.R. Fairclough, I: 300–335.

ULYSSES: [ULIXES]

URBAN. Pope Urban I, fl. third century A.D., reigned A.D. 222–230. He was martyred in 230, during the reign of Alexander Severus. The *Liber pontificalis* makes him a martyr during the reign of Diocletian (A.D. 285–305) and thus mistakenly associates him with Cecelia (*NCE* XIV: 477). The story of his life appears in *Legenda aurea* LXXVII.

Urban is the pope in *The Second Nun's Tale*. Cecile sends her husband Valerian to seek the old pope Urban, who lives in a cave near the Via Appia, *SNT* 141–189, and Urban explains to him the nature of Cecile's vocation, *SNT* 190–215; he baptizes Valerian, *SNT* 215–217. Valerian leads his brother Tiburce to Urban, *SNT* 253–280. Pope Urban baptizes Tiburce, *SNT* 344–357. Urban buries Cecile's body and sanctifies her church, *SNT* 540–550. [**Almache: Cecile: Maxime: Tiburce: Valerian**]

Urban appears once initially, *SNT* 189; ten times in medial positions, *SNT* 177, 179, 185, 217, 306, 309, 350, 541, 547, 551; and once in final rhyming position, *SNT* 305.

Jacobus de Voragine, *GL*, trans. G. Ryan and H. Ripperger, 299–300; *ibid., LA*, ed. Th. Graesse, 341–342.

URSA is the first word of the name of the constellation Ursa Major, or the Great Bear, also known as the Big Dipper, which dominates the North Pole. It never goes below the horizon. In mythology the Great Bear is the huntress Callisto, whom Juno, through jealousy, changed into a bear because Jupiter loved her. When Jupiter set her in the heavens as the Great Bear, Juno decreed that the constellation would never set (*Met* II.407–530; *OM* II.1365–1694).

Boethius remarks that Ursa is never washed in the deep western sea; that is, the constellation never sets, *Bo* IV, *Metr* 6.8–15. [**Arctour: Boëtes: Calistopee**]

Ovid, *Met*, ed. and trans. F.J. Miller, I: 94–97; *OM*, ed. C. de Boer, I, deel 15: 201–208.

V

VACHE. Sir Philip de la Vache, 1346–1408, married the daughter of Sir Lewis Clifford, one of Chaucer's closest friends. Edith Rickert gives a history of the Vache family and includes an account of their various difficulties. Philip de la Vache was made a Knight of the Chamber in 1378 and a Knight of the Garter in 1399. A country gentleman with a reputation for lavish hospitality, he may have been the model for the Franklin in the *General Prologue.*

Chaucer addresses him in the Envoy of *Truth* 22. Since this envoy exists in only one of the twenty-two manuscripts of the poem, it may have been added at a later date.

A. David, "The Truth about Vache." *ChauR* 11 (1977): 334–337; E. Rickert, "Thou Vache." *MP* 11 (1913–1914): 209–225; *Riverside Chaucer*, ed. L. Benson, 1084.

VALENTINE: [VALENTYN]

VALENTYN, VALENTYNE, VALENTYNES. Three martyrs named Valentine, who have nothing to do with love, are commemorated on February 14. Two of them were beheaded on February 14: a priest of Rome, whose shrine was established near the Flaminian Way, and the other, a bishop of Terni, to whom a basilica was dedicated in the eighth century. The earliest passions of the two Valentines were written in the sixth or seventh centuries. The third is Valentine of Rhetie, a seventh-century itinerant bishop, buried near Merano in the Italian Tyrol. Jacobus de Voragine recounts a life of St. Valentine in *Legenda aurea* XLII, and a life appears in the *South-English Legendary* 16 (late thirteenth century).

Spring begins when the sun enters the zodiacal sign Aries. Many birds mate in February and in some western European countries flowers bloom by February 23. Chaucer seems to have been the first author in English to connect St. Valentine's Day with the mating birds, and the *Parlement of Foules* appears to be the first Valentine poem. The chronology of the Valentine poems of Graundson, Gower, and Clanvowe is uncertain. The poet lists *The Book of St. Valentynes Day,* probably *The Parlement of Foules* among those he retracts, *ParsT* 1086. *The Complaint of Mars* is sung by a bird on St. Valentine's Day, *Mars* 13–14. On the first day of May the birds sing to St. Valentine, *LGW F* 108–146, *LGW G* 89–1330.

Valentyn occurs in a medial position, *PF* 683; *Valentyne* occurs in a medial position, *Mars* 13, and in final rhyming position, *LGW F* 145, *LGW G* 131. *Valentynes,* the ME genitive case, appears in *ParsT* 1086, and four times in medial positions, *PF* 309, 322, 386; *Compleynt d'amours* 85.

Jacobus de Voragine, *GL,* trans. G. Ryan and H. Ripperger, 165–166; *ibid., LA,* ed. Th. Graesse, 176–177; A. Kellogg and R.C. Cox, "Chaucer's St. Valentine: a Conjecture." *Chaucer, Langland, and Arthur: Essays in Middle English Literature,* 108–145; J.B. Oruch, "St. Valentin, Chaucer, and Spring in February." *Speculum* 56 (1981): 534–565; *The South-English Legendary,* ed. C. D'Evelyn and A.J. Mill, I: 61–62.

VALERIA. Jerome tells the story of Valeria, who would not remarry when her husband died, *Epistola adversus Jovinianun (Letter Against Jovinian)* I.46 *(PL* 23: 276).

Dorigen mentions Valeria among her examples of true wifehood, *FranklT* 1456. **[Dorigen]**

The name occurs in final rhyming position.

G. Dempster, "Chaucer at Work on the Complaint in *The Franklin's Tale." MLN* 52 (1937): 6–16; K. Hume, "The Pagan Setting of *The Franklin's Tale* and the Sources of Dorigen's Cosmology." *SN* 44 (1972): 289–294; J. Sledd, "Dorigen's Complaint." *MP* 45 (1947): 36–45.

VALERIAN, VALERIANS. Valerian is the noble youth married to Cecilia, who converts him and his brother Tiburce to Christianity. They all suffer martyrdom for the faith *(Legenda aurea* CLXIX).

Valerian, married to Cecilia, respects her requests on their wedding night. She tells him that to see the angel who protects her, he must be converted and seek out Pope Urban in a cave near the Via Appia, *SNT* 141–217. Valerian accompanies his brother Tiburce to Urban, *SNT* 253–280. Pope Urban baptizes them both, *SNT* 344–357. On Almachius's orders, Valerian and Tiburce are beheaded, *SNT* 379–406.

Jacobus de Voragine does not give an etymology of *Valerian.* Like the name *Tiburce, Valerian,* the name of a Roman clan, suggests that the bearer was of noble birth. *Valerian* occurs six times initially, *SNT* 148, 162, 183, 204, 218, 253; eight times in medial positions, *SNT* 203, 224, 232, 235, 262, 266, 350, 408; and three times in final rhyming position, *SNT* 129, 213, 306.

Valerians, the ME genitive case, appears in medial position, *SNT* 277.

Jacobus de Voragine, *GL*, trans. G. Ryan and H. Ripperger, 689–695; *ibid.*, *LA*, ed. Th. Graesse, 771–777.

VALERIE, VALERYE[1]. This is the familiar name for Walter Map's *Dissuasio Valerii ad Rufinum philosophum ne uxorem ducat*, which forms Distinction IV, chapter 3, of *De nugis curialium* (1180–1183). A Welsh cleric, Map (c. 1140–c. 1209), became archdeacon of Oxford. During the medieval period some scholars, among them Nicholas Trevet, believed the *Dissuasio* to be the work of Valerius Maximus. The work gives details of the disadvantages of marriage and illustrates the unhappiness that, the author claims, lies in store for the man who marries.

Alys of Bath refers to the treatise simply as "Valerye," *WBP* 671, a work bound up in Jankyn's anthology. The God of Love's reference to "Valerye," *LGW G* 280, may indicate the *Dissuasio*, with its mention of Lucretia, Penelope, and the Sabine Women. Chaucer may also have meant Valerius Maximus, as in the entry below. [**Crisippus: Jerome: Jovinian: Tertulan: Theofraste: Trotula: Valerius**]

Valerie, the English variant of Latin *Valerius*, is derived in this case through pronunciation of the Latin genitive case *Valerii*. It appears once medially, *WBP* 671; *Valerye*, a spelling variant, appears once medially, *LGW G* 280.

R.J. Dean, "Unnoticed Commentaries on the *Dissuasio Valerii* of Walter Map." *MRS* 2 (1950): 128–150; Walter Map, *De nugis curialium: Courtiers' Trifles*, ed. and trans. M.R. James, 288–311.

VALERIUS, VALERYE[2]. Valerius Maximus was a Roman historian during Tiberius's reign (A.D. 14–37), to whom he dedicated his handbook for rhetoricians, *Factorum dictorumque memorabilium libri novem* (*Nine Books of Memorable Deeds and Sayings*). Published after A.D. 31, it consisted mostly of moral and philosophical stories.

Dame Alys tells two stories found in *Factorum dictorumque memorabilium, Liber* VI.3: *De severitate*: the story of Metellius, who beat his wife because she drank wine, *WBP* 460–462, and that of Simplicius Gallus, who left his wife because she looked out the door bareheaded, *WBP* 643–646. She specifically mentions Valerius's story of Tullus Hostilius, *WBT* 1165–1167, from *Liber* III.4: *De humili loco natis qui clari evaserunt*, where the name is spelled *Tullius*. R.A. Pratt points out that these stories also appear in the thirteenth-century *Communiloquium sive summa collationum* of John of Wales, which Chaucer may have known.

Valerius is one of the Monk's authorities on Caesar, *MkT* 2720. Anecdotes about Caesar appear in *Liber* IV.4 and *Liber* VIII.5. Chauntecleer apparently puns on Maximus, "oon of the gretteste auctour that men rede," *NPT* 2984–3049, when he tells a story from *Liber* I.7.10 of the *Factorum dictorumque memorabilium libri novem.* The story also appears in Cicero's *De divinatione* I.27. The God of Love mentions Valerie as a writer of noble deeds of faithful wives, *LGW G* 280–281, an ambiguous reference, which could indicate Walter Map's *Dissuasio Valerie ad Rufinum philosophum ne uxorem ducat* (1181-1183), with its mention of Lucretia, Penelope, and the Sabine Women, as well as the work of Valerius Maximus. **[Tullius Hostillius: Valerie]**

Valerye, the English variant of Latin *Valerius*, appears once medially, *LGW G* 280; *Valerius* appears once in medial position, MkT 2720, and once in final rhyming position, *WBT* 1165.

Cicero, *De divinatione*, ed. and trans. W.A. Falconer, 284–287; Walter Map, *De nugis curialium: Courtiers' Trifles*, ed. and trans. M.R. Rhodes, 288–311; *OCD*, 1106; K.O. Petersen, *On the Sources of the* Noones Preestes Tale, 109; R.A. Pratt, "Chaucer and the Hand That Fed Him." *Speculum* 41 (1966): 619–642; Valerius Maximus, *Factorum dictorumque memoralibilium libri novem*, ed. J. Valpy, I: 202, 373–374, 472–473, 717–718.

[VALERIUS FLACCUS.] Little is known about Valerius Flaccus, fl. first century A.D. He is famous for his work, *Argonauticon*. His *agnomen* or title of place, Setinus, indicates that he was a native of Setia, either in Campania or in Spain. He probably began his *Argonauticon* c. A.D. 70, but it remained unfinished when he died, c. A.D. 90. The poem tells of the voyage of the ship *Argo* and its occupants, the Argonauts, led by Jason in search of the Golden Fleece.

Chaucer does not mention Valerius Flaccus but seems to have known *Argonauticon* at firsthand; he mentions the title in *LGW* 1457 and directs the reader to it for the names of those who went in search of the Golden Fleece. *Argonauticon* I.353–483 lists the heroes who accompanied Jason on the quest. The influence of the poem appears in *HF* III.1572, 1585–1587, where Thrace is given as the home of Aeolus, god of the winds. Virgil, in contrast, says that Aeolus's home is in Aeolia (*Aeneid* I.50–59). Phebus is described as "golden tressed," *Tr* V.8. Shannon points out that no ancient poet, except Valerius Flaccus, has used this epithet for Phoebus. The stories of Hypsipyle and Medea, *LGW* 1368–1679, appear in *Argonauticon* II and VII. The *Valerie* of *LGW G* 280 is ambiguous and may indicate Valerius Flaccus, Valerius Maximus, or the Valerius of Walter Map's *Dissuasio Valerii ad Rufinum philosophum ne uxorem ducat* (1181-1183). **[Isiphile: Jason: Medea]**

E.P. Shannon, *CRP*, 340–355; Valerius Flaccus, *Argonauticon*, ed. and trans. J.H. Mozley; Virgil, *Aeneid*, ed. and trans. H.R. Fairclough, I: 244–245.

VALERIUS MAXIMUS: [VALERIUS]

VENUS, the daughter of Jupiter and Dione, was at first the goddess of gardens (*Met* XIV.585–595). The *vinalia rustica*, the wine festival of August

19, was dedicated to Venus and Jupiter (Varro, *De lingua Latina* [*On the Latin Tongue*] VI.20). She was Vulcan's wife but had many lovers. By Bacchus, she was mother of Hymenaeus, god of marriage (Martianus Capella, *De nuptiis Mercurii et Philologiae* I.1), and of Priapus, god and guardian of gardens (Pausanias, *DG* IX.31.2). By Mars, she was Cupid's mother; by Hermes (Mercury), she was mother of Hermaphroditos, whose name denotes his parentage (*Met* IV.288–388). By Antigamus, Venus was mother of Jocus or Sport (*De planctu Naturae*, X.142–154, Prose V). Ovid calls her *geminorum mater amorum* (mother of the twin loves), as the mother of Eros and Anteros (*Fasti* IV.1).

Venus, Saturn's daughter, was born of the foam of his severed testicles, which his son Jupiter cut off and threw into the sea. This story is told of Aphrodite Urania, who represents chaste love in Plato, *Symposium* 180D–181. Medieval mythographers, including Isidore (*Etym* VIII.xi.77), say that Venus's father is the mutilated god Saturn, instead of Uranus. One version of the myth says that as Venus emerged from the sea, she landed at Paphos in Cyprus; another version says that she first landed at Cythera off the Laconian coast. Both islands claimed her as their goddess. She is also called *Venus Anadyomene* (Venus rising from the sea). Both Venus, Jove's daughter, and Venus, Saturn's daughter, represent multiple connotations, including the *vita voluptuosa* or the voluptuous life, in Chaucer's poetry. The dove and the sparrow are her birds, Friday her day, and copper her metal. Her devotees are Alys of Bath, Aurelius, Chauntecleer, Damyan, Januarie, Palamon, and Troilus.

Palamon is devoted to Venus in *The Knight's Tale*. He thinks he sees Venus walking in the garden below his prison window, but it is Emelye, *KnT* 1102–1111. Venus slays him with jealousy, *KnT* 1332–1333; she is "gerry" or fickle, *KnT* 1535–1539. Theseus builds her an oratory above the east gate of the stadium, *KnT* 1902–1905, on the walls of which are pictures that indicate the goddess is a conflation of her mythological and planetary aspects. Venus dwells on Mount Citheron, *KnT* 1918–1936. Her effect on lovers is their destruction, *KnT* 1940–1954. She floats on the sea, *KnT* 1955–1958. From the navel down, she is covered with waves as green as glass; she holds a citole or cithara in her right hand, and on her head she wears a garland of fresh roses. Her doves fly above her head, and her son Cupid—winged, blind, and armed with bow and arrows—precedes her, *KnT* 1957–1966. Chaucer describes Venus in this passage in almost the same words as Petrus Berchorius in *De formis figurisque deorum*, fol. 5ᵛa. 41–44: *Fingebatur igitur Venus puella pulcherrima nuda & in mari natans & in manu sua dextera concham marinam continens atque ges[ta]ns, que rosis erat ornata, a columbis circumvolantibus comitata* ("Venus is painted as a very beautiful girl, nude, swimming in the sea, and holding a seashell in her right hand; she is ornamented with roses, with a train of doves flying around her"). Berchorius links the seashell with music and, by substituting the *citole* or cithara for the seashell, Chaucer continues the tradition that music is part of the voluptuous life. Palamon worships Venus at the twenty-third hour of Sunday, two hours before sunrise on Monday, *KnT* 2209–2216. He addresses Venus as Jove's daughter and Vulcan's spouse when he prays to her, *KnT* 2221–2386. Strife erupts between Venus and Mars in heaven, which Saturn eventually settles, *KnT* 2438–2482.

Venus dominates Dame Alys, *WBP* 464–710. Venus laughs because Januarie has become her knight and dances with her firebrand in her hand before the bride, *MerchT* 1723–1728; this fire hurts Damyan, the squire, *MerchT* 1777. The firebrand is borrowed from *RR* 15778. Damyan burns in Venus's fire, *MerchT* 1875. Perhaps because of destiny or happenstance, or because the time is appropriate for the works of Venus, May pities Damyan, *MerchT* 1968–1981. Wine and youth increase Venus's influence, *PhysT* 59. Friday is Venus's day; she is the goddess of pleasure, and Chauntecleer is her servant, *NPT* 3342–3348. The Dreamer finds himself in a temple of glass, where he sees a portrait of the Venus, naked and floating in the sea, wearing a garland of red and white roses, holding a comb; her doves, her blind son Cupid, and her husband Vulcan accompany her, *HF* I.130–139. Jove's Venus causes Dido to fall in love with Eneas, with unhappy results, *HF* I.213–432. The Eagle tells the Dreamer that Jupiter will reward him for his service to Venus, *HF* II.615–618. On a tablet of brass is painted the story of Troy, as Venus warns Eneas to flee, *HF* III.162–165. Ovid, Venus's clerk, stands on a pillar of copper, *HF* III.1486. Copper is Venus's metal, *CYT* 829, and in *Confessio Amantis* IV.2473.

The inscription above the garden gate acknowledges the dual nature of Venus, *PF* 127–140. The sparrow is Venus's bird, *PF* 351. In the darkened temple Venus lies half-naked on her bed; painted on the walls are stories of love's martyrs and the manner of their deaths, *PF* 246–294. The formel eagle does not want to serve Venus or Cupid just yet, *PF* 652–653. Pandarus serves Venus, *Tr* II.234, 1524. The narrator of the *Troilus* invokes Venus in the Prohemium, *Tr* III.1–49. Chauncey Wood shows that multiple Venuses appear in this passage: the goddess of concupiscence, the goddess of generation, the patron deity of friendship, and the source of filial and patriotic love. Troilus invokes Venus, whose servant he is, Venus, *Tr* I.1014, II.972–973, III.706–719, but curses Cipride, *Tr* V.208. Venus is the God of Love's mother, *LGW F* 338, *LGW G* 313.

Venus, the mother of Aeneas, was called *Venus Genetrix* or *Venus Erycina* and was regarded as the mother of the Roman people. The Julian clan (gens Iulia), of which Julius Caesar was the most famous member, traced their descent from Iulus (Ascanius), her grandson (*Fasti* IV.19–60, 123–124). A temple on Mount Eryx, on the northwest coast of Sicily, was dedicated to her as ancestress of the Roman people (*Met* V.363)

As Aeneas's mother, Venus appears in *HF* I.162–252, *LGW* 940–1086.

Venus is also the planet of the third circle, counting away from the earth, between Mercury and the sun (see Ptolemaic map). Mars is lord of the third heaven, Venus's sphere. Libra is her day house, and Taurus her night house. Pisces is her exaltation or sign of maximum power, and Virgo is her depression, or sign of minimum power (*Tetrabiblos* I.19). She is Hesperus, the evening star, and Lucifer, the morning star (*Amores* I.vi.65–66; *Heroides* XVIII.112).

Dame Alys says that she is all Venerien and her heart is Martian, *WBP* 609–610. Venus has given her great desire; she cannot withdraw her chamber of Venus from the man who pleases her, *WBP* 611–618. The children of Venus (*i.e.*, those born under her influence) are contrary to Mercury's children: Venus's children love riot and extravagance, while Mercury's children are clerks or scholars, *WBP* 697–700. Ptolemy remarks that when Mars and Venus are allied, their subjects are pleasing, cheerful, erotic, fond of dancing, and pleasure loving, among other qualities (*Tetrabiblos* III.13). Venus and Mercury occupy opposite positions, so that Venus is exalted in Pisces (the depression of Mercury) and depressed in Virgo (the exaltation of Mercury), *WBP* 704; *SqT* 272–273; Venus falls where Mercury is raised, *WBP* 705. Venus sits in her seventh house (the division of the celestial sphere just above the horizon) at Troilus's birth, *Tr* II.680–686. She adorns the third heaven, *Tr* III.2. She represses the malice of Mars and Saturn, *Tr* III.715–721, *LGW* 2589–2595. She is the "wel-nilly" or well-meaning planet, *Tr* III.1257. She rises as Cynthia sets, *Tr* V.1016–1019. Venus gives Ypermystra her great beauty, and Venus, allied with Jupiter in Ypermystra's horoscope, influences her behavior, *LGW* 2584–2588. Jupiter allied with Venus makes the subject pure, of good character, guileless, religious, moderate, and decorous in matters of love (*Tetrabiblos* III.13). Ypermystra cannot hold the knife to kill Lino because Venus has repressed Mars's venom at her birth, *LGW* 2589–2595. Venus weeps in her sphere and causes the downpour, *Scogan* 11–12.

The Complaint of Mars, a Valentine poem, is an astrological interpretation of *Met* IV.171–189; J.D. North shows how the poem accords with medieval astronomy. The narrator, bidding the birds awaken, points to Venus rising, *Mars* 2. The poem will tell how Mars had to leave Venus when Phebus rose in the morning, *Mars* 22–28. Mars, lord of the third heaven, wins Venus's love, *Mars* 31. Venus reigns in bliss because she governs Mars, *Mars* 44, and Mars sings in his happiness with Venus, who causes him such pleasure, *Mars* 45–46. Mars enters Venus's palace to live there, *Mars* 50–56, and in great joy Venus kisses Mars, *Mars* 71–75. Phebus, torch in hand, knocks on Venus's chamber, *Mars* 81–84, and Venus weeps and embraces Mars, *Mars* 85–91. Venus flees to Cilenios's tower; that is, Venus enters the first 2 degrees of Gemini, Mercury's mansion or house, *Mars* 113–114. Mars is now disconsolate and addresses Venus in the language of courtly love, *Mars* 136–146.

The Complaint of Venus is based on three French *balades* by Otes de

Graunson, the first, fourth, and fifth from his *Cinq balades ensuivans* (Braddy 61–64). The fifth and twelfth hours of Saturday belong to Venus, *Astr* II.12. The degree of longitude of Venus is the sixth degree of Capricorn, *Astr* II.40. [**Bachus: Cipride: Citherea: Dido: Dyone; Eneas: Esperus: Fyssh: Graunson: Imeneus: Libra: Lucifer[1]: Mars: Mercurie: Palamon: Pisces: Priapus: Taur: Troilus: Virgo: Vulcano**]

Venus occurs three times initially, *WBP* 611; *Tr* III.1257; *HF* I.213; seventy-eight times in medial positions: *KnT* 1102, 1104, 1332, 1536, 1904, 1918, 1937, 1949, 1955, 2216, 2265, 2272, 2386, 2440, 2453, 2480, 2487, 2585, 2663; *WBP* 464, 604, 618, 700, 704, 705, 708; *MerchT* 1777, 1875, 1971; *SqT* 272; *CYT* 829; *PhysT* 59; *MkP* 1961; *NPT* 3342; *PF* 261, 351, 652; *HF* I.130, 219, 227; *HF* II.618; *HF* III.1487; *Tr* II.234, 680, 972, 1524; *Tr* III.48, 187, 705, 712, 951, 1257; *Tr* IV.1601; *Tr* V.1016; *LGW F* 338; *LGW G* 313; *LGW* 1021, 1072, 1086, 2584, 2591, 2592; *Mars* 2, 26, 31, 46, 77, 84, 89, 104, 113, 136, 141, 143, 145, 146; *Scogan* 11; nine times in final rhyming position, *KnT* 2221; *WBP* 697; *FranklT* 937, 1304; *HF* I.162, 465; *LGW* 940, 998; *Mars* 43.

Alan of Lille, *De planctu Naturae*, ed. N.M. Häring, 849; *ibid., The Plaint of Nature*, trans. J.J. Sheridan, 164–165; Petrus Berchorius, *Ovidius Moralizatus* XV, ed. J. Engels, 22; H. Braddy, *Chaucer and the French Poet Graunson*, 61–64; Fulgentius, *Fulgentius the Mythographer*, trans. L.G. Whitbread, 105–160; John Gower, *The Complete Works*, ed. G.C. Macaulay, II: 368; R. Hollander, *Boccaccio's Two Venuses*, 51–52; Isidore, *Etymologiae*, ed. W.M. Lindsay, I; Martianus Capella, *De nuptiis Mercurii et Philologiae*, ed. A. Dick, 3–4; *ibid., The Wedding of Mercury and Philology*, trans. W.H. Stahl, 3; J.D. North, "Kalenderes Enlumyned Ben They." *RES*, 20 (1969): 137–142; Ovid, *Amores and Heroides*, ed. and trans. G. Shower-man, 250–253, 340–341; *ibid., Fasti*, ed. and trans. J.G. Frazer, 188–193, 196–197; *ibid., Met*, ed. and trans..F.J. Miller, I: 198–205, 262–263, II: 340–343; E. Panofsky, *Studies in Iconology*, 142–144; Pausanias, *DG*, ed. and trans. W.H.S. Jones, IV: 306–307; Plato, *Symposium*, ed. and trans. W.R.M. Lamb, 106–111; Ptolemy, *Tetrabiblos*, ed. and trans. F.E. Robbins, 90–91, 349–351, 352–355; B.N. Quinn, "Venus, Chaucer, and Pierre Bersuire." *Speculum* 38 (1963): 479–480; E.G. Schreiber, "Venus in the Medieval Mythographic Tradition." *JEGP* 74 (1975): 519–535; J. Steadman, "Venus' Citole in Chaucer's *Knight's Tale* and Berchorius." *Speculum* 34 (1959): 620–624; Varro, *De lingua Latina (On the Latin Tongue)*, ed. and trans. R.G. Kent, I: 192–193; E.H. Wilkins, "Descriptions of Pagan Divinities from Petrarch to Chaucer." *Speculum* 32 (1957): 511–522; C. Wood, *Chaucer and the Country of the Stars*, 103–160; *ibid., The Elements in Chaucer's Troilus*, 99–128.

VERGIL: [VIRGIL]
VERGINIA: [VIRGINIA]
VERGINIUS: [VIRGINIUS]

VINCENT OF BEAUVAIS was born between 1190 and 1200. Sometime after 1250, when he became librarian of the Royal Library of Louis IX of France, he began his *Speculum majus*. He wrote three parts: *Speculum naturale*, based on the works of Plato, Pliny, ibn-Sina, and Isidore of Seville;

Speculum doctrinale, which combines theology and the history of art, industry, society, and learning; and *Speculum historiale,* a history of the world from the Christian point of view, published by Caxton in 1490 as *The Myrrour of the World.* A fourth part, the spurious *Speculum morale,* was added between 1310 and 1325. This huge work establishes Vincent as chief of medieval encyclopedists (*NCE* XIV: 679).

Chaucer shows some acquaintance with this work, especially in *The Monk's Tale* and the *Legend of Good Women.* The old wife quotes from a passage in *Speculum historiale,* X.71, *WBT* 1195–1200. The God of Love refers to Vincent's *Estoryal Myrour,* which gives examples of virtuous women in Book VI.cviii–cxxii, *LGW G* 307.

Vincent occurs once, medially, *LGW G* 307.

P. Aiken, "Chaucer's Legend of Cleopatra and the *Speculum Historiale.*" *Speculum* 13 (1938): 232–236; *ibid.,* "Vincent of Beauvais and Chaucer's Knowledge of Alchemy," *SP* 41 (1944): 371–389; *ibid.,* "Vincent of Beauvais and Chaucer's *Monk's Tale.*" *Speculum* 17 (1942): 56–68; *ibid.,* "Vincent of Beauvais and Dame Pertelot's Knowledge of Medicine." *Speculum* 10 (1935): 281–287; Vincent of Beauvais, *Speculum majus.*

VIRGIL, VIRGILE, VIRGILIUS. Publius Vergilius Maro, 70–19 B.C., was born at Andes near Mantua in Cisalpine Gaul. His clan name *Vergilius* and his family name *Maro* are Etruscan. He is commonly known as Virgil, although the Roman *Vergil* is being used increasingly. His *Eclogues,* his first work in ten pastoral poems, became very famous during the Middle Ages, especially the Fourth, which was held to be a prophecy of Christ's birth. Besides several shorter poems, his other main works are the *Georgics,* consisting of four books on agriculture, and his great work, *Aeneid,* an epic in twelve books begun about 26 B.C. and left almost unfinished at his death in 19 B.C. He was buried near Naples, where his tomb became a shrine and a place of pilgrimage shortly afterward.

During his lifetime Virgil's poetry was highly esteemed. As the study of grammar became highly developed, his work was used to illustrate the categories of rhetoric, in which form it was generally known during the medieval period, when his poetry became the backbone of medieval Latin studies. In the fourth century there appeared *Vita Vergili,* published by Aelius Donatus, Jerome's teacher, followed by *Interpretationes Vergilianae,* a commentary in twelve books by Tiberius Claudius Donatus, and a detailed commentary on all Virgil's work by Marius Severus Honoratus. In the early fifth century Macrobius devoted Books 3–6 of his *Saturnalia* to Virgilian criticism; in the later fifth century Fabius Planciades Fulgentius wrote his *Expositio Vergilianae continentiae secundum philosophos moralis (Exposition of the Content of Virgil According to Moral Philosophy)* giving allegorical interpretation to the *Aeneid.* In Dante's *Commedia* Virgil is called the supreme virtue, Reason (*Inf* X.4). In the twelfth century, John of Salisbury presented the first six books of the *Aeneid* as the development of the human soul (*Policraticus* VIII.24). The story of Aeneas developed into romance with the *Eneas,* written by a Norman cleric between 1150 and 1160, a poem that exerted enormous influence on poets of the time and was imitated by the Flemish poet Heinrich von Veldeke in his German *Eneide* (1170–1185). Virgil himself appeared as clerk, poet, and astrologer in the *Dolopathos* (late twelfth century). Virgil also developed the attributes of a magician, especially in Naples near his tomb, then throughout Europe. In Wolfram von Eschenbach's *Parzival* (twelfth century) Klingsor the magician is Virgil's descendant, and Virgil the magician appears in *Cléomades,* written near the end of the thirteenth century, and in *Renart le Contrefait,* written in the fourteenth century.

Although Virgil's name appears only eight times in Chaucer's works, his influence is pervasive. The fiend tells the accursed summoner that, after he has experienced hell, he will be able to hold a chair in the subject, better than Dante or Virgile, *FrT* 1517–1520. The story of Dido held Chaucer's imagination more than any other in Virgil; he recounts it in *HF* I.140–378 and gives it fuller treatment in *The Legend of Dido,* but there he follows Ovid rather than Virgil. Whoever wants to know the torments of hell must read Virgile, or Claudian, or Daunte, *HF* I.445–450, a reference to *Aeneid* VI, *De raptu Proserpinae,* and *Inferno.* The poet hears Messenus's trumpet, which Virgilius has mentioned, *HF* III.1243–1244, referring to *Aeneid* VI.162–176. Virgile stands on a pillar of "tynned iren," *HF* III.1481–1485. Tin is Jupiter's metal, and iron belongs to Mars. E. Nitchie interprets this image to mean that Jupiter controls Mars in the *Aeneid.* The narrator bids his little book to kiss the steps of "Virgile, Ovyde, Omer, Lucan, and Stace," *Tr* V.1786–1792. The narrator gives glory and honor to "Virgil Mantoan" at the beginning of Dido's story, *LGW* 924–925. The narrator says he could follow Virgile but then the story would be too long, *LGW* 1002–1003.

Chaucer refers to *Eneydos,* the *Aeneid,* three times: the death of Priam in *Aeneid* II.532–558, *NPT* 3355–3361; and two references for the story of Dido, *HF* I.377–378 and *LGW* 928. [**Achate: Ascanius: Dido: Eneas: Iulo: Venus**]

Virgil, the English contraction of Latin *Vergilius,* occurs once, medially, *LGW* 924; *Virgile,* with syllabic final -e, occurs in *FrT* 1519; with silent final -e, in *HF* I.378, 449; and twice in final rhyming position, *HF* III.1483; *LGW* 1002. *Virgilius,* the English variant of Latin *Vergilius,* occurs once, in final rhyming position, *HF* III.1244.

D. Comparetti, *Vergil in the Middle Ages;* E.R. Curtius, *ELLMA,* 36; Dante, *The Divine Comedy,* ed. and trans. C.S. Singleton, I, 1: 98–99; *Eneas, roman du XIIe siècle,* ed. J.-J. Salverda de Grave; Fulgentius, *Fulgentius the Mythographer,* trans. L.G. Whitbread, 103–152; Macrobius *Saturnalia,* trans. P.V. Davies, 188–439; *ibid., Saturnalia,* ed. J. Willis, I: 161–395; E. Nitchie, *Vergil and the English Poets,* 57–59; J.F. Spargo, *Virgil the Necromancer: Studies in Virgilian Legends;* Virgil, *The Complete Works,* ed. and trans. H.R. Fairclough; Heinrich von Veldeke, *Eneide,* ed. G. Schub and T. Frijs.

VIRGILE: [VIRGIL]
VIRGILIUS: [VIRGIL]

VIRGINIA. Verginia, daughter of the Roman consul Verginius, was the young Roman maiden for whom Appius the judge conceived a violent lust. He commissioned Marcus Claudius his client to claim the girl as his own, while her father was away at the front. Marcus Claudius followed Appius's plan and claimed that the girl, who belonged in his house, had been stolen away by Verginius. Appius ruled that Claudius could keep her as his own until her father arrived the next day. Her fiancé claimed her, but his claim was ignored. Verginia was surrendered to Claudius. Her father Verginius returned posthaste from the front and, leading his daughter to the marketplace, he pleaded with the populace to strengthen his claim to his daughter. Appius appeared and, ignoring Verginius's pleas, awarded Verginia to Claudius. Verginius thereupon stabbed his daughter in the heart, asserting that only thus could he proclaim her freedom (Livy, *Ab urbe condita liber* III.xliv-lviii; *Confessio Amantis* VII.5131–5306; *RR* 5589–5658).

Virginia is Virginius's daughter in *The Physician's Tale*. She is Nature's masterpiece, *PhysT* 7–29, over whom Venus and Bacchus have no power, *PhysT* 58–60. Because he feels passionate lust for her, Apius hires the villain Claudius to swear in his court that Virginia is Claudius's slave, *PhysT* 121–129. Apius awards Virginia to Claudius, *PhysT* 144–174, and Virginius pleads for his daughter, *PhysT* 175–190, but to no avail, *PhysT* 191–202. Virginius goes home and tells his daughter that he intends to kill her rather than give her to Claudius, *PhysT* 203–230. Virginia pleads for her life and laments her death as Jeptha's daughter lamented her death, *PhysT* 238–250. Virginius beheads his daughter and sends her head to Apius, *PhysT* 251–259. The people cast Apius in prison, where he hangs himself, and they hang Claudius on a tree, but they exile Virginius for slaying his daughter, *PhysT* 260–276. M.S. Waller suggests that Chaucer may have been influenced by *De eruditione filiorum nobilium*, by Vincent of Beauvais, and by an abridged version of Aegidius Romanus's *De regimen principum*, done about 1344. This work may have been brought to England by Constance of Castile, John of Gaunt's second wife. [Apius: Claudius²: Virginius]

Virginia, the English variant of Latin *Verginia*, the feminine form of the family's clan name, appears once, medially, *PhysT* 213. The English variant emphasizes the heroine's chastity.

J.D.W. Crowther, "Chaucer's *Physician's Tale* and its 'Saint.'" *ESC* 8 (1982): 125–137; John Gower, *The Complete Works*, ed. G.C. Macaulay, III: 377–382; Livy, *Ab urbe condita libri*, ed. and trans. B.O. Foster, II: 142–199; *RR*, ed. E. Langlois, II: 263–265; *RR*, trans. C. Dahlberg, 114; Vincent of Beauvais, *De eruditione filiorum nobilium*, ed. A. Steiner; M.S. Waller, "*The Physician's Tale*: Geoffrey Chaucer and Fray Juan Garcia de Castrojriz." *Speculum* 51 (1976): 292–306; K. Young, "The Maidenly Virtues of Chaucer's Virginia." *Speculum* 16 (1941): 340–349.

VIRGINIUS. Verginius was Verginia's father in Livy's account, *Ab urbe condita liber* III.xliv-lviii, who stabs his daughter in the marketplace to save her from the lecherous judge Appius. **[Apius: Claudius²: Virginia]**

Virginius, the English variant of Latin *Verginius*, the family's clan name, occurs twice initially, *PhysT* 175, 191; once medially, *PhysT* 272; and five times in final rhyming position, *PhysT* 2, 167, 180, 197, 203.

John Gower, *The Complete Works*, ed. G.C. Macaulay, III: 377–382; Livy, *Ab urbe condita libri,* ed. and trans. B.O. Foster, II: 142–199; *RR,* ed. E. Langlois, II: 263–265; *RR,* trans. C. Dahlberg, 114.

VIRGO, the constellation the Virgin, is the sixth sign of the zodiac and lies in the northern hemisphere between Leo and Libra. It is the day house of Mercury, the exaltation or sign of maximum power of Mercury, and the depression or sign of minimum power of Venus (*Tetrabiblos* I.19), and the dry and cold sign (*Confessio Amantis* VII.1082).

Venus falls where Mercury is raised, *i.e.*, in the sign of Virgo, *WBP* 705. Virgo lies opposite Pisces, *Astr* II.6.17–18. All the signs from the head or beginning of Aries to the end of Virgo are called signs of the north, *Astr* II.28.13–15. Virgo is the "sovereign" or western sign that Aries obeys, *Astr* II.28.37. **[Mercurie: Venus]**

The name appears only in the *Astrolabe.*

John Gower, *The Complete Works,* ed. G.C. Macaulay, II: 262; Ptolemy, *Tetrabiblos*, ed. and trans. F.E. Robbins, 91.

VISCONTE: [VISCOUNTE]

VISCOUNTE. Bernabo Visconti, lord of Milan in Lombardy and a powerful member of the Ghibelline party, was a contemporary of Richard II and well known at the English court. Lionel, Duke of Clarence, married his daughter Violanta, and Sir John Hawkwood, English commander of Milan's forces, married another daughter, Donnina. Records show that Chaucer went to Milan in 1378 on a diplomatic mission for Richard II, where he met Bernabo and Sir John. In 1385 Bernabo's nephew treacherously deposed him, and he died in prison in December 1385.

In his short stanza on Bernabo, the Monk recounts the story of Bernabo's death, *MkT* 2399–2406. Bernabo is the "scourge of Lumbardye" because at the time of his fall he was besieging Verona and his soldiers were ravaging the countryside.

Viscounte occurs in final rhyming position, *MkT* 2399.

D.K. Fry, "The Ending of *The Monk's Tale.*" *JEGP* 71 (1972): 355–368; R.A. Pratt, "Geoffrey Chaucer, Esq., and Sir John Hawkwood." *ELH* 16 (1949): 188–193.

VITULON. Witelo the Polish physicist was born c. 1230; the date of his death is unknown. His most important work is a treatise based on optics, *Perspectiva*, written between 1270 and 1278, incorporating the work of the Arab physicist ibn al-Haitham, *Kitab al-manazir* or *The Book of the Telescope*. The work contains chapters on experiments with concave mirrors. Witelo also wrote a philosophical treatise, *De natura daemonorum* or *On the Nature of Demons*, and a religious treatise, *De primaria causae poenitentiae* or *On the Primary Cause of Penitence*.

The magic mirror reminds Cambyuskan's courtiers of the works of Alocen, Vitulon, and Aristotle dealing with unusual mirrors, *SqT* 232–235. **[Alocen: Aristotle]**

Vitulon, the ME variant of the Latin genitive case *Vitellonis*, appears in final rhyming position, *SqT* 232.

D.C. Lundberg, "Lines of Influence in Thirteenth-Century Optics: Bacon, Witelo, Pecham." *Speculum* 46 (1971): 66–83; W. Thiesen, "Witelo's Recension of Euclid's *De visu*." *Traditio* 33 (1977): 394–402; L. Thorndike, *A History of Magic and Experimental Science*, II: 454–456; Witelo, *Perspectivae liber quintus: An English Translation with Introduction and Commentary and Latin Edition of the First Catoptrical Book*, ed. and trans. A.M. Smith.

VULCAN: [VULCANO]

VULCANO, VULCANUS. Vulcan was the Roman counterpart of the Greek god Hephaestus, god of fire and of blacksmiths. He was thrown from the battlements of Olympus and thereafter limped. He fell on the island of Lemnos, where the women nursed him; later, the inhabitants worshipped him. He became Venus's husband and suffered accordingly. When he discovered her affair with Mars, he forged a net of fine bronze and rigged it up above her bed. As she lay with Mars, the net descended and prevented their escape. Vulcan then called the gods to witness their confusion (*Met* IV.173–189; *OM* IV.1268–1371; *Confessio Amantis* V.636–746). Vulcan was called Mulciber (*Fasti* VI.626–627), a name known to medieval mythographers, but Chaucer does not use it.

Palamon addresses Venus as spouse of Vulcanus, *KnT* 2222. Arcite reminds Mars that he, too, has suffered the pain of love for Venus and that Vulcan has caught him in his net, *KnT* 2383–2391. A gold image of Vulcan appears in the temple of glass, *HF* I.119–139. **[Mars: Venus]**

Vulcano appears once in final rhyming position, *HF* I.138; *Vulcanus*, the Latin form, occurs once medially, *KnT* 2389, and once in final rhyming position, *KnT* 2222.

John Gower, *The Complete Works*, ed. G.C. Macaulay, II: 419–422; Ovid, *Fasti*, ed. and trans. J.G. Frazer, 366–367; *ibid.*, *Met*, ed. and trans. F.J. Miller, I: 190–191; *OM*, ed. C. de Boer, II, deel 21: 39–41.

VULCANUS: [VULCANO]

WADE, WADES. The Piðrikssaga or *Thidreks Saga* tells that Wade was the son of King Wilkinus and a sea-woman. He grew to be a giant and became Weyland's father. He took Weyland, while he was still very young, to the dwarfs to be educated and agreed to return for him after one year. Weyland learned so quickly and became so expert in all kinds of smith work that the dwarfs decided to kill his father and to keep him in bondage to them. Wade returned early for his son, but the dwarfs killed him in a landslide. When Weyland discovered this deed, he killed the dwarfs and escaped from their country in a wonderful boat, which he constructed himself (*Thidreks Saga* II. Cantos 2 and 3). In the Anglo-Saxon poem *Widsith* 22, Wade is called "Wada Haelsingam." Wade's courtship of Hild for his king, Hetel, also involves a boat, but this one is not magical.

Januarie says that he does not want a thirty-year-old woman for his wife, for old wives know much craft "on Wades Boot," *MerchT* 1423–1424. The emphasis seems to be on the special qualities of the boat. The story of Weyland may have been transferred to Wade by Chaucer's time. Januarie is tricked and deceived by the twenty-year-old May just as successfully as Wade deceived Hagen, Hild's father. After dinner at Pandarus's house, Pandarus sings, Criseyde plays, and Pandarus tells the tale of Wade, *Tr* III.610–615. Pandarus is also deceiving Criseyde, for she does not know of the plan he has in mind for her.

Wade occurs in final rhyming position, *Tr* III.614. *Wades*, the ME genitive case, occurs in the penultimate position, *MerchT* 1424.

E.J. Boshe, "Some Notes on the Wade Legend." *PQ* 2 (1923). 282–288; *Widsith*, ed. R.W. Chambers, 95–103; K.P. Wentersdorf, "Theme and Structure in the *Merchant's Tale*: The Function of the Pluto Episode." *PMLA* 80 (1965): 522–527.

WALTER is the name of the young marquis of Saluzzo who marries Griselda, then torments her in *The Clerk's Tale*. In Petrarch's Latin story, *De obedientia ac fide uxoria mythologia* (1373–1374), the marquis is named Valterius; in the anonymous French source, *Le Livre Griseldis*, his name is Wautier. **[Griselde]**

Although Walter is one of the main characters in *The Clerk's Tale*, the name occurs only ten times, twice initially with initial stress, *ClT* 1107, 1111; seven times in medial positions, *ClT* 77, 421, 631, 761, 722, 986, 1044; and once in final position where the second syllable is given primary stress to emphasize the rhyme, *ClT* 612.

Boccaccio, *Decameron*, trans. J. Payne, rev. and annotated C.S. Singleton, II: 780–794; E.P. Kadish, "Petrarch's Griselda: An English Translation." *Mediaevalia* 3 (1977): 1–24; N. Lavers, "Freud, *The Clerk's Tale*, and Literary Criticism." *CE* 26 (1964): 180–187; Petrarch, *De insigni obedientia et fide uxoris*; *Le Livre Griseldis*, ed. J.B. Severs, *S&A*, 296–331.

WATTE is the diminutive for *Walter*.

The Summoner repeats the few Latin terms he knows as a jay repeats "Watte," *Gen Prol* 639–643.

WILLE. This daughter of Cupid does not appear in Greek or Roman mythology. She is called *Voluttade* in Boccaccio's *Tes* VII.54, and Chaucer translates the name as *Wille* (Skeat, I: 343 and 513).

The Dreamer sees Wille, Cupid's daughter, tempering the heads of his arrows in a well; she then files them, some to slay and some to wound, *PF* 214–217. **[Cupide]**

Boccaccio, *Tutte le opere*, ed. V. Branca, II: 473; K. Malone, "Chaucer's Daughter of Cupid." *MLR* 45 (1950): 63.

WILLIAM, Duke of Normandy, was called the Conqueror after the Battle of Hastings in 1066, when he defeated Harold of England. He ruled England from 1066 to 1087.

The Sargeant of the Law knows all the cases and judgments since the time of King William, *Gen Prol* 323–324.

The name occurs medially, *Gen Prol* 324.

D.C. Douglas, *William the Conqueror*.

WITELO: [VITULO]

XANTIPPA. Xantippe, the second wife of Socrates, developed the reputation of a shrew during the Middle Ages and appears as a scolding wife in the antifeminist literature of the period. Jerome mentions her in this context, *Epistola adversus Jovinianum* (*Letter Against Jovinian*) I.48 (*PL* 23: 278–279). Christine de Pizan, however, presents Xantippa and Socrates in a loving marriage in *The Book of the City of Ladies* (1405) II.21.1.

Jankyn reads to Dame Alys how Xantippa "caste pisse upon his head," *WBP* 727–732. Jerome says it was water. **[Socrates]**

The name, a pronunciation variant, occurs in medial position, *WBP* 729.

Christine de Pizan, *The Book of the City of Ladies*, trans. E.J. Richards, 130–131.

XANTIPPE: [XANTIPPA]
XRISTUS: [CRIST]

Y

YARBAS. Iarbas, king of Gaetulia, was the son of Jupiter Ammon. He fell in love with Dido when she came to North Africa and built her city of Carthage. But Dido refused his offer of marriage and chose Aeneas instead. When she realized that Aeneas was determined to leave her, she feared that Iarbas and the neighboring kings would attack and destroy her (*Heroides* VII; *Aeneid* IV.198–201, 325–326).

Yarbas is distressed when he hears the rumor that Dido is in love with Eneas, *LGW* 1244–1257. Dido fears that he will destroy her, *LGW* 1316–1318.
[Dido: Eneas]
The name appears medially, *LGW* 1245.

Ovid, *Her*, ed. and trans. G. Showerman, 82–99; Virgil, *Aeneid*, ed. and trans. H.R. Fairclough, I: 408–409; 416–419.

YKARUS. Icarus, Daedalus's son, accompanied his father when he fled from Athens to Crete. When Daedalus angered Minos by constructing the cow in which Pasiphae enjoyed her passion for the bull, Daedalus had to leave Crete as quickly as possible. He constructed huge wings, held together with wax, for Icarus and himself. Icarus flew too near the sun; the wax melted, and he plunged into the sea that bears his name (*Met* VIII.183–235; *OM* VIII.1579–1960; *RR* 5215–5233).

Not even unhappy Dedalus and his foolish child Ykarus have flown as high as the eagle says he will take the frightened dreamer, *HF* II.919–924.

Ykarus, the OF variant, appears in final rhyming position, *HF* II.920.

Ovid, *Met*, ed. and trans. F.J. Miller, I: 418–423; *OM*, ed. C. de Boer, III, deel 30: 146–156; *RR*, ed. E. Langlois, II: 249; *RR*, trans. C. Dahlberg, 108.

YMENEUS: [MENEUS]

YOLE. Iole, daughter of King Eurytus of Oechalia, fell in love with Hercules, and he took her home with him. His wife Dejanira discovered the affair and, hoping to regain his love, smeared Hercules's shirt with the blood of Nessus, the centaur Hercules had killed. The poison ate into his flesh when he put on the shirt, and Hercules knew that he would die. He ordered the pyre built and, climbing onto it, called on his son Hylas to apply the torch (*Heroides* IX; *Met* IX.1–272; *RR* 9192–9202).

Ercules's infidelity to Yole appears in a catalogue of false lovers, *HF* I.402–403. [**Dianira: Ercules**]

Yole, the French variant, appears in final rhyming position, *HF* I.402.

Ovid, *Her,* ed. and trans. G. Showerman, 118–121; *ibid., Met,* ed. and trans. F.J. Miller, II: 2–23; *RR,* ed. E. Langlois, III: 111–112; *RR,* trans. C. Dahlberg, 166.

YPERMYSTRA, YPERMYSTRE. Hypermnestra was one of the fifty daughters of Danaus and married her cousin Lynceus. Danaus feared his brother Egyptus and ordered his daughters to slay their husbands on their wedding night. Hypermnestra helped Lynceus escape, and Danaus imprisoned her (*Heroides* XIV).

The Man of Law says that Chaucer commends the wifehood of Ypermystra, Penelope, and Alceste, *MLI* 75–76. In his version of the story Chaucer switches the fathers and children: Ypermystra is Egiste's daughter, and Lyno is Danao's son, *LGW* 2561–2575. Venus gave Ypermystra great beauty, but since Jupiter is part of her horoscope, she values conscience, truth, fear of shame, and true wifehood, *LGW* 2584–2585. Mars's influence was feeble when Ypermystra was born, and she cannot handle the knife to slay Lyno, her husband, *LGW* 2589–2595. Because of the bad aspects of Saturn, she dies in prison, *LGW* 2595–2722. [**Danao: Egiste: Jupiter: Mars: Saturn**]

Chaucer may have been indebted to an Italian translation of the *Heroides* for the variant form *Ypermystra.* Latin initial *h* was not pronounced. *Ipermystre,* a spelling variant, occurs once, in a medial position, *LGW* 2663, with elided final -e. *Ypermystra* occurs once initially, *LGW* 2575; twice in medial positions, *MLI* 75; *LGW* 2594; *Ypermystre* occurs three times in medial positions with elided final -e, *LGW F* 268, *LGW G* 222; *LGW* 2604, and twice medially with syllabic final -e, *LGW* 2632, 2647.

S.B. Meech, "Chaucer and an Italian Translation of the *Heroides.*" *PMLA* 45 (1930): 123; Ovid, *Her,* ed. and trans. G. Showerman, 170–181; *OM,* ed. C. de Boer, I, deel 15: 268–273.

YPOCRAS. Hippocrates of Cos, fl. fifth century B.C., was the first scientific physician and the founder of Greek medical science. Several works were attributed to him, among them the *Aphorisms,* which included the famous *dictum*: "Life is short, but art is long, the opportunity fleeting, the experiment perilous, the judgment difficult." Between 1360 and 1385 Merton College owned a copy of the *Aphorisms* in a Latin translation from the Arabic of Constantinus Africanus.

Ypocras is among the Physician's authorities, *Gen Prol* 431. Neither Ypocras nor Galen can cure the Man in Black of his grief, *BD* 571; the line reflects *RR* 15959. A summary of the famous dictum appears in *PF* 1–2. Ypocras is also the name of an aphrodisiac made of wine, sugar, and spices, *MerchT* 1807.

Ypocras, the OF variant, occurs medially, *Gen Prol* 431; *BD* 571.

Hippocrates, *Hippocrates,* ed. and trans. W.H.S. Jones and E.T. Withington; P. Kibre, "Hippocratic Writings in the Middle Ages." *Bulletin of the History of Medicine* 18 (1946): 371–412; F.M. Powicke, *The Medieval Books of Merton College*, 139; *RR*, ed. E. Langlois, IV: 126; *RR*, trans. C. Dahlberg, 271.

YPOMEDOUN: [IPOMEDON]

YPOTIS is the Wise Child hero of the Middle English dialogue poem of the same name, a conversation between Ypotis and the Emperor Hadrian, translated from the Latin version, *Altercatio Hadriani Augusti et Epicteti philosophi* (probably from the third century A.D.). The earliest manuscripts of the poem date from the fourteenth century, and fourteen manuscripts have survived.

Sir Thopas surpasses Ypotis, *Thop* 898. [**Thopas**]

Ypotis, the ME variant of Epictetus, occurs in final rhyming position.

D. Everett, "A Note on 'Ypotis.'" *RES* 6 (1930): 446–448; L.H. Loomis, ed., "Sir Thopas." *S&A*, 503; C. Horstmann, ed., *Ypotis. Altenglische Legenden*; F.E. Utley, "Dialogues, Debates, and Catechisms." J.E. Wells, *A Manual of Writings in Middle English*, ed. A. Hartung, III: 740–741.

YSAAC, YSAAK. Isaac was Abraham's son, born when both he and his wife Sarah were very old. God tested Abraham by commanding that he sacrifice Isaac, and Abraham determined to obey. He took the lad, a bundle of wood for the fire, and led the way to Mount Moriah. But as he laid Isaac on the altar and raised the knife, the angel of the Lord appeared and stopped him. He showed him a ram caught in a thicket, which Abraham sacrificed instead of Isaac (Genesis 22:1–14). Isaac's two sons were Esau and Jacob, twins by his wife Rebecca. When Isaac grew old and blind, Rebecca advised Jacob, the younger twin, to dress in animal skins and to pretend to be Esau and so defraud his older brother of Isaac's blessing (Genesis 24–26).

Jacob, by the good counsel of his mother Rebecca, won Isaac's blessing, *Mel* 1098. Isaac, who thought it nothing to be slain, prefigures the death of Christ, *ABC* 169–176. [**Abraham: Jacob: Rebekka**]

Ysaac, the medieval Latin variant, appears initially, *ABC* 169; *Ysaak* appears in Mel 1098.

"The Abraham and Isaac Plays." *The Corpus Christi Plays of the Middle Ages*, ed. R.T. Davies; A. Lancashire, "Chaucer and the Sacrifice of Isaac." *ChauR* 9 (1975): 320–326; "The Play of Isaac and Rebecca." *The Drama of the Medieval Church*, ed. K. Young, II: 259–264.

YSAYE: [ISAYE]

YSIDIS. Isis was the Egyptian mother goddess and the wife of Osiris. Valerius Maximus tells a brief story about a man who was caught attempting to burn down the temple of Diana at Ephesus so as to gain fame. The citizens decreed that his name should never be known, *Factorum dictorumque memorabilium liber* VIII.14. Valerius does not give the man's name, but refers the reader to Theopompus, a Greek historian and a contemporary of Philip II and Alexander the Great. It is historically true that Diana's temple at Ephesus was burned down in 356 B.C., on the night Alexander was born. The histories of Theopompus are lost, but the man's name, Herostratus, appears in Solinus's *Polyhistoria* XL. 2–3, sometimes called *Collectanea rerum memorabilium* and written soon after A.D. 200.

A man comes forward, claiming that he had burned down the temple of Isis at Athens in order to become famous, *HF* III.1842–1858. In keeping with ancient and medieval traditions, Chaucer does not mention the man's name. Although the sources say that the temple in question is Diana's temple at Ephesus, Chaucer makes the temple that of Isis at Athens.

Ysidis, the Latin genitive singular of *Isis*, occurs in final rhyming position, *HF* III.1844.

Caius Julius Solinus, *Polyhistoria*, ed. C. Salmas, 236; Valerius Maximus, *Factorum dictorumque memorabilium libri novem*, ed. J. Kappy, I: 807–808.

YSIDRE (saint). Isidore of Seville, c. A.D. 560–636, was born into a noble family at Cartagena, Spain. He was bishop of Seville from 600 to 636, the year of his death. One of the most learned and prolific men of his age, he is best known for *Etymologiarum sive originum libri XX,* also called *Etymologiae or Etymologies,* an encyclopedia in twenty books, covering the seven liberal arts, the myths of the pagans, geography, law, medicine, gems, trees, foods, and much else, heavily influenced by Pliny's *Natural History.* One of the most important transmitters of classical learning during the medieval period, Isidore earned the name "Schoolmaster of the Middle Ages." He also wrote *Historia Gothicum, Vandalorum, Suevorum* or *A History of the Goths, Vandals, and Suevi.*

The Parson quotes Ysidre, *ParsT* 89. Skeat (V: 448) suggests as a source Isidore's *Sententiarum libri tres*, II.13, but also points out that the two quotations are not identical. The Parson uses Ysidre's comparison of the fires of rancor with the fire made from the kindling of the juniper tree, *ParsT* 550–552. A fire made from the wood of this tree will last a year or more if the coals are covered with ash, *Etymologiae* XVII.vii.35.

Ysidre, the OF variant, occurs *ParsT* 89, 551.

E. Bréhaut, *An Encyclopaedist of the Dark Ages, Isidore of Seville*; Isidore, *Etymologiarum sive originum libri XX*, ed. W.M. Lindsay, I; *ibid., The History of the Goths, Vandals and Suevi*, trans. with introd. G. Donini and G.B. Ford, Jr.; *ibid., The Medical Writing*, trans. W.D. Thorpe; M.L.W. Laistner, *Thought and Letters in Western Europe*, 89–94; K.N. Macfarlane, *Isidore of Seville on the Pagan Gods*.

YTAKUS, the Ithacan, is used as a name for Ulysses, who came from Ithaca, *Bo* IV, *Metr* 7.18. **[Ulixes]**

YVE. Three saints named Yves appear in European martyrology: St. Yves, a mythical Persian bishop of the seventh century, who became patron saint of Huntingdonshire; St. Yves, patron saint of Brittany, canonized in 1347; St. Yves, bishop of Chartres in the twelfth century.

The greedy friar, *SumT* 1943, and the merchant of St. Denys, *ShipT* 227, swear by St. Yve. R.H. Cline suggests the Bishop of Chartres for both references.

The name occurs in final rhyming position, *SumT* 1943, *ShipT* 227.

R.H. Cline, "Four Chaucer Saints." *MLN* 60 (1945): 482.

Z

ZACHARIE, ZAKARIE. Zechariah was a prophet in Israel from the second year of King Darius's reign to the end of that reign, 520–485 B.C.

The Parson, condemning the rich adornment of horses, quotes Zechariah 10:5: "God seith by Zacharie the Prophete, 'I wol confounde the ryderes of swich horses,'" *ParsT* 434. The passage may have been influenced by Peraldus, *Tractatus de viciis* (1236). Zacharie calls the Virgin an open well to wash the sinful soul of his guilt, *ABC* 177–178. This is an interpretation of Zechariah 13:1: "In that day there shall be a fountain opened to the house of David and to the inhabitants of Jerusalem for sin and for uncleanness." The *ABC* is a translation of the hymn to the Virgin in Guillaume de Deguilleville's *Le Pèlerinage de la vie humaine* (c. 1355).

Zacharie, the OF and ME variant, appears initially, *ABC* 177; *Zakarie*, a spelling variant, appears in *ParsT* 434.

K.O. Petersen, *The Sources of* The Parson's Tale, 40.

ZANZIS. Zeuxis, fl. 397 B.C., was a painter from Heraclea. He was well known to Socrates and his circle; Plato mentions his work in *Gorgias* 453C, 453D. Zeuxis added the use of highlights to shading. Pliny mentions his paintings of Penelope, Helen, and the infant Hercules strangling two snakes as outstanding (*HN* XXXV.xxxvi.61–66).

Nature says that neither Apelles or Zanzis could imitate her Virginia, *PhysT* 15–18. Pandarus quotes a proverb from Zanzis, "the newe love chaceth ofte the olde," *Tr* IV.414–415. Skeat (II: 487–488) suggests Ovid, *Remedia amoris* 462; J. Kreuzer suggests Rule 17 of Book III, *De amore* by Andreas Capellaneas. D.K. Fry points out that Zeuxis is mentioned in Cicero's *De inventione* II.1.12 in a story that values individual qualities in separate ladies rather than all qualities in just one, as Pandarus points out,

Tr IV.407–413. Fry suggests further that, in ascribing the proverb to Zanzis (an old sage), Chaucer follows the device used elsewhere in the poem. Just as he ascribes the work to one Lollius, so he quotes a well-known proverb from Ovid but attributes it to the source of the idea in the previous stanza, Zeuxis or Zanzis. Zeuxis's fame as a painter appears in *RR* 16185.

Zanzis is a Chaucerian variant; *Zeuzis* also occurs in manuscripts and is closer to the Greek *Zeuxis.* The name occurs twice medially, *PhysT* 16; *Tr* IV.414.

D.K. Fry, "Chaucer's *Zanzis* and a Possible source for *Troilus and Criseyde* IV.407–413." *ELN* 9 (1971): 81–85; Manly-Rickert, VII.6; *RR,* ed. E. Langlois IV: 137; *RR,* trans. C. Dahlberg, 274.

ZARQALA, AL-: [ARSECHIELE]

ZECHARIA: [ZACHARIE]

ZENO of Elea, fl. c. 460 b.c., became a follower of Parmenides the philosopher. He invented the art of Dialectic and was adept at pointing out the paradoxes and contradictions of other philosophical systems. Among his works were *Life According to Nature, Of Emotions, Of Rhetoric.* With Parmenides, he founded the Eleatic school of philosophy. He died after great torture for refusing to divulge the names of his accomplices in a plot to overthrow tyranny (Diogenes Laertius, IX).

Lady Philosophy reminds Boethius of the torments of Zeno, that good men suffer for their ideas and their principles, *Bo* I, *Prosa* 3.55. **[Achademycis: Eleaticis: Parmanydes]**

Diogenes Laertius, *Lives of the Eminent Philosophers,* ed. and trans. R.D. Hicks, II: 434–439.

ZENOBIA: [CENOBIA]
ZEPHERUS: [EOLUS]
ZEPHIRUS: [EOLUS]
ZEPHYRUS: [EOLUS]
ZEUSIS: [ZANZIS]
ZEUXIS: [ZANZIS]

Appendix

Glossary of Astronomical and Astrological Terms

Alpha, the first letter of the Greek alphabet, used to designate the brightest star in a constellation; *e.g.,* Castor is the alpha or the brightest star in the constellation Gemini.

Ascendent, that point of the ecliptic or the sun's path that rises in the east at the time of one's birth.

Beta, the second letter of the Greek alphabet, used to designate the second brightest star in a constellation; *e.g.,* Pollux is the beta or second brightest star of the constellation Gemini.

Conjunction, derived from Latin *conjunctio,* "a joining together," the alignment of two planets or celestial bodies in the same longitude.

Constellation, a number of fixed stars grouped together in the form of an imaginary figure.

Constellation, also the position of the planets with regard to one another at the time of one's birth.

Declination, the celestial equivalent of latitude, measured in degrees; *e.g.,* Cancer is called the sun's summer declination. In Chaucer's time, the sun entered Cancer on June 12; in our time, the sun enters Cancer on June 21, the longest day of the year.

Dejection or **Depression,** the sign of the zodiac in which a planet has minimum power, the sign in which the planet is least effective; *e.g.,* Virgo is the dejection or the depression of Venus.

Dignity, a sign in which a planet acquires strength.

Direct signs, those signs in the western semicircle of the zodiac; *e.g.*, Cancer, Leo, Virgo, Libra, Scorpius, Sagittarius. They are also called **sovereign** signs or **signs of right ascension** and ascend in more than two hours.

Ecliptic, the great invisible circle or path of the sun, tilted at 27 degrees from the earth's equator, described by the sun in the course of a year.

Equator, an imaginary line circling the earth, halfway between the North and South Poles.

Equinox, that time of the year when the sun crosses the celestial equator, when the lengths of day and night are equal. In Chaucer's time, the sun entered Aries on March 12 and Libra on September 12. In modern times, the sun enters Aries on March 21, the spring equinox, and it enters Libra on September 21, the autumn equinox.

Exaltation, a sign of the zodiac in which a planet has its maximum power, the sign in which it is most effective; *e.g.*, Pisces is the exaltation of Venus.

Face, of a zodiacal sign, 10 degrees of the sign. Each sign has three faces.

Gamma, the third letter of the Greek alphabet, used to designate the third brightest star in a constellation; *e.g.*, Alnath is the gamma or third brightest star of the constellation Auriga.

Head of a planet, the beginning of a planet.

House of a planet, one of two signs in which the planet intensifies its effects, one a solar or day house and the other a lunar or night house. The sun and the moon have one sign for both houses. Each house covers a space of 30 degrees and is divided into three faces. Scorpio is the day house of Mars, and Aries is its night house. A house is also one of twelve additional houses (*Astrolabe* II. 36 and 37). The houses are named as follows: *vita* (life), *lucrum* (gain), *fratres* (brothers), *genitor* (parent), *nati* (birth), *valetudo* (health), *uxor* (wife), *mors* (death), *pietas* (piety), *regnum* (rule), *benefacta* (benefactor), *carcer* (prison).

Inequal hours, planetary hours in which each planet has its special influence.

Latitude, an imaginary horizontal line, running from east to west, parallel to the equator, which serves as a measure of distance from the equator.

Longitude, an imaginary vertical line, parallel with the meridian of Greenwich, itself an imaginary line, running from north to south, which serves as a measure of distance from Greenwich, England.

Magnitude, a measure of brightness of a star; the average of the 20 brightest stars defines the first magnitude. A star of the sixth magnitude is the faintest we can see without binoculars.

Mansion, also called a **house** or domicile.

Nadir, a point in the celestial sphere diametrically opposite the **zenith** of a planet.

Oblique signs, the signs in the eastern semicircle of the zodiac: Capricorn, Aquarius, Pisces, Aries, Taurus, and Gemini, which are said to obey the **direct** or western signs They are also called **tortuous** signs and ascend in less than two hours.

Planet, a wandering star as opposed to a fixed star.

Primum mobile or the First Movement, the ninth sphere, which contains no heavenly bodies and revolves from east to west in 24 hours. Its movement is so powerful that it causes the other spheres to revolve with it.

Sovereign or **direct** signs, the signs in the western semicircle of the zodiac.

Term, one of certain inequal divisions of the signs, each segment governed by one of the planets and none by the sun and the moon.

Tortuous signs, also called **oblique** signs, the signs in the eastern semicircle of the zodiac; they obey the signs in the western semicircle.

Zenith of a planet, that point directly above the planet; every planet has its own zenith.

Zodiac, the "circle of animals" or the "circle of beasts" in the celestial sphere about 8 or 9 degrees on each side of the ecliptic. It is divided into twelve parts called signs, beginning with the sign Aries or the Ram. Each sign occupies 30 degrees on the line of the ecliptic, through one of which the sun passes each month. The signs are named after twelve constellations with which, in former times, they coincided approximately, but in Chaucer's time the constellation and the sign no longer occupied identical positions in the celestial sphere. When we speak of the twelve signs, we mean the signs of the zodiac.

This Glossary is composed of definitions taken from J.D. North, "Kalenderes Enlumyned Ben They," *RES*, new series 20 (1969): 136–137; Valerie Illington, ed., *The Facts on File Dictionary of Astronomy* (New York: 1979), and Charles A. Whitney, *Whitney's Star Finder* (New York: 1975), 73–75. All are used by permission.

Planets

Their Houses

Each planet has a solar or day house ruled by the sun, found in the semicircle from Leo to Capricorn, and a lunar or night house, ruled by the moon, found in the semicircle from Cancer to Aquarius (see Map 5). The following order of the planets follows the Ptolemaic system (see Maps 4 and 5).

Planet	Solar or Day House	Lunar or Night House
Saturn	Capricorn	Aquarius
Jupiter	Sagittarius	Pisces
Mars	Scorpio	Aries
Sun	Leo	Leo
Venus	Libra	Taurus
Mercury	Virgo	Gemini
Moon	Cancer	Cancer

Their Exaltations and Their Depressions

The following order follows the Ptolemaic System (see Map 4).

Planet	Exaltation	Depression
Saturn	Libra	Aries
Jupiter	Cancer	Capricorn
Mars	Capricorn	Cancer
Sun	Aries	Libra
Venus	Pisces	Virgo
Mercury	Virgo	Pisces
Moon	Taurus	Scorpio

NORTHERN AND SOUTHERN SIGNS

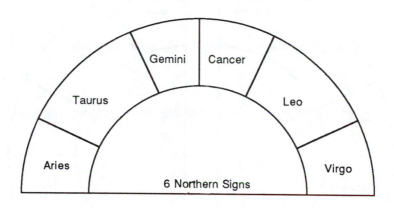

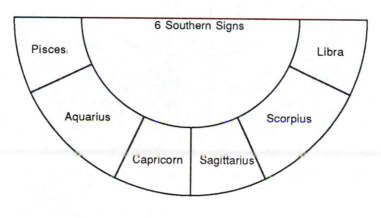

MAP 1

EASTERN AND WESTERN SIGNS

North

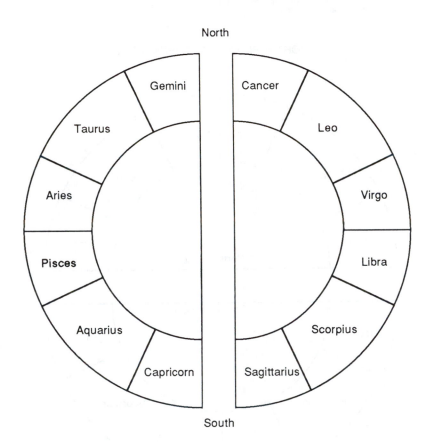

South

6 Eastern Signs
also called "tortuous" signs
or "oblique" signs

6 Western Signs
also called "direct" signs
or "sovereign" signs
or "signs of the right ascension"

MAP 2

EQUINOXES AND TROPICS

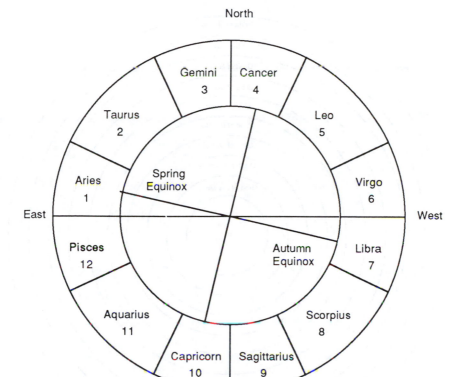

Aries is the Spring Equinox
Cancer is the Summer Tropic

Libra Is the Autumn Equinox
Capricorn is the Winter Tropic

The Equinoxes are exactly opposite each other; the Tropics are also exactly opposite each other.

MAP 3

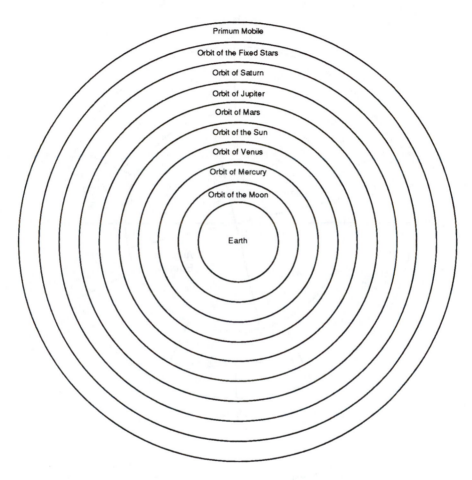

Primum Mobile

Orbit of the Fixed Stars

Orbit of Saturn

Orbit of Jupiter

Orbit of Mars

Orbit of the Sun

Orbit of Venus

Orbit of Mercury

Orbit of the Moon

Earth

THE PTOLEMAIC SYSTEM OF THE UNIVERSE

MAP 4

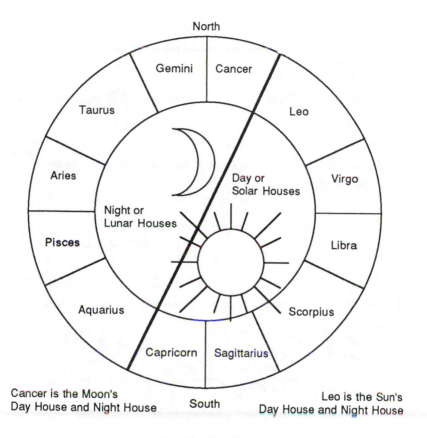

North

Gemini | Cancer

Taurus

Leo

Aries

Virgo

Day or
Solar Houses

Night or
Lunar Houses

Pisces

Libra

Aquarius

Scorpius

Capricorn | Sagittarius

Cancer is the Moon's
Day House and Night House

South

Leo is the Sun's
Day House and Night House

PLANETARY HOUSES

MAP 5

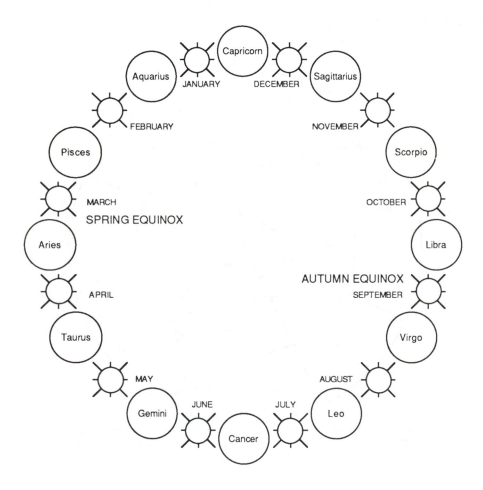

Capricorn

Aquarius

JANUARY   DECEMBER

Sagittarius

FEBRUARY   NOVEMBER

Pisces

Scorpio

MARCH   OCTOBER

SPRING EQUINOX

Aries

Libra

APRIL   AUTUMN EQUINOX

SEPTEMBER

Taurus

Virgo

MAY   AUGUST

Gemini   JUNE   JULY   Leo

Cancer

THE EQUINOXES AND THE SIGNS OF THE ZODIAC

MAP 6

The Sun ☼

Bibliography

Primary Sources

Abelard, Peter. *Historia calamitatum*. Ed. J. Monfrin. 2nd ed. Paris: J. Vrin, 1959.

——. *The Story of Abelard's Adversities*. Trans. with notes of the *Historia calamitatum* by J.T. Muckle. With a preface by E. Gilson. Rev. ed. Toronto: Pontifical Institute of Mediaeval Studies, 1986.

Alain de Lille. *De planctu Naturae*. Ed. N.M. Häring. *Studi Medievali*, 3, serie 19.2 (1978): 797–879.

Alan of Lille. *Anticlaudianus, or The Good and Perfect Man*. Trans. and commentary by J.J. Sheridan. Toronto: Pontifical Institute of Mediaeval Studies, 1973.

——. *The Plaint of Nature*. Trans. and commentary by J.J. Sheridan. Toronto: Pontifical Institute of Mediaeval Studies, 1980.

Alanus de Insulis. *Anticlaudianus*. Texte critique avec une introduction et des tables par R. Bossaut. Paris: J. Vrin, 1955.

Albertanus Brixiensis. *Liber consolationis et consili*, ex quo hasta est fabula de Meilbeo et Prudentia. Ed. Thor Sundby. The Hague: A.F. Host, 1873.

Alexandre du Pont. *Roman de Mahomet en vers du XIIIe siècle*, . . . accompagnés de notes par M. Reinaud et Francesque Michel. Paris: Silvestre, 1831.

Alhazen (ibn al-Haytham). *De Aspectibus; Opticae thesaurus Alhazeni arabus libri septem*. Ed. Friedrich Risner. Basel: 1572; rpt., with introd. by David C. Lundberg. New York: Johnson Reprint, 1972.

Der Anglonormannische Boeve de Hamtone. Ed. A. Stimming. Halle: M. Niemeyer, 1899.

The Anglo-Saxon Chronicle. Trans. with introd. by G.N. Garmonsway. London: Dent; New York: Dutton, 1954, 1965.

Apuleius Madaurensis. *Apologia.* Trans. H.E. Butler. Oxford: Clarendon Press, 1909, rpt. Westport, Conn.: 1970.

——. *Pro se de magia liber (Apologia).* Ed. Rudolf Helm. Leipzig: B.G. Teubner, 1959.

Aristotle. *Historia animalium.* Ed. and trans. A.L. Peck. Cambridge, Mass.: Harvard Univ. Press; London: W. Heinemann, 1965.

——. *Metaphysica (Metaphysics).* Ed. and trans. H. Tredennick. 2 vols. Cambridge, Mass.: Harvard Univ. Press; London: W. Heinemann, 1933, 1968.

——. *Metereologica (Meteorology).* Ed. and trans. H.D.P. Lee. Cambridge, Mass.: Harvard Univ. Press; London: W. Heinemann, 1952, 1962.

——. *On the Heavens (De caelo et mundo).* Ed. and trans. W.K.C. Guthrie. Cambridge, Mass.: Harvard Univ. Press; London: W. Heinemann, 1939.

——. *On the Soul (De anima).* Ed. and trans. W.S. Hett. Cambridge, Mass.: Harvard Univ. Press; London: W. Heinemann, 1936, 1974.

——. *Parva naturalia.* Ed. and trans. W.S. Hett. Cambridge, Mass.: Harvard Univ. Press; London: W. Heinemann, 1936, 1964.

——. *Physics (Physica).* Ed. and trans. P.H. Wicksteed and F.M. Cornford. 2 vols. Cambridge, Mass.: Harvard Univ. Press; London: W. Heinemann, 1929, 1963.

——. *Posterior Analytics (Analytica Posterior).* Ed. and trans. H. Tredennick. Cambridge, Mass.: Harvard Univ. Press; London: W. Heinemann, 1960.

Arrian. *Anabasis Alexandri.* Ed. and trans. E.I. Robson. 2 vols. Cambridge, Mass.: Harvard Univ. Press; London: W. Heinemann, 1967.

Athanasius. *La plus ancienne version Latine de la vie de Saint Antoine.* Etude critique textuelle par H. Hoppenbrouwers. Nijmegen: Dekker & van de Vegt, 1960.

Augustine [Aurelius Augustinus]. *The City of God Against the Pagans.* Ed. and trans. G.E. McCracken. 7 vols. Cambridge, Mass.: Harvard Univ. Press; London: W. Heinemann, 1957–1972.

——. *Concerning the City of God Against the Pagans.* Trans. H. Bettenson, with an introd. by D. Knowles. Harmondsworth: Penguin, 1972.

Averroes (ibn-Rushd). *On Aristotle's* De generatione et corruptione: *Middle Commentaries and Epitome.* Trans. from the original Arabic and the Hebrew and Latin versions with notes and introd. by S. Kurland. Cambridge, Mass.: Medieval Academy of America, 1958.

Avicenna. *The General Principles of Avicenna's* Canon of Medicine. Ed. and trans. Masher H. Shah. Karachi: Nameed Clinic, 1966.

Babrius and Phaedrus. *[Fables of] Babrius and Phaedrus.* Ed. and trans. B.E. Perry. Cambridge, Mass.: Harvard Univ. Press; London: W. Heinemann, 1965.

Baudouin de Condé. *Dits et contes de Baudouin de Condé et de son fils Jean de Condé*, publiés d'après les manuscrits de Bruxelles, Turin, Rome, Paris, et Vienne et accompagnés de variantes et de notes explicatives par A. Scheler. 3 vols. Bruxelles: V. Devaux, 1864–1867.

Bede. *Opera historica.* Ed. and trans. J.E. King. 2 vols. Cambridge, Mass.: Harvard Univ. Press; London: W. Heinemann, 1954.

——. *A History of the English Church and People.* Trans. with introd. by L. Sherley-Price. Baltimore: Penguin, 1965.

The Belles Heures of Jean, Duke of Berry. Commentaries by Millard Meiss and Elizabeth H. Beatson. New York: George Braziller, 1974.

Benedict of Nursia. *The Rule of St. Benedict.* The Abingdon Copy. Ed. J. Chamberlain. Toronto: Pontifical Institute of Mediaeval Studies, 1982.

Benoît de Sainte-Maure. *Le Roman de Troie.* Ed. L. Constans. 6 vols. SATF. Paris: Firmin-Didot, 1904–1912.

Berchorius, Petrus. *Reductorium morale, liber XV: Ovidius moralizatus, Cap.i: de formis figurisque deorum.* Textus et codice Brux. Bibl. Reg. 863–869 critice editus. Ed. J. Engles. Utrecht: Instituut voor Laat Latijn der Riksuniversiteit, 1966.

Bernard of Clairvaux. *Opera, ad fidem codicum recensuerunt.* Ed. Jean LeClercq *et al.* 5 vols. Rome: Editiones Cisterciensis, 1957–1968.

Bernard Silvester. *Cosmographia.* Ed. with introd. and notes by P. Dronke. Leiden: E.J. Brill, 1978.

——. *Megacosmos.* Ed. Carl S. Barach and Johan Wrobel. Innsbruck: 1876.

al-Biruni, Muhammad ibn-Ahmad. *The Chronology of Ancient Nations.* An English version of the Arabic text of the *Athar-il-Bakiya* of al-Biruni or "Vestiges of the Past." Trans. and ed. C.E. Sachau. London: W.H. Allen, 1879.

Boccaccio, Giovanni. *L'Ameto.* Trans. J. Serafini-Saulis. New York: Garland Publishing, Inc., 1984.

——. *The Book of Theseus: Teseida delle nozze d'Emilia.* Trans. Bernadette Marie McCloy. New York: Medieval Text Association, 1974.

——. *Concerning Famous Women.* Trans. with introd. and notes by Guido Guarino. New Brunswick: Rutgers Univ. Press, 1966.

——. *De casibus virorum illustrium.* Ed. P.G. Ricci and V. Zaccaria. *Tutte le Opere di Giovanni Boccaccio*, IX. Milan: A. Mondadori, 1983.

——. *De claris mulieribus.* Ed. V. Zaccaria. *Tutte le Opere di Giovanni Boccaccio*, X. Milan: A. Mondadori, 1967.

——. *De genealogia deorum gentilium libri.* Ed. Vincenzo Romano. 2 vols. Bari: Laterza, 1951.

——. *The Decameron.* Trans. John Payne, rev. and annotated by C.S. Singleton. 3 vols. Berkeley: Univ. of California Press, 1982.

——. *The Fates of Illustrious Men.* Trans. and abridged by Louis B. Hall. New York: Ungar, 1965.

——. *Il Filocolo.* Ed. and trans. D.S. Cheney and T.G. Bergin. New York: Garland Publishing, Inc., 1985.

——. *Le Rime; L'Amorosa visione; La caccia di Diana.* Ed. V. Branca. Bari: G. Laterza, 1931.

——. *Tutte le opere di Giovanni Boccaccio.* Ed. Vittorio Branca. 10 vols. Milan: A. Mondadori, 1967–1983.

——. *Vita di Dante,* di texte della *Poesia.* Ed. Carlo Muscetta. Rome: Edizione dell'Ateneo, 1963.

Boethius. *Tractates and The Consolation of Philosophy.* Ed. and trans. H.F. Stewart, E.K. Rand, and S.J. Tester. Cambridge, Mass.: Harvard Univ. Press; London: W. Heinemann, 1973.

The Book of the Quinte Essence. Ed. F.J. Furnivall. EETS, O.S. 16. London: N. Trübner, 1866.

Bradwardine, Thomas. *Thomas of Bradwardine, Tractatus de proportionibus: Its Significance for the Development of Mathematical Physics.* Ed. and trans. H. Lamar Crosby, Jr. Madison: Univ. of Wisconsin Press, 1955.

Calcidius. *Calcidius on Matter, His Doctrines and Sources, and a Chapter on the History of Platonism by J.C.M. van Winden.* Leiden: E.J. Brill, 1959.

Cassiodorus, Flavius M.A. *Institutiones.* Ed. R.A.B. Mynors. Oxford: Clarendon Press, 1937.

——. *Cassiodori Senatoris Variae: I. Epistolae Theodoricianae Variae.* Ed. Th. Mommsen. Berlin: Weidmannos, 1894.

——. *Introduction to Divine and Human Readings.* Trans. with introd. and notes by L.W. Jones. New York: Columbia Univ. Press, 1946.

——. *The Letters of Cassiodorus.* A condensed translation of *Variae epistolae,* with an introd. by T. Hodgkin. London: H. Frowde, 1886.

Catullus. *Carmina.* Ed. R.A.B. Mynors. Oxford: The Clarendon Press, 1958.

——. *Catullus: A Critical Edition.* Ed. and introd. by D.F.S. Thomson. Chapel Hill: Univ. of North Carolina Press, 1978.

Caxton, W. *Caxton's Aesop.* Ed. with introd. and notes by R.T. Lenaghan. Cambridge, Mass.: Harvard Univ. Press, 1967.

——. *The History of Renard the Fox.* Trans. and printed by Caxton in 1481. Ed. with introd. and notes by D.B. Sands. Cambridge, Mass.: Harvard Univ. Press, 1960.

La Chanson de Roland. Ed. Cesare Segre. Milan: R. Ricciardi, 1971.

Chaucer, Geoffrey. *The Book of Troilus and Criseyde*. Ed. R.K. Root. Princeton: Princeton Univ. Press, 1926.

——. *Chaucer's Translation of Boethius' "De consolatione philosophiae."* Edited from the additional MS 10.340 in the British Museum, collated with the Cambridge University Library MS Ii.3.21 by Richard Morris. London: Early English Text Society, 1868.

——. *The Complete Works of Geoffrey Chaucer*. Ed. W.E. Skeat. 7 vols. Oxford: Clarendon Press, 1894–1897.

——. *The Minor Poems: Part One*. Ed. G. Pace and A. David. Norman: Univ. of Oklahoma Press, 1982.

——. *The Riverside Chaucer*. 3rd ed. Ed. Larry Benson, based on *The Works of Geoffrey Chaucer*. 2nd ed. Ed. F.N. Robinson. Boston: Houghton Mifflin, 1987.

——. *The Tales of Canterbury*. Ed. Robert A. Pratt. Boston: Houghton Mifflin, 1974.

——. *The Text of the Canterbury Tales*. Studied on the Basis of all Known Manuscripts by John M. Manly and Edith Rickert. 8 vols. Chicago: Chicago Univ. Press, 1940.

——. *A Treatise on the Astrolabe*. Ed. W.W. Skeat. London: Published for the Chaucer Society by N. Trübner, 1872; rpt. New York: Johnson Reprint, 1967.

The Chester Mystery Cycle: Essays and Documents. Ed. R.M. Lumiansky and D. Mills. Chapel Hill: Univ. of North Carolina Press, 1983.

Chrétien de Troyes. *Erec und Enid*. Ed. Wendelin Foerster. Amsterdam: Editions Rodopi, 1965.

——. *Lancelot or The Knight of the Cart (Le chevalier de la charrette)*. Ed. and trans. W.W. Kibler. New York: Garland Publishing, Inc., 1981.

——. *Perceval; or The Story of the Grail*. Trans. Ruth Harwood Cline. New York: Pergamon Press, 1983.

——. *Le Roman de Perceval ou Le Conte du Graal*. Texte établi en français moderne par Henri de Briel. Paris: C. Klincksieck, 1971.

Christine de Pizan. *The Book of the City of Ladies*. Trans. Earl J. Richards. New York: Persea Books, 1982.

——. *The Epistle of Othea*. Trans. Stephen Scrope. Ed. Curt Bühler. London: Oxford Univ. Press, 1970.

Cicero. *De natura deorum*. Ed. and trans. H. Rackham. Cambridge, Mass.: Harvard Univ. Press; London: W. Heinemann, 1951.

——. *De officiis*. Ed. and trans. Walter Miller. Cambridge, Mass.: Harvard Univ. Press; London: W. Heinemann, 1913, 1975.

——. *De oratore*. Ed. and trans. E.W. Sutton and H. Rackham. 2 vols. Cambridge, Mass.: Harvard Univ. Press; London: W. Heinemann, 1942.

——. *De re publica. De legibus: Somnium Scipionis*. Ed. and trans. C.W. Keyes. Cambridge, Mass.: Harvard Univ. Press; London: W. Heinemann, 1952.

——. *De senectute. De amicitia. De divinatione*. Ed. and trans. W.A. Falconer. Cambridge, Mass.: Harvard Univ. Press; London: W. Heinemann, 1953.

——. *Tusculan Disputations*. Ed. and trans. J.B. King. Cambridge, Mass.: Harvard Univ. Press; London: W. Heinemann, 1950.

Claudian. *De raptu Proserpinae*. Ed. with an introd. and commentary by J.B. Hall. Cambridge: Cambridge Univ. Press, 1969.

——. *De raptu Proserpinae*. Ed. and trans. Maurice Platnauer. 2 vols. Cambridge, Mass.: Harvard Univ. Press; London: W. Heinemann, 1922, 1963.

The Corpus Christi Play of the English Middle Ages. An edition with introd. and notes by R.T. Davies. Totowa, N.J.: Rowman and Littlefield, 1972.

Cursor Mundi. Ed. Richard Morris. EETS, O.S. 57, 59, 62, 66, 68, 99, 101. London: K. Paul, Trench, Trübner, 1874–1893.

Cynewulf. *Elene*. Ed. P.O.E. Gradon. London: Methuen, 1958.

Dante Alighieri. *Il convivio*. Ed. M. Simonelli. Bologna: R. Patrón, 1966.

——. *The Divine Comedy*. Ed. and trans. C.S. Singleton. 3 vols. in 6. Princeton: Princeton Univ. Press, 1970–1975.

——. *De monarchia*. Ed. Pier Giorgio Ricci. Milan: A. Mondadori, 1965.

Dares Phrygius. *De excidio Troiae historia*. Ed. F. Meister. Leipzig: B.G. Teubner, 1873.

—— and Dictys Cretensis. *The Trojan War: The Chronicles of Dictys of Crete and Dares the Phrygian*. Trans. R.M. Frazer. Bloomington, Ind.: Indiana Univ. Press, 1966.

Deguilleville, Guillaume de. *The Pilgrimage of the Life of Man*. Englysht by John Lydgate. Ed. F.J. Furnivall. EETS, ex. ser. 77, 83, 92. 3 vols. London: K. Paul, Trench, Trübner, 1901–1904.

Dictys Cretensis. *Ephemeridos belli Troiani libri, a Lucio Septimio ex Graeco in Latinum sermonen translati*. Ed. Werner Eisenhut. Leipzig: B.G. Teubner, 1973.

Diodorus of Sicily. *The Library of History*. Ed. and trans. C.B. Welles. 12 vols. Cambridge, Mass.: Harvard Univ. Press; London: W. Heinemann, 1933, 1968.

Diogenes Laertius. *Lives of the Eminent Philosophers*. Ed. and trans. R.D. Hicks. 2 vols. London: W. Heinemann, 1925, 1972.

Dioscorides. *The Greek Herbal of Dioscorides*. Englished by John Goodyear, A.D. 1655. Ed. Robert T. Gunther. London: Hafner Publishing Company, 1934, 1968.

The Distichs of Cato: A Famous Medieval Textbook. Ed. and trans. W.J. Chase. Madison: Univ. of Wisconsin Press, 1922.

Dives and Pauper. Ed. P.H. Barnum. EETS, O.S. no. 275. London: Oxford Univ. Press, 1976.

The Earliest Life of Gregory the Great. Ed. B. Colgrave. Cambridge: Cambridge University Press, 1985.

The Early South-English Legendary of Lives of the Saints. I. MS. Laud. 108 in the Bodleian Library. Ed. C. Horstmann. EETS, O.S. 87. London: N. Trübner, 1887.

Eilhart von Oberge. *Tristrant.* Trans. with an introd. by J.W. Thomas. Lincoln: Univ. of Nebraska Press, 1978.

Eneas, roman du XIIe siècle. Ed. J.-J. Salverda de Grave. 2 vols. Paris: H. Champion, 1973.

Epicurus. *Letters, Principal Doctrines and Vatican Sayings.* Trans. by Russel M. Greer. Indianapolis: Univ. of Indiana Press, 1964.

Euripides. *The Plays of Euripides.* Trans. R. Lattimore and D. Green in *The Complete Greek Tragedies.* 4 vols. Chicago: University of Chicago Press, 1959.

Eusebius. *The Ecclesiastical History.* Ed. and trans. J.E.L. Oulton. London: W. Heinemann, 1932.

The Fleury Play of Herod. Text and music edited with translations from the Fleury Manuscript by T. Bailey. Toronto: Pontifical Institute of Mediaeval Studies, 1965.

Florus, Lucius Annaeus. *Epitome of Roman History.* Ed. and trans. Edward Seymour Forster. Cambridge, Mass.: Harvard Univ. Press; London: W. Heinemann, 1929, 1967.

Froissart, Jean. *L'Espinette Amoureuse.* Ed. avec introd., notes, et glossaire par A. Fournier. Paris: C. Klincksieck, 1963.

——. *Froissart's Chronicles.* Trans. and ed. John Jolliffe. New York: The Modern Library, 1968.

Fulgentius, Fabius Planciades. *Fulgentius the Mythographer.* Trans. from the Latin by Leslie George Whitbread. Columbus, Ohio: Ohio State Univ. Press, 1971.

Furnivall, F.J. *A Parallel Text Print of Chaucer's* Troilus and Criseyde. From the Campsall ms. of Mr. Bacon Frank. . . . Put forth by F.J. Furnivall. London: For the Chaucer Society by N. Trübner, 1881–1882.

Galen. *On the Natural Faculties.* Ed. and trans. A.J. Brock. Cambridge, Mass.: Harvard Univ. Press; London: W. Heinemann, 1957.

——. *On the Passions and Errors of the Soul.* Trans. by Paul W. Harkins, with introd. and interpretation by Walther Riese. Columbus, Ohio: Ohio State Univ. Press, 1963.

Garnier de Pont-Sainte-Maxence. *Vie de Saint Thomas le Martyr de Cantorbire.* Trans. Janet Shirley. London: Phillimore, 1975.

Gautier de Châtillon. *Alexandreis.* Ed. F.A.W. Mueldner. Leipzig: B.G. Teubner, 1863.

Geoffrey de Vinsauf. *Poetria nova.* Trans. Margaret F. Nims. Toronto: Pontifical Institute of Mediaeval Studies, 1967.

Geoffrey of Monmouth. *Historia regum Britanniae.* A variant version edited from manuscripts by Jacob Hammer. Cambridge, Mass.: The Medieval Academy of America, 1951.

——. *Historia regum Britanniae.* Ed. A. Griscom. Trans. R.E. Jones. London: Longmans Green, 1929.

——. *The History of the Kings of Britain.* Trans. with introd. by Lewis Thorpe. Harmondsworth: Penguin, 1966.

——. *Vita Merlini.* Ed. and trans. J.J. Parry. Urbana: Univ. of Illinois Press, 1925.

Geoffrey of Vitry. *The Commentary of Geoffrey of Vitry on Claudian's "De raptu Proserpinae."* Transcribed by A.K. Clarke and P.M. Giles, with an introd. and notes by A.K. Clarke. Leiden: E.J. Brill, 1973.

Gesta Romanorum or Entertaining Moral Stories. Trans. Charles Green. Rev. and corrected by Wynnard Hooper. New York: 1894; rpt. AMS Press, 1970.

Gesta Romanorum. Ed. Hermann Oesterley. Hildesheim: G. Olms, 1963.

Gilbert of Poitiers. *The Commentaries on Boethius.* Ed. N.M. Häring. Toronto: Pontifical Institute of Mediaeval Studies, 1966.

Gottfried von Strassburg. *Tristan,* with the *Tristan* of Thomas. Trans. with an introd. by A.T. Hatto. Baltimore: Penguin, 1960.

Gower, John. *The Complete Works.* Ed. G.C. Macaulay. 4 vols. Oxford: Clarendon Press, 1899–1902.

Gratian. *Decretum,* in *Corpus iuris canonici* I, 2nd ed., . . . fidem recognovit et adnotatione critica instruxit Aemilius Friedberg. 2 vols. Leipzig: B. Tauchnitz, 1879–1881.

Gregory of Tours. *The History of the Franks.* Trans. with an introd. by L. Thorpe. Harmondsworth: Penguin, 1974, 1982.

Gregory the Great. *The Dialogues of Gregory the Great. Book II: Saint Benedict.* Trans. with introd. and notes by Myra L. Uhlfelder. Indianapolis: Bobbs-Merrill, 1967.

——. *Pastoral Care.* Trans. and annotated by Henry Davis. Westminster, Md.: Neuman Press, 1950.

Gui de Warewic, roman du XIIIe siècle. Ed. Alfred Ewert. 2 vols. Paris: E. Champion, 1932–1933.

Guido delle Colonne. *Guido de Columnis: Historia destructionis Troiae*. Ed. Nathaniel E. Griffin. Cambridge, Mass.: Medieval Academy of America, 1936.

——. *Historia destructionis Troiae*. Trans. with an introd. and notes by Mary Elizabeth Meek. Bloomington, Ind.: Indiana Univ. Press, 1974.

Guillaume de Lorris and Jean de Meun. *Le Roman de la Rose*. Ed. Ernest Langlois. 5 vols. SATF. Paris: Firmin-Didot, 1914–1924.

——. *Le Roman de la Rose*. Ed. Felix Lecoy. 2 vols. Paris: H. Champion, 1966–1970.

——. *The Romance of the Rose*. Trans. Charles Dahlberg. Princeton: Princeton Univ. Press, 1971.

Guillaume de Machaut. *Oeuvres*. Ed. E. Hoepffner. 3 vols. SATF. Paris: Firmin-Didot, 1908–1921; rpt. New York: Kraus Reprints, 1965.

——. *La Prise d'Alexandrie*. Ed. M.L. de Mas Latrie. Geneva: Librarie Droz, 1877.

Guy of Warwick. Ed. J. Zupita. The Second or Fifteenth-century Version. EETS, ex. ser. 26, 42, 49, 59. London: K. Paul, Trench, Trübner, 1875–1879.

Ham, Edward Billings, ed. *Five Versions of the Venjance Alexandre*. Elliott Monographs of the Romance Languages and Literatures, vol. 34. Princeton: Princeton Univ. Press; Paris: Presses universitaires de France, 1935.

Heinrich von Veldeke. *Eneide*. Ed. G. Schub and T. Friijs. 3 vols. Berlin: G. de Gruyter, 1964–1970.

Hermes Trismegistus. *Corpus Hermeticum*. Texte établi par A.D. Nock et traduit par A.M.J. Festugière. 4 vols. Paris: Société d'edition "Les Belles-Lettres," 1945–1954.

——. *Hermetica; the Ancient Greek and Latin Writings which Contain Religious or Philosophic Teachings Ascribed to Hermes Trismegistus*. Ed. and trans. with notes by Walter Scott. Oxford: The Clarendon Press, 1924–1938.

Herodotus. *Histories*. Ed. and trans. A.D. Godley. 2 vols. London: W. Heinemann, 1928.

Hesiod. *The Homeric Hymns and Homerica*. Ed. and trans. H.G. Evelyn-White. Cambridge, Mass.: Harvard Univ. Press; London: W. Heinemann, 1914, 1967.

Higden, Ranulph. *Polychronicon Ranulphi Higden Monachi Cestrensis*. Together with the English Translations of John Trevisa and of an unknown writer of the fifteenth century. Ed. J.R. Lumby and C. Babington. 8 vols. London: Her Majesty's Stationery Office, 1869; rpt. New York: Kraus, 1964.

Hippocrates. *Hippocrates.* Ed. and trans. W.H.S. Jones and E.T. Withington. 3 vols. London: W. Heinemann, 1923–1927.

Historia Apollonii regis Tyri. Ed. Alexander Riese. Leipzig: B.G. Teubner, 1893.

Homer. *Iliad.* Ed. and trans. A.T. Murray. 2 vols. Cambridge, Mass.: Harvard Univ. Press; London: W. Heinemann, 1924, 1971.

——. *Odyssey.* Ed. and trans. A.T. Murray. 2 vols. Cambridge, Mass.: Harvard Univ. Press; London: W. Heinemann, 1953.

The Hours of Catherine of Cleves. Introd. and commentaries by John Plummer. New York: George Braziller, 1966.

ibn-Ridwan. *Medieval Islamic Medicine: Ibn-Ridwan's Treatise "On the Prevention of Bodily Ills in Egypt."* Trans. with introd. by Michael W. Dols. Arabic text by Adil S. Gamal. Berkeley, Calif.: Univ. of California Press, 1984.

ibn-Rushd. *The Epistle on the Possibility of Conjunction with the Active Intellect,* with the "Commentary" of Moses Narboni. Ed. and trans. Kalman P. Bland. New York: Jewish Theological Seminary, 1982.

ibn-Sina. *Remarks and Admonitions, Part One: Logic.* Trans. Shams Constantine Inati. Medieval Sources in Translation, 28. Toronto: Pontifical Institute of Mediaeval Studies, 1984.

Innocent III. *De miseria condicionis humanae.* Ed. and trans. Robert E. Lewis. Athens, Ga.: Georgia Univ. Press, 1978.

——. *De miseria condicionis humane.* Ed. and trans. M. Maccarrone. Lugano: Thesaurus Mundi, 1955.

Iscanus, J. *Werke und Briefe.* Ed. Ludwig Gompf. Leiden: E.J. Brill, 1970.

Isidore. *Etymologiarum sive originum libri XX.* Ed. W.M. Lindsay. 2 vols. Oxford: Clarendon Press, 1911, 1962.

——. *The History of the Goths, Vandals, and Suevi.* Trans. from the Latin with an introd. by G. Donini and G.B. Ford, Jr. 2nd rev. ed. Leiden: E.J. Brill, 1970.

——. *The Medical Writings.* Trans. with introd. and commentary by William D. Sharpe. Transactions of the American Philosophical Society, new series 54, Part 2. Philadelphia: American Philosophical Society, 1964.

Jacobus de Voragine. *The Golden Legend.* Trans. and adapted from the Latin by Granger Ryan and Helmut Ripperger. New York: Arno Press, 1969.

——. *Legenda aurea.* Ed. Th. Graesse. 3rd ed., 1890. Osnabrück: Otto Zeller, 1965.

Jean de Meun. *Traduction de la première épître de Pierre Abelard (Historia calamitatum).* Ed. Charlotte Charier. Paris: H. Champion, 1934.

Jehan de Tuim. *Li hystore de Julius Cesar*. Ed. F. Settegast. Halle: M. Niemeyer, 1881.

Jerome. *The Principal Works of St. Jerome*. Trans. W.H. Freemantle. New York: Christian Literature Company, 1893.*Select Letters of St. Jerome*. Ed. and trans. F.A. Wright. London: W. Heinemann, 1933.

——. *Select Letters of St. Jerome*. Ed. and trans. F.A. Wright. London: W. Heinemann, 1933.

Joannes Scotum. *Annotationes in Marciam*. Ed. Cora Lutz. Cambridge, Mass.: Medieval Academy of America, 1939.

John of Salisbury. *Frivolities of Courtiers and Footprints of Philosophers*. Translation of the first, second, and third books . . . of the *Policraticus*, by J.B. Pike. Minneapolis: Univ. of Minnesota Press; London: Oxford University Press, 1938.

Jordanes. *The Gothic History*. Trans. C.C. Mierow. Princeton: Princeton Univ. Press, 1915.

Josephus, Flavius. *The Jewish War*. Ed. and trans. H. St. J. Thackeray, R. Marcus, A. Wikgren, and L.H. Feldman. 9 vols. Cambridge, Mass.: Harvard University Press; London: W. Heinemann, 1926, 1976.

——. *Jewish Antiquities*. Ed. and trans. R. Marcus and A. Wikgren. Cambridge, Mass.: Harvard Univ. Press; London: W. Heinemann, 1926, 1956–1965.

Juvenal. *Satires*. Ed. and trans. G.G. Ramsay. Cambridge, Mass.: Harvard Univ. Press; London: H. Heinemann, 1950.

al-Khwarizmi. *The Astronomical Tables of al-Khwarizmi*. Trans. with commentary of the Latin version by O. Neugebauer, ed. H. Suter. Copenhagen: Munksgaard, 1962.

King Horn. Ed. J. Hall. Oxford: Clarendon Press, 1901.

Kyng Alisaunder. Ed. G.V. Smithers. 2 vols. EETS, no. 237 and 227. London: Oxford University Press, 1957.

Langland, W. *The Vision of Piers Plowman*. A critical edition of the B-Text based on Trinity College Cambridge MS. B.15.17 with selected variant readings, an introd., glosses, and a textual and literary commentary by A.V.C. Schmidt. London: J.M. Dent; New York: E.P. Dutton, 1978.

"Launcelot do Lac," the Non-Cyclic Old French Prose Romance. Ed. Elspeth Kennedy. 2 vols. I: Text, 2: Introduction, Bibliography, Notes and Variants, Glossary, and Index of Proper Names. Oxford: Clarendon Press; New York: Oxford University Press, 1980.

Layamon. *Brut*. Ed. G.L. Brooke and R.F. Leslie. EETS, no. 250. London, New York: Oxford University Press, 1963, 1978.

——. *Brut*. Ed. and trans. Frederick Madden. 3 vols. London: Society of Antiquaries, 1847.

The Letters of Heloise and Abelard. Trans. with introd. by Betty Radice. Harmondsworth: Penguin, 1974, 1979.

Libeaus Desconus. Ed. M. Mills. EETS, O.S. 261. London, New York: Oxford Univ. Press, 1969.

Livy (Titus Livius). *Livy (Ab urbe condita libri).* Ed. and trans. B.O. Foster, F.G. Moore, E.T. Sage, A.C. Schlesinger, and R.M. Greer. 14 vols. Cambridge, Mass.: Harvard Univ. Press; London: W. Heinemann, 1959.

Lost Books of the Bible. Trans. William Hone. New York: Bell Publishing, 1926; rpt. 1974.

Lucan, M.A. *Pharsalia.* Ed. and trans. J.D. Duff. London: W. Heinemann; Cambridge, Mass.: Harvard Univ. Press, 1928, 1969.

Lucretius. *De rerum natura.* Ed. and trans. W.H.D. Rouse. Rev. with a new text, introd., notes, and index by M.F. Smith. Cambridge, Mass.: Harvard Univ. Press; London: W. Heinemann, 1924, 1975.

The Lyf of Oure Lady: the Middle English Translation of Thomas of Hales' "Vita Sanctae Mariae." Ed. S.M. Horall. Heidelberg: C. Winter, 1985.

Macrobius. *Macrobius's Commentary on the Dream of Scipio.* Trans. with introd. and notes by W.H. Stahl. New York: Columbia Univ. Press, 1952.

——. *The Saturnalia.* Trans. with introd. and notes by P.V. Davies. New York: Columbia Univ. Press, 1969.

——. *Saturnalia. In Somnium Scipionis Commentarius.* Ed. J. Willis. 2 vols. Leipzig: B.G. Teubner, 1963.

Malory, Sir Thomas. *Le Morte d'Arthur.* Ed. J. Cowen, introd. J. Lawlor. 2 vols. Baltimore: Penguin, 1969.

——. *Works.* Ed. Eugène Vinaver. 2nd ed. 3 vols. Oxford: Clarendon Press, 1967; rev. 1973.

Mandeville, John. *Mandeville's Travels.* Ed. M.C. Seymour. Oxford: Clarendon Press, 1967.

La Maniere de Language que t'enseigners bien adroit parler et escrire doulz françois selon l'usage et la coustume de France (1396). Ed. P. Meyer. *Revue critique* (1873).

Map, Walter. *De nugis curialium: Courtiers' Trifles.* Ed. and trans. M.R. James, rev. C.N.L. Brooke and R.A.B. Mynors. Oxford: Clarendon Press, 1983.

Marbode of Rennes. *Marbode of Rennes.* De lapidibus. Ed. John M. Riddle. Considered as a medical treatise with text, commentary, and C.W. King's translation, together with text and translation of Marbode's minor works on stones. Wiesbaden: Franz Steiner, 1977.

Martianus Capella. *Martianus Capella.* Ed. Adolphus Dick. Addenda adiecit Jean Préaux. Stuttgart: B.G. Teubner, 1925, 1969.

——. *Martianus Capella and the Seven Liberal Arts.* Trans. W.H. Stahl and Richard Johnson with E.L. Burge. 2 vols. New York: Columbia Univ. Press, 1977.

Martin of Braga. *Opera Omnia.* Ed. Claude W. Barlow. New Haven: Yale Univ. Press, 1950.

The Middle English Stanzaic Versions of the Life of St. Anne. Ed. R.E. Parker. EETS. London: Oxford Univ. Press, 1928.

Muhammad ibn-Umail. "Three Arabic Treatises on Alchemy." Ed. Muhammad Turabi 'Ali, trans. H.E. Stapleton and M. Hidayat Hosain. *Memoirs of the Asiatic Society of Bengal* 12 (1933): 147–197.

Mythographi Latini. Ed. T. Munckerus. Amsterdam: Ionnis et Someren, 1681.

Nicholas of Lynne. *The Kalendarium of Nicholas of Lynne.* Ed. Sigmund Eisner. Trans. G. McEoin and S. Eisner. Athens, Ga.: Georgia Univ. Press, 1980.

Octavian. Ed. Gregor Sarrazin. Heilbronn: G. Henninger, 1885.

Octavian. Ed. F. Sparran. EETS. New York: Oxford University Press, 1986.

Origen. *The Song of Songs: Commentary and Homilies.* Trans. and annotated by R.P. Lawson. Westminster, Md.: Neuman Press, 1957.

Orosius, Paulus. *Seven Books of History Against the Pagans;* the *Apology* of Paulus Orosius. Trans. with introd. and notes by Irving W. Raymund. New York: Columbia Univ. Press, 1936.

Ovid (Publius Ovidius Naso). *The Art of Love and Other Poems (Ars amatoria).* Ed. and trans. J.H. Mozley. 2nd ed. rev. G.P. Goold. Cambridge, Mass.: Harvard Univ. Press; London: W. Heinemann, 1979.

——. *Fasti.* Ed. and trans. J.G. Frazer. Cambridge, Mass.: Harvard Univ. Press; London: W. Heinemann, 1931, 1967.

——. *Fasti.* Ed. and trans. with notes by J.G. Frazer. 5 vols. Cambridge, Mass.: Harvard Univ. Press, 1931.

——. *Heroides* and *Amores.* Ed. and trans. G. Showerman. 2nd ed. rev. G.P. Goold. Cambridge, Mass.: Harvard Univ. Press; London: W. Heinemann, 1977.

——. *Metamorphoses.* Ed. and trans. F.J. Miller. 2nd ed. 2 vols. Cambridge, Mass.: Harvard Univ. Press; London: W. Heinemann, 1921.

——. *Tristia; Epistulae ex Ponto.* Ed. and trans. A.L. Wheeler. Cambridge, Mass.: Harvard Univ. Press; London: W. Heinemann, 1924, 1965.

Ovide Moralisé, poème du commencement du XIVe siècle. Publié d'après tous les manuscrits connus. Ed. C. de Boer. Verhandlungen der Koninklyke Nederlandische Akademie van Wetenschappen, deel 15, 21, 30, 37, 43. Amsterdam: 1915–1938.

The Parlement of the Thre Ages. Ed. M.Y. Offord. EETS, no. 246. London: Oxford Univ. Press, 1959.

Pausanias. *Description of Greece*. Ed. and trans. W.H.S. Jones. 5 vols. London: W. Heinemann; New York: G.P. Putnam, 1918–1935.

Peter Riga. *Aurora: Petri Rigae Biblia Versificata,* A Verse Commentary on the Bible. Ed. Paul E. Beichner. 2 vols. Notre Dame: Univ. of Notre Dame Press, 1965.

Petrarch, Francesco. *Africa*. Trans. and annotated by Thomas G. Bergin and Alice S. Wilson. New Haven: Yale Univ. Press, 1977.

——. *Letters from Petrarch*. Selected and trans. by Morris Bishop. Bloomington, Ind.: Indiana Univ. Press, 1966.

——. *Rerum familiarium libri ix-xvi: Letters on Familiar Matters*. Trans. Aldo S. Bernardo. Baltimore: Johns Hopkins Univ. Press, 1982.

——. *Le Rime Sparse et i Trionfi*. Ed. Ezio Chiorboli. Bari: G. Laterza, 1930.

——. *The Triumphs of Petrarch*. Trans. Ernest H. Wilkins. Chicago: Univ. of Chicago Press, 1962.

Petrus Alfonsi. *The 'Disciplina Clericalis' of Petrus Alfonsi*. Trans. and ed. Eberhard Hermes; trans. into English P.R. Quarrie. London and Henley: Routledge and Kegan Paul, 1970.

——. *The Scholar's Guide*. Trans. J.R. Jones and J.E. Keller. Toronto: Pontifical Institute of Mediaeval Studies, 1969.

Philostratus. *The Life of Apollonios of Tyana*. Ed. and trans. F.C. Conybeare. 2 vols. Cambridge, Mass.: Harvard Univ. Press; London: W. Heinemann, 1912, 1969.

Piramus et Tisbé, poème du XIIe siècle. Ed. C. de Boer. Paris: H. Champion, 1921.

Plato. *Meno*. Ed. and trans. W.R.M. Lamb. Cambridge, Mass.: Harvard Univ. Press; London: W. Heinemann, 1924, 1977.

——. *Phaedo*. Ed. and trans. H.N. Fowler. Cambridge, Mass.: Harvard Univ. Press; London: W. Heinemann, 1914, 1982.

——. *Republic*. Ed. and trans. P. Shorey. 2 vols. Cambridge, Mass.: Harvard Univ. Press; London: W. Heinemann, 1937, 1969.

——. *Symposium*. Ed. and trans. W.R.M. Lamb. Cambridge, Mass.: Harvard Univ. Press; London: W. Heinemann, 1925, 1961.

——. *Timaeus*. Ed. and trans. R.G. Bury. Cambridge, Mass.: Harvard Univ. Press; London: W. Heinemann, 1959.

The Play of Antichrist. Trans. with an introd. by J. Wright. Toronto: Pontifical Institute of Mediaeval Studies, 1967.

Pliny (G. Plinius Secundus). *Historia Naturalis (Natural History)*. Ed. and trans. R. Rackham, W.H.S. Jones, D.E. Eichholz. 10 vols. Cambridge, Mass.: Harvard Univ. Press; London: W. Heinemann, 1938.

Plutarch. *Moralia*. Ed. and trans. F.C. Babbitt, H. Cherniss, P.A. Clement, P.H. De Lacy, B. Einarson, H.N. Fowler, W.C. Helmbold, E.L. Minar, L. Pearson, F.H. Sandbach, W.C. Sandbach. 15 vols. Cambridge, Mass.: Harvard Univ. Press; London: W. Heinemann, 1926–1980.

——. *Parallel Lives*. Ed. and trans. Bernadotte Perrin. 11 vols. Cambridge, Mass.: Harvard Univ. Press; London: W. Heinemann, 1914.

Polybius. *The Histories*. Trans. from the text of F. Hultsch by Evelyn S. Shuckburgh, with a new introd. by F.W. Walbank. 2 vols. Bloomington, Ind.: Indiana Univ. Press, 1962.

——. *The Histories*. Ed. and trans. W.P. Paton. 2 vols. Cambridge, Mass.: Harvard Univ. Press; London: W. Heinemann, 1954.

Ptolemy (Claudius Ptolemaeus). *Tetrabiblos*. Ed. and trans. F.E. Robbins. Cambridge, Mass.: Harvard Univ. Press; London: W. Heinemann, 1940, 1980.

Publilius Syrus. *The Moral Sayings of Publilius Syrus*. Trans. D. Lyman. Cleveland: [n.p.], 1856.

——. *Publilii Syri mimi, similesque senteniae, selectae ae poetis antiquis, Latinis*. Ed. J.F. Kremsiev. Leipzig: J. Sommer, 1818.

——. *Publilii Syri Sententiae*. Ad fidem codicum optimorum primum recensuit Eduardus Woelfflin. Leipzig: B.G. Teubner, 1869.

Pyrame et Thisbé. Texte normand du XIIe siècle. Ed. critique avec introduction, notes, et index de toutes les formes par C. de Boer. Amsterdam: J. Müller, 1911.

La Querelle de la Rose. Letters and Documents. Ed. and trans. J.L. Baird and J.R. Kane. Chapel Hill: Univ. of North Carolina Press, 1978.

Remigius Autissiodorensis. *Commentum in Martianum Capellam*. Ed. with an introd. by Cora Lutz. 2 vols. Leiden: E.J. Brill, 1962.

Renard the Fox. Trans. from the Old French by Patricia Terry. Boston: Northeastern Univ. Press, 1983.

Renaud de Beaugeu. *Le bel inconnu, ou, Giglain fils de Messire Gauvain et de la fée aux blanches mains*. Publié d'après les manuscrits uniques de Londres avec une introd. et un glossaire par C. Hippeaux. Geneva: Slatkin Reprints, 1969.

Rhazes (al-Razi). *A Treatise on the Smallpox and Measles*. Trans. by William A. Greenhill. London: 1848; rpt. Baltimore: Williams & Wilkins, 1939.

Le Roman de Cassidorus. Ed. J. Palermo. 2 vols. SATF. Paris: A.J. Vrin, 1963–1964.

Le Roman de Helcanus. Ed. critique d'un texte en prose du XIIIe siècle par H. Nieddzielski. Genève: Droz, 1966.

Le Roman de Renard (Branches I, II, III, IV, V, VIII, X, XV). Chronologie, préface, bibliographie, notes, et lexique par Jean Dufournet. Paris: Garnier-Flammarion, 1970.

Le Roman de Renart. Transcrit par Jacques Haumont. Paris: H. Piazza, 1966.

Le Roman de Thèbes. Publié d'après tous les manuscrits par Léopold Constans. 2 vols. SATF. Paris: Firmin-Didot, 1890.

Le Roman de Thèbes (The Story of Thebes). Trans. John Smart Coley. New York, London: Garland Publishing, Inc., 1986.

Le Roman de Tristan en Prose. Ed. Renée L. Curtis. Woodbridge, Suffolk; Dover, N.H.: Baydell & Brewer, 1985.

Le Roman de Tristan par Thomas. Ed. J. Bédier. 2 vols. SATF. Paris: Firmin-Didot, 1903–1905.

The Romance of Beves of Hamtoun. Ed. E. Kölbing. EETS, ex. ser. 46, 48, 65. London: K. Paul, Trench, Trübner, 1885–1894.

The Romance of Guy of Warwick. Edited from the Auchinleck manuscript in the Advocates' Library, Edinburgh, and from Ms. 107 in Caius College, Cambridge, by John Zupita. EETS, ex. ser. 42, 49, 59. London: Oxford Univ. Press, 1883, 1887, 1891, rpt. 1966.

The Romance of Perceval in Prose. A translation of the P manuscript of the Didot Perceval by Dell Skuls. Seattle: Univ. of Washington Press, 1961.

The Romance of the Emperor Octavian. Now first published from Mss. at Lincoln and Cambridge. Ed. James Orchard Halliwell. London: The Percy Society, 1844.

The Romance of Tristan by Beroul. Ed. Alfred Ewert. 2 vols. Oxford: B. Blackwell, 1967–1970.

The Romance of Tristan and Ysolt by Thomas of Britain. Trans. from the Old French and Old Norse by R.S. Loomis. New York: E.P. Dutton, 1923.

Rose, M., ed. *The Wakefield Mystery Plays.* London: Evans, 1961.

Rossignol. Ed. and trans. J.L. Baird and John R. Kane, with an introductory essay on the Nightingale tradition. Kent, Ohio: Kent State Univ. Press, 1978.

The Rule of St. Benedict: The Abingdon Copy. Ed. John Chamberlain. Toronto: Pontifical Institute of Mediaeval Studies, 1982.

Scriptores historiae Augustae. Ed. and trans. D. Magie. 3 vols. London: W. Heinemann, 1922–1932.

Seneca, Lucius Annaeus. *Ad Lucillum epistulae morales.* Ed. and trans. R.M. Gummere. 3 vols. Cambridge, Mass.: Harvard Univ. Press; London: W. Heinemann, 1920, 1953.

——. *Moral Essays*. Ed. and trans. J.W. Basore. 2 vols. Cambridge, Mass.: Harvard Univ. Press; London: W. Heinemann, 1932, 1970.

Les Sept Sages de Rome. Ed. Gaston Paris. 2 vols. SATF. Paris: Firmin-Didot, 1876.

Seven Medieval Latin Comedies. Trans. Alison Goddard Elliott. New York: Garland Publishing, Inc., 1984.

Sir Gawain and the Green Knight. A new critical edition by Theodore Silverstein. Chicago and London: Univ. of Chicago Press, 1984.

Sir Orfeo. Ed. A.J. Bliss. London: Oxford Univ. Press, 1954.

Sir Perceval of Galles. Ed. J. Champion and F. Holthausen. Heidelberg: C. Winter; New York: G.E. Stechert, 1913.

Solinus, C.J. *Polyhistoria*. Ed. C. Salmas. Leipzig: [n.p.], 1777.

The Song of Roland. Fragment from Lansdowne MS 388, Leaf 381. Ed. S.J. Herrtage. EETS, ex. ser. 35. London: N. Trübner, 1880.

The Song of Roland. Trans. D. Sayers. Harmondsworth: Penguin, 1937, 1971.

The South-English Legendary. Ed. from Corpus Christi College, Cambridge, MS. 145 and British Museum MS. Harley 2277, with variants from Bodley MS. Ashmole 43 and British Museum MS. Cotton Julius D. IX by Charlotte D'Evelyn and Anna J. Mill. EETS, nos. 235–236, 244. 3 vols. London: Oxford Univ. Press, 1956, 1967.

Statius. *Thebaid* and *Achilleid*. Ed. and trans. J.H. Mozley. 2 vols. London: W. Heinemann, 1928.

——. *The Medieval* Achilleid *of Statius*. Ed. Paul M. Clogan, with introd., variant readings, and glosses. Leiden: E.J. Brill, 1968.

Strabo. *Geography*. Ed. and trans. H.L. Jones. 8 vols. Cambridge, Mass.: Harvard Univ. Press; London: W. Heinemann, 1932, 1967.

Strode, Ralph. *Consequentiae et obligationes cum commentis*. Venice: Octavianus Scolis, 1493.

——. *An Edition and Translation of the* Tractatus de consequentiis *by Ralph Strode,* fourteenth-century logician and friend of Geoffrey Chaucer, by Wallace Knight Seaton. Berkeley: Univ. of California Press, 1973.

Suetonius. *De vita Caesarum*. Ed. and trans. J.C. Rolfe. 2 vols. Cambridge, Mass.: Harvard Univ. Press; London: W. Heinemann, 1951.

Susannah. An Alliterative poem of the fourteenth century. Ed. Alice Miskimin. New Haven: Yale Univ. Press, 1969.

Sutherland, R., ed. *The* Romaunt of the Rose *and* Le Roman de la Rose: A Parallel-Text edition. Berkeley: Univ. of California Press, 1968.

Tacitus. *The Annals*. Ed. and trans. John Jackson. 2 vols. Cambridge, Mass.: Harvard Univ. Press; London: W. Heinemann, 1937, 1951.

——. *Annals of Imperial Rome*. Trans. Michael Grant. Baltimore, Md.: Penguin, 1956.

Tertullian. *Apology. De spectaculis*. Ed. and trans. T.R. Glover. London: W. Heinemann; New York: G.P. Putnam, 1931.

Theodulus. *Theoduli eclogam*. Ed. J. Osternacher. Urfahr: Ripariae prope Lentiam, 1902.

Thomas of Bradwardine: His Tractatus Proportionibus. Ed. H. Lamar Crosby. Madison: Univ. of Wisconsin Press, 1955.

Thomas of Celano. *The Life of St. Clare*. Trans. Pascal Robinson. Philadelphia: Delphin Press, 1910.

Three Old English Prose Texts. In MS Cotton Vitellius A.xv. Ed. with introd. and glossarial index by Stanley Rypins. EETS, O.S. 161. London: Oxford Univ. Press, 1924 for 1921.

Three Ovidian Tales of Love. Ed. and trans. Raymond Cormier. New York: Garland Publishing, Inc., 1981.

Trotula of Salerno. *The Diseases of Women by Trotula of Salerno*. Trans. Elizabeth Mason-Hohl. Los Angeles: Ward Ritchie Press, 1940.

Two Lives of St. Cuthbert: A Life by an Anonymous Monk of Lindisfarne and Bede's Prose Life. Ed. B. Colgrave. Cambridge: Cambridge Univ. Press, 1985.

Valerius Flaccus, E. *Argonauticon*. Ed. and trans. J.H. Mozley. Cambridge, Mass.: Harvard Univ. Press; London: W. Heinemann, 1934.

Valerius Maximus. *De dictiis factisque memorabilium*. Ed. B. Hase. 3 vols. Paris: N.E. Lemaire, 1822.

——. *Factorum dictorumque memorabilium libri novem*. Ed. J. Kappy. 2 vols. London: A.J. Valpy, 1823.

Varro. *On the Latin Tongue*. Ed. and trans. R.G. Kent. 2 vols. Cambridge, Mass.: Harvard Univ. Press; London: W. Heinemann, 1951.

Villon, François. *The Complete Works*. Trans. J.U. Nicholson. New York: Covici, Friede, 1931.

Vincent of Beauvais. *De eruditione filiorum nobilium*. Ed. A. Stever. Cambridge, Mass.: Medieval Academy of America, 1938.

——. *Speculum Majus*. Venice: 1591.

Virgil (P.M. Vergilius). *The Complete Works: Eclogues, Georgics, Aeneid, and Minor Poems*. Ed. and trans. H.R. Fairclough. Rev. ed. 2 vols. Cambridge, Mass.: Harvard Univ. Press; London: W. Heinemann, 1932.

Wace. *Le Roman de Brut*. Ed. J. Ivor Arnold. 2 vols. SATF. Paris: Firmin-Didot, 1938–1940.

——. *Le Roman de Brut.* Branche I–V, VIII, X, XV. Chronologie, préface, bibliographie, notes, et lexique par Jean Dufouret. Paris: Garnier-Flammarion, 1970.

—— *Le Roman de Rou de Wace.* Ed. A.J. Holden. 3 vols. SATF. Paris: A. & J. Picard, 1970–1973.

The Wakefield Pageants in the Towneley Cycle. Ed. A.C. Cawley. Manchester: Manchester Univ. Press, 1958, 1968.

Walsingham, Thomas. *Historia brevis Thomae Walsingham ab Edwardo primo ad Henricum quinto.* London: H. Binneman, 1574.

Widsith. Ed. R.W. Chambers. Cambridge: Cambridge Univ. Press, 1912.

Witelo. *Perspectivae liber quintus: An English Translation with Introduction and Commentary and Latin Edition of the First Catoptrical Book.* Ed. and trans. A. Mark Smith. Studia Copernica, 23. Warsaw: The Polish Academy of Sciences, 1983.

Woods, M.C., ed. *An Early Commentary on the* Poetria nova *of Geoffrey of Vinsauf.* New York: Garland Publishing, Inc., 1983.

Xenophon. *Cyropaedia.* Ed. and trans. Walter Miller. 2 vols. London: W. Heinemann; New York: Macmillan, 1914, 1925.

The York Plays. Ed. Richard Beadle. London: Edward Arnold. 1982.

Ypotis. Altenglische Legenden. Ed. C. Horstmann. Heilbronn: G. Henninger, 1881.

Secondary Sources

Aers, D. "Criseyde: Woman in Medieval Society." *ChauR* 13 (1979): 177–200.

Afnan, S.M. *Avicenna: His Life and Works.* London: G. Allen & Unwin, 1958.

Aiken, Pauline. "Chaucer's *Legend of Cleopatra* and the *Speculum Historiale.*" *Speculum* 13 (1938): 232–236.

——. "Vincent of Beauvais and Chaucer's Knowledge of Alchemy." *SP* 41 (1944): 371–389.

——. "Vincent of Beauvais and Chaucer's *Monk's Tale.*" *Speculum* 17 (1942): 56–68.

——. "Vincent of Beauvais and Dame Pertelote's Knowledge of Medicine." *Speculum* 10 (1935): 281–287.

——. "Vincent of Beauvais and the Green Yeoman's Lecture on Demonology." *SP* 35 (1938): 1–9.

Allan, Donald J. "Mediaeval Versions of Aristotle: *De Caelo* and the Commentary of Simplicius." *MRS* 2 (1950): 82–120.

Allen, Judson B., and Patrick Gallagher. "Alisoun Through the Looking Glass: Or Every Man his Own Midas." *ChauR* 4 (1970): 99–105.

——. "Herman the German's Averroistic Aristotle and Medieval Literary Theory." *ChaucR* 9 (1976): 67–81.

Allen, R.H. *Star Names and their Meanings.* New York: G. Stechert, 1899.

Anderson, M. "Blanche, Duchess of Lancaster." *MP* 45 (1947–1948): 152–159.

Arberry, Arthur J. "Rhazes on the Philosophic Life." *Asiatic Review* 45 (1949): 703–713.

Archer, J.W. "On Chaucer's Source for 'Arveragus' in the *Franklin's Tale.*" *PMLA* 65 (1950): 318–322.

Arn, Mary-Jo. "Three Ovidian Women in Chaucer's *Troilus*: Medea, Helen, Oenone." *ChauR* 15 (1980): 1–10.

Atwood, E.B. "Two Alterations of Virgil in Chaucer's Dido." *Speculum* 13 (1938): 454–457.

Auerbach, E. *Literary Language and its Public in Late Latin Antiquity.* Trans. R. Mannhein. New York: Pantheon Books, 1965.

Ayres, H.M. "Chaucer and Seneca." *Romanic Review* 10 (1919): 1–15.

Badel, Pierre-Yves. *Le Roman de la Rose au XIVe siècle. Etude de la reception de l'oeuvre.* Genève: Droz, 1980.

Baird-Lange, Lorrayne Y. "Trotula's Fourteenth-Century Reputation, Jankyn's Book, and Chaucer's Trot." *Studies in the Age of Chaucer,* Proceedings 1 (1984): 245–256.

Baker, Howard. *Persephone's Cave: Cultural Accumulations of the Early Greeks.* Athens, Ga.: Univ. of Georgia Press, 1979.

——. "Pythagoras of Samos." *Sewanee Review* 80 (1972): 1–38.

Barrett, C.K. *Luke the Historian in Recent Study.* London: Epworth Press, 1961.

Bassan, M. "Chaucer's 'Cursed Monk,' Constantinus Africanus." *MS* 24 (1962): 127–140.

Beare, F.W. *Saint Paul and His Letters.* New York: Abingdon Press, 1962.

Beichner, P.E. "Absolon's Hair." *MS* 12 (1950): 222–233.

——. "Chaucer's 'Hende Nicholas.'" *MS* 14 (1952): 151–153.

——. "Daun Piers, Monk and Business Administrator." *Speculum* 34 (1959): 611–619.

——. *The Medieval Representative of Music, Jubal or Tubalcain?* Notre Dame: Univ. of Notre Dame Press, 1954.

Bennet, H.S. *Chaucer and the Fifteenth Century.* New York: Oxford Univ. Press, 1947, 1966.

Bennett, J.A.W. *Chaucer at Oxford and at Cambridge*. Toronto: Toronto Univ. Press, 1974.

——. "Chaucer, Dante and Boccaccio." *MAE* 22 (1953): 114–115.

——. *Chaucer's Book of Fame*. Oxford: Clarendon Press, 1968.

Benson, C. David. *The History of Troy in Middle English Literature: Guido delle Colonne's Historia destructionis Troiae in Medieval England*. Woodbridge, Suffolk: D.S. Brewer, 1980.

——. "King Thoas and the Ominous Letter in Chaucer's *Troilus*." *PQ* 58 (1979): 364–367.

——. " 'O Nyce World': What Chaucer Really Found in Guido delle Colonne's *History of Troy*." *ChauR* 13 (1979): 308–315.

Benson, L., ed. *The Learned and the Lewed: Studies in Chaucer and Medieval Literature*. Harvard English Studies, 5. Cambridge, Mass.: Harvard Univ. Press, 1974.

Benson, R.L., and G. Constable, eds. *Renaissance and Renewal in the Twelfth Century*. Cambridge, Mass.: Harvard Univ. Press, 1982.

Bergin, T.G. *Boccaccio*. New York: Viking Press, 1981.

Bethurum, P., ed. *Critical Approaches to Medieval Literature*. New York: Columbia Univ. Press, 1960, 1967.

Bevan, E. *A History of Egypt Under the Ptolemaic Dynasty*. London: Methuen, 1927.

Boer, C. de. "Guillaume de Machaut et l'*Ovide Moralisé*." In *Ovide Moralisé*, deel 15 (1915): 28–43.

Boitani, P. *Chaucer and Boccaccio*. Oxford: Clarendon Press, 1977.

Boshe, E.J. "Some Notes on the Wade Legend." *PQ* 2 (1923): 282–288.

Bourdillon, F.W. *The Early Editions of the* Roman de la Rose. London: The Bibliographical Society, 1906.

Braddy, H. *Chaucer and the French Poet Graunson*. Baton Rouge: Louisiana State University, 1947.

——. "The Two Petros in *The Monk's Tale*." *PMLA* 50 (1935): 69–80.

Bradley, D.R. "Fals Eneas and Sely Dido." *PQ* 39 (1960): 122–125.

Brehaut, E. *An Encyclopaedist of the Dark Ages, Isidore of Seville*. New York: Columbia Univ. Press, 1912, 1964.

Brennan, John P. "Reflections on a Gloss to the *Prioress's Tale* from Jerome's *Adversus Jovinianum*." *SP* 70 (1973): 243–251.

Brittain, Frederick. *Saint Giles*. Cambridge: W. Heffer, 1928.

Brown, C. "Chaucer and the 'Hours of the Blessed Virgin.'" *MLN* 30 (1915): 231–232.

Brown, Emerson, Jr. "Chaucer and a Proper Name: Januarie in *The Merchant's Tale.*" *Names* 31 (1982): 79–87.

——. "Epicurus and Voluptas in Late Antiquity: The Curious Testimony of Martianus Capella." *Traditio* 38 (1982): 75–106.

——. "Hortus Inconclusus: The Significance of Priapus and Pyramus and Thisbe in *The Merchant's Tale.*" *ChauR* 4 (1970): 31–40.

——. "Priapus and *The Parlement of Foulys.*" *SP* 72 (1975): 258–274.

——. "Why Is May called 'Mayus'?" *ChauR* 2 (1967): 273–277.

Brown, Peter R.L. *Augustine of Hippo.* Berkeley: Univ. of California Press, 1967.

Brusendorff, A. *The Chaucer Tradition.* London: Oxford University Press; Copenhagen: V. Pio, 1925.

Busard, H.L.L., ed. *The First Latin Translation of Euclid's "Elements" Commonly Ascribed to Adelard of Bath, Books I–VIII and Books X.36–XV.2.* Toronto: Pontifical Institute of Mediaeval Studies, 1983.

Byers, J.R. "Harry Bailly's St. Madrian." *ELN* 4 (1966): 6–9.

Bush, D. "Chaucer's Corinne." *Speculum* 4 (1929): 106–107.

Caldwell, Robert A. "Wace's *Roman de Brut* and the Variant Version of Geoffrey of Monmouth's *Historia regum Britanniae.*" *Speculum* 31 (1956): 675–682.

Campbell, F.W.G. *Apollonius of Tyana: A Study of his Life and Times.* Chicago: Argonaut, Inc., 1908, 1968.

Carmody, Francis J. *Arabic Astronomical and Astrological Sciences in Latin Translation.* Berkeley: Univ. of California Press, 1956.

——. "The Planetary Theory of Ibn Rushd." *Osiris* 10 (1952): 556–586.

Cary, G. *The Medieval Alexander.* Ed. D.J.A. Ross. Cambridge: Cambridge Univ. Press, 1967.

Cesareo, G.A. *Le origini della poesia lirica e la poesia sciliana sotto gli Suevi.* 2nd ed. Milan: R. Sandron, 1924.

Charnier, Charlotte. *Héloise dans l'histoire et dans la légende.* Paris: H. Champion, 1933.

Cholmeley, H.P. *John Gaddesden and the Rosa Medicinae.* Oxford: The Clarendon Press, 1912.

Chrysostomus, B. *John Chrysostom and his Times.* Trans. M. Gonzaga. Westminster, Md.: Newman Press, 1960.

Clagett, Marshall. "The Medieval Latin Translation from the Arabic of the *Elements* of Euclid with Special Emphasis on the Versions of Adelard of Bath." *Isis* 44 (1953): 16–42.

Clasby, E. "Chaucer's Constance: Womanly Virtue and the Heroic Life." *ChauR* 13 (1979): 221–233.

Clemen, W. *Chaucer's Early Poetry.* Trans. C.A.M. Sym. New York: Barnes and Noble, 1963.

Cline, R.M. "Four Chaucer Saints." *MLN* 60 (1945): 480–482.

Clogan, P.M. "Chaucer and the *Thebaid* Scolia." *SP* 61 (1964): 599–619.

——. "Chaucer's Cybele and the *Liber Imaginum Deorum.*" *PQ* 43 (1964): 272–274.

——. "Chaucer's Use of the *Thebaid.*" *EM* 18 (1967): 9–31.

Clouston, W.A. *On the Magical Elements in Chaucer's Squire's Tale, with Analogues.* Chaucer Society, 2nd series, no. 26. London: Chaucer Society, 1890.

Coffman, G.R. "John Gower, Mentor for Royalty." *PMLA* 69 (1954): 953–964.

Cohen, Gustave, ed. *La "Comédie" latine en France au XIIe siècle.* 2 vols. Paris: Société d'Edition "Les Belles-Lettres," 1931.

Colledge, E. *Renard the Fox and Other Netherlands Secular Literature.* Leiden: A.W. Sijthooff, 1967.

Comparetti, D. *Vergil in the Middle Ages.* Trans. E.F.M. Benecke. Hamden, Conn.: Archon Books, 1966.

Conley, John. "The Peculiar Name *Sir Thopas.*" *SP* 73 (1976): 42–61.

Cook, A.S. "The Date of the Old English 'Elene.'" *Anglia* 15 (1893): 9–20.

Cook, Robert G. "Chaucer's Pandarus and the Medieval Ideal of Friendship." *JEGP* 69 (1970): 407–424.

Cooper, Geoffrey. " 'Sely John' in the 'Legend' of *The Miller's Tale.*" *JEGP* 79 (1980): 1–12.

Cope, J.I. "Chaucer, Venus, and the Seventh Sphere." *MLN* 67 (1952): 245–246.

Corbin, H. *Avicenna and the Visionary Recital.* Trans. W.R. Trask. New York: Pantheon Books, 1960.

——. *Histoire de la philosophie islamique.* Paris: Gallimard, 1964.

Cordie, C. "Geoffrey Chaucer e Giovanni da Legnano." *Letterature Moderni* 2 (1951): 82–85.

Correale, Robert M. "Nicholas of Clairvaux and the Quotation from 'St. Bernard' in Chaucer's *The Parson's Tale,* 1130–1132." *AN&Q* 20 (1981): 2–3.

——. "The Source of the Quotation from 'Crisostom' in *The Parson's Tale.*" *N&Q* 225 (1980): 101–102.

Corson, H. *Index of Proper Names and Subjects to Chaucer's Canterbury Tales.* Chaucer Society, no. 72. London: Chaucer Society, 1911.

Coville, A. *La Vie intellectuelle dans les domaines d'Anjou-Provence de 1380 à 1435.* Paris: E. Droz, 1941.

Cowgill, B.K. "The *Parlement of Foules* and the Body Politic." *JEGP* 74 (1975): 315–335.

Cowper, B.H. *The Apocryphal Gospels.* [n.p.]: 1981.

Cross, J.E. "Mary Magdalene in the Old English Martyrology: The Earliest Extant 'Narrat Josephus' variant of her Legend." *Speculum* 53 (1978): 16–25.

Crow, M.M., and C.C. Olson, eds. *Chaucer-Life Records.* Compiled by John M. Manly and Edith Rickert, with the assistance of Lilian J. Redstone and others. Oxford: Clarendon Press, 1966.

Crowther, J.D.W. "Chaucer's *Physician's Tale* and its 'Saint.'" *ESC* 8 (1982): 125–137.

Cummings, H.M. "Chaucer's Prologue 1–7." *MLN* 37 (1922): 86–90.

——. *The Indebtedness of Chaucer's Work to the Italian Works of Boccaccio.* New York: Phaeton Press, 1967.

Curry, W.C. "Astrologizing the Gods." *Anglia* 47 (1923): 213–243.

——. *Chaucer and the Mediaeval Sciences.* Rev. and enl. ed. New York: Barnes and Noble, 1960.

——. "O Mars, O Atazir." *JEGP* 22 (1923): 347–368.

Curtius, E. *European Literature and the Latin Middle Ages.* Trans. W.R. Trask. Bollingen Series 36. Princeton: Princeton Univ. Press, 1967.

Dahlberg, C.R. "Macrobius and the Unity of the *Roman de la Rose.*" *SP* 58 (1961): 573–582.

d'Alverny, Marie-Thérèse. "L'Explicit du 'De animalibus' d'Avicenne traduit par Michel Scot." *Bibliothèque de l'Ecole des Chartes* 115 (1957): 32–42.

——. "Translations and Translators." *Renaissance and Renewal in the Twelfth Century.* Ed. R.L. Benson and G. Constable. Cambridge, Mass.: Harvard Univ. Press, 1982, 421–462.

Dane, J.A. "Chaucer's Eagle's Ovid's Phaeton: A Study in Literary Reception." *JMRS* 11 (1981): 71–82.

Daniels, R.J. "Uxor Noah: Raven or Dove?" *ChauR* 14 (1979–1980): 23–32.

David, A. "The Truth About Vache." *ChauR* 11 (1977): 334–337.

Davidson, G. *A Dictionary of Angels.* New York: Macmillan, 1967.

Davies, R.T. "Chaucer's Madame Eglantine." *MLN* 67 (1952): 400–402.

Dean, R.J. "The Earliest Medieval Commentary on Livy." *Medievalia et Humanistica* 3 (1945): 86–98; 4 (1946): 110.

——. "Unnoticed Commentaries on the *Dissuasio Valerii* of Walter Map." *MRS* 1 (1950): 128–150.

Dear, F.M. "Chaucer's *Book of the Lion.*" *MAE* 7 (1938): 105–112.

Le Débat sur Le Roman de la Rose. Edition critique avec introd., traductions, et notes. Notes by Erick Hicks. Paris: H. Champion, 1977.

Dedeck-Héry, V.L. "Le Boèce de Chaucer et les Manuscrits français de la *Consolation* de Jean de Meun." *PMLA* 59 (1944): 18–25.

——. "Boethius' *De consolatione* by Jean de Meun." *MS* 14 (1952): 165–275.

——. "Jean de Meun et Chaucer, traducteurs de la *Consolation* de Boèce." *PMLA* 52 (1937): 967–991.

Delany, P. "Constantinus Africanus' *De Coitu:* A Translation." *ChauR* 4 (1971): 55–65.

——. "Constantinus Africanus and Chaucer's *Merchant's Tale.*" *PQ* 46 (1967): 560–566.

Delany, S. "Doer of the Word: The Epistle of St. James as a Source for Chaucer's *Manciple's Tale.*" *ChauR* 17 (1982–1983): 250–254.

——. "Womanliness in *The Man of Law's Tale.*" *ChauR* 9 (1974): 63–72.

Demaître, L.E. *Doctor Bernard de Gordon: Professor and Practitioner.* Toronto: Pontifical Institute of Mediaeval Studies, 1980.

Dempster, G. "Chaucer at Work on the Complaint in *The Franklin's Tale.*" *MLN* 52 (1937): 16–23.

Donaldson, C. *Martin of Tours: Parish Priest, Mystic, and Exorcist.* London and Boston: Routledge and Kegan Paul, 1980.

Donaldson, E.T. "Briseis, Breseida, Criseyde, Cresseid, Cressid: Progress of a Heroine." *Chaucerian Problems and Perspectives.* Ed. E. Vasta and Z. Thundy. Notre Dame: Univ. of Notre Dame Press, 1979, 3–12.

——. "Chaucer's Final *-E.*" *PMLA* 63 (1948): 1101–1124; 64 (1949): 609.

——. *Speaking of Chaucer.* New York: W.W. Norton, 1970.

——. "Venus and the Mother of Romulus: *The Parliament of Fowls* and the *Pervigilium Veneris.*" *ChauR* 14 (1980): 313–318.

Donaldson, Ian. *The Rapes of Lucretia: A Myth and its Transformations.* Oxford: Clarendon Press, 1982.

Donovan, M.J. "The Image of Pluto and Proserpina in *The Merchant's Tale.*" *PQ* 36 (1957): 49–60.

——. "Chaucer's January and May: Counterparts in Claudian." *Chaucerian Problems and Perspectives.* Ed. E. Vasta and Z. Thundy. Notre Dame: Univ. of Notre Dame Press, 1979, 59–69.

Douglas, D.C. *William the Conqueror.* Berkeley: Univ. of California Press, 1964.

Dronke, P. "Chaucer and Boethius' *De Musica.*" *N&Q* 211 (1966): 92.

——. "A Note on *Pamphilus.*" *JWCI* 42 (1979): 225–230.

Duckett, E.A. *St. Dunstan of Canterbury: A Study of Monastic Reform in the Tenth Century.* New York: W.W. Norton, 1955.

Duls, L.D. *Richard II in the Early Chronicles.* The Hague: Mouton, 1975.

Duncan, E.H. "The Literature of Alchemy and Chaucer's *Canon's Yeoman's Tale:* Framework, Theme, and Characters." *Speculum* 43 (1968): 633–656.

——. "Chaucer and 'Arnald of Newe Toun': A Reprise." *Interpretations* (1977): 7–11.

Dunlop, D.M. "The Work of Translation at Toledo." *Babel* 6 (1960): 55–59.

Dwyer, R. *Boethian Fictions: Narratives in the Medieval French Versions of the Consolatio Philosophiae.* Cambridge, Mass.: Medieval Academy of America, 1976.

The Earliest Lives of Dante. Trans. from the Italian of Giovanni Boccaccio and Leonardo Bruni Aretino by James Robinson Smith. New York: Russell and Russell, 1968.

Ehrhart, M.J. "Machaut's *Dit de la Fonteinne Amoureuse,* the Choice of Paris, and the Duties of Rulers." *PQ* 59 (1980): 119–139.

Eliason, N.E. *The Language of Chaucer's Poetry.* Anglistica 17. Copenhagen: Rosenkelde & Bagger, 1973.

——. "Personal Names in the *Canterbury Tales.*" *Names* 21 (1973): 137–152.

Ellinwood, L. "A Further Note on 'Pilates Voys.'" *Speculum* 8 (1933): 526–528.

Emerson, F.W. "Cambalus in *The Squire's Tale.*" *N&Q* 203 (1958): 461.

Emerson, O.F. "Some of Chaucer's Lines on the Monk." *MP* 1 (1903): 105–115.

Emmerson, R.K. *Antichrist in the Middle Ages: A Study of the Medieval Apocalypticism, Art, and Literature.* Seattle: Univ. of Washington, 1981.

Encyclopaedia Judaica. 16 vols. New York: Macmillan, 1947–1972.

Encyclopaedia of Islam. New ed., edited by an editorial committee consisting of H.A. Gibb (and others). 4 vols. Leiden: E.J. Brill, 1954–1960.

Epstein, H.J. "The Identity of Chaucer's 'Lollius.'" *MLQ* 3 (1942): 391–400.

Evans, G.R. *Alan of Lille: The Frontiers of Theology in the Later Twelfth Century.* Cambridge: Cambridge Univ. Press, 1983.

——. *The Thought of Gregory the Great.* Cambridge: Cambridge Univ. Press, 1986.

Everett, D. "A Note on 'Ypotis.'" *RES* 6 (1930): 446–448.

Fairchild, H.N. "Active Arcite, Contemplative Palamon." *JEGP* 26 (1927): 285–293.

Fansler, D.S. *Chaucer and the* Roman de la Rose. New York: Columbia Univ. Press, 1914.

Faral, E. *Les Arts poétiques du XIIe et du XIIIe siècles.* Paris: H. Champion, 1924, 1958.

——. *"Pyrame et Thisbé*: Texte normand du XIIe siècle." *Romania* 41 (1912): 294–305.

——. *Recherches sur les sources Latines des contes et romans courtois du moyen âge.* Paris: H. Champion, 1967, 1983.

Farmer, D.H. *The Oxford Dictionary of Saints.* Oxford: Clarendon Press, 1978, 1979.

Ferguson, M.A.H. *Bibliography of English Translations from Medieval Sources, 1943–1967.* New York: Columbia Univ. Press, 1974.

Fisher, J.H. *John Gower: Moral Philosopher and Friend of Chaucer.* New York: New York Univ. Press, 1964.

Fisher, R.M. " 'Cosyn' and 'Cosynage': Complicated Punning in Chaucer's *Shipman's Tale.*" *N&Q* 210 (1965): 168–170.

Fleming, J.V. "Daun Piers and Dom Pier: Waterless Fish and Unholy Hunters." *ChauR* 15 (1981): 287–294.

——. *The* Roman de la Rose: *A Study in Allegory and Iconology.* Princeton: Princeton Univ. Press, 1969.

Förster, Max. "Eine Nordenglische Cato-Version." *Englische Studien* 36 (1906): 1–55.

Fordyce, C.J. *Catullus: A Commentary.* Oxford: Clarendon Press, 1961.

Foster, B. "Chaucer's Seynt Loy: An Anglo-French Pun?" *N&Q* 213 (1968): 244–245.

Fox, R.C. "Chaucer and Aristotle." *N&Q* 203 (1958): 523–524.

Frank, R.W. *Chaucer and the* Legend of Good Women. Cambridge, Mass.: Harvard Univ. Press, 1972.

French, W.H. *Essays on King Horn.* Ithaca: Cornell Univ. Press, 1940.

Friedman, J.B. "Eurydice, Heurodis, and the Noon-Day Demon." *Speculum* 41 (1966): 22–29.

——. *Orpheus in the Middle Ages.* Cambridge, Mass.: Harvard Univ. Press, 1970.

Friend, A.C. "Chaucer's Version of the *Aeneid.*" *Speculum* 28 (1953): 317–323.

Frost, G.L. "That Precious Corpus Madrian." *MLN* 57 (1942): 177–179.

Fry, D.K. "Chaucer's Zanzis and a Possible Source for Troilus and Criseyde IV.407–413." *ELN* 9 (1971): 81–85.

——. "The Ending of *The Monk's Tale*." *JEGP* 71 (1972): 355–368.

——. "Polyphemus in Iceland." *Acta* 4 (1977): 65–86.

Fyler, J.M. *Chaucer and Ovid.* New Haven: Yale Univ. Press, 1979.

Galway, M. "Chaucer's Sovereign Lady: A Study of the Prologue to the Legend and Related Poems." *MLR* 33 (1938): 145–199.

Garbaty, T.J. "*Pampihilus, De Amore*: An Introduction and Translation." *ChauR* 2 (1967–1968): 108–134.

——. "The *Pamphilus* Tradition in Ruiz and Chaucer." *PQ* 46 (1967): 457–470.

Gardner, W.B. "Chaucer's 'Unworthy Sone of Eve.'" *Texas University Studies in English* 25 and 26 (1946–1947): 77–85.

Garrett, R.M. " 'Cleopatra the Martyr' and her Sisters." *JEGP* 22 (1923): 64–74.

Garth, H.M. *Saint Mary Magdalene in Medieval Literature.* Baltimore: Johns Hopkins Univ. Press, 1950.

Gaylord, A.T. "Dido at Hunt, Chaucer at Work." *ChauR* 17 (1982): 300–315.

——. "The Moment of Sir Thopas: Towards a New Look at Chaucer's Language." *ChauR* 16 (1981–1982): 311–329.

——. "The Promises in the *Franklin's Tale*." *ELH* 31 (1964): 331–365.

Gelbach, M. "On Chaucer's Version of the Death of Croesus." *JEGP* 6 (1907): 657–660.

Ghisalberti, F., ed. "Giovanni del Virgilio Espositore delle 'Metamorphosi.'" *Il Giornale Dantesco* 34 (1933): 1–110.

——. "Medieval Biographies of Ovid." *JWCI* 9 (1946): 10–59.

Gibson, M., ed. *Boethius, His Life, Thought, and Influence.* Oxford: B. Blackwell, 1981.

Gibson, M.T. "The Study of the *Timaeus* in the Eleventh and Twelfth Centuries." *Pensamiento* 25 (1969): 183–194.

Giffin, M.E. *Studies in Chaucer and his Audience.* Quebec: Les Editions "L'Eclair," 1956.

Gilliat-Smith, E. *St. Clare of Assisi: Her Life and Legislation.* London: J.M. Dent, 1914.

Gillingham, J. *Richard the Lionheart.* London: Weidenfeld and Nicolson, 1978.

Goldin, F. *The Mirror of Narcissus in the Courtly Love Lyric.* Ithaca: Cornell Univ. Press, 1967.

Gordon, R.K. *The Story of Troilus as told by Benoît de Sainte-Maure, Giovanni Boccaccio, Geoffrey Chaucer, and Robert Henryson.* Toronto: Univ. of Toronto Press, 1934, 1978.

Gore, J.E. *An Astronomical Glossary.* London: 1919.

Grant, E. "Bradwardine and Galileo: Equality of Velocities in the Void." *Archive for History of Exact Sciences* 2 (1965): 344–364.

Green, M.H. "The *De genecia* Attributed to Constantine the African." *Speculum* 62 (1987): 299–323.

Green, R.F. *Poets and Prince Pleasers.* Toronto: Univ. of Toronto Press, 1980.

Green, R.H. "Alan of Lille's *De planctu Naturae.*" *Speculum* 31 (1956): 649–674.

——. "Classical Fable and English Poetry." *Critical Approaches to Medieval Literature.* Ed. D. Bethurum. New York: Columbia Univ. Press, 1960, 113–135.

Grennen, J.E. "The Calculating Reeve and his *Camera obscura.*" *JMRS* 14 (1984): 245–259.

——. "Chaucer's 'Secree of Secrees': an Alchemical Topic." *PQ* 42 (1962): 562–566.

——. " 'Sampsoun' in *The Canterbury Tales*: Chaucer Adapting a Source." *NM* 47 (1966): 117–222.

Griffin, M.T. *Seneca.* Oxford: Clarendon Press, 1976.

Griffin., N.E. *Dares and Dictys: An Introduction to the Study of Medieval Versions of the Story of Troy.* Baltimore: J.H. Furst, 1907.

——. "The Greek Dictys." *American Journal of Philology* 29 (1908): 329–335.

Griffith, R.H. *Sir Perceval of Galles: A Study of the Sources of the Legend.* Chicago: Univ. of Chicago Press, 1911.

Gunther, R.W.T. *Early Science at Oxford.* 14 vols. Oxford: Clarendon Press, 1922–1945.

Hall, L.B. "Chaucer and the Dido and Aeneas Story." *MS* 25 (1963): 148–159.

Haller, S. "*The Knight's Tale* and the Epic Tradition." *ChauR* 1 (1966): 67–84.

Hallmundsson, M.N. "Chaucer's Circle: Henry Scogan and his Friends." *Medievalia et Humanistica,* new series 10 (1981): 129–139.

Hamlin, B.F. "Astrology and the Wife of Bath: A Re-Interpretation." *ChauR* 9 (1973–1974): 153–165.

Hamilton, A. "Helowys and the Burning of Jankyn's Book." *MS* 34 (1972): 196–207.

Hamilton, G.L. *The Indebtedness of Chaucer's* Troilus and Criseyde *to Guido delle Colonne's* Historia Trojana. New York: Columbia Univ. Press, 1903.

——. "Chauceriana I: The Date of the *Clerk's Tale.*" *MLN 23* (1908): 171–192.

Hamilton, M.P. "Chaucer's 'Marcia Catoun.'" *MP* 30 (1932): 361–364.

——. "Bernard the Monk: Postscript." *MLN* 62 (1947): 190–191.

Hammond, E.P. *Chaucer: A Bibliographical Manual.* New York: Peter Smith, 1933.

Hamp, E.P. "St. Ninian/Ronyan Again." *Celtica* 3 (1956): 290–294.

Harder, H.L. "Livy in Gower's and Chaucer's Lucrece Stories." *PMPA* 2 (1977): 1–7.

Harder, K.B. "Chaucer's Use of the Mystery Plays in *The Miller's Tale.*" *MLQ* 17 (1956): 193–198.

Hardison, O.B. "The Place of Averroes' Commentary on the *Poetics* in the History of Medieval Criticism." *MRS* 4 (1970): 57–81.

Harty, K. "Chaucer's Man of Law and the 'Muses that Men Clepe Pierides.'" *SSF* 18 (1981): 75–77.

——. "The Reputation of Queen Esther in the Middle Ages: *The Merchant's Tale* IV (E) 1742–45." *BSUF* 19 (1978): 65–68.

Haskell, A.S. *Essays on Chaucer's Saints.* The Hague: Mouton, 1976.

——. "The Host's Precious Corpus Madrian." *JEGP* 67 (1968): 430–440.

——. "The St. Joce Oath in the Wife of Bath's Prologue." *ChauR* 1 (1966): 85–87.

——. "The St. Simon in *The Summoner's Tale.*" *ChauR* 5 (1971): 218–224.

——. "Sir Thopas: The Puppet's Puppet." *ChauR* 9 (1974–1975): 253–261.

Haskins, C.H. *Studies in the History of Mediaeval Science.* Cambridge, Mass.: Harvard Univ. Press, 1924.

Hawkes, J. *Man and the Sun.* London: Cresset Press, 1962.

Hawkins, J.E. "Chaucer and the *Pervigilium Veneris.*" *MLN* 49 (1934): 80–83.

Hazelton, R. "Chaucer and Cato." *Speculum* 35 (1960): 357–380.

——. "The Christianization of Cato." *MS* 19 (1957): 157–173.

Helterman, J. "The Dehumanizing Metamorphoses of the Knight's Tale." *ELH* 38 (1971): 493–511.

Henkin, L.J. "Jacob and the Hooly Jew." *MLN* 55 (1940): 254–259.

Henning, S. "Chauntecleer and Taurus." *ELN* 3 (1965): 1–4.

Hervieux, L. *Les Fabulistes Latins depuis le siècle d'Auguste jusqu'à la fin du moyen âge.* 5 vols. Paris: 1893–1899; New York: Burt Franklin, 1965.

Heym, G. "Al-Razi and Alchemy." *Ambix* 1 (1938): 184–191.

Hibbert, E. *The Plantagenet Prelude.* New York: G.P. Putnam, 1976, 1980.

Hieatt, A.K. "Eve as Reason in a Tradition of Allegorical Interpretations of the Fall." *JWCI* 42 (1980): 221–226.

Hill, D.M. "An Interpretation of *King Horn.*" *Anglia* 75 (1957): 157–172.

Hillis, N.D. *David the Poet and King.* Chicago: F.H. Revell, 1901.

Hilton, R.H. *Bond Men Made Free: Medieval Peasant Movements and the English Uprising of 1381.* London: Temple Smith, 1973.

——. *The English Peasantry in the Later Middle Ages.* Oxford: Clarendon Press, 1975.

Hinckley, H.B. "The Grete Emetreus King of Inde." *MLN* 48 (1933): 148–149.

Hodgkin, T. *Theodoric the Goth.* New York: G.P. Putnam, 1900, 1912.

Hoffman, R.L. "Jephthah's Daughter and Chaucer's Virginia." *ChauR* 2 (1967): 20–31.

——. "Mercury, Argus, and Chaucer's Arcite: *Canterbury Tales* I (A) 1384–90." *N&Q* 210 (1965): 128–129.

——. "Ovid and Chaucer's Myth of Theseus and Pirithous." *MLN* 1 (1965): 252–257.

——. *Ovid and the* Canterbury Tales. Philadelphia: Univ. of Pennsylvania Press, 1967.

——. "Ovid and the Monk's Tale of Hercules." *N&Q* 210 (1965): 406–409.

——. "Ovid's Argus and Chaucer." *N&Q* 210 (1965): 213–216.

——. "Ovid's Priapus in the *Merchant's Tale.*" *ELN* 3 (1966): 169–172.

——. "Pygmalion in the *Physician's Tale.*" *AN&Q* 5 (1967): 83–84.

——. "Two Notes on Chaucer's Arcite." *ELN* 4 (1967): 172–175.

Hollander, R. *Boccaccio's Two Venuses.* New York: Columbia Univ. Press, 1977.

Hone, W., ed. *The Lost Books of the Bible.* New York: Abingdon Press, 1926, rpt. 1974.

Hornstein, L.H. "Petrarch's Laelius, Chaucer's Lollius?" *PMLA* 63 (1948): 64–84.

Howser, H.S. *Richard the First in England.* Las Colinas, Tex.: Tangelwüld Press, 1986.

Hume, K. "The Pagan Setting of *The Franklin's Tale* and the Sources of Dorigen's Cosmology." *SN* 44 (1972): 289–294.

Huppé, B.F., and D.W. Robertson, Jr. *Fruyt and Chaf.* Princeton: Princeton Univ. Press, 1963.

Hurd-Mead, K. "Trotula." *Isis* 14 (1930): 349–367.

Illingworth, V., ed. *The Facts on File Dictionary of Astronomy.* New York: Facts on File, 1979.

Immaculate, Sister M. "Fiends as 'servant unto man' in the *Friar's Tale.*" *PQ* 21 (1942): 240–244.

Isaacs, N.D. "Constance in Fourteenth-Century England." *NM* 59 (1958): 260–277.

Jennings, F.C. *Satan, His Person, Work, Place, and Destiny.* Neptune, N.J.: Loizeaux Brothers, 1975.

Jennings, M. "The Art of the Pseudo-Origen Homily *De Maria Magdalene.*" *Medievalia et Humanistica*, new series, no. 5 (1974): 139–152.

Jones, A.H.M. *The Herods of Judaea.* Oxford: Clarendon Press, 1938, 1967.

Kadish, E.P. "Petrarch's Griselda: An English Translation." *Mediaevalia* 3 (1977): 1–24.

Kahane, H., and R. Kahane. "Akritas and Arcita: A Byzantine Source of Boccaccio's *Teseida.*" *Speculum* 20 (1945): 415–425.

Karpinsky, L.C., and J.C. Winter, eds. *Contributions to the History of Science.* Ann Arbor: Univ. of Michigan, 1930; rpt. New York: Johnson Reprints, 1972.

Kaske, R.E. "*Clericus Adam* and Chaucer's *Adam Scriven.*" *Chaucerian Problems and Perspectives.* Ed. E. Vasta and Z. Thundy. Notre Dame: University of Notre Dame Press, 1979, 114–118.

Kellogg, A.L. "An Augustinian Interpretation of Chaucer's Pardoner." *Speculum* 26 (1951): 465–481.

——. "St. Augustine and *The Parson's Tale.*" *Traditio* 8 (1952): 424–430.

——. "Susannah and *The Merchant's Tale.*" *Speculum* 35 (1960): 275–279.

——, and R.C. Cox. *Chaucer, Langland, and Arthur: Essays in English Literature.* New Brunswick: Rutgers Univ. Press, 1972.

Kelly, J.N.D. *Jerome: His Life, Writings and Controversies.* London: Duckworth, 1975.

Kennedy, E.S., and Walid Ukashah. "Al-Khwarizmi's Planetary Latitude Tables." *Centaurus* 14 (1969): 86–96.

Kibre, P. "Hippocratic Writings in the Middle Ages." *Bulletin of the History of Medicine* 18 (1946): 371–412.

Kittredge, G.L."Chaucer and Froissart (with a discussion of the date of *Meliador*)." *Englische Studien* 26 (1879): 321–336.

——. "Chauceriana I." *MP* 7 (1910): 465–483.

——. "Chaucer's Alceste." *MP* 6 (1908): 435–439.

——. "Chaucer's Lollius." *Harvard Studies in Classical Philology* 28 (1917): 47–133.

——. "Guillaume de Machaut and *The Book of the Duchess.*" *PMLA* 30 (1915): 1–24.

——. "Henry Scogan." *Harvard Studies and Notes in Philology and Literature* 1 (1892): 109–117.

——. "Lewis Chaucer or Lewis Clifford." *MP* 14 (1916–1917): 513–518.

——. *Observations on the Language of Chaucer's Troilus*. London: The Chaucer Society, 1891; rpt. New York: Russell and Russell, 1969.

——. "The Pillars of Hercules and Chaucer's 'Trophee.'" *Putnam Anniversary Volume*. New York: Stechert, 1909, 545–566.

Klibansky, R. *The Continuity of the Platonic Tradition during the Middle Ages: Plato's Parmenides in the Middle Ages and Renaissance*. Rev. ed. Millwood, N.Y.: Kraus International, 1984.

Koch, R.A. "Elijah the Prophet, Founder of the Carmelite Order." *Speculum* 24 (1959): 547–560.

Koonce, B.G. "Satan the Fowler." *MS* 21 (1959): 176–184.

Kritzeck, J. *Peter the Venerable and Islam*. Princeton: Princeton Univ. Press, 1964.

Kuhl, E.P. "Chaucer's 'My Maister Bukton.'" *PMLA* 38 (1923): 115–132.

——. "Chaucer's Madame Eglantine." *MLN* 60 (1945): 325–326.

Lacy, N., ed. *The Arthurian Encyclopedia*. New York: Garland Publishing, Inc., 1986.

Laistner, M.L.W. "Martianus Capella and his Ninth Century Commentators." *Bulletin of the John Rylands Library* 9 (1925): 130–138.

——. *Thought and Letters in Western Europe A.D. 500 to 900*. New ed., rev. Ithaca: Cornell Univ. Press, 1957.

Lancashire, A. "Chaucer and the Sacrifice of Isaac." *ChauR* 9 (1975): 320–326.

Langlois, E. *Les manuscrits du* Roman de la Rose: *Description et classement*. Lille: Tallandier, 1910.

——. *Origines et sources du* Roman de la Rose. Paris: E. Thorin, 1891.

Langmuir, G.I. "The Knight's Tale of Young Hugh of Lincoln." *Speculum* 47 (1972): 459–482.

Lavers, N. "Freud, *The Clerk's Tale*, and Literary Criticism." *College English* 26 (1964): 180–187.

Lee, A.T. "A Woman Free and Fair: Chaucer's Portrayal of Dorigen in *The Franklin's Tale*." *ChauR* 19 (1984–1985): 169–178.

Leff, G. *Bradwardine and the Pelagians*. Cambridge: The Univ. Press, 1959.

Legge, M.D. "The Gracious Conqueror." *MLN* 68 (1953): 18–21.

Lenaghan, R. "Chaucer's *Envoy to Scogan*: The Uses of Literary Convention." *ChauR* 10 (1975–1976): 46–61.

Levey, M. "Ibn Masawaih and his Treatise on Simple Aromatic Substances." *Journal of the History of Medicine* 16 (1961): 394–410.

Levinson, W. *England and the Continent in the Eighth Century.* Oxford: Clarendon Press, 1946.

Lewis, R.E. "Chaucer's Artistic Use of Pope Innocent III's *De Miseria Humane Condicionis* in the Man of Law's Prologue and Tale." *PMLA* 81 (1966): 485–492.

——. "Glosses to the Man of Law's Tale from Pope Innocent III's *De Miseria Humane Conditionis.*" *SP* 64 (1967): 1–16.

Lobineau, G.A. *Histoire de Bretagne.* 2 vols. Paris: F. Muguet, 1707.

Loomis, D.B. "Saturn in Chaucer's *Knight's Tale.*" *Anglia* 14 (1968): 149–161.

Loomis, L.H. *Medieval Romance in England.* New York: B. Franklin, 1965.

Loomis, R.S. *Arthurian Tradition & Chrétien de Troyes.* New York: Columbia Univ. Press, 1949.

——, ed. *Arthurian Literature in the Middle Ages: A Collaborative History.* Oxford: Clarendon Press, 1959.

——. "Verses on the Nine Worthies." *MP* 15 (1917): 19–27.

Loschiane, L.A. "The Birth of 'Blanche the Duchess': 1340 Versus 1347." *ChauR* 13 (1978): 128–132.

Lounsbury, T.R. *Studies in Chaucer.* 3 vols. New York: Harper, 1892.

Lowes, J.L. "Chaucer and Dante." *MP* 14 (1916–1917): 705–735.

——. "Chaucer and the *Ovide Moralisé.*" *PMLA* 33 (1918): 302–325.

——. "The Dragon and his Brother." *MLN* 28 (1913): 229.

——. "The Prioress's Oath." *Romanic Review* 5 (1914): 368–385.

——. "The Tempest at Hir Hoom-comynge." *MLN* 19 (1904): 240–243.

Lumiansky, R.M. "The Story of Troilus and Briseida According to Benoît and Guido." *Speculum* 29 (1954): 727–733.

Lundberg, D.C. "Lines of Influence in Thirteenth-Century Optics: Bacon, Witelo, Pecham." *Speculum* 46 (1971): 66–83.

Luria, M. *A Reader's Guide to the* Roman de la Rose. Hamden: Archon Books, 1982.

Lutz, C.E. "The Commentary of Remigius of Auxerre on Martianus Capella." *MS* 19 (1957): 137–156.

Lynch, J.J. "The Prioress's Greatest Oath, Once More." *MLN* 72 (1957): 242–249.

Lyon, E.D. "Roger of Ware, Cook." *MLN* 52 (1937): 491–494.

McCall, J.P. "Chaucer and John of Legnano." *Speculum* 40 (1965): 484–489.

——. "Chaucer and the Pseudo-Origen *De Maria Magdalena:* A Preliminary Study." *Speculum* 46 (1971): 491–509.

MacDonald, A. "Absolon and Neot." *Neophilologus* 848 (1964): 235–237.

MacFarlane, K.N. *Isidore of Seville on the Pagan Gods (Origines VIII.11)*. Philadelphia: The American Philosophical Society, 1980.

McKeehan, B. "The Book of the Nativity of St. Cuthbert." *PMLA* 48 (1933): 981–999.

MacNeile, A.H. *An Introduction to the Study of the New Testament*. 2nd ed., rev. C.S.C. Williams. Oxford: Clarendon Press, 1952.

McPeek. J.A.S. "Did Chaucer Know Catullus?" *MLN* 46 (1931): 293–301.

McVaugh, M.R. "The *Experimenta* of Arnold of Villanova." *JMRS* 1 (1971): 107–118.

Madeleva, Sister M. *Chaucer's Nuns and other Essays*. New York: Appleton, 1925.

Magoun, F.P., Jr. *A Chaucer Gazetteer*. Chicago: Univ. of Chicago Press, 1961.

——. "Chaucer's Summary of Statius' *Thebaid* II–XII." *Traditio* 11 (1955): 409–420.

——. *The Gests of King Alexander of Macedon*. Cambridge, Mass.: Harvard Univ. Press, 1929.

Makarewicz, Sister M.R. *The Patristic Influence on Chaucer*. Washington, D.C.: Catholic Univ. of America Press, 1953.

Malone, Kemp. "Chaucer's Daughter of Cupid." *MLR* 45 (1950): 63.

——. "Harry Bailey and Godelief." *English Studies* 31 (1950): 209–215.

Manly, J.M. *Chaucer and the Rhetoricians*. London: Oxford Univ. Press, 1926.

——. "Chaucer's Scrivener." *TLS*, May 16, 1929, 403.

——. "Litel Lowis my Sone." *TLS*, June 7, 1929, 430.

——. "Marco Polo and *The Squire's Tale*." *PMLA* 11 (1896): 349–362.

——. *Some New Light on Chaucer*. New York: Holt, 1926.

Mascall, E.L.. and H.S. Box. *The Blessed Virgin Mary: Essays by Anglican Writers*. London: Darton, Longmans, Todd, 1963.

Masi, M., ed. *Boethius and the Liberal Arts*. Berne: Peter Lang, 1981.

Mathew, G. *The Court of Richard II*. London: John Murray, 1968.

Matthews, L.J. "The Date of Chaucer's *Melibee* and the Stages of the Tale's Incorporation in *The Canterbury Tales*." *ChauR* 20 (1985–1986): 221–234.

Meech, S.B. "Chaucer and an Italian Translation of the *Heroides*." *PMLA* 45 (1930): 110–128.

——. "Chaucer and the *Ovide Moralisé* —A Further Study." *PMLA* 46 (1931): 182–204.

Metlitzki, D. *The Matter of Araby in Medieval England.* New Haven: Yale Univ. Press, 1977.

Meyer, P. "Les Manuscrits français de Cambridge." *Romania* 32 (1903): 88–91.

Meyer, P. "Notice et Extraits du MS. 8336 de la Bibliothèque de Sir Thomas Phillipps, No. 12." *Romania* 13 (1885): 510–511.

Michel, F., ed. *Tristan: Receuil de ce qui reste des poèmes relatifs à ses aventures.* Paris: Tochener, 1835–1839.

Migne, J.P., ed. *Patrologiae cursus completus, series Graeca.* 157 vols. Paris: 1857–1866.

——, ed. *Patrologiae cursus completus, series Latina.* 221 vols. Paris: 1844–1864.

Miller, A.D. "Chaucer's 'Secte Saturnyn.'" *MLN* 47 (1932): 99–102.

Minnis, A.J. "A Note on Chaucer and the *Ovide Moralisé.*" *MAE* 48 (1979): 254–257.

Moland, L., and C. d'Héricault. *Nouvelles françaises en prose du XIVe siècle.* Publié d'après les manuscrits avec une introd. et des notes. Paris: P. Jannet, 1858.

Moorman, C. "The Prioress as Pearly Queen." *ChauR* 13 (1978): 25–33.

Murdoch, J.E. "*Euclides graeco-latinus*: A Hitherto Unknown Medieval Latin Translation of the Elements Made Directly from the Greek." *Harvard Studies in Classical Philology* 71 (1967): 249–302.

Murray, G. *Euripides and his Age.* Oxford: Clarendon Press, 1946.

Muscatine, C. *Chaucer and the French Tradition.* Berkeley and Los Angeles: Univ. of California Press, 1969.

——. "The Name of Chaucer's Friar." *MLN* 70 (1955): 169–172.

Mycoff, D.A. *A Critical Edition of the Legend of Mary Magdalene from Caxton's "Golden Legende" of 1483.* Salzburg: Institut für Anglistik und Amerikanstik, Unversität Salzburg, 1985.

Neville, M. "Chaucer and St. Clare." *JEGP* 55 (1956): 423–430.

New Catholic Encyclopedia. 15 vols. New York: McGraw-Hill, 1967.

Nitchie, E. *Vergil and the English Poets.* New York: AMS Press, 1966.

Norris, D.M. "Herry Bailey's Corpus Madrian." *MLN* 48 (1933): 146–148.

North, J.D. "Kalenderes Enlumyned Ben They." *RES* 20 (1969): 129–154, 257–283, 418–444.

Norton-Smith, J. "Chaucer's *Etas Prima.*" *MAE* 23 (1963): 117–124.

——. *Geoffrey Chaucer.* London: Routledge & Kegan Paul, 1974.

Oberman, H.A. *Forerunners of the Reformation: The Shape of Late Medieval Thought; Illustrated Key Documents.* Trans. P.L. Nyhus. New York: Holt, Rinehart and Winston, 1966.

O'Donnell, J.J. *Cassiodorus.* Berkeley: Univ. of California Press, 1979.

Oruch, J.B. "St. Valentine, Chaucer, and Spring in February." *Speculum* 56 (1981): 534–565.

Owen, C.A. "One Robyn or Two?" *MLN* 67 (1952): 336–338.

Oxford Classical Dictionary. Ed. N.G.L. Hammond and H.H. Scullard. 2nd ed. Oxford: Clarendon Press, 1970.

Oxford Companion to Classical Literature. Compiled and ed. Paul Harvey. Oxford: Clarendon Press, 1937, 1955.

Palmer, J.N. "The Historical Context of *The Book of the Duchess*: A Revision." *ChauR* 8 (1974): 253–261.

Palomo, D. "What Chaucer Really Did to *Le Livre de Mellibee.*" *PQ* 53 (1974): 304–320.

Panofsky, E. *Studies in Iconology.* New York: Harper & Row, 1962.

——. *Renaissance and Renascences in Western Art.* New York: Harper & Row, 1972.

Pannekoek, A. *A History of Astronomy.* New York: Interscience Publishers, 1961.

Parr, J. "Chaucer's Semiramis." *ChauR* 5 (1970): 57–61.

——, and N.A. Holtz. "The Astronomy and Astrology in Chaucer's *The Complaint of Mars.*" *ChauR* 15 (1981): 255–266.

Parry, T. *A History of Welsh Literature.* Trans. I. Bell. Oxford: Clarendon Press, 1955.

Parsy, P. *Saint Eloi (590–659).* Paris: J. Gabalda, 1907.

Patch, H.R. *The Tradition of Boethius: A Study of His Importance in Medieval Culture.* New York: Oxford Univ. Press, 1935; rpt. Russell and Russell, 1970.

Peck, R. "The Idea of 'Entente' and Translation in Chaucer's *Second Nun's Tale.*" *AnM* 8 (1967): 23–35.

Peters, F.E. *Aristoteles Arabus.* Leiden: E.J. Brill, 1968.

Petersen, J.M. *The Dialogues of Gregory the Great in Their Late Antique Cultural Background.* Toronto: Pontifical Institute of Mediaeval Studies, 1984.

Petersen, K.O. *On the Sources of the* Nonnes Preestes Tale. Radcliff College Monographs no. 10. New York: Haskell House, 1966.

——. *On the Sources of* The Parson's Tale. Radcliff College Monographs no. 12. Boston: Ginn, 1901; rpt. New York: AMS Press, 1973.

Pfeffer, Wendy. *The Change of Philomel: The Nightingale in Medieval Literature.* New York: Peter Lang, 1985.

Phillips, J.A. *Eve, The History of an Idea.* New York: McGraw-Hill, 1984.

Piggott, S. "The Sources of Geoffrey of Monmouth." *Antiquity* 15 (1941).

Powicke, F.M. *The Medieval Books of Merton College.* Oxford: The Clarendon Press, 1931.

Pratt, R.A. "Chaucer and *Le Roman de Troyle et de Criseide.*" *SP* 53 (1956): 509–539.

——. "Chaucer and *Les Cronicles* of Nicholas Trevet." *Studies in Language, Literature, and Culture of the Middle Ages and Later,* ed. E. Bagby Atwood and A.A. Hill (1969): 303–311.

——. "Chaucer and the Hand that Fed Him." *Speculum* 41 (1966): 619–642.

——. "Chaucer and the Pillar of Hercules." *Studies in Honor of Ullman.* St. Louis: The Classical Bulletin (1960): 118–125.

——. "Chaucer's Claudian." *Speculum* 22 (1947): 419–429.

——. "Chaucer's 'Natal Jove' and 'Seint Jerome . . . agayn Jovinian.'" *JEGP* 61 (1962): 244–248.

——. "Chaucer's Use of the *Teseida.*" *PMLA* 62 (1947): 508–621.

——. "Conjectures Regarding Chaucer's Manuscript of the *Teseida.*" *SP* 42 (1945): 743–763.

——. "Geoffrey Chaucer, Esq., and Sir John Hawkwood." *ELH* 16 (1949): 188–193.

——. "The Importance of Manuscripts for the Study of Medieval Education, as Revealed by the Learning of Chaucer." *Progress in Medieval and Renaissance Studies, Bulletin* no. 20 (1949): 43–51.

——. "Jankyn's Book of Wikked Wyves: Antimatrimonial Propaganda in the Universities." *AnM* 3 (1962): 5–27.

——. "Karl Young's Work on the Learning of Chaucer." *A Memoir of Karl Young.* New Haven: Privately printed, 1946.

——. "A Note on Chaucer's Lollius." *MLN* 65 (1950): 183–187.

——. "Saint Jerome in Jankyn's Book of Wikked Wyves." *Criticism* 5 (1963): 316–322.

——. "Three Old French Sources of the Nonnes Preestes Tale." *Speculum* 57 (1972): 422–444; 646–668.

——. "Was Robin the Miller's Youth Misspent?" *MLN* 59 (1944): 47–49.

Quinn, B.N. "ps. Theodolus." *Catalogus translationium et commentariorum: Medieval and Renaissance Translations and Commentaries,* ed. P. O. Kristellar, 2 (1971): 383–397.

——. "Venus, Chaucer, and Peter Bersuire." *Speculum* 38 (1963): 479–480.

Raby, F.J.E. *Christian Latin Poetry.* 2 vols. Oxford: Clarendon Press, 1927.

Rand, E.K. *Founders of the Middle Ages.* Cambridge, Mass.: Harvard Univ. Press, 1928.

Rathbone, E. "Master Alberic of London." *MRS* 1 (1941): 35–38.

Raynaud, G., and H. Lemaître, eds. *Le Roman de Renart le Contrefait.* 2 vols. Paris: H. Champion, 1914.

Rea, J.A. "An Old French Analogue to *General Prologue* 1–18." *PQ* 46 (1967): 128–130.

Reames, S.L. *The* Legenda aurea: *A Re-examination of its Paradoxical History.* Madison: Univ. of Wisconsin Press, 1985.

Réau, L. *Iconographie de l'art chrétien.* lst ed. Paris: Presses Universitaires de France, 1955–1959.

Reiss, E. "The Story of Lamech and its Place in Medieval Drama." *JMRS* 2 (1971): 35–48.

Reynolds, L.D. *The Medieval Tradition of Seneca's Letters.* Oxford: Clarendon Press, 1965.

Richards, M.P. "The Miller's Tale: 'By Seinte Note.'" *ChauR* 9 (1975): 212–215.

Rickert, E. "Chaucer at School." *MP* 29 (1932): 257–274.

——. "Chaucer's 'Hodge of Ware.'" *TLS*, October 20, 1932, 761.

——. "Goode Lief, my Wyf." *MP* 25 (1927): 79–82.

——. "A Leaf from a Fourteenth-Century Letter Book." *MP* 25 (1927): 249–255.

——. "Thou Vache." *MP* 11 (1913–1914): 209–225.

Robbins, R.H. "Chaucer's Rosemounde." *Studies in the Literary Imagination* 4 (1971): 73–81.

——, ed. *Secular Lyrics of the XIVth and XVth Centuries.* 2nd ed. Oxford: Clarendon Press, 1955.

Roberts, J.H. "The Nine Worthies." *MP* 19 (1922): 297–305.

Robertson, D.W., Jr. *A Preface to Chaucer.* Princeton: Princeton Univ. Press, 1962.

Robinson, I. *Chaucer's Prosody: A Study in Middle English Verse Tradition.* Cambridge: Cambridge Univ. Press, 1971.

Robinson, J.A. *The Times of St. Dunstan.* Oxford: Clarendon Press, 1969.

Robinson, P. *The Rule of St. Clare: Its Observance in the Light of Early Documents.* Philadelphia: The Dolphin Press, 1912.

Ronan, M.V. *St. Anne: Her Cult and Her Shrines.* New York: P.J. Kenedy, 1927.

Root, R.K. "Chaucer's Dares: Joseph of Exeter." *MP* 15 (1917–1918): 1–22.

——. "Chaucer's Legend of Medea." *PMLA* 24 (1909): 124–154.

Rose, H.J. *A Handbook of Greek Mythology, Including its Extension to Rome.* London: Methuen, 1928.

Rosen, E. "The Invention of Eye–Glasses." *Journal of the History of Medicine and Allied Sciences* 11 (1956): 13–46; 183–218.

Ross, D.J.A. *Alexander Historiatus.* London: The Warburg Institute, Univ. of London, 1963.

Rowland, B., ed. *Chaucer and Middle English Studies in Honor of Rossell Hope Robbins.* London: G. Allen and Unwin, 1974.

——. "Exhuming Trotula, *sapiens matrona* of Salerno." *Florilegium* 1 (1979): 42–57.

Royster, J.F. "Chaucer's 'Colle Tregetour.'" *SP* 23 (1926): 380–384.

Rudat, W.E.H. "Aurelius' Quest for Grace: Sexuality and the Marriage Debate in the *Franklin's Tale*." *CEA Critic* 45 (1982): 16–21.

Ruggiers, P.G. "Platonic Forms in Chaucer." *ChauR* 17 (1983): 366–381.

Ruska, J. "Chaucer und sein Buch Senior." *Anglia* 61 (1937): 136–137.

Russell, J.B. *Lucifer: The Devil in the Middle Ages.* Ithaca: Cornell Univ. Press, 1984.

Russell, P.E. *The English Intervention in Spain and Portugal in the Time of Edward III and Richard II.* Oxford: Clarendon Press, 1955.

Samuel, I. "Semiramis: The History of a Legend in the Middle Ages." *Medievalia et Humanistica,* Fasc. III (1944): 32–44.

Sanderlin, G. "Quotations from St. Bernard in the *Parson's Tale*." *MLN* 54 (1939): 447–448.

Sarton, G. *An Introduction to the History of Science.* 3 vols. in 5. Baltimore: Wilkins and Wilkins, 1927–1948.

Savage, H.L. "Chaucer and the 'pitous deeth' of 'Petro, Glorie of Spayne.'" *Speculum* 24 (1949): 357–375.

——. "Arcite's Maying." *MLN* 55 (1940): 207–209.

Scattergood, V.J. "Perkyn Revelour and The Cook's Tale." *ChauR* 19 (1984–1985): 14–23.

Schibanoff, S. "Argus and Argyve: Etymology and Characterization in Chaucer's *Troilus*." *Speculum* 51 (1976): 647–658.

Schjellerup, H.C.F.C. *Description des étoiles fixés composée au milieu du dixième siècle de notre ère par l'astronome abd-l-Rahman al-Sufi.* St. Petersburg: Comité de l'Academie Imperiale de Science, 1874.

Schlauch, M. *Chaucer's Constance and Accused Queens.* New York: New York Univ. Press, 1927.

Schless, H. *Chaucer and Dante: A Revaluation.* Norman, Okla.: Pilgrim Books, 1984.

Schmidt, A.V.C. "Chaucer and the Golden Age." *Essays in Criticism* 26 (1976): 99–115.

Schoeck, R.J. "Chaucer's Prioress: Mercy and Tender Heart." *The Bridge: A Yearbook of Judaeo-Christian Studies,* ed. J. Oesterreicher, 2 (1956): 239–255.

Schofield, W. "The Story of Horn and Rimenhild " *PMLA* 18 (1903): 1–83.

——. *Studies in Libeaus Desconus.* Boston: Ginn, 1895.

Scholz, W. "The Canonization of Edward the Confessor." *Speculum* 36 (1961): 38–60.

Schreiber, E.G. "Venus in the Medieval Mythographic Tradition." *JEGP* 74 (1975): 519–535.

Scullard, H.M. *Scipio Africanus: Soldier and Politician.* Ithaca: Cornell Univ. Press, 1970.

Seaton, E. "Goode lief my wife." *MLR* 41 (1946): 196–202.

Sedgwick, W.B. "The *Bellum Troianum* of Joseph of Exeter." *Speculum* 5 (1930): 49–76.

Septimus, B. "Petrus Alfonsi on the Cult at Mecca." *Speculum* 56 (1981): 517–533.

Severs, J.B. "The Source of Chaucer's *Melibeus.*" *PMLA* 50 (1935): 92–99.

Seznec, J. *The Survival of the Pagan Gods.* Trans. B.F. Sessions. New York: Harper and Row, 1961.

Shannon, E.F. *Chaucer and the Roman Poets.* Cambridge, Mass.: Harvard Univ. Press, 1929.

Silverstein, H. T. "Chaucer's 'Brutus Cassius.'" *MLN* 47 (1932): 148–150.

Silvia, D.S., Jr. "Glosses to the *Canterbury Tales* from St. Jerome's *Epistola adversus Jovinianum.*" *SP* 62 (1965): 28–39.

Singer, A.E. "Chaucer and Don Juan." *WVUPP* 13 (1961): 25–30.

Sisam, C. "An Early Fragment of the *Old English Martyrology.*" *RES* 4, new series 15 (1953): 209–220.

Sledd, J. "*Canterbury Tales* C 3100, 320: By Seint Ronyan." *MS* 13 (1951): 226–233.

——. "*The Clerk's Tale*: The Monsters and the Critics." *MP* 51 (1953–1954): 73–82.

——. "Dorigen's Complaint." *MP* 45 (1947): 36–45.

Slocum, S.K. "How Old Is Chaucer's Pandarus?" *PQ* 58 (1979): 16–25.

Smalley, B. *The Becket Conflict and the Schools.* Oxford: Clarendon Press, 1973.

——. *English Friars and Antiquity in the Early Fourteenth Century.* Oxford: Basil Blackwell, 1960.

Smith, R.M. "Five Notes on Chaucer and Froissart." *MLN* 66 (1951): 27–32.

——. "The Limited Vision of St. Bernard." *MLN* 61 (1946): 38–44.

Smyser, H.M. "A View of Chaucer's Astronomy." *Speculum* 45 (1970): 359–373.

Sources and Analogues of Chaucer's Canterbury Tales. Ed. W.F. Bryan and G. Dempster. New York: The Humanities Press, 1958.

Southern, R.W., ed. and trans. *The Life of St. Anselm, Archbishop of Canterbury, by Eadmer.* Oxford: Clarendon Press, 1962.

——. *Saint Anselm and his Biographer.* 2nd ed. Cambridge: Cambridge Univ. Press, 1986.

——. *Western Views of Islam in the Middle Ages.* Cambridge, Mass.: Harvard Univ. Press, 1962.

Spargo, J.F. *Virgil the Necromancer: Studies in Virgilian Legends.* Cambridge, Mass.: Harvard Univ. Press, 1934.

Spencer, T.H. "Chaucer's Hell: A Study in Medieval Convention." *Speculum* 2 (1927): 177–200.

——. "The Story of Ugolino in Dante and Chaucer." *Speculum* 9 (1934): 295–301.

Spisak, J.W. "Chaucer's *Pyramus and Thisbe.*" *ChauR* 18 (1983–1984): 204–210.

Stahl, W.H. "The *Quadrivium* of Martianus Capella: Its Place in the Intellectual History of Western Europe." *Arts libéraux et philosophie au moyen âge. Actes du quatrième congrès international de philosophie médiévale.* Montreal: Institut d'études médiévales, 1969, 959–967.

——. "Toward a Better Understanding of Martianus Capella." *Speculum* 40 (1965): 102–115.

Steadman, J.M. "Chauntecleer and Medieval Natural History." *Isis* 50 (1959): 236–244.

——. " 'Goddes Boteler' and 'Stellifye' (*The House of Fame*, 581, 592)." *Archiv* 197 (1960): 16–18.

——. " 'Hir Grettest Path': The Prioress, St. Eligius, and St. Godebertha." *Neophilologus* 43 (1959): 49–57.

——. "Simkin's Camus Nose: A Latin Pun in *The Reeve's Tale?*" *MLN* 75 (1960): 4–8.

——. "Venus' Citole in Chaucer's *Knight's Tale* and Berchorius." *Speculum* 34 (1959): 620–624.

Stephen, L., and S. Lee, eds. *The Dictionary of National Biography.* 22 vols. London: Oxford Univ. Press, 1921–1922.

Stevens, M. "Malkyn in the Man of Law's Headlink." *Leeds Studies in English* 1 (1967): 1–5.

Stewart, H.F. *Boethius: An Essay*. Edinburgh and London: W. Blackwood, 1891.

Stillwell, G. "Convention and Individuality in Chaucer's *Complaint of Mars*." *PQ* 35 (1956): 69–89.

Stokes, M. "The Moon in Leo in Book V of *Troilus and Criseyde*." *ChauR* 17 (1982–1983): 116–129.

Strong, C. "Sir Thopas and Sir Guy." *MLN* 23 (1908): 73–77; 102–106.

Struder, P., and J. Evans. *Anglo-Norman Lapidaries*. Paris: H. Champion, 1924.

Strunk, O., ed. *Source Readings in Music History*. New York: W.W. Norton, 1950.

Sundwall, M. "Deiphobus and Helen: A Tantalizing Hint." *MP* 73 (1975): 151–156.

Sutherland, R. "*The Romaunt of the Rose* and Source Manuscripts." *PMLA* 74 (1959): 178–183.

Sypherd, W.O. *Studies in Chaucer's* Hous of Fame. Chaucer Society, 2nd series, no. 39. London: Chaucer Society, 1907.

Taggie, B.F. "John of Gaunt, Geoffrey Chaucer, and 'O Noble, O Worthy Petro of Spayne.'" *FCS* 10 (1984): 195–228.

Tatlock, J.S.P. *Development and Chronology of Chaucer's Works*. London: 1907; Gloucester, Mass.: Peter Smith, 1963.

——. "Astrology and Magic in Chaucer's *Franklin's Tale*." *Anniversary Papers by Colleagues and Pupils of George Lyman Kittredge*. Boston: Ginn, 1913, 339–350.

——. "St. Cecilia's Garlands and their Roman Origin." *PMLA* 45 (1930): 129–168.

——. "Chaucer's Elcanor." *MLN* 36 (1921): 95–97.

——, and A.G. Kennedy. *Concordance to the Complete Works of Geoffrey Chaucer and the Romaunt of the Rose*. Washington, D.C.: Carnegie Institution, 1927.

——, and P. MacKaye. *The Scene of The Franklin's Tale Visited*. London: K. Paul, Trench and Trübner, 1914.

Taylor, B. "The Medieval Cleopatra: The Classical and Medieval Tradition of Chaucer's *Legend of Cleopatra*." *JMRS* 7 (1977): 249–269.

Theisen, W. "Witelo's Recension of Euclid's *De visu*." *Traditio* 33 (1977): 394–402.

Thorndike, L. *A History of Magic and Experimental Science*. 8 vols. New York: Columbia Univ. Press, 1923–1958.

——. "Latin Manuscripts of Works by Rasis at the Bibliothèque Nationale, Paris." *Bulletin of the History of Medicine* 32 (1958): 54–67.

Toomer, G.J. "A Survey of the Toledan Tables." *Osiris* 15 (1968): 5–174.

Toynbee, P. *Dante Alighieri: His Life and Works.* Ed. with an introd., notes, and bibliography by C.S. Singleton. Gloucester, Mass.: Peter Smith, 1971.

——. *A Dictionary of Proper Names and Notable Matters in the Works of Dante.* Rev. C.S. Singleton. Oxford: Clarendon Press, 1968.

Tryon, R.W. "Miracles of Our Lady in Middle English Poetry." *PMLA* 38 (1923): 308–388.

Tupper, F. "Chaucer and Trophee." *MLN* 31 (1916): 11–14.

Turab 'Ali, M., ed. "Three Arabic Treatises on Alchemy by Muhammad ibn Umail (10th century A.D.), with Excursus, an edition of the Latin Rendering of the Ma' al-Waraqi by E. Stapleton and M. Hidayat Husain." *Memoirs of the Royal Asiatic Society of Bengal* 12 (1933).

Turner, C.H. "Latin Lists of the Canonical Books, I, The Roman Council Under Damasus, A.D. 382." *Journal of Theological Studies* 1 (1899–1900): 554–560.

——. "St. Peter in the New Testament." *Theology* 13 (1926): 66–78.

Upton, J. "A Manuscript of the Book of the Fixed Stars by Abd-ar-Rahman as Sufi." *Metropolitan Museum Studies* 4 (1933).

Varty, K. *Reynard the Fox: A Study of the Fox in Medieval English Art.* Leicester: Leicester Univ. Press, 1967.

Vasta, E., and Z. Thundy. *Chaucerian Problems and Perspectives.* Notre Dame: Univ. of Notre Dame Press, 1979.

Vaughan, A.C. *Zenobia of Palmyra.* New York: Doubleday, 1967.

Vinge, Louise. *The Narcissus Theme in Western European Literature up to the Early Nineteenth Century.* Trans. R. Dewsnap and Nigel Reeves. Lund: Skånska Centryckeriet, 1967.

von Balthasar, H.U. *Origen, "Spirit and Fire": A Thematic Anthology of his Writing.* Trans. R.J. Daly, S.J. Baltimore: Catholic Univ. of America Press, 1984.

von Kriesler, N.A. "An Aesopic Allusion in *The Merchant's Tale.*" *ChauR* 6 (1971): 30–37.

Wallace, D. *Chaucer and the Early Writings of Boccaccio.* Woodbridge, Suffolk, and Dover, N.J.: Boydell & Brewer, 1985.

Wallace-Hadrill, A. *Suetonius: The Scholar and his Caesars.* New Haven: Yale Univ. Press, 1984.

Waller, M.S. "*The Physician's Tale:* Geoffrey Chaucer and Fray Juan Garcia de Castrojeriz." *Speculum* 51 (1976): 292–306.

Walwin, P.C. *St. Christopher Today and Yesterday.* Gloucester: A.E. Smith, 1968.

Watson, E.W. *The Cathedral Church of Christ in Oxford.* London: R. Tuck & Sons, 1935.

Wells, J.E. *A Manual of Writings in Middle English.* Ed. A. Hartung. 8 vols. New Haven: Modern Language Association, 1967.

Wentersdorf, K.P. "Theme and Structure in the *Merchant's Tale:* the Function of the Pluto Episode." *PMLA* 80 (1965): 522–527.

Wenzel, S. "Chaucer and the Language of Contemporary Preaching." *SP* 73 (1976): 138–161.

——. "The Source of Chaucer's Seven Deadly Sins." *Traditio* 30 (1974): 351–378.

Weston, Jessie. *The Legend of Sir Lancelot du Lac.* London: Nutt, 1901.

Wetherbee, W. "The Function of Poetry in the 'De planctu Naturae' of Alain de Lille." *Traditio* 25 (1969): 87–125.

——. *Platonism and Poetry in the Twelfth Century.* Princeton: Princeton Univ. Press, 1972.

Whaite, H.C. *St. Christopher in English Medieval Wall Painting.* London: E. Benn, 1929.

White, R.B. "Chaucer's Daun Piers and the Rule of St. Benedict: The Failure of an Ideal." *JEGP* 70 (1971): 13–30.

Whiting, B.J. *Chaucer's Use of Proverbs.* Cambridge, Mass.: Harvard Univ. Press, 1934.

——. *Gawain: his Reputation, his Courtesy, and his Appearance in Chaucer's Squire's Tale. MS* 9 (1947): 189–234.

Whitney, C.A. *Whitney's Star Finder.* New York: A.A. Knopf, 1975.

Wilkins, E.H. "Criseida." *MLN* 24 (1909): 65–67.

——. "Descriptions of Pagan Divinities from Petrarch to Chaucer." *Speculum* 32 (1957): 511–522.

——. *Petrarch's Eight Years in Milan.* Cambridge, Mass.: Medieval Academy of America, 1958.

——. *Petrarch's Later Years.* Cambridge, Mass.: Medieval Academy of America, 1959.

——. *Studies in the Life and Works of Petrarch.* Cambridge, Mass.: Medieval Academy of America, 1955.

Willard, C.C. *Christine de Pizan: Her Life and Works.* New York: Persea, 1984.

Willard, R. "Chaucer's 'text that seith that hunters ben nat hooly men.'" *Studies in English* (1947): 209–251.

Wilson, K.M. "Chaucer and St. Jerome: The Use of 'Barley' in the Wife of Bath's Prologue." *ChauR* 19 (1985): 245–251.

Wimsatt, J.I. "The Apotheosis of Blanche in *The Book of the Duchess*." *JEGP* 66 (1967): 26–44.

——. "Guillaume de Machaut and Chaucer's Love Lyrics." *MAE* 47 (1978): 66–87.

——. "Guillaume de Machaut and Chaucer's *Troilus and Criseyde*." *MAE* 45 (1976): 277–293.

——. *The Marguerite Poetry of Guillaume de Machaut*. Chapel Hill: Univ. of North Carolina Press, 1970.

——. "The Sources of Chaucer's 'Seys and Alcyone.'" *MAE* 36 (1967): 231–241.

Wimsatt, W.K. "Vincent of Beauvais in Chaucer's Cleopatra and Croesus." *Speculum* 12 (1937): 375–381.

Windeatt, B.A., ed. and trans. *Chaucer's Dream Poetry: Sources and Analogues*. Cambridge: D.S. Brewer, 1982; Totowa, N.J.: Rowman and Littlefield, 1982.

Wingate, S.D. *The Medieval Latin Versions of the Aristotelian Scientific Corpus*. London: The Courier Press, 1931.

Winny, J. *Chaucer's Dream Poems*. New York: Harper and Row, 1973.

Wise, B.A. *The Influence of Statius upon Chaucer*. Baltimore: J.H. Furst, 1911.

Witlieb, B.L. "Chaucer and the *Ovide Moralisé*." *N&Q* 215 (1970): 202–207.

——. "Jupiter and Nimrod in *The Former Age*." *Chaucer Newsletter* 2 (1980): 12–13.

Wood, C. *Chaucer and the Country of the Stars: Poetic Uses of Astrological Imagery*. Princeton: Princeton Univ. Press, 1970.

Wynn, P. "The Conversion Story in Nicholas Trevet's 'Tale of Constance.'" *Viator* 13 (1980): 259–274.

Young, K. "Chaucer and Geoffrey of Vinsauf." *MP* 41 (1943–1944): 172–182.

——. "Chaucer and Peter Riga." *Speculum* 12 (1937): 299–303.

——. "Chaucer's Aphorisms from Ptolemy." *SP* 34 (1937): 1–7.

——, ed. *The Drama of the Medieval Church*. 2 vols. Oxford: Clarendon Press, 1933, 1962, 1967.

——. "The Maidenly Virtues of Chaucer's Virginia." *Speculum* 16 (1941): 340–349.

——. *The Origin and Development of the Story of Troilus and Criseyde*. Chaucer Society, 2nd series, no. 40. London: The Chaucer Society, 1908; New York: The Gordian Press, 1968.

——. "The 'Secree of Secrees' of Chaucer's Canon's Yeoman." *MLN* 58 (1943): 605–607.

Ziolkowski, J. *Alan of Lille's Grammar of Sex: The Meaning of Grammar to a Twelfth-Century Intellectual.* Cambridge, Mass.: Medieval Academy of America, 1985.